Citizenship Reimagined

The United States is entering a new era of progressive state citizenship, with California leading the way. A growing number of states are providing expanded rights to undocumented immigrants that challenge conventional understandings of citizenship as binary, unidimensional, and exclusively national. In *Citizenship Reimagined*, Allan Colbern and Karthick Ramakrishnan develop a precise framework for understanding and measuring citizenship as expansive, multidimensional, and federated – broader than legal status and firmly grounded in the provision of rights. Placing current immigration battles in historical context, they show that today's progressive state citizenship is not unprecedented: US states have been leaders in rights expansion since America's founding, including over the fights for Black citizenship and for women's suffrage. The book invites readers to rethink how American federalism relates to minority rights and how state laws regulating undocumented residents can coexist with federal exclusivity over immigration law.

Allan Colbern is Assistant Professor of Political Science at Arizona State University. He is a Presidential Award recipient from the Russell Sage Foundation and Carnegie Corporation, and his research has been featured in the *Washington Post* and the *Los Angeles Times*.

S. Karthick Ramakrishnan is Professor of Public Policy at the University of California, Riverside and founding Director of its Center for Social Innovation. He is a trustee of The California Endowment, a Frederick Douglass 200 honoree, and the recipient of major grants from the National Science Foundation, Robert Wood Johnson Foundation, Bill & Melinda Gates Foundation, James Irvine Foundation, and other national and state foundations.

Citizenship Reimagined

A New Framework for State Rights in the United States

ALLAN COLBERN
Arizona State University

S. KARTHICK RAMAKRISHNAN
University of California, Riverside

CAMBRIDGE
UNIVERSITY PRESS

CAMBRIDGE
UNIVERSITY PRESS

University Printing House, Cambridge CB2 8BS, United Kingdom

One Liberty Plaza, 20th Floor, New York, NY 10006, USA

477 Williamstown Road, Port Melbourne, VIC 3207, Australia

314–321, 3rd Floor, Plot 3, Splendor Forum, Jasola District Centre, New Delhi – 110025, India

79 Anson Road, #06–04/06, Singapore 079906

Cambridge University Press is part of the University of Cambridge.

It furthers the University's mission by disseminating knowledge in the pursuit of education, learning, and research at the highest international levels of excellence.

www.cambridge.org
Information on this title: www.cambridge.org/9781108841047
DOI: 10.1017/9781108888516

© Cambridge University Press 2021

First published 2021

A catalogue record for this publication is available from the British Library.

ISBN 978-1-108-84104-7 Hardback
ISBN 978-1-108-74472-0 Paperback

To Shima, Maya, and Kilian;
Brinda, Omjivan, and Millan.

Contents

Figures

Tables

Acknowledgments

The spark for this book originated in 2009, while Allan was a graduate student at the University of California, Riverside, and Karthick had recently gotten tenure and started the Immigration Research Group (IRG). The IRG included Allan, Chris Haynes, Andrea Silva, and Tom Wong, all of whom are professors now and are carrying on the tradition of community-engaged and policy-relevant research that we began over a decade ago.

Our research group embarked on two projects. The first was to produce an introduction to immigration concepts and scholarship that would be accessible to journalists and community partners alike. Allan volunteered to produce a review of key concepts and traditions related to citizenship – his graduate training had included a heavy dose of coursework in political theory, and he was looking for ways to merge his budding interests in immigration policy with his prior undergraduate work in Black history. The other project entailed research on punitive state laws on immigration in Arizona and elsewhere, as well as variations in the law enforcement practices of sheriff and police departments closer to home. Much of this research informed the book *The New Immigration Federalism*, which Karthick coauthored with Pratheepan Gulasekaram in 2015 focusing on immigration law and politics.

All along, however, Allan kept encouraging Karthick to think bigger, to consider not only law and politics but also, more fundamentally, notions of membership and citizenship. That insistence and persistence inspired a new line of research that led to the production of this book. First, we decided to dig more deeply into the implications of California's advancements in immigrant rights and produced our first policy report, *The California Package* (2015). In the report, we laid out a roadmap modeled on the state's pro-immigrant laws from 1996 to 2015 and used the term "state citizenship" for the first time. We hit a narrative jackpot almost immediately, as we elaborated these ideas in a June 2015 op-ed in the *Los Angeles Times* and, a few months later, the newspaper featured a front-page story on immigrant integration that referenced the notion of a "California citizenship."

Energized, we reached out in August 2015 to the Center for American Progress and the MacArthur Foundation to organize a strategic policy conversation on immigrant rights that would take state policy more seriously. The timing for such a convening was fortuitous – President Obama's renewed push for immigration reform had already ground to a halt in 2014, as had his attempts to expand Deferred Action for Childhood Arrivals (DACA) and create a new program for Deferred Action for Parents of Americans (DAPA). The prospects for a favorable Supreme Court decision were looking grim, and there was an increasing recognition, among funders and advocates alike, that state-level policy innovation was an idea whose time had come.

Interestingly, and perhaps a bit audaciously, we held this convening on state policy innovation not in Washington, DC, New York, Sacramento, or Los Angeles but in downtown Riverside. We organized a full-day meeting of a prominent set of national funders, immigrant rights leaders, and researchers – where everyone could learn about the twenty-year fight to expand immigrant rights in California from activists and scholars alike, and also gain important insights about policy reforms elsewhere in the country, including in New York, Connecticut, and Illinois. In addition to another two other convenings – in Sacramento with SEIU California and the California Immigrant Policy Center, and at UC Riverside with the Presley Center for Crime and Justice Studies—this meeting formed the basis of another coauthored report, *State Policies on Immigrant Integration: An Examination of Best Practices and Policy Diffusion* (2016). We drew insights from these various policy conversations to outline innovative strategies that advance immigrant rights, from legislation to implementation and policy diffusion. Throughout this process, we began to sketch out a more complete framework on state citizenship and progressive federalism.

We began our book project in earnest at that time, and have since benefited tremendously from ideas and feedback from our colleagues in academia, philanthropy, and the nonprofit sector. First, we are grateful to the California Immigrant Policy Center (CIPC) and the New York Immigrant Coalition (NYIC), who are not only doing the tireless work of building statewide coalitions to advance immigrant rights but have also provided us valuable access to archival materials and interviews. At CIPC, we thank Reshma Shamasunder, Cythia Buiza, Almas Sayeed, Carmen Chang, Orville Thomas, Sandhya Nadadur, Sandhya Nadadur, Sumeet Bal and Andre Barrios, for including us in their strategic meetings and events and for their feedback at various stages of this book project. At NYIC, we thank Steven Choi, Muzna Ansari, and Betsy Plum, for engaging us in their state policy blueprint and for their many helpful discussions around past challenges and recent successes in New York on immigration policies.

In addition, we thank legislators and other policy practitioners for their feedback and engagement over the last several years. These include Ricardo Lara (in his capacity as California state senator and sponsor of many laws advancing immigrant rights); Jesse Melgar, Lara's then-communications director and now press secretary for Governor Gavin Newsom; Angelica Salas and Joseph Villela from the Coalition of Humane Immigrant Rights Los Angeles; Marielena Hincapie from the National Immigration Law Center; Linda Lopez, who served as chief of the Office of Immigrant Affairs in Los Angeles; Eliana Kaimowitz, from her days at SEIU to the California Department of Social Services; Javier Hernandez at the Inland Coalition for Immigrant Justice; Chris Newman at the National Day Labor Organizing Network; Jonathan Mehta Stein at the Asian Law Caucus; Phil Wolgin at the Center for American Progress; and Alex Nowrasteh at the Cato Institute.

We also benefited from various conversations with philanthropic leaders working on immigrant rights including Cathy Cha at the Evelyn and Walter Haas Jr. Fund, Geri Mannion at The Carnegie Corporation of New York, Tara Magner at the MacArthur Foundation, Aixa Cintron at the Russell Sage Foundation, Vik Malhotra at the Ford Foundation, Efrain Escobedo at the California Community Foundation, Marshall Fitz and Kavitha Sreeharsha at the Emerson Collective; Marlon Cuellar at The California Endowment; Sandra Martinez at the California Wellness Foundation; and Daranee Petsod at Grantmakers Concerned with Immigrants and Refugees.

We also owe a boatload of thanks to our various academic colleagues. First, we thank our colleagues and friends at the University of California, Riverside. For their feedback on early outlines and chapters, we give our thanks to Jennifer Merolla, Francisco Pedraza, Loren Collingwood, Ben Newman, Ben Bishin, David Pion Berlin, Danielle Lemi, Andrea Silva, and Sono Shah. We also owe special thanks to Deep Gulasekaram, for his feedback and support on our early work, and to Dan Tichenor, for inviting Karthick to a Carnegie-funded workshop in Portland, Oregon, in December 2017 to get feedback on our book's initial chapters. There, we gained invaluable feedback from Dan, Elizabeth Cohen, Debra Thompson, Cybelle Fox, Saladin Ambar, and Alison Gash, who not only helped sharpen our concept of state citizenship but also provided references to expand our engagement with a broader range of scholarship.

We are also grateful for the opportunity to present this work at the Immigration Initiative workshop sponsored by the Social Science Research Council and headed by Deborah Yashar, Nancy Bermeo, and Michael Jones-Correa. In addition to getting valuable feedback from the organizers, we benefited from the insights and recommendations from all the workshop participants, including Sara Wallace Goodman, Amada Armenta, Shannon Gleeson, and Cecilia Menjivar. Finally, Karthick's January 2019 presentation at the Race, Ethnicity, and Politics workshop at Northwestern University proved critical in helping to expand our book's scope from a predominant focus on immigrant rights and progressive state citizenship to encompassing the history of regressive state citizenship and Black citizenship rights. For that, we are grateful for incisive feedback from Traci Burch, Julie Lee Merseth, Thomas Ogorzalek, Andrew Roberts, Reuel Rogers, and Al Tillery.

We owe significant gratitude to many more scholars from various disciplines who have offered their thoughts, encouragement, questions, and critiques over the years. In addition to those already mentioned, we give our deep and sincere thanks to Cecilia Ayón, Ming H. Chen, Els de Graauw, Laura E. Enriquez, Miriam Feldblum, David FitzGerald, Michael Fortner, Megan Ming Francis, Paul Frymer, Angela Garcia, Marcela García-Castañon, Heather K. Gerken, Cyril Ghosh, Ron Hayduk, Jennifer Hochschild, Christopher Lasch, Anna O. Law, Jennifer Lee, Bruce Link, Willem Maas, John Mollenkopf, Hiroshi Motomura, Mireille Paquet, Manuel Pastor, Doris Marie Provine, Cristina Rodriguez, John Skrentny, Yuhki Tajima, Veronica Terriquez, Christine Thurlow Brenner, Monica Varsanyi, Daisy Vasquez Vera, Jackie Vimo, Qingfang Wang, Mary Waters, Janelle Wong, and Tom Wong.

The ideas in this book also benefited greatly from opportunities to present at various conferences and meetings, including the 2015 Annual Meeting of the Law and Society Association, the 2016 Annual Meeting of the Southern California Law and Social Sciences Forum (SoCLASS), the 2016 and 2018 Annual Meetings of the American Political Science Association (APSA), the 2017 Annual Meeting of the Association for Public Policy Analysis & Management (APPAM), the 2017 Annual Meeting of the Western Political Science Association (WPSA), the 2018 Welcoming San Diego Summit, the 2018 International Political Science Association (IPSA) World Congress Conference, the Winter 2018 Politics of Race, Immigration and Ethnicity Consortium, and the 2019 European Consortium for Political Research (ECPR).

We are also grateful to the staff at Cambridge University Press and especially to Sara Doskow, for her enthusiasm and guidance in bringing this book to fruition, and to Wade Guyitt, for his careful copyediting. We hope that the insights from this book will be useful in both the short term and the longer duration, informing not only theory and empirical scholarship but also the strategic work of social movement and policy leaders.

From Allan:
I owe special thanks to a few people who have supported every step of my young academic career. Thank you to Dan Tichenor, whose *Dividing Lines: The Politics of Immigration Control in America* first inspired me to specialize in American political development as a graduate student. Gaining his mentorship and support early in graduate school has been a true blessing. Thank you to Elizabeth Cohen, whose *Semi-Citizenship in Democratic Politics* opened my eyes to citizenship studies and sparked my early conversations with Karthick that, years later, led to coauthoring this book. I am incredibly thankful to Elizabeth's mentorship, feedback, and advice. Thanks also to David FitzGerald and John Skrentny for opening their doors and inviting me as a visiting graduate student to join University of California, San Diego's Center for

Comparative Immigration Studies. My time at CCIS and their mentorship helped me navigate academia and grow as an interdisciplinary scholar. Thanks to my close friends Cale Crammer, Steven Cauchon, Diego Esparza, James Cemo, Michael Prather and Kevin Sitz, for providing an incredible support system during and after our time together in graduate school. I am grateful to Arizona State University's support, especially School Director Scott Barclay, Dean Todd Sandrin and Associate Dean Patricia Friedrich for providing me the opportunity to present the book manuscript at the 2018 New College faculty colloquium. Natasha Behl, your mentorship and friendship and our collaborations on methods and citizenship studies have made transitioning to ASU as a new assistant professor meaningful and productive; Shawn Walker, Julie Murphy Erfani, Jennifer Keahey, Amit Ron, Suzanne Vaughan, Kishonna Gray, and Carol Mueller, thank you for your encouragement, support, and friendship, which made writing this book at ASU easier.

Thank you to Karthick Ramakrishnan. Having him as a dissertation chair and as a mentor has been invaluable to my identity and success as a scholar. Karthick is inspiring. So many of our conversations have energized my passion for advocacy, teaching, and research. And I am thankful for our growing friendship. This has made coauthoring this book my most memorable academic experience thus far.

Deserving special recognition, thanks to my parents (Cindy and Gregg), sister (Ashley) and parents-in-law (Susan and Kiomars) for caring enough to support my education, work and family. Above all, I owe my deepest thanks to my loving wife, Shima Kalaei. I cherish all of our discussions about politics and life, and learning about her experience of being a Persian Jewish refugee and integrating as a young child. Without Shima's support, this book would not have been possible. She sacrificed time to support every step with incredible patience and encouragement, for which I will always be thankful. And thanks to my little ones, Maya (four years old) and Kilian (newly born), for making our home an exciting place.

From Karthick:

To Allan: I am grateful to have been on this journey with you, from being your advisor to being a colleague, friend, and collaborator on this book. Your background in political theory and your prior research on runaway slaves was invaluable for this project, and it has been a treat to be able to riff with you and to challenge ourselves and support each other every step of the way.

My professional life now spans multiple institutions and contexts, and I am grateful for the support and patience of colleagues and institutions in the many years it took to complete this project. In addition to colleagues already mentioned at UC Riverside, I am grateful for the support of Anil Deolalikar in his capacity as dean, John Medearis as chair of political science, and Kurt Schwabe as chair of public policy. I am also very thankful for the support of colleagues at the Center for Social Innovation at UCR, including Paola Avendano, Michael Bates, Marlenee Blas, Eric Calderon, Karla Lopez del Rio, Francisco Pedraza, Ellen Reese, and Gary Rettberg. Thanks also to my colleagues at AAPI Data, including Jennifer Lee, Janelle Wong, Sono Shah, Sunny Shao, and Mai Do for helping us maintain progress on that work. I also draw strength and community from the support and collaboration of civic leaders in the Inland Empire (thank you to Sky Allen, Pastor Samuel Casey, Mike Chavez, Tom Dolan, Luz Gallegos, Michael Gomez-Daly, Javier Hernandez, Corey Jackson, Felicia Jones, Sheheryar Kaoosji, Gabriel Maldonado, Celene Perez, Andrea Vidaurre, Dina Walker, Torie Weiston-Serdan, the Saturday morning group, and more). Thaks also to my philanthropic colleagues in the region including Paulette Brown-Hinds, Celia Cudiamat, Michelle Decker, Max Espinoza, Randall Lewis, Margarita Luna, Nicole Pritchard, Amy Sausser, and Patricia Watkins.

My colleagues at The California Endowment have heard me discuss different aspects of this book over the years, and I am grateful for the feedback and advice of Bob Ross, Daniel Zingale, Beatriz Solis, Margarita Luna, Hanh Cao Yu, Marion Standish, and my Board colleagues including Shawn Ginwright, Bishop Minerva Carcaño, Stephen Bennett, Hector Flores, Michelle Siqueiros, and Vien Truong. I am also grateful for the friendship and thought partnership of other leaders in government and philanthropy working to advance the rights of disenfranchised populations, including Fred Ali, Fatima Angeles, Judy Belk, Ludovic Blain, Rob Bonta, Cathy Cha, Max Espinoza, Kaying Hang, Chet Hewitt, Don Howard, Alex Johnson, Kathleen Kelly Janus, Jeff Kim, Sandra Martinez, Lenny Mendonca, Cat Nou, Chris Punongbayan, Julie Su, Aditi Vaidya, and Sue Van.

Of course, all of my work is heavily subsidized by the kindness, understanding, and help from my parents (Tarakad and Rani) and from Brinda, Omji, and Millan. Thank you, thank you, thank you.

Introduction

October 5, 2013, was a big day for immigration and citizenship in the United States. Tens of thousands of protesters – undocumented immigrants, naturalized citizens, and native-born alike – rallied across more than forty states around the country, from large cities like Los Angeles, New York, and Boston to smaller places like Reading, Pennsylvania; Hobbs, New Mexico; and Yakima, Washington.[1] In Minneapolis, nearly 2,000 demonstrators "marched from the Basilica of St. Mary, after an interfaith prayer service, to the plaza, hoisting flags and placards and chanting empowerment cries, including 'Si se puede!'"[2] In Birmingham, Alabama, hundreds of rally participants listened to "the president of the N.A.A.C.P. in Alabama, [who] portrayed the immigration effort as part of broader civil rights activism in the state,"[3] while in Reading, Pennsylvania, "demonstrators demanded that the congressmen sign onto or co-sponsor bipartisan immigration reform, speak on the House floor about the urgency of reform and oppose laws that promote racial profiling."[4] These protests were all part of the National Day of Immigrant Dignity and Respect, as thousands of Americans joined President Barack Obama's call for Congress to pass immigrant legalization as part of a comprehensive reform package.

Even though the nationwide rallies for immigrant legalization were sizable and widespread, they were not the most important development on immigrant rights and citizenship happening that day. An even more consequential action on citizenship took place on October 5, 2013, in Sacramento and primarily involved just one individual: Governor Jerry Brown of California. That day, Governor Brown signed a set of eight bills that sought to expand immigrant rights in the state. Prominent among them was the California TRUST Act (AB 4), which would significantly constrain the circumstances under which state and local law enforcement could "[detain] an individual on the basis of a United States Immigration and Customs Enforcement hold after that individual becomes eligible for release from custody."[5] Other bills the governor signed that day included a measure that would allow unauthorized immigrants to practice law in California and gain admission to the State Bar, another bill suspending or revoking an employer's business license "for retaliation against employees and others on the basis of citizenship and immigration status," and yet another measure that would allow extortion charges against those who threaten to "report the immigration status or suspected immigration status of an individual or the individual's family."[6] Importantly, Jerry Brown signed these immigration bills two days after signing another landmark piece of legislation, AB 60, that would allow unauthorized immigrants to move more freely across the state by applying for driver's licenses and obtaining auto insurance.[7]

Taken together, these various state laws in 2013 advanced immigrant rights on several key dimensions, such as the right to free movement, the right to due process and legal protection, and the right to human capital formation (including allowing people to practice their profession and to be immune from workplace retaliation). The governor recognized the symbolic importance of his actions that day, even as thousands were marching on streets across the country. "While Washington waffles on immigration, California's forging ahead," he said, adding, "I'm not waiting."[8] What Brown did not realize, however, was that his actions were propelling California toward a new era of progressive state citizenship in the United States. Not only did these laws provide a meaningful measure of protection for undocumented residents, but they also marked a pivotal moment in the state's ability to provide residents with access to a panoply of rights. These citizenship rights were not only constitutionally permissible but also politically feasible. As we shall demonstrate in this book, California had made sufficient progress on key dimensions of citizenship that, by the summer of 2013, had reached a tipping point. The various legislative measures that Governor Brown signed in October pushed it over the edge, accelerating it toward a new era of progressive state citizenship. Today, California's example inspires many advocates across the country to reimagine citizenship for a new era, with states playing a critical role in the advancement of civil rights.

CALIFORNIA IS NOT ALONE

While California has gone the farthest in advancing the rights of its immigrant residents, it is by no means alone. As of this writing, sixteen states and the District of Columbia offer all residents access to state driver's licenses, regardless of their immigration status.[9] These include not only Democratic states with long-established immigrant populations, like Washington, Illinois, and Hawaii, but also politically mixed states with relatively newer immigrant populations, like Nevada, Utah, and Vermont. In addition, nineteen states and the District of Columbia provide in-state tuition to residents regardless of their immigration status, and six states plus the District of Columbia provide immigrant children access to health insurance, regardless of their immigration status. Finally, in addition to California, seven other states (Connecticut, Illinois, New Jersey, New York, Oregon, Vermont, and Washington) and the District of Columbia have so-called sanctuary policies that limit cooperation between law enforcement and US Immigration and Customs Enforcement.[10]

California was by no means the first state to pass strong policies protecting immigrants and meaningfully advancing their rights. Earlier in 2013, Connecticut Governor Dannel Malloy signed both a driver's license bill and a TRUST Act limiting the state's cooperation with immigration enforcement.[11] And more than twenty-five years prior, on July 7, 1987, Oregon enacted one of the country's first state sanctuary policies, severing their enforcement of federal immigration law. The Oregon bill had easily passed the Senate, twenty-nine votes to one, as well as the House, fifty-eight votes to one, and was signed into law by Governor Neil Goldschmidt. It remains in effect today, stating:

No law enforcement agency of the State of Oregon or of any political subdivision of the state shall use agency moneys, equipment or personnel for the purpose of detecting or apprehending persons whose only violation of law is that they are persons of foreign citizenship present in the United States in violation of federal immigration laws.[12]

Oregon's state sanctuary law was born out of happenstance. In 1977, Delmiro Trevino was dining with three other Chicano men at the Hi Ho Restaurant in Independence, Oregon. Without showing a warrant or properly identifying themselves, sheriff's deputies entered the restaurant and began interrogating the men about their citizenship status. According to a news account, "a deputy grabbed [Trevino] by the arm and forced him to stand in the middle of the restaurant in front of other customers. Trevino, a U.S. citizen of Mexican descent, later filed what would become a class action lawsuit in which he said being publicly called out left him feeling humiliated."[13]

Trevino enlisted the help of a trial lawyer in Salem, Oregon, and together they filed suit against law enforcement agencies in Oregon for engaging in "a pattern and practice of stopping, detaining, interrogating, searching and harassing" people of Mexican origin because of their appearance.[14] Although the case was dismissed, Trevino's lawyer Rocky Barilla ran for state assembly nearly a decade later and won. Once there, Barilla convinced his colleagues to pass a law that would end local police abuses and limit state and local cooperation with immigration authorities. Importantly, Oregon's sanctuary law in 1987 was not an outgrowth of the Central American sanctuary movement in the 1980s, nor was it part of a broader effort by Oregon to pass a litany of immigrant rights measures. Indeed, as Barilla noted, "this was not meant to be a sanctuary law . . . It was meant to protect local city resources from using them to supplant federal spending."[15] Still, the law was meaningful in that it provided immigrants and Mexican Americans in Oregon the rights to due process and free movement in the state.

What do these examples tell us about the evolving nature of citizenship in the contemporary era? And what accounts for the expansion and contraction of state citizenship rights in the United States? These are two of the central questions motivating this book. In answering these questions, we will have more to say about Oregon, Connecticut, and other states that are pushing toward what California has already achieved – a durable, multifaceted, and meaningful form of state citizenship. We call this development "progressive state citizenship," where states provide rights and protections that exceed those provided at the national level. At the same time, we also seek to shed greater light on what we call "regressive state citizenship," where states remove or erode citizenship rights that are supposed to be guaranteed at the national level.

STATE CITIZENSHIP?

Many may balk at the notion that California, or any other state, can provide citizenship to its resident populations. Our claims rub against the conventional legal view of citizenship in the United States today – as an exclusive and formal membership controlled by the federal government, with sovereign power over its borders and people. This legal conception of citizenship – as predominantly or exclusively national – is prevalent well beyond the United States. National citizenship has become intuitive and normalized as *the* dominant type of rights-based citizenship across the world. National articulations of citizenship draw heavily on Max Weber's framework of modern political citizenship as membership in national states, with varying emphases such as the process of state formation through war-making and the creation of welfare states with strict rules defining insiders who are entitled to benefits and outsiders excluded from those same benefits. Regardless of the emphasis, the conventional view of citizenship today is still one that is largely tied to a framework where national governments reign supreme within their territories and where the world is divided into mutually exclusive jurisdictions.

The conventional view of citizenship today has three hallmark features: citizenship is binary, unidimensional, and exclusively national. First, citizenship is viewed as binary – one is either a citizen or one is not, with no gradations in between. Furthermore, this binary view of citizenship is often tied to just one dimension: legal status. Citizenship is largely seen as a unidimensional gateway, as rules concerning birthright citizenship and naturalization prove to be authoritative in providing individuals access to a comprehensive set of political, social, and legal rights. Without legal status, the thinking goes, one cannot hope to draw upon any kind of citizenship rights. Finally, the conventional view sees citizenship as exclusive to national governments, with state and local forms of citizenship rendered irrelevant with the rise and consolidation of the modern national state. Thus, most scholars and practitioners today still see national governments as having a monopoly over the use of legitimate force. They also see national governments as having the exclusive ability to define and control citizenship – with documents such as passports, birth certificates, and naturalization certificates serving as important markers of legal presence and controlling access to a variety of rights. We say more about the conventional view of citizenship in Chapter 2.

In recent years, scholars and practitioners alike have offered alternative conceptualizations of citizenship, but they have largely done so outside a rights-based framework. Scholars in urban studies have challenged the traditional model of citizenship over its claims to national exclusivity.[16] For example, Michael Javen Fortner (2016) develops the concept of "effective citizenship," emphasizing city-level autonomy and governmental ties to the local community and particularly the capacity of local actors to work together to achieve collective goals.[17] Rogers Smith (2016) has a similar, expansive view of urban citizenship. As he explains, cities play three specific roles that have an upward impact on American citizenship: "as sites of political activity embedded in larger [national] structures, as political actors in those larger structures, and as political symbols."[18] In this formulation, citizenship is a generalized concept that has both local and national dimensions, with policies, actions, and symbols that can provide individuals with varying levels of representation, empowerment, and sense of belonging. Scholars of global cities go even further. Decentering citizenship studies away from national boundaries, these scholars point to multiple, overlapping, and coexisting memberships, including urban, local, national, global, transnational, postnational, and dual-national membership.[19]

In addition to urban scholars, immigration researchers have also challenged the conventional view of citizenship for its fixation on legal status as: (1) a binary distinction providing a sharp line between noncitizen from citizen; and (2) an authoritative distinction that lords over all other dimensions of citizenship by controlling access to a variety of political, social, legal, and economic rights. This challenge has a long tradition. Writing in 1965, T. H. Marshall traced full citizenship as an evolving concept, beginning with civil rights and then expanding to include political and social rights.[20] Writing more recently, Elizabeth Cohen builds on Marshall's foundational work by developing a more precise and concise framework of multidimensional citizenship that is grounded in the provision of rights.[21]

Other scholars of multidimensional citizenship go beyond a focus on rights, drawing attention to factors like legal status, political participation, and sense of belonging. Importantly, Irene Bloemraad, Anna Korteweg, and Gokce Yurdakul (2008) argue that these dimensions can operate semi-independently from each other and that citizenship need not be collapsed into one single dimension of rights.[22] By presenting these four general dimensions shared by state-centered and human rights approaches alike, Bloemraad, Korteweg, and Yurdakul provide a broad foundation for addressing the substance of citizenship that is sorely lacking in the national citizenship framework.

Others, writing in traditions as varied as postnationalism, multiculturalism, and feminism, have also offered expansive notions of citizenship, moving beyond rights to include the exercise of sovereign power and the lived experiences of people.[23] As we note in Chapter 2, these broader frameworks present compelling critiques of the conventional view of citizenship. At the same time, they also run the risk of "conceptual stretching" by combining such disparate ideas as access to rights, the exercise of those rights, and psychological notions of identity and emotional attachment.

We believe that it is possible to preserve a multidimensional view of citizenship that is entirely grounded in rights, including the provision of rights by governments and access to those rights by members of social groups. We also argue that citizenship rights are not exclusive to the federal government and that states have acted in various ways throughout American history to expand or contract those rights. Finally, we produce a set of indicators showing expansion and contraction in various dimensions of citizenship rights. We do all of this while drawing attention to important federalism dynamics involving *constitutional frameworks* as interpreted through courts, *legal actions* pushed by political parties and social movements, and the *bureaucratic capacity and political will* of national and state governments to enforce citizenship rights. Importantly, we show that, even though state citizenship may be moving in a progressive direction in many places today, the United States has also seen many periods of regressive state citizenship, where states have used the cover of federalism to contract citizenship rights.

THE DARK SIDE OF FEDERALISM

Federalism does not have a great reputation in the history of U.S. civil rights. Vivid images from the Civil Rights era to the present day capture the dark side of states' rights: the Arkansas National Guard preventing nine black students from entering an all-White high school in 1957; Southern sheriffs turning loose attack dogs and firehoses on civil rights protesters in 1963; a county clerk in Kentucky refusing to issue marriage licenses to gays in 2015. All of these images, and their associated stories, powerfully depict the attempts by states and localities to claw back rights that were won at the national level.

The concern about federalism as a cover for eroding civil rights is reflected not only in popular understandings of the topic but also in much scholarship on federalism and civil rights. Writing in 1964, William Riker concluded that "if in the United States one disapproves of racism, one should disapprove of federalism," and that, by contrast, "if in the United States one approves of Southern White racists, then one should approve of American federalism."[24] Since Riker's provocative statement, a large body of scholarship in the post–Civil Rights era has called out federalism for preserving the power of states to enforce racially punitive policies, making little mention of the ability of states to push for progressive reforms that promote the rights of immigrants and racial minorities.[25]

Scholars have also noted how racial politics continue to shape the politics of federalism and poverty in the post–Civil Rights era. For example, Joe Soss, Richard Fording, and Sanford Schram explain that federal cuts to welfare programs, such as Aid to Families with Dependent Children (AFDC) and General Assistance programs, led to the reassertion of state control over welfare provision. Removing federal rules in 1996 that previously blocked states from preventing who has access to welfare, states are now able to employ a principle of "less eligible" to discipline the poor and to disproportionately target racial minorities.[26] Lisa Miller's *The Perils of Federalism* also highlights how the structure of federalism favors interest groups like the National Rifle Association and prevents national solutions to local crime in primarily Black and poorer neighborhoods, leaving them even more vulnerable to gun violence.[27]

In *Federalism and the Making of America*, David Brian Robertson argues that federalism creates a double battleground of: (1) whether the government should act and by what means; and (2) which level of government should have the power to act.[28] This has often benefited racial inequity, Robertson explains: "Federalism's powerful influence on American political development is most clear in the enduring political battles about race," from preserving slavery and Jim Crow–era racial order under the banner of states' rights to paving the road to racial disparities in employment, housing and education in modern times.[29] According to Robertson, states rights' have been invoked time and again to prevent national interference and to preserve particular kinds of racial orders or regimes. He depicts federalism as a weapon, one that White supremacists have successfully wielded to prevent and slow progress on racial equality and even reverse gains from the Civil Rights era. Federalism's effectiveness in these racial battles, he explains, has had the unintended consequence of legitimatizing the concept as a conservative weapon for other issues, including fights against environmentalism, abortion, and same-sex marriage.

Finally, Jamila Michener's *Fragmented Democracy: Medicaid, Federalism and Unequal Politics* advances a new line of critique against federalism and its harmful effects on racial minorities. Examining differential access to Medicaid, a program funded by both the federal government and the states, Michener argues that federalism acts as an institutional "purveyor of political inequality" that erodes political capacity among low-income people, especially Black and Latino minorities who are low-income, because they reside in states with restrictive Medicaid policies.[30] Thus, not only does federalism allow for massive inequalities in welfare provision, but it also produces significant disparities in political participation among low-income, minoritized residents. In addition to these indirect harmful effects of federalism on minority participation, states have placed even more direct constraints on voting by passing strict voter identification and felon disenfranchisement laws that have been particularly prevalent in states with expanding Black and Latino populations.[31]

Critiques of federalism are not confined to the Civil Rights era and its aftermath. Scholars have shown that federalist accommodations in the Progressive and New Deal eras strengthened racial conservatives and White supremacists in state and local governments. Eileen L. McDonough shows that progressive national reforms in the 1910s and 1920s emerged as welfare policy initiatives, but developed distinctly from civil rights issues, as states and local governments continued to erode the rights of racial minorities.[32] Similarly, Margaret Weir explains that, contrary to conventional wisdom, Progressive-era reforms did not bear a direct relationship to New Deal reforms. The Progressive movement ran parallel to the New Deal, but had different goals. Essential to the Progressive movement was a devolution in political participation, away from party control. Thus, the movement sought to advance structural reforms to constrain political participation and corruption, while opening pathways to new forms of democratic political participation at the state and local level. The New Deal, by contrast, sought to establish federal reforms that would empower and mobilize new national constituencies. According to Weir, "states, fundamentally, were not part of the New Deal regime."[33] As a result, "the [national] reform impulse that transformed the federal government in the 1930s had no enduring counterpart in the states" and soon lost steam.[34] With their own distinctive capacities and political logics, states thus set their own pathways of development, often focusing around exclusionary and racist policies.[35]

Patterns of racial exclusion at the state level can be seen across the literature on New Deal federalism. James T. Patterson shows that liberal New Deal reforms at the federal level developed alongside conservative movements at the state level.[36] The few states that aligned with federal reforms, including New York and Massachusetts, experienced successful and enduring reforms in the administration of relief and labor laws. Cybelle Fox reveals, however, that these Northeastern states' inclusive welfare policies only benefited White European immigrants. The devolution of New Deal relief administration to states also provided new tools for Southern and Southwestern states to exclude, target, and marginalize racial minorities, regardless of their citizenship or immigration status.[37] Similarly, Robert Lieberman's *Shifting the Color Line: Race and the American Welfare State* and Michael Brown's *Race, Money, and the Welfare State* highlight state-level dynamics that undercut the aspirations of federal reformers to provide broad social protection, in both North and South. Finally, Suzanne Mettler shows us that states used their police power after New Deal federal reforms to restrict social welfare to women and minorities through the 1960s, until federal judicial rulings began to narrow the scope of this power.[38]

From the New Deal reforms and beyond, much scholarship on federalism has shown how conservative state and local governments exploited the framework of federalism to create authoritarian enclaves, uphold White supremacy, and hinder the progress of federal reforms.[39] It is thus abundantly clear that federalism can significantly worsen racial and gender inequality, labor relations, social welfare, health, voting rights, and civil liberties.[40]

PROGRESSIVE FEDERALISM

The dark side of federalism offers a cautionary tale, but it is not the only story about states and the advancement of civil rights. As both the historical and contemporary records show, federalism can also provide structural opportunities for states and localities to advance progressive reforms. These developments have occurred both within states and across states, building momentum toward national reforms. As we discuss in Chapter 3, the expansion of women's suffrage was a state-led affair, starting in the Mountain West during the late 1800s and expanding rapidly across other Western states in the 1910s before snowballing into a federal constitutional amendment by the end of the decade. The right of same-sex marriage went through a different process of state diffusion – starting with state court decisions in Massachusetts (2004), California (2008), Connecticut (2008), and Iowa (2009) and followed by a series of state legislative expansions from 2009 through 2014 before finally becoming a nationally guaranteed right with the Supreme Court's 2015 decision in *Obergefell v. Hodges*.

These examples point to the possibility of progressive federalism, where states serve as political and policy laboratories that advance the rights and interests of disenfranchised populations. Our work on state citizenship thus builds on a growing body of scholarship on progressive federalism. A cornerstone of the progressive view of federalism is that states can move the country forward by advancing equality and justice, and particularly so when progress is stalled at the federal level. This flips the script of "states' rights," showing that federalism and devolution of authority are not exclusively a conservative rallying cry to block progressive reforms and enforce racially exclusive policies and norms. Advocates of progressive federalism also employ state's rights arguments but in a modified manner – arguing for federal laws and constitutional provisions that set a durable floor upon which states can build additional protections.

At the same time, most contemporary writing on progressive federalism has focused not on the expansion of rights but rather on the diffusion of social welfare spending and state regulatory policies such as smoking bans, environmental protections, and minimum wage increases. Indeed, in "The Promise of Progressive Federalism,"[41] one of the most influential contemporary pieces on the topic, Richard Freeman and Joel Rogers conceive of rights as being set primarily at the national level, with states being allowed to innovate and expand on federal standards primarily through regulation and the provision of benefits. The authors note that devolution of authority does not have to lead inevitably to a "race to the bottom" where exclusion is the norm, as the dark side of federalism might suggest. Instead, the federal government can set an important "floor" upon which states can build further benefits and protections, rather than a "ceiling" that limits state progress through the power of federal preemption. At the same time, most of the innovations that Freeman and Rogers envision involve pro-worker laws at the state level, including state minimum wages, welfare eligibility, and collective bargaining, although they also briefly consider state-led environmental regulations, progressive voting reforms, and expansions in health care access, reproductive rights, and antidiscrimination laws based on sexual orientation. More recently, Lenny Mendonca and Laura Tyson (2018) have argued more generally for progressive federalism as a strategy for encouraging social innovation that can scale up to the national level. Indeed, they use the analogy of the federal government as "a venture capitalist, soliciting, supporting, and scaling innovative solutions developed by state and local governments."[42]

Heather Gerken and others advance the concept of progressive federalism even further, calling it "the new nationalism" and reenvisioning the American state in its federalist form as beginning from the state to the federal level.[43] Gerken and colleagues collectively show that federalism is a tool for progress in national politics, national power, national policymaking, and national norms. They argue that progressive states can advance a "well-functioning *national* democracy" in many ways that go beyond policy diffusion from the bottom up to also include pushing the nation forward by overcoming political gridlock, cultivating discourse and agenda setting, and diffusing policy upward as a model for national reform.[44]

In other work, Gerken pushes against that long-held view of states' rights and federalism as being intrinsically opposed to progressive reforms. The federal government, she explains, "has plenty of power to protect racial minorities and other groups," but to do so requires "political will."[45] Viewing states' role in federalism as progressive, Gerken explains, "upends conventional thinking that the federal government is the backstop for maintaining progressive policy."[46] According to this view, local and state politics do not undermine national policies – rather, they fuel national reforms. Moreover, as Gerken explains, viewing progressive change from the bottom up centers the analysis on racial minorities, who may now have greater access to political power in local and state government than at the national level. Similarly, Jessica Bulman-Pozen argues that federalism provides a "durable and robust scaffolding" for political parties to compete, with national parties using state and local jurisdictions to wage partisan fights.[47]

Progressive federalism thus paints the interconnection between local, state, and national government differently than what we see from the conservative view of federalism. States become core parts of the nationalist vision rather than serving as barriers to it. States seek to integrate rather than divide the nation state. As Gerken explains: "Federalism-all-the-way-down is not your father's federalism. It cannot be invoked to shield local discrimination from national interference, but it may play a role in promoting equality .... [It] can provide a structural means for achieving goals traditionally associated with right-protecting amendments like the First and Fourteenth."[48]

Finally, progressive federalism can be equally powerful as a form of state resistance to restrictive national developments. Progressive state governments can provide rights and protections to citizens and noncitizens that exceed the federal floor, temporarily anchoring the country to progressive values and ideals during times of restrictive national regimes. Decades prior to the contemporary concept of progressive federalism, Robert Cover advanced a state-centric concept of "combative federalism" to capture federalism dynamics where states and localities check federal power by refusing to cooperate in the administration of federal programs.[49] In their recent collaboration, Jessica Bulman-Pozen and Heather Gerken advance a similar concept of "uncooperative federalism" to capture how states use regulatory power conferred by the federal government to then resist federal policy on issues of immigration, health, and education.[50] Lastly, Peter Markowitz contributes to Freeman and Rogers' idea that states are not preempted from being able to exceed an established federal floor on rights and protections, speaking more directly to the contemporary roles of states in advancing immigrant rights.[51] The current trend in progressive federalism thus runs counter to dominant historical narrative of federalism as one that empowers states and localities to block national progress and entrench regressive racial orders. Perhaps not coincidentally, these calls for progressive federalism have grown louder with conservatives in charge of the White House, one or both houses of Congress, and the US Supreme Court.

Our work on state citizenship builds on this growing scholarship on progressive federalism while still acknowledging the regressive and reinforcing[52] forms that federalism can take. We show that, regardless of what policies are pushed federally or how national citizenship is defined, there is still room for states and localities to build distinctive forms of state citizenship. We acknowledge that regressive state policies can conflict with national developments in citizenship, and that insufficient enforcement of the Fourteenth Amendment can enable regressive regimes even today. These sorts of tensions and complementary relations, between state and national paths of political development, are an inherent feature of federalism, and they lead to distinctive and parallel forms of national and state citizenship.

WHY STATE CITIZENSHIP (AND NOT LOCAL CITIZENSHIP)?

While federalism involves the interplay between various levels of government – including local, state, and national – our book focuses on citizenship at the state level and not the local level, for several reasons. First, it is important to recognize that the US Constitution gives significant powers to states, from provisions such as the Tenth Amendment, which reserves to "the State or the people" those powers that are "not delegated to the United States by the Constitution, nor prohibited by it to the States," to designing institutions such as the US Senate that put states on equal footing. No such provisions exist for localities in the US Constitution. State authority is rooted in the origin of American federalism, and it changes as the Supreme Court, Presidency, Congress, and states continually attempt to redefine the balance of power between federal government and states in the provision of rights.[53] Importantly, the Founders of the US Constitution were concerned with placing too much power into federal hands, and they saw states – not local governments – as the primary counterweight to federal power. Not only did they wish to avoid a strong central government that could restore a British-style monarchy, many Founders also wanted to preserve state control over slavery in the South.[54]

State authority was not only guaranteed through the Constitution: it was also enabled through actions and decisions by the president, the Supreme Court, and Congress. Throughout much of the nineteenth century, the federal government's hands-off approach to regulating slavery, immigration, and social welfare placed states in control, not only in defining the contours of state citizenship but also in denying national citizenship to Blacks. The US Constitution gave Congress the power to establish a "uniform Rule of Naturalization," which it first passed in 1790 to include free white persons living in the United States for more than two years. By contrast, the US Constitution and federal law were silent on the national citizenship rights of Black persons. Moreover, states held sovereign power over granting their own forms of state citizenship, even to non–federal citizens.[55] National developments on citizenship in the antebellum period emerged in reaction to state tensions over slavery and freedom. Most notably, in *Dred Scott v. Sanford* (1857), the Supreme Court denied that any Black person, enslaved or free, could be recognized as a national citizen. Chief Justice Taney stated: "[W]e must not confound the rights of citizenship which a state may confer within its own limits and the rights of citizenship as a member of the Union."[56] While the Taney court excluded Blacks from national citizenship, it recognized the constitutional legitimacy and autonomy of states to expand or contract state citizenship rights to Blacks.

The passage of the Fourteenth Amendment following the Civil War limited the power of states to infringe on the rights of individuals. However, this was largely a matter of principle rather than practice, as the Supreme Court continued to give wide berth to Southern states to infringe on the civil rights of Blacks through the legal doctrine of "separate but equal." Supreme Court jurisprudence after the end of Reconstruction and the weakness of the Republican Party in the South further strengthened the ability of states to restrict voting rights.[57] It took nearly a century after the Civil War for court decisions, social movement activity, and Congressional action to strengthen the hand of the federal government vis-à-vis states in the provision and guarantee of civil rights. At the same time, states have not receded from the scene with respect to civil rights. As the extensive literature on federalism in the post–Civil Rights era has shown, states remain significant actors in the provision and restriction of rights and benefits to low-income groups and communities of color.[58]

While the Constitution and Courts have provided varying leeway to states vis-à-vis the federal government with respect to citizenship rights, they have consistently given state governments near-total authority over the actions of local governments. States may recognize the need to delegate authority to local governments to address local concerns, needs, and objectives. However, the power of local government is not inherent. Thus, for example, Dillon's rule makes clear that local governments are neither equal nor independent from state government. Rather, they are political subdivisions of the state (often referred to as "creatures of the state"). Iowa Supreme Court Justice John Dillon helped establish the doctrine of state sovereignty over local governments when he ruled in 1868 that "[m]unicipal corporations owe their origin to, and derive their powers and rights wholly from, the [state] legislature. It breathes into them the breath of life, without which they cannot exist. As it creates, so may it destroy. If it may destroy, it may abridge and control."[59] This doctrine was later upheld by the United States Supreme Court in *Hunter v. Pittsburgh* (1907)[60] and was articulated perhaps most clearly in a 1982 anti-trust case where the Court declared:

Ours is a "*dual* system of government," ... which has no place for sovereign cities. As this Court stated long ago, all sovereign authority "within the geographical limits of the United States" resides either with "the Government of the United States, or [with] the States of the Union. *There exist within the broad domain of sovereignty but these two.* There may be cities, counties, and other organized bodies with limited legislative functions, but they are all derived from, or exist in, subordination to one or the other of these."[61]

While we typically think of the federal government as having supreme power on immigration, the last two decades have seen a significant uptick in state regulations, including those that preempt local policies on immigration. On the pro-immigrant side, California has passed laws that prevent localities from mandating businesses to comply with the E-Verify system of employment verification. It has also passed legislation banning local ordinances that require landlords to check on the immigration status of their tenants (see Chapter 5). State preemption of local policies can also be restrictive in nature, however, as several states, including Mississippi, North Carolina, South Carolina, and Georgia, have enacted laws that compel local jurisdictions to cooperate with federal immigration enforcement.[62] More recently, in May 2017, Texas passed a law, SB 4, that prohibited local sanctuary policies and authorized law enforcement to check on the legal status of anyone they arrest. It also made local officials who refuse to aid in federal immigration enforcement requests criminally liable and subject to removal from office. Soon after SB 4 passed, US District Judge Orlando Garcia held an injunction on key parts of the law, pending a decision by the Fifth Circuit Court of Appeals. On March 13, 2018, however, the appeals court largely upheld the state law,[63] including its provisions banning local governments from adopting noncooperation policies on immigration enforcement and others imposing fines, jail time, and removal from office for local officials who violate any part of the law.[64]

Finally, states in recent years have also played a significant role in shaping voting rights. While constitutional and federal protections on voting provide a minimum baseline of rights, states can expand or contract access through their own set of voting and identification laws. In 2004, Arizona passed Proposition 200, the "Arizona Taxpayer and Citizen Protection Act," changing voter registration procedures to require residents to prove US citizenship prior to registering to vote and requiring state and local agencies to verify proof of immigration status to provide access to public benefits. In *Arizona v. Inter Tribal Council of Arizona, Inc* (2013), the Supreme Court ruled that Prop 200's voter requirement was preempted by federal law on voter registration. However, it also left intact the law's restrictions on state public benefits and left open the door for citizenship identification requirements for state elections, which Arizona and Kansas subsequently implemented.[65] On the progressive side of state citizenship, states are permitted to develop state driver's licenses that do not meet federal security requirements, even as they are mandated to comply with the federal REAL ID Act in order for licenses to be eligible for domestic travel verification. Similarly, despite federal mandates that prohibit the employment of unauthorized immigrants, states have the power to grant business licenses and professional licenses to residents regardless of their immigration status.

We will have a lot more to say in future chapters about what states can do with respect to expanding or contracting citizenship rights. For now, it is abundantly clear that states have considerable authority over the provision of rights to their residents, including the power to overrule local decisions that expand or contract citizenship rights. To be clear, we are not making a normative claim that states *should* have the ability to preempt local citizenship rights or that this kind of state preemption is necessarily good. Our claim is merely a descriptive one that captures essential features of American federalism, with states preserving the ability to preempt local policies on citizenship rights. Indeed, in many cases, the exercise of preemptive authority of states may actually reflect the successful spread of local efforts to expand citizenship rights, such in the case of women's voting rights (Chapter 3), Black civil rights in the antebellum North (Chapter 4), and immigrant rights in California and elsewhere (Chapter 5 and 6).

OUR APPROACH TO THE STUDY OF STATE CITIZENSHIP

State authority exists in complex arrangements that are not easily captured by individual-level processes. We use a historical institutional approach to the study of state regimes of citizenship, in line with the broad analytic tradition of

American Political Development (APD). This tradition in political science focuses on the development and transformation of political orders, defined loosely as the political arrangement of institutions, policies, and groups, that span long periods of time. It provides a way to capture issues and institutions evolving across several dimensions, over time, and helps to understand and explain "durable shifts in governing authority."[66] APD originated as a movement to develop stronger analytical tools for understanding the American state as a federated and constitutive arrangement of institutions, laws, parties, actors, and social movements. Prior conceptions of strong and weak nation-states in the state-building scholarship privileged Max Weber's concepts of centralization and professional bureaucracy, and inappropriately applied them to the American context. By contrast, APD places federalism front and center of American state-building and has grown into an important subfield for explaining the complexities in the political development of race, power, and citizenship.

We build from the well-established tradition of APD scholarship, where political development is not assumed to be linear and federalism is not assumed to be static. As Anna Law notes, state control over slavery also extended to immigration control, which helps explain why the federal government avoided playing a more active role in immigration policy prior to the Civil War.[67] Similarly, Richard Valelly shows why it took two separate Reconstructions – one after the Civil War and one a century later – before Blacks meaningfully achieved voting rights.[68] Despite the landmark reforms of the 1960s, however, civil rights and Black suffrage remain open to erosion and backsliding. Indeed, some scholars have referred to the contemporary period as a "second nadir" of Black rights, similar to the erosion of rights under Jim Crow,[69] while others have suggested that we are seeing the early stirrings of a third Reconstruction, with social movements mobilizing against the removal of voter protections for racial minorities following the US Supreme Court decision in *Shelby County v. Holder* (2013).[70]

APD scholars have long argued that race is intimately and inextricably connected to American state-building, citizenship, and inequality.[71] As Desmond King and Rogers Smith have noted, the American state has multiple racial orders, and national, state and local governments act as an oppressor and protector of racial equality in different periods of history.[72] Richard Valelly shows how LGBT politics is a contingent and historically evolving construct – as he explains, "[i]t is not, consequently, rooted in an unchanging straight/gay binary."[73] Scholarship in American Political Development thus captures both federalism dynamics and citizenship dynamics of expanding and contracting rights of different groups throughout American history, all while examining the role of courts, parties, social movements, presidents, and Congress in passing legislation and implementing them.[74] We employ the APD approach to explain the historical development of state citizenship in a federalist framework.

Prior to any analysis of state citizenship, however, it is important to be clear about our concepts and indicators – and especially so for a field that is still in relative infancy. Scholars of federated citizenship have adapted concepts from national citizenship to state and local policies, often on an individual and ad hoc basis, without first considering fundamental questions related to concept formation. We provide new answers by turning to the well-developed scholarship on concept formation found in comparative politics and the literature on democratization, including the seminal works of Giovanni Sartori, John Gerring, and David Collier. We draw inspiration from the democracy literature to more systematically assess how we can best draw external distinctions between citizenship and other forms of membership, internal distinctions for different types of citizenship, and intersections between citizenship and federalism. We use this conceptual framework to consider the full range of state citizenship policies in the United States. Specifically, we map distinctive periods in the historical development of state citizenship regimes, from the antebellum period to the Reconstruction and Jim Crow eras to the Civil Rights period and its partial unraveling. We then apply our framework of federated citizenship to provide a deeper and more precise understanding of Black civil rights and immigrant rights in the United States, with federalism conflict and accommodation at its core. We end with some consideration of future implications for progressive state citizenship, based on what is constitutionally permissible and what is politically likely given current trends in federal–state conflicts.

Our analysis proceeds as follows: in Chapter 2, we outline the history of citizenship as a political concept, with important variations between republican and liberal traditions from Greece and Rome to the present day. Despite this rich variation, the dominant view of citizenship today is still something that emerged from the period of nation-state–building in the nineteenth century: citizenship is still primarily seen as nationally provided and tied inextricably to legal status. This exclusive and unidimensional view of citizenship remains dominant even as urban scholars challenge its claims of exclusivity and immigration scholars challenge its singular focus on legal status. We argue that these critiques are limited, in part, because they move away from a rights-based framework and run the risk of conceptual stretching by adding such dimensions as identities, feelings of belonging, and the exercise of political power. We believe it is possible to counter the dominant, rights-based model of national citizenship without falling into the trap of conceptual stretching.

We make a fresh start in the systematic conceptualization of citizenship, drawing on the rich theoretical tradition of concept formation in the comparative study of democratic politics. The framework we advance takes apart "legal status" as a national litmus test, showing that legal status is not the gateway to rights as is often assumed. In its place, we develop a parallel set of rights along five key dimensions, with the provision of those rights varying by jurisdiction – federal, state, and local. We also lay out important differences between *progressive citizenship*, where states expand rights beyond those provided at the national level; *regressive citizenship*, where states restrict or erode rights provided at the national level; and *reinforcing citizenship*, where states reinforce or mirror federal rules on rights provision. Finally, we move from concept formation to the development of indicators for state citizenship regimes, something that becomes very important in subsequent chapters as we analyze the evolution of citizenship across states and over time.

While Chapter 2 lays out a general framework for reimagining citizenship in a federated polity, Chapter 3 focuses on the particular case of the United States and the development of national citizenship and state citizenship over time. Following the lead of other works in American history and political development, we lay out three major periods in federated citizenship that follow significant developments in the US Constitution and federal law: the *Framers' period*, stretching from the Articles of Confederation and the founding constitution through sectionalism and the Civil War; the *Reconstruction period*, starting with the major constitutional amendments that set the stage for citizenship rights guarantees, followed by the establishment and subsequent collapse of national control ensuring the provision of those rights; and the *Civil Rights period*, starting with the Twenty-Fourth Amendment and the Civil Rights Act of 1964, the Voting Rights Act of 1965, the Immigration and Nationality Act of 1965, the Fair Housing Act of 1968, and subsequent extensions and contractions in citizenship rights provided at the national and state levels along lines of race, gender, immigrant status, and sexual orientation. For each historical period, we outline the *constitutional opportunities* that emerge from amendment activity and court interpretation, the *legislative actions* pushed by political parties and social movements to take advantage of those opportunities and constraints, and the *executive actions* of national and state governments to enforce citizenship protections.

With the American constitutional and legal framework as a backdrop, the rest of this book dives deeper into the political histories of African Americans and immigrants, applying our multidimensional framework to the provision of progressive, regressive, and reinforcing state citizenship over time. Chapter 4 begins with a stark reminder that Blacks had no access to national citizenship rights in the antebellum period, even though there were more than 435,000 free Blacks living in the United States at the time of the Supreme Court's 1857 *Dred Scott* ruling. The Framers' constitution had accommodated the interests and demands of slaveholding states at the time of ratification and thus gave much greater power to states than the federal government in setting citizenship rights. The constitutional framework structuring Black citizenship changed significantly after the Civil War, as new forms of state citizenship emerged against the backdrop of Reconstruction and decades of Jim Crow, followed by rapid changes in the Civil Rights period that continues until today. Throughout this chapter, we train our focus on the role of the Constitution and courts in defining and constraining the citizenship rights of Blacks, as well as the role of parties and social movement actors in propelling legislative action toward rights expansion and contraction.

Next, Chapter 5 turns to California, to carefully assess where it currently stands with respect to state citizenship and to situate its present configuration in a sweep of the state's history. As we show, California pioneered and championed anti-Chinese and anti-immigrant legislation from its founding through the late 1990s, and only recently began to move toward a more pro-immigrant stance. We then explore key milestones in immigrant rights over the past decade and pinpoint 2015 as the year when progressive state citizenship got consolidated. Finally, we trace pivotal factors that incubated and enabled the development of progressive state citizenship in California, including voter backlash against racial propositions, partisan shifts in the state legislature, and the growing strength of social movement actors aided by long-term investment strategies by private foundations.

While certain developments in federalism were necessary conditions for California's progress on state citizenship, they were by no means sufficient. In Chapter 6, we draw attention to comparisons between California and other states with respect to their provision of immigrant citizenship rights. We start with the border dividing California and Arizona, two states that lie on opposite ends of the spectrum on progressive and regressive state citizenship, respectively. And yet, Arizona is not the only exclusionary state on immigrant rights today. Indeed, our analysis reveals that Alabama is about as exclusionary as Arizona, and states like Georgia and Tennessee are not too far behind. In this chapter, we situate various states along a continuum from the most inclusionary to the most exclusionary with respect to each of our five dimensions of citizenship rights. We also conduct a fifty-state statistical analysis to identify the reasons why some states have proceeded farther than others in the development of progressive state citizenship.

Finally, in Chapter 7, we look more deeply into the dynamics that produce advancements in progressive state citizenship, with examples from both the historical and contemporary periods. Using the Advocacy Coalition Framework (ACF) of policy change, we argue that some of the most notable legislative advancements in progressive state citizenship have occurred because of the intersection of two key factors: state advocacy coalitions that unite strong social movement actors and legislative champions, as well as policy openings generated by federalism tensions. We illustrate our argument using three examples: the two-decade push for driver's licenses in New York, the timing and spread of immigration sanctuary laws since 2005, and a historical examination of Black state citizenship in the antebellum North. After reviewing these examples, we end our book by offering thoughts on the future of citizenship rights in a politically polarized United States.

2

Citizenship in a Federated Framework

Since the early 2000s, several states have passed immigrant integration policies, on matters ranging from in-state tuition and financial aid to undocumented students, expanded health benefits, and access to driver's licenses. Despite federal plenary power over immigration law in the United States, it is clear that states and localities can facilitate, or restrict, the lives of their undocumented immigrant residents, beyond what is prescribed under federal law.[1] National and state policies present some stark contrasts with respect to unauthorized immigrants. At the federal level, these individuals lack the legal right to remain in the United States and often live in perpetual fear of deportation. At the same time, several states welcome these same individuals, granting them social, economic, and political opportunities that are routinely granted to US citizens or legal permanent residents. States that engage in progressive policymaking have not only mitigated the enforcement of federal immigration law; they have also constructed more inclusive models of political membership. What is emerging today in the United States, we argue, is the construction of a type of state citizenship that exists alongside national citizenship, with potential for harmonious coexistence as well as conflict.

In order to understand state citizenship, we first need to address the question *what is citizenship?* History offers many forms of citizenship.[2] To grasp how the concept has developed, this chapter compares the original city-state construction of citizenship in ancient Greece and Rome to modern constructions of the nation-state after the American and French Revolutions. We demonstrate that state-building traditions from Max Weber to Charles Tilly and Rogers Brubaker have led to an uncritical and problematic acceptance of citizenship as an exclusively national concept, with legal status sharply demarcating citizen from noncitizen. This exclusive and unidimensional view remains dominant in the "common sense" understanding of citizenship today, even as urban scholars challenge its claims of exclusivity and immigration scholars challenge its singular focus on legal status.

As we argue in this chapter, national citizenship remains predominant because the alternatives leave unchallenged some of the core claims regarding rights and offer in their place a fuzzier set of categories. Studies of multidimensional citizenship, for example, tend to combine different types of concepts like *rights*, which are provided by government institutions, with others concepts like *political behavior*, such as acts of political participation, and *political attitudes*, such as sense of belonging. Similarly, studies of urban citizenship have explored rights alongside concepts and processes such as local representation, empowerment, sense of belonging, and "effective citizenship." In addition, these studies pay insufficient attention to structures and dynamics of federalism that include accommodation as well as conflict.

We believe it is possible to counter the dominant model of national citizenship without falling into the trap of conceptual fuzziness. After reviewing the contemporary literature on urban citizenship and multidimensional citizenship, we offer a conceptual framework that incorporates these two perspectives while still retaining a focus on rights as a foundational basis. Importantly, this allows us to offer a framework of state citizenship that can coexist with traditional understandings of national citizenship without being dismissed as fanciful or wishful thinking. The framework we advance takes apart "legal status" as a national litmus test, showing that legal status is not the gateway to rights as is often assumed. In its place, we develop a parallel set of rights alongside five key dimensions, with the provision of those rights varying by jurisdiction (federal, state, and local). We also provide indicators of state citizenship for each of these five dimensions, something that becomes very important in future chapters as we analyze the evolution of citizenship across states and over time.

THE CONSOLIDATION OF NATIONAL CITIZENSHIP

For over a century, we have been accustomed to thinking of citizenship as exclusive to the nation-state. Despite the growth of supranational governing structures such as the United Nations and the European Union, or the decentralization of power in places like Spain, Canada, and the United Kingdom, the dominant conception of citizenship today is still fixated on rights granted by national-level governments. Importantly, citizenship is largely viewed as exclusive *within* nation-states, even if it may not be exclusive *across* nation-states. For example, several countries allow for residents to be "dual citizens," meaning that they are allowed to hold legal status and documents that permit them access to political, social, and economic rights in more than one country. In this sense, citizenship is not exclusive across nation-states. At the same time, these same countries do not formally acknowledge citizenship from subfederal jurisdictions such as states, provinces, or cities. This makes citizenship exclusive within the nation-state.

In addition to being seen as an exclusively national phenomenon, the dominant view of citizenship among many scholars and practitioners is also largely binary: either one is a citizen or one is not, with no room in the middle for partial forms of citizenship. In addition, this binary view of citizenship is centrally tied to one dimension: legal status. As we elaborate, traditional scholarship on citizenship views legal status as the key that unlocks various protections, rights, and benefits that broadly and collectively constitute citizenship. In the United States, for example, national citizenship is automatically granted to all persons born inside the country through the principle of *jus soli*, meaning "right of soil" or birthright citizenship. It is also granted to children born abroad to American parents through the principle of *jus sanguinis*, or "right of blood," and to naturalized immigrants through rules set by the federal government. Anyone else residing in the country – such as a tourist, a student, an unauthorized immigrant, or a legal permanent resident – lacks access to the full complement of economic, social, and political rights that include voting, running for political office, and obtaining certain types of public sector jobs.

As we argue in this chapter, this binary, unidimensional, and exclusively national view of citizenship is deeply flawed. It does injustice to the etymological and historical roots of the concept, which grew out of cities in ancient Greece and Rome and continued to hold sway through the Middle Ages in Europe and through the nineteenth century in many other parts of the world. The dominant view of citizenship-as-legal-status also fails to recognize the multiple dimensions of citizenship that emerge from liberal, republican, and ascriptive traditions in political philosophy. We will consider each of these limitations in greater detail as we outline a brief history of the development of citizenship from ancient Greece to the contemporary period.

Political theorists generally pinpoint the origins of citizenship in ancient Greece, where the city of Athens set up the first space for residents to become civically engaged in politics, all while adhering to basic principles of political equality and rule of law among those who participated. As Aristotle noted, Athenian citizenship emerged as a de facto political identity belonging only to city patriarchs who participated in politics, and not formally granted as a legal status based on birth or residence.[3] Access to participation was the key step separating new Athenian citizens from city residents. No formal litmus test defined who qualified for citizenship; instead, Athenian citizenship was rooted in a shared cultural understanding of what it means to be a citizen and who was deserving of it. By contrast, Roman city-states developed a basis for citizenship rooted in legal status. As the historian J. G. A. Pocock explained, Roman cities made "citizen" into a legal term, which legally defined a person's relation to the state as being "free to act by law, free to ask and expect the law's protection, a citizen of such and such a legal community, of such and such a legal standing in that community."[4] Rainer Bauböck similarly notes that citizenship was a status provided under Roman law, rather than an attachment based on participation according to Athenian tradition.[5] Importantly, the Roman model considered property and material possessions to be the key factors allowing entry into the legal status of citizen, a requirement that was lacking in the Athenian model.

Despite their differences on who is a citizen – as a political being or as a person with legal rights – Athens and Rome set the philosophical foundations for republican and liberal traditions, respectively, that shape our contemporary understandings of citizenship. Thus, for example, the republican tradition has grown to emphasize not only participatory acts such as voting but also civic virtues such as obeying laws and being informed and engaged in public affairs.[6] Meanwhile, the liberal tradition of citizenship has grown to include John Locke's notion of consent and contracts in the *Second Treatise* (1680), where the state provides citizens with legal access to privileges and protections while at the same time obligating citizens to follow laws, pay taxes, and serve in the military.[7] Importantly, neither the republican nor the liberal tradition specifies the level of statehood that is capable of providing citizenship. Each focuses instead on the question of what connects states to citizens in a meaningful way and, in particular, what differentiates citizens from residents and noncitizens. Athenian and Roman notions of citizenship point to citizens' access to political participation or their rights to full legal protection, respectively, as key factors that differentiate citizens from other types of individuals residing in the territory.

How, then, did citizenship become narrowly identified with national government, as a "unitary and homogenous" legal status[8] granted by a sovereign state? In order to answer that question, we need to understand more generally the rise of the nation-state as a dominant political formation. After Athens and Rome, European feudalism brought an end to citizenship, as residents became the subjects of monarchs and lords with no legal rights or political voice. City-states reemerged in Europe's Renaissance period and began to combine Athenian and Roman notions of citizenship with modern characteristics of military service. What soon became dominant, however, was the expansive power of particular monarchs who were successful in exerting control and securing loyalty over progressively larger swaths of territory. As Max Weber famously noted in *Politics as a Vocation*,

the modern state is a compulsory association which organizes domination. It has been successful in seeking to monopolize the legitimate use of physical force as a means of domination within a territory. To this end the state has combined the material means of organization in the hands of its leaders, and it has expropriated all autonomous functionaries of estates who formerly controlled these means in their own right. The state has taken their positions and now stands in the top place.[9]

Importantly, in Weber's framework, legitimacy plays as important a role in the rise of the modern state and modern citizenship as does its administrative strength and military might.[10]

More recent articulations of citizenship draw heavily on Max Weber's framework of equating modern political citizenship as membership in national states, with varying emphases. Charles Tilly's conceptualization of citizenship is centrally tied to his model of state formation as rooted in the war-making capacities of expansionary states. Most notably, Tilly argued in his 1975 book *The Formation of National States in Western Europe* that "[w]ar made the state, and the state made war."[11] According to Tilly, war-making was important not only because it allowed the sovereign to eliminate rivals within a territory but also because "the building of an effective military machine imposed a heavy burden on the population involved: taxes, conscription, requisitions, and more. The very act of building an effective military machine produced arrangements which could deliver resources to the government for other purposes."[12] In *Coercion, Capital and European States* (1992), Tilly expands on this argument, noting that citizenship rights "began first over the means of war, and then over enforceable claims outside of the area of war, and thereby helped to enlarge the obligations of states to their citizens."[13] Finally, in his 1996 *Citizenship, Identity, and Social History*, Tilly develops the concept of citizenship further, arguing that it is "a certain kind of tie: *a continuing series of transactions between persons and agents of a given state in which each has enforceable rights and obligations uniquely by virtue of (1) the person's membership in an exclusive category, the native-born plus the naturalized and (2) the agent's relation to the state rather than any other authority the agent may enjoy.*"[14] Citizenship can range from "thin" to "thick" based on the level of "transactions, rights and obligations sustained by state agents and people living under their [national] jurisdiction."[15] Thus, according to Tilly, modern citizenship is centrally tied to the specific logic and dynamics that established national states as the dominant political unit.

Rogers Brubaker writes of citizenship in a similar vein, although for him welfare state provision – not war-making – is paramount in the establishment of national citizenship. He deepens the identification of citizenship with national statehood by tying it to processes of what he calls "social closure," with dimensions that are both international (territorial closure) and domestic (domestic closure). First, Brubaker notes that the international system is, in reality, an interstate system, and "citizenship is an international filing system, a mechanism for allocating persons to states ... In a world divided among exhaustive and mutually exclusive jurisdictions of sovereign states, it is axiomatic that every person ought to have a citizenship, that everyone ought to belong to one state or another."[16] At the same time, the allocation of citizenship is not merely an administrative convenience. According to Brubaker, territorial closure became essential in an era where states were expected to provide relief for poor residents and had to devise rules to coordinate who they could expel from their territory. And they did so "following two basic principles: a state could expel into the territory of another state only a person belonging to that state; and a state was obliged to admit to its territory its own members.

This made it urgent to specify who belonged to the state."[17] Even today, citizenship becomes essential in differentiating those who are able to remain unconditionally within a state from those whose ability to remain is subject to state discretion.

In addition to interstate dynamics, domestic politics also made it important to demarcate insiders and outsiders, particularly with the advent of nationalism. Indeed, Brubaker notes that it is now taken for granted that the goal of national states is "to express the will and further the interests of distinctive and bounded nations," which in turn often entails excluding nonnationals from valued goods such as the franchise, participation in costly social programs, and employment in public administration.[18] Thus, citizenship is a form of social closure that becomes essential to preserving not only the territorial integrity of a state in a coordination game with other countries but also the social integrity of the national state by demarcating clear boundaries between insiders and outsiders within each territorial state.

Like Brubaker, Jonathan Torpey employs Max Weber's concept of (national) states as monopolizing the legitimate use of force in a territorial jurisdiction, adding a critical dimension of control over free movement. The creation and provision of international passports, Torpey argues, enabled nation states to monopolize control over the movement of people within borders and across them, as well as to identify and differentiate citizens from residents and noncitizens for purposes other than border enforcement.[19] The French Revolution threatened the security of the French state, sparking its need to begin controlling the movement of foreigners across its borders and to build its military through conscription. The passport system addressed both of these fundamental needs of building a nation-state, according to Torpey, and facilitated the development of stable national identities in France. While Torpey's focus on passports was novel, the idea that control over free movement is essential to nation-states is not new. Writing on state formation much earlier, Stein Rokkan also argued that the capacity to regulate "the movement of men, commodities, and ideas" is fundamental to the project of building a nation-state.[20]

Recent scholars in comparative politics have challenged Brubaker's classic treatment of France and Germany's divergent historical pathways, pointing to convergence in national citizenship policies in Europe and elsewhere. Yet, even these critiques tend to reaffirm national citizenship as the dominant concept today, with comparative scholars noting that nation-states have actually gained control over citizenship by adding civic integration requirements and tests (on language proficiency and cultural, political, and legal knowledge) to their naturalization process. Sarah Goodman Wallace's work, for example, shows that these integration policies provide a formal process for national identity formation to be linked to the binary process of providing legal status. She also shows that cross-national variation is rooted, in part, in how and to whom nation-states have historically granted citizenship.[21] These emerging trends prompt Goodman to warn "against faddish postnational, supranational and transnational predictions" on the next evolutionary step for citizenship, as a replacement of national citizenship.[22] Goodman builds from a rich comparative politics scholarship that unpacks legal status into different types of naturalization policy but still uses the binary of legal status as the key reference point of comparison in national citizenship.[23] Taken together, comparative work on citizenship in contemporary Europe is largely silent on federated citizenship within nation states, and on multidimensional rights beyond the provision of legal status.[24]

Many legal scholars draw similarly rigid boundaries around the nation-state, treating citizenship as nationally exclusive and tied intimately to legal status. Peter Schuck, for example, argues that citizenship is defined not only by what it includes but also by those it excludes.[25] On the one hand, Schuck's legal scholarship on immigration law employs a federalist view of a strong nation-state, emphasizing that states and localities ought to have larger roles in "employment-based admissions, immigration enforcement, and employer sanctions, to strengthen federal immigration policy."[26] At the same time, these states and localities act primarily to enforce national citizenship. As Schuck explains, the "'federalist default' arrangement is for federal programs to rely on state and local involvement, including in the enforcement of federally promulgated rules."[27] When paired with his normative arguments about the value of US citizenship and rights, Schuck sees state and local governments as enabling and servicing an exclusionary national regime of citizenship.

Peter Spiro, a coauthor on many works with Schuck, argues that there has been a general devaluation of national citizenship because its distinctive privileges, obligations, values, and attachments have been diluted by membership rules (*jus soli,* or birthright citizenship), low thresholds for naturalization, toleration of plural nationality, procedural due process and equal protection rights for immigrants, international law, and international human rights norms.[28] While national citizenship retains some measure of prestige, Spiro's central claim is that globalization has led to a dilution of the value of citizenship: "the boundaries of human community transcend territorial ones, in a way that citizenship cannot process."[29] Similar to Schuck's stance on immigration federalism, Spiro argues that states should be able to function as "demi-sovereigns" to restrict the rights of immigrants, and thereby preserving exclusionary citizenship's value, until Congress expressly preempts these laws.[30]

Several legal scholars have pushed back against Schuck and Spiro's view of immigration federalism for its exclusionary bent and its overly narrow focus on plenary powers. Hiroshi Motomura and Linda Bosniak explore immigrants' rights that already exist in federal, state, and local laws and make broader claims for why these rights are essential to welcoming immigrants as "Americans in waiting." Although these arguments vary significantly from the restrictive views of citizenship by Schuck and Spiro, they nevertheless reinforce the notion of national citizenship as the ideal or archetype, with formal citizenship and legal status serving as a gateway to a full range of rights.[31]

Taken together, the scholarship on state formation has led to a common set of understandings regarding the nature of modern citizenship, with three hallmark features: as exclusive, as a gateway to various rights, and as starkly binary. First, citizenship is exclusive to national governments, with state and local forms of citizenship rendered irrelevant with the rise and consolidation of the modern national state. The view of citizenship as exclusive is not merely historical. Contemporary scholars in this tradition note that nation-states still have a monopoly over the ability to define and control citizenship, with documents such as passports, birth certificates, and naturalization certificates serving as important markers of legal access and identification. Citizenship is also seen as a unidimensional gateway, as rules concerning birthright citizenship and naturalization prove to be authoritative and determinative to providing individuals with access to a comprehensive set of political, social, and legal rights (see Figure 2.1).

Indeed, the consequences of not possessing citizenship can be significant. Without the same legal status as citizens, other residents such as temporary authorized migrants, legal permanent residents, and unauthorized immigrants do not have access to the same complement of political, social, and legal rights. Thus, for example, noncitizens can be prevented from voting, from entering the country without a visa, and from entering certain types of occupations or running for political office. Noncitizens lack access to full legal rights and protection from deportation, which also applies to legal permanent residents convicted of nonviolent crimes.[32] Finally, according to this tradition, citizenship is binary. There are no degrees of citizenship; either one is a citizen or one is not. And the determination of citizenship usually involves litmus tests such as certificates of birth, naturalization, and parentage to determine eligibility.

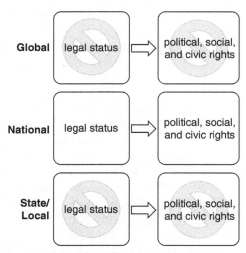

FIGURE 2.1 Citizenship as binary, unidimensional, and exclusively national

Despite its continued dominance among scholars and practitioners alike, the national model of citizenship has faced strong challenges to its hallmark features of exclusivity and unidimensionality. Scholars of urban politics, either in the American context or writing with respect to global cities, have challenged the traditional model and its claims to national exclusivity. Similarly, immigration scholars have challenged the unidimensional view of citizenship, where legal status lords over all other dimensions of citizenship by purportedly controlling access to a variety of political, social, legal, and economic rights. In the following sections, we elaborate on each of these challenges to national citizenship, which in turn provide the foundation for our novel framework of federated and multidimensional citizenship.

AN EMERGING LITERATURE ON URBAN CITIZENSHIP

Scholars of urban politics and local immigrant incorporation have challenged the conventional model of citizenship over its claims of national exclusivity. Like traditions from early Athens and Rome, local concepts of citizenship today continue to develop from republican and liberal traditions, and with a focus on local political projects, processes, and policies instead of national ones. Thus, for example, urban scholar Michael Fortner develops the concept of "effective citizenship," emphasizing city-level autonomy and governmental ties to the local community and particularly the capacity of local actors to work together to achieve collective goals. In the tradition of Athenian participation, "effective citizenship" is actively and collectively constructed by city governments and local communities, which, Fortner argues, means going beyond "individual loyalty and sense of belonging to cities" to include practices with real value, city politics engagement, and "capacity of residents to determine the fate of their communities."[33] Given America's historical struggle to overcome second-class citizenship and the particular significance of urban spaces for minorities, urban scholars argue that cities can either expand or contract the meaning of citizenship, both in its local and national orientations. As Rogers Smith explains, cities play three specific roles that have upward impact on American citizenship: "as sites of political activity embedded in larger [national] structures, as political actors in those larger structures, and as political symbols."[34] In this formulation, citizenship is a concept that has both local and national dimensions, with policies, actions, and symbols that can provide individuals with varying levels of representation, empowerment, and sense of belonging.

Scholars of global cities go even further.[35] Decentering citizenship studies away from national boundaries, these scholars point to diverse memberships beyond national boundaries as well as within – including urban, local, global, transnational, postnational, and dual-national membership.[36] Saskia Sassen explains that citizenship rooted to the state is a historical construction constituted as a "tightly packaged bundle of what were in fact often rather diverse elements," one that is being destabilized by "the emergence of new types of political subjects and new spatialities for politics."[37] Despite assumptions of exclusivity in the national conception of citizenship, the growing scholarship effectively pushes us to become more open in considering different types of jurisdictions and spatial levels in which citizenships can form.

Local citizenship takes on a different character when applied to the study of immigrant populations, since immigrants face a different set of opportunities and constraints than their native-born, minority counterparts. As a result, immigration scholars have drawn attention to the vital role of cities in promoting the integration of immigrants and protecting them from federal enforcement. At the same time, there is vigorous debate in this emerging literature as to whether these policies should be considered a form of local citizenship. On the one hand, legal scholars of immigration like Rose Cuison-Villazor argue that local citizenship bears important similarities and differences from national citizenship. Drawing on the work of Yishai Blank, Cuison-Villazor argues that "local citizenship, similar to national citizenship, involves questions of membership, rights, and privileges attendant to citizenship. Yet, it is descriptively different because much of the negotiations for membership and rights occur at the municipal level, which give rise to the opportunities that shape the rights, privileges, and obligations of local citizenship."[38] Villazor then considers the case of San Francisco and its robust policies on immigrant sanctuary, arguing that they sever local enforcement of federal immigration law and, by doing so, construct a new local status for undocumented residents. In addition to creating a distinctive local status, the process of crafting sanctuary policies provides unauthorized immigrants a new sense of belonging and new access to participation, all of which bundle together to make up a meaningful type of local citizenship.[39]

Even more critical of national exclusivity, Peter Markowitz notes that the US Constitution only vaguely defines national citizenship and is much more precise and protective of state citizenship.[40] Using normatively grounded and constitutionally grounded analyses, Markowitz argues that states today can provide a formal state citizenship, even to unauthorized immigrants. This is only possible because state citizenship fundamentally differs from national citizenship. Markowitz argues that, contrary to popular belief, the Fourteenth Amendment did not set up a preemption scenario, where national citizenship constitutionally replaced state citizenship. It instead preserved both types of citizenship, but layered them in important ways. Thus, for example, federal law (such as the Voting Rights Act of 1965) provides a floor that protects rights from being infringed upon by state or local governments, but federal law does not set a ceiling on the ability of state or local governments to expand rights. Rather than critiquing national citizenship, Markowitz shows that state citizenship can model itself after national citizenship, as a formal and legal gateway to various rights and protections.

By contrast, scholars of immigration federalism like Els de Graauw and Cristina Rodriguez find notions of subfederal citizenship to be normatively loaded and analytically unhelpful. De Graauw notes, for example, that urban citizenship has "strong normative undertones" about the equality of "all urban residents, regardless of their immigration or citizenship status."[41] Still, federal immigration law severely constrains how cities can expand equality for local immigrant residents, especially those who are undocumented. Thus, she opts for the broader concept of "membership" rather than citizenship, arguing that city municipal ID cards given to undocumented immigrant residents create a "local bureaucratic membership," which expands their sense of local belonging and local access to participation. De Graauw is careful not to oversell the power of local integration policies, noting that cities may not be able to constitutionally expand "the *de jure* rights and benefits of undocumented immigrants," but they do welcome them as "*de facto* members" of their local communities and "confer societal membership."[42] Importantly, De Graauw shines a light on the constraints faced by local efforts at immigrant integration and immigrant rights, even in progressive cities such as New Haven and San Francisco.[43] In a similar vein, Cristina Rodriguez draws attention to the growth of immigration federalism in the age of globalization but reverts to national citizenship as the gold standard. Rodriguez notes that "the promise of state and local strategies for integration, particularly because of local progressive resistance to enforcement, has given rise to an optimistic but romantic notion of local citizenship," adding: "The citizenship status that can only be granted by the federal government, like legal status itself, will be indispensable to the long-term stability that promotes investment in the community and adaptation to the country."[44]

Finally, scholars of "multilevel citizenship" echo urban and local critiques, but their conceptualization is purposely contingent on national citizenship.[45] Sub- and supra-state institutions like the rise of European Union citizenship, or regional and subnational integration efforts, partly decenter the concept of citizenship away from its national focus. As Willem Maas explains, "the intention [here] is to question taken-for-granted assumptions currently embedded in the [citizenship] concept" and to broaden analysis to other levels.[46] Elizabeth Cohen and Jenn Kinney advance a disaggregated "American" citizenship concept as multilevel and constitutive of federal/state/local rights and status – "rooted simultaneously in legally assigned statuses and geographic location."[47] Noncitizens share a federal legal status but are provided differential sets of rights from their state and city of residence, which creates multilevel semi-citizenships. Rogers Smith similarly explains that dynamics in immigration federalism, including restrictive state and local policies called "attrition though enforcement" and integrationist policies seeking to expand immigrant rights, are a type of multitiered governance that create "moderate" forms of political peoplehood.[48]

Collectively, the proliferation of citizenship subtypes – from urban, local, global, transnational, postnational, and multilevel citizenship, among others – offer important challenges to national exclusivity. These subtypes capture the potential inclusion of nationally marginalized and excluded minorities and immigrants, which is a normative selling point. However, these citizenship subtypes are also often indistinct from one another and from national citizenship, causing problems of conceptual stretching and blurring. In addition, the expansion of rights in many treatments of local citizenship often remains more aspirational than substantive, which is why de Graauw and Rodriguez raise caution and avoid using the term "local citizenship" altogether. In order to sufficiently address these critiques, it is important for scholarship on state and local citizenship to be grounded in dimensions that are distinct and well measured. A strong conceptualization of subfederal citizenship should also enable systematic comparisons to national citizenship and should provide for dynamic interactions between local, state, and federal governments. Without stronger conceptual clarity and consistency, the proliferation of citizenship subtypes risks being dismissed as exceedingly vague and merely aspirational.

MULTIDIMENSIONAL CITIZENSHIP AND CONCEPTUAL STRETCHING

The conventional model of citizenship has been criticized not only for its exclusive focus on national-level citizenship but also for its unidimensional fixation on legal status. As outlined earlier, the traditional model views citizenship as a binary distinction, with legal status providing a sharp line that demarcates noncitizen from citizen. It also privileges legal status over all other dimensions of citizenship, making it authoritative in controlling access to a variety of political, social, legal, and economic rights. This unidimensional focus on legal status has received considerable pushback among citizenship scholars, ranging from early works by T. H. Marshall to more recent studies by Linda Bosniak, Irene Bloemraad, Elizabeth Cohen, and others. As we will elaborate, these works have produced a broader and richer understanding of how citizenship is actually practiced today. At the same time, the push toward multidimensionality has also introduced new problems in the conceptualization of citizenship by bundling together disparate types of concepts under the same label, a phenomenon that social scientists call "conceptual stretching." We believe that is possible to reimagine citizenship in a way that preserves the virtues of conceptual clarity and consistency from the traditional model of citizenship while also reflecting the greater diversity of how citizenship is understood and practiced in a multidimensional context.

There is by now a well-developed scholarship in Europe on citizenship and its multiple dimensions. Irene Bloemraad, Anna Korteweg, and Gökçe Yurdakul provide an important summary of the contemporary literature on multidimensional citizenship, all while orienting the field toward a focus on four dimensions that capture both empirical and normative dimensions.[49] They argue that the vigorous debate between nation-state and human rights approaches to citizenship has neglected to raise pressing questions related the content or substance of citizenship.[50] As Bloemraad, Korteweg, and Yurdakul explain, human rights–based arguments are primarily "outlining a normative desire" and often identify rights that are "already present in liberal democratic practices."[51] They also highlight that "nation-states continue to hold substantial power over the formal rules and rights of citizenship and to shape the institutions that provide differentiated access to participation and belonging, with important consequences for immigrants' incorporation and equality."[52] Thus, the premise upon which the human rights critique has been waged against the nation-state, by attaching rights to persons and pointing to international institutions and norms as protecting those natural rights, is unable to provide a robust distinction between human rights from other rights, and to counter the claim to sovereignty by national governments over citizenship.[53]

Importantly, Bloemraad, Korteweg, and Yurdakul steer the debate away from citizenship's location and toward unpacking the contents of citizenship: "The evolution of different Western definitions of citizenship has led to a conception of citizenship that includes four different dimensions: legal status, rights, (political) participation, and a sense of belonging."[54] Concepts have proliferated in isolation, often imposing unitary assumptions about what citizenship is and what it ought to be. By presenting these four broad dimensions (Figure 2.2), shared by state-centered and human rights approaches alike, the authors provide a broad foundation for addressing the substance of citizenship.

The multidimensional framework developed by Bloemraad, Korteweg, and Yurdakul captures many normative traditions and approaches to citizenship and is a welcome departure from the rigid and binary features of the traditional model of citizenship. At the same time, this move toward multidimensionality also introduces a new set of challenges. In particular, it bundles together dissimilar concepts and approaches, leading to a considerable reduction in conceptual consistency and clarity. First, this multidimensional view combines four different types of political phenomena: *rights* (political, social, and civil rights), the *exercise of rights* (participation in society), the *right to rights* (legal status), and *political identification* (sense of belonging). Some of these concepts veer into root concepts[55] that are distinct from citizenship, like political power, nationalism, participation, and representation. This multidimensional

| legal status | political, social and civic rights | participation in society | sense of belonging |

FIGURE 2.2 Citizenship as multidimensional

framework also bundles together the provision of rights, which is typically found in state-centered approaches to citizenship, with access to rights, which is typically found in individual-centered approaches to citizenship. Thus, for example, participation can include the right to vote, which is a provision of the state, or it can be considered the individual exercise of voting and differential access to this right. Finally, it is unclear whether these four dimensions are to be valued equally and whether there are any important thresholds to degrees of citizenship.

Some degree of conceptual stretching is also evident in the conflation of citizenship and citizenship regimes. The notion of regimes in comparative politics has created new flexibility in applying the citizenship concept to varying levels of analysis (transnational, national, local), groups, policies, and historical periods. Jane Jenson and Martin Papillon helped to launch this extension of citizenship studies by building on Gøsta Esping-Andersen's state welfare regimes concept to develop the concept of citizenship regime.[56] As Aude-Claire Fourot, Mireille Paquet, and Nora Nagels explain, citizenship regimes show how citizenship is tethered to power and inequality, and can be applied to different levels of analysis and with respect to formal and informal features of citizenship.[57] Jensen and Papillon define citizenship regime as "the institutional arrangements, rules and understandings that guide and shape concurrent policy decisions and expenditures of states, problem definitions by states and citizens, and claims-making by citizens."[58] Scholars like Deborah J. Yashar also analyze contested citizenship in the framework of democratic regimes, revealing how Indigenous groups can make political claims to, and simultaneously contest, national citizenship. Moreover, Yashar shows contradictory citizenship processes at play in Latin America, with policies that expand Indigenous rights that simultaneously result in a loss of Indigenous group autonomy, identity and power.[59] Regimes, or the kinds of institutional rules and power arrangements that uphold various types of citizenship, are important to examine in their own right. Indeed, we devote considerable attention to rules like constitutional frameworks and the power of social movements and political parties in much of this book. However, we also believe that it is important to distinguish certain types of citizenship in a federated framework (progressive, regressive, or reinforcing) from the kind of regimes that uphold them.

Just as it is possible to avoid the problem of conceptual stretching when speaking of regimes that uphold particular configurations of citizenship rights, it is also possible to produce a multidimensional framework on citizenship that is grounded in rights. First, it is instructive to remember that multidimensionality is not new to citizenship. Writing in 1965, T. H. Marshall traced full citizenship as an evolving concept, beginning as civil rights and then expanding to include political and social rights. Elizabeth Cohen correctly argues, however, that Marshall's normative commitments to full equality prompt him to make the elements of citizenship contingent upon one another rather than treating them as potentially independent concepts and processes.[60] Thus, Marshall's historical and normative approaches reduce civil, political, social, and nationality rights rather than reveal their distinctive value. "In Marshall's telling, there is a dependent relationship between types of rights. Social rights allow the exercise of civil and political rights that in turn ground support for the kinds of equality embodied by social rights."[61] Rather than fully develop a multidimensional concept, Marshall intentionally blurs the different sets of rights that he sets up.[62]

Elizabeth Cohen's significant intervention is that she builds on Marshall's rights tradition to develop a more parsimonious framework of multidimensional citizenship that is grounded in rights. By doing so, she addresses concerns raised by a range of citizenship scholars, including human rights and multicultural scholars critical of legitimating state authority, as well as civil rights and second-class citizenship scholars seeking stronger state roles over equal rights. For example, the legal scholar Linda Bosniak is critical of what it means to privilege national citizenship over other notions of membership because it considers noncitizen rights to be in conflict with binary presumptions of a fully enclosed system of rights. Noncitizen rights, Bosniak argues, make possible the "paradoxical idea of 'noncitizen citizenship'" or "hybrid condition of alienage" and forces scholars to reconsider citizenship's conceptual utility and privileged position.[63] The conventional concept of citizenship as national and binary is severely limited in this regard. It only captures the binary process of naturalization but misses the range of dimensions Bloemraad, Korteweg, and Yurdakul highlight as essential and, therefore, cannot reconcile second-class citizenship or states' provision of noncitizen rights (they are simply bracketed as contradictory to citizenship).

Similar to Bloemraad, Korteweg, and Yurdakul, Cohen criticizes binary notions of citizenship as overly narrow and advances a multidimensional framework that draws on various traditions shaping citizenship rights. She employs a positivist approach, "locating the authority to define citizenship outside the realm of solely normative theory and within practices that draw on plural sources, including the politically relevant practices of states in their capacity as generators of rights that themselves constitute political relationships."[64] Thus, Cohen establishes rights as a conceptual bedrock to multidimensional citizenship and avoids mixing in associative activity or civic virtues. This has the advantage of being more conceptually consistent than Bloemraad, Korteweg, and Yurdakul's framework. As Cohen explains, a focus on rights provides a "conceptually useful starting place for analyzing forms of membership that fall between citizenship and non-citizenship."[65] She builds a positivist concept of citizenship on the actual provision of and access to rights, rather than normative ideas of who ought to have rights. Disaggregating Marshall's contingent rights into multiple independent and fundamental citizenship rights, Cohen advances a concept of semicitizenship composed of "rights [that] are unbundled and rebundled in packages."[66] In particular, she repackages rights into two broad, abstract dimensions of *relative rights* such as the right to vote, which are dependent on particular types of political systems to render them intelligible, and autonomous rights, such as the right to one's bodily integrity, which are not similarly constrained.

Cohen's approach shows us that it is possible to have a rights-based framework on citizenship that breaks with the oversimplification of the traditional model, with states providing citizenship in a fully enclosed system of rights. Cohen's rights-based framework also maintains conceptual consistency by keeping the focus on states rather than trying to group states and individuals together in a definition of citizenship. States are the ones that provide differential bundles of rights to groups like children, felons, racial minorities, and various classes of foreign-born residents. Thus, it is possible to incorporate inequality in a definition of citizenship without having to combine the *exercise* of rights with the *provision* of rights. Finally, as Cohen points out, this kind of multidimensional approach grounded in rights also frees us from the assumption "that nation-states generate only one kind of citizenship."[67]

At the same time, Cohen's rebundling of citizenship rights – into broad, abstract categories of autonomous rights and relative rights – is insufficiently precise for our purposes. Indeed, Cohen's framework turns out to be two-dimensional rather than multidimensional as found in the works of Marshall, Bloemraad, and many other scholars on citizenship in Europe and North America. In the following section, we sketch out a novel framework of citizenship that is consistently grounded in rights and their provision by states (like Cohen's), while at the same time capturing the level of multidimensional detail found in the works of Bloemraad and others. We believe that such a multidimensional framework offers us a way to overcome the major limitations of the traditional model of citizenship (with its strong assumptions of national exclusivity and unidimensionality), while at the same time retaining conceptual consistency on rights and the provision of those rights by political institutions.

STATE CITIZENSHIP IN A FEDERATED FRAMEWORK: OUR DEFINITION

Given recent advancements in state-based immigrant rights in the United States, we believe that the time is ripe for a new model of multidimensional citizenship that intersects with federalism. The conventional model of citizenship still has considerable appeal because of its clear focus on rights and its clear declaration that nation-states have ultimate authority to confer or deny political membership and rights to individuals. At the same time, the traditional model problematically ties legal status to all other citizenship rights and is unhelpful to understanding the provision of rights by governments in a federated framework. While the literatures on multidimensional citizenship and urban citizenship have made some important strides in pushing for alternative conceptions of citizenship, many studies within these traditions have failed to achieve the same kind of conceptual clarity that is a hallmark of the traditional model. We believe that it is possible to preserve a multidimensional view of citizenship while maintaining a focus on rights – their provision by governments and access to those rights by individuals and members of social groups. We also believe that it is possible to embed these rights in a multilevel framework of federalism, with legal arrangements and political dynamics structuring the relationship between federal rights and those granted at the state and local level.

We define citizenship quite simply as *the provision of rights by a political jurisdiction to its members*. Our approach is in the tradition of T. H. Marshall, Irene Bloemraad, and Elizabeth Cohen, but our empirical and theoretical goals differ. First, we maintain a focus on rights even as we allow for a multidimensional understanding of citizenship. Thus, we conceptualize and operationalize citizenship as the provision of rights (and access to those rights) along five dimensions: (1) right to free movement; (2) right to due process and legal protection; (3) right to develop human capital; (4) right to participate and be represented; and (5) the right to identify and belong. Some of these dimensions have been explored outside of a rights-based framework, and we believe that it is possible, and indeed preferable, to keep a consistent focus on rights – their provision by governments and their differential access by members of particular social groups. Our work also bridges citizenship studies with the fast-growing literature on immigration federalism, with states and localities playing important roles in regulating the lives of immigrants.[68] We define *state citizenship* as the provision of rights by states in a federal framework. State citizenship does not signify secession or other forms of outright conflict with federal citizenship; indeed, the two can be complementary even as they push and pull with changes in broader dynamics of federalism.

We devote the rest of this chapter to laying out our rights-based, multidimensional framework of citizenship, building a case for state citizenship that cannot simply be reduced to state residency, and providing a robust set of indicators to measure citizenship rights at the federal, state, and local levels. Finally, we also map out three types of state citizenship in a federalism framework: (a) *regressive state citizenship*, where states erode rights that granted to individuals at the federal level; (b) *restrictive state citizenship,* where states enforce federal limitations on rights to particular types of individuals; and (c) *progressive state citizenship,* where states exceed the rights granted to particular types of individuals at the federal level. As we shall see in Chapter 3 and beyond, these concepts and indicators are especially helpful in understanding contemporary dynamics in immigrant rights at the state and local levels. At the same time, our conceptual framework is designed in a way that it can be more broadly applicable to understanding citizenship rights as they involve race, ethnicity, gender, LGBT identity, religion, and disability.

CITIZENSHIP IS A PARTICULAR KIND OF MEMBERSHIP

Citizenship is the provision of rights by a political jurisdiction to its members.
This is a simple definition that relies on a few key assumptions: (1) that
citizenship involves *political* membership, as opposed to other types of
membership; (2) that this membership is rooted in political *jurisdictions*, as
opposed to other types of political entities like parties and interest groups; and
(3) that it involves the *provision of rights*, as opposed to other types of dynamics
involving states and social actors such as political participation, political
influence, or feelings of patriotism and other types of political attachment.
While these assumptions may seem eminently reasonable, each needs further
discussion and justification.

In systematizing our definition of citizenship, we draw heavily on the
tradition of concept formation as pioneered by the political scientist Giovanni
Sartori and refined in recent decades by John Gerring and Steve Levitsky as
applied to the study of democratization and democracy. Writing in 1970,
Sartori penned a foundational article about the problem of "conceptual
stretching," whereby scholars in comparative political science were taking
specific concepts from particular places and applying them to new political
jurisdictions across the globe, regardless of their context.[69] Thus, for
example, concepts like "participation" and "mobilization" developed in the
context of established, competitive democracies like the United States or
England would not hold the same meaning in authoritarian systems like
China and the Soviet Union. Sartori did not view this translation problem as
one of measurement but rather as a more fundamental one of conceptualization:

> Let it be stressed, therefore, that long before having data which can speak for themselves,
> the fundamental articulation of language and of thinking is obtained logically – by
> cumulative conceptual refinement and chains of coordinated definitions – not by mea-
> surement. Measurement of what? We cannot measure unless we know first what it is that
> we are measuring.[70]

Sartori noted that there was an inverse relationship between a concept's specific
attributes (intension) and its applicability across a range of cases (extension),
and he argued that scholars would need to make their concepts more abstract
(lower in intension) if they were to apply them across a broader range of cases
across the world.

Sartori's foundational work on concept formation took on new urgency in
the 1990s, as political scientists grappled with trying to understand a new wave
of democratization in the wake of the collapse of the Soviet Union and the
backsliding toward authoritarianism happening in many parts of Latin America
and Africa. This period also saw a proliferation of different types of democratic
regimes, such as "neopatrimonial democracy," "authoritarian democracy,"
"illiberal democracy," and confusion among political scientists about what,
exactly, each term meant and how they were comparable to or different from

each other. In the tradition of Sartori, David Collier and Steve Levitsky wrote a seminal article in 1997 that brought a significant degree of order to the chaos of conceptualization around democracy.[71] And in so doing, they produced a systematic framework on concept formation and conceptual hierarchies that have proved useful in other domains.[72] Key to the Collier and Levitsky framework is a differentiation between *root concepts* such as "democracy," *overarching concepts* such as "regimes" that are more general, and two kinds of *subtypes*: classical subtypes such as "parliamentary democracy" that entail the addition of adjectives to the root concept to describe a particular form of democracy; and diminished subtypes such as "illiberal democracy" where one or more key attributes of democracy are missing.

While the field of democracy studies has benefited from a concerted effort to provide conceptual clarity amidst a proliferation of concepts, there has not been a similarly ambitious effort in the field of citizenship studies. Certainly, efforts by Bloemraad, Korteweg, and Yurdakul and by Cohen, which we have described extensively in this chapter, and Cohen and Ghosh's recent theoretical overview on the topic have helped the field think more systematically about different concepts of citizenship that have proliferated over the last two decades.[73] Still, citizenship scholars have rarely undertaken efforts, similar to those by democracy scholars, to embed related notions in a conceptual hierarchy, with Wallace Goodman's 2014 book a notable exception that conceives citizenship as a type of political membership with "formal legal status, conveying protection and access to rights under state rules."[74] We build on this effort and seek to provide a comprehensive conceptual map on citizenship that: (1) enables us to differentiate citizenship from various other types of political memberships; (2) allows for multiple dimensions while still remaining solidly within a framework of rights provision; and (3) allows us to conceive of citizenship at different scales – local, state, and national – and critically examine their tensions and interrelationships in a framework of federalism.

In Figure 2.3, we provide a simplified concept hierarchy on citizenship, which we define as *the provision of rights by a political jurisdiction to its members*, with key assumptions at each stage of specification. Note that, in a concept hierarchy, a term can be defined as a "root concept" at any stage, with overarching concepts at higher levels in the ladder of abstraction and subtypes at lower levels of abstraction. Thus, for instance, we can think of citizenship as a root concept, with various other stages as overarching concepts in climbing up the ladder of abstraction (Figure 2.3, version 1). Alternatively, we can think of political membership as a root concept, with citizenship and state citizenship as subtypes much farther below in the ladder of abstraction. We will elaborate on each of these stages in turn, but it is important to note that, regardless of where we begin in the concept hierarchy, we conceptualize citizenship most broadly as a kind of membership. Even though our concept of citizenship privileges political jurisdictions and their provision of rights, it is impossible to speak of

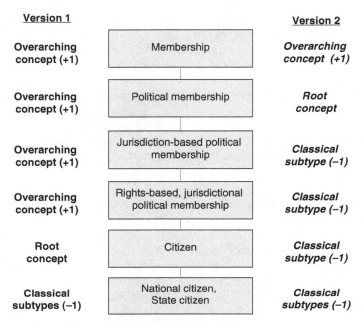

FIGURE 2.3 Simplified concept hierarchy on citizenship

citizenship without referring to members who are embedded in these jurisdictions and have access to those rights.

The basic notion of membership transcends various types of citizenship traditions. Michael Walzer defines the general notion of membership as a "primary good that we [as humans] distribute" to form a sense of community and belonging. Citizenship, by contrast, is a type of bounded membership that concerns "present and future populations."[75] Thus, while membership universally included all Athenians into one community, Athenian citizenship was an exclusive membership of men who actively participated in self-governance, the defining feature of citizenship's republican tradition. All members of the Roman empire, even slaves, were included in the same general community, while Roman citizenship, defined by the provision of rights, created more exclusive political ties between citizens and the city-state.[76]

Another way that scholars have noted membership to be an overarching concept is through the idea of a state of nature (where a general pre-state membership forms) and a state of government (where a state-type of political membership forms). In his *Second Treatise*, John Locke refers first to a state of nature where humans are created equal and then begins to narrow his analysis from this general state of humans to one of legitimate governance and consent of the people, built on the liberal notion of citizenship rights.[77] Similarly,

Hannah Arendt's post–World War II critique of statelessness in *Origins of Totalitarianism* is rooted in the overarching idea of membership as belonging through inalienable human rights, which is distinctive from and conceptually prior to membership as citizenship through the state's provision of rights.[78] Finally, Linda Bosniak is critical of employing the concept of citizenship without considering alternative parallel forms of membership types largely because it does not easily capture the inclusion and rights of noncitizens.[79] As we note earlier, Els de Graauw avoids using the term "citizenship" and prefers the overarching concept of membership in her study of local identification cards and integration of immigrants, for the same reasons.[80]

Of course, citizenship is not just any kind of membership: it is a political membership that is distinct from other types of social membership (Figure 2.4). Thus, for example, while residents of the United States might have US citizenship as their form of political membership, they can also simultaneously hold other types of social memberships as defined by race (Black), ethnicity (Korean American), religion (Mormon), and many other factors such as gender, sexual orientation, and the like. Indeed, as many scholars have pointed out, these identities are often intersectional,[81] and it is certainly possible for aspects of political membership to intersect with various aspects of social membership. It is important to note, however, that politics is not simply something that can be reduced to social relations; the state, broadly defined, and related institutions such as political parties are critical.[82] Thus, it would be impossible to speak of political membership without making any mention of political institutions such as courts, legislatures, political parties, and the executive branch or of attempts to influence those political institutions through mechanisms such as voting, making campaign contributions, or protesting.

While the narrowing of membership to political membership is a step in the right direction, it is insufficiently precise to declare it as citizenship. As we can see in Figure 2.4, there are other types of political membership such as those involving political parties (someone can be a registered Republican or

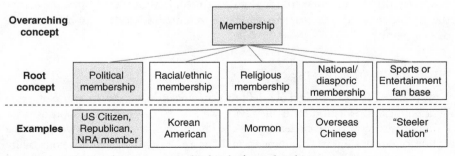

FIGURE 2.4 Citizenship as a particular kind of membership

Democrat, for example, and thus be qualified to vote in a party primary) and interest groups (someone can be a member of groups such as the National Rifle Association or United We Dream that are designed primarily to mobilize members to get involved in political action and policy debates). In order to be able to differentiate between membership in these types of political institutions, it is important to keep citizenship's focus on political membership that is based on jurisdictions. As the *Oxford English Dictionary* notes, a jurisdiction is "the extent or range of judicial or administrative power; the territory over which such power extends."[83] Of course, jurisdictions often overlap, with cities, counties, states, and national governments often holding sway over the same member. And countries can vary in the extent to which higher-level jurisdictions can preempt or overrule actions undertaken at lower-level jurisdictions. However, as long as a country has some kind of federalism arrangement, with states, provinces, counties, or municipalities having jurisdiction over the lives and livelihood of members, there is no reason why citizenship needs to be limited to the national level. We will have much more to say about citizenship in a federated framework later in this chapter.

While a focus on jurisdiction-based political membership gets close to our definition of citizenship, it is still insufficiently precise. For example, one can be a citizen of the United States, which is a jurisdiction-based political membership. But so, too, are memberships like "voter," "protester," "constituent," and "American," as shown in Figure 2.5. Thus, in order to avoid the problem of conceptual stretching, it is important to find one additional feature that can differentiate "citizen" from these other related concepts. We adopt the liberal convention of a grounding citizenship in rights, which allows us to differentiate citizenship from other political concepts like participation, representation, power, and influence. A rights-based approach to citizenship is also critical to our attempt to situate citizenship in a federalism framework, where structural relationships between federal, state, and local governments vary in the extent to which they can independently, or conditionally, confer different types of rights to members. Our concept of citizenship deliberately excludes the actual exercise of citizenship rights by individual members, such as political participation or feelings of identification or belonging. As we shall discuss shortly, however, this framework still enables us to think about how rights structure the ability of citizens to participate, get represented, identify, and have a sense of belonging.

WHAT KIND OF RIGHTS?

Now that we have established our definition of citizenship as the provision of rights by a political jurisdiction to its members, we turn to tackle the question of what kind of rights constitute citizenship. As we have already discussed, we reject the notion of citizenship as a unidimensional construct, with legal status controlling access to a host of rights. In the United States, it is possible for those without legal

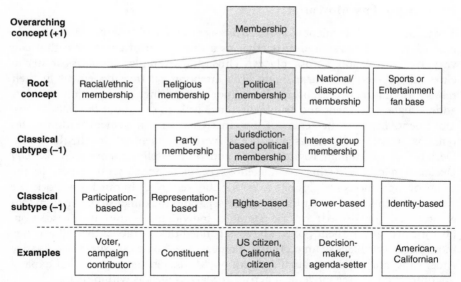

FIGURE 2.5 Elaborated concept hierarchy on citizenship

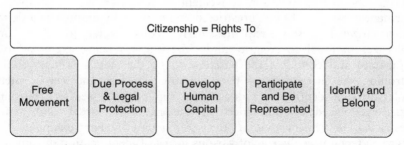

FIGURE 2.6 Multidimensional citizenship in a rights-based framework

status to nevertheless gain access to meaningful political rights such as freedom of speech and the ability to gain representation through the decennial process of apportionment and redistricting. At the same time, we also find significant limitations to existing multidimensional frameworks of citizenship, as they tend to mix varied concepts together, including rights, the right to have rights, the exercise of rights, political identification, and sense of belonging.

We believe it is possible to have a multidimensional framework for citizenship while still preserving rights as the basis for each dimension. In Figure 2.6, we sketch out five main dimensions to citizenship, with reference to prior literature and concepts in international human rights and American jurisprudence where relevant. First, the right to free movement is an essential aspect of citizenship.

Dimension 1: Free Movement

The right to free movement is assumed as essential to citizenship, but it is largely underdeveloped or ignored altogether as a dimension of citizenship that can vary over time and across places. Thus, for example, scholars of urban citizenship have spent surprisingly little attention on free movement in their rebuke of national citizenship. Even more surprising, immigration scholars addressing enforcement and criminality have little to say about the right to free movement. Even in the realm of human rights, free movement within states remains underdeveloped as a concept, with no mention in the Universal Declaration of Human Rights (1948) and only implied mention in the UN Declaration of the Rights of Indigenous Peoples (2007) with respect to the rights of indigenous peoples not to be forcibly removed. In our framework, we develop the concept of free movement as a separate core dimension, as a right that is provided (or denied) by the state to individuals within its jurisdiction. Historically, government policies have expanded or contracted the right to free movement, for Blacks, immigrants, paupers, the homeless, the poor, Native Americans, and other marginalized groups. Moreover, the policies that expand or contract cover free movement across borders as well as within them.

Conventional understandings of national citizenship conflate free movement with legal status. Furthermore, by assuming that the power of national governments over population movement is sovereign and exclusive, free movement is assumed to be unrestricted and universally granted as a de facto right of citizenship. As we explained early in this chapter, Jonathan Torpey emphasizes national sovereignty and citizenship as being exclusive to the nation-state and considers the passport to be the state's primary tool for controlling the movement of people within borders and across them.[84] Scholarship on identification documents similarly stresses free movement restrictions placed on foreigners at the national border and assumes unrestricted movement within the nation-state.[85] For example, Craig Robertson recognizes the role of various forms of identification documents as targeting marginalized groups in American history but emphasizes the general acceptance after World War I of the American passport as the primary document signaling authority over free movement.[86]

A review of American history reveals, however, that the right to free movement was by no means standardized across the entire country, nor was it a right provided exclusively by the federal government. In early America, federal, state, and local governments often contracted this right to free movement. Most states passed laws broadly restricting convicted criminals and paupers from entry into state borders, placed sanctions on persons responsible for unlawfully transporting convicts and paupers into state borders, and granted state and local authorities the power to remove unauthorized persons to their "place of lawful settlement."[87] Beginning in the 1820s, states expanded their control by passing laws that further contracted the right to free movement by requiring masters of vessels to post bonds, pay a head tax, or pay commutation fees before state officials would admit immigrants into state borders, requiring the reporting of passengers to track all new arrivals, and establishing almshouses and workhouses as an alternative solution to removing immigrants who became public charges.[88]

State governments also contracted rights of free movement for free and enslaved Blacks. Restrictions placed on entry/exit and removal of Blacks were paired with robust internal migration controls. Southern states passed laws restricting Blacks' movement involving trade and bartering of goods, carving out specific Black travel routes and curfews, and blocking access to public resources. Government policies established slave and freedmen passes (and metal tags in some jurisdictions), which functioned both as identification documents and as work visas to regulate which Blacks could freely move. Moreover, government policies established local militias and slave patrols to enforce laws on the free movement and activities of enslaved and free Blacks.[89] Several federal, state, and local laws on fugitive slaves sought to limit the movement of runaway slaves and made it a punishable crime to harbor Blacks considered to be unlawfully present, although some Northern states enacted more progressive legislation expanding free movement starting in 1820 with Pennsylvania's personal liberty law.[90]

Following the Civil War, federal, state, and local policies continued to contract the right to free movement, using debt to physically restrict Blacks to plots of land as exploited tenant farmers and sharecroppers, and using criminal status under a convict leasing system to contract Blacks out as laborers on public infrastructure projects and to private entities.[91] Moreover, the removal of federal troops from the South in 1877 ended Radical Reconstruction and ushered in a new era of regressive and restrictive state and local policies.[92] Though Blacks were recognized as US citizens under the Fourteenth Amendment, 1877 nevertheless marked an end to federal protection. As C. Vann Woodward explains of this moment, "What the new status of the Negro would be was not at once apparent."[93] Black codes proliferated, followed by Jim Crow segregation, a comprehensive set of racialized policies that contracted Black rights to free movement and presence. Segregation contracted their right to free movement by separating Blacks from Whites in private and public spaces – public transportation (trains, buses, and other common carriers), housing, workplaces, restaurants, theaters, hospitals, playgrounds, public parks, swimming pools, organized sports, the armed services, and public schools.

While Jim Crow ended in the 1960s, stop-and-frisk policies, the war on drugs, and mass incarceration continues to contract the right of African Americans to free movement, among other rights.[94] For example, the NYPD's stop and frisk policy allows a police officer to stop, question, and search any pedestrian if they "reasonably suspect" that the pedestrians may commit, or may have already committed, a crime. From 2001 to 2010, New York City created and enforced an electronic database of the names and addresses of individuals subject to a stop-and-frisk, regardless of whether they were charged with any crimes."[95] Framed as a policy to maintain law and order, stop-and-frisk contracts the right to free movement of Blacks and other minorities. Indeed, stop-and-frisk was even recognized as a "policy of indirect racial profiling" in *Floyd v. City of New York* (2013), but the court did not order an end to stop-and-frisk.[96] Moreover, research shows that persons of African and Hispanic descent were stopped more frequently than Whites.[97]

Much like stop-and-frisk, states and cities have enacted a range of policies to contract the free movement of minority and immigrant populations.[98] Arizona's SB 1070 was a comprehensive law that not only contracted the rights of undocumented immigrants in the state but also set up a de facto racialized restriction on free movement against Mexican-origin individuals. It targeted immigrants for removal through requiring alien registration and made it a state crime to fail to carry proof of lawful status. The state law also prevented cities in Arizona from expanding the right to free movement by banning local noncooperation ordinances (or so-called sanctuary policies). It also limited free movement by defining the transporting of an undocumented person as harboring.

The concept of free movement has not been entirely neglected by citizenship scholars, as it is often assumed to be an essential feature of citizenship. Elizabeth Cohen provides some clarity on this significance and addresses free movement as falling within a nationality dimension, where differential rights of free movement are given to citizens and noncitizens. She explains that "nationality typically entails the right to live within the borders of, and the right to travel freely within, a particular nation-state. In the case of the foreign-born, these rights are disaggregated by placing conditions on the circumstances and timing of residence and travel. Temporary workers, refugees, and economic immigrants, among others, all have different elements of rights associated with nationality."[99] Moreover, Cohen's concept of time intersects with the right to free movement, and she argues that "[t]emporal boundaries carve up populations into hierarchically ordered groups with different rights. It is not just residency and free movement rights that are affected when one's visa expires, but eligibility for a host of other rights that legal non-citizen residents enjoy."[100] Free movement here, however, remains undefined as a dimension of citizenship rights.

Finally, there is a question about whether the right to free movement entails the right to stay, exit, or to have shelter. Tracing how homeless US citizens today are criminalized and then legally stripped of their right to shelter, Leonard Feldman argues that we should move away from viewing homelessness as a social or economic problem and reconceptualize it as "problem of sovereign state power" and the provision of rights.[101] Homeless populations have faced vagrancy laws in the past and are now being displaced and criminalized by local anti-homeless policies. One might also consider the dislocation caused by gentrification to be an infringement on the right to free movement,[102] although we do not consider the "right to stay" in the face of gentrification to be an essential feature of citizenship. Furthermore, we consider the right to housing or shelter as more centrally related to another dimension of citizenship rights that we articulate later in this chapter: the right to develop human capital.

We develop "free movement" as a dimension that is generalizable to national, state, and local provision of rights. Even without federal legal status, undocumented immigrants are granted a right to free movement in a variety of ways and contrary to our dominant understanding of national citizenship and immigration law. Whereas history has more examples of contracting this right for minoritized populations like Blacks, Asian Americans, Hispanics, and Native Americans, expansions in the right to free movement also emerge, and particularly so with respect to the right to free movement for runaway slaves.[103] States today can provide expansions in the right to free movement for undocumented immigrants through laws granting access to driver's licenses and auto insurance, laws limiting the impounding of cars for those without driver's licenses, and laws expanding access to public transportation, public buildings, and safe spaces from federal immigration enforcement.

Dimension 2: Right to Due Process and Legal Protection

The idea that states protect their members is central to citizenship. Nation-states protect citizens through a domestic police force, an international military force, and diplomacy. National governments also protect citizens at home by setting up a constitution and access to the courts in order to secure civil rights. While this kind of protection is often provided to those with "legal status," we expand the concept into a broader dimension of "due process and legal protection" that is applicable to national, state, and local governments. In the immigration context, legal status becomes especially important for understanding state and local citizenship. Not only can states pass policies that limit their cooperation with federal immigration enforcement: they can also expand access to constitutional and legal protections to residents who lack legal status at the federal level.

The provision of due process rights by states to racial minorities predated the Civil War and the Fourteenth Amendment that followed the end of the war. Much like undocumented immigrants today, slaves lacked constitutional and federal rights and protections. The US Constitution and federal Fugitive Slave Laws passed in 1793 and 1850 granted slave owners the right to capture and reclaim their "property," made it a crime to harbor runaway slaves, and created a federal body to administer warrants, removal, and fines for interference. Nevertheless, some Northern states and cities passed a range of personal liberty laws – forbidding and punishing state and local officials from enforcing the federal fugitive slave law, making the removal of *any* Black person from the state without court approval a crime, and granting all Blacks equal due process protections under state law (including: appointing special state commissioners to defend fugitive slaves in court, placing the burden of proof on slave owners, and providing all Blacks with the right of habeas corpus, trial by jury, and testimony against Whites).[104]

Controlled by White mobs, state courts sanctioned Jim Crow segregation and contractions in due process by denying Blacks legal protection from physical violence and lynching. As Megan Ming Francis shows us, it took decades of the NAACP fighting vigorously to get the federal government to step in and end lynching, first by employing strategies to influence civil society and the executive branch to push for national legislation.[105] The US Supreme Court eventually ruled in *Moore v. Dempsey* (1923) that state courts' criminal procedure infringed on Blacks' due process rights. However, it wasn't until the 1960s that federal law dismantled Jim Crow segregation.

The right to due process and legal protection is related to the right of free movement, but they are not identical. In the case of unauthorized immigrants today, expansions in the right to free movement are achieved through policies like providing access to driver's licenses, while expansions in the right to legal protections are achieved through laws that ban police officers from inquiring about federal legal status during regular traffic stops. Similarly, states and localities are expanding the right to due process and legal protections of undocumented immigrants by making them less vulnerable to immigration enforcement. These include laws that prevent cooperation in immigration enforcement, prevent the use of federal legal status in civil and criminal cases, protect immigrant confidentiality, and provide legal representation in court. Expansions of these rights are also achieved by decoupling federal immigration law and criminal law through policies that change sentencing practices and use of gang databases. States can further expand due process rights of undocumented immigrants by limiting detentions to forty-eight hours, providing full disclosure of immigration detainer requests, and providing legal resources to aid immigrants in court. Beyond enforcement consequences, states and localities expand the due process rights of immigrants by offering legal resources for DACA applications, visa applications, or petitions for naturalization.

Dimension 3: Right to Develop Human Capital

Next, we add the right to develop human capital, or the fundamental resources and capacities that individuals need to thrive. While we can speak separately about the right to public education and basic medical care, we find that these rights are exceedingly specific, and insufficiently inclusive, to be useful as a conceptual category of rights. Much like Henry Shue's notion of basic rights of subsistence that are necessary for the exercise of other rights,[106] and Amartya Sen's notion of substantive freedoms that include not only protections from hunger and disease but also against deprivations of capabilities,[107] our broad notion of a right to develop human capital includes not only the right to basic education and medical care but also other rights and protections provided by law that are the fundamental building blocks for individuals to thrive. These include the right to work,[108] the right to property,[109] the right to basic shelter,[110] the right to marry,[111] and the right to adopt.[112] Most of these rights derive from the principle of equal protection that arose from struggles involving discrimination on the basis of race, disability status, and sexual orientation; we discuss these in greater detail later in this chapter.

America has a long history of contracting the right to education for marginalized citizens and immigrants, followed by expansion of these rights, perhaps most notably when the US Supreme Court ruled in *Brown v. Board of Education* (1954) to secure access to equal education for Blacks.[113] Education remains an evolving right essential to the development of human capital. In 1975, Texas passed a law that denied state education money to local school districts for undocumented children and gave discretionary power to districts to ban these children from public schools or charge them tuition. *Plyler v. Doe* (1982) quoted *Brown v. Board of Education* (1954) to emphasize that denying the right to education disadvantages undocumented children for their entire life and places them into a permanent subcaste.[114] All of the Supreme Court justices in *Plyler* agreed that the US Constitution protected undocumented immigrants to some extent, and five of the nine ruled on equal protection grounds that "Texas violated the children's constitutional right of access to public education and secondary schools," by making access depend on their legal immigration status.[115] *Plyler* is considered the high-water mark for immigrants' constitutional rights, but it is not the end point.[116] Beyond K–12 education, which *Plyler* established as a universal constitutional baseline, the right to education can be expanded or contracted through policies on access to postsecondary education, in-state tuition, and financial aid. And beyond education access, the right to develop human capital is expanded or contracted through federal, state, and local policymaking and jurisprudence on health care, work, assets, shelter, and family.

All individuals in the United States have minimal access to emergency medical care through the Emergency Medical Treatment and Active Labor Act (EMTALA) of 1986. EMTALA requires hospitals receiving Medicare payments to "provide for an appropriate medical screening examination" to individuals regardless of whether or not they are eligible for any public benefits.[117] In addition, hospitals are prevented from transferring the individual to another medical facility unless the patient has been stabilized or the hospital has obtained the informed consent of the patient or a doctor who authorizes the transfer. Generally, federal law denies health care benefits and insurance to undocumented immigrants and places limits on legally residing immigrants. The Personal Responsibility and Work Opportunity Reconciliation Act (PRWORA) of 1996 barred many legal immigrants from federally funded public benefit programs, including Temporary Assistance for Needy Families (TANF), the Supplemental Nutrition Assistance Program (SNAP, often referred to as "food stamps"), Supplemental Security Income (SSI), and Medicaid and Children's Health Insurance Program (CHIP). Federal policy also stipulates that individuals may be determined a "public charge" if they rely on, or are likely to rely on, public cash assistance such as SSI and TANF or long-term institutional care. More recently, the Affordable Care Act of 2010 excluded undocumented immigrants from health insurance coverage.

Given these federal contractions in health care and health insurance, states are tasked with an important role in expanding eligibility for federal benefits or creating separate state and local alternative forms of health care coverage. States can expand access to federal programs for individuals classified under "permanently residing under color of law" (PRUCOL) with Deferred Action for Childhood Arrivals (DACA). Similar to policies on noncooperation in immigration enforcement, states can also create separate, more inclusive state-funded health insurance and health care programs that expand health access to undocumented immigrants.

Much like on health care, policies on employment are extensive and can either expand or contract the right to human capital. For the first time, in 1971, an amendment was proposed to the Civil Rights Act that would have added disability as grounds for discrimination. The bill failed, but it led to antidiscrimination language in the 1973 Rehabilitation Act, which stated, "No otherwise qualified handicapped individual in the United States shall, solely by reason of his handicap, be excluded from the participation in, be denied the benefits of, or be subjected to discrimination under any program or activity receiving Federal financial assistance." This law greatly expanded access for individuals with disabilities by preventing discrimination in all programs led by federal agencies or receiving federal money, as well as in federal employment and employment practices of federal contractors. The Americans with Disability Act of 1990 expanded access and protection from discrimination to individuals with disabilities in all areas of employment, in schools, in transportation, and in all public and private places open to the general public. ADA's expansions in the right to develop human capital paralleled what the Civil Rights Act of 1964 accomplished, ending segregation in public places and banning employment discrimination on the basis of race, color, religion, sex, or national origin.

With respect to employment rights involving immigrants, federal law has contracted rather than expanded access to employment for unauthorized immigrants. Congress passed the Immigration Reform and Control Act in 1986, which required all employers to verify the identity and federal work authorization of all paid employees by using an I-9 form and made it illegal for employers to knowingly hire or recruit undocumented immigrants. Congress later established an Internet-based verification system, E-Verify, in 1997 which required a social security number and the provision of a photo on identity documents. Importantly, while all employers are required to comply with the I-9 requirements, the same is not true for E-Verify. States and localities can expand access to employment and worker protections by limiting E-Verify requirements and thereby creating a legal safety net for immigrants. States can also expand or contract access to business licenses and professional licenses, and they can expand access to labor protections like wage theft and create new baselines in state and local labor law that go beyond these federal protections.

The right to shelter or affordable housing is also central to the ability to develop one's human capital. Some aspects of housing, such as anti-homeless policies and gentrification dynamics, can be considered contractions in the right to free movement (as we have articulated earlier), while housing segregation policies that limit access to affordable housing for Blacks, immigrants, and other marginalized populations are contractions in their right to develop human capital. As Douglass Massey and Nancy Denton explain, racial segregation not only impacts access to housing: it also impacts access to the schools, hospitals, and other institutions.[118] In *Dark Ghetto: Dilemmas of Social Power* (1965), Kenneth B. Clark writes that "the dark ghetto's invisible walls have been erected by the white society, by those who have power, both to confine those who have no power and to perpetuate their powerlessness. The dark ghettos are social, political, educational, and – above all – economic colonies."[119] Segregation severely constrains opportunities and perpetuates inequalities in the right to develop human capital, even physical availability of healthy foods.[120]

Contractions in the development of human capital rights have earlier roots in alien land laws and other restrictions on property ownership and employment (see Chapter 5). Housing discrimination has also included a broader range of exclusionary policies related to banking and lending that have limited minority access to capital. Passed in 1934, the National Housing Act formalized redlining under federal law and established the Federal Housing Administration (FHA), which made it official policy to withhold mortgage capital from racialized minorities. Residential security maps were created by the Federal Home Loan Bank Board (FHLBB) in 1935 as a way to grade neighborhoods as good or bad investments; they targeted Black neighborhoods as bad investments and at risk of mortgage default, preventing access to bank loans and other opportunities.

State and local laws on housing covenants have also constrained the rights to human capital formation. In response to the Great Migration of Southern Blacks, from the 1920s to 1948, White property owners, real estate boards, and neighborhood associations drew up contracts called housing covenants that prohibited the purchase, lease, or occupation of property to Blacks and other groups. In *Corrigan v. Buckley* (1926), the US Supreme Court validated racial housing covenants, and by 1940 an estimated 80 percent of property in Chicago and Los Angeles had restrictive covenants barring Black families.[121] By the late 1960s, federal law and court decisions swung in the opposite direction, as the Supreme Court barred discrimination in all housing in *Jones v. Mayer* (1968), and federal, state and local fair housing laws began to expand the right to develop human capital through housing.[122] Expansion in rights have also emerged through reverse redlining and intentional affordable access to marginalized groups in designated areas.

Federal and state laws and court decisions provide differential rights to LGBT and racial communities related to human capital by regulating marriage, sexual conduct (or intimacy), employment discrimination, and adoption. State laws in antebellum America permitted owners to forbid slave marriage and strictly regulate their sexual activities. Following the Civil War and new freedom of Blacks, states and local governments enacted Black Codes that included so-called anti-miscegenation laws, which forbade marriages between Blacks and Whites. Upheld in *Pace v. Alabama* (1883), these laws prohibiting interracial marriage and punishing Black sexual conduct outside of marriage were core features of Jim Crow segregation.[123] It was not until the Supreme Court decision *Loving v. Virginia* (1967) that interracial marriage was permitted.[124]

Gay rights have similarly been contracted, then expanded, with respect to human capital development. President Clinton instituted the policy of "Don't ask, don't tell" in 1994, leaving LGBT service members without a right to open sexual conduct or identification. Similar to anti-miscegenation laws, many states enacted regressive laws that ban same-sex sexual conduct and marriage. In *Lawrence v. Texas* (2003), the US Supreme Court struck down a Texas law and those of thirteen other states known as sodomy laws, ruling that they violated due process under the Fourteenth Amendment, which protects intimate consensual sexual conduct.[125] More recently, the US Supreme Court ruled in *Obergefell v. Hodges* (2015) that same-sex couples also have a fundamental right to marry under the Fourteenth Amendment's equal protection and due process clauses.[126] While no Congressional law bars employment discrimination on the basis of sexual orientation or gender identity, the US Supreme Court upheld this right in *Bostock v. Clayton County* (2020), preempting laws in twenty-eight states that have contracted gay rights by allowing a person to be fired for being lesbian, bisexual, or gay.[127]

Finally, the right to marriage itself is often linked to other rights related to human capital formation. These include inheritance and property rights, succession of marriage when moving across states, medical decision-making authority, adoption rights, birth and death certificates, health insurance, and child custody.[128] Outside of marriage, US lawful permanent residents can adopt children in the United States, which falls under state adoption laws.[129]

Dimension 4: Right to Participate and Be Represented

States holds considerable sway over the right to vote. Federal territories, states, and localities in early America attracted immigrants by expanding them access to suffrage and holding political office, while enacting policies that contracted these same rights for non-Whites and women.[130] Ron Hayduk shows that the progression and regression of noncitizen voting were political choices, not constitutional ones.[131] Until the 1920s, many states granted voting to white immigrants who were "declarant aliens," meaning that they had declared their intent to become US citizens. Some scholars have made a normative case for the continuation of immigrant access to voting. Gerald Rosberg links noncitizen voting rights to the Fourteenth Amendment, arguing that, because aliens are a suspect class and voting is a fundamental right, noncitizens should have a right to vote under the Constitution under the principle of strict scrutiny.[132] Jamin Raskin similarly defends the constitutionality of noncitizen voting through "one person, one vote" jurisprudence and court precedent but makes clear that states get to decide whether to expand or contract immigrant access to voting.[133]

Government policies and court rulings play a significant role in shaping the right to participate and be represented. Contractions in the voting rights of US citizens and immigrants have emerged through many types of policies. State and local policies, especially in the heyday of Jim Crow segregation and exclusion, disenfranchised eligible voters through literacy testing, poll taxes, early registration, and residency requirements for voting. Today, states constrain the right to participate through voter-ID laws and policies that require proof of US citizenship, reduce early voting access, restrict same-day registration, restrict voter registration drives, purge voter files, restrict voting among felons and ex-felons, limit voter assistance, and limit student voter registration efforts on college campuses.[134] Finally, the right to vote can be expanded to US noncitizens and, indeed, there is a storied history of states in the Midwest and the South during the 1800s and early 1900s that allowed noncitizens to vote, as long as they declared their intention to become US citizens.[135]

Importantly, the 1996 Illegal Immigration Reform and Immigrant Responsibility Act (IIR-IRA) prohibited, for the first time, noncitizens from being able to vote in national elections. At the same time, the law continued to allow states to provide for noncitizen voting in state elections, as provided in the US Code (18 USC 611):

§611. Voting by aliens
    (a) It shall be unlawful for any alien to vote in any election held solely or in part for the purpose of electing a candidate for the office of President, Vice President, Presidential elector, Member of the Senate, Member of the House of Representatives, Delegate from the District of Columbia, or Resident Commissioner, unless –

    (1) the election is held partly for some other purpose;

    (2) aliens are authorized to vote for such other purpose under a State constitution or statute or a local ordinance; and

    (3) voting for such other purpose is conducted independently of voting for a candidate for such Federal offices, in such a manner that an alien has the

opportunity to vote for such other purpose, but not an opportunity to vote for a candidate for any one or more of such Federal offices.

Finally, the right to participate also often includes a related right to be represented. The US Constitution stipulated that apportionment would be based on a count of persons. Of course, not all persons were treated equally for purposes of apportionment: slaves were counted as three-fifths of a person until the abolition of slavery and the passage of the Fourteenth Amendment, which stipulated that representation would be based on a count of all persons; likewise, "Indians not taxed" were excluded from being counted by the Census until 1870, and they were not counted for purposes of apportionment until the Indian Citizenship Act of 1924.[136] The Supreme Court has also upheld the principle of equality of representation based on one person, one vote in *Reynolds v. Sims* (1964) and upheld recently in *Evenwel v. Abbott* (2016) that maps would be based on all individuals and not merely US citizens.[137] In addition to Congressional apportionment and redistricting based on a count of persons, all individuals in the United States who are not incarcerated have the right to engage in acts of political participation such as encouraging others to vote, educating them about the political process, and engaging in protest activity. In addition, legal permanent residents are allowed to make campaign contributions, even as they are not allowed to vote in federal elections. Finally, a few municipalities and school boards today provide the right to vote to residents and parents, respectively, regardless of their legal or immigration status.[138]

Dimension 5: Right to Identify and Belong

Finally, governments can also enact policies that expand or contract the right to identify and belong. This feature of citizenship is too often conflated with other concepts such as nationalism, patriotism, or symbolic images of the nation-state's heritage. Often missing in these perspectives is how the state itself can create a sense of belonging for its citizens. Similarly, urban scholars and human rights scholars conflate race, ethnicity, and pan-ethnicity by emphasizing cross-border communal identities or local identities in their concepts of citizenship. We seek to preserve this important dimension of belonging but to recast it in a rights framework, with states playing an active role in enacting a range of policies that either expand or contract the right to identify and belong.

Citizenship commonly invokes a bounded sense of belonging or inclusion, yet, despite having legal citizenship status, many minority groups lack fundamental rights and protections. Federal, state, and local government policies can either expand or contract the right to identify and belong, especially those that expressly address racial and ethnic identities, language, and histories. For example, states and localities can expand access to this right by removing alienating language from laws and removing English-only provisions and policies. They can also grant identification documents that, in addition to having functional uses like driving or access to banking (affecting the right of free movement and right to human capital development), also establish a proof of identity and right to belong in the jurisdiction. Thus, for example, San Francisco, Oakland, New Haven, and a few other cities provide municipal ID cards to all of its residents, including undocumented immigrants, as part of its local vision of membership.[139] Governments also have the ability, through identification documents, Census forms, and other data collections, to grant or refuse official recognition to particular groups such as transgender communities and racial/ethnic groups.

Finally, expansions in the right to identify include official government acts, statement, or apologies that seek to recognize past policy discriminations and to acknowledge groups as being valued. For example, after the Japanese attacked Pearl Harbor in 1942, President Roosevelt issued Executive Order 9066 to detain an estimated 120,000 Japanese Americans and place them into internment camps. In 1998, the federal government formally apologized by enacting the Civil Liberties Act, which granted reparations to Japanese Americans who had been interned. Similarly, on June 18, 2012, the US House of Representatives passed House Resolution 683, formally apologizing for the federal government's Chinese Exclusion Act of 1883. Listing the history of the Burlingame Treaty of 1868, which not only encouraged Chinese immigration to the United States but also afforded certain rights and protections to Chinese once they arrive, the resolution cites key provisions of the Chinese Exclusion Act. It then formally apologizes, stating that "the House of Representatives regrets the passage of legislation that adversely affected people of Chinese origin in the United States because of their ethnicity."[140]

STATE CITIZENSHIP AND AMERICAN FEDERALISM

Despite the emergence of federal plenary power over US immigration policy in the late 1800s, states and localities have continued to play important roles in regulating the lives of immigrants. Our work bridges citizenship studies with the fast-growing literature on immigration federalism, which examines the recent proliferation of state and local restrictive and integrationist immigration policies. American federalism intersects with citizenship and immigration in important and related ways. We therefore examine how federalism structures state and local citizenships, including the types of policies that emerge to provide a range of rights to immigrants, and relative thresholds for determining inclusion and exclusion. Federal immigration law targets undocumented immigrants for removal, and enforcement takes place within federal, state, and local jurisdictions. It is therefore necessary to consider how federalism – through Constitutional developments, federal law, and court decisions – shape state and local provision of rights before being able to claim that separate state and local citizenships exist.

We employ our concept of citizenship to systematically disaggregate national, state and local provisions of rights to their respective members and argue that each level forms distinctive regimes of citizenship: national, state, and local citizenships (see Figure 2.7). All of three citizenship subtypes emerge in a federalist framework as conceptually distinctive in their provision of the five core citizenship rights. Each citizenship subtype runs parallel to the others.

Our notion of citizenship is constitutionally rooted and constrained by federalism. States do not have an inherent right to pass policies that provide rights in each of the five dimensions. Their power to do so is subject to federalism dynamics. In the remainder of this book, we employ an American political development approach to explain how state citizenship develops, and we argue that it is constitutive, meaning that it expands and contracts over time. Key institutions and political movements shape state citizenship, including: the role of courts in shaping constitutional state and local powers, federal law's intersections with state and local powers, and the role of political parties and social movements. Also, as we elaborated in Chapter 1, our focus in this book is on the development of state citizenship in the United States. We do this not only

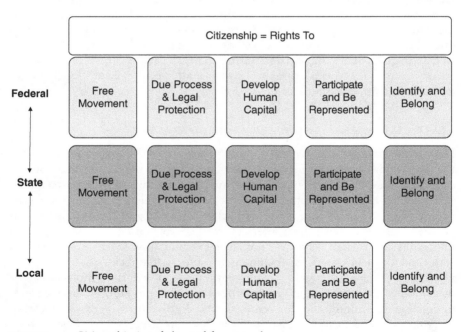

FIGURE 2.7 Citizenship in a federated framework

with an eye toward simplicity but also because of the special role for states (and not localities) accorded by the US Constitution and the deference given by courts to allowing states virtually free rein in how they structure the power of local governments within their jurisdictions.

Finally, it is important to note that state citizenship is not semi-citizenship. Cohen's concept of *semi-citizenship* reveals differential rights across groups that do not have the full bundle of citizenship rights. Her analytical framework adds precision to the concept of citizenship by identifying two types of rights – autonomous rights and relative rights – found in the core dimensions of civil, political, social, and nationality rights that Cohen argues are essential to national citizenship. Different types of semi-citizenship can emerge from this framework, which illustrates that citizenship is not an all-or-nothing venture or simply defined by legal status. Through multiple semi-citizenship subtypes, Cohen captures some of the important fault lines separating groups, with each subtype containing different core rights but not all of the core rights of national citizenship.[141]

Our concept of state citizenship builds on the tradition of T. H. Marshall, Irene Bloemraad, and Elizabeth Cohen, but our empirical and theoretical goals differ. Bloemraad, Korteweg, and Yurdakul reveal common dimensions across the diverse citizenship literature, and Cohen reveals differential access to citizenship rights. We employ our state-centric and rights-based definition to develop a generalizable and systematic concept of citizenship, with consistent rules. We argue that robust regimes of (full, not semi-) citizenship emerge as the bundling of the five core dimensions of rights, after each dimension meets specific thresholds.

Our concept of state citizenship falls under a "kind hierarchy" with *classical* subtypes, as advanced by Giovanni Sartori and elaborated by David Collier and others.[142] Moving up and down Sartori's ladder of abstraction, we systematically develop our concept of state citizenship along a vertical array of concepts to increase analytical differentiation and avoid conceptual stretching.[143] As a classical subtype, state citizenship has the attributes of the superordinate concept of citizenship, plus attributes that differentiate it from national citizenship and local citizenship.[144] At both the superordinate (citizenship) level and classical subtype level (state citizenship), we add conceptual precision by setting a consistent rule on what the dimensions ought to be and how to operationalize and measure them. By contrast, Cohen's concept of semi-citizenship falls under a "part-whole hierarchy" with *diminished* subtypes of full citizenship rights.[145] Semi-citizenships are diminished subtypes of full citizenship, and, as we show in Figure 2.8, one can speak of semi-citizenship at varying levels of government – national, state, or local.

Our American political development approach speaks to semi-citizenship in important ways but avoids conflating it with state citizenship. We trace expansions and contractions in rights across all five dimensions, over time, to

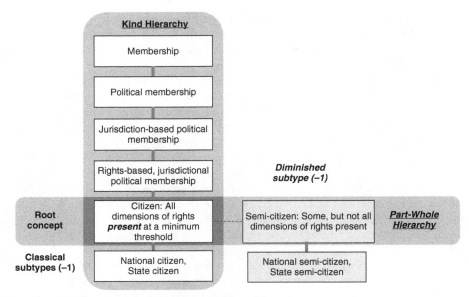

FIGURE 2.8 State citizenship and semi-citizenship

explain the development of state citizenship. In the process of cumulating rights across all five dimensions, one can speak of the semi-citizenship of different groups, at different historical periods, and at any level of government. Our theoretical focus is on state citizenship emerging through this historical process, where rights cumulate and reach a tipping point that pushes toward robust regimes of state citizenship.

WHAT IS PROGRESSIVE STATE CITIZENSHIP?

We conceptualize and operationalize citizenship as the expansion or contraction in the provision of rights by states and also allow for the possibility of discriminatory practices and other barriers to meaningfully access those rights among different groups in society. Governments can either *expand* or *contract* its provision of rights to its members along all five of citizenship's core dimensions. Building from our concept of citizenship in a federalist framework, as laid out in this chapter, we develop a typology of state citizenship regimes that relate the provision of state rights to those provided at the national level (Figure 2.9). For instance, states have, in various periods, expanded rights for protected classes beyond those provided at federal level or have established state-level protected classes in the absence of federal rights. We classify these instances as regimes of *progressive state citizenship*. Examples include the provision of Black voting rights in

Types of State Citizenship	Relation to Federal Citizenship	Examples
Progressive	*Expand rights above those provided at federal level, and/or establish state-level protected classes in the absence of federal rights*	Black voting rights in antebellum North Noncitizen voting pre-World War II Women's suffrage in states pre-1919 Gay marriage in states pre-2015 Immigrant rights regime in CA post-2014
Reinforcing	*Reinforce or mirror federal rules on rights provision*	*Inclusionary:* State anti-discrimination laws that reinforce federal rules *Exclusionary:* State driver's licenses requiring federal legal presence Naturalization requirements for state employment; State restrictions on welfare eligibility
Regressive	*Restrict or erode rights provided at federal level, and/or establish state-level pariah classes*	Bans on black voting in antebellum North; Slavery and re-enslavement laws in antebellum South Jim Crow laws Voter ID laws post-2006 Immigrant rights regimes in AZ, GA

FIGURE 2.9 Variants of state citizenship in a federated framework

antebellum North (see Chapter 4), White noncitizen voting in many Midwestern states and territories prior to World War I (see Chapter 6), state-level voting rights for women before the passage of the Nineteenth Amendment in 1920, state rights on gay marriage before the Supreme Court decision in *Obergefell v. Hodges* in 2015, and California's regime on immigrant rights after 2015 (see Chapter 5).

States have also restricted or eroded rights that were supposed to be guaranteed to protected classes at the federal level, or they have established state-level pariah classes in the absence of federal declarations on the matter. We classify these as instances of *regressive state citizenship*. Examples of regressive state citizenship include bans on Black voting in the antebellum North (see Chapters 3 and 4), Jim Crow–era laws excluding Blacks from equal rights to participation, free movement, and due process in violation of the Fourteenth Amendment (see Chapters 3 and 4), and laws eroding immigrant rights in states like Arizona and Georgia today (Chapter 6).

Finally, state laws can also reinforce or mirror federal rules on the provision of rights, expanding their applicability and reach by attaching them to state-level privileges and penalties. Thus, for example, most states today provide driver's licenses only to those residents who have federal legal presence. Many states have also prevented undocumented immigrants from accessing state welfare benefits and access to public colleges and universities, and most states require US citizenship as a requirement for employment in certain types of professions such as law enforcement. These are examples of *reinforcing state citizenship* that move in an exclusionary direction – using federal rights restrictions as a template to enact state-level restrictions. At the same time, states can also reinforce federal rules in a manner that promotes inclusionary citizenship. Thus, for instance, states laws can mirror federal rules on nondiscrimination in employment and housing and attach state-level enforcement mechanisms and penalties that deepen the provision of federal rights.

It is important to note that our notions of progressive and regressive citizenship, which are based in a federated framework, are related to notions of inclusive and exclusionary citizenship but are not identical to them. Inclusive and exclusionary notions of citizenship take on absolute measures and operate at any level of government. By contrast, our notion of progressive, restrictive, and regressive citizenship looks at rights provided at the state level *relative* to those provided at the federal level. Thus, for example, if citizenship policies are identically inclusive at the federal level and at the state level, we can speak of inclusive citizenship policy at the state level but not progressive citizenship at the state level, because there is no difference between the federal "floor" on inclusion and what the state is able to provide. A similar logic would apply to exclusive regimes of citizenship: those regimes would be characterized as regressive only if the state regime were more exclusive than the federal one.

As we illustrate in Figure 2.9, most driver's licenses policies today can be considered a form of reinforcing state citizenship that is exclusionary, as most states use federal guidelines on lawful presence to determine access to this important state right to free movement. Meanwhile, California and other states have enacted policies that grant undocumented immigrants access to state driver's licenses, which is progressive on the right to free movement. By contrast, Jim Crow laws on voting (such as literacy tests, poll taxes, early registration, and residency requirements) can be considered regressive forms of state citizenship because they restrict access to federally guaranteed rights and are not simply reinforcing or mirroring federal restrictions. By contrast, state laws that allow local extension of voting rights to noncitizens are considered progressive because they exceed federal rights.

We noted in our introductory chapter that most scholars of race and civil rights in the United States tend to provide a pessimistic view of federalism. Jamila Michener, for example, argues that federalism acts as an institutional "purveyor of political inequality" that erodes the political capacity among low-income people, especially Black and Latino minorities who are low-income, because they reside in the wrong states, counties, or neighborhoods – with restrictive Medicaid policies.[146] Skepticism began with William Riker's 1964 statement about federalism promoting racism and discrimination, especially in the South: "if in the United States one disapproves of racism, one should disapprove of federalism," and by contrast, "if in the United States one approves of Southern white racists, then one should approve of American federalism."[147]

Our study explores the three variants of *regressive, reinforcing,* and *progressive* state citizenship, revealing how American federalism can either hinder or improve racial equality. We show how early American federalism placed states into a central and exclusive role in the provision of rights. For example, Chapter 5 shows how California's statehood and entry into the Union happened in a short span of a year, largely as a result of finding gold during the moment of the Mexican American war. Even before statehood, California began to enact robust contractions in the rights of Blacks, Native Americans, Mexican Americans, and immigrants. It soon placed some of these exclusions into its state constitution, developed a robust *regressive* state citizenship through anti-Chinese laws before the federal Chinese Exclusion Act of 1882, and then, up until 1998, formed a robust *exclusionary* state citizenship reinforcing federal immigration law's restrictions on Mexican immigrants.

While California dramatically shifted after 1998 toward forming a *progressive* regime of state citizenship by 2015, innovating and expanding immigrant rights, Arizona and other states developed *reinforcing and exclusionary* regimes of state citizenship, advancing a "mirror theory" of immigration enforcement by the states. Most notably Arizona's defense of S.B. 1070 was to mirror federal immigration status definitions and pursue the same general goals of federal immigration law of identifying and removing unlawfully present persons. Arizona's law created a state immigration enforcement scheme to coexist and mirror federal schemes.[148] One of the authors of S.B. 1070, former Kansas Secretary of State Kris Kobach, championed the "mirror image theory" of Arizona's law as a way to protect federal plenary authority under Article I of the US Constitution.[149]

Through a historical-institutional approach, we explain the formation of these three state citizenship subtypes in a federalist framework. We contribute to the well-established federalism scholarship that reveals regressive and restrictive elements around race, but we challenge the notion that these pathways of political development are linear or inescapable. We also build on and advance the concept of progressive federalism, which has provided a much-needed pivot to focusing on the positive role of states and localities in advancing progress but remains underdeveloped – only focusing on states' progressive role in pushing national-level reforms. We contribute to this emerging scholarship on progressive federalism, broadening the conceptualization beyond its nationalist orientation. Progressive federalism does not only filter up to national reforms. Regardless of what is pushed federally, we show that there is still room for states and localities to advance autonomous subnational reforms and innovations.

One of our core arguments is that federalism creates room for states and localities to develop divergent pathways that runs parallel to federal-level developments, occasionally conflicting with national policy but also complementing it. Tensions are an inherent feature of federalism. Progressive state citizenship provides a hopeful and viable story about inclusive possibilities in federalism, race, and citizenship. It also advances a broader conception of progressive federalism as having national, state, and local orientations – national reforms can progress from bottom-up diffusion (per Gerken and Bullman-Pozen),[150] but state and local progressive reforms can also remain distinctive and separate from national level developments.

INDICATORS OF PROGRESSIVE STATE CITIZENSHIP

So far, we have laid out our concept of citizenship as the provision of rights (and access to those rights) along five dimensions: (1) right to free movement; (2) right to due process and legal protection; (3) right to develop human capital; (4) right to participate and be represented; and (5) the right to identify and belong. We have also introduced three variants of state citizenship that emerge from expanding or contracting the provision of these rights, in a federalist framework. In this section, we operationalize our concept of progressive state citizenship by identifying the full set of possible indicators and thresholds in all five dimensions of rights.

Progressive state citizenship is a classical subtype that exists only when all five dimensions are present. Concept formation in the tradition of Giovanni Satori requires clear standards for determining when state governments expand or contract its provision of rights in each dimension and when all five dimensions cumulate to create a regressive, restrictive, or progressive form of state citizenship. To capture this variation, we advance an additive scheme of indicators with unique minimum thresholds for determining whether an expansion or contraction of rights takes place in each dimension. Our approach goes well beyond an arbitrary categorization of rights as citizenship, offering an additive scheme that reveals the timing and sequencing of each dimension's development and possible tipping points toward regressive or progressive state citizenship. In Chapters 4 through 6, we provide a detailed look at how states perform on various indicators of state citizenship for Blacks and immigrants in the historical and contemporary period (see Table 2.1). Our aim here is to provide a broad set of indicators that enable us to *operationalize* state citizenship before we get to scoring particular states, in particular time periods, and for particular populations.

TABLE 2.1 *Indicators of state citizenship: D1 right to free movement*

Dimension 1: Right to Free Movement	Threshold for Progressive State Citizenship	Preempted
Right to drive		
Driver's license	*Minimum requirement*	
Auto insurance	*Minimum requirement*	
No car impounds	*Minimum requirement*	
Right to take public transportation	*Minimum requirement*	
Right to access government building	*Minimum requirement*	
Right to access safe spaces from federal enforcement		
Schools	*Minimum requirement*	
Hospitals	*Minimum requirement*	
Courts	*Minimum requirement*	
Right to go freely after law enforcement stops/holds	*Minimum requirement*	
Right to access international airports		*Preempted*
Right to safely pass through immigration checkpoints		*Preempted*
Right to stay		*Preempted*

Right to free movement: Obtaining a driver licenses today has become an essential feature of the right to free movement that has immediate impacts on areas of rights. In states that deny undocumented residents access to a driver's license, local police officers can partner with federal immigration officers by setting up driver's license checkpoints, and sobriety checkpoints can lead to immigration consequences.[151] The risks in driving without a license range from deportation to financial consequences of being cited or having their car impounded.[152] In addition to requiring a policy enacted that grants undocumented residents driver's licenses, we also require a policy providing access to auto insurance and preventing car impounds as minimum thresholds on the right to drive.

More broadly, we require a minimum threshold on a basic right to take public transportation, either as a *de jure* expansion of this right or as a *de facto* practice. We also consider a basic right to access state government buildings and designated spaces free of enforcement to be critical to free movement. These indicators and policies bundle together to distinguish the formation of a right to free movement in the contemporary period. Meanwhile, there are many areas today that are federally regulated and preempted. States cannot determine or regulate international airports, federal immigration checkpoints, or the right to stay. America's contemporary federalist framework of federal immigration regulations and enforcement practices significantly constrain many of state citizenship's rights, especially on free movement. Finally, we also include indicators of free movement rights from the antebellum period with respect to free Blacks, runaway slaves, and Southern slaves. While most individuals are not subject to similar restrictions in the United States today, it is nevertheless important to include those free movement rights in our general set of indicators that can span across various periods in American history.

Right to due process and legal protection: Federal immigration agents have access to law enforcement databases at the state and local levels. States and localities can enact polices that limit access to certain types of crimes, and they can enact policies that change their own sentencing – lowering a sentence to less than a year, for example – in order to avoid immigration consequences. Moreover, there are a range of policies highlighted in Table 2.2 that states can enact to expand undocumented immigrants' due process rights once they are detained. While unauthorized immigrants lack constitutional and federal due process protections in immigration court, state policies that limit holds to forty-eight hours, inform people in their custody of a detainer request, and create legal protections of attorney confidentiality, among other expansions in rights, can be critical to preventing possible transfers to ICE and deportation consequences. Whereas the state can legally and financial innovate more robust immigrant rights protections, we identify only the most critical baseline of due process and legal protections as setting the cumulative threshold for Dimension 2. Despite being considered inalienable rights in

TABLE 2.2 *Indicators of state citizenship: D2 right to due process and legal protection*

Dimension 2: Right to Due Process and Legal Protection	Threshold for Progressive State Citizenship	Preempted
Right not to be profiled against for *presumed* legal status	*Minimum requirement*	
Right not to be asked about legal status	*Minimum requirement*	
Noncooperation in federal immigration enforcement	*Minimum requirement*	
Absence of state and local deportation practices	*Minimum requirement*	
Right not to have enforcement information shared (with fed.)	*Minimum requirement*	
Right not to have any information shared	*Above minimum*	
Right to be informed of immigration detainer request	*Above minimum*	
Right to testify in court	*Minimum requirement*	
Right to enter into contracts	*Above minimum*	
Right to due process		
Against unconstitutional detentions (forty-eight hours)	*Minimum requirement*	
Against unreasonable search and seizure	*Minimum requirement*	
Entitled to phone calls when detained	*Minimum requirement*	
Right to attorney confidentiality	*Minimum requirement*	
Right to attorney ethical representation	*Minimum requirement*	
Right to post bail, pardoning, commutation, and rehabilitation	*Minimum requirement*	
Right to crime victim protections	*Minimum requirement*	
Financial assistance for legal counsel involving immigration	*Above minimum*	
Sentencing to prevent immigration implications	*Above minimum*	
Right to federal immigration relief services	*Above minimum*	

criminal court, these same rights are not provided to immigrants charged for civil violations in immigration court, making state policies especially critical.

Sometimes, policies can simultaneously expand the right to due process and free movement. For example, the California Values Act (AB 54) passed in 2017 expanded due process rights, expanding legal protection by limiting whom state and local law enforcement can hold, question, and transfer to federal immigration authorities. At the same time, it also expanded the right of free movement by creating more safe spaces for unauthorized immigrants. AB 54 states:

The Attorney General, by October 1, 2018, in consultation with the appropriate stakeholders, shall publish model policies limiting assistance with immigration enforcement to the fullest extent possible consistent with federal and state law at public schools, public libraries, health facilities operated by the state or a political subdivision of the state, courthouses, Division of Labor Standards Enforcement facilities, the Agricultural Labor Relations Board, the Division of Workers Compensation, and shelters, and ensuring that they remain safe and accessible to all California residents, regardless of immigration status. All public schools, health facilities operated by the state or a political subdivision of the state, and courthouses shall implement the model policy, or an equivalent policy. The Agricultural Labor Relations Board, the Division of Workers' Compensation, the Division of Labor Standards Enforcement, shelters, libraries, and all other organizations and entities that provide services related to physical or mental health and wellness, education, or access to justice, including the University of California, are encouraged to adopt the model policy.[153]

We consider AB 54 to be a milestone expansion in noncooperation, absence of police in deportation practices, and right not to be asked about legal status – and qualify this policy as meeting the minimum thresholds for those particular indicators highlighted in Table 2.2. Nevertheless, the law could have done even more to decouple state and local resources from federal immigration law. The bill's author, Senate leader Kevin De León, amended it to allow police officers to work on federal task forces not focused on immigration enforcement, to allow for transferring and sharing information with federal officials about felons with violent or serious convictions, granting immigration authorities access to state and local jails to interview inmates but denying them permanent office spaces in jails.[154] Finally, as in the case of free movement, our framework on the rights to due process and legal protection can also be used outside of the contemporary immigration context, as we shall see with the example of Blacks during the antebellum and Jim Crow periods.

Right to develop human capital: Beginning in 1996, new federal laws made many groups of noncitizens ineligible for important federal health care benefits and prohibited states from conferring public benefits, including professional licenses and in-state tuition, among others, to unauthorized immigrants unless the state affirmatively enacted a new state law providing these benefits. Thus, while *Plyer v Doe* (1982) provides a universal constitutional right to K–12 education, states control the right to postsecondary education, equity, and financial aid. They are central to all aspects of health care from lawfully residing immigrants and undocumented immigrants alike. Moreover, given the vulnerability of undocumented workers – of threats by employers to report them to federal immigration agents, despite federal labor law protections – states play an important role in filling gaps in labor protection, particularly in limiting how legal status can be used by placing legal sanctions and fines on employers for labor violations, exploitation, and use of legal status reporting as a form of retaliation.

Expanding access, equity, and protection in education, health, and work critically determine the right to develop human capital (see Table 2.3).

TABLE 2.3 *Indicators of state citizenship: D3 right to develop human capital*

Dimension 3: Right to Develop Human Capital	Threshold	Preempted
Right to K–12 education	*Minimum requirement*	
Right to public higher education		
Access equal to US citizens	*Minimum requirement*	
In-state tuition	*Minimum requirement*	
Financial aid	*Minimum requirement*	
Right to health care		
Emergency care	*Minimum requirement*	
Private care	*Minimum requirement*	
Subsidized for free health insurance	*Minimum requirement*	
Food and nutrition assistance	*Minimum requirement*	
Right to work		
No wrongful termination	*Minimum requirement*	
Labor protections equal to US citizens	*Minimum requirement*	
Access to practice professions with a license	*Minimum requirement*	
Access to public employment	*Above minimum*	
Access to private work contracts	*Above minimum*	
Right to property, assets, and wealth		
Banking	*Minimum requirement*	
Land and home ownership	*Minimum requirement*	
Estates, wills, trusts, beneficiary	*Minimum requirement*	
Right to shelter		
Access to affordable rent equal to US citizens	*Minimum requirement*	
Right to marriage	*Minimum requirement*	
Right to child custody	*Minimum requirement*	
Right to adopt	*Above minimum*	
Right to family reunification	*Above minimum*	

Similarly, states can ensure that undocumented immigrants have a right to shelter and can access this right, by legally preventing local landlords from requiring proof of legal status – a legal tactic employed by anti-immigrant restrictions in the early 2000s. Lastly, state laws regulate the right to marriage and adopt, and they can shape the right to family reunification. As we shall see in Chapters 3 and 4, these state-controlled rights pertaining to family formation have been particularly salient in the case of Blacks and other racial minorities prior to the 1960s and for LGBT individuals in the contemporary period.

Right to participate and be represented: We have already noted that the US Constitution allows for the representation of all persons, regardless of their legal status. In addition, the First Amendment's free speech protections set up a constitutional right to participate, including a right to protest, engage in consumer activism, sign petitions, mobilize and educate voters, and contact public officials. Nevertheless, given the vulnerability of undocumented immigrants and other marginalized groups, states can enact policies that contract these rights. Interior immigration enforcement can threaten or physically prevent undocumented immigrants from engaging in protests or other activities. Similarly, local law enforcement can prevent or limit racial minority citizens from their rights to organize, protest, or even contact officials. We therefore consider state-level safeguards to these rights to be a minimum requirement for the right to participate and be represented to exist (see Table 2.4).

In early America, settlers had to be attracted to new territories, and extending the right to vote was a strategy to attract new immigrants: in many cases, immigrants were also allowed to hold office without becoming a citizen. Most states continued to allow immigrants to vote elections until the 1920s.[155] From 1920 until 1968, immigrants were generally barred from voting through state and local laws. In 1968, New York City passed a law to provide noncitizen parents of schoolchildren the right to vote in community school board elections and to hold office on school boards.[156] In 1991, Takoma Park, Maryland, became the first city to provide noncitizens the right to vote in city government elections, not only expanding participation but also providing important representation to the city's majority immigrant population. In 2016, San Francisco joined these progressive cities by passing Proposition N, allowing noncitizen parents or guardians to vote in school board elections. States control local voting laws, and we consider these local rights to be an extension of state policy. For example, states like Maryland expressly recognizing "home rule" – the idea that municipalities have authority to pass laws relating to the incorporation, organization, government, or other affairs within its jurisdiction – allow cities to provide noncitizens the right to vote in local elections.[157] Moreover, it is constitutionally possible for states to once again provide voting rights to noncitizens, and, since 1990, many states have proposed legislation to do so.[158]

TABLE 2.4 *Indicators of state citizenship: D4 right to participate and be represented*

Dimension 4: Right to Participate and Be Represented	Threshold	Preempted
Right to contact public officials	*Minimum requirement*	
Right to mobilize voters	*Minimum requirement*	
Right to educate voters	*Minimum requirement*	
Right to attend public hearings	*Minimum requirement*	
Right to serve on a jury	*Above minimum*	
Right to Be counted in US Census (apportionment)	*Minimum requirement*	
Right to contribute to electoral campaigns		
Local	*Minimum requirement*	
State	*Minimum requirement*	
Federal	*Above minimum*	*Preempted (except LPRs)*
Right to be represented on law enforcement–related task force		
Local	*Above minimum*	
State	*Above minimum*	
Federal	*Above minimum*	
Right to vote in elections		
Local	*Minimum requirement*	
State	*Above minimum*	
Federal		*Preempted*
Right to serve in appointed office		
Local	*Minimum requirement*	
State	*Above minimum*	
Federal		*Preempted*
Right to run for elected office		
Local	*Above minimum*	
State	*Above minimum*	
Federal		*Preempted*

Elections and office holding at the state and local government levels go beyond voting, and we set the minimum thresholds requirement as the right to contribute money to campaigns and the right to serve on a locally appointed office in government. States can extend rights above these minimum levels, deepening the state's provision of the right to participate by: granting the right to vote in school board elections, local elections, and state elections; granting the right to serve on a jury; and granting the right to serve as an appointed or elected state government official. State and local governments have begun to provide noncitizens a right to be appointed to political office. For example, Huntington Park in California appointed two undocumented immigrant residents to political commissions in 2015.[159] More recently, in 2018, California similarly appointed an undocumented immigrant to serve on the California Student Opportunity and Access Program Project Grant Advisory Committee, to advise on ways to increase college access to low-income or underserved communities in the state. While we consider local political appointments as minimum threshold requirements, state appointments go above the threshold to deepen the right to participate.[160]

Right to identify and belong: Lastly, indicators of expanding the right to identify and belong certainly require at a minimum level some form of official government-sanctioned identification documented – whether this is a driver's license or other state ID – for nonimmigration-related purposes within the state. Moreover, a minimum level of state policies and practices is required to demonstrate equal public accommodation, as well as a similarly minimum level removal of alienating language from policies and, when historically relevant, governmental apologies and recognition of past alienating practices and formal acts of exclusion or harm (see Table 2.5). While these policies do not need to be robust in scope and total number, they should signal through official government policies a right to identify and belong equal to US citizens.

TABLE 2.5 *Indicators of state citizenship: D5 right to identify and belong*

Dimension 5: Right to Identify and Belong	Threshold	Preempted
Public accommodation equal to US citizen (bedrock principle)	*Minimum requirement*	
Right to identification document	*Minimum requirement*	
Absence of alienating language in policy	*Minimum requirement*	
Absence of alienating language in society	*Above minimum*	
Absence of English-only policy	*Minimum requirement*	
Acts of apology for historical exclusions	*Minimum requirement*	
Acts of symbolic inclusion	*Minimum requirement*	
Acts of reparations for historical injustices	*Above minimum*	

In 1937, California's state legislature began to use the term "alien" in its labor code for employed non-US citizens. Most of its Labor Code statutes were repealed in 1970, but California's definition for "alien" remained in place. In 2015, the chair of the Senate Labor and Industrial Labor Relations Committee, California Senator Tony Mendoza, introduced S.B. 432. A core argument in support of the law made in the Senate Rules Committee was that "any derogative references to foreign-born individuals be repealed from state law" and that "the word 'alien' has no place in the laws of our state and more importantly, should never be the basis of an employment hiring protocol."[161] Passed on August 10, 2015, S.B. 432 deleted the outdated and discriminatory reference to "aliens" in state law, marking an important step forward in welcoming and embracing immigrants as integral to California's culture, society, and economy. Outside of the immigration context, recent state laws allowing transgendered individuals to indicate a gender other than male or female on government forms, and driver's licenses present a powerful example of states providing, and controlling, the right of particular groups to identify and belong.

Only when all five dimensions reach their theoretical, minimally required thresholds do they cumulate to form a robust regime of state citizenship. This section illustrated the thresholds for progressive dimensions on progressive state citizenship and focused on contemporary examples expanding rights through state policies on undocumented immigrants. However, as we show in Chapters 3 and 4, these indicators can also apply to state expansions of rights for other groups of US citizen and noncitizen alike and to other historical periods. And they can also apply, in reverse, to notions of regressive state citizenship, as we illustrate with our examples involving Blacks (Chapter 4) and immigrants (Chapters 5 and 6). Our additive scheme of indicators is grounded in minimum thresholds for determining whether an expansion or contraction of rights takes place, providing important conceptual precision to the meaning of progressive state citizenship as well as analytical clarity on the timing and sequencing of each dimension and their formation of state citizenship.

CONCLUSIONS

Our notion of *state citizenship* rubs against the dominant representation of national citizenship as an exclusion-based, formal, and unitary membership, set up by sovereign nations that have exclusive power over their borders and people. Impressive as state integration policy gains are, some may dispute the very notion that states (within a nation) are able to create a new form of citizenship. State citizenship makes sense in a federalist framework and as a parallel concept to national citizenship. It does not refer to state secession by another name, nor is it meant to highlight states' rights as in the context of the American Civil War. We argue that federalism has lasting consequences for citizenship, which we define quite simply as the provision of rights by a political jurisdiction to its members.

What happens at the national level directly impacts state citizenship's dimensions, indicators, and thresholds. Furthermore, our federalist framework considers state citizenship to be complementary to national level dynamics rather than in conflict with national citizenship. Specifically, state citizenship emerges from the expansion or contraction of core rights (and access to those rights) along five dimensions: (1) the right to free movement; (2) the right to due process and legal protection; (3) the right to develop human capital; (4) the right to participate and be represented; and (5) the right to identify and belong.

We also uncover three types of state citizenship in a federalism framework: (a) regressive state citizenship, where states erode rights that granted to individuals at the federal level; (b) reinforcing state citizenship, where states enforce federal limitations on rights to particular types of individuals; and (c) progressive state citizenship, where states exceed the rights granted to particular types of individuals at the federal level. As we shall see in Chapter 3 and beyond, these concepts and indicators are especially helpful in understanding contemporary dynamics in immigrant rights at the state and local levels. At the same time, our conceptual framework is also designed in a way that it can be more broadly applicable to understanding citizenship rights as they involve race, gender, and LGBT identity. So far, we have laid out a general framework for federated citizenship, where national, state, and local forms of citizenship can coexist, with the potential for federalism conflict and accommodation over time. We now turn to examine the development of federated citizenship in the United States, where courts, parties, social movements, and political institutions have played a significant role in shaping the evolution of state citizenship and national citizenship over time.

3

National and State Citizenship in the American Context

Conventional wisdom might suggest that national citizenship in the United States began with its founding Constitution. After all, the country had experimented with the Articles of Confederation for a few years and found it to be so lacking in national power that the Founders pushed for a constitutional convention to form a stronger national government. Interestingly, however, the original constitution makes only three mentions of "Citizens of the United States," and all of them relate to eligibility for serving as president, as a member of the House of Representatives, or as a member of the US Senate. In addition, the original constitution also requires that the president be a "natural born Citizen," meaning someone who is a citizen at birth and not someone who acquires citizenship through naturalization.[1] All other mentions of citizenship in the original Constitution relate to state citizenship, noting that "[t]he Citizens of each State shall be entitled to all Privileges and Immunities of Citizens in the several States"[2] and that the judicial power of the United States extends to adjudicating disputes involving "a State and Citizens of another State, between Citizens of different States, between Citizens of the same State claiming Lands under Grants of different States, and between a State, or the Citizens thereof, and foreign States, Citizens or Subjects."[3] The founders' Constitution, via the Bill of Rights, did specify various rights and liberties to persons regardless of their nativity or status as state citizens or citizens of the United States, but those rights were confined to only those involving the national government. Indeed, the Tenth Amendment to the US Constitution, which noted that "[t]he powers not delegated to the United States by the Constitution, nor prohibited by it to the States, are reserved to the States respectively, or to the people," was largely interpreted by Congress and the courts as giving wide latitude to states to determine the rights of citizens and persons in relation to state government authority.

It was not until the passage of the Fourteenth Amendment after the Civil War that the US Constitution harmonized the rights of individuals involving federal and state government alike, with important provisions protecting individual rights through birthright citizenship, equal protection, and due process. Ironically, these guarantees of national citizenship also meant that the stage was set for regressive state citizenship. As we show in this chapter, the Fourteenth Amendment established a new constitutional foundation for the federal government to preempt or overrule state laws that limited rights of its residents. However, the Fourteenth Amendment's safeguards were largely a matter of principle rather than practice, a political reality determined by Supreme Court jurisprudence and the weakness of the Republican Party in the South. The state of courts and parties after Reconstruction strengthened the ability of states to take over control of the rights of Blacks. As a result, the Fourteenth Amendment effectively set the stage for a new form of federated citizenship – what we call "regressive state citizenship."

Our concept of citizenship as multidimensional and federated captures the tensions between major developments in national citizenship, such as the Fourteenth Amendment, that still allow for states to expand or contract rights. We employ the American Political Development (APD) approach to ground our conceptual framework on multidimensional and federated citizenship in the particulars of the American legal, political, and historical context. As noted in our introductory chapter, APD is an approach that focuses on the development and transformation of political orders, defined loosely as the political arrangement of institutions, policies, and groups – capturing "durable shifts in governing authority."[4] The explanatory framework that we develop reveals how American federalism shapes state governments' authority to expand and contract citizenship rights. Specifically, we argue that federalism shapes the contours of state citizenship through: (1) *constitutional opportunities* that arise from amendment activity and court interpretation; (2) *legislative actions* that emerge from the work of political parties and social movements; and (3) *executive actions* that result from the bureaucratic capacity and political will of national and state governments to enforce citizenship rights (Figure 3.1). Put another way, constitutional

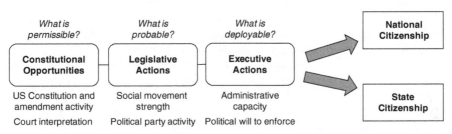

FIGURE 3.1 Explanatory framework for changes in state citizenship

opportunities set the constraints on what is *permissible* for states and the federal government to legislate on citizenship rights; legislative actions animate what is *probable* on citizenship rights; and executive actions guide what is *deployable* and ultimately enforced on citizenship rights at the national and state levels.

What is permissible, probable, and deployable combine together at key moments in time to expand or contract multiple dimensions of citizenship rights as laid out in Chapter 2. The US Constitution and courts set the opportunity for state citizenship to exist, while federal institutions and actors' legislative and executive actions shape the scope and forms that state citizenship takes. At times in American history, there is a strong alignment between the two levels of government as states reinforce what is occurring nationally with respect to the expansion or contraction of rights for certain groups. Importantly, alignment between federal and state visions for citizenship is rarely static. Regressive state citizenship under Jim Crow was only possible after passage of the Fourteenth Amendment, and it took nearly a century after the Civil War for court decisions, social movements, and Congressional action to strengthen the hand of the federal government vis-à-vis states in guaranteeing Black citizenship rights. Even so, during this same period in American history, states did not recede from the scene with respect to advancing progress on rights, particularly women's rights.

As we show in this chapter, state citizenship has emerged in specific US political contexts and broadly affects immigrants and the native-born alike, as well as disenfranchised populations including communities of color, women, and sexual minorities. The transition from state to federal citizenship rights are neither linear nor permanent, nor do they apply equally to all groups. It is often the case that some groups experience major expansions in their rights at the same time that other groups face contractions in rights at either the federal or state levels or both. Nevertheless, in grounding our concept of state citizenship in an explanatory framework specific to the US context, we seek to show that major developments in *constitutional opportunities* and *legislative action* do translate into major transformations in the rights of most groups (such as Blacks, immigrants, women, and LGBT communities). The conceptual framework we develop in Chapter 2 and the explanatory framework developed in this chapter inform the rest of the book – where we provide a deeper examination of the evolving nature of state citizenship as it pertains specifically to Black citizenship (Chapter 4) and immigrant citizenship (Chapters 5 and 6) in the United States.

STATE CITIZENSHIP AND AMERICAN POLITICAL DEVELOPMENT

In the tradition of APD scholarship, we argue that the boundaries of national and state citizenship are structured or constrained by the American constitutional framework as interpreted by courts. And yet, the constitutional framework only lays out the broad contours of what is permissible; it is the activism of Congress and state legislatures, often propelled by party and social movement activism, that animates and fills in the details of how state citizenship and national citizenship operate in relation to each other. On rare occasions, activism by parties and social movements are so significant that they prompt changes in the constitutional framework itself, either through constitutional amendments or by shaping court perceptions of super-majoritarian opinion. And rarer still are pivotal moments in American political development that define key periods of rights expansion and contraction that shape national citizenship and state citizenship alike.

Constitutional Opportunities

Our explanatory framework offers an understanding of how the US Constitution frames authority and power, similar to the work of Anna Law, and is grounded in a larger scholarship in history and law by Eric Foner, Paul Finkelman, David Brian Robertson, and James H. Kettner, among others.[5] We situate broader analyses of the Constitution to fully unpack how federated citizenship was built on the Framers' Constitution and how the US Constitutional framework has developed with respect to citizenship over time. For example, in addressing the early role of states in controlling immigration law, our constitutional focus is on how immigration intersects with the citizenship rights of various groups, including free Blacks, slaves, runaway slaves, and immigrants – at national, state, and local levels of government. We show that the transition from state to federal citizenship rights are neither linear nor permanent.

The US Constitution, we argue, frames but does not animate the expansion or contraction of citizenship rights. Congress, parties, and social movement, as well as federal capacity and willingness to enforce federal law – all within the limits set by the US Constitution – can either propel, stall, or roll back citizenship rights at varying levels of government (Table 3.1). These animating factors allowed for the regression of Black rights under Jim Crow and more recently, have allowed for the progression of undocumented immigrants' rights in California, despite federal plenary power over immigration law. The interplay between the Fourteenth and Tenth Amendments, we argue, provides the constitutional framework that shapes the boundaries of citizenship today, including divergence in regressive, reinforcing, and progressive regimes of citizenship across states and across groups. In line with scholars of citizenship and American political development, we also argue that nation-building (i.e. the project of building national state capacity and the willingness of the federal government to enforce federal law) plays a critical role in the development of national citizenship and state citizenship. Nation-building layers on top of the structural framework of the American constitution to set the conditions and

TABLE 3.1 *State citizenship in the context of American federalism*

	Key Features	Net Effects
Constitutional opportunities	US Constitution • Art. 1. Congressional "necessary and proper" clause • Art. 2. President's "inherent power" • Article IV, Section 2, "privileges and immunities" • Tenth Amendment's anti-commandeering clause • Tenth Amendment's reserved powers clause • Fourteenth Amendment's equal protection clause	• Constraints on preemptive power of federal government • Constraints on federal government's rights in relation to individuals • Constraints on states' rights in relation to individuals
	Courts • Constitutional interpretation • Judicial review	
Legislative action	Congressional leadership • Legislative role of president • Legislative role of states • Social movement strength	• Propels and animates action through federal and state legislation • Federal legislation enables and constrains preemptive authority

(*continued*)

TABLE 3.1 *(continued)*

	Key Features	Net Effects
Executive action	Capacity • Budgetary resources and constraints • Federal bureaucratic resources and footprint • Cooperative arrangements with subfederal bureaucracies Willingness to deploy capacity • Control federal territories and terms of new state admissions • Enforce federal law within states • Sue states • Apply budgetary constraints on states	• Enables and constrains ability of states to expand or contract individual rights

boundaries for what is permissible and probable with respect to citizenship rights at the federal, state, and local level.

As Anna Law explains, the US Constitution "purposely 'did not resolve' the question of how to balance national and state power," setting a limit on the federal government's broad Constitutional claims to plenary powers over immigration law.[6] Specifically, regional conflicts over slavery prevented leaders at the Constitutional Convention from clearly defining who had authority to regulate the movement of people within and across national, state, and local territorial borders. While slavery hampered the development of national control over international and internal migration, the original constitutional framework actually allowed for nation-building to occur and for national sovereignty to grow greater than state sovereignty under new federal laws and court rulings. For example, David Brian Robertson explains, "The Constitution left the dividing line between national and state power ambiguous, inviting endless political conflict over the rules of federalism in the United States," and that these tensions existed in both the antebellum and post–Civil War eras.[7] William Riker similarly explained that political parties have played a critical role in maintaining federalism by choosing which level of government should control policy.[8] We build from this extensive literature to show that both the Tenth Amendment and the Fourteenth Amendment are the key constitutional instruments in shaping federated citizenship today, for progressive and conservative reform movements alike.

Legislative Action

Beyond the US Constitution, we build our explanatory framework from the rich scholarly traditions of APD, historical institutionalism, and comparative politics that have used terms like racial alliances, authoritarian enclaves, and political and racial orders or regimes to reveal moments of consolidated power by coalitions that wield governing authority over minority groups, broadly speaking.[9] In doing so, we also clarify how our analytical purposes differ, and what specifically we draw from this scholarship. Analytically, our focus for this chapter is to set up an explanatory framework of the key institutions and actors that shape the development of multidimensional citizenship rights in a federated political system (as detailed in Chapter 2). Thus, rather than identifying regime consolidation or entrenchment, we employ the APD approach to trace and reveal how the US Constitution, courts, parties, and social movements combine together at key moments in time to expand or contract citizenship rights at varying levels of government. Our focus is not on regimes or authoritarian enclaves, but it is important to note that our analysis of institutions and actors, and our concept of multidimensional citizenship at the state level, speaks to similar concerns over race, power, and identity.

Key political actors that operate within this federal system are critical to the timing and scope in the provision of federal, state, and local rights to various groups. Thus, in addition to accounting for eras of nation-building, our explanatory framework builds on the work of Richard Valelly, Paul Frymer, Sidney Milkis, and Daniel Tichenor, and others, to explain how courts, parties, and social movements work together to maintain or change state citizenship. Whereas this scholarship focuses primarily on national-level reforms, we argue that this same set of actors operates strategically to shape rights in a federated system based on political opportunity structures. The political alignment of courts, parties, and social movements allows for nation-building eras to differ with respect to the provision of federated rights. Moreover, who is in control during critical moments of nation-building determines not only whether the federal government is willing to enforce the federal baseline of rights but also which groups are included or excluded from their provision via national bureaucratic institutions. In addition, state courts, parties, and social movements can also play an independent role in expanding rights, contracting them, or creating a parallel set of rights that reinforce those provided at the federal level (see Chapter 2, Figure 2.9).

Within APD, scholars who focus on the critical role of institutional actors often privilege national and formal institutions and pay scant attention to social movements. Notably, Richard Valelly examines the role of courts and parties to explain key differences between the First and Second Reconstructions, with little focus on how variations in social movement-building influenced these institutions during each period.[10] Jeffrey Jenkins, Justin Peck, and Vesla Weaver devote critical attention to Congressional legislative activity on anti-lynching and other civil rights measures between the two Reconstructions, although the role of social movement actors receives comparatively little attention.[11] Similarly, Paul Frymer does not pay much attention to the role of social movements in his analysis of how race shapes the strategies of political parties and their electoral capture of Black voters.[12] Finally, APD scholars with a state or regional bent – including David A Bateman, Ira Katznelson, and John S. Lapinski, Robert Mickey, and Morgan J. Kousser – tend to privilege the calculations and actions of political elites rather than social movement actors.[13] Thus, while race is central to long-standing scholarship in American Political Development, social movements and activists on the front lines of reform politics are mostly invisible. Social movements may be central in the scholarship on race among historians, sociologists, and critical race scholars,[14] but they receive comparatively little attention among APD scholars.

There are, however, some notable recent exceptions.[15] In their recent 2019 book, Sidney Milkis and Daniel Tichenor recognize a strong role for social movement leadership by examining how their uneasy alliances with US presidents have shaped civil rights expansion and conservative backlash.[16] Among APD scholars, Megan Ming Francis's is one of the first to seriously engage social movements, shedding new light on the development of the national civil rights movement, tracing the history and tactics employed by the NAACP starting in the early 1900s that laid the organizational and legal groundwork for subsequent gains in the 1960s.[17] Much like Francis, Chloe Thurston aptly and critically attends to the work of social movement actors who render "the state's role in their lives visible and legible" and contest "statebuilding" at the margins.[18] Addressing the American welfare state, Thurston's work also places civil rights and feminist organizations at the forefront of American political development in the mid-twentieth century.[19] This scholarship builds on an earlier tradition, including W. E. B. Du Bois, who famously argued in *Black Reconstruction* that Blacks were essential actors in the fight to expand voting rights and officeholding, establish free public schools, and create social welfare in the South.[20]

Similar to these efforts, our explanatory framework considers both social movements and formal government institutions as central to understanding changes in citizenship over time. Importantly, we also posit an important role for federalism tension – ranging from outright conflict to accommodation and avoidance – in shaping the contours of state citizenship and national citizenship. Indeed, federalism conflicts have played a transformative role in American political development, waged not only as a conservative political tactic to contract rights and decrease the size of the federal government but also as a progressive tactic to expand rights and create pressures for national-level transformation. Jessica Bulman-Pozen explains that America's federalist system provides the scaffolding for partisan debate to emerge and shape policy formation at both the national and state levels.[21] Similarly, Rose Pickerill and Cythnia Bowling explain that when political parties are polarized, as they are today, federalism creates the context for unified state governments to lead the country in passing policies on issues of immigration, health, education, marijuana, and same-sex marriage.[22] Gulasekaram and Ramakrishnan similarly describe the role of immigration "issue entrepreneurs" who exploit party polarization and the multilevel playing field of American federalism to stall federal immigration reform and simultaneously push for particular types of state-level immigration policy.[23]

While party polarization in the context of federalism clearly matters, so too does the work of social movement actors, particularly at the state level. As we show in Chapters 6 and 7, public policy theories of advocacy coalitions are best suited to explain how legislative action on immigrant rights and civil rights draw upon the coordinated work of social movements, their legislative champions, and party leaders including state governors to push state citizenship in either a progressive or a regressive direction.

Executive Action

Karen Orren and Stephen Skowronek define political development as "a durable shift in governing authority," and "governing authority," in turn, as "the exercise of control over persons or things that is designated and enforceable by the state."[24] We build on this definition to show that nation-building has two components – federal capacity and federal willingness to enforce – that have fundamentally shaped the scope and inclusionary features of federated citizenship. Stephen Skowronek described the federal government of the nineteenth century as a "state of courts and parties" and little else. This is because political parties coordinated national government through appointments, while insulated federal courts minimally redefined what state and local governments could do.[25] Federal capacity gradually increased after the Civil War out of Progressive-era regulations, but it was not until the 1930s and 1940s, in response to the Great Depression and WWII, that federal activities dramatically expanded. Nation-building, once underway, fundamentally altered citizenship at all levels of the federalist system and continues to do so today.

The limits to administrative capacity and political will are non-trivial, as Anna Law has shown with respect to US immigration law. As she explains, "One may have adequate administrative capacity and still no authority to act, just as much as one may have authority but no capacity to carry it out. The former characterization better explains nineteenth-century migration policy [in the United States] being housed at the subnational level."[26] After the formation of the US Constitution, the federal government had full authority to expand its control on matters such as immigration, as Congress quickly established the Departments of War, Foreign Affairs, Treasury, and Navy, as well as the Post Office, and asserted its constitutional authority to regulate navigation and create seamen's hospitals, the Customs Service, and the Bank of the United States.[27] Additionally, national agencies and administrative officials grew during this early period, and presidents starting with Thomas Jefferson exercised their authority to ban American ships from sailing to foreign ports without federal permission, using the power of the US Navy to do so.[28] Yet, despite early growth in the federal government's administrative capacity and willingness to use it in some areas, regional differences over race and slavery prevented the federal government from taking control of immigration law. Instead, it permitted states and localities to take the reins in passing and enforcing laws on immigration until the post–Civil War period, understanding that this would allow it to avoid irreconcilable regional political conflicts.[29]

Expanded federal capacity through nation-building, however, does not automatically entail federal willingness to enforce new rights. Robert Lieberman, Suzanne Mettler, Richard Benzel, Ira Katznelson, and Cybelle Fox, among others, have shown us that federalism has, time and again, been waged as a constitutional and political instrument by courts, parties, and social movements seeking to redefine racial and gender politics.[30] Desmond King's recent work goes even further in showing the essential role of political will in what he terms "forceful federalism," where the federal government actively coerces state and local governments to become active enforcers of federal civil rights.[31] Changes to American federalism through sweeping, durable expansions and contractions in national governance, which we define as both bureaucratic capacity and willingness to enforce, have occurred through various eras in American political history, including the Progressive era (1890s through 1910s), the New Deal (1930s), the Great Society (1960s), and, more recently, a conservative era ushered in by Nixon and Reagan (1970s and 1980s). Within the bounds set by constitutional jurisprudence involving the Tenth and Fourteenth Amendments, these American nation-building projects have fundamentally shaped the bounds of federated citizenship for Blacks, immigrants, women, and LGBT communities over time.

KEY PERIODS IN THE DEVELOPMENT OF STATE CITIZENSHIP

APD's focus on orders, defined loosely as the political arrangement of institutions, policies, and groups, provides a historical framework grounded in periodizing significant changes in governmental authority and power.[32] Our explanatory framework grounds analysis of multidimensional and federated citizenship by breaking up American history into three distinctive periods, all anchored to sweeping national reforms to the US Constitution and civil rights.[33] These three periods of state citizenship – (1) the Framers' Constitution; (2) the "Separate and Unequal" period; and (3) the Civil Rights period – align with the periods covered by Richard Valelly's two reconstructions, Vann C. Woodward's demarcation of antebellum and post–Reconstruction era segregation laws, and an emerging scholarship on the rise of the carceral state following the 1960s civil rights reforms by Vesla Weaver and others.[34]

Additionally, the periodization on immigration federalism corresponds roughly to these same three periods, although the dynamics of federal preemption vastly differ, resulting in different types of state citizenship forming for contemporary Blacks and immigrants (see Figure 3.2). Starting in the 1870s, the Supreme Court enabled the federal government to take on the exclusive authority to control immigration entry and exit, placing stronger restrictions on states with respect to immigration control than with respect to Black populations after the Civil War. In addition, as Gulasekaram and Ramakrishnan have shown, 1965 emerges as an important moment in inaugurating a new era of immigration federalism not because of changes in federal–state dynamics but because of new limits on Mexican migration that created the conditions for states to enter more fully into the realm of controlling immigrant lives.[35]

Our explanatory framework builds upon (and in some respects breaks from) other scholarship on race in the United States. Our first departure is that, because we see American racial politics as recurrently structured in terms of rival racial alliances, each in control of some governing institutions, we think for many purposes it is not useful to speak of the United States as having a "racial state" or a single "racial order," as many other scholars do. These authors are right to contend that, despite the American state's internal divisions,

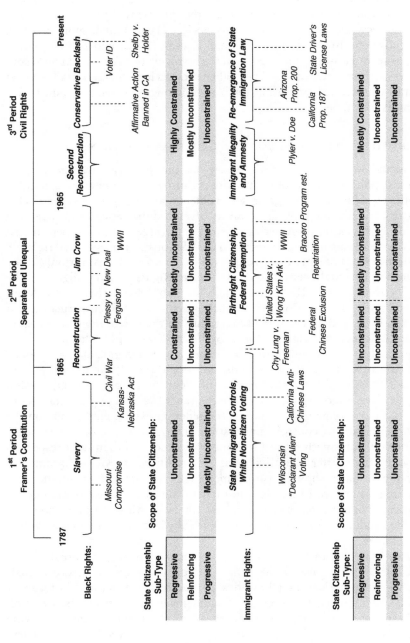

FIGURE 3.2 Periodization of state citizenship in the United States

in any given period it does play an aggregate role in generating a particular overall national pattern of racial identities, statuses, and policies. That is why we can speak in shorthand of the "slavery" era and the "Jim Crow" era. Importantly, these periods should be understood as the eras of struggles over slavery and over Jim Crow laws and practices, even if these struggles usually did not take place between the leaders of the two major parties. To our ears, language suggesting a unitary character to the American state or "racial order" fails to capture the complexity of contestation over racial politics, citizenship rights, and federalism.

Similarly, the terminology of a "racial state" fails to call attention to the reality that particular institutions of "the state" have always been found on both sides of these contests, even if in highly unequal proportions at different times. For example, in their influential book *Racial Formation in the United States*, Michael Omi and Howard Winant contend that the "central elements" in American struggles over race are "the state and social movements" – a formulation that can suggest "the state" is captured and recaptured as a whole by one racially motivated social movement or another, with political parties playing relatively little role. But as their ensuing discussions reveal, in fact the story of American racial contests cannot be told without recognizing that, in the complex governing system of federalism and separation of powers in the United States, different governing institutions have often been controlled by proponents of different racial policies, in ways bound up with, though rarely identical to, partisan politics.[36]

Federalism Tensions Inherent in the US Constitution

The US Constitution created the political conditions for federalism tensions to emerge and to become driving forces behind American political development. For our explanatory framework, the potential for conflict is a critical feature of federalism that allows for parallel national and state citizenships to coexist, thereby setting different levels of rights for the same populations. Importantly, however, these federalism tensions only emerge within the prescribed boundaries set by the US Constitution and clarified by court rulings of what is constitutionally permissible. As we note later, the Civil War was a notable exception of a conflict that spilled outside the boundaries of the US Constitution and was an outright institutional crisis.

The US Constitution firmly established that it and federal laws are supreme over state and local laws in Article 6:

This Constitution, and the laws of the United States which shall be made in pursuance thereof; and all treaties made, or which shall be made, under the authority of the United States, shall be the supreme law of the land; and the judges in every state shall be bound thereby, anything in the Constitution or laws of any State to the contrary notwithstanding.

This established a federal legislative baseline, where federal law preempts state and local laws wherever they conflicted. It also empowered the US Supreme Court and the federal court system to strike down federal, state, and local laws by ruling that they were unconstitutional or preempted by federal law. Furthermore, Article 1, Section 8, gave Congress broad authority to make all laws "necessary and proper" for executing all its enumerated powers.

Indeed, the framers considered alternative plans that would have empowered the federal government even further. The Virginia Plan of 1787, laid out by James Madison of Virginia, included empowering Congress with the authority to veto "all laws passed by the several States," regardless of whether a conflict between federal and state law existed.[37] This meant that the federal government would be able to control states' prerogatives and legislative authority, resulting in a fundamentally different federalist system with only the national government considered sovereign. Alexander Hamilton of New York supported Madison's vision for a strong, centralized national government, arguing that the new national government required enough power to preserve itself and that national power "must swallow up the State powers" or be "swallowed up by them."[38] While the Virginia Plan was not adopted, its nationalist vision helped to form the basic constitutional framework for federal power, including the Supremacy Clause and the "necessary and proper" clause.

Even as the Framers' Constitution allowed for the possibility of expanding the power of the federal government, it also provided a mechanism to preserve the authority of states via the Tenth Amendment: "The powers not delegated to the United States by the Constitution, nor prohibited by it to the states, are reserved to the states respectively, or to the people." This fairly simply worded Amendment has provided the framework for most "states' rights" arguments, which have been to defend both the contraction of citizenship rights (as in the case of American slavery and Jim Crow) as well as the expansion of rights (as in the case of sanctuary policies involving runaway slaves in the antebellum period and those involving undocumented immigrants today). The Tenth Amendment continues to shape the basic contours of federalism debates today, although the tensions now involve not only the Supremacy clause and the "necessary and proper" clause but also the Fourteenth Amendment, passed in 1868.

The Fourteenth Amendment fundamentally reshaped federalism by establishing national citizenship as a right of all persons born in the United States and setting a framework for individuals to enjoy the same guarantees of rights vis-à-vis state government as they enjoyed with respect to the federal government. This "equal protection" clause of the Fourteenth Amendment has been critical to the expansion of state citizenship rights in many instances, including *Brown v. Board of Education*'s (1954)[39] ban on laws permitting racial discrimination in public schools, *Loving v. Virginia*'s (1967)[40] ban on laws restricting and criminalizing interracial marriage, *Roe v. Wade*'s (1973)[41] ban on laws infringing on women's reproductive rights, *Plyler v. Doe*'s (1982)[42] extension of the *Brown* decision to ban laws restricting undocumented children from attending K–12 public schools, and *Obergefell v. Hodges*'s (2015)[43] invalidating of state bans on same-sex marriage. As we shall discuss later in this chapter, it took nearly a century for "equal protection" to begin eliminating regressive forms of state citizenship. For our purposes here, we argue that the Fourteenth Amendment together with the Tenth Amendment provide the basic constitutional structure for federalism tensions to emerge, shaping the realm of what is permissible with respect to national citizenship and state citizenship.

The Fourteenth Amendment still allows key aspects of the Tenth Amendment to remain in force, as long as states do not violate federally guaranteed individual rights. Thus, courts have continued to rule that the federal government cannot compel state governments to enact, enforce, or administer federal policies or programs, upholding what is often referred to as the Tenth Amendment's "anti-commandeering" principle. In *New York v. United States* (1992), the US Supreme Court ruled that Congress could not order state legislatures either to regulate low-level radioactive waste in accordance with federal instructions or to take title to the waste.[44] Similarly, in *Printz v. United States* (1997), it ruled that Congress could not order state executive officials to help conduct background checks on would-be handgun purchasers on an interim basis.[45] A provision in President Obama's Affordable Care Act (ACA) (2010) was blocked by the US Supreme Court in *National Federation of Independent Business (NFIB) v. Sebelius* (2012) because it mandated that states expand eligibility requirements or face federal withholding of funding. The court ruled that this provision was coercive in nature and was therefore in conflict with the Tenth Amendment's anti-commandeering principle.[46]

While the US Constitution sets the stage for federalism tension to develop, the conflicts themselves are propelled by the political activity of parties and social movement actors operating at the national, state, and local levels. Federalism tensions and conflicts over the provision of citizenship rights are not new. Deep federalism conflicts emerged over slavery in the antebellum period, fueled in part because Southern control over Congress prevented openings for discussing federal laws that might safeguard the rights of free Blacks or limit the spread of slavery. As we show in Chapter 4, abolitionists turned to Northern state legislatures to enact a variety of laws to protect free Blacks and runaway slaves because they could effectively pressure state and local governments to pass such reforms, even as they got stymied at the federal level on abolition and fugitive slave rendition. The federalism tensions that emerged between federal and state laws related to slavery were within the bounds of the Framers' Constitution, and the Court allowed some of these laws to stand. By the 1840s and 1850s, however, states began enacting laws that were in defiance of federal law and pushed the country to more open conflict, ultimately provoking a constitutional crisis and a civil war.

THE FRAMERS' CONSTITUTION

By the time of the American Revolution, the thirteen original colonies had developed relatively unique histories, economies, and cultures. For example, the Southern states of Georgia, South and North Carolina, and Virginia thrived on large plantation economies of tobacco, rice, and indigo that relied on slave labor. Middle states like Maryland, New Jersey, New York, Pennsylvania, and Delaware had smaller farms, operated mostly by families without slaves, and began to diversify into manufacturing. Further north, in New England states like Connecticut and Massachusetts, the harsh climate led to an economy based on shipbuilding, fishing, and commerce linked to Southern agricultural goods. The vast size differences among states and their different stages of economic development also fueled tensions within and across these regions. Even within the South, tensions emerged over the possibility of ending the international slave trade, with Georgia and South Carolina seeking to fuel their newly emerging plantations with slaves from the Caribbean and Africa, while the older established states of Virginia and North Carolina, who already had a large slave population, sought to limit the forced migration of new Blacks.[47]

America's first experiment in a shared national government was thus largely deferential to the power of states. In the Articles of Confederation, ratified in 1781, states' sovereignty overshadowed the formation of the national government, preventing it from having an executive, its own court system, or the power to impose taxes. Article 3, for example, described the national government as "a firm league of friendship" among the states, to defend the nation from foreign threats and to provide for a united foreign policy. Article 9 checked national power by requiring nine states (of the thirteen) to assent to Congress's declarations of war. More importantly, without being able develop its own revenues and resources, which requires the power of taxation, the new national government went bankrupt in its first years. The Articles of Confederation failed to provide the national sovereignty required for nation-building.

The new US Constitution ratified in 1787 created a vastly different constitutional framework and a stronger foundation for nation-building. Still, as with the Articles of Confederation, Southern states were organized and well positioned to push for a constitutional framework based on "states' rights" that safeguarded their control over domestic slavery, even as the rest of the world was moving toward an elimination of the slave trade. At the same time, forces pushing towards abolition, led by activists like Anthony Benezet, were sufficiently strong to introduce tensions and contradictions in the original Constitution. Indeed, tensions over slavery would also ultimately doom the original Constitution's silent arrangement on slavery. In 1850, Congress passed a compromise on slavery by guaranteeing that much of the vast western land gained from Mexico in the war of 1846–1848 would be open to the possibility of slavery and of strengthening existing federal fugitive slave laws to effectively extend Southern power into the free states north of the Mason-Dixon line. Two years later, in 1854, Stephen Douglas from Illinois introduced the Kansas–Nebraska Act, allowing slavery to continue its extension in the western territories on the principle of "squatter sovereignty." As Chapter 4 explains, Northern Democrats sought to accommodate Southern Democratic demands, with President Franklin Pierce ordering the US military to enforce the fugitive slave law in the North.

These events helped spark the rise of the new Republican Party, which ran on the platform of confronting Southern power in national politics and stopping the spread of slavery. The prolonged fight over Kansas's entrance as either a slave or a free state symbolized the looming constitutional crisis facing America. Pro- and anti-slavery forces entered the state, falsely claiming to be residents with the right to vote for officials in the new territorial legislature and on the fate of slavery. Between 1855 and 1859, under dual governments led by pro- and anti-slavery officials, Kansas proposed both pro- and anti-slavery state constitutions. It was only after the Civil War had begun that Kansas was formally admitted to the Union as a free state. Strong reactions in the North following the Kansas–Nebraska Act of 1854 led to the rise of the Republican Party, with a platform of confronting Southern power in national politics. When Abraham Lincoln won the presidency in 1860, Southern states began to push for proslavery amendments to the US Constitution under the threat of secession.

The Civil War was the result of a constitutional crisis. Southern officials sought to change the US Constitution's structure of American federalism even more in their favor, with state sovereignty replacing federal supremacy but with added constraints placed on Northern progressive state citizenship. For example, US Senator Robert Tooms of Georgia introduced an amendment to constitutionally protect slavery in federal territories and slave states, require federal enforcement of these protections against insurrections, and constitutionally deny free states the power to provide state-level rights of writs of habeas corpus and trial by jury in fugitive slave cases. Southern officials also sought to require federal enforcement of their slave codes or to pass a comprehensive federal slave code. Unable to amend the US Constitution, South Carolina declared Southern secession and was soon followed by Mississippi, Florida, Alabama, Georgia, Louisiana, and Texas.

State Citizenship in Antebellum America

With Southern officials controlling the US Congress for much of the antebellum era, federal reforms to protect Blacks or limit slavery proved to be intractable. Constitutional openness and national inaction created the conditions for Southern and Northern states to enact a range of policies that shaped the rights of free Blacks and alleged runaway slaves very differently. Blacks without proof of their freedom on hand were presumed to be slaves by the federal government, Southern states, and some Northern states. The US Constitution, however, did not require Northern states to follow suit on verification (much like it does not require states today to verify whether all individuals in their jurisdiction are in compliance with federal immigration law). And as we discuss more in Chapter 4, decisions like *Dred Scott* (1857) reaffirmed state citizenship in the antebellum period by expressly denying national citizenship to free Blacks.

While the North is known for paving the road to freedom, some Northern states had, in fact, developed highly exclusionary forms of state citizenship. While many state constitutions formally banned slavery, they nevertheless still included provisions permitting indentured servitude and denying Blacks the ability to vote, hold public office, or testify in court.[48] Exclusions grew in scope from Northern state laws requiring Blacks to show proof of freedom before entering, residing in, or searching for employment in the state and requiring Blacks to register with their county of residence—a practice not required for White immigrant residents. Regarding runaway slaves, some Northern state laws mandated state institutions, schools, employers, and officials to actively enforce federal fugitive slave laws and check for freedom papers; such laws also criminalized interfering in the capture of runaway slaves. By the mid-1800s, some Northern states passed laws to create colonization programs to remove their Black residents. The exclusionary regimes of state citizenship that spread throughout the South, of course, were far harsher and even more extensive than those in the North.

By contrast, progressive state citizenship in the free North emerged from a range of laws to protect and integrate all Blacks within their territorial borders, including runaway slaves. Northern states passed laws automatically freeing any slave brought into their borders by slave owners – referred to as "slaves in transit."[49] They passed laws that protected their Black residents from being kidnapped and sold into slavery, banned state and local officials from participating in enforcing federal fugitive slave law, and denied the federal government the right to use state and local courts and resources to hear cases that might lead to returning a Black person to slavery. Blacks were even granted the right to vote in some Northern states. Finally, as we detail later in this chapter, progressive state citizenship in the antebellum period also included the expansion of voting rights for White immigrants in territories and states eager to promote population growth and westward expansion.[50]

Constitutional Opportunities and Interpretation

The framers' constitutional framework empowered the federal government to enact naturalization law with varying requirements that allowed national citizenship to slowly develop and evolve. In Federalist Paper 39, Alexander Hamilton, James Madison, and John Jay stressed the importance of a uniform naturalization law, laying the foundation for Article 1, Section 8, Clause 4, of the US Constitution, empowering Congress with authority to set the rules for national citizenship. The Naturalization Act of 1790 limited naturalization to "any alien, being a free white person," who resided in the US for at least two years; and it effectively barred Blacks, Native Americans, and women from acquiring citizenship. While this federal law formed an exclusionary national citizenship, the federal government was mostly inactive with regard to providing rights to its populations. Equally important, naturalization law applied only to new immigrants. Congress was silent on the citizenship status of persons born in the United States, and, therefore, state citizenship emerged as the more dominant form of rights-based membership with much clearer exclusionary boundaries.

While the US Constitution granted Congress authority over many national matters, it was silent on the question of national citizenship. Instead, it referred to *all persons* when setting up the basic foundations for national governance, including its provisions on the census and taxation, with direct implications for Congressional and Presidential representation. In drafting the US Constitution, Southern states benefited from having all persons counted, especially slaves, because this would inflate the number of Congressional representatives assigned to the state. Pierce Butler and Charles Pinckney of South Carolina both proposed at the Constitutional convention that "blacks be included in the rule of Representation, equally with the Whites." Butler argued that "the labour of a slave in South Carolina was as productive and valuable as that of a freeman in Massachusetts," and, since the national government "was instituted principally for the protection of property," slaves should be counted fully when determining the South's representation in national government.[51]

The Framers protected the balance between free and slave states through compromise, adding in Article 1, Section 2, that the decennial Census would count slaves as three-fifths of a person for purposes of apportioning Congressional seats, and it stipulated that apportionment would be based on a count of persons, not citizens:

Representatives and direct taxes shall be apportioned among the several states which may be included within this union, according to their respective numbers, which shall be determined by adding to the whole number of free persons, including those bound to service for a term of years, and excluding Indians not taxed, three fifths of all other Persons. The actual Enumeration shall be made within three years after the first meeting of the Congress of the United States, and within every subsequent term of ten years, in such manner as they shall by law direct.

Nationally, the constitutional gaps between who the Census would count for purposes of apportionment (all persons excluding Native Americans) and laws stipulating those who were able or eligible to vote (White, adult males) largely remained in place until women's suffrage (1920), the granting of voting rights to Native Americans through the 1924 Indian Citizenship Act, and the 1965 Voting Rights Act.

With apportionment allowing states to count slaves as persons, Southern leaders at the Constitutional Convention widely rejected proposed schemes to have the president elected by direct popular vote. For example, Hugh Williamson of Virginia argued that, under such a scheme, the South would be unable to elect their own leaders as president because "her slaves will have no suffrage."[52] To resolve the immediate conflict over how to elect the president, James Madison compromised by turning away from strongly supporting direct election by the people to supporting the creation of the electoral college – a system where a number of electors are assigned to each state equal to its total congressional and senatorial representation. Madison explained that the "right of suffrage was much more diffusive in the Northern than the Southern States; and the latter could have no influence in the election on the score of the Negroes."[53] Unable to vote, Blacks who were free and enslaved were nevertheless counted for the purposes of determining the number of a states' electors for the presidency.

What might seem to be the most controversial proslavery addition to the US Constitution – the Fugitive Slave Clause established under Article 4 – was in fact an already well-established compromise. The Northwest Ordinance of 1787 set up the first federal fugitive slave law, which was rewritten into the US Constitution as Article 4, stating: "No person held to service or labour in one state, under the laws thereof, escaping into another, shall, in consequence of any law or regulation therein, be discharged from such service or labour, but shall be delivered up on claim of the party to whom such service or labour may be due."[54] "Slavery" was never actually referred to directly in the Constitution in order to avoid a conflict with Northern officials. Instead, fugitive slaves were called "persons owing service or Labour," with no mention of their formal, legal status as slaves.[55]

The use of "persons" throughout the US Constitution was strategic and necessary to ratification. Southern and Northern officials alike were able to agree on the same constitutional provisions because they were anchored to state-based legal definitions of citizenship, freedom, indenture, and slavery. The US Constitution's vague references to national citizenship, prior to the Fourteenth Amendment's passage in 1868, starkly contrasted with the bright lines of state citizenship and its exclusionary and inclusionary features. Only state and local laws regulated virtually all aspects of antebellum life, ranging from defining a person's legal status as a slave or freed person to regulating who could freely move or reside in the state and who could attend public schools, work, or vote. The only clear rules on "national citizenship" during this period entailed Constitutional provisions on qualification for federal elected office and federal laws pertaining to naturalization.

Federalism was also structured in such a way as to preserve states' authority over the legal status and rights of its populations. The US Constitution's diversity jurisdiction clause – established in Article III, Section 2, Paragraph I – limited the right to sue in federal courts to "Citizens of different States." As a result, federal judges were able to deny slaves and free Blacks alike access to federal due process, since access to this fundamental right was based on whether a person was granted citizenship status by their residing state.[56] Finally, the Bill of Rights provided protections to individuals only with respect to the federal government, and the Tenth Amendment specified that "powers not delegated to the United States by the Constitution, nor prohibited by it to the States, are reserved to the States respectively, or to the people." In short, the US Constitution did not provide a uniform direction on national citizenship, nor did it resolve the deep tensions over race, slavery, and federalism. The broad national coalition required to draft and ratify the US Constitution meant that slavery would be protected, national citizenship would be largely unspecified, and federalism would be molded around Northern and Southern tensions on slavery, leaving determination and control over citizenship largely to the states.

Legislative Action: Parties and Social Movements

Slavery and economic development set the path for the Framers' Constitution to launch the newly united states into joint nationhood without stripping them of their former power as colonial states. This constitutional conservatism had important consequences for how political parties formed in early America and prevented the new federal government from passing policies that might preempt state or local policy, especially on the rights of resident populations. Moreover, strong state and local political parties emerged largely separated from national political parties, further strengthening the decentralized states' rights federal-legal framework.[57]

Without having access to a strong national party until the Republican Party's emergence in the late 1850s, abolitionists were unable to influence Congress to alter the status quo. Led by key figures like William Lloyd Garrison and Frederick Douglass, the abolitionists' goal was to slowly weaken slavery through a moral campaign and to build a broad national coalition to push federal laws or Constitutional amendments that would sever the federal government's connection to slavery. This social movement included Northern abolitionists circulating massive amounts of anti-slavery literature to the South; New York alone mailed 175,000 separate items to slave states in the summer of 1835.[58]

Abolitionists also regularly petitioned Congress to train the national spotlight on slavery. In 1834, the American Anti-Slavery Society led a large national petition campaign that gathered 34,000 signatures for a House bill to end slavery in the District of Columbia. This incident led Southern Democrats, who were the majority in Congress for much of the antebellum period, to institute the infamous gag rule, which "stipulated that all petitions or resolutions 'relating in any way, or to any extent whatsoever, to the subject of slavery or the abolition of slavery' were to be automatically and indefinitely 'laid on the table.'"[59] The gag rule was enforced from 1836 to 1844, essentially stopping any national progress from being made on slavery. Despite this setback, abolitionists continued to petition for national abolition in the District of Columbia, abolition in federal territories, a ban on slavery in new states, prohibition of slavery at federal forts and on the high seas, and prohibition of the extensive interstate slave trade.[60] On fugitive slave law, after failing to pressure for national reforms, abolitionists turned their legislative efforts to pressuring Northern state governments to resist federal law by passing personal liberty laws (this is a topic we explore in greater detail in Chapter 4).

As the federal government acted to preserve the balance between free and slave states, it also began to articulate, for the first time, the exclusions of national citizenship. In 1820, the legislature of Missouri, a slaveholding federal territory gained under the Louisiana Purchase, submitted its request to the US Congress for statehood. Missouri's petition for admission threatened the existing balance. Not only did Missouri seek to enter as a slave state, it proposed a state constitution that mandated laws "to prevent free negroes and mulattoes from coming to and settling in the State, under any pretext whatsoever."[61] For the first time, the US House and Senate had to debate whether the US Constitution's "privileges and immunities" clause applied to free Blacks.[62]

Officials from Northern states took Missouri's petition as an opportunity to define free Blacks as US citizens, arguing that the US Constitution's "privileges and immunities" protected their right to travel freely across state borders. Congress chose to allow Missouri's constitution to retain the clause banning the in-migration of free Blacks to the state. Congress left unaddressed the question of whether free Blacks had national citizenship rights. However, by allowing exclusive bans on Black entry to the state of Missouri, Congress made it clear that free Blacks were not protected by the US Constitution's "privileges and immunities" clause.

The last decade of the antebellum era formalized what abolitionists and Blacks had already known: that Blacks were not national citizens. In *Dred Scott v. Sandford* (1857), Chief Justice of the Supreme Court Justice Taney warned that if free Blacks were entitled to the "privileges and immunities" of national citizens, then state Black codes would be invalid. Taney explained that free Blacks would have "the right to enter every other State whenever they pleased, singly or in companies, without pass or passport, and without obstruction, to sojourn there as long as they pleased, to go where they pleased at every hour of the day or night without molestation."[63] The use of "persons" throughout the US Constitution anchored legal definitions of citizenship, freedom, indenture, and slavery exclusively to state laws at the time. Taney went further to clarify the racist underpinnings of national citizenship by referencing the *Passenger Cases* (1849) and explaining that the Constitution "protected a slave owner's right to interstate travel – the right 'to enjoy a common country' – such that movement between two states could not give rise to the deprivation of his property in persons.[64] We say more about *Dred Scott* and the Taney Court in Chapter 4.

Executive Action: Administrative Capacity and Political Will

When the nation was founded, states retained all of their previous laws and prerogatives that made governance possible. By contrast, the federal government emerged as a legislative blank slate. It was also an administratively weak state, and its capacity was largely reliant on the cooperation or assistance of states to carry out basic federal governance. This included granting national citizenship: lacking capacity, Congress gave state courts the power to confer federal citizenship under the Naturalization Act of 1790.[65] Moreover, several of the explicit powers granted to the federal government in the US Constitution – of taxation, militia, and commerce – were powers also preserved for state governments. The Framers' considered these powers essential for nation-building to occur, but they made them concurrent to states' powers in order to secure the sovereignty of both federal and state governments. Federal power did develop, but it was limited. Federal revenues from taxation were used to provide grants-in-aid to the states that would allow federal control over new policy areas.[66]

The limited administrative capacity of the federal government also extended to matters of law and order. During the Constitutional Convention, General Sherman argued that states' sovereignty required having their own "Militia for defense against invasions and insurrections, and for enforcing obedience to their laws."[67] Indeed, the US Constitution expressly limited the US president's role as Commander in Chief from being able to commandeer states' militia in Article 1, Section 2, Clause 1:

> The President shall be Commander in Chief of the Army and Navy of the United States, and of the Militia of the several States, when called into the actual Service of the United States; he may require the Opinion, in writing, of the principal Officer in each of the executive Departments, upon any Subject relating to the Duties of their respective Office, and he shall have Power to grant Reprieves and Pardons for Offences against the United States, except in Cases of Impeachment.

States' sovereignty was so strong that, even during crises of internal rebellions, the national government required state permission in order to intervene domestically and protect the nation.

THE "SEPARATE BUT UNEQUAL" PERIOD

The Framers' proslavery Constitution had allowed restrictive as well as permissive regimes of state citizenship to proliferate. Without Constitutional boundaries on what states could do with respect to the rights of Blacks, Northern abolitionists were able to construct progressive state citizenship through their own policy experiments that expanded the rights of free Blacks and runaway slaves – through state abolition, anti-kidnapping protections, due process rights, resistance to federal fugitive slave law, and more. The prescribed boundaries of the original US Constitution also allowed Southern states to enslave Northern free Blacks unlawfully entering their borders.

While the Civil War had ended slavery, state citizenship provisions still varied fairly dramatically. President Andrew Johnson had allowed Southern states to reenter the Union largely unregulated, which led to states passing a range of Black codes that retained White control over Black labor. These laws also banned Blacks from voting, having access to public services, having free movement, and having access to public accommodations, transportation, and education. States also passed anti-miscegenation laws that barred interracial marriage and restricted Black custody rights over their children. The period of "radical Reconstruction" provided only a temporary lull in the development of regressive state citizenship; most of these laws reemerged after 1877, in some cases even stronger than before.

Constitutional Opportunities and Interpretation

In contrast to the Framers' Constitution, the postbellum constitution set clear boundaries on state citizenship that compelled revisions to Northern and Southern constitutions alike. Meanwhile, at the national level, the US House and Senate approved the Fourteenth Amendment, which prohibited "states from abridging equality before the law," provided for a reduction of a state's congressional representatives if Black voting rights were denied, and barred ex-Confederates from holding state or national office. Federal capacity and willingness was at a historic high mark: not only were the ex-Confederate state constitutions required to recognize the Thirteenth Amendment's abolition of slavery, but Congress required the states to ratify the Fourteenth Amendment before they could rejoin the Union – shedding the old version of states' rights. Soon after, Congress added the Fifteenth Amendment in 1870 to provide constitutional guarantees of voting rights for all male citizens.

For a brief period, the courts aligned with the Republican-led Congress, enforcing the Fourteenth and Fifteenth Amendments to expand Black citizenship rights in resistant states. In *US v Hall* (1871), in Alabama, federal Circuit Court judge William B. Woods declared that "the right to freedom of speech and other rights enumerated in the first eight articles of the amendment" were national rights under the Fourteenth Amendment's privileges and immunities clause. This meant not only that states were prohibited from infringing on the rights of US citizens but also that they were required to actively protect the rights of US citizens equally. Justice Woods interpreted equal protection to encompass states' "inaction as well as action."[68] Until 1873, the US Supreme Court had refused to take on a case that would allow it to provide a national interpretation of the Fourteenth Amendment, making *Hall* the primary precedent.

In a case involving Klan members who raided the home of Amzi Rainey for voting for the Republican Party, physically assaulting and raping his family members, US Attorney General David T. Corbin sought to make a much broader impact on federalism and the rights of federal citizens.[69] Corbin argued to the Fourth Circuit Court that the Fourteenth Amendment's immunities and privileges clause had nationalized the Bill of Rights. This included the Fourth Amendment right to due process (preventing illegal searches and seizures) and the Second Amendment right to bear arms. Known as the "Ku Klux Klan Trials" of 1871–1872, Corbin led in prosecuting Southern KKK members under the federal Enforcement Acts, while seeking a way to bring to the US Supreme Court the deeper constitutional changes to federalism made possible by the Fourteenth Amendment. These trials marked the high-water mark of federal court willingness, under the new Constitutional amendments, to significantly constrain states' exclusion of Blacks from federal rights.

At the same, the Fourteenth and Fifteenth Amendments did not fully extend federal citizenship to all minority groups. Women were not granted the right to vote until the Nineteenth Amendment passed in 1920, and Native Americans continued to be restricted from citizenship until the Indian Citizenship Act of 1924. Moreover, the Naturalization Act of 1870 extended the right to naturalize to "aliens of African nativity and to persons of African descent" but barred other non-Whites from naturalizing and strengthened federal citizenship requirements for voting in federal elections.[70] Mexican immigrants gained the right to naturalize in *In re Rodriguez* (1897) but were also denied voting rights under Jim Crow.[71] Most Asian immigrants did not gain the right to naturalize until the 1940s, when the United States expanded eligibility to meets its foreign policy goals during World War II and the early Cold War.

Federal Supremacy on Immigration Control and Birthright Citizenship: Even as the courts were redefining federalism with regard to civil rights in the post-Civil War prior, they were also altering the landscape of immigration control and immigrant rights in the United States. Federal plenary power over immigration law first emerged in 1849 and then continued to expand through the late 1800s and early 1900s. Beginning with *Smith v. Turner* (1849), the US Supreme Court struck down state laws in New York and Massachusetts imposing an entry tax on alien passengers arriving from foreign ports as preempted by federal exclusivity over foreign commerce.[72] In *Chy Lung v. Freeman* (1875), it struck down California's state law imposing an entry bond on Chinese immigrants, ruling that control over the admission of foreigners into the country was exclusively a federal responsibility.[73] Federal control expanded under *Chae Chan Ping v. United States* (1889), which interpreted the US Constitution as providing for federal immigration control and describing such control as absolute, exclusive, and beyond judicial review.[74] Meanwhile, federalism was being redefined through the distinction made by the courts between federal immigration law and state/local alienage law. For example, at the local level, *Yick Wo v. Hopkins* (1886) struck down a San Francisco ordinance regulating laundry establishments in the city that discriminated against Chinese immigrants for violating the Fourteenth Amendment's equal protection clause.[75] By contrast, at the federal level, *Fong Yue Ting v. United States* (1893) expanded power by allowing federal deportation of Chinese immigrants, even long-term residents.[76]

Court interpretation of federal immigration law and the Constitution was mostly exclusionary but did provide some glimmers of inclusion. As the Chinese immigrant population increased to over 100,000 in 1880, with a large presence in the Western states, the federal court ruled in *In re Ah Yup* (1878) that "a native of China" was not considered White and that Asians were prohibited from naturalization, despite not being explicitly banned in federal naturalization law.[77] Soon thereafter, Congress passed its Chinese Exclusion Act of 1882, banning any new migration of Chinese immigrants (see Chapter 5). At the same time, Chinese exclusion would not apply to those born in the United States. In 1898, the US Supreme Court in *United States v. Wong Kim Ark* extended the Fourteenth Amendment's birthright citizenship to the children of Chinese immigrants. Thus, even if Ark had migrated to China after being born in the United States, he could not be excluded from returning to the United States under the Chinese Exclusion Act.[78] This was a significant expansion through court interpretation of the national right of birthright citizenship, which had previously only been applied to Blacks. Nevertheless, this expanded application did little to remedy the erosion of minority citizenship rights at the state level, including Jim Crow policies in the South and the proliferation of state "alien land laws" targeting Asian immigrants during the early twentieth century (see Chapter 5).

Reconstruction's End and Backsliding on Citizenship Rights: Like in the Reconstruction's expansionary period, courts and parties were essential to legitimizing post-Reconstruction contractions in rights. For over two-and-a-half decades, from 1873 to 1898, the US Supreme Court took center stage striking down Reconstruction-era gains in federal laws that were built on the Thirteenth, Fourteenth, and Fifteenth Amendments, and it established a new interpretation of rights that devolved power back to the states. It also minimized the Fourteenth Amendment's equal protection to allow for "separate but equal" provisions and weakened the enforcement of the privileges and immunity clause.

In 1873, the US Supreme Court made its first official ruling that narrowed rather than expanded the Fourteenth Amendment's safeguards. The *Slaughter House Cases* (1873) ruled that federal protection of national citizens' civil rights did not extend to property rights, which were under the control of states.[79] Although this decision had nothing to do with race, the Court opened the window for White supremacy to rise again under the banner of states' rights. Soon after, court rulings on federalism enabled more direct assaults by states on Black civil rights. In *United States v. Reese* (1876), Chief Justice Morrison Waite declared that the Fifteenth Amendment did not establish a right to vote, only a right against racial discrimination, and ruled that Sections 3 and 4 of the 1870 Enforcement Act were unconstitutional.[80] That same day, Waite also ruled in *United States v. Cruikshank* (1876) that the Enforcement Act was an unconstitutional overreach of Congressional power.[81] Specially, the Court narrowed the power of the federal government to safeguard Fourteenth Amendment constitutional rights only against state action, not against private actions. This decision placed broad constraints on the Fourteenth Amendment's privileges and immunities and made enforcement against individual acts of racial discrimination, segregation, and violence the exclusive power of state and local governments.[82]

As Richard Valelly explains, Waite "systematically shattered the implicit justification in Reconstruction constitutionalism of every count, except for those based on the Fifteenth Amendment."[83] The US Supreme Court went on to further weaken the federal government by building a states' rights precedent, with its 8–1 landmark decision in the *Civil Rights Cases* (1883). Taking on and enjoining five separate court cases from the South and the North on racial segregation, the US Supreme Court struck down critical provisions in the Civil Rights Act of 1875 that had prohibited racial discrimination in public accommodations (hotels, restaurants, theatres, and railroads). Importantly, this decision narrowed the meaning of the Fourteenth Amendment's enforcement clause in Section 5 by making it the exclusive jurisdiction of states, rather than of the federal government.[84]

Following this erosion of federal power to protect Black rights, the courts turned their energy to upholding state laws that explicitly endorsed racial segregation. In *Louisville, New Orleans, and Texas Railroad v. Mississippi* (1890), the Court overturned its prior ruling in *Hall v. de Cuir* (1877) to allow state constitutions to require segregation on public carriers.[85] In its landmark decision of *Plessy v. Ferguson* (1896), the US Supreme Court established the doctrine of "separate but equal" to legitimize Jim Crow under guise of the Fourteenth Amendment.[86] Finally, in *Williams v. Mississippi* (1898), the US Supreme Court upheld Mississippi's constitutional voter requirements that disenfranchised Blacks in the state.[87] From 1900 until the 1950s, the courts simply denied Blacks full protection under the Thirteenth, Fourteenth, and Fifteenth Amendments, even when state laws were blatant constitutional violations, with rare exceptions (Chapter 4 provides a fuller overview of Jim Crow's origin).[88]

Patchwork Constitutional Expansion on Rights

The Supreme Court made some progress in the early twentieth century by chipping away at racial segregation, although this was done in a halting and piecemeal manner. The Court invalidated public laws imposing residential segregation in *Buchanan v. Warley* (1917).[89] At the same time, its subsequent validation of racially restrictive covenants in *Corrigan v. Buckley* (1926) permitted public enforcement of pervasive private discrimination in housing markets.[90] There was tentative progress on educational segregation, too. In 1938, in *Missouri ex rel. Gaines v. Canada*, the Court struck down a Missouri law allowing the state university to bar state residents who were Black from being admitted.[91] Importantly, the court rejected the state's offer to pay out-of-state fees for the Black students to attend a peer institution outside of Missouri as an inadequate defense of equal protection under the Fourteenth Amendment. *Gaines* was a stepping stone to reversing "separate but equal," but it did not itself rule segregated schooling unconstitutional. A decade later, Mexican Americans' right to attend California's public schools was also upheld by the US Court of Appeals for the Ninth Circuit ruled in *Mendez v. Westminster* (1947), which ruled: "By enforcing the segregation of school children of Mexican descent against their will and contrary to the laws of California, respondents have violated the federal law as provided in the Fourteenth Amendment to the Federal Constitution by depriving them of liberty and property without due process of law and by denying to them the equal protection of the laws."[92]

Gaines was later used as precedent in a similar case of admission to a Texas law school in *Sweatt v. Painter* (1950) and, even more remarkable, served as precedent in *McLaurin v. Oklahoma State Regents for Higher Education* (1950) to strike down separate classroom, library, and dining tables for Black students at the University of Oklahoma.[93] In the landmark *Brown v. Board of Education in Topeka* (1954), the Supreme Court built on these Fourteenth Amendment precedents to abolish the Plessy "separate but equal" doctrine. However, equal protection remained largely confined to public education.[94] To uproot Southern regimes of regressive state citizenship, the United States would need legislative activism and national enforcement on the order of a "Second Reconstruction."

Legislative Action: Parties and Social Movements

Federal civil rights acts and enforcement acts were passed by Congress in 1866, 1867, 1870, 1871, and 1875 to reinforce the Fourteenth Amendment birthright citizenship protections and the Fifteenth Amendment's right to vote. Majority-Black districts provided a new solid base for Republican success, and the party did much to foster its relationship with Black voters. From 1867 to 1877, these legislative and partisan dynamics together led to more than 600 Blacks being elected to state and local offices, and sixteen were elected to the US Congress. Indeed, Southern Black officials joined their Northern Republican allies in the US Congress to help pass the federal Civil Rights Act of 1875, which guaranteed to all persons full and equal access to "inns, public conveyances on land and water, theaters, and other places of public amusement" and prohibited exclusion of Blacks from jury duty.[95]

Until 1877, national Republicans still sought to maintain "an active southern policy" to protect voting rights through "Republican-led Senate investigations of southern electoral fraud and intimidation."[96] Yet, as we show in Chapter 4, the weakening of Republican control at the national level and weakening of the social movement fighting for Black civil rights set the stage for Reconstruction's end. After 1870, with the passage of the Fifteenth Amendment, many Whites viewed the Black civil rights struggle as a success, creating deep tensions within the North over the Republican Party's continued leadership on Reconstruction in the South. White women in particular redirected their activism after the Fifteenth Amendment passed in 1870 to fight for their own suffrage. Meanwhile, faced by a sharp contraction in the national economy in 1874, Northern Whites more generally began to turn away from the costly, nationalist Reconstruction vision of racial equality – and the Republican Party began to fracture as a result.

White-supremacist Democratic control returned to the South in 1877 without federal oversight and overtook the US Congress in the mid-1890s, causing the Republican Party to abandon its Black base in order to compete in national elections. The spread of Jim Crow–era voting restrictions in the early 1900s secured this desertion of Black rights by both national political parties. As Jim Crow emerged in full at the beginning of the twentieth century, the Democratic Party used its majority control over the US Senate, often through filibuster, to prevent federal laws from passing that might interfere with Jim Crow policy. Social movements emerged as early as 1909, but they were largely cut off from Congress and experienced minimal success in changing constitutional interpretation through litigation (as we detail in Chapter 4). It wasn't until the 1950s and 1960s that civil rights grew into a large enough social movement to shake loose Southern Democrats' stronghold over the federal government.

Finally, restrictions on women's reproductive rights and the temperance movement emerged, in part, out of the Progressive movement but with a focus on perceived corruptions in the family unit rather than in government. The New York Society for the Suppression of Vice, the first "purity society" in the country, founded by Anthony Comstock in 1872, pushed for tougher federal laws against abortion. Comstock also gained support from Vice President Henry Wilson and Supreme Court Justice William Strong in drafting a federal obscenity law – The Comstock Act – banning the circulation and importation of obscene materials through national mail. Congress easily passed the law without much debate on March 1, 1873.

The Comstock Act banned every article designed, adapted, or intended "for preventing conception or producing abortion, or for indecent or immoral use; and every article, instrument, substance, drug, medicine, or thing which is advertised or described in a manner calculated to lead another to use or apply it for preventing conception or producing abortion, or for any indecent or immoral purpose"; it included a severe penalty of up to a $5,000 fine and ten years in prison for violators of the law.[97] Following this federal victory, anti-vice societies emerged across the country, creating the Social Purity Alliance in 1885 that successfully pressured twenty-two states to enact obscenity laws that banned promotion of contraceptives and twenty-four states to enact laws banning birth control and abortion. These anti-vice movements merged with the early temperance movement; in Connecticut, for example, Phineas T. Barnum, who was the chairman of the Joint Standing Committee on Temperance, led the drafting of the obscenity statute without much involvement by Comstock. Congress amended the Comstock Act in 1897 to also ban the importation of contraceptives and their deposit at freight offices for interstate shipment and strengthened the law once again in 1908.

By the mid-1930s, eight states mirrored federal law by prohibiting the flow of contraceptive information, adding to their existing laws on obscenity.[98] Importantly, the Supreme Court upheld the constitutional validity of these laws, giving little recognition of rights to privacy and reproductive control. In *Commonwealth v. Allison* (1917), the Court upheld the 1879 Comstock law of Massachusetts.[99] In the case, pro-contraception advocates argued unsuccessfully that medical necessity required contraception. Chief Justice Samuel Ruggs argued that anti-contraception laws were "designed to promote the public morals and in a broad sense the public health and safety. Their plain purpose is to protect purity, to preserve chastity, to encourage continence and self-restraint, to defend the sanctity of the home, and thus engender in the state and nation a virile and virtuous race of men and women."[100]

Expansions in White Female and Immigrant Suffrage: Even as states in the post-Reconstruction era institutionalized regimes of regressive state citizenship with respect to Black residents and voters, the same period also saw the rapid diffusion of progressive state citizenship for White women. In 1868, during Congressional Reconstruction, two distinct movements were formed: the National Woman Suffrage Association (NWSA) fought nationally for an amendment to the US Constitution, while the American Woman Suffrage Association (AWSA) led by abolitionist Lucy Stone pursued amending state constitutions and passing state laws.[101] NWSA found its efforts at national reform roadblocked not only by Southern leaders' fear of extending voting rights to Black women, which they saw as further tipping the scales toward racial equality, but also by party machines in the North worried that they would lose their control if women could vote. Meanwhile, for AWSA, success at the state level was slow and limited to the Mountain West, in Utah (1870) and Colorado (1893). AWSA faced numerous close defeats in state legislatures across the country from 1868 to 1890 but continued to organize a grassroots movement.

With national reform intractable and state bills continuing to fall just under the required vote for passing, NWSA and AWSA merged in 1890 to form the National American Woman Suffrage Association (NAWSA) with a strategy of forming local offices in towns, cities, wards, and precincts across the country, building a mass following and partnerships with organized labor, and engaging in new tactics of pressuring political leaders through demonstrations and door-to-door canvassing. Early success in extending voting rights for women in school board elections between 1890 and 1910 helped chapters build local capacity and build towards statewide victories. Female suffrage at the statewide level soon followed, starting with Washington (1910) and followed soon by California (1911), Arizona (1912), Kansas (1912), Oregon (1912), and Illinois (1913).[102] Meanwhile, Congress continued to resist, voting down constitutional amendments in 1914 and 1915. By then, women's suffrage had turned their mass movement of the early 1900s into an advocacy coalition with state and local ties. The National Women's Party (NWP), which formed in 1916 and, as a national partner organization to NAWSA, focused on a "Winning Plan" that built support in thirty-six states to amend the US Constitution, finally succeeding in 1920.[103]

Thus, expansion of women's suffrage was a state-led affair, starting in the Mountain West during the late 1800s and expanding rapidly across other Western states from 1910 to 1917 before snowballing into a federal constitutional amendment. Still, there were limits to these gains in citizenship rights. Even in the 1930s, women could be legally kept off of juries, thus limiting their right to participate and be represented. They were also given different work hours, paid less money, and imprisoned for using birth control, all of which fall under our citizenship dimension of rights to develop human capital.[104] It was not until the emergence of "second-wave" feminism in the 1960s and 1970s that women made further advancements in citizenship rights.

Much like the contrast between Black rights and women's rights, the rights of other minority groups also waxed and waned from 1900 to the 1950s. The Jones-Shafroth Act of 1917 granted US citizenship to all Puerto Ricans born after the US incorporated the island as a federal territory. Domestically, the Indian Citizenship Act of 1924 extended national citizenship to Native Americans. Yet, unlike White women, racial minorities including Native Americans and Mexican Americans were regularly denied rights under Jim Crow state laws, despite their US citizenship.[105]

Race often mattered more than citizenship, especially when it came to the right to vote. The US Constitution did not forbid noncitizens from voting in federal elections and, until the 1920s, twenty-two states and federal territories had at some point allowed noncitizens to vote in various types of elections.[106] As the legal scholar Jamin Raskin has noted, these laws "reflected both an openness to newcomers and the idea that the defining principle for political membership was not American citizenship but the exclusionary categories of race, gender, property, and wealth."[107] States and territories in the Northwest permitted alien suffrage as an incentive for immigrants to settle there, and the practice evolved over time: in the early 1800s, the new states of Illinois, Indiana, Michigan, and Ohio allowed voting for all male residents twenty-one years or older, but after the War of 1812 and its accompanying rise in nativist sentiment, most new territories restricted the franchise to citizens. Then, in 1848, Wisconsin provided an innovation that helped overcome nativist opposition, by allowing voting for "declarant aliens" who had declared their intention to become US citizens, and thirteen states adopted this policy after the Civil War, including several Southern states eager to grow their resident populations.[108]

By the 1920s, however, all states had repealed such policies, as nativist sentiment reached a fever pitch following America's entry into World War I and rising labor unrest at home.[109] As John Hope Franklin explains, following the Great Migration of Blacks to Northern States and the return of Black veterans after WWI ended, "the greatest period of interracial strife the nation had ever witnessed" unfolded with twenty race riots in the last six months of 1919 alone.[110] During the same period that women gained the right to vote, anti-immigrant nativism led to national legislation shutting down immigration to a trickle,[111] as well as eliminating any remaining state laws allowing for "declarant aliens" to vote in places like Texas, Mississippi, and Arkansas.[112]

The impetus for immigration restriction in the 1920s also prompted an unprecedented attempt by Congress to tinker with the counting of aliens for purposes of apportionment, as Southern representatives sought to introduce amendments to a much-delayed reapportionment bill in 1929 that would exclude aliens from the population count for apportionment.[113] Many of these states stood to lose representation after the 1920 count, as the westward expansion of the United States had effectively come to a close. Furthermore, Congress had voted to stop expanding the size of the US House, a measure that had previously helped slow-growing states with smaller immigrant populations to minimize losses in Congressional apportionment. Ultimately, these amendments were defeated, but it is quite likely that, even if they had passed, they would have not withstood judicial review, given the explicit provisions for the counting of persons in the US Constitution.[114]

Whereas World War I marked a high point for racism and nativism, World War II helped to usher in some national changes that expanded national voting rights and naturalization rights. An uneasy alliance between Democrats and Republicans during World War II enabled Congress to pass a federal law expanding Black voting rights for the first time since Reconstruction. The Soldier Voting Act of 1942, which eliminated the poll tax for military personnel, passed with nationwide, bipartisan support. As we explain in Chapter 4, Southern Democratic support for this inclusionary voting law was strategic: it protected Jim Crow by cutting short any attempt to pass legislation that would preempt state control over the domestic voting rights of Blacks. World War II also spurred new social movement tactics to gain presidential leadership on civil rights. As

Christopher Parker explains, the NAACP used incidences of White violence on Black veterans to pressure President Harry S. Truman to take bolder federal action in fighting racism and promote civil rights.[115] This led Truman to issue Executive Order 9981 in 1948, banning discrimination "on the basis of race, color, religion or national origin" in the United States Armed Forces.

US foreign policy considerations also played an important role during World War II and the Cold War that soon followed. With China as an important ally in the Pacific theater during World War II, Congress passed the Magnuson Act in December 1943, repealing all prior measures of Chinese exclusion from the United States, allowing up to 150 Chinese immigrants to enter the country annually, and finally allowing Chinese immigrants to naturalize as US citizens.[116] Sensing an opening, immigrant activists such as Dalip Singh Saund pushed for further expansions in the right to naturalize Asian immigrants. In 1946, Congress passed the Luce-Celler Act allowing Indian and Filipino immigrants to naturalize and providing for a quota of 100 immigrants from each country annually.[117] Finally, the 1952 McCarran-Walter Act removed all remaining racial bans on naturalization and allowed up to 100 individuals per year to migrate to the United States from other Asian countries.[118]

Executive Action: Bureaucratic Capacity and Political Will

Federal administrative capacity grew significantly during Reconstruction and during the early twentieth century. Following the Civil War, the federal government had authority over the readmission of ex-Confederate states into the Union, including the ability to require that they add constitutional provisions to state constitutions related to abolition and Black civil rights. However, it would take some time for the federal government to consistently employ its administrative capacity to enforce federal law.

Reconstruction under President Andrew Johnson's leadership was purposely inactive, likely the result of Johnson being a Southerner and a Democrat, who stepped into the presidency after Lincoln's assassination. On May 29, 1865, Johnson issued a general proclamation of pardon and amnesty for most Confederates and authorized the provisional governor of North Carolina to proceed in reorganizing its state's constitution. The only requirement Johnson set for state constitutional conventions to proceed was that it was chosen by the voters who pledged future loyalty to the US Constitution and to accept the Thirteenth Amendment (1865) by abolishing slavery. Most noteworthy, by not renewing former President Lincoln's Freedmen's Bureau Bill in 1866, President Johnson ended the federal government's leadership on the provision of food, housing, health care, reuniting Black families, and setting up and overseeing employment contracts with private landowners through the Freedmen's Bureau. He also vetoed the Civil Rights Bill of 1867.

Appalled, moderate Republicans joined the Radicals of their party in formalizing a Congressional vision for reconstruction by overturning Johnson's vetoes in 1866 (Freedmen's Bureau) and 1867 (Civil Rights Act). Taking over the process of Reconstruction in 1867, the Republican Congress shifted the federal government's stance, expanding protections for federally guaranteed rights and setting significant limits on state power. Most notably, Congress reversed the President Johnson's actions by passing the Reconstruction Act of 1867, placing former Confederate states back under federal military control, requiring Black participation in elections, and barring former Confederate leaders from electing or becoming delegates for a new state constitutional convention. Administrative capacity and political will to reinforce federal rights remained strong for a decade under Congressional Republican leadership. When Reconstruction formally ended in 1877, federal willingness to enforce federal law also deteriorated and Democratic electoral gains soon redirected national governance away from protecting minority rights.

Federal capacity grew tremendously at the beginning of the twentieth century, but equal rights did not automatically follow. Foreshadowing the Progressive movement to reform a corrupt and inefficient bureaucracy, the Pendleton Act of 1883 established competitive entrance exams for federal agency recruitment and establishing a meritocratic system for hiring and promotion.[119] It also established the US Civil Service Commission, which "supervised examinations, made investigations, recommended rules to govern federal personnel, and requested disciplinary action."[120]

The next major expansion in the size and role of federal government in the economy, social welfare, employment, and housing came in response to the Great Depression.[121] President Roosevelt's New Deal (1932–1941) provided the needed massive undertaking and transformation by the federal government. However, as many scholars have uncovered in great detail, the New Deal largely excluded racial minorities from many of the benefits given to Whites. The Social Security program established in 1935 included old-age insurance that excluded agricultural and domestic workers, which made up the majority of the nation's Black labor force. In 1933, the Wagner-Peyser Act created the United States Employment Service (USES) designed to help job-seekers find work throughout the country and recruit workers to New Deal public works programs, a massive federal undertaking.[122] Federal programs for old age insurance, unemployment compensation, housing aid, the Civilian Conservation Corps, federal housing mortgage support, and new labor laws all expanded the size and scope of the federal government significantly. While these expansions certainly could have benefited all residents, we explain in greater detail in Chapter 4 (for Blacks) and Chapter 5 (for immigrants) that New Deal expansions in rights were racially exclusive, in part because Southern and Western states lobbied to give states greater control in the administration of many federal welfare schemes.

Moreover, federal executive actions that expanded Black civil rights went against the legislative actions of Congress at the time and thus had limited impact on the regressive state citizenship regimes erected during Jim Crow. World War II provided another opening for nation-building under presidential leadership. In 1946, President Truman addressed the nation after an assault on a Black veteran gained national attention: "When a major and a City Marshal can take a negro Sergeant off a bus in South Carolina, beat him up and put out one of his eyes, and nothing is done about it ... something is radically wrong with the system." He went on, saying, "I am going to try to remedy it."[123] Truman appointed a commission on civil rights that year, which issued a 1947 report recommending federal desegregation of the armed forces, the creation of a permanent Fair Employment Practices Committee, and passage of federal laws to combat lynching and ban state poll taxes.[124]

Still, presidential leadership on civil rights through executive action waxed and waned. When *Brown* ended the constitutional and legal legitimacy of segregated schools in 1954, it would take three years of state-sanctioned violent resistance preventing racial integration of schools before President Eisenhower in 1957 deployed the federal military to the South. Indeed, Eisenhower's support of federal civil rights bills in 1957 and 1960 was strategic with respect to geopolitics; he was concerned about securing America's reputation as an egalitarian democracy to fight the spread of communism. A general lack of willingness to lead in civil rights enforcement permitted regressive state citizenship to continue, in clear violation of constitution's equal protection of all federal citizens.

THE CIVIL RIGHTS ERA

The Civil Rights Act of 1964, and related legislation championed by social movement activists through 1968, ushered in a new era in US citizenship rights. While Congress had made prior attempts to legislate on civil rights, those efforts lacked much enforcement authority. The Civil Rights Act of 1957 in its original form provided the US Justice Department preemptive power to litigate any civil rights suit in the country, unconstrained by whether violations were under federal, state, or local jurisdiction. The final passed version established the Civil Rights Section of the Justice Department, but the proposed provision to empower it with a litigation mechanism was removed by Southern Democrats in the US Senate, after South Carolina's pro-segregationist Strom Thurmond led a Senate filibuster. The law established a federal Civil Rights Commission with authority to investigate discriminatory conditions, but it was empowered only to recommend corrective measures, not to enforce federal law.

The Civil Rights Act of 1960 also fell short due to Democratic resistance. It authorized federal judges to oversee racial discrimination but only through requiring local authorities to maintain and provide voting records. We explain in Chapter 4 that local authorities resisted court oversight by not keeping records, and Jim Crow remained firmly in place. Social movement pressure continued to build nationally, with the March on Washington in 1963 amassing the largest demonstration on the nation's capital up to that point in American history, with more than 200,000 people walking in protest to the Lincoln Memorial. There, Martin Luther King Jr. addressed the peaceful, nonviolent protesters in his televised "I Have a Dream" speech, viewed by millions of Americans at home. This helped to usher in a new era of Civil Rights reform, referred to by some scholars as the Second Reconstruction.[125]

The passage of the Civil Rights Act of 1964 provided the legal framework for ending Jim Crow segregation nationwide. It banned discrimination (based on race, color, religion, sex, or national origin); segregation in schools, employment, and public accommodations; and unequal use of voter registration requirements. In addition, the Twenty-Fourth Amendment was ratified in 1964, banning poll taxes in federal elections. The Supreme Court soon extended the ban on poll taxes to state and local elections in *Harper v. Virginia State Board of Elections* (1966).[126] Finally, the Voting Rights Act (VRA) of 1965 stopped all voter restrictions for a five-year period in jurisdictions with histories of voter suppression, created federal "preclearance" with the Justice Department placed in charge of authorizing new electoral rules, and appointed federal officials to monitor compliance.

Following these legislative successes, Dr. King shifted from voting rights advocacy in 1966 to leading nonviolent marches and lobbying efforts (in partnership with the NAACP and the National Committee Against Discrimination) to fight for fair housing and residential desegregation.[127] The Fair Housing Act, passed in 1968, prohibited discrimination concerning the sale, rental, and financing of housing based on race, religion, national origin, or sex. This law represented the high-water mark of the civil rights legislation and was followed by a decade of court rulings extending equal protection jurisprudence to upholding race-conscious affirmative action laws and policies. Thus, from 1964 onward, state regimes of regressive and exclusionary citizenship were highly constrained by court rulings, new legislation, and a strong willingness on the part of the federal government to enforce federal law.

At the same time, the 1970s also marked an important decade for consolidating conservativism within the Republican Party, which, by the 1980s, fueled court reversals of precedent to a colorblind approach, along a loss of federal willingness to enforce all of federal law. While Barry Goldwater's presidential candidacy in 1964 had introduced state's rights to the Republican Party mainstream, the Nixon and Reagan presidencies consolidated its place in both electoral campaigns and presidential administration. As we detail later in this chapter, conservative rollbacks on civil rights started in the Nixon administration and accelerated during the Reagan years. President Reagan's court nominees began rolling back prior decisions on equal protection, and the federal government devolved power to states on affirmative action rather than vigorously expanding and enforcing federal civil rights law. At the same time, the federal government expanded its role in the carceral state, in the War on Drugs, and in immigration law and enforcement, further impinging on the civil rights of communities of color.

The struggle for gay citizenship rights emerged in this context of erosion in both state and federal protections. Utah passed the first state Defense of Marriage statute in 1995, stipulating that it does not have to recognize out-of-state marriages that violate state public policy. Soon thereafter, Democratic President Bill Clinton signed the Defense of Marriage Act in 1996, defining under federal law that a legal union was between one man and one woman and barring same-sex couples from receiving federal benefits, rights, or privileges. Meanwhile, that same year, California passed Proposition 209, amending the state constitution to prohibit state governmental institutions from considering race, sex, or ethnicity, specifically in the areas of public employment, public contracting, and public education. Prop. 209 officially marked the end of uniform national support for affirmative action and the turn in American federalism to a states' rights vision of the federal Civil Rights Act of 1964. The year 1996 was also a watershed moment in federalism and immigrant rights, as Clinton signed laws that authorized state cooperation with federal authorities on immigration enforcement, wiped the slate clean on state welfare provisions to immigrants, and required state legislative approval for any future benefits (we cover in depth the aftermath of 1996 federal restriction for immigrant rights in Chapter 6).[128] By the late 1990s, it was clear that any advancements in citizenship rights would need to be driven from the state level upward.

Constitutional Opportunities and Interpretation

Civil Rights jurisprudence in the 1960s breathed new life into the Reconstruction Amendments and used them as powerful tools to eliminate most forms of regressive state citizenship involving Blacks and to expand rights to new populations. Most of the judges appointed were racial liberals, who applied the US Constitution to strengthen federal laws, old and new. This was especially important for how Title VII of the 1964 Civil Rights Act would be interpreted to support race-conscious remedies and to add new categories of protection including religion and gender.[129] As John Skrentny explains,[130] Title VII was written as a classic liberal policy intended to erase racial differences in order to achieve equality in the workplace:

It shall be an unlawful employment practice for an employer –

(1) to fail or refuse to hire or to discharge any individual, or otherwise to discriminate against any individual with respect to his compensation, terms, conditions, or privileges of employment, because of such individual's race, color, religion, sex, or national origin; or

(2) to limit, segregate, or classify his employees or applicants for employment in any way which would deprive or tend to deprive any individual of employment opportunities or otherwise adversely affect his status as an employee, because of such individual's race, color, religion, sex, or national origin.[131]

By the 1970s, the federal courts had begun to expand Title VII into a legal tool for advancing racial justice based on the Fourteenth Amendment provisions of due process and equal protection. Similar constitutional developments occurred from court decisions expanding their interpretation of protections under the Thirteenth Amendment (abolishing slavery) and the Fifteenth Amendment (Black suffrage) to cover contemporary issues of federal rights. Federal capacity also grew during the Civil Rights period, expanding the size of the federal judiciary to handle the growth of civil rights litigation.[132] However, many of these advancements in civil rights jurisprudence stalled in the mid-1980s and began rolling back soon thereafter.

The Right to Participate

The 1965 Voting Rights Act (VRA) marks the formal transition into the Civil Rights period, with important implications for the US Constitution and federalism. The VRA suspended voting tests and systems in state and local jurisdictions with less than 50 percent registration or turnout of their resident voting-age population during the recent 1964 election and put in place a system of federal oversight over state election rules.[133] Section 5 required all new subfederal jurisdictions with known legacies of voter suppression to submit any new voting rules to the Justice Department for "preclearance." The VRA, as a result of its enforcement sections, struck at the heart of regressive voting laws that had epitomized White supremacy's hold on political parties and formal government through the Jim Crow period. It fundamentally shifted power over voting rights to the federal government, without actually ending states' control over the voting process for federal, state, and local elections.

It is no coincidence that the Civil Rights period was ushered in by the courts having to uphold the VRA against challenges by Southern states on the grounds that it violated Tenth Amendment protections of state prerogatives. In *South Carolina v. Katzenbach* (1966), the Warren Court, with a near unanimous decision, ruled that the Voting Rights Act was a valid exercise of Congress's power under the enforcement clause of the Fifteenth Amendment, which gave Congress full powers to stop discrimination in voting.[134] Justice Hugo Black of Alabama wrote a partial dissent arguing that Section 5 was a unconstitutional overreach of federal power that required some, but not all, states to gain federal approval before passing a state law or constitutional amendment on voting. In his dissent, Black argued:

Section 5, by providing that some of the States cannot pass state laws or adopt state constitutional amendments without first being compelled to beg federal authorities to approve their policies, so distorts our constitutional structure of government as to render any distinction drawn in the Constitution between state and federal power almost meaningless.... Certainly if all the provisions of our Constitution which limit the power of the Federal Government and reserve other power to the States are to mean anything, they mean at least that the States have power to pass laws and amend their constitutions without first sending their officials hundreds of miles away to beg federal authorities to approve them.[135]

The Court rejected the claims of South Carolina and state attorneys general from Virginia, Louisiana, Alabama, Mississippi, and Georgia that the law lacked a rational basis and intruded on state prerogatives protected by the Tenth Amendment. In a companion case, *Katzenbach v. Morgan* (1966), the US Supreme Court also upheld Section 4(e)'s protection of the right to register and vote to those with limited English proficiency.[136] In a similar vein, the US Supreme Court held in *White v. Regester* (1973) that a 1970 redistricting scheme for two urban counties in Texas represented a form of "vote dilution" affecting Mexican Americans and African Americans violated VRA and the Fifteenth Amendment.[137] Looking at the "totality of circumstances" that included the state's history of political and economic discrimination against minorities, the court struck down the state's entire reapportionment scheme.

Due Process and Human Capital Rights

From 1965 to the 1980s, Jim Crow's legacy was overturned by court rulings that expanded the constitutional framework's meaning and created an entirely new role for federal law, past and present. More robust sets of federal rights emerged, not just for political representation (including voting and redistricting) but also for due process and legal protections (through criminal justice reforms) and human capital formation (via antidiscrimination protections in the workplace, housing, and elsewhere). In *Jones v. Alfred Mayer Co.* (1968), Desmond King and Rogers Smith explain that the US Supreme Court had even given "new life to provisions in the Civil Rights Act of 1866,"[138] which was a Reconstruction-era federal law passed by the Radical Republican Congress over the veto of President Andrew Johnson in order to enable the full integration of newly freed Blacks. The 1866 federal law prohibited both private and state discrimination in the rights of federal citizens to "inherit, purchase, lease, sell, hold, and convey real and personal property," hallmark features of what we describe as the right to human capital formation.[139]

In the *Jones* decision, Justice Potter Steward upheld the 1866 federal law, ruling that the Thirteenth Amendment's abolition of slavery empowered Congress with authority to pass legislation banning private racial discrimination that would perpetuate "badges and incidents of slavery," and clarified Congress's authority to "determine what are the badges and incidents of slavery, and the authority to translate that determination into effective legislation."[140] Stewart's ruling in *Jones* was wide-reaching for recently enacted federal laws as well. It "meant that federal anti-discrimination laws applied to *all* real estate transactions," essentially striking down exemptions provided to resident owners under the Fair Housing Act of 1968, which had banned discrimination concerning the sale, rental, and financing of housing based on race, religion, national origin, or sex, while also strengthening federal enforcement of the 1968 law.[141] *Jones*'s precedent has also led modern Fourteenth Amendment court rulings on racial discrimination by landlord's unequal treatment of tenants, local zoning ordinances, the practice of "blockbusting," "redlining" in home loans, and unequal access to homeowners' insurance – providing a net of protections under the federal right to human capital formation.[142]

While Thirteenth and Fifteenth Amendment jurisprudence loomed large during the Civil Rights period, the court's extension of the Fourteenth Amendment's meaning is arguably the most significant for national citizenship. In 1971, the US Supreme Court in *Griggs v. Duke Power Co.*, ruled that Duke Power Company, a utility corporation that provided services to North Carolina, South Carolina, and the federal government, had violated Title VII of the Civil Rights Act of 1964 by requiring employees to take performance tests that did not provide a "reasonable measure of job performance."[143] King and Smith explain that, while federal law was designed to prevent *intentional* racial discrimination under Title VII, the court ruling in *Griggs* extended its protection under a new category of disparate racial impacts, regardless of their intent.[144] The company's intelligence tests were considered to be a form of racial discrimination because they disparately affected Black employees. In addition to adding this meaning of protection to existing federal law, *Griggs* held that employers face the burden of producing and proving the necessity of any tests they require for employees.

When the conservative US Supreme Court ruled in *Wards Cove Packing Co. v. Atonio* (1989) to reduce this employer-based burden, replacing "proving the necessity" with simply showing evidence of business-relevant justification, Congress responded by passing the Civil Rights Act of 1991 that amended federal law to expressly include *Griggs*'s burden of proof for employers.[145] Importantly, Paul Frymer explains that federal courts began to rule on employment protections under the National Labor Relations Act (1935) and Title VII (1964).[146] Antidiscrimination lawsuits, as a result, dramatically increased during the Civil Rights period with increased access to federal courts for protection.

The courts also upheld race-conscious policies in employment.[147] In *Steelworkers v. Weber* (1979), the US Supreme Court explicitly upheld a collective bargaining agreement that reserved 50 percent of a company's training program's positions exclusively to Blacks.[148] Recognizing that there was a very low number of Black employees in an area with a high Black population, the corporation worked with African American, Latino, and Asian American civil rights organizations and women's groups to form the collective bargaining agreement.[149] The following year, in *Fullilove v. Klutznick* (1980), the US Supreme Court also upheld the federal Public Works Employment Act of 1977's provision that set aside 10 percent of federal contracts to minority-owned businesses.[150]

Other Human Capital Rights: Marriage, Privacy Protections, and Education

In the same year that Congress passed the Voting Rights Act, the US Supreme Court in *Griswold v. Connecticut* (1965) struck down Connecticut's Comstock law, which prohibited any person from using "any drug, medicinal article or instrument for the purpose of preventing conception," arguing that the law effectively denied only disadvantaged citizens from having access to medical assistance and information on proper legal methods of birth control.[151] The court invalidated the law on the grounds that it violated the "right to marital privacy" from governmental intrusion. In their concurring opinions, Justice Byron White and Justice John Marshall Harlan II argued that privacy was also protected under the Fourteenth Amendment's due process clause. Soon after, in *Eisenstadt v. Baird* (1972), the court extended this right to unmarried couples on the Fourteenth Amendment's equal protection grounds.[152]

In *Loving v. Virginia* (1967), the US Supreme Court struck down all state laws banning interracial marriage as violations of the Fourteenth Amendment's equal protection and due process clauses.[153] Virginia's Racial Integrity Act of 1924 had criminalized marriage between people classified by the state as "White" and as "colored." The court argued that no "distinctions drawn according to race" can be used to outlaw marriage under state laws and overruled the post-Reconstruction case of *Pace v. Alabama* (1883), which had previously opened the window for Jim Crow segregation laws to include restrictions on the family unit.[154] Of course, this right to marriage and protections over the family unit did not extend to everyone. The US Supreme Court only recently extended the right to marriage to include same-sex couples in *Obergefell v. Hodges* (2015), after decades of restrictive state laws followed by a flurry of state marriage expansions starting in 2004.[155]

Expanded rights to human capital formation also included the reproductive rights of women. In 1972, in *Eisenstadt v. Baird*, the US Supreme Court extended *Griswold*'s right-to-privacy decision to include unmarried couples, based on the Fourteenth Amendment's equal protection clause.[156] The following year, in the landmark case on women's reproductive rights, *Roe v. Wade* (1973), the US Supreme Court struck down a Texas law that criminalized aiding a woman in getting an abortion, arguing:

This [women's] right of privacy, whether it be founded in the Fourteenth Amendment's concept of personal liberty and restrictions upon state action, as we feel it is, or ... in the Ninth Amendment's reservation of rights to the people, is broad enough to encompass a woman's decision whether or not to terminate her pregnancy.[157]

The same day as *Roe* was decided, the court also released its decision to overturn an abortion law of Georgia, in *Doe v. Bolton* (1973).[158] The *Roe* court struck a trimester-based balance for prioritizing women's reproductive rights (first trimester), medical expertise (second trimester), and fetal viability (third trimester), the latter defined as the potential for a fetus to live outside the mother's womb, with or without artificial life support. Thus, while *Roe* opened the door for restrictive state laws to deny reproductive rights during the third trimester, it also safeguarded this right during the first two trimesters.

The following decades presented a mixed picture with respect to women's rights to human capital formation. Just after *Roe* was decided, in *Weinberger v. Wiesenfeld* (1975), the court invalidated a Social Security provision established in 1935 that permitted widows, but not widowers, to collect special benefits while caring for minor children. The Court ruled that this disparity violated equal protection.[159] That same year, in *Stanton v. Stanton* (1975), the Court invalidated a statute requiring parents to support their sons until age twenty-one but their daughters only until age eighteen.[160] Gender equality continued to expand under the Fourteenth Amendment's equal protection in *Orr v. Orr* (1979), with the Court invalidating a law permitting alimony payments to be imposed only on husbands upon divorce.[161] After its conservative shift during the 1980s, in *Planned Parenthood v. Casey* (1992), the Supreme Court revised *Roe* by replacing the trimester balancing framework altogether with a standard based solely on fetal viability.[162] The 1992 ruling also, importantly, reversed the strict scrutiny standard established by *Roe* of state or local laws, further weakening women's reproductive rights.

The right to privacy expanded protections to sexual minorities as well. *Lawrence v. Texas* (2003) struck down a Texas sodomy law that prohibited certain forms of intimate sexual contact between members of the same sex. Without stating a standard of review in the majority opinion, the court overruled *Bowers v. Hardwick* (1986)[163] declaring that the "Texas statute furthers no legitimate state interest which can justify its intrusion into the personal and private life of the individual."[164] Justice O'Connor, who wrote a concurring opinion, framed it as an issue of rational basis review. Justice Kennedy's majority opinion, based on the liberty interest protected by the due process clause of the Fourteenth Amendment, stated that the Texas anti-sodomy statute touched "upon the most private human conduct, sexual behavior, and in the most private of places, the home." Thus, the Court held that adults are entitled to participate in private, consensual sexual conduct. While *Lawrence* was framed in terms of the right to liberty, Kennedy described the "right to privacy" found in *Griswold* as the "most pertinent beginning point" in the evolution of the concepts embodied in *Lawrence*.[165]

The court's expansion of human capital rights went beyond employment, housing, and the family unit. After *Brown* (1954) had struck down segregation in public schools, courts also upheld affirmative action policies in postsecondary admissions and extended the right to K–12 education to undocumented children. In *Regents of the University of California v. Bakke* (1978), the US Supreme Court upheld college admissions' affirmative action policies but ruled that specific racial quotas in admissions were unconstitutional.[166] Affirmative action was not only important to integrating minorities into the nation's public schools after *Brown*; it also began to address material racial inequalities of past discrimination and exclusion. John Skrentny rightly explains that affirmative action in higher education could be justified under the Fourteenth Amendment: "institutional structures in society often work to maintain or worsen the subordinated positions of individuals in nonwhite groups. Moreover, just and responsible lawmaking and judging interprets the Fourteenth Amendment's guarantee of the 'equal protection of the laws' as requiring that these institutional hierarchies be recognized and that attempts to break them up be undertaken."[167] Indeed, for postsecondary education where admissions is mostly merit based, *Brown* provided an insufficient constitutional framework.

Bakke helped fill this constitutional gap and was later upheld in *Grutter v. Bollinger* (2003), where the US Supreme Court argued that the state has a compelling interest to ensure that students of a minority group reach a "critical mass" that would guarantee their full integration and representation.[168] In *Gratz v. Bollinger* (2003), the court simultaneously struck down the University of Michigan's more rigid, point-based undergraduate admission policy as an unconstitutional quota system that made race the primary factor for admissions.[169] Importantly, as with abortion laws, court decisions upholding affirmative action in postsecondary education left open whether or not states could legally permit these policies – indeed, *Grutter* specifically upholds affirmative action as a state interest (not an individual's right). In 2006, after *Grutter*, the Michigan Civil Rights Initiative (Proposal 2) was passed, prohibiting the use of race in the University of Michigan's Law School admissions processes. This law was upheld by the US Supreme Court in *Schuette v. Coalition to Defend Affirmative Action* (2014).[170]

On immigrant rights, in *Graham v. Richardson* (1971), the US Supreme Court invalidated restrictive welfare schemes in Pennsylvania and Arizona that barred legal immigrants from being able to access public benefits, ruling they violated the Fourteenth Amendment's equal protection clause.[171] Importantly, while *Graham*'s expansion of legal immigrant's rights generally aligned with the court's expansion of other groups' rights, including those of Blacks, women, and the LGBT community, it did not include undocumented immigrants. In fact, the distinction between legal and undocumented rights to human capital formation had become much more distinctive and exclusionary, beginning with *De Canas v. Bica* (1976), which upheld a restrictive California employer sanction law to prevent undocumented residents from gaining employment in the state.[172] Gulasekaram and Ramakrishnan point out that, while the majority opinion in *De Canas* was based on a federal preemption rationale, "it concurrently clarified that states maintained the constitutional authority to structure the everyday lives of its residents, which could include, under certain circumstances, regulating on the basis of unlawful immigration status."[173] This authority of states over the rights of their immigrant residents, both legal and undocumented, continued to be redefined by the courts.

In *Sugarman v. Dougall* (1973), the court struck down a state law that discriminated "against resident aliens seeking permanent positions in the competitive class of the state civil service, but [opined] that states may discriminate against noncitizens with regard to participation 'in the [state's] political community.'"[174] Indeed, courts during the Civil Rights period have ruled that states have authority to grant or restrict the political rights of noncitizens, including for voting, holding elected office, performing jury service, and obtaining public employment (e.g., state police officers, public school teachers).[175] At the same time, in *Toll v. Moreno* (1982), the court made it clear that states could not discriminate between legal permanent residents and other visa holders that Congress had allowed to establish residence in the United States.[176] Importantly, court rulings like *Toll* protected the rights of legal immigrants on the grounds of preemption, with the federal government having broad constitutional authority over states in the determination of immigration policy. Immigrant rights, as a result, have developed along a separate line of court precedent than minorities who are citizens of the United States.

The only ruling by the court on immigration-related laws that is grounded explicitly in an equal protection framework, rather than a federal preemption framework, was *Plyler v. Doe* (1982).[177] In *Plyler*, the US Supreme Court struck down a Texas state law passed in 1975 that withheld state funds for educating undocumented children and permitted school districts to deny enrollment to undocumented children.[178] Texas officials argued that undocumented children were unprotected under the US Constitution because they were in the country in violation of federal law. The court countered, arguing that, once inside the country, every person (not just citizens) fall within the jurisdiction of the US Constitution and of federal, state, and local governments. Importantly, the court dismissed the plaintiff's first claim that the state law was preempted and ruled entirely on their second claim, that the state law violated the Fourteenth Amendment's equal protection of the laws guaranteed to "all persons." It ruled that no state can limit a child's access to K–12 public education under the Fourteenth Amendment, regardless of their legal status. Hiroshi Motomura highlights that the court not only referred to the landmark *Brown* (1954) decision in justifying its ruling, but it also drew on the principle of immigrant integration into American society.[179]

Since *Plyler* (1982), the courts have applied the plenary powers framework, rather than constitutional rights, in adjudicating restrictive state and local laws on immigration. In *Chamber of Commerce of the United States v. Whiting* (2011), the US Supreme Court upheld Arizona's 2007 law that requires the use of E-Verify by Arizona employers, punishable by suspension or revocation of the employer's business license.[180] At issue was whether revocation of a business license constituted an employer sanction, which the 1986 Immigration Reform and Control Act (IRCA) made exclusive to the national government, or whether it fell under the authority of states to regulate business licenses, which remained under the purview of state control. The court ruled in favor of the latter, noting that IRCA preempted the ability of states to impose fines on employers for violations of federal immigration law but not the ability to revoke business licenses. By contrast, in *Arizona v. United States* (2012), the US Supreme Court struck down most, but not all, of Arizona's SB 1070 as preempted by federal immigration law. This included striking down provisions making it a state-level crime for noncitizens to not have federal identity documents or to seek employment in the state, as well as striking down the provision authorizing warrantless arrests of persons that an officer believed to be in the country unlawfully. In justifying preemption, the Court referred back to century-old cases on Chinese exclusion and other decisions upholding the exclusive right of the United States to control immigration as part of its foreign-policymaking powers.[181] Importantly, the court upheld one provision, allowing local law enforcement to ask for proof of legal status during routine traffic stops. Its provision requiring cooperation with federal immigration officers, including transferring custody to federal authorities of any person suspected or known to be in the country unlawfully, were never even placed under court scrutiny.

In Chapter 6, we provide a detailed analysis of the current legal landscape of immigration federalism, including how recent court rulings have shaped the various state laws in place today. Importantly, following changes to federal immigration law in 1996 that opened the doors for states to restrict immigrant access to public benefits and resources and expanded federal–local immigration enforcement partnerships, the courts have allowed many types of state and local laws that expand or contract the rights of undocumented immigrants. Recently, the US Supreme Court ruled in *Hoffman Plastic Compounds, Inc. v. National Labor Relations Board* (2002) that undocumented workers are not entitled to back pay under federal law, making them more vulnerable to employer abuse and severing their protection under the National Labor Relations Act of 1935.[182] This rollback in immigrant rights transcends the immigration context; since the 1980s, a conservative takeover of the US Supreme Court has led to important reversals weakening the constitutional rights of national citizens, including the right to vote in 2013.

Conservative Backsliding in Court Interpretation

Conservative backsliding on civil rights jurisprudence gained steam in the 1980s, starting with President Reagan's appointment of three justices and the elevation of William Rehnquist to chief justice. Part of the erosion of civil rights hinged on the distinction between intentions to discriminate and discriminatory impacts regardless of intent. For example, in *General Building Contractors Association v. Pennsylvania* (1982), Black engineers filed a discrimination lawsuit after being denied access to an exclusive hiring hall and to an apprenticeship program formed by their local union and the trade association. The district court had found the union guilty under Title VII and also found the contractors' association to be in violation of 42 USC §1981, a provision derived from the 1866 Civil Rights Act and the 1870 Enforcement Act, which the lower court interpreted as banning actions with racially disparate impacts. Overturning the district court ruling, the new conservative US Supreme Court argued that the 42 USC §1981, "like the equal protection clause, must be read in color-blind fashion as banning only intentional racial discrimination" and ruled that no evidence of discriminatory practices existed.[183]

In *Wards Cove Packing Co. v. Atonio* (1989), the Supreme Court ruled that Title VII did not prevent an "Alaskan salmon cannery from hiring mostly whites for skilled jobs and mostly non-whites for unskilled jobs."[184] As a conservative move, *Wards Cove* fundamentally weakened racially disparate impact protections in discrimination cases: it did this by switching the burden from being placed on the employer (as the *Griggs* ruling did in 1971) to being placed on employees who are possible victims in the case. Moreover, the court ruled that employees' evidence must show that their company's hiring practices were unreasonable wherever a disparate impact claim is made. According to King and Smith, at the heart of this shift in court interpretation were conservative litigation groups, the Reagan Justice Department, the US Chamber of Commerce, and the Equal Employment Advisory Council, who all filed briefs in support of the Alaskan company to alter how the court approached racially disparate impact claims.[185]

As court interpretation weakened protections discrimination by racial minorities, it also began to interpret the Fourteenth Amendment more narrowly. The same year as *Wards Cove*, the US Supreme Court in *Richmond v. J. A. Croson Co.* (1989) ruled that Richmond City Council's Minority Business Utilization Plan, which required "white contractors who received city contracts to employ minority subcontractors for at least 30 percent of the total dollar amount of each contract," was unconstitutional because the city of Richmond lacked Congress's power to enforce the Fourteenth Amendment's equal protection clause.[186] Meanwhile, the court began to apply the Fourteenth Amendment's equal protection clause as a constitutional ceiling preventing race-conscious policies. Some progress was made in *Metro Broadcasting, Inc. v. FCC* (1990), where the court reduced equal protection challenges against race-conscious federal laws to intermediate scrutiny, arguing that strict scrutiny could only apply to state or local laws. However, *Adarand Constructors, Inc. v. Peña* (1995) returned to strict scrutiny to federal, state or local governments alike. Thus, whenever any level of government created racial classifications for its contracts or other hiring practices, court precedent requires strict scrutiny of whether these classifications are narrowly tailored to further compelling governmental interests; otherwise, the they are considered to be violating the Fourteenth Amendment's equal protection clause.[187] In other words, contemporary courts have interpreted antidiscrimination protections in the constitution as supporting race-neutral policies and opposing race-conscious ones even if they are intended as remedies to help communities of color.

Indeed, just weeks before Justice Sonia Sotomayor was confirmed to be a member of the US Supreme Court in 2009, the Court issued another ruling striking at the heart of affirmative action. After the New Haven Fire Department in Connecticut issued a test for determining promotions to management positions and none of the Black employees passed, the city chose to invalidate the test to avoid a future lawsuit. Nineteen White employees and one Hispanic employee passed, however, and filed a suit under Title VII of the Civil Rights Act of 1964 against the city. The US Supreme in *Ricci v. DeStefano* (2009) ruled in favor of the firefighters, noting: "Although the city had not adopted any racial quota or formal 'affirmative action' promotion system, the fact that it decided not to use the test it had administered due to its racial consequences still represented a form of 'race-conscious' policymaking that the Court saw as requiring heightened judicial scrutiny."[188] Beginning in 1986, decades before the *Ricci* ruling, King and Smith explain that the conservative court was already applying a "strong basis in evidence" standard in affirmative action cases that made it hard to defend race-based "hiring, school admissions, [and] school attendance" as remedies for past racial discrimination.[189]

Justice Ruth Bader Ginsburg's wrote in her dissent to *Ricci* that the "heavier burden of proof the majority was imposing on those who wished to shift to more racially inclusive employment tests might well undermine voluntary efforts to alter selection methods for hiring in order to combat 'pre-existing racial hierarchies.'"[190] She went on to raise concerns about the fact that the city only considered written tests, rather than other performance-based assessments, in their determinations for promotions. Ginsburg's dissent was reflective of how far the court had moved on civil rights jurisprudence; the choice *not to* use particular employment assessments for hiring or promotions because they might be exclusionary in nature, possibly causing racially disparate impacts, was ruled to be a form of race-conscious (or affirmative action) policy requiring strict scrutiny – a policy that the court struck down in *Ricci*.

Legislative Action: Parties and Social Movements

The nonviolent protest march, led by civil rights leader Martin Luther King Jr., in 1964 from Selma to Montgomery, Alabama's capital, shocked the country as television screens filled with images of Alabama's state troopers and local sheriffs using tear gas and billy clubs to violently assault the peaceful protesters. President Lyndon Johnson responded to the crisis of what became "Bloody Sunday," addressing Congress in the following week to push for a federal voting rights bill.[191] As Valelly explains, the 1957, 1960, and 1964 Civil Rights Acts, which "sought to strengthen litigation remedies" and "were the vehicle for the Justice Department's litigation program," were unable to secure voting rights despite federal capacity and resources.[192] Selma and Johnson's subsequent pressure on Congress to pass the Voting Rights Act (VRA) of 1965 provided somewhat of a clean slate, with Section 4, Title 1, stopping all voter restrictions for a five-year period in jurisdictions with histories of voter suppression, including

Alabama, Alaska, Georgia, Louisiana, Mississippi, South Carolina, and Virginia, twenty-six North Carolina counties, three Arizona counties, one Hawaii county, and one Idaho county. The act also prevented the state of New York from enforcing its English-language competence test against voting-age Puerto Ricans residing in New York.[193]

In addition, Section 5 of the Act created federal "preclearance" with the Justice Department placed in charge of authorizing new electoral rules, while Section 6 appointed federal officials to monitor compliance electoral processes in jurisdictions covered by Section 4.

Just prior to the VRA, the Twenty-Fourth Amendment to the US Constitution (passed in 1962) was officially ratified in 1964, following decades of movement-building that began during the New Deal era by Southern liberals to ban state and local poll taxes. Importantly, this constitutional amendment only banned poll taxes for federal elections, leaving state and local elections untouched, with the tax still in effect in Alabama, Arkansas, Mississippi, Texas, and Virginia. As Valelly explains, "Mississippi's administration of the tax was particularly onerous. The county sheriff collected it; payment was legally restricted to the Christmas season. New registrants had to pay not only the current year's levy but also that for the previous year and the following year. That amount, eight dollars, captured about 20 percent of monthly family income in some rural areas."[194] Section 2 of the VRA, modeled after the Fifteenth Amendment, prohibited discriminatory voting practices or procedures on the basis of race, color, or membership in one of the language minority groups identified in Section 4(f)(2) of the Act, thereby extending the Twenty-Fourth Amendment ban on poll taxes to all elections nationwide.

Politically, during the mid-1960s, the Democratic Party faced internal divisions over its future as the party of civil rights. Alabama's Democratic Governor George Wallace, who was allowed violent attacks on civil rights protesters in Selma, ardently championed segregation and ran against incumbent President Lyndon Johnson in the 1964 Democratic Primaries. Losing to Johnson, Wallace ran again in 1968 on a third-party ticket, this time winning the electoral college votes of five Southern states. With Johnson choosing not to run for reelection, Democratic nominee Hubert Humphrey contrasted his run with Wallace's anti-desegregation campaign, promising to continue the Democratic Party's War on Poverty and support for civil rights.

Meanwhile, Richard Nixon won the presidency through a less explicitly racist Southern strategy than Wallace. Nixon appealed to dissatisfied White voters with a promise to restore law and order, in response to rioting in cities and the rise of the Black Panther Party, as well as ending the war in Vietnam. In short, the mid-1960s provided the origin of today's division between the two parties on race; the Democratic Party took on the lead of expanding civil rights and effectively captured the Black voting base, and the Republican Party turned to a Southern strategy and rule-of-law approach to criminal justice, the war on drugs, and immigration enforcement that helped build its White, conservative voting base through racial dog-whistles.[195]

In 1966, King shifted from voting rights to leading nonviolent marches for open housing Northern cities like Chicago, demanding President Johnson and Congress pass federal law that would not only ban housing discrimination but also actively enforce residential desegregation. King partnered with the GI Forum, the NAACP, and the National Committee Against Discrimination in Housing to effectively lobby Congress for legislation, but multiple fair housing bills failed to pass in 1968. President Lyndon Johnson had previously ordered a Commission on Urban Housing and the Kerner Commission Report on civil disorders, which concluded residential segregation in fact created "separate and unequal" conditions for Whites and Blacks, despite the legal abolition of Jim Crow.[196] During this campaign for fair housing legislation, Martin Luther King Jr. was assassinated, ramping up momentum in Congress to speedily pass the Fair Housing Act of 1968 without further debate – prohibiting discrimination concerning the sale, rental, and financing of housing based on race, religion, national origin, or sex.

Congressional legislation was soon followed by administrative action. The Department of Housing and Urban Development (HUD), established in 1965, created a Title VIII Field Operations Handbook to implement the new federal law, which stated that

it shall be unlawful, because of race, color, religion, sex, handicap, familial status, or national origin, to restrict or attempt to restrict the choices of a person by word or conduct in connection with seeking, negotiating for, buying or renting a dwelling so as to perpetuate, or tend to perpetuate, segregated housing patterns, or to discourage or obstruct choices in a community, neighborhood or development.[197]

At the same time, the 1968 law was unable to roll back housing desegregation or end racial discrimination in public and private housing. As King and Smith explain, a compromise with the Republican Senate leader Everett Dirksen prevented the law from covering "single-family homes sold or rented directly by their owners and small apartment buildings with resident owners, and it again did not provide any federal agency with authority to issue cease-and-desist orders."[198] HUD was empowered only to investigate housing complaints and negotiate voluntary agreements, and the Department of Justice and individual victims were empowered by the law to pursue litigation of discrimination cases.[199] Douglas Massey and Nancy Denton explain that Black–White segregation remained "high and virtually constant" and has even continued to expand in most cities from 1970 (estimated at 70 percent) to 1990 (estimated at 90 percent).[200]

Conservative countermovements led by Republicans in Congress under President Nixon's leadership led to the passage of the Housing and Community Development Act of 1974, which cut funding for all federal grant programs structured to decrease residential racial segregation.[201] Rolling back desegregation efforts through legislation was followed by the US Supreme Court's ruling, in *Arlington Heights v. Metropolitan Housing Development Corporation* (1977), that the Fourteenth Amendment's equal protection clause only banned "racially discriminatory intent or purpose" and not "racially disproportionate impact" in single-family housing policy, making litigation efforts by racial minorities and civil rights organizations harder to win.[202] The court's ruling narrowed the meaning of the 1968 federal law's antidiscrimination protections but allowed for state and local governments to expand the right to human capital in housing. Congressional legal action in 1968 and the court ruling made presidential willingness key to the federal government's presence in shaping housing policy at the state and local levels.

Democratic partnerships with civil rights organization and outreach to Black voters clearly contrasted with Republican Party positions on employment, education, housing, redistricting, criminal justice practices, and much more. The Republican presidential platforms of the 1970s and 1980s rejected affirmative action, rejected "forced busing" to achieve racial integration in public schools, and began to apply a narrow understanding of the Fourteenth Amendment's equal protection clause, upholding only colorblind approaches to equal protection and striking down race-conscious remedies as themselves discriminatory. Democratic Presidential platforms, by contrast, ran on the promise of enforcing all equal opportunity laws, affirmative action, and mandatory "transportation" of students to schools (up until 1996). In 1972, Democratic nominee George McGovern (who lost to Nixon) ran on a platform with the expressed goal of achieving "proportional representation" for racial minorities within the party through affirmative action rules, and he explicitly supported the emergence of Black pride and Ethnic Studies programs in schools.[203]

The Democratic Party's new partnership with civil rights organizations helped to a create a legislative roadblock to constitutional backsliding in the early 1980s. In *Mobile v. Bolden* (1980), the US Supreme Court had upheld an at-large election system in the White-majority city of Mobile, Alabama, which had made it nearly impossible for Black candidates to win.[204] The court employed a colorblind approach to interpreting the Fourteenth Amendment's equal protection clause, the Fifteenth Amendment, and the VRA of 1965, ruling that "electoral systems not only had to have 'disproportionate impact' on racial minorities" but must also have been enacted "demonstrably with an invidious 'discriminatory purpose.'"[205] The court was moving away from the precedent set under *White v. Regester* (1973), where a reapportionment scheme was struck down on the basis that it would dilute racial minority votes: *Mobile* created a higher standard for proving discrimination, requiring proof of "discriminatory purpose."

Following this conservative turn by the courts, civil rights groups and Congressional Democrats quickly mobilized to push, not only to renew the VRA in 1982, but also to amend Section 2 so that it would mandate federal action against "state districting plans that made the election of blacks or Latinos improbable."[206] In drafting the amendment, Democrats turned to *White v. Register* to include the language of "results oriented" as a way to align the implementation in Section of the VRA with how the courts ruled prior to *Bolden*. As King and Smith explain, this also worked to "foster the creation of majority-minority districts" and was supported by a bi-partisan coalition, but with different purposes.[207] Importantly, increased litigation by the NAACP and other civil rights organizations quickly led to this expanded federal voting rights law being applied by the US Supreme Court in *Rogers v. Lodge* (1982), which invalidated an at-large system in rural Georgia.[208] With litigation a key strategy of civil rights organizations, even the conservative court in *Thornburg v. Gingles* (1986) actively expanded voting rights by providing a new set of guidelines for courts, in addition to Section 2, to strike down state schemes that dilute racial minority votes through redistricting and other devices.[209] After 1986, Republicans continued their assault on race-conscious approaches to expanding citizenship rights, especially with respect to human capital formation and political representation.

The US Supreme Court ruling of 5–4 in *Shaw v. Reno* (1993), with all five conservative appointees from Presidents Reagan and Bush forming the majority, restricted the use of race altogether as a factor for state redistricting schemes.[210] Conservative Justice O'Connor held that North Carolina's new Congressional district drawn after the 1990s census could only be understood "as an effort to segregate voters into separate voting districts because of their race," which violated the Fourteenth Amendment's equal protection clause. The *Reno* precedent was expanded by the court throughout the 1990s and 2000s, striking down similar redistricting schemes and clarifying that there did not need to be a "bizarre" shape for a new scheme to be ruled unconstitutional, when race was used a factor in its design.[211] In *Miller v. Johnson* (1995), for example, Justice Kennedy ruled that, if race was the "predominant, overriding factor," there must be a strong showing of necessity to remedy proven discrimination against racial minorities.[212] When Section 4 of the VRA came up for renewal in 2006, conservative court rulings after *Reno* created political conditions for bipartisan support to renew it without any changes.

Indeed, Republican-controlled state legislatures were able to use redistricting to their advantage and had begun to carve out new restrictions on voting that built on its racialized rule-of-law approach. Throughout the 2000s, felon disenfranchisement laws stripping voting rights from people with prior criminal convictions spread alongside the rise of new voter ID requirements at polls. In *Shelby County* v. *Holder* (2013), the US Supreme Court left the structure of the VRA in place, including Section 5's "preclearance" process, but it struck down the forty-year-old coverage formula established in Section 4(b).[213] The court argued that the tradition of equal sovereignty among the states required Congressional action to come up with an updated formula that would justify the disparate treatment of particular states or local jurisdictions. With partisan polarization preventing Congress from passing a new coverage formula, the new court ruling opened the door for state and local voting rules to reemerge.

The post-1980s conservative era has gone well beyond rolling back civil rights gains. We have also seen the strengthening of punitive measures that were seeded in the 1960s and accelerated during the decades that followed. As Vesla Weaver explains, the Civil Rights era saw the reinstatement of the death penalty, felon disenfranchisement, and the expansion of prison labor. In addition, the Law Enforcement Assistance Act of 1965, the Crime Control and Safe Streets Act of 1968, and other measures related to the "war on drugs" and capital crimes "had an exceptional and long-lasting effect, with imprisonment increasing six-fold between 1973 and the turn of the century."[214]

Executive Action: Bureaucratic Capacity and Political Will

By the 1960s, the federal government's administrative capacity was very strong and capable of carrying out desegregation and enforcement of new federal civil rights laws. Indeed, even before the VRA, President Kennedy's administration partnered with civil rights groups, like the NAACP, the Southern Christian Leadership Conference (SCLC), the Student Nonviolent Coordinating Committee (SNCC), and the Congress on Racial Equality (CORE), to launch a Voter Education Project throughout the South. Under Kennedy, the federal government had gained a new willingness to enforce voting rights under the Fifteenth Amendment, helping Black voter registration to increase from 29 percent to 43 percent of voting-age Black Southerners in the span of two years, between 1962 and 1964.[215] Moreover, prior to the VRA, the US Census Bureau's Current Population Survey began to investigate, for the first time, voter turnout through its biennial Voting and Registration Supplement in 1964.[216] These legal, administrative, and research tools provided tremendous capacity for the federal government to support expansions in Black citizenship rights.

Presidential willingness, however, has always remained critical for enforcing federal law. After the Civil Rights Act of 1964 passed, President Johnson issued Executive Order 11246 in 1965 to establish the general principle of affirmative action and to mandate all federal agencies to instruct contractors "to take affirmative action to ensure that applicants are employed, and that employees are treated during employment, without regard to their race, color, religion, sex or national origin."[217] With Title VII of the 1964 Civil Rights Act and the Equal Employment Opportunity Commission (EEOC) in place, President Johnson issued an executive order creating an Office of Federal Contract Compliance (OFCC) under the authority of the Department of Labor. OFCC was directed to oversee employers doing business with the federal government and required them to demonstrate racial integration of their workforces and subcontractors. Johnson also appointed Howard Samuels in charge of the Small Business Administration (SBA), originally created in 1953, to use the SBA's Section 8 (a) program to provide contracts to companies comprising "socially or economically disadvantaged persons."[218] In short, President Johnson was able to build from Congressional legislation to expand the federal government's direct role in affirmative action programs that promoted race-conscious hiring, promotion, and contracting.

Sidney Milkis and Daniel Tichenor also show how unwilling presidents can do the opposite, roadblocking civil rights enforcement and rolling back significant gains through weakening the administration of federal programs.[219] After Congress passed a law on fair housing in 1968 with strong bipartisan support, the initial enforcement from President Nixon was limited. The new president actively roadblocked his own administration, particularly HUD secretary George Romney, from formulating a plan that would place the federal bureaucracy in a leadership role on housing integration. While HUD and White House staff resisted Nixon by enforcing the 1968 federal law, regulations were slow to develop. By 1971, Nixon removed Romney from having authority on fair housing. He directed White House aides to develop a policy that would prevent mandates on affordable housing in suburban areas, explaining that an "open society does not have to be homogeneous, or even fully integrated."[220] Similarly, Nixon prevented his Justice Department from actively pursuing litigation under the Fair Housing Act.

The Ford and Reagan administrations built on this legacy of administrative resistance, with goals of "reducing the degree of direct federal involvement in housing" (1976), providing housing assistance "without federal subsidies" or via "decentralized block grants" (1980), and developing a "voucher system" to return "public housing to the free market" (1984).[221] Skrentny and others show that the Reagan administration made the colorblind approach a central feature of federal administration in the 1980s, removing race as a factor and focusing exclusively on individual ability and qualification for employment or education.[222] Republican President George H. W. Bush was similarly unwilling to fully enforce the VRA through the Department of Justice's Civil

Rights Division. After the 1990 census, redistricting schemes spread throughout the Southern states, but Bush's DOJ only challenged Alabama, Georgia, and North Carolina's schemes under Section 4's preclearance, leaving schemes in thirteen other states unchallenged.[223]

In direct contrast to Republicans' general lack of willingness to use federal power to ensure racially equitable outcomes, Democratic presidents have made various attempts to strengthen the federal government's enforcement authority. For example, Jimmy Carter and Democrats in Congress passed the Community Reinvestment Act of 1977, which required federal regulators to oversee whether banks were providing housing loans to urban areas in an attempt to fight against discriminatory redlining. Under Carter's leadership, Democrats worked with the NAACP, the AFL-CIO, the League of Women Voters, and the ACLU to propose a bill in 1980 that would have strengthened the enforcement provisions of the Fair Housing Act (from 1968), but President Reagan's election roadblocked the bill from succeeding.

In addition, President Bill Clinton in 1993 launched a "fair lending" initiative expanding HUD's grants to private groups and established fair lending divisions in regional offices with federal regulatory officials overseeing lending practices on the ground. Finally, the Obama administration advancing rights to housing via litigation against discrimination and promotion of residential racial integration through federal policies. For example, the Justice Department's Civil Rights Division created a new unit that focused on reversing redlining, including negotiating a settlement for discriminatory lending practices involving the American International Group (AIG) and nearly 2500 African Americans.[224] Presidential willingness thus spans the full range of federal civil rights laws on employment, education, housing, and voting, among others.

CONCLUSIONS

State citizenship is not simply an abstract concept. As our review of American constitutional history and political development has shown, state citizenship was part of the original US constitution and, indeed, received greater treatment than discussions of national citizenship. And state citizenship remains relevant today even after passage of the Fourteenth Amendment, which guaranteed individuals access to the same set of nationally guaranteed rights across all states. Despite these guarantees of the Fourteenth Amendment, states retain the ability to expand protections beyond those guaranteed at the federal level, as many states have done periodically with respect to women's rights, reproductive rights, immigrant rights, and LGBT rights. Finally, states have also frequently engaged in regressive forms of citizenship, by enacting laws and policies that restrict or erode rights that are supposed to be guaranteed under federal law.

It is important for us to view rights expansions and contractions not only with respect to the framework of the US Constitution and state constitutions, which shape what is *permissible* on citizenship rights at any given time, but also to the activities of political parties and social movements that animate what is *probable* through legislative activity, as well as to the bureaucratic capacity and political will of federal government and state governments alike that shape what is *deployable* and ultimately enforced. The general conceptual framework that we developed in Chapter 2, which can be applied to various country contexts, combined with the explanatory framework in this chapter that applies it to the US context, guides our historical and institutional analysis for the rest of the book, as we examine more deeply the evolving nature of state citizenship as it pertains to Black rights and immigrant rights.

4

State Citizenship for Blacks

Dred Scott v. Sandford (1857) has been long understood as a deeply flawed Supreme Court decision on civil rights that helped propel the nation into civil war. When the Supreme Court ruled that states, and not the federal government, were the ultimate arbiters of citizenship rights, it established a critical constitutional moment clarifying the meaning of Black citizenship in the United States.[1] The Court's interpretation of citizenship, as primarily a state matter, was not simply a reflection of the limitations in the US Constitution. Even after the Reconstruction amendments invalidated *Scott* and established citizenship rights at the national level, Black citizenship rights at the state level continued to be constrained and contested in the century that followed – and often made worse under critical moments of federal expansion. This chapter takes a fresh look at the well-established history of Black civil rights in the United States, using our framework of multidimensional citizenship and federated citizenship to better understand the expansion and contraction of rights during the pre–Civil War, Jim Crow, and Civil Rights eras.

Dred Scott was born into slavery circa 1799 and lived in various Southern states before moving to the "free state" of Illinois in 1830. He also moved to the free federal territory of Wisconsin from 1836 through 1840 under the ownership of John Emerson, a US army surgeon. Later, after Dred Scott and his family were brought back to Missouri, he attempted to purchase freedom for himself, his wife, and their two children. When his owner refused, Scott filed a lawsuit in 1846 with the Missouri court, arguing that their prior residence in free territories required their emancipation.[2] Lower courts ruled in Scott's favor, in line with the Missouri Compromise of 1820, which demarcated Northern freedom and Southern slavery along the 36°30′ parallel. A decade later, the Supreme Court in a 7–2 decision reversed the lower court ruling, denying freedom to Scott and his family.

In writing the majority opinion, Chief Justice Taney went well beyond deciding the fate of the Scott family's freedom, declaring that "no black person could ever be a citizen of the United States and thus blacks could not sue in federal courts." The immediate implications of the Taney court's ruling were profound. The 1850 Census had counted about 435,000 free Blacks in the United States, about 198,000 of whom were living in the North, 200,000 in the South, and the remainder in the West.[3] Regardless of whether a Black person was legally residing in a free federal territory or free Northern state, the Taney Court's ruling denied them national citizenship and the right to federal due process. Although the *Dred Scott* decision is widely known for its national implications, denying Black freedom and hastening the cause of abolition, it also had significant implications for state citizenship as the exclusive jurisdiction for Black rights. This constitutional moment in 1857 formalized distinctions between national citizenship and state citizenship that were already implicit in the legal framework of American slavery – clarifying that there was no basis for national citizenship for Blacks under the US Constitution and that any additional rights and protections for Blacks could only be accorded at the state level.

Prior to the *Dred Scott* decision, the federal government was largely silent on the citizenship rights of Blacks, with no provisions for them in the US Constitution. Rights provisions in federal law were also limited, confined to legislation establishing freedom from servitude in Northern territories and for new Northern states entering the Union. Consequently, even though Black citizenship rights were mostly nonexistent in the South and severely constrained in many Northern states, they were largely consonant with the meager rights and protections offered to Blacks at the national level. More pointedly, slavery in Southern states was not an instance of regressive state citizenship, because there was virtually no guarantee of rights to Blacks at the national level, save their being counted as three-fifths of a person for Congressional apportionment.

Ultimately, the Civil War, Reconstruction, and the growth of the national state under the New Deal and the Great Society would erect an edifice of national citizenship that would dwarf the state citizenship regimes of the antebellum period. However, as Table 4.1 shows, regressive forms of state citizenship began to emerge after the Civil War and passage of the Reconstruction amendments. Federalism dynamics during Reconstruction and afterwards meant that national rights did not simply supersede or replace citizenship at the state level. Instead, they altered the type of state citizenship capable of forming. Using the five core dimensions of citizenship developed in Chapter 2 and the APD framework outlined in Chapter 3, we show how constitutional opportunities, legislative actions, and executive actions combined to drive competing visions for Black citizenship rights at both federal and state levels.

TABLE 4.1 *Black state citizenship in the United States*

A. Black citizenship in a multidimensional framework of rights

1) Free movement	Freedom papers and anti-harboring laws (*pre–Civil War*); segregated trains and buses (*Jim Crow*); stop and frisk (*post–Civil Rights*)
2) Due process and legal protection	Limitations on habeas corpus, Black testimony, trial by jury (*pre–Civil War*); convict-lease system and lynching (*Jim Crow*); drug laws, three strikes laws (*post–Civil Rights*)
3) Develop human capital	Marriage bans, anti-miscegenation laws, segregated schools, housing covenants (*Jim Crow*); affirmative action, workforce protections, "ban the box" laws (*Civil Rights* and *post–Civil Rights*)
4) Participate and be represented	Voting eligibility laws (*pre–Civil War*); poll tax, literacy tests (*Jim Crow*); Voting Rights Act protections (*Civil Rights*); voter ID laws (*post–Civil Rights*)
5) Identify and belong	Installation of Confederate statues, flags, and other symbols (*Jim Crow, Civil Rights*); removal of some Confederate symbols (*post–Civil Rights*)

B. Black citizenship subtypes in a federated framework

Progressive state citizenship	Free movement, noncooperation with enforcing federal fugitive slave law, and voting rights in PA, NY, and MA (*pre–Civil War*); rights expansions by Black-led state legislatures in the South (*reconstruction*); state criminal justice reforms, including felon voting rights and "ban the box" policies (*post–Civil Rights*)
Reinforcing (inclusionary) state citizenship	Freedom from servitude in Northern territories (*pre–Civil War*); New Deal (e.g., FERA) benefits administration in states such as NY and IL; Harlem Renaissance, unionism, and rise of National Negro Congress (1935–1946) (*post-Reconstruction*); state antidiscrimination laws mirroring federal laws (*Civil Rights* and *post–Civil Rights*)
Reinforcing (exclusionary) state citizenship	Slavery in the South (*pre–Civil War*); disparate-impact drug enforcement laws (*post–Civil Rights*)
Regressive state citizenship	Black codes in Southern states (*Reconstruction*); Jim Crow south restrictions on all dimensions; segregation and housing rights limits in Northern states (*post-Reconstruction and Jim Crow*); state voter ID laws; Three Strikes laws (*post–Civil Rights*)

Note: Periods are indicated in *italics*: pre–Civil War (1789–1865), Reconstruction (1865–1877), post-Reconstruction and Jim Crow (1878–1964), Civil Rights (1965–1971), post–Civil Rights (1972–present).

America's early Constitution and federal laws preserved and protected slavery while expressly depriving Blacks of national rights. Consequently, varying forms of reinforcing state citizenship emerged throughout the South and in parts of the free North. Indeed, during antebellum America, Blacks without proof of their freedom were presumed to be slaves, including by the federal government, Southern states, and some Northern states. At the same time, compromises made in passing the US Constitution also permitted several Northern states to develop what we call progressive state citizenship (see Chapter 2, including Figure 2.9). States like Massachusetts and New York offered voting rights to their Black residents (Dimension 4 of our conceptual framework) that far exceeded rights afforded at the national level (see Table 4.1). More rare, states like Massachusetts and Pennsylvania actively resisted enforcing federal fugitive slave law (Dimension 1) and created new categories of rights and protections for their free and self-emancipated Black residents (Dimensions 1 and 2). These competing visions of Black citizenship set the stage for the Civil War and continued to inform subsequent fights over Black citizenship rights in a federated context.

Immediately following the Civil War, Reconstruction Amendments to the US Constitution created a new national framework for Black rights, with the Fourteenth Amendment securing national citizenship for all Blacks and requiring states to honor all aspects of federally provided rights through the equal protection clause. Concurrent with Black national citizenship, Reconstruction also paved the way for inclusionary forms of state citizenship that reinforced federal expansions in rights. As Table 4.1 shows, the types of state citizenship varied as a result: reinforcing federal laws during the antebellum era had meant that states were exclusionary by mirroring federal *contractions* in rights. By contrast, reinforcing federal laws during the Reconstruction era meant that states were inclusionary by mirroring federal *expansions* in rights.

Moreover, a strong federal presence and willingness to enforce federal law – from federal military occupation to legislative mechanisms such as the Civil Rights Act of 1875 – directly enabled rights expansion in state citizenship. Thus, for nearly a decade, Republican and Black-majority legislatures in the South expanded Black rights in the face of strong resistance by White supremacists and Southern Democrats. These expansions collapsed, however, when the federal government withdrew from the South, paving the way for Whites to violently take control of Southern state legislatures and usher in a new era of regressive Black citizenship. Modest progress on Black citizenship in the South was, indeed, wholly inadequate and fleeting. Several prominent post-Reconstruction scholars, including C. Vann Woodward, W. E. B. DuBois, and Richard Vallely, have amply shown that the contraction of Black rights returned with a vengeance in a matter of years. However, this was not simply a reversion to a prior status quo. As we argue in this chapter, it was a worsening of state-provided rights in relation to the federal government, taking the form of regressive state citizenship where states restrict or erode rights provided at the national level.

Thus, while scholars and observers alike point to Reconstruction and its demise as pivotal moments in the development of civil rights in the United States, our focus on state citizenship reveals an even more complex and insidious form of regressive citizenship. As federalism evolved to include greater cooperation between national and state government programs, states remained the central power for determining who would receive federal benefits and rights. This meant that despite the Fourteenth Amendment's guarantees of equal protection, national citizenship grew to have a fundamentally distinctive inclusionary meaning for Whites, who directly benefited from New Deal expansions in federal social welfare in response to the Great Depression. At the same time, with states positioned as gatekeepers to federal programs, the model of cooperative federalism that benefited Whites also ensured the exclusion of Blacks and other racial minorities from those same benefits and rights. Importantly, unlike in the case of immigrant rights today (see Chapters 5 and 6), examples of progressive state citizenship for Black residents have been rare in the contemporary period. Whereas states during the twentieth century played critical roles in the expansion of rights for women (on voting), for same-sex couples (on marriage equality), and for a number of other marginalized groups, the record of "state's rights" and Blacks has been overwhelmingly restrictive.

We focus our conceptual and explanatory frameworks (from Chapters 2 and 3, respectively) to foreground the contested nature of Black citizenship and to explain that state-level progress was possible but often fleeting. Unlike for other groups throughout American history, Black citizenship since the Civil War has mostly required activism and change on a national scale in order to replace regressive regimes of state citizenship. Fortunately, the growth of Black activism and other aspects of the modern civil rights movement proved powerful enough to provide for a Second Reconstruction. The Civil Rights Act of 1964 and the Voting Rights Act (VRA) of 1965 wiped away the Constitutional doctrine of "separate but equal" and paved the way for federal action against most forms of regressive state citizenship.

However, federated citizenship did not simply vanish after the 1960s. Vigorous enforcement of new civil rights measures held the forces of regressive state citizenship at bay for nearly five decades, even as the Republican Party began pursuing a "Southern strategy" to woo White Democrats back toward the Republican Party and proposing mechanisms to dilute Black voting power after gaining control of various Southern statehouses. This was perhaps most notable in the realm of voting rights (Dimension 4 in our framework). The renewal of VRA in 1970 and 1975, and its strengthening through amendment in 1982, were followed by an erosion in voting rights through the passage of state disenfranchisement laws and voter ID laws. In 2013, the US Supreme Court in *Shelby County v. Holder* invalidated the need for Southern states to get preclearance from the federal government before making any changes to voting rights laws such as switching from district to at-large systems or adding new requirements to the processes of voter registration and voting.[4] As in the post-Reconstruction era, this contemporary ruling opened the floodgates to reinstating new state policies on voter identification cards, voter registration purges, and use of unreliable databases to verify identity.

The erosion of Black citizenship rights began much earlier with President Nixon's administration, under which many of the national expansions on the right to legal protection and due process (Dimension 2) were unravelled, through a systematic War on Drugs that legally empowered local law enforcement to criminalize entire Black communities. Deepening the backsliding on Black citizenship rights was mass incarceration, which put in place a new federalism arrangement for regressive state citizenship to emerge, based on denying Black citizenship rights across several dimensions, including the right to free movement while on parole or after being released (Dimension 1); the right to housing, child custody, and employment (Dimension 3); and by framing Black ex-convicts as outsiders (Dimension 5). As the total number of people incarcerated increased from roughly 500,000 in 1980 to more than 2.2 million in 2015, the racial implications of mass incarceration for Black citizenship rights has become evident and clear.[5] This systematic targeting has led to Black majorities in both the incarcerated population and the correctional population, with important implications for citizenship rights.

Thus, despite sweeping national gains in rights during the 1960s, regressive state citizenship has reappeared, albeit in a weaker and more indirect form than during Jim Crow. Only recently have civil rights organizations begun focusing again on state-level rights strategies involving criminal justice, housing, and education. For example, the American Civil Liberties Union (ACLU) in 2019 launched its fifty-state blueprint to end mass incarceration in the United States.[6] In addition, California has been leading several criminal justice reform efforts, passing a range of policies that are beginning to expand Black citizenship rights in the state. Still, many of these reforms have started decades after conservative backsliding on Black citizenship rights, and it will likely take several more years for states to establish durable regimes of progressive state citizenship.

CONSTITUTIONAL FORMATION AND BOUNDARIES OF STATE CITIZENSHIP (1787–1789)

As we detailed in Chapter 3, the US Constitution was relatively silent on the issue of national citizenship, confining it to discussions on the eligibility to serve in Congress and the presidency, and devoting far more attention to the privileges and immunities that flowed out of state citizenship. Here, we briefly overview the

Constitutional framework that led to various forms of early state citizenship and the political compromises forged in 1787 that helped to define antebellum politics over who has rights.

Southern delegates aimed to create a weak national government to prevent the abolishment of slavery. In setting up political representation, for example, Southern Whites fought for a political balance between Northern free states and Southern slave states to ensure that slavery would be protected. Pierce Butler and Charles Pinckney of South Carolina both proposed at the convention that "blacks be included in the rule of Representation, equally with the Whites."[7] While Northern delegates balked at this power grab, the "three-fifths compromise" ended up ensuring the disproportionate representation of pro-slavery interests in the US House of Representatives.[8] As noted in Chapter 3, James Madison also helped protect pro-slavery interests by ensuring that the president would be chosen by the Electoral College rather than by direct popular vote. Finally, the Framers' Constitution also included a Fugitive Slave Clause in Article 4, which enabled Southern slaveholders to reclaim runaway slaves, even if they had fled to free states or territories. Sectional differences caused by slavery thus led to a peculiar structuring of American federalism ripe with conflict, especially over the rights of Blacks, that was foundational to the formation of national and state citizenship.

The Uneven Nature of Black Freedom

Emancipation in the North revealed deep concerns over citizenship that go well beyond the binary of free person or slave. In line with our multidimensional framework of citizenship rights, Black emancipation proceeded in an incremental and halting fashion *within each state*, with advancements in certain types of rights and stalling and regression in others. Emancipation also spread unevenly *across Northern states*, with some states as leaders in certain dimensions and laggards in others. Our citizenship framework provides new meaning to northern emancipation laws as foundational for America's first experiments in progressive state citizenship. We argue that state emancipation laws did more than simply abolish northern institutions of slavery: they also laid the foundation of Black citizenship rights to emerge and grow. Indeed, these laws extended rights for the first time to previously enslaved Blacks across four of five the core dimensions of our conceptual framework, leaving only the right to participate and be represented untouched. Still, emancipation schemes were nowhere near comprehensive, and, under our framework, they are considered starting points for more robust provisions of rights along each dimension.

In this section, we show that state officials, social movement actors, and occasionally courts were critical to the early development of progressive state citizenship, with emancipation laws establishing the first basis for Black citizenship rights. During America's founding moment, state officials in what would become the free North were forced to confront broader questions about what freedom meant. This included raising debates over whether newly freed Blacks ought to also gain the right to participate and be represented alongside their White counterparts. Thus, while the US Constitution and federal laws denied rights to most Blacks, Northern emancipation laws were effectively setting the basis for Black citizenship rights to grow at the state level.

Progress on Black rights originated with anti-slavery movements well before the US Constitution, led first by White Quakers who formed Society of Friends organizations. As early as 1758, the Society of Friends unanimously agreed that "Friends should be advised to manumit their slaves, and that those who persisted in holding them should not be allowed to participate in the affairs of the Society."[9] Soon after establishing these individual pledges, anti-slavery activists began to file so-called freedom suits, whereby enslaved Blacks could gain their freedom through filing legal manumission in the courts.[10] The global anti-slave trade movement and the increased salience of Revolutionary-era values for equality and freedom provided new opportunities for abolitionism to spread. For example, Anthony Benezet (1713–1784), a French Huguenot who joined the Society of Friends in 1772, sought to merge the global anti-slave trade movement to the abolition movement within the United States. This further empowered enslaved Blacks in Massachusetts to mobilize around global and national events by petitioning the Massachusetts legislatures for their freedom in 1773, casting American resistance to British rule as an attempt to "free [itself] from slavery."[11] Black and White abolitionists continued to draw on the larger framework of American freedom to push for Northern emancipation laws in the late 1770s and early 1780s.[12]

Blacks also forged varying footholds in state abolition politics through military ties with America's fight for independence. An estimated 30,000 Blacks served during the Revolutionary War, mostly on the side of England, which promised their freedom.[13] Northern colonies, many of which were actively debating whether to pass emancipation laws, enlisted enslaved Blacks through a trade of service agreement, giving Blacks their freedom and compensating slave owners.[14] Massachusetts in particular allowed Blacks to serve in militia units alongside Whites and formed the all-Black Bucks of America company. Meanwhile, in southern colonies like South Carolina and Georgia, where slaves constituted nearly half of the entire population, the legislatures prevented militias from arming any Black person. Only Maryland allowed militias to recruit enslaved Blacks for its war efforts, and Virginia allowed free Blacks to enlist in its militias.[15] Thus, while Blacks' service during the Revolutionary War further encouraged emancipation and abolition of slavery in the North, it had the opposite effect in the South of instilling fear in Whites and prompting even more restrictive slavery laws.

As the US Constitution protected Southern slavery, activists pursued different approaches to securing Black freedom and rights. Notably, William Lloyd Garrison led America's immediate abolitionist movement, arguing that slavery's deep ties to the US Constitution and to institutions had created a moral vacuum in the country. Under Garrison's leadership, immediate abolitionists sought reform only at the national level and through building a moral case among the general public, avoiding formal politics altogether for being corrupt. By contrast, other activists working within the Constitution's design of federalism fought to pass state laws ending slavery and advancing the rights of newly freed Blacks within Northern states. At the same time, emancipation created more legal questions than answers when it came to the rights of Blacks because it occurred in many forms (through constitutions, laws, and court rulings) and even prolonged slavery in some instances by making emancipation gradual rather than immediate.

Northern states were not united in their vision for what Black freedom would look like. Vermont's 1777 constitution led as the first state to abolish slavery, which included revolutionary language of equality and unalienable rights: "no male person, born in this country, or brought from over sea, ought to be holden by law, to serve any person, as a servant, slave or apprentice, after he arrives to the age of twenty-one Years, nor female, in like manner, after she arrives to the age of eighteen years, unless they are bound by their own consent, after they arrive to such age, or bound by law, for the payment of debts, damages, fines, costs, or the like."[16]

Pennsylvania went even further. With a much larger Black population, and bordering the South, the state's Quakers and radical legislature of 1780 made an even stronger statement when it led in passing the nation's first legislated emancipation act, declaring slavery to be "repugnant" to natural liberties. A bold step forward at the time, Pennsylvania's gradual "postnati" emancipation law freed newborn slaves only after they had served twenty-eight years of their life in legalized bondage, thus prolonging the institution of slavery. Moreover, slave owners in Pennsylvania were legally able to sell their slaves into neighboring states, including young Blacks before they turned twenty-eight, and could send female slaves out-of-state when pregnant so that the child would not be born free.[17] Seeking to address some of these problems, in 1788, White Quaker abolitionists led the state in passing a new law requiring that all births and children from slaves be registered, preventing enslaved husbands and wives from being separated more than ten miles without their consent, banning the practice of sending pregnant slaves out of the state for their delivery, and fining residents caught trading slaves £1,000.[18]

And yet, total abolition remained elusive in Pennsylvania. Facing legislative constraints to entirely ending slavery in the state, Quaker abolitionists pursued abolition through the courts, arguing that the state's 1790 state constitution's declaration of rights applied to all men. Beginning in 1795, abolitionists took on a test case for a freedom suit relying on their interpretation of the state constitution, which would supersede state law. The case, *Negro Flora v. Joseph Graisberry*, made its way to the High Court of Errors and Appeals, which ruled in 1802 that slavery was legal within the boundaries of the 1780 and 1788 state laws, and that the state's constitution did not end slavery.

Despite constant legislative efforts led by the Pennsylvania Society for the Abolition of Slavery, who petitioned the state in 1793 and regularly sent memorials on the horrors of slavery to the state legislature, officials were unable to form the consensus needed to pass immediate abolition. From 1797 to 1800, abolition bills were considered but were never voted on in both the House and the Senate.[19] Pennsylvania continued to expand the categories of who was freed from slavery, slowly but never absolutely. Only by 1816 were the children of runaway slaves considered to be free under state law.[20]

Rhode Island banned the sale of slaves out of the state without their permission in 1779, but it made little headway on general emancipation after the war. Moses Brown, a Quaker and future leader in state politics (including in Rhode Island's ratification of the US Constitution in 1790), petitioned the General Assembly of Rhode Island in 1783 but failed to secure an emancipation law. Over the next year, Brown pursued anti-slavery activism through the local press and pamphlets through New England, and in 1784 he succeeded in passing Rhode Island's gradual emancipation law in 1784, freeing all children born of slaves and freeing girls at age eighteen and boys at twenty-one. Brown continued his anti-slavery activism in state politics by pushing a 1787 law banning Rhode Island's participation in the international and domestic slave trades, followed by creating the Providence Society for Abolishing the Slave Trade in 1789 to enforce the state's anti-slave trade legislation. Connecticut's gradual emancipation act passed in 1784 and was appended to the state's revised slave code as a measure providing for "post-nati" emancipation, freeing newborn slaves only after they had reached the age of twenty-five.

In Pennsylvania (1780; effective in 1784), Rhode Island (1784), and Connecticut (1784), reforms were led by political leaders favoring gradual emancipation laws. Meanwhile, officials in the Massachusetts Assembly sought to avoid making public their views on slavery, letting all proposed abolition bills die before even being debated.[21] Instead, a statewide campaign led by Quakers virtually ended slavery through private emancipations across the state in the 1780s, and soon after the courts stepped in. Thomas Sedgwick, a prominent attorney and delegate to the Continental Congress, led in freedom suits against the state claiming that Massachusetts's 1780 constitution's inclusion of natural equality essentially abolished slavery in the state. On July 8, 1783, the Massachusetts Supreme Court's ruling in *Commonwealth v. Jennison* effectively abolished slavery in a case where a slave named Quock Walker sued his owner for his freedom. William Cushing, the chief justice of Massachusetts's Supreme Court, instructed the jury that, because of the state constitution's declaration that "[a]ll men are born free and equal," slavery was "as effectively abolished as it can be by the granting of rights and privileges wholly incompatible and repugnant to its existence."[22]

These different approaches to emancipation had consequences for state citizenship. Most Northern states followed the gradual emancipation framework, often compensating slave owners for the property value of their slaves.[23] According to the US Census, slaves continued to exist under Pennsylvania's gradual scheme as late as 1840, while Massachusetts's private manumissions and court ruling completely ended the presence of slavery by 1790. New York's legislature began considering gradual emancipation measures in 1784 but did not pass a decisive bill until 1799. Historian Patrick Rael explains: "For sixteen years the fate of enslaved New Yorkers hung in the balance as politicians debated everything from former masters' responsibility for the moral instruction of the free to the emancipated's right to hold political office."[24] New York's 1799 gradual emancipation law freed slave children born after July 4, 1799, and indentured women to their former owners until the age of twenty-five and men until twenty-eight.[25] New Jersey followed in 1804.

BLACK CITIZENSHIP IN THE ANTEBELLUM PERIOD

The US Constitution, court decisions, and federal legislative action set the constraints and opportunities for state citizenship to emerge. From Northern emancipation laws onward, we see dynamics in federalism shape the contours of progressive state citizenship, with expansions in rights limited as the sole source of protections offered to free Blacks and at odds with corresponding national legislation on the rendition of fugitive slaves. American federalism prevented Northern states and residents from being isolated from the evils of slavery.

Even as Northern state legislatures debated emancipation laws to free Blacks within their borders, they faced the prospect of federal preemption. The Fugitive Slave Clause in the US Constitution noted that runaway slaves shall be "delivered up on claim of the party to whom such service or labour may be due," but it did not compel states to capture them or render them to their former masters. Thus, abolitionists soon attempted to carve out state legal protections for Blacks that could counteract provisions in federal law. After the Massachusetts Supreme Court ruled in *Commonwealth v. Jennison* (1783) to abolish slavery, state officials led the North in expanding the rights of free Blacks in 1785 by passing two legal protections: the first anti-kidnapping law in the country, making it a state crime to remove any free Black person; and the first habeas corpus law, ensuring that state and local judges investigated recaption claims and afforded them a full hearing. Two years later, in 1787, the Massachusetts legislature expanded free Blacks' right to due process by passing the first writ of replevin law, ensuring that all detained Blacks were brought to a state court before being removed under federal law.[26]

Soon thereafter, Northern states began to see the limits of providing state protections without corresponding national legislation. Following an incident where slave catchers had kidnapped a free Black citizen in Pennsylvania in 1791 and took him to Virginia to be sold into slavery, the Pennsylvania Abolitionist Society (PAS) pressured the governor of Pennsylvania to request that the slave catchers be extradited to Pennsylvania to be tried in court for kidnapping, but a national law protecting free Blacks did not exist.[27] Meanwhile, the PAS led Northern US officials to introduce the first federal anti-kidnapping bill to the US House of Representatives in 1791.

In response, the Southern-led Congress passed the first federal Fugitive Slave Act in 1793. The Act went beyond the US Constitution by expanding the rights of slave owners to recapture runaway slaves in Northern states and federal territories by penalizing "any person" from obstructing their efforts at recaption.[28] Section 4 of the federal law stated

[t]hat any person who shall knowingly and willingly obstruct or hinder such claimant, his agent, or attorney, in so seizing or arresting such fugitive from labor, or shall rescue such fugitive from such claimant, his agent or attorney, when so arrested pursuant to the authority herein given and declared; or shall harbor or conceal such person after notice that he or she was a fugitive from labor, as aforesaid, shall, for either of the said offences, forfeit and pay the sum of five hundred dollars.[29]

The 1793 federal law gave no protections from kidnapping to free Northern Blacks, which set the foundation for sectionalism in the antebellum period to worsen. All Blacks, regardless of their status, lacked federal protections or the right to be free from enslavement. Meanwhile, the Fugitive Slave Act's anti-harboring provision clarified that Northern states and residents were not isolated from the evils of slavery, despite enacting emancipation laws.

As we explained in Chapter 3, the Framers' Constitution introduced the potential for strong national institutions, but it also preserved states' rights through compromises that balanced the interests and representation of free states and slave states alike. Southern Democrats wielded their majority control over the US House of Representatives to put in place a gag rule from 1836 to 1844, making all petitions, memorials, or resolutions regarding slavery automatically tabled. Thus, unable to reform national policy, abolitionists pursued state-level strategies to expand the rights of Black residents, often in response to federalism conflicts reminding the free North of slavery's reach far beyond the South.

Progressive State Citizenship in the North

As Northern states continued to develop more robust visions for what it means to be free and to be a rights-bearing citizen within their jurisdictions, especially regarding where Black residents fit into their vision of formal belonging and protection, a deep federalism conflict emerged. Neither the federal government nor states and localities were specified in the US Constitution or in the 1793 fugitive slave law as having the authority to enforce federal law. From 1793 to 1850, fugitive slave law only provided slave owners the right of recaption, including hiring slave catchers to remove runaway slaves and *requesting* federal and northern officials to aid in recaption. Equally important, the

Tenth Amendment prevented the federal government from being able to commandeer or otherwise compel Northern states and localities to enforce federal law. The seeds for federalism conflict were thus sown in both the US Constitution and federal law.

After failing repeatedly to reform federal law to include anti-kidnapping protections for free Blacks in the late 1790s and again from 1817 to 1819, the PAS turned its focus to expanding Black rights at the state level instead. Led mostly by White abolitionists with strong allies in state government, the PAS built a statewide coalition capable of mobilizing popular support in the state when major national events related to slavery emerged. Two weeks after the Missouri Compromise passed, extending slavery into federal territories and allowing Missouri to enter the Union as a slave state, the PAS led a massive petition campaign to pressure the state legislature to pass what were called "personal liberty laws," including an immediate emancipation law, an anti-kidnapping law, and the first Northern law to sever the state's role in enforcing the federal fugitive slave law (Dimensions 1 and 2 of our framework).[30] Total abolition in the state remained elusive under its gradual emancipation scheme, but Pennsylvania achieved a major transformation by providing rights to free Blacks and ending its role in capturing runaway slaves.[31]

With the US Constitution vague, and federal law silent, on the rights of free Blacks to avoid being kidnapped or sold into slavery, Pennsylvania made these rights very explicit for the first time in American history with the passage of its anti-kidnapping and its personal liberty laws in 1820. Pennsylvania's anti-kidnapping law established a maximum sentence of twenty-one years of hard labor for kidnapping any Black person in the state and included seizing a man by "force or violence" as an act of kidnapping (Dimension 2). Furthermore, its personal liberty law denied the federal government the right to use state officials in slave rendition (Dimensions 1 and 2), made it a misdemeanor crime for state officials to participate in federal enforcement (Dimension 2), and banned state courts from hearing rendition cases that might lead to the return of an alleged runaway slave to Southern slavery (Dimension 2).[32] As our explanatory framework clarifies, progressive state citizenship fell within the boundaries of the US Constitution, and it emerged from coalitions led by social movement and partisan actors that strategically leveraged federalism to push for transformative changes in state citizenship rights.

Soon after these transformations took hold in Pennsylvania, the political conditions for progressive state citizenship would be tested and clarified by the courts and generally upheld under the Tenth Amendment. Following the passage of Pennsylvania's 1820 laws, strong opposition emerged from neighboring slave states. Commissioners from Maryland drafted and introduced a pro-slavery bill to the state of Pennsylvania, leading the PAS to respond by organizing a special meeting around drafting a stronger personal liberty law to further clarify the role of its state courts in rendition cases. The bill introduced by the PAS prevented "interested or ex parte testimony" to be used as evidence in recaption cases and clarified that state officials were not obligated to accept southern states' "jurisdiction of claims to alleged runaways."[33] In 1826, the Pennsylvania legislature passed the law, essentially acquiring full state control over the recaption process while preserving its earlier model of severing its participation in enforcing federal law. The new law created strict standards for issuing certificates of removal that were controlled by the state, established an equal protection clause making it a crime to seize any Black person without a warrant, and implemented the PAS's amendment for securing state control over all Blacks within its jurisdiction (Dimensions 1 and 2 of our framework).[34]

Progressive state citizenship had evolved in Pennsylvania to include a range of due process and legal protection rights for both free Blacks and runaway slaves. Yet these developments, occurring in 1826, overstepped the state's constitutional reach. In 1842, the Supreme Court in *Prigg v. Pennsylvania* placed the constitutionality of Pennsylvania's laws into the national spotlight.[35] Four professional slave catchers – Edward Prigg, Nathan Bemis, Jacob Forward, and Stephen Lewis – seized Margaret Morgan in Pennsylvania in 1837 after successfully completing pre-seizure procedures by making a demand for recaption to Pennsylvania state officials.[36] Morgan's former slave owner, John Ashmore, had allowed her to live freely, and, in 1832, Morgan moved to Pennsylvania, where she married a free Black man and had one child. State officials refused to grant the slave catchers a certificate of removal, and the slave catchers responded by abducting Morgan and her child and taking them to Maryland. The governor of Maryland extradited Prigg to the governor of Pennsylvania for kidnapping after agreeing that the state of Pennsylvania would expedite the case to the US Supreme Court for a uniform rule on extradition cases.

The Supreme Court ruled in *Prigg* that the federal government has plenary powers over fugitive slave law, thus declaring unconstitutional any form of state interference in recaption. Pennsylvania's courts could not take over control of the fugitive slave rendition process, which was exclusive to the federal government, taken on when US Congress enacted the Fugitive Slave Law of 1793. Writing the majority opinion, Judge Joseph Story stated: "[I]t might well be deemed an unconstitutional exercise of the power of interpretation, to insist that the states are bound to provide means to carry into effect the duties of the national government [as prescribed in federal law], nowhere delegated or intrusted to them by the Constitution."[37] *Prigg* ruled that states could not interfere in federal recaption but provided no clear legal definition of what constitutes interfering. Importantly, *Prigg* also applied the Tenth Amendment, ruling that, while states could voluntarily aid in the enforcement of federal law, the federal government could not mandate states to enforce federal law. Prigg thus set a new, albeit ambiguous, precedent for how Northern progressive state citizenship could provide protection to runaway slaves.

Prigg accelerated the development of progressive state citizenship in other states. In the 1840s, the formation of the Massachusetts Abolition Society (MAS) and the anti-slavery Liberty Party strengthened ties between the abolitionist movement and state officials in Massachusetts.[38] Elizur Wright led MAS to quickly mobilize around *Prigg v. Pennsylvania* (1842) and the George Latimer Case (1842) to build a statewide network of public support and petition campaign for the state's first law severing its role in enforcing federal fugitive slave law. Slave catchers arrested runaway slave George Latimer, who fled from Norfolk, Virginia, with his wife to Boston on October 21, 1842. Massachusetts Chief Justice Lemuel Shaw denied abolitionists and Latimer's attorney's request for a writ of personal replevin, which would stop Latimer's removal and provide Latimer a jury trial (among his peers) to determine if in fact he was a fugitive or not.[39] Facing a short window, the Liberty Party quickly established a Latimer Committee, purchased Latimer's freedom, and led in a targeted state petition campaign.[40] Wright's coalition used political seats won by the Liberty Party as leverage to align themselves with House Whigs, agreeing to elect H. A. Collins (Whig) as speaker in return for Whig support in passing the 1843 personal liberty law – banning all state officials and state resources from being used to enforce the Fugitive Slave Law of 1793 and avoiding overreaching the state's power by not seeking to take control over federal fugitive slave rendition.[41]

Black rights in Massachusetts reached a high point in 1855, when a comprehensive law passed that was essential to establishing the right to free movement (Dimension 1), the right to due process and legal protection (Dimension 2), and the right to identify and belong (Dimension 5). Specifically, the new state law forbade state officials from enforcing the federal fugitive slave law, established a strict anti-kidnapping law, and provided additional due process protections, including appointing special state commissioners to defend runaway slaves in court, placing the burden of proof on slave owners and providing all Blacks with the right of habeas corpus, of trial by jury, and of giving testimony against Whites.[42] Although this law did not explicitly include a right to identify and belong, the activism over the capture and extradition of Anthony Burns in 1854 and the associated movement rhetoric over the state's landmark law made it very clear: runaway slaves were citizens of Massachusetts. Rising tensions further enabled Massachusetts's law to become the model for five other Northern legislatures (Connecticut, Vermont, Rhode Island, Michigan, and Maine), who passed similar laws that same year.[43]

It is important to note, however, that enacting progressive state citizenship in a federated context did not automatically translate into equal citizenship rights for Blacks and Whites in the antebellum North. "To most northerners," the historian Leon Litwack explains, "segregation constituted not a departure from democratic principles, as certain foreign critics alleged, but simply the working out of natural laws, the inevitable consequence of the racial inferiority of the

Negro."[44] As C. Vann Woodward's seminal work *The Strange Career of Jim Crow* (1955) makes clear, segregation proliferated first in the antebellum North, but it fundamentally differed from the Jim Crow that emerged after the Reconstruction era.[45] Segregation in the antebellum North was more of the laissez-faire variety; it was largely driven by the private sector, receiving tacit acceptance from state and local governments. By contrast, Jim Crow segregation in the postwar South was driven by state law and embedded and enforced in all aspects of government and society.

Segregation in the antebellum North originated in exclusion from residential areas as well as in railway cars, omnibuses, stagecoaches, and steamboats, where Blacks were either assigned to their own sections or barred entirely.[46] Jim Crow emerged in part as a private system of segregation and exclusion, including most hotels, restaurants, and White churches (where Blacks could attend but had their own "Negro pews"). Segregated schools, hospitals, and cemeteries also ensured that Blacks would be systematically separated from Whites.[47] Indeed, Litwack notes that, where schools were integrated in progressive cities like Boston, teachers often punished their White students by threatening to place them in the "n***er-seat" [our edits] or into the "Negro class." Moreover, beginning as early as 1832, multiple large-scale anti-Black riots erupted in Philadelphia, Columbia, and other parts of Pennsylvania, where Whites stormed Black sections of cities, destroyed their homes, churches, and meeting halls, and forced hundreds of Blacks to permanently flee or to become homeless.[48] Minstrel shows emerged in the 1840s as a popular form of White entertainment across the North, including in its most progressive states like Massachusetts, Pennsylvania, and New York and in progressive cities like Boston, Philadelphia, and New York City. Strong abolitionist groups like the Massachusetts Anti-Slavery Society (MASS) were unable to mobilize the state to act against these popular and institutionalized forms of White racism.

However, in 1841, MASS led a campaign to legally integrate railways in the state, "for a law declaring equal rights of persons in the use of the means of conveyance furnished under charters from the State," and to repeal that state's anti-miscegenation law that barred interracial marriage.[49] Wendell Phillips of Massachusetts, in 1842, argued to the state legislature that it was "a right, not a privilege to be transported in the cars of the corporations ... [and] it surely ought to be an equal right." Phillips added that Jim Crow cars are "an injury to his rights, and insult to his person."[50] Despite gaining support from the joint legislative committee, the state legislature refused to pass a railroad integration law in 1842. A member of the committee proposing the legislation, Representative Charles Francis Adams of Boston, pressured corporations to end their Jim Crow policies or face a state legislative ban the following year. The strategy seemed to have worked, as MASS and other abolitionists reported by 1843 that the state's railways no longer practiced segregation as a result. While segregation remained a significant counterforce for full Black inclusion,

Massachusetts continued to make legislative advancements in Black citizenship rights through the Civil War.

By contrast, in Pennsylvania, where the first personal liberty law passed to protect runaway slaves (in 1820 and 1826), the forces of racism and segregation were even stronger than in Massachusetts, and they ultimately ended up eroding gains in Black citizenship rights. Most notably, at the state's constitutional convention in 1837, White delegates recognized the importance of equality under the law but then went on to explain: "you can never force the citizens of this commonwealth to believe or practice it; we can never force our constituents to go peaceably to the polls, side by side with the negro."[51] Other delegates at the convention questioned if Whites were "willing to extend to the blacks his social equality and rights; to receive him in his family or at his table, on the same footing and terms with his wife and friends and acquaintances; allow them to marry with his children, male and female?"[52] At the time of this constitutional convention, the Pennsylvania Supreme Court reinterpreted the state's early constitution, ruling that "Negroes could not legally exercise the right to vote," but offered no tangible evidence other than hearsay about what the state's framers had intended when establishing equal rights in the state constitution.[53] Importantly, as Leon Litwack notes, this decision reaffirmed what White delegates at the 1837 convention were already planning: Black disenfranchisement. The following year, in 1838, voters approved the new state constitution, which formally barred Blacks from the right to vote.

Thus, as we explained in Chapter 2, progress on one dimension of Black citizenship rights did not automatically translate to progress on others and could indeed stop well short of equality with Whites. Still, the forms of progressive state citizenship that emerged in the antebellum North were notable achievements given the context of federalism – in relation to both the nonexistent rights provided to Blacks at the national level and the various ways that several Northeastern states resisted Southern attempts to recapture runaway slaves and re-enslave free Blacks.

Reinforcing (Exclusionary) State Citizenship in the Midwest

The US Constitution provided no direction on slavery and freedom in the states or in federal territories, with the exception of the fugitive slave clause protecting slaveowner's right to property. Without Constitutional direction, northern territories were subject to Article 6 of the Northwest Ordinance of 1787, which stated that slavery would not exist in the states that would be created from that territory. The US Congress approved new state admissions with a very low bar of preserving the ratio of free states to slave states, adding no new constitutional requirements. This allowed exclusionary laws to emerge in the Midwest. As we noted in Chapter 3, the relative silence of the US Constitution on the rights of national citizenship paved the way for state citizenship regimes that were consonant with federal law but were nevertheless restrictive in the provision of rights to their Black residents.

Exclusionary moves on Black citizenship in the Midwest were quick to develop because state leaders had long-established roadmaps set by Southern political developments for how to constrain the rights of Blacks. Ohio entered the Union in 1803 with a state constitution that banned slavery, in accordance with federal law. But it also legalized indentured servitude of both Whites and Blacks until the age of twenty-one for males and eighteen for females, as well as denying free Blacks the right to vote and to hold public office.[54] The most populated region was southern Ohio, which was made up primarily of White Democrats with strong ties to slave states. Throughout the antebellum period, and despite a strong abolitionist movement in northern Ohio, the southern part of the state controlled the legislature and passed numerous restrictive laws. After its admission to the Union, Ohio's legislature quickly moved to enact a range of restrictions on Black migration modeled after slavery laws and Black laws of the South. In 1804, it passed a comprehensive law requiring all Blacks to show proof of freedom before entering, residing in, or searching for employment in the state, as well as requiring Blacks to register with their county of residence (Dimensions 1, 3, and 5). The 1804 law also mandated state officials and formal institutions to aid in recaption and made it a misdemeanor for anyone in the state to interfere in the recaption process, with fines of up to $1,000 (Dimension 2).[55]

As Paul Frymer shows, westward expansion in Ohio and elsewhere was achieved through homestead laws establishing different forms of racial control, particularly policies to restrict Black immigration aimed at creating exclusively White populated states.[56] In 1807, Ohio expanded its restrictions on entry by requiring Blacks to attain two sponsors who were property owners and willing to post a $500 bond that guaranteed future good behavior of new Black residents (Dimension 1). This law also banned Black testimony against Whites (Dimension 2), increased fines for interfering in runaway slave recaption (Dimension 2), and mandated that employers and schools aid in recaption and verify certificates of freedom of all Blacks in the state (Dimensions 2 and 3).[57] The state's restrictive laws were enforced selectively, leaving Blacks in northern Ohio in a constant position of vulnerability. For example, in 1829, a campaign to remove Blacks in Cincinnati was led by White mobs, overseers of the poor, and state officials who issued a proclamation for "illegal" Blacks to leave the state by June 29. All Blacks lacking proof of freedom and registration in their county of residence were subject to being detained by state officials under the federal fugitive slave law. Abolitionists responded by securing support from the lieutenant governor of Upper Canada for Cincinnati Blacks to find safe haven across the international border. Over 1,200 Blacks migrated north to Canada.[58]

Despite the state's anti-Black laws, Northern Ohio had a large Black population and abolitionist movement that was active in the Underground

Railroad, protecting runaway slaves through local and extralegal mechanisms. Between 1790 and 1840, the Black population doubled its size every ten years, and by 1860 Ohio had reached over 36,000 Black residents, establishing it as the third most Black-populated state in the North. Yet, Ohio Democrats and conservative Republicans denied Black's from voting, holding office, or testifying in court (Dimension 2 and 4). Moreover, state leaders also ignored Black petitions for reforms in state policy (Dimension 4). Despite these setbacks, Blacks strategically aligned with White abolitionists and sympathetic White officials in northern Ohio to form large petition campaigns, most of which were oriented toward repealing existing state restrictions. Abolitionists' unsuccessful petition to repeal Ohio's Black testimony law led Democrats to propose a constitutional amendment in 1819 that, if passed, would have legalized slavery in the state.

Rising sectional tensions occasionally led to competing developments on Black citizenship rights in Ohio, Indiana, and Illinois. All three states passed anti-kidnapping laws to protect their free Black residents. In 1816, Indiana passed an anti-kidnapping law requiring slave catchers to attain a warrant from a justice of the peace or judge of the supreme circuit (Dimension 2). Failing to expand rights more broadly, Ohio abolitionists were able to gain enough support from the state's Democratic leaders to pass its first anti-kidnapping law in 1819 and expanded legal protections for free Blacks from kidnapping in 1831 (creating a new procedural rule requiring the use of recaption claims through justices of the peace) and in 1843 (establishing a sentence of up to seven years of hard labor for kidnapping).[59] Similarly, in 1833, Illinois passed an anti-kidnapping law that "provided sanctions against anyone who forcibly arrested anyone else to remove him from the state without having established a claim according to the laws of the United States."[60] Importantly, these inclusionary laws provided only a minimum level of rights to free Black residents, and all three states simultaneously passed strict state laws to enforce federal fugitive slave law (Dimension 2), while Indiana passed a stricter anti-harboring law in 1816 regulating the false documentation and harboring of runaway slaves (Dimension 2).[61] Indeed, Stephen Douglass, a Democratic US senator from Illinois and resident of Chicago, was chairman of the Congressional Committee on Territories and led in the passage of the new Fugitive Slave Act of 1850.[62]

White supremacists in Illinois and Indiana used the same national events – that abolitionists had leveraged in Massachusetts to expand rights – to mobilize around further restricting Black rights. Siding with Southern Democrats, Illinois and Indiana's state leaders responded to the Fugitive Slave Act of 1850 and the Kansas-Nebraska Act in 1854 by shutting their doors entirely to Blacks. In 1851, Indiana passed a new state constitution banning all Blacks from entering the state (Dimension 1) and gaining lawful employment (Dimension 3). The state enforced employer sanctions and applied any fines toward the state's colonization program to remove resident Blacks.[63]

The following year, in 1852, Indiana passed another law requiring all Blacks residing in the state prior to November 1, 1851, to register or face removal (Dimensions 1 and 5).[64] Again, in 1852, 1853, and 1855, Indiana passed laws strengthening its colonization program to remove Black residents from the state (Dimension 1).[65] Illinois similarly passed laws banning Black immigration into the state in 1852, but it did not go so far as to enforce its immigration ban or to remove resident Blacks (see Table 4.2).[66]

Reinforcing (Exclusionary) State Citizenship in the South

It would be a profound and obvious understatement to say that the US Constitution and federal law allowed Southern states to restrict the rights of Black residents even further than those in the Midwest. Various Congressional laws and compromises demarcating the lines of free states and slave states and territories provided Southern states with even more autonomy than their Northern counterparts to develop highly exclusionary forms of state citizenship. At the same time, debates over emancipation were not exclusive to the North. Upper regions of the South received petitions for abolishing slavery, with advocates appealing to religious and revolutionary values of American freedom. Virginia, Delaware, and Maryland responded by passing laws to allow for private manumission by slave owners, but they did not impose a state emancipation scheme.[67] These manumission laws led to the increased presence of free Blacks and debates over their rights in Southern states.

The US Constitution gave enormous power to the national government but also instilled political safeguards to prevent national legislation that might preempt or alter the institution of slavery. Whereas federal legislative action was a blank slate at the founding of the United States, the Tenth Amendment safeguarded states' colonial laws to preserve Southern slavery and further preserved states' control over passing restrictive laws, absent federal action. Thus, in sharp contrast to the conflict in the North over fugitive slave rendition, Southern forms of state citizenship reinforced existing federal restrictions on who had rights. Importantly, Southern states could rely on their colonial laws on the treatment of slaves, but they did not have a clear roadmap when it came to free Blacks and manumitted slaves. Moreover, throughout the antebellum era, Southern states developed robust exclusionary regimes of state citizenship with some progressive elements on the rights of free Blacks. Like the most progressive states of the free North, the slave state of Maryland went so far as to provide free Blacks the right to vote, to own property, to due process protections in court, and to attend public schools.

Sectionalism and regional political constraints within the North and South thus created different pathways in the development of Black state citizenship. Variations in the South emerged on the rights of enslaved Blacks and free Blacks, driven in part by regional developments toward a more diverse, urbanized economy in Maryland, Virginia, and North Carolina and the

TABLE 4.2 *Variants of state citizenship in antebellum America, 1878–1861*

Policy Type	Citizenship Dimensions 1–5*	Slave South	Free North
Inter-state entry	1	*Exclusionary reinforcing* • Michigan (1820) state constitution closes state border to free Blacks	*Progressive* • Philadelphia, New York, Massachusetts allowed for entry without restrictions *Exclusionary reinforcing* • Ohio (1804) state law requires bond for free Black entry
International entry	1	*Regressive (but, federalism conflict)* • South Carolina (1820) Seaman Act closed international ports to foreign free Blacks	*Progressive* • Philadelphia, New York, Massachusetts allowed for entry without restrictions *Exclusionary reinforcing* • Ohio (1804) state law requires bond for free Black entry
Manumission papers *proof of freedom*	1, 5	*Exclusionary reinforcing*	*Progressive* • Philadelphia, New York, Massachusetts (presumption of free status) *Exclusionary reinforcing* • Ohio (1804) state law requires proof of freedom for entry (presumption of slave status)
Sunset curfew	1	*Exclusionary reinforcing*	

(*continued*)

TABLE 4.2 *(continued)*

Policy Type	Citizenship Dimensions 1–5*	Slave South	Free North
Passes/tags	1, 3	*Regressive* • Charleston, SC	*N/A*
Vagrancy laws	1, 3	*Exclusionary reinforcing*	
Gathering restrictions	1, 2	*Exclusionary reinforcing*	
Public transportation	1	*Exclusionary reinforcing* • Fugitive slave enforcement in all Southern states	*Progressive* • Massachusetts de-facto end to Jim Crow segregation on railways (1843) *Regressive* • Precursors to Jim Crow separation *Exclusionary reinforcing* • Ohio, Indiana, Illinois legal status check on public waterways
Fugitive Slave Law	2	*Exclusionary reinforcing* • Mandated private fugitive slave enforcement in South Carolina	*Progressive* • Philadelphia (1820, 1826, 1847), Massachusetts (1843, 1855) personal liberty laws barring state and local resources and officials from enforcing fugitive slave law *Exclusionary reinforcing* • Ohio, Indiana, Illinois

(continued)

TABLE 4.2 *(continued)*

Policy Type	Citizenship Dimensions 1–5*	Slave South	Free North
Anti-Harboring Law *on fugitive slave enforcement in state institutions, employment, schools, and private spaces (homes)*	1, 2	*Exclusionary reinforcing* • Fugitive slave enforcement in all southern states • Slave patrols established in South Carolina, Michigan, Georgia, Virginia	*Exclusionary reinforcing* • Ohio, Indiana, Illinois
State-led removal *fugitive slave enforcement in the North; colonization schemes*	1, 2	*Regressive* • Colonization schemes in South Carolina	*Exclusionary reinforcing* • Fugitive slave enforcement in Ohio, Indiana, Illinois *Regressive* • Colonization schemes in Indiana (1850s), Illinois (1850s)
Court access rights *slave freedom suits; habeas corpus; writ of replevin; black Testimony; burden of proof in fugitive rendition cases*	2	*Regressive* • Blacks were allowed to file suits for their freedom (e.g., Dred Scott) but were denied basic due process rights in court	*Progressive* • Philadelphia: habeas corpus (1785; 1847) • Massachusetts: habeas corpus (1785); writ of replevin (1787); trial by jury (1837); Black testimony (1855); burden of proof on slave owners in fugitive rendition cases (1855)

(continued)

TABLE 4.2 (*continued*)

Policy Type	Citizenship Dimensions 1–5*	Slave South	Free North
Court testimony rights *trial by jury*	2	*Regressive*	*Progressive* • Massachusetts (1855)
Interracial sexual relations *anti-miscegenation laws* *bastardy laws* *sodomy laws*	2, 5	*Progressive* • Interracial intimacy permitted de facto *Regressive* • Criminalized Black intimacy as immoral; barred interracial marriage	
Right to marriage	3	*Regressive* • Legal marriages require slave-owner consent and have no contractual or property rights	
Right to vote	4	*Progressive* • Maryland provided voting rights to free Blacks (pre-1810) *Regressive* • Most states barred Blacks from voting	*Progressive* • Philadelphia (before 1828), New York, Massachusetts *Regressive* • Northern states also barred Blacks from voting or placed certain restrictions
Right to elected office	4	*Regressive* • No Black elected officials	*Regressive* • No Black elected officials (due to political party preference or state bans)

*The provision of rights to: (1) free movement; (2) due process and legal protection; (3) develop human capital; (4) participate and be represented; and (5) identify and belong.

emergence of a Deep South economy ever more reliant on plantation slave labor. In the Upper South, state and local governments began to redefine the rights of enslaved Blacks hired in cities and no longer bound by the watchful eye of slaveowners on the plantation. Further South, slave owners retained nearly unfettered control over the lives of enslaved Blacks on their plantations.[68] Our citizenship framework helps to situate these variations occurring between the Upper and Deep South as dimensions of slaves' rights, with more exclusionary forms of state citizenship emerging in the latter.

Progressive and Reinforcing Elements in the Border State of Maryland

As a Southern state bordering the North, and growing less reliant on slave labor, Maryland developed a decidedly mixed approach to the political status and rights of free Blacks in the state. The state soon began restricting the rights of free Blacks, drawing lines separating those who were free before or after 1783, with newly freed Blacks denied the right to vote, hold public office, or testify against Whites.[69] Nevertheless, some free Blacks wielded political power through voting, until Maryland amended its state constitution in 1801 to limit voting rights to "free white male citizens, and no other." Responding to its free Black population more than doubling in the span of one decade, from 8,000 (1790) to 19,000 (1800), in 1806 Maryland passed its first restriction on the in-migration of free Blacks from other states by imposing a $10 fine for entering and making Blacks who failed to pay subject to being sold into slavery outside of Maryland (Dimensions 1 and 2).[70] Thus, while Maryland sought to limit Black migration, it preserved elements of progressive state citizenship for its Black residents – who were legally allowed to hold property (Dimension 3), seek due process in courts (Dimension 2), and attend schools (Dimension 3) – until the 1830s and 1840s.

Bordering the free North, Blacks in Baltimore, Maryland, were only 100 miles from Philadelphia by coach and grew in size from just 323 in 1790 to more than 10,000 in 1820, with Black households making up 23.5 percent of the total for the city.[71] Baltimore is where Benjamin Lundy published his treatise on Black rights, *The Genius of Universal Emancipation*, and where he mentored abolitionist leader William Lloyd Garrison in 1829.[72] Thus, the progressive state citizenship that formed early in Maryland provided free Blacks the capacity to develop strong links to the North, through abolitionist networks, regional church and fraternal order networks, and newspapers.[73]

The strength of its free Black population in turn led Maryland to separate the state legislature from the church in ways that expanded Black rights significantly. In 1802, the state enacted a law severing its legislative control over Christian-specific congregations seeking to add or incorporate congregations, "without any exception."[74] The law expressly forbade state officials from abridging or affecting "the rights of conscience or private judgment, or in the least to alter or change the religious constitution or government of any church, congregation or society, so far as respects, or in anywise concerns, doctrine, discipline or worship."[75] Starkly contrasting with other Southern states, Maryland's free Blacks were able to legally purchase land and create independent Black churches (Dimension 3 of our framework). By contrast, in other Southern cities like Charleston, Richmond, and Saint Louis, free Blacks caught gathering for religious purposes outside the supervision of White authorities were threatened with forced removal from the state or enslavement.[76]

The 1820 Missouri Compromise, however, shifted Maryland in a more restrictive direction. Recall that, as discussed in Chapter 3, the Missouri Compromise effectively denied freed Blacks the rights of US citizenship by allowing a state (Missouri) to ban the entry of free Blacks from other states, effectively ignoring the Constitution's privileges and immunities clause. Soon, other Southern states like Maryland followed suit. Facing a fast-growing Black population and three new railroad projects (the Baltimore and Susquehanna, the Baltimore and Washington, and the Baltimore and Ohio) that made Black interstate travel easier, Maryland enacted its own 1820 ban on Black in-migration (Dimension 1).[77] More than a decade later, in response to the slave uprising of more than sixty slaves led by Nat Turner in 1831 in neighboring Virginia, Maryland fundamentally changed its relations with its own free Black residents by mirroring the restrictions of Southern states. In 1831, it passed a law banning all Blacks from "assembling or attending religious meetings unless the gathering was led by a licensed White clergyman or other respectable White person" (Dimension 3).[78]

In early 1832, Octavius Taney, a member of Maryland's Senate Committee on the "condition of the colored population," sought new restrictions toward free Blacks by linking them to slave unrest.[79] Taney hatched out Maryland's first plan for removing all Blacks from the state, going so far as to propose that Congress fund the effort, stating:

In my opinion South Carolina or any other slaveholding state has a right to guard itself from the danger to be apprehended from the introduction of free people of colour among their slaves – and have not by the constitution of the US surrendered the right to pass the laws necessary for that purpose. I think this right is reserved to the states & cannot be abrogated by the US either by legislation or by treaty.[80]

A joint committee of the Maryland Senate and House of Delegates were unwilling to go as far as Taney's proposal, but supported the state legislature in passing a comprehensive law in 1832 that barred Black in-migration and made Maryland's free Black residents who left the state for more than thirty days "aliens" (Dimension 1 and 5). It also created new requirements for free Blacks to acquire gun licenses, required Black religious meetings to have White supervision, banned Whites from purchasing staple crops from Blacks, and banned Blacks from selling "spirits" (Dimension 3).[81] While the law did not touch on Taney's primary goal of removing Blacks, state lawmakers created the Maryland State Colonization Society in 1832, which pursued and funded consensual removal of Blacks to Liberia up through the Civil War.

In passing its 1835 Black Law, Maryland had clearly ended its progressive state citizenship and joined the rest of the South in the fight against abolition. The new state law prohibited all Blacks from "knowingly call[ing] for, etc., any abolition handbill, etc., having a tendency to create insurrection, etc., among the people of color," subject to up to twenty years' imprisonment (Dimension 4).[82] In December of that same year, Representative James Hammond of South Carolina and Speaker James Polk of Tennessee proposed the infamous gag rule in the US House of Representatives – making all petitions, memorials, or resolutions regarding slavery automatically tabled and preventing all further action upon them. With Southern control of Congress, this gag rule was in force from 1836 to 1844, until Representative John Quincy Adams of Massachusetts was able to repeal it. In 1841, Maryland further restricted the circulation and possession of abolitionist literature by barring any person from "knowingly taking part in the preparation or circulation of printed or written materials having a tendency to create discontent among Black Marylanders, or to stir them to insurrection."[83]

Soon after, in 1844, Maryland began to regulate the out-of-state travel of its free Black residents, passing a law that required them to obtain travel papers from the criminal court (Dimension 1). This permit established their "legal personhood" but also subjected Blacks' right to travel to the court's discretion and required Black applicants to provide the written endorsement of "three respectable White persons, known to be such by the judge or judges of said court."[84] Under the law, any Black person who entered Maryland without travel papers authorizing their entry were "subject to arrest, fine, or sale into servitude if apprehended."[85] The only exceptions were "sailors, wagon drivers and messengers in the actual service of a non-resident, [who] could stay over two weeks, under penalty of ten dollars a week."[86]

Maryland debated a new state constitution in 1850, led in part by radical colonization activists seeking to remove the state's entire free Black population.[87] A committee on the Free Negro Population justified removal on the grounds that statewide the free Black population had reached 73,000 in 1850, exceeding the White population in eleven counties. It went on to state that all free Blacks were "reared in all the vices, ignorance, wants and degradations, characterizing a class of our population called free, but in reality the veriest slaves on earth."[88] With this backdrop, the committee recommended a comprehensive removal plan: mandating all Blacks to register and ending Black property and due process rights, followed by state-led removal of all Black residents. The constitutional proposal also required manumitted slaves to leave within thirty days or be re-enslaved, as well as banning future in-migration of Blacks. In the end, Maryland's 1851 constitution ignored all of these measures and left the future of Blacks in the state unaddressed.

Reinforcing (Exclusionary) State Citizenship in the Slaveholding South

Exclusion via reinforcing state citizenship emerged as the general pattern of Black citizenship in the South, with South Carolina (previously Carolina) providing an important archetype that Southern states modelled their policies after. As a colonial global hub for rice and indigo commodity crops and cotton on the sea islands, Carolina's dependence on slave labor set the stage for restrictive measures on the rights of enslaved, newly freed, and free Blacks. In 1686, Carolina created the first legal requirement inside the US for slaves to carry passes, or "tickets," while publicly trading goods outside of their owner's plantation or residence, which also established a nighttime curfew for all slaves in the state (Dimensions 1, 3 and 5).[89] Shortly after, Carolina passed a law in 1691 setting up slave control duties for the states' colonial militia and a special town watch in the city of Charleston to enforce slavery law and its slave pass system (Dimension 1).[90] All Whites were required under the new law to enforce slave passes, slave bartering restrictions, and fugitive slave laws to return runaway slaves. Making the racial regime more complete, in 1696 the state passed a law explicitly protecting all Whites in the event that they assaulted or killed slaves who resisted being arrested or detained (Dimension 2).[91] To increase enforcement capacity, the state also established in 1704 a slave patrol militia that operated independently from the colonial militia.[92]

Free Blacks largely held the same rights as Whites until 1721. Then, Carolina passed one of its early Negro Acts restricting voting to only "free White men" and quickly followed up with laws closing off future expansions in the free Black population. The following year, Carolina passed a Negro Act requiring freed slaves to leave the province within twelve months of being manumitted by their owners or be re-enslaved (Dimensions 1, 2, and 5). Soon, Carolina's restrictions on black life would escalate dramatically. On September 9, 1739, twenty slaves gathered near the Stono River, located 20 miles from Charlestown. After breaking into a local store where they stole guns and ammunition, the runaway slaves killed an estimated twenty-five Whites. This incident marked the largest slave uprising to occur in colonial America. Carolina responded by dealing a final blow to the rights of Blacks. The Negro Act (1740) stripped free Blacks of any due process or legal protections by relegating all criminal cases against free Blacks to the "same second-class judicial process designed for slaves" (Dimension 2). It also formally placed manumission under the control of state courts, completing Carolina's oversight and regulation of requirements for freed Blacks to leave the state or be re-enslaved (Dimensions 1 and 5).[93] Most freed Blacks subsequently left the state. As historian Peter Wood explains, these restrictive slavery laws and Negro Acts ensured that the proportion of free Blacks in South Carolina never exceeded 1 percent of the total Black population before the American Revolutionary War.[94]

While the US Constitution set up a new Union, colonial laws became the legal foundation upon which American states built their legal institutions of slavery and state citizenship after the Revolutionary War. South Carolina continued to pass laws expanding control over the movement and activities of Blacks, including requiring freedmen passes and tags for free Blacks that had to be renewed in the city or county of residence each year (passing such a law in 1783 and again in 1800) (Dimensions 1 and 5); passing a Seaman Act banning free Blacks in other states from entering its borders in 1822 (Dimension 1); and creating local patrol committees to oversee slave patrols in 1830 (Dimension 2). Slave or free, all Black persons caught infringing on South Carolina's state laws were subject to penalties, including possible removal, forced labor, imprisonment, enslavement, or re-enslavement (Dimension 2).

Throughout the antebellum era, Southern states passed laws that invested significant power in slave patrols, laws restricting Black involvement in the trade and bartering of goods (Dimension 3), laws designating specific Black travel routes and curfews (Dimensions 1 and 3), and laws restricting Black access to public resources (Dimension 3). Slave and freedmen passes functioned both as an identification document and a work visa (Dimensions 1, 3, and 5), and both local militias and slave patrols actively enforced Southern laws on and off the plantation.[95] Southern regimes of reinforcing state citizenship were also composed of anti-harboring laws, making it a crime to harbor Blacks considered to be unlawfully present, as defined under federal, state, and local laws. Finally, restrictions on free movement extended to the very design of Southern cities after 1820, especially as the Upper South's economy diversified away from staple crops, with urban housing plans that confined slaves to bordered backyards and a municipal legal system designed to limit slaves' freedom outside of their master's house.[96] In addition, Southern state and local governments legally sanctioned the separation of Black families through slave auctions to facilitate the growth of slavery in the Deep South.[97]

Southern criminal justice subjected free Blacks to the same exclusions under slavery laws, including denying them from having due process or legal protection, which extended to denying them protection from being wrongfully enslaved and, often, legally punishing free Blacks with enslavement.[98] Thus, at the heart of the debates over state citizenship were fundamental questions about whether Blacks could have any meaningful rights at all.[99]

Black Citizenship and Federalism Conflict in the Run-Up to Civil War

The depth to which antebellum states were able to create varying regimes of state citizenship for Blacks continued to increase in the lead-up to the Civil War. South Carolina's declaration of secession referenced Northern personal liberty laws as the cause for the nation's sectional crisis. Yet, states in the North and South expanded and contracted the rights of Blacks, both enslaved and free, with a patchwork of rights that generated significant federalism conflict. These included attempts by Northern states to protect and even legally free Southern slaves crossing their borders (including slaves in transit and runaway slaves), as well as attempts by Southern states to expel Northern free Blacks and even enslaving those unlawfully entering their borders. The 1850s marked the critical tipping point for sectionalism. A comprehensive law opened federal territories up to slavery and hardened fugitive slave law even further. Northern states responded by expanding their protections of Blacks at the state level while creating the Republican Party to confront the growing slave power in national government. The last decade of the antebellum era was marked by the Supreme Court formalizing what abolitionists and Blacks had already known: that Blacks were not national citizens.

The Compromise of 1850 had guaranteed that much of the vast western land gained from Mexico in the war of 1846–1848 would be open to the expansion of slavery into new states and territories. It also strengthened existing fugitive slave laws, effectively extending southern power into the free states north of the Mason-Dixon line. The dissolution of the Whig Party had left the presidency open to a series of pro-South northern Democrats (known as "doughfaces" in the political slang of the day), while political opposition to slave-owner power had only slowly coalesced around marginal third parties. By the mid-1850s, important figures in the South had called to reopen the slave trade as well as to wrest the Caribbean sugar island of Cuba from Spanish control for the purposes of expanding the footprint of American slavery.[100]

On July 5, 1852, in Rochester, New York, Frederick Douglass addressed the Rochester Ladies' Anti-Slavery Society about how the American Revolution and notions of freedom were not the same for Blacks and Whites. In his "What to the Slave is the Fourth of July" speech, he said: "The sunlight that brought life and healing to you, has brought stripes and death to me. This Fourth [of] July is yours, not mine. You may rejoice, I must mourn. To drag a man in fetters into the grand illuminated temple of liberty, and call upon him to join you in joyous anthems, were inhuman mockery and sacrilegious irony."[101] Two years later, in 1854, Stephen Douglas from Illinois introduced the Kansas-Nebraska Act with the goal of opening the West for expansion. The Act permitted slavery in the western territories on the principle of "squatter sovereignty," effectively repealing the Missouri Compromise of the 1820s. This elicited a strong reaction in the North that led to the rise of the Republican Party, with a platform of confronting the power of Southern slavery in national politics and stop the spread of slavery into Western territories.

Meanwhile, in 1854, a federal marshal had arrested abolitionist editor Sherman Booth for violating the Fugitive Slave Act of 1850 by aiding in the rescue of Joshua Glover, a runaway slave. With the help of abolitionists, Glover succeeded in fleeing to freedom across the Canadian border. Meanwhile, in Wisconsin, Booth was granted a writ of habeas corpus from a state judge to be released from federal custody, prompting US Marshal Stephen V. R. Ableman to appeal to Wisconsin's Supreme Court to prevent Booth's release. The court not only affirmed Booth's release in 1855, but it also ruled that the federal fugitive slave law was unconstitutional, despite the Supreme Court's decision in *Prigg v. Pennsylvania* (1842). The Supreme Court soon stepped in to issue two important decisions in 1857 and 1858 that solidified states' full control over the rights of Blacks and the federalism conflict over fugitive slave law, further fanning the flames of sectionalism.

In *Dred Scott v. Sandford* (1857), Supreme Court Chief Justice Taney warned that if free Blacks were entitled to the "privileges and immunities" of national citizens, then state Black codes would be invalid. Taney explained that free Blacks would have "the right to enter every other State whenever they pleased, singly or in companies, without pass or passport, and without obstruction, to sojourn there as long as they pleased, to go where they pleased at every hour of the day or night without molestation."[102] The US Constitution treated Blacks fundamentally differently. Whereas the constitution directed the federal government to protect the rights of Whites, "states' rights" prevented the same federal protections from being given to Blacks. Taney went further to clarify this distinction by referencing the *Passenger Cases*, according to Martha S. Jones, by explaining that the Constitution "protected a slave owner's right to interstate travel – the right 'to enjoy a common country' – such that movement between two states could not give rise to the deprivation of his property in persons."[103]

During the 1850s, a Congress controlled by Southern Democrats enacted a series of compromises, opening up the possibility of extending slavery into federal territories and new states and strengthening the enforcement of federal fugitive slave law in the North. These events helped spark the rise of the new Republican Party, which ran on the platform of confronting Southern power in national politics and stopping the spread of slavery. When Abraham Lincoln won the presidency in 1860, Southern states began to push for pro-slavery amendments to the US Constitution (as we detailed in Chapter 3). The constitutional requirement of three-fourths of the states to ratify ensured that these Southern amendments failed. Soon thereafter, South Carolina declared secession, followed by Mississippi, Florida, Alabama, Georgia, Louisiana, and Texas.

BLACKS AND FEDERATED CITIZENSHIP UNDER RECONSTRUCTION (1865–1877)

The Civil War ended in April, 1965, sparking a decade-long national project of Reconstruction. The US Constitution was revolutionized by the Thirteenth Amendment's national abolition (1965) and by the Fourteenth and Fifteenth Amendments' (1868 and 1870, respectively) guarantee of birthright citizenship and voting rights to Blacks. In contrast to the antebellum era, the postbellum US Constitution set clearer boundaries on state citizenship, compelling revisions to Northern and Southern constitutions alike. Northern states held new constitutional conventions to reset the rights of Blacks in accordance with changes to the US Constitution. Northern states were also able to build upon their antebellum regimes of progressive state citizenship and help shape the national direction on Black rights. Meanwhile, Confederate states faced greater hurdles set by the federal government during Reconstruction to be readmitted as full members of the national community while making similar reforms to their constitutions and laws.

This section will reveal, however, that state citizenship continued to evolve out of competing visions and conflict over Black rights. For two decades (1865 to 1877), contradictions emerged from varying forms of state citizenship. Southern states enacted Black codes despite a strong federal military presence and segregationist policies in the North as well as the South. At the same time, Blacks were also gaining the right to vote and hold office for the first time in much of America's history, including in Southern states and in the national government. Following the end of Reconstruction in 1877, however, state-level progress on Black rights was swiftly replaced with strongly regressive regimes of state citizenship by the early twentieth century under Jim Crow.

Competing National Visions for Black Citizenship (1865–1866)

Essential to the emergence of progressive state citizenship, especially in the South, was strong national leadership (executive action in our APD framework), combined with constitutional opportunities for expansion in Black citizenship rights and legislative actions to help secure these rights. Notably, Reconstruction marked a moment in American history in the advancement of Black citizenship rights, not only nationally but also in several states. For a short while, the South provided a hopeful, albeit contentious, model for progressive federalism to advance Black rights; however, this promise was short lived. With the end of Reconstruction and the emergence of Jim Crow, the South took an alarming turn in the opposite direction, going from building on federal rights (progressive state citizenship) to instituting regimes that robbed Blacks of citizenship rights that were supposed to be guaranteed at the federal level (regressive state citizenship).

The prospects for Reconstruction were not immediately obvious after the end of the Civil War. Andrew Johnson, a Southerner and War Democrat appointed as the military governor of Tennessee, stepped into the presidency after Lincoln's assassination at a critical time in the shaping the postwar legacy. Guided by his allegiance to the Democratic Party and his desire to secure Southern support for his reelection in 1868, on May 29, 1865, Johnson issued a general proclamation of pardon and amnesty for most Confederates. He also authorized the provisional governor of North Carolina to proceed in reorganizing the state's constitution. New state constitutions were expected to repeal their ordinances of secession, to repudiate the Confederate debt, and to accept the Thirteenth Amendment (1865) by abolishing slavery.

President Johnson reversed wartime gains in Black rights by revoking General Sherman's Special Field Orders from January 16, 1865, which provided land and mules to former Black slaves, known as "forty acres and a mule" – returning the land to its previous White owners. The following year, in 1866, Johnson vetoed the bill to renew the Freedmen's Bureau (formally known as the Bureau of Refugees, Freedmen and Abandoned Lands), which led in the provision of food, housing, and health care, the reuniting of Black families, and the setting up and overseeing of employment contracts with private landowners. Johnson made his vision for Black rights even more clear, vetoing the Civil Rights Bill of 1867, the first attempt by the US Congress after the war to define all persons born in the United States as national citizens who were to enjoy equality before the law. Sharing the same White supremacist views as Southern Democrats, President Johnson thus sought to preserve "states' rights" and exclusionary Black citizenship.

Appalled, moderate Republicans joined the Radicals in formalizing a Congressional vision for reconstruction by overturning the presidential vetoes in 1866 (Freedmen's Bureau) and 1867 (Civil Rights Act), setting the stage to impeach President Johnson from office.[104] The Senate acquitted Johnson, but by then Radical Republicans had taken over control of Congress and approved the Fourteenth Amendment, which prohibited "states from abridging equality before the law," provided for a reduction of a state's congressional representatives if Black voting rights were denied, and barred ex-Confederates from holding state or national office. They then turned their sights on reversing Johnson's Southern Reconstruction, passing the Reconstruction Act of 1867, which put the former Confederate states back under federal military control and temporarily divided the South into five military districts. Southern states were required to hold elections that would include Blacks and barred former Confederate leaders in the process of electing and becoming delegates for a new state constitutional convention. Not only were the constitutions required to recognize the Thirteenth Amendment's abolition of slavery, but Congress also required all Southern states to ratify the Fourteenth Amendment before they could rejoin the Union.

The presidency of Ulysses S. Grant enabled Congress to deepen inclusive moves on state citizenship in ways that benefited Black residents. Congress passed the federal Enforcement Acts in 1870 and 1871, which prohibited discrimination by state officials in voter registration on the basis of race, color, or previous condition of servitude and empowered the president with the legal authority to enforce voting rights throughout the country, which included physically protecting Blacks from vigilante violence.[105] As we detail in this section, Congressional Reconstruction set up Constitutional opportunities and legislative actions that enabled progressive state citizenship at a time when national Radical-Republicans were committed to federal enforcement of voting rights, labor protection, and due process.

Executive Actions Enable Regressive State Citizenship (1865–1867)

The future of state citizenship for Blacks depended on strong national leadership, and progressive citizenship in particular faced significant challenges from Southern Whites. From 1865 to 1867, under President Johnson's vision of states' rights, Black codes replaced slavery law in the South to ensure White supremacy over Black labor and access to public services.[106] These codes recreated Black dependency on White-owned land and plantations through new legal mechanisms other than slavery, including contract-based apprenticeships, debt peonage, sharecropping, and state-led convict leasing (Dimensions 1, 2, and 3). The Thirteenth Amendment banned slavery, yet these codes sought to reinstall a form of lifetime bondage by enforcing Black labor contracts that were void of labor protections. Unable to repay their loans with high interest rates, Black labor was made legally subject to White control. Similarly, antebellum vagrancy laws were revamped as the primary state law restricting Black travel (Dimension 1), which soon conflicted with the Fourteenth Amendment's extension of privileges and immunities to all Black US citizens. In short, immediately following the Civil War, the future of Black citizenship became highly contested, and the Constitutional opportunities short of freedom from being enslaved remained unclear.

Mississippi led the South's development of regressive citizenship immediately after the Civil War, passing a law in 1865 that forbade "any freedman, negro, or mulatto to ride in any first-class passenger cars, set apart, or used by and for White persons" (Dimensions 1 and 5).[107] The only exception to the restriction were Blacks "travelling with their mistress in the capacity of maids."[108] Florida also passed a law, that same year, stipulating that "if any negro, mulatto or other person of color shall intrude himself into ... any railroad car or other public vehicle set apart for the exclusive accommodation of white people, he shall be deemed guilty of a misdemeanor and, upon conviction, shall be sentenced to stand in pillory for one hour, or be whipped."[109] The following year, in 1866, Texas enacted the third Southern law restricting Black travel on railroads by requiring all railroad companies to "attach to passenger trains one car for the special accommodation of freedmen" to separate Blacks from Whites.[110]

States in the South were also able to preserve control over segregating public education, marriage, and sexual relations under Black codes. Southern states legally segregated their public schools (Dimension 3), led first by Tennessee, Arkansas, and Texas in 1866, spreading soon to fifteen more states from 1868 to 1888, and followed by another wave of thirteen state laws passed from 1889 to 1915 that included several in the North.[111] Bans on interracial marriage also developed in parallel (Dimensions 3 and 5). South Carolina's 1866 Black code reaffirmed its antebellum policy, stating, "Marriage between a White person and person of color shall be illegal and void."[112] In addition, Black mothers were legally banned from having custody of their interracial children, and antebellum state bastardy laws made Black fathers financially responsible for their interracial children (Dimension 3). During the time of President Johnson's control over Reconstruction (1865–1867), five states (Alabama, Georgia, Mississippi, South Carolina, and Arizona) had passed anti-miscegenation laws banning racial intermarriage and interracial sexual relations, which spread to a total of nine states by 1884, embodying what Cohen explains is the "very essence of the beliefs southern whites held about race: that whites were racially superior to blacks and that any mixing of the two groups was bound to sully the whites."[113]

Legislative Action Enables Progressive State Citizenship (1867–1874)

Congress invalidated many of the regressive moves on state citizenship once it wrested power back from President Johnson. The Reconstruction Act of 1867 fundamentally altered the development of state citizenship in the South by requiring Confederate states to go back to the drawing board under stricter federal rules for readmission. The Republican Party also took hold of Southern state and local offices during a critical time of their new constitutional and legal developments. The Radical Republican national party led in federal oversight of Reconstruction in the South, and the Republican Party in the South provided Blacks a place to cast their vote and to run for political office, with political participation rights enforced by the US military. In addition to empowering Blacks politically, Congressional Reconstruction banned former Confederate leaders from voting or holding office, placing new constraints on countermovements by White supremacists and the Democratic Party attempting to prevent progress in the South. These factors were the key to propelling the development of progressive state citizenship in the South. However, while constitutional law and federal law enabled progressive state citizenship to emerge, actual changes to Southern laws required Black activism and political power at the state level. Variations in Black political power across Southern states thus generated a new patchwork of state citizenship, with progressive, regressive, and reinforcing elements.

The immediate shift after the Radical Congress took over Reconstruction is illustrated by South Carolina, where Black delegates led in designing a bill of rights for its 1868 state constitution, which stated: "Distinction on account of race or color, in any case whatever, shall be prohibited, and all classes of citizens shall enjoy equally all common, public, legal and political privileges."[114] Following its constitution, a Radical Republican majority took hold of the state legislature of South Carolina for the first time, eager to advance and enforce legal equality. According to the US Census of 1870, Blacks were the majority population in Mississippi, South Carolina, and Louisiana, were more than 40 percent of the population in Alabama, Florida, Georgia, and Virginia, and were roughly 25 percent of the population in Arkansas, North Carolina, Tennessee, and Texas.[115] Black voter turnout during this period was also very high: up to 90 percent when there was an absence of violent campaigns to prevent Black participation in the South.[116]

Republicans carefully navigated around violence from White supremacists to build up a Black membership within the party and to support Blacks in getting elected into new roles as sheriffs, judges, school board members, city council officials, state legislators and governors, and national representatives (Dimension 4). Majority-Black districts provided a new solid base for Republican success, and the party did much to foster its relationship with Black voters. Richard Vallely explains: "Governors Powell Clayton of Arkansas (1868–1871), Robert Scott of South Carolina (1868–1872), Edmund Davis of Texas (1870–1873), Henry Warmoth of Louisiana (1868–1872), and Ossian Hart of Florida (1873–1874) all developed partly effective state policies in response to violence, deploying biracial militias to protect Black voters. Warmoth, in particular, built a vast police and militia establishment consisting of three separate forces."[117] From 1867 to 1877, more than 600 Blacks were elected to state and local offices, and sixteen were elected to the US Congress. Hiram Revels of Mississippi became the first Black senator in 1870, and P. B. S. Pinchback of Louisiana became the first African-American governor in 1872.

Under Republican leadership at the state level, Southern states within a short span of time passed robust laws advancing the rights of Blacks to develop human capital (a core tenet of the Thirteenth Amendment) and equal access to public accommodations. For example, South Carolina in 1868 passed a law prohibiting "licensed businesses" from racially discriminating against Blacks, with violations incurring fines of up to $1,000 or a one-year prison sentence.[118] South Carolina continued to enact a range of labor protections for Black workers on plantations, protecting workers rights against liens (in 1869), limiting liens to one-third of the total crop produced (in 1874), and ending the state's convict leasing system (in 1874). These laws critically improved the economic opportunities of Blacks at a time when White landowners were seeking to entrench systems of debt peonage on plantations.

In addition to these economic protections (Dimension 3), South Carolina and Louisiana also passed state laws prohibiting racial segregation in the South's first public school systems and in public accommodations. Integrating the public schools from 1868 to 1877 succeeded as a result of federal military partnership with states to enforce state law (also Dimension 3). One of the most prominent examples of educational integration under Reconstruction was the admission of Blacks to one of the South's premier institutions, the University of South Carolina in 1873. Mississippi and Florida passed similar state laws prohibiting segregation in public accommodations (but not schools).[119] Newly empowered urban Blacks led protests and sit-ins to push for additional antidiscrimination municipal laws (Dimension 5). Two months after passage of the Reconstruction Act of 1867, Blacks succeeded in repealing New Orleans's military order of 1864, banning discrimination on streetcars, and repealing similar laws in Richmond, Charleston, and other Southern cities (Dimension 1).[120]

Despite making important progress on desegregation, antidiscrimination, and civil rights, South Carolina continued to segregate many state-run institutions, including its penitentiary and insane asylums.[121] However, this was also the norm in many Northern states. The rapid development that emerged in the South toward a progressive state citizenship was certainly shaped by national trends, especially ongoing debates over the Reconstruction Amendments from 1865 to 1870, as well as the capacity and willingness of the Radical Republican Congress to actively support progressive changes at the state level. This allowed Southern progressive state citizenship to often exceed, and outpace, legislative gains at the national level. Indeed, Southern Black officials joined their Northern Republican allies in the US Congress to champion for a federal civil rights bill as early as 1870, but it took more than five years for this effort to succeed as law.

The federal Civil Rights Act of 1875 guaranteed to all persons full and equal access to "inns, public conveyances on land and water, theaters, and other places of public amusement" and prohibited exclusion of Blacks from jury duty.[122] Originally included in the 1870 bill, proposed bans on discrimination in public schools and at cemeteries were removed before the 1875 law was passed. Progressive state laws passed under Republican leadership in the South preceded this federal law, and some exceeded this federal standard by including integrating schools. State laws also faced fewer enforcement barriers than federal law because they were not subject to constitutional scrutiny on the grounds of jurisdiction-based or enforcement-based powers under federalism. As Historian Eric Foner explains, the Civil Rights Act of 1875 was weak because it did not provide for clear federal enforcement mechanisms.[123]

Yet Republican control of Southern legislatures, maintained by support from Black voters, also faced a strong countermovement. Fearing White vigilante violence, Blacks were forced to join secret Union League meetings and develop their own private militias to protect Black communities. In 1870, when an estimated 2,500 armed Whites engaged in violent protests of election results in 1870 in Laurens County, South Carolina, Governor Scott (Republican) responded by establishing a state militia that could protect Blacks and Republicans.[124] The following year, in 1871, the growing Constitutional crisis over Black voting rights caused Governor Scott to appeal to President Grant to intervene. Under powers established by the Enforcement Act of 1871, President Grant declared nine counties (out of thirty-one total) in South Carolina to be in a state of rebellion, allowing him to temporarily suspend the writ of habeas corpus in order to make mass arrests of KKK members without having to seek court warrants. Over 1,000 arrests were made, and President Grant further supported the effort to arrest those who fled South Carolina through extradition.[125] Still, active enforcement by the national government was not enough. As we discuss later in this chapter, progressive state citizenship in the South began to unravel as the Courts began closing Constitutional opportunities for Black citizenship rights starting in 1873 and as Black political power waned with the rise of White supremacists and Democratic Redeemer governments.

Contrasting Progressive State Citizenship in the North and South

Congressional Reconstruction and Republican control over state legislatures had in some ways allowed for progressive state citizenship in the South to outpace the North. Republicans in the North faced electoral challenges, foremost a much larger White majority and a resurgence of the Democratic Party that benefited from White animosity over changes brought on by postbellum race relations. The Republican Party itself was focused on issues of national policy reforms and Southern Reconstruction rather than Northern state-level reforms. This left many Northern states more isolated from the forces essential to forging more inclusive forms of state citizenship. In fact, after 1870, with the passage of the Fifteenth Amendment, many Northern Whites viewed the Black civil rights movement as a national success, creating tensions within the Republican Party over its continued leadership on Reconstruction in the South.

In the year Congress took control over Reconstruction, New York's convention (1867–1868) provided an opportunity to remove the racial barriers to voting put in place originally in 1821, under a Republican majority and governor, Reuben Fenton. Visiting New York in 1867, Sojourner Truth appealed to Republican officials for the establishment of racial equality, highlighting the legacies of the 1821 racial restrictions on voting as one of the key barriers (Dimension 4). Black religious leaders and labor leaders also continued to organize for state expansions on rights in employment, land ownership, and cooperative workshops (Dimension 3).[126]

Yet, this robust Northern civil rights movement was met with strong resistance, with Tammany Hall in Manhattan, New York, in 1868 hosting the Democratic National Convention, where several Southern ex-Confederate delegates participated. A resurgent postbellum White supremacist movement had also been underway in the state, led by Samuel J. Tilden, the state's future governor and leader of the state's Democratic Party, who argued in 1868 that New York's "policy must be *condemnation and reversal of negro supremacy.*"[127] Four days before the 1869 state elections took place, two of the Black ministers leading the civil rights movement were nearly beaten to death by White supremacists on Hudson Street. New Yorkers voted days later to uphold the 1821 property qualifications, denying equal suffrage for the third time.[128] The following year, in 1870, the passage of the Fifteenth Amendment had nationalized voting rights, which New York officials treated as nullifying the state's property qualification. Still, from 1870 to 1874, armed militias on both the federal and state sides were required to oversee the ballot box, until New York in 1874 gave way, amending its state constitution to include equal male suffrage (Dimension 4).[129]

Maryland fits somewhere between the Southern and Northern experiences with progressive state citizenship. As we explain of the antebellum era, Baltimore, Maryland, was home to one of the nation's largest free Black populations, and state laws had provided a range of rights to its original free Black populations. Yet, the state also followed South Carolina and Georgia, among other Southern states, in closing its borders to the in-migration of free Blacks, and it later proposed plans for the removal of all Black residents through colonization schemes. Importantly, unlike the rest of the South, Maryland joined the Union as a loyal border state, making them exempt from President Lincoln's wartime Emancipation Proclamation and the Congressional actions during Reconstruction of military occupation. Indeed, like New York and the rest of the North, Maryland was partly unconstrained by the legislative and executive actions essential to forming progressive state citizenship during the Reconstruction era.

Maryland revised its state constitution in 1864 during the war, providing for the immediate, unconditional abolition of slavery prior to the Thirteenth Amendment. Nevertheless, the state entered the postwar era with its antebellum Black laws in full force. Maryland ended up repealing its Black in-migration ban in 1865 (Dimension 1), but it preserved a criminal code originating under slavery law that allowed for Blacks to be either whipped or imprisoned (Dimension 2). The state also denied due process protections to Blacks, including maintaining imprisonment for Blacks convicted under old slavery laws, and preserving long-standing limits on Black testimony against Whites (Dimension 2). The state also preserved its antebellum apprenticeships, which legally bound Black labor to White employers while remaining within the bounds of the US Constitution's Thirteenth Amendment (Dimension 3). As historian Martha Jones explains, the state's apprenticeship law even empowered the Orphan's Court to deny Blacks from having rights over the custody of their children (Dimension 3).[130] The federal government managed to put some constraints in place; in 1867, the federal circuit court in Baltimore intervened, ruling that Maryland's apprenticeship laws violated the Civil Rights Act of 1866.[131] Yet Maryland and the rest of the North remained mostly unconstrained by Reconstruction compared to their Southern counterparts.

Exclusion of Blacks through segregation began early in Maryland, including laws banning Black admission into its newly created public education system meant for Whites (Dimension 3). Interracial marriage bans were struck down, and marriages of former slaves were recognized under state law, but the state preserved its sodomy laws that criminalized the sexual relations and behaviors of Blacks, as well as preserving its pre–Civil War ban on Blacks serving in the state militia (Dimensions 2, 3, and 5).[132] Responding to their exclusion, Blacks formed their own schools and organizations, and secured arms from the US military to establish their own armories.[133] Importantly, in Baltimore, Blacks successfully petitioned the state legislature to earmark Black tax money to be used exclusively to fund Black schools – and effectively opened up twenty-five all-Black schools by the end of 1866 (Dimension 3).[134]

END OF RECONSTRUCTION AND THE RISE OF JIM CROW (1877–1900)

After the Civil War, the Radical Republican US Congress forged a strong set of Constitutional provisions to prevent restrictive regimes of state citizenship from reemerging. Indeed, abolitionists from the North had instructed Republicans to look to their personal liberty laws of the antebellum period when drafting the Fourteenth Amendment's equal protection and due process clauses.[135] By securing national citizenship for Blacks, the Fourteenth Amendment ended the power of states to legally restrict Blacks from freely migrating across states. Moreover, federal civil rights acts and enforcement acts were passed in 1866, 1867, 1870, 1871, and 1875 to reinforce the Fourteenth Amendment birthright citizenship protections and the Fifteenth Amendment's right to vote.

Nevertheless, Supreme Court rulings following the end of Reconstruction ended up watering down these Constitutional rights. The Court established an interpretation of the Fourteenth Amendment that undermined national citizenship by upholding an older logic of "states' rights." The Court minimized equal protection to mean "separate but equal," weakened the privileges and immunity clauses, and began to strike down major federal civil rights legislation achieved during Reconstruction. The years 1896 and 1898 marked tipping points for states in developing regressive regimes that essentially denied Blacks their nationally provided rights. Meanwhile, White-supremacist Democratic control returned to the South in 1877, without federal oversight, and proceeded to overtake the US Congress in the mid-1890s. The spread of Jim Crow–era voting restrictions in the early 1900s secured the desertion of Black rights by both national political parties.

The historian C. Vann Woodward, in his book *The Strange Career of Jim Crow* (1955), was among the first to challenge the idea that segregation laws were merely throwbacks to antebellum slavery laws.[136] As Woodward and others have explained, White supremacists had to develop new legal strategies to preserve racial hierarchies, and Blacks faced evolving constitutional safeguards and federal, state, and local laws in their fight for equal citizenship.[137] Our state citizenship framework is in line with Woodward's thesis, supporting his argument that Jim Crow was indeed a distinctive development after 1877. While racial segregation had existed in colonial and antebellum America, it took on new meaning against the backdrop of the Fourteenth Amendment. Southern states did not simply maintain the laissez-faire segregation of many Northern states in the antebellum period. Instead, they invested considerable judicial, legislative, executive, and social power to build and maintain systems that actively removed Black rights that were

TABLE 4.3 *Contrasting state citizenship in Reconstruction and Jim Crow, 1867–1954*

Policy type	Citizenship dimensions 1-5*	Reconstruction	Jim Crow
Segregated carriers	1, 3, 5	*Progressive* • 1869–1875 South (civil rights laws guaranteeing equal access)	*Regressive* • 1881–1914 South first, then spread nationwide (railroads, passenger cars, waiting room)
Segregated public accommodations	1, 3, 5	*Progressive* • 1869–1875 South (civil rights laws guaranteeing equal access)	*Regressive* • 1881–1954 South first, then spread nationwide
Vagrancy laws *Criminalized unemployed Blacks and vagrancy*	1, 3	*Regressive* • 1865–1910 South	*Regressive* • 1865–1910 South
Enticement laws *Prohibited Black labor from being competitive or recruited*	1, 3	*Regressive* • 1865–1905 South	*Regressive* • 1865–1905 South
Contract enforcement laws *Bound Black labor by limiting competition in the labor market to the beginning of each contract year*	1, 2, 3	*N/A*	*Regressive* • 1885–1907 South
Emigrant-agent law *Restricted recruitment of Black labor*	3	*N/A*	*Regressive* • 1875–1925 South
Convict-lease system *Forced Black labor*	1, 2, 3	*N/A*	*Regressive* • 1880–1920 in the South

(continued)

TABLE 4.3 (*continued*)

Policy type	Citizenship dimensions 1-5*	Reconstruction	Jim Crow
Lynching	2	*Regressive* • 1865–1877 infrequent in the South	*Regressive* • 1880–1964 Mostly South, but Nationwide
Segregated schools *Separate and Unequal*	3	*Regressive* • 1865–1913 South	*Regressive* • 1865–1913 South, then Nationwide
Workforce protections	3	*Progressive*	*Regressive*
Housing restrictions *Residential segregation ordinances* *Housing covenants*	3	*Progressive*	*Regressive* • 1892–1950s
Interracial sexual relations and marriage *Anti-miscegenation laws* *Sodomy laws*	2, 3, 5	*Regressive* • 1865–1908 South, then Nationwide	*Regressive* • 1865–1908 South, then Nationwide
Right to apportionment	4, 5	*Progressive*	*Regressive* • 1882 Texas law
Right to vote *Poll tax* *Literacy test* *Residency requirement* *Multiple ballot box* *Secret ballot*	4	*Progressive*	*Regressive* • 1885–1907 (poll tax); 1890–1908 (literacy test; residency requirement)
Right to elected office	4	*Progressive*	*Regressive (but legally allowed)*
Right to serve on jury	4	*Progressive*	*Regressive*
Right to organize/ protest	4		*Regressive* • 1950–1964 NAACP banned from Southern states

*The provision of rights to: (1) free movement; (2) due process and legal protection; (3) develop human capital; (4) participate and be represented; and (5) identify and belong.

supposed to be guaranteed nationally. The erosion of Black citizenship rights at the state level was so complete that, even as the federal government rose in prominence during the New Deal era, it allowed states to continue enforcing their regimes of exclusionary citizenship and expanding their policy tools to maintain White supremacy.

The Rise of Redeemer Governments in the South

Faced by a sharp contraction in the national economy in 1874, Northern Whites began to turn away from the Reconstructionist vision of racial equality. White women, in particular, redirected their activism after the passage of the Fifteenth Amendment in 1870 to fight for their own suffrage. In the 1872 presidential election, the liberal wing of the Republican Party nominated its own candidate, Horace Greeley (New York), who ran against the incumbent, President Ulysses Grant (Illinois). Grant won with a strong majority, but the Republican Party split placed new political constrains on President Grant, limiting his ability to strongly enforce military Reconstruction in the South. Republicans succeeded in passing the Civil Rights Act in 1875, barring state segregation of public accommodations, but it was a weak and hollowed-out version of the original 1870 proposed bill. Disagreements over the bill further fractured the Republican Party's Northern and Southern White base, enabling the Democratic Party to pick up ninety-six seats and become the majority in the US House of Representative in 1874 for the first time since the Civil War.[138]

This change in Republican control at the national level, and a decline among the general public for continuing Reconstruction, opened the door for Democratic Redeemer governments to retake the South. Democrats had taken control much earlier in Southern states officially readmitted by President Grant and the Republican Congress, including in Virginia (1869), North Carolina (1870), Georgia (1871), Texas (1873), Alabama (1874), and Arkansas (1874). By 1875, President Grant's position had changed on the issue of enforcing military Reconstruction in the South, allowing Democrats to successfully wage violent campaigns to retake Mississippi and Tennessee in 1875, without federal intervention. Only Florida, Louisiana, and South Carolina remained under Republican control at the state level.

Against this backdrop, the presidential election of 1876 became the most disputed in American history and led to a political compromise to end Reconstruction. Republicans had nominated Rutherford B. Hayes, a moderate from Ohio with deep sympathy for the South. Democratic candidate Samuel J. Tilden (New York) won the popular vote, but no clear winner could be determined because both Democrats and Republicans disputed the electoral results of Florida, Louisiana, and South Carolina. The twenty electoral votes from these three states were required by both candidates to reach the 270 needed to win the election. In January 1877, in an 8–7 vote along party lines, the Electoral Commission's fifteen members declared Hayes the winner, but only after Hayes negotiated with Southern Democrats to form the Compromise of 1877.

Under the 1877 Compromise, President Hayes agreed to remove all remaining federal troops from the South and to provide federal subsidies to help Southern states build levees and railroads. Ending federal Reconstruction meant that the North would no longer interfere in Southern elections to protect Blacks. The Democratic Party quickly cemented "Redeemer" governments throughout the South by violently removing Republican officials from office. Once the "Solid South" emerged, distinctive political constraints were placed on progressive state citizenship: Black Republicans continued to elect candidates to local office, but White Democrats gained controlled over statewide political offices and developed policy regimes that systematically advanced the rights and interests of Whites to the exclusion of Blacks.

Indeed, the US Congress formally recognized Democratic electoral victories over Republicans in contested elections for state government in Louisiana and Florida.[139] Meanwhile, in South Carolina, "rival armed governments faced off against one another."[140] These political changes provided ripe conditions for regressive regimes of state citizenship to proliferate across the South. Over the next two decades, the US Supreme Court took center stage, reversing the federal government's power to enforce the Thirteenth, Fourteenth, and Fifteenth Amendments. A new interpretation of states' rights provided the backbone for regressive state citizenship to emerge and dominate for nearly a century.

Courts Open the Door to Jim Crow (1873–1889)

In 1873, the US Supreme Court made its first official ruling on the Fourteenth Amendment, narrowing rather than expanding its safeguards. The *Slaughter House Cases* (1873) ruled that federal protection of citizens' civil rights did not extend to property rights, which were under the control of states.[141] Other key cases soon followed. In *United States v. Cruikshank* (1876), the US Supreme Court ruled that the federal government did not have jurisdiction to charge private individuals of depriving other US citizens of their constitutional rights under the Enforcement Act of 1870, thereby returning the task of Black protection from White violence to state governments and state courts.[142] The court went further, ruling that the Fourteenth Amendment's due process and equal protection clauses only applied to states, not individuals, and placed exclusive jurisdiction over the First and Second Amendments in state governments.[143] That very same day, the court ruled in *United States v. Reese* (1876) that the Fifteenth Amendment did not establish a right to vote, only a right against racial discrimination, and ruled that sections 3 and 4 of the 1870 Enforcement Act specific to voter protections were unconstitutional.[144]

Court interpretation thus recast the Reconstruction amendments in ways that enabled new forms of regressive state citizenship. By voiding the Enforcement Act of 1870, the key federal mechanism for enforcing the

Fourteenth and Fifteenth Amendments, the Supreme Court enabled Southern states to begin passing restrictions on voting and White vigilante groups to engage in state-sanctioned campaigns to violently disenfranchise Blacks and remove Republican leaders from political office. The Ku Klux Klan, the Knights of the White Camelia, and the White Leagues, groups that had emerged across the South during the Reconstruction era, were no longer constrained by the federal government and federal law.[145] The Supreme Court thus instituted a new framework for federalism that placed most rights under the control of states and that subjected Blacks, who continued to fight for their right to vote and hold political office, to greater physical threats and intimidation from White supremacists. Meanwhile, in the *Civil Rights Cases* (1883), the US Supreme Court struck down critical provisions in the Civil Rights Act of 1875 that prohibited racial discrimination in public accommodations (hotels, restaurants, theatres, and railroads), narrowing the meaning of the Fourteenth Amendment's enforcement clause in Section 5 to the exclusive jurisdiction of states (see Table 4.3).[146] By the late 1880s, the South was well on its way to erecting regimes of regressive state citizenship, with erosion of Black citizenship rights across all dimensions.

The Emergence of Jim Crow

When the US Supreme Court removed the decade-long progress under the Reconstruction Amendments and federal law, it enabled a new era of regressive state citizenship to emerge starting in the late 1870s. By 1896, the landmark decision *Plessy v. Ferguson* had officially established the doctrine of "separate but equal" that legitimized Jim Crow under the guise of the Fourteenth Amendment. Homer Plessy had challenged the constitutionality of Louisiana's 1890 law requiring racially segregated railway cars as a violation of equal protection. By a 7–1 ruling, the US Supreme Court rejected the argument, noting that it was reasonable for state legislatures to "act with reference to the established usages, customs, and traditions of the people, and with a view to the promotion of their comfort and the preservation of the public peace and good order."[147] The Court also ruled that separation does not stamp "the colored race with a badge of inferiority. If this be so, it is not by reason of anything found in the act, but solely because the colored race chooses to put that construction upon it."[148]

In providing this race-neutral rationale for segregation, the Court also provided a key opening for the Southern regime of Jim Crow to quickly spread to the North and to the federal government. The race-neutral language helped to align Southern Jim Crow with the national political agendas of Progressive-era reformers. As John David Smith explains, the Jim Crow regime outside of the South was partly built on the logic that racial separation would "maintain law, order and stability" and "cleanse the political system by eliminating them as a source of corruption among Democrats, Republicans, and

Populists."[149] Most of the "work" of Jim Crow, however, occurred in the South. As Whites began to reestablish control over Southern legislatures, they began to pass restrictions on Black labor, education, marriage, and transportation, even during the height of military Reconstruction (Dimensions 1 and 3). By the early 1870s, Southern states also began to enact a range of voter restrictions, beginning with Georgia's poll tax in 1871 (Dimension 5). Not long after, Redeemer governments gained full control over the South and quickly enacted regressive state constitutions and laws in the 1880s and 1890s. These developments provided test cases used by the US Supreme Court to formalize Jim Crow as a new constitutional order: "separate but equal."

The effects of Jim Crow were not confined to the South. As we will show, Southern Democrats also gained critical leverage over the presidency and the US Congress during moments of federal expansion in social welfare, jobs, and housing. These moments included World War I, the Great Depression, and World War II. The federal government thus shifted from simply accommodating Southern states to giving them a central role in restricting Black citizenship rights – inserting race-based exclusions into New Deal policies, modelling federal agencies and law on Jim Crow segregation, and creating federal–state partnerships that placed states (not the federal government) in charge of federal programs.

Lynching and Other Violations of Due Process and Legal Protection

As Southern Democratic governments regained power in the late 1870s, regressive state citizenship solidified, in part, from the legal sanctioning of White violence against Black citizens. Military Reconstruction merely held White Supremacy at bay and often failed. Whites in Louisiana, for example, had led in routine vigilante killings of Blacks, illustrated by the dramatic episode of Whites leading a "n***er hunt" [our edits] in 1868 of 120 Blacks.[150] Changing Constitutional interpretation under *United States v. Cruikshank* (1876) and the withdraw of the federal government from the South in 1877 placed White Southern officials in full control of the criminal justice system. It also made the sanctioning of vigilante violence the primary tool of White supremacy in the South: Southern Blacks were effectively denied from having any meaningful Constitutional rights under the Fourteenth Amendment because the federal government could not act against private individuals or interfere in state criminal proceedings.

Southern lynching played a critical role in shaping the early transition to regressive state citizenship and changes in black activism. Lacking federal rights and protection enabled lynching to become the means by which Southern states denied Blacks the right to free movement (Dimension 1 of our framework), the right to legal protection and due process (Dimension 2), and the right to identify and belong (Dimension 5). Lynching grew into a commercialized and advertised form of popular White entertainment in the South, meant to establish a culture of White supremacy: Black body parts were sold as souvenirs, children were released early from school to attend, and Whites considered their participation as a sign of Southern status. Richard Vallely, for example, describes the North as having "its boardwalks" and the South as having "its lynchings."[151] Indeed, from 1880 to 1920, over 700 Blacks on average were lynched each decade, with a peak occurring between 1890 and 1900 of over 1,000 Blacks lynched – mostly in the South.[152] As an extension of regressive state citizenship, lynching emerged from Southern states' extralegal sanctioning of "private" violence, enabled by the US Supreme Court's "states' rights" interpretation of the Fourteenth Amendment.

Importantly, regressive elements from the South spread, with lynching showcasing the horrors of Jim Crow in the North as well. Progressive elements of the North, however, provided necessary political foundations for reform movements to emerge and push back. In the 1890s, Ida B. Wells's activism through the media sought to reveal the horrors of lynching and its racial logic.[153] Nearly two decades later, a biracial coalition formed the National Association for the Advancement of Colored People (NAACP) in the North in response to a 1908 incident of mob violence in Springfield, Illinois – in which more than 2,000 Blacks were forced to flee the city and two were lynched – which grew into the nation's predominant civil rights organization.[154] As Megan Francis Ming explains, the newly formed NAACP pursued a three-pronged strategy of educating the national public, lobbying for federal legislation, and seeking new constitutional constraints through court litigation. After laying the groundwork of a decade-long education campaign, the NAACP shifted strategy to lobbying the US Congress and the presidency to sponsor the first federal anti-lynching bill in 1921. The NAACP developed into a strong lobbying organization able to pressure lawmakers to support the bill, which included a bipartisan coalition of Republicans and Northern Democrats in Congress and early presidential support from Democrats like Woodrow Wilson. Yet, from 1882 to 1951, a total of 248 federal anti-lynching bills were introduced to the US Congress without success. Southern Democratic opposition and their heightened power to filibuster in the Senate remained a steadfast barrier.[155]

Regressive state citizenship gained a stronger national foothold once Southern lynching was tied to Northern race riots and reframed as an issue of "law and order." Southern and Northern officials together preserved states' control over criminal justice, allowing them to pursue different paths for excluding Blacks from having basic rights to legal protection and due process. When the NAACP had amassed strong support to ban lynching in the 1930s, Thomas Connally of Texas led Southern senators to formalize their opposition strategy, viewing a federal anti-lynching law as the gateway to broad civil rights legislation that would end Jim Crow. In Senate debates and speeches, lynching was strategically disconnected from White supremacy and connected to race riots occurring in the North as a larger national crisis. Connally argued in 1937 that no Southern state had a law that sanctioned lynching, thereby giving the appearance of separation between the state and acts by private individuals or mobs. With Northern Republicans convinced, Southern senators were able to strike at the heart of the NAACP's argument that the Fourteenth Amendment's equal protection clause provided constitutional grounds for federal jurisdiction on Southern lynching.[156] Moreover, the general decrease in lynching by the 1930s and fallacious Southern state laws on anti-lynching (that were never enforced) created an appearance of progress that further legitimized Southern and Northern opposition to federal legislation.

Presidential leadership also failed. In 1934 and 1935, White vigilantes in Florida and Mississippi transported their Black victims across state borders before lynching them, violating the Lindbergh Kidnapping Act of 1932. Yet, when the federal government could intervene by enforcing existing federal laws over criminal acts that crossed interstate borders, it chose not to. President Roosevelt showed some interest in 1942 during World War II, ordering the Justice Department to automatically explore, where federal jurisdiction existed, any new lynching cases, but this failed to produce any change in state control over the cases. President Truman similarly responded to race riots and violence by ordering the FBI to investigate lynching cases, but he was met with resistance by Director J. Edgar Hoover, who insisted that "a considerable amount of manpower investigating murders, lynchings and assaults, particularly in the Southern states, in which there cannot conceivably be any violation of a federal statute" was a waste.[157] Federal judges, legislators, and bureaucrats were unwilling to challenge the perceived sovereignty of Southern states over their domestic affairs.

States' rights persevered, but regressive state citizenship in the South was forced to provide the appearance of racial progress in order to preserve Jim Crow. International and national pressure after World War II increased the publicization of lynching and vigilante violence. Woodward explains: "The Nazi crime against the minority race, more than anything else, was the offense against the Western moral code that branded the Reich as an outlaw power. Adolf Hitler's doctrine of the 'master race' had as its chief victim the Jew, but the association of that doctrine with the creed of White supremacy was inevitably made in the American mind."[158] White supremacist Strom Thurmond, governor of South Carolina, proclaimed in 1947 that Black lynchings were "flagrant violations of every concept of law and order."[159] This shift safeguarded regressive state citizenship from federal legislation and provided an important rhetorical weapon used by Southern leaders to retain control over criminal law and proceedings. As long as the state appeared legitimate, which meant not expressly sanctioning lynching or violence, it was constitutionally safeguarded from federal interference. The Fourteenth Amendment's equal protection clause, at this time, only empowered the federal government if states themselves were the aggressors.

In the midst of leading its national fight for anti-lynching legislation, the NAACP was also making headway on due process rights through the courts. In 1919, a case known as the Phillips County 12 opened the door to NAACP litigation. Black tenant farmers in rural Arkansas had gathered in a Black church to discuss how to pressure White landowners to pay them market price for their cotton. White law enforcement officials put a violent end to the meeting and were soon joined by a multistate White mob of vigilante groups in Arkansas and neighboring states, who led in killing over 200 Black men, women, and children and in driving thousands of Blacks out of Phillips County, Arkansas. Seventy-two Black men were arrested, and twelve were sentenced to death. As Meghan Ming Francis explains: "Each member of the Phillips County 12 received a trial that was no longer than an hour. In the courtroom was a bloodthirsty mob that had agreed to let the legal proceedings take place only after the courts had promised that the accused would be found guilty and executed."[160]

Taking on litigation for the first time, the NAACP defended the Phillips County 12's due process right to a fair trial, eventually leading to the US Supreme Court decision in *Moore v. Dempsey* (1923), which ruled that a fair trial must be free from mob domination and that the federal government could interfere in state criminal court proceedings to ensure due process under the Fourteenth Amendment.[161] This legal victory, as Megan Ming Francis notes, provided a critical juncture for the development of the NAACP's legal strategy. Subsequent victories won by the NAACP would expand due process rights for Blacks through the US Supreme Court, with *Powell v. Alabama* (1932) ruling that, under the Fourteenth Amendment's due process clause, defendants in capital cases have a right to state-appointed counsel; *Hollins v. Oklahoma* (1935) ruling that race-based exclusions for state jury selection was unconstitutional; and *Brown v. Mississippi* (1936) ruling that confessions gained through torture were unconstitutional.[162] Thurgood Marshall began work for the NAACP leading the case of *Chambers v. Florida* (1940), where the US Supreme Court ruled that any confessions that police officers obtain under duress were considered to be illegal.[163] That same year, Marshall founded the NAACP's Legal Defense and Educational Fund and began his career as their chief counsel; he led civil rights victories for the next two decades, culminating with *Brown v. Board of Education of Topeka* (1954).[164]

Despite this progress in constitutional interpretation, regressive state citizenship in the South and elsewhere in the country remained fully intact. Blacks remained completely vulnerable to the horror of Southern White violence, only able to seek federal court intervention after their due process rights were denied by lower courts. The NAACP's inability to influence federal legislation illustrates how intractable national politics were for challenging the entrenchment of Jim Crow laws and "states' rights." The rise of mass protests during the 1950s and the 1960s returned the South to brutal episodes of state violence and de facto sanctioning of White vigilante violence. The NAACP was legally banned from organizing in many Southern states, and desegregation under *Brown* (1954) was met with violent resistance. Indeed, regressive state citizenship was still deeply anchored by court precedent on how federalism shaped civil rights, and private violence remained under the jurisdiction of states.

Restrictions on Free Movement

Like with the anti-lynching campaign of the NAACP, Jim Crow segregation went largely unscathed from federal legislative action and was placed under minimal constitutional scrutiny by the court. Between 1900 and 1906, Blacks led in an estimated twenty-five boycotts of Jim Crow streetcars, with a focus on causing economic disruption to pressure for ending local segregation policy.[165] W. E. B. du Bois launched the Niagara Movement in 1905 attacking separate Jim Crow cars because they charged Blacks the same price as Whites. These early efforts were unsuccessful but provided a critical model for the tactics employed in the 1950s and the 1960s by coalitions between churches and organizations like the NAACP, the Congress on Racial Equality (CORE), and the Student Nonviolent Coordinating Committee (SNCC). In the South, where the majority of the US Black population resided, disenfranchised and confined to harsh Jim Crow segregation, churches (especially those located in urban areas) provided civil rights organizations with access to an already organized Black base, respected Black leadership, and physical infrastructure for activism.[166]

Federal power over interstate commerce made the fight to desegregate interstate public carriers (trains and buses) relatively easy. The NAACP's legal strategy, developed from its anti-lynching campaign, provided a clear pathway through the courts to challenge state segregation laws and private company policies. The first challenge to Jim Crow was achieved in *Morgan v. Virginia* (1946), where the US Supreme court ruled that state segregation policies on interstate carriers infringed on the federal government's exclusive power of interstate commerce.[167] Virginia Governor William M. Tuck responded to the ruling in his inaugural address to the state in January, 1946, stating: "If this policy of expansion of Federal activities into state fields continues it will result in the virtual abolition of the states." The following year, in 1947, the Congress of Racial Equality (CORE) and the Fellowship of Reconciliation (FOR) joined together to lead the "Journey of Reconciliation," to test whether states or private companies upheld the *Morgan* ruling. Leaving from Washington, DC, White and Black activists travelled together on a Greyhound bus and Trailways bus through four states of the Upper South, including Virginia, with no real incidences. The Freedom Rides of the 1960s built on these earlier "Journey of Reconciliation" interstate rides to protest segregation on all public carriers, under Dr King's nonviolent model.

In 1950, the US Supreme Court, in *Henderson v. United States*, outlawed segregation in the dining cars of interstate railroads.[168] Then, in 1955, just after *Brown v. Board of Education*, two rulings by the Interstate Commerce Commission effectively integrated all interstate buses and trains.[169] In *Boynton v. Virginia* (1960), the US Supreme Court ruled that segregated services, such as shelters and restaurants, intended for the use of interstate bus passengers were also unconstitutional.[170] Segregation of public carriers that did not cross state lines were insulated under the *Plessy* "separate but equal" doctrine and states' rights, requiring strong grassroots mobilizing to pressure state and local government to reform their segregation policies. While the NAACP remained a vital lifeline, Black activists developed robust mass mobilizations from the bottom up that were highly local in nature. Disruption through economic boycotts and direct-action demonstrations were a key grassroots tactics employed by civil rights organizations. The yearlong bus boycott in Montgomery, Alabama, provided the needed watershed in 1955 for the civil rights movement.

The Montgomery boycott built from a year of planning by the Women's Political Council (WPC), formed in 1949, who met with the city commission in 1954 to express their grievance with the city's segregation ordinance. Blacks were forced to stand over empty White-only seats, enter at the rear of the bus, and walk long distances to bus stops placed by the city far from Black neighborhoods. Local Black community leaders provided the primary organization to the mass boycott, partnering with the WPC and churches. They chose not to wait for the NAACP headquarters in New York to provide local support to the movement.[171] On December 1, 1955, Rosa Parks refused to give up her seat to a White man, which was a crime under the city's segregation law. Parks had served as a secretary for the NAACP, was experienced in Black protest, and was deeply tied to the Black church. Once the boycott began, the national collaboration between the NAACP and Black churches provided significant financial support, creating an important regional link between the South and the North that remained throughout the civil rights movement. White labor and peace organizations throughout the North also provided support, including the United Automobile Workers Union in Detroit and the War Resisters League.[172]

Even as Montgomery police made it illegal for taxi drivers to provide cheap rides in support of the boycott, movement leaders innovated and adapted. Joining the movement, Reverend Martin Luther King Jr. helped to set up a private carpool system for the entire Black community and connected the boycott with the Black church's ideological foundations of nonviolent protest. Through this combination, Montgomery created tremendous local pressure for change and paired it with the nationwide support needed for the court to intervene. On November 13, 1956, the US Supreme Court in *Browder v. Gayle* struck down Alabama's state and local segregation laws on busing under the Fourteenth Amendment's equal protection clause.[173]

The civil rights movement entered a new era in the mid-1950s. After the NAACP's victory in *Brown* (1954), which ruled to desegregate all public schools, pro-segregationists enacted state and local laws banning the organization and used the apparatus of state and local enforcement to crack down on its activities. Importantly, this sparked the emergence of new organizations in the South that provided local support for direct action movements. For example, concurrent with the Montgomery victory, Black activists in Tallahassee and other cities created new local organizations to lead their own boycotts of buses. Reverend Steele, president of the NAACP local in Tallahassee, explained that fear of the NAACP being outlawed under state or local law led them to create the Inter Civic Council (ICC) in 1955. Importantly, ICC served as an organizational nexus linking local bus boycotts to national organizations.[174] Indeed, the NAACP remained critical national allies to local movement, providing much-needed funding support and public education support that allowed for such movements to gain national and international attention. The most important role the NAACP played was leading in litigation against state and local laws after the US Supreme Court struck them down.

Similarly, after Alabama banned the NAACP in 1956, Reverend Shuttleworth organized the Alabama Christian Movement for Human Rights (ACMHR), built from and funded by church leadership and the Black base of Birmingham. The ACMHR led the charge in confronting the White power structure in Birmingham to change state and local policies in compliance with changes under the US Supreme Court. The ACMHR organized bus-riding by Blacks to defy local de facto segregation and then filed federal lawsuits after Blacks were illegally arrested. It similarly protested segregation at the railroad station and enrolled Black children in White schools to confront the problem of state and local noncompliance with the *Brown* decision. In 1956, Shuttleworth pressured the Birmingham Personnel Board to end its White-only policy to allow Blacks to take the civil service exam and become police officers in Black communities. This ushered in a decade-long fight over hiring Black officers between Shuttleworth and the commissioner on Public Safety, Eugene "Bull" Connor, who worked closely with the White Citizens' Council and the KKK to police Black residents.[175]

Even as the civil rights movement built more capacity by developing into a complex network of national, regional and local organizations, Congressional legislation and federal enforcement were noticeably absent. This gap enabled regressive state citizenship in the South to continue apace. President Eisenhower avoided intervening to desegregate buses and schools, arguing that these Southern problems had to be solved locally.[176] In response, the civil rights movement continued to grow connections nationally and regionally. In 1957, Black leaders across the South (along with allies in New York) created the Southern Christian Leadership Conference (SCLC) to connect the civil rights movements of the sixteen Southern states, with Dr King as the president.[177] Headquartered in Atlanta, the SCLC had a robust affiliate structure partnering with existing Black organizations like the ICC and the ACMHR, as well as deep roots in the Black church and leadership, all of which combined to make it a highly effective social movement organization.

Restrictions on Participation and Representation

One-party rule, and the "Solid South," did not emerge immediately following Reconstruction's end. Blacks continued to vote and hold office. After Reconstruction had ended and troops were removed, Black state officials continued to serve in Virginia (until 1891), North Carolina (until 1894), and South Carolina (until 1902). At the time when Louisiana passed its segregation law for railways in 1890, which led to *Plessy v. Ferguson*, the state had sixteen Black officials serving as its General Assembly.[178] Moreover, the Democratic Party itself faced formidable opposition from a growing populist movement and from fusionist governments. North Carolina's Fusion Party from 1894 to 1900, composed of a coalition of Black Republican and Populist Party members, were still able to win state elections. Mississippi's Republican Party, in 1889, had nominated a "complete state ticket for the first time since 1875," providing new competition with Democrats running for office that year.[179] Indeed, as we explained in Chapter 3, Constitutional constraints posed by the Fifteenth Amendment, the Fourteenth Amendment, and federal elections laws posed a critical barrier to Democratic Redeemer governments that were in power.

White supremacists and Democrats began to roll out voter restrictions across Southern states, beginning with Georgia's poll tax law (1868, 1871, and 1877), Texas's registration law (1874) and secret ballot (1879), and South Carolina's multiple box law (1882). As a result of the Supreme Court's changing Constitutional interpretation, every Southern state by 1903 had enacted some form of restriction, avoiding constitutional scrutiny by not explicitly denying the right to vote on the basis of race or class. In 1885, Florida held a convention to reform its "Carpetbag" constitution from 1868, by granting power to the state legislature to pass a law requiring a poll tax for voting and to redraw districts, while also mandating racial segregation of public schools and prohibiting interracial marriage. Soon after, state legislators passed the poll tax law in 1889, just prior to elections that year, effectively preventing majority-Black districts in Florida's rural Black-belt areas from being able to afford to vote. That same year, under the state's new constitution, the legislature was reapportioned to weaken Republican opposition, and registering to vote in person was added as a requirement to further deny Blacks their right to vote.[180]

In Mississippi, once the Republican Party began to push for the federal Lodge Election Bill in 1889, seeking to establish federal oversight over elections to ensure the protection of Black voting rights and party competition, US Senator James Z. George of Mississippi began to campaign for a state constitutional convention.[181] The possibility of federal intervention threatened de facto voting restrictions through ballot-box stuffing and voter intimidation, regular practices in Mississippi and across the South at the time. George thus raised alarms that, in order to ensure Democratic dominance in the US House and Senate, Mississippi needed to follow Florida's lead and quickly reform its constitution.

Yet, tensions emerged because the same legal mechanism that would prevent Blacks from voting also applied to poor, illiterate Whites. The segregationists found a workaround. They reapportioned Mississippi's districts so that Black belt countries, controlled by White plantation owners, made up the majority for Senate votes. Meanwhile, they safeguarded White voting rights by providing voter registrars, all of whom were Democrats and White, with authority to register any illiterate person as long as they understood the constitution. The convention added a one-year residency requirement and a $2 annual poll tax, and it authorized local governments to pass their own voter restrictions in the future.[182] This accelerated the demise of the Republican and Populist parties and the rise of one-party Democratic rule in 1892.

A vital constitutional safeguard to Black voting was the Fourteenth Amendment's Section 2, which reduces congressional representation for states that deny suffrage on racial grounds. However, this protection was never included in federal legislation or enforced. Meanwhile, the Fifteenth Amendment (1870) granted Congress the power to pass legislation to establish federal enforcement mechanisms. Using that power in 1871, the Radical Republican Congress established "voting supervisors" under the Enforcement Act of 1871, granting federal courts in the South the power to appoint local elections supervisors and to call on federal marshals to criminally prosecute interference in elections.[183] In a last-ditch effort, in 1890, Republican Congressmen, with the support of President Benjamin Harris, proposed the Federal Elections Bill in the House and the Senate that built upon the Enforcement Act's voting rights provision from the Reconstruction era. If passed, the bill would have provided teeth to the Fifteenth Amendment by authorizing federal circuit courts to appoint federal supervisors on congressional elections to oversee the entire voting process, including registration with the power to administer oaths to new voters. It would have also given federal officials the power to overturn election results declared and certified by state officials. Yet, while Southern Democrats in the Senate played an important role in defeating the bill, it was division within the Republican Party that led to its death.

Fractures began to occur within the Republican Party over continuing to support Black equal rights as early as the mid-1870s. Pennsylvania Senators Matthew S. Quay and J. Donald Cameron sought to direct the party toward economic policies and tariffs that made the Republican Party more appealing to White voters nationally, resulting in Republican-led delays in voting on the Elections Bill in 1890.[184] Once Senate Republicans brought the bill up for a vote in 1891, Southern Democrats filibustered and Republicans acquiesced. Gaining control of the presidency in 1892 and both Houses of Congress, Democrats repealed the voting rights portions of the Enforcement Acts in 1894 and eliminated most remaining civil rights measures not already undermined by the Court.[185] Federal inaction in 1891 provided momentum to Southern states, who were carefully tracking how federal legislation might impact the future of voting rights in the South.

Mississippi's 1890 constitution was reaffirmed by federal inaction on the Elections Bill that year and, later, by federal repeal of the Enforcement Acts. Other states took notice. Between 1890 and 1910, ten of the eleven former Confederate states followed Mississippi's model of passing new constitutions or amendments that effectively disfranchised most Blacks and tens of thousands of poor Whites through a combination of poll taxes, literacy and comprehension tests, and residency and record-keeping requirements. Grandfather clauses permitted illiterate Whites to vote, while local Democratic control ensured that state and local laws were enforced to deny Blacks the right to vote. Other rights were attached to voting rights, making those who could not vote ineligible to serve on juries or to run for office. These federalism dynamics enabling state regressive policies help to explain the timing of policy learning and diffusion by the late 1890s and early 1900s.[186] The US Supreme Court's unanimous ruling in *Williams v. Mississippi* (1898) upholding the literacy test and poll tax voting restrictions of Mississippi's 1890 constitution signaled the final Southern victory for states' rights and twentieth-century Jim Crow. States' laws, the court ruled, did not violate the Fifteenth Amendment because they were not explicitly discriminating based on race.

Black Resistance to Regressive Voting and Representation in Georgia

Georgia's place in Southern history is central, and helps illustrate how Black activism and political leadership fought the rise of regressive state citizenship. Home to Atlanta University, where W. E. B. du Bois was a professor in history and economics from 1897 to 1910, Georgia grew into a hub for Black intellectual leadership. Under his lead, the Atlanta Conference of Negro Problems was held each year, bringing together Black leaders and activists. For example, in 1898, Du Bois published a report on the current state of black activism, highlighting the organizing capacity of 236 distinctive churches, secret societies, and beneficial societies across major cities of the South.[187] Building on this work, Du Bois launched the Niagara Movement in 1905, with a focus on challenging Booker T. Washington's accommodationist approach to Black social progress. Finally, in 1910, Du Bois joined the newly formed NAACP, launching himself as one of the nation's most important civil rights activist. Thus, in many ways, Georgia was the epicenter of Black-led resistance to regressive state citizenship.

Similar to many other Southern states, Georgia went from enacting regressive state citizenship to progressive (under Reconstruction) to regressive once again after the end of Reconstruction. Georgia revised its state constitution in 1868, establishing the first Southern poll tax, which required "each male adult to pay $1 poll tax each year or lose the right to vote."[188] Republicans' takeover of Reconstruction ensured that state officials in Georgia suspended this poll tax requirement in 1868, up until Democrats regained power over the state legislature in 1871. As Morgan Kousser explains, this poll tax requirement allowed for others, including political parties, to pay the tax for large numbers of Black voters – making it a weak mechanism for excluding Blacks from the right to political participation (Dimension 5).[189]

Meanwhile, a decade of progress empowered Black activism. John H. Deveaux founded the *Colored Tribune* in 1875 (renamed *Savannah Tribune* in 1876), with the purpose of defending "the rights of the colored people, and their elevation to the highest plane of citizenship," through providing newspaper coverage of Jim Crow injustices to Georgia and Florida.[190] Black political leaders were also beginning to take on more active leadership within states' Republican parties. After running for the US House of Representatives on the Republican ticket, William A. Pledger started the movement within his home state of Georgia to push for including more Black leadership and patronage in the state's Republican Party.[191]

Signs that regressive state citizenship would return were apparent throughout the South, but Georgia's Black activists were able to delay this inevitability. Georgia's transition to a Redeemer Democratic state legislature occurred in 1875, and ex-Confederate leaders, like Robert Augustus Toombs, pushed for a constitutional convention in 1877 that enshrined a harsher, cumulative poll tax (Dimension 5). As Kousser explains, this regressive constitutional provision caused a steady decline in Georgia's Black voting that spanned over two decades.[192] Georgia's new constitution also coincided with the end of Reconstruction and the Republican Party's abandonment of Black citizenship rights. These federalism dynamics placed significant constraints on Black leaders like Pledger seeking to strengthen their role in the state's Republican Party. Indeed, Georgia's GOP fractured into separate White and Black caucuses in 1882 and the national Republican Party formally disassociated itself from Georgia's Black GOP leadership.[193]

Still, Atlanta's growing Black activism provided a strong resistance to the state politics of Georgia under solid Democratic control, even after the 1877 constitution and abandonment by both national and state Republicans. When State Representative Thomas W. Hardwick proposed a literacy test bill with a grandfather clause for Whites, it failed to pass the House in 1899 and again in 1901 due to a combination of Black protests, White labor opposition, and lack of a united Democratic support for another voter restriction. From 1907 through 1908, Black activists led massive voter registration campaigns in the face of the state's poll tax, Democratic control of the election process, and vigilante Whites burning their churches and lynching their loved ones, but it failed to challenge the passage of the literacy test. Eventually, and only after decades of Black resistance, Georgia followed other Southern states by amending its constitution to add a literacy test in 1908.[194] Following the spread of constitutional and legal restrictions on Black voting rights, all Southern Democrats had adopted the White-only primary by 1915, entrenching regressive state citizenship under a regional blanket referred to as the Solid South.[195]

Black voters in the South were disenfranchised until 1965 for several reasons. Activism for Black voting rights at the national level had significantly weakened after the passage of the Fifteenth Amendment, and by the late 1800s the Republican Party had begun to entirely abandon Black voters. The women's suffrage movement moved away from its supportive role for Black civil rights, leading a long movement of its own from 1875 through 1920, when it finally succeeded with a "Winning Plan" to build enough support in thirty-six states to ratify the Nineteenth Amendment. Notably, this constitutional amendment came after years of battling for national legislation, state legislation, and court intervention.[196]

Furthermore, single-party rule in the South had entirely disconnected the Republican Party from the electoral incentives motivating them to advocate for Black rights.[197] This factor, in addition to broader changes across the country fueled by industrialization and immigration, prompted the Republican Party not only to move away from supporting federal voting rights laws but also to join Southern Democrats by enacting their own restrictive voting laws in the industrial North, excluding immigrants and working-class Whites.[198] Race mattered, however. Whereas illiterate immigrants in Northern states could effectively gain the franchise through education, Southern Blacks were systematically excluded from politics and placed into a subjugated caste as an inferior race.[199]

Limited Progress on Voting Rights

The Jim Crow era did provide some openings. Oklahoma's admission to the United States in 1907 enabled the NAACP to challenge some of the legal voting restrictions established across the South. Oklahoma's legislature in 1910 amended its constitution to include a "good understanding clause" and a grandfather clause in order to exempt Whites from its literacy-test restriction on voting. The amendment stated that "[n]o person shall be registered ... or be allowed to vote ... unless he be able to read and write any section of the Constitution of the state of Oklahoma; but no person who was, on January 1, 1866, or any time prior thereto, entitled to vote under any form of government ... and no lineal descendant of such person, shall be denied the right to register and vote because of his inability to so read and write sections of such Constitution."[200] In *Guinn v. United States* (1915), the US Supreme Court ruled that the "old soldier" and "grandfather" exemptions from literacy tests were unconstitutional under the Fifteenth Amendment.[201] These sections of Oklahoma and Maryland's state constitutions – and state laws in Alabama,

Georgia, Louisiana, North Carolina, and Virginia – were all struck down under *Guinn*.

However, the ruling was too little, too late. All tangible barriers to voting were already in place by 1915, and one-party rule, protected by the all-White primary, was fully entrenched in the South. Just prior to the ruling in *Quinn*, Oklahoma passed a state law "automatically registering everyone qualified to vote in 1914, when the grandfather clause was in effect," thereby sidestepping the court's ruling by dramatically increasing White voter registration while making Black voter registration nearly impossible through other state laws.[202] Indeed, when Alabama passed its new constitution in 1901, it replaced the reference to suffrage as a "right," calling voting a "privilege" – a clear rhetorical rebuke of the Fifteenth Amendment.[203]

Meanwhile, the US Supreme Court left intact state poll taxes, state registration laws, state-appointed Democratic oversight of all Southern elections, among other Jim Crow–era legal mechanisms intended (but not expressly written) to target Blacks while exempting similarly situated Whites. The US Supreme Court unanimously upheld Georgia's poll tax in *Breedlove v. Suttles* (1937), explaining that it did not violate the Fourteenth Amendment's equal protection or privileges and immunities clauses, nor did it violate the Nineteenth Amendment.[204] In a rare showing, Black activists found an ally in Georgia's liberal Democratic Governor Ellis Gibbs Arnall, who passed a new state constitution in 1945 that abolished the poll tax, making Georgia the second Southern state following Florida's lead in 1937. Arnall also was one of the only Southern governors to adhere to the US Supreme Court's *Smith v. Alright* (1944), which struck down the all-White primary as violating the Fourteenth Amendment's equal protection clause.[205] This Georgian alliance for civil rights proved to be short-lived, however, as White supremacist leaders resumed control.

Court interpretation eventually prevented state laws and party rules from explicitly banning Blacks from the right to vote under the Fourteenth Amendment's equal protection, though not the Fifteenth Amendment. Even with these court rulings, White state and party leaders found ways to circumvent them and protect their regimes of regressive state citizenship. In *Nixon v. Herndon* (1927), the US Supreme Court ruled against Texas's White-only primary as a violation of the Fourteenth Amendment's equal protection clause, because state law barred voting on the basis of race.[206] In response, Texas quickly amended its law so that the Democratic Party was able to preserve the race-based primary system: it made the party, not the state itself, responsible for setting voting qualifications. Followed this move by Texas, the US Supreme Court upheld the party's rule for an all-White primary in *Grovey v. Townsend* (1935), ruling that the Fourteenth Amendment did not apply to discrimination by private organizations such as political parties.[207] Importantly, while *Smith v. Allright* (1944) ended the all-White primary and *Guinn* (1915) ended the grandfather clause, regressive state citizenship stood strong. Success through activism at the state level was exclusive to Florida's repeal of the poll tax in 1937 and Georgia's in 1945. At no time before 1965 was Jim Crow or states' rights seriously threatened on the issue of voting rights.

Southern Democrats were able to effectively block any consideration for federal reforms, until World War II politicized the rights of Black soldiers. This was perhaps best exemplified by Senator Thomas Connally of Texas. After leading Southern senators' opposition strategy to anti-lynching legislation, Connolly devised a new wartime strategy of legislative delay in the Senate to prevent the federal anti-poll tax law from passing. Critical to this success, he convinced his Southern Democratic colleagues not to filibuster the Soldier Voting Act of 1942, which eliminated the poll tax for only military personnel – a policy that had gained nationwide, bipartisan support. This move was strategic on Connolly's part: he avoided being seen as unpatriotic and created goodwill among his Northern Republicans that proved critical to defeating attempts to abolish poll taxes entirely.[208]

Indeed, Connolly led in two successful Senate filibusters blocking bills that would ban the poll tax nationwide. He argued that Article I, Section 2, of the US Constitution granted states the power to determine voter qualifications in both federal and state elections. Meanwhile, his close colleague, Theodore Bilbo of Mississippi, sowed doubt among Northern Republicans, arguing that poor Whites of the North had even more to benefit from the poll tax being abolished.[209] Additionally, the Senators argued that a federal voting law violated the Tenth Amendment which protected states and localities from such federal overreach. These arguments gained enough sympathy from Northern Republicans to prevent the votes required for Senate cloture, and the bills proposed in 1942 and 1944 both died. Still, even if the poll tax had been abolished nationwide, Southern states would still have maintained their regimes of regressive state citizenship. It would take a comprehensive effort to advance Black citizenship rights to ensure the critically important dimension of Black voting rights.

Restrictions on Human Capital Formation

Many features of Southern political development were uniquely draconian, but regressive Black state citizenship was also prevalent in the North, particularly in response to the Great Migration. In 1914, Northern industries experienced a wartime boom in manufacturing that coincided with a national reduction in White immigrants from Southeastern Europe due to nativist immigration laws. This produced a need for new Black labor in the North. Meanwhile, in the South, plantations were facing a crisis from the spread of the Mexican boll weevil that destroyed cotton products from Louisiana in 1906 to Mississippi in 1913 and Alabama in 1916. Natural disasters also simultaneously prompted the South to move away from producing cotton to less labor-intensive uses of land such as growing food crops and livestock. These pull-and-push factors prompted the mass migration of Blacks to Chicago, Detroit, Cleveland, Philadelphia, and New York, including an estimated 525,000 between 1910 and 1920 and nearly double this number in the 1920s.[210] Black migrants from the South joined a prior wave of Black laborers in Northern cities, many of whom had been recruited and transported from the South to serve as strikebreakers during labor disputes in New York (in 1895), Cleveland (in 1896), Detroit (in 1919), Milwaukee (in 1922), and Chicago (in 1904 and 1905).[211]

Northern states and cities soon began forging a Jim Crow of their own. This was enabled by similar exclusionary national developments and by a new "scientific" justification of Black inferiority spreading across the country that legitimized Jim Crow.[212] Thus, across the North, middle-class Whites began to view migrating Southern Blacks as having "uncouth manners, unclean habits, slothful appearance, and illicit behavior of poorly educated, poverty-stricken migrants who had only recently been sharecroppers," and working-class Whites feared the economic competition from their new Black residents. With employment in blue-collar jobs controlled by labor unions, in the Northeast and the Midwest, Black workers were excluded from being hired or trained under apprenticeships in trade industries.[213] Unions that did hire Blacks faced backlash from White union members through mass strikes that forced unions to either exclude Blacks or place Blacks into segregated local affiliates. Most notably, the American Federation of Labor and its affiliates excluded Blacks until the 1929 crash, and the Congress of Industrial Organizations only represented Blacks in segregated locals, through poorly devised contracts and low-level job assignments.[214] Across the Northeast and Midwest, regressive state citizenship emerged from state and local governments segregating Black employees on their public works projects (Dimension 3), as well as enabling private businesses to categorically exclude Blacks from their hiring processes (Dimension 3).

Activism emerged to confront these exclusions. Multiracial groups like the Urban League, the Socialist Party of America, and the Communist Party advocated for the rights of Black workers at the local levels but were themselves targets of the federal government for being too radical. As early as 1900, Blacks employed as Pullman porters in major cities across the county began to fight for their own national union – the Brotherhood of Sleeping Car Porters (BSCP). Under the leadership of A. Philip Randolph, the union was officially launched in 1925 but met considerable resistance from Pullman Company, who countered by creating its own union to represent its employees. Randolph and the BSCP were unable to gain support from the heart of the Black community and Black churches because Pullman effectively framed the BSCP as having foreign roots in socialism and communism that were counter to Black interests. Local political officials, especially in the South, worked together with Pullman Company to ban BSCP meetings.

In 1927, the BSCP filed a case with the federal government's Interstate Commerce Commission to investigate Pullman Company on employee wages and working condition, but the ICC chose not to take the case on their basis of not having jurisdiction. The following year, in 1928, the BSCP faced another hurdle: it considered striking and mobilizing for federal intervention through the Railway Labor Act (RLA; passed in 1926), but the Great Depression made striking impossible for Black employees. Recognizing its limitations, Randolph in 1929 succeeded in gaining affiliated status for the BSCP with individual chapters of the American Federation of Labor, including Chicago, Cleveland, Denver, Detroit, Fort Worth, Kansas City, Los Angeles, New Orleans, New York City, Oakland, St. Louis, St. Paul, and Washington, DC. These affiliations enabled Randolph to gain greater access to President Roosevelt, who, in 1934, amended the RLA and then passed the Wagner-Connery Act (1934), banning company unions and expressly covering porters as a protected union under federal law. After three decades, the BSCP was finally certified in 1935 as the official union for Pullman workers. Yet, on the whole, Black citizenship remained highly regressive, subject to harsh exclusions in the right to human capital formation at both federal and state levels of government.

Black Exclusion under the US Presidency and Congress (1913–1941)

Regressive state citizenship under Jim Crow had a significant impact on the direction of national development. As David A. Bateman, Ira Katznelson, and John S. Lapinski all explain, Southern Democrats formed a cohesive voting bloc in the US Congress in the early 1900s that essentially "remade the American state in its image" with a regulatory regime that was bureaucratically weak and delegated implementation of federal programs either to the states or to public-private entities.[215] Prior to this ascendancy of the Southern bloc, Blacks were initially welcomed under new expansions in federal civil service jobs. However, as Jim Crow grew more entrenched in the South and then spread North, the federal government began to adopt similar racial exclusions from human capital formation (Dimension 3).

During the short window between Reconstruction and Jim Crow, and before the federal government aligned itself with Southern states, the US Congress passed the Pendleton Act of 1883. This foreshadowed the movement toward progressivism (1897–1914) to reform a corrupt and inefficient bureaucracy, by establishing competitive entry exams for federal agency recruits and basing these agencies on a meritocratic system.[216] For example, Congress established the US Civil Service Commission, which "supervised examinations, made investigations, recommended rules to govern federal personnel, and requested disciplinary action."[217] This version of federal employment tended to privilege the educated elite, which meant that Black graduates from major universities like Howard, Fisk, and Atlanta were able to compete for federal civil service careers equal to Whites (Dimension 3). As Desmond King explains, "invoking the meritocratic principles and ideology shaping civil service reform in most Western democracies and integral to Progressivism, it is clearly envisaged that

Black American employees will benefit from these opportunities in the same way as White workers."[218] According to King, the number of Black civil servants rose significantly, from 620 in 1883 (Blacks appointed to positions after the Civil War) to 2,393 in 1893.[219] For ten years, Black recruitment through the Pendleton Act was highly successful, nearly tripling the number of Blacks employed by the federal government in the span of a single decade.

However, federal policy on Black employment changed under the same Southern forces that led to the entrenchment of Jim Crow. Between 1913 and 1914, multiple Jim Crow bills were introduced in the US Congress: HR 5968 proposed to segregate clerks and employees of the "White race from those of African blood or descent;" HR 13772 proposed to segregate all Black employees in the federal government; and HR 17541 proposed to make it unlawful for Black recruits to obtain either commissioned or noncommissioned positions in the Army or the Navy.[220] While these laws did not pass, new restrictions in federal employment began to emerge that both excluded Blacks entirely from competitive civil service position (placing Blacks only in custodial and junior clerical positions) and segregated Black federal employees. President Woodrow Wilson, a Southern Democrat, led the charge. In 1914, the US Civil Service Commission made photographs mandatory on all application forms (later replaced with fingerprints in 1940).[221] This enabled racial discrimination to formalize in USCSC recruitment practices and aligned it with segregated departments like the Post Office and the Treasury. Writing to President Woodrow Wilson in 1913, the NAACP had already expressed strong concerns about Jim Crow practices developing in the federal civil service, which the organization argued created "two classes among its civilian employees. It has set the colored people apart as if mere contact with them were contamination."[222] Unfortunately, these legislative and executive actions by Southern Democrats under Wilson were only the beginning of Jim Crow nation-building.

A decade later, federal policies formed what Ira Katznelson accurately depicts of the 1930s New Deal as an affirmative action program for Whites only.[223] When Democrats gained control of Congress during the 1930s, they set a much lower federal baseline for Black rights: they entirely exempted most agencies from USCSC oversight and made racially exclusionary forms of patronage the core practice for filling approximately 100,000 federal positions that opened in 1934.[224] More importantly, federal erosions in Black rights occurred simultaneously with federal expansions in the right to human capital formation for Whites. In response to recovery efforts from the Great Depression, the federal government dramatically escalated its size and role in the economy, social welfare, employment, and housing – a major shift that ironically provided even more opportunities for states to deepen their regimes of regressive citizenship. President Roosevelt's (1932–1941) New Deal, as many scholars have uncovered in great detail, largely excluded Blacks from the many benefits given to Whites. The Social Security program established in 1935 included old-age insurance that excluded agricultural and domestic workers, who made up of the majority of nation's Black labor force. Jim Crow laws, lack of labor union representation, and private discrimination in employment made unemployment disproportionately concentrated among Blacks, who were similarly excluded under the New Deal's social security program.[225]

In passing the Wagner-Peyser Act in 1933, which created the United States Employment Service (USES) to help job-seekers find work to fill New Deal public works programs, the Democratic-controlled Congress intended for the USES to reinforce rather than oppose Jim Crow segregation and states' rights. Its funding was originally set by states and matched by federal funding (1933–1946), its state offices operated under the control of state commissioners, and it effectively employed mostly Whites because state and local laws determined the positions available for the USES to recruit Blacks. Meanwhile, the Fitzgerald Act passed in 1937 further increased racial disparities by creating a committee to administer and monitor federal apprenticeship programs led by the secretary of labor in an attempt to nationalize training for new industry skills that benefited Whites only.[226]

A Glimmer of Hope: Wartime Presidency (1941–1945)

From 1914 to 1940, the NAACP had led the effort to expose discrimination in USES recruitment and lobbied to end requiring photographs on civil service application forms. This effort proved successful in 1940, when Senator James Mead led the initiative in Congress to replace photographs with fingerprints, but the USES continued its regressive recruitment and hiring practices because of its federalist structure: its commissioners were state-appointed (not federal) and operated out of local offices to recruit workers. World War II had provided the first real glimmer of hope for expanding the right to human capital formation, with new presidential leadership. Yet, legislative actions proved fleeting.

President Roosevelt entered World War II facing great pressure from the NAACP and from A. Philip Randolph of the Brotherhood of Sleeping Car Porters. In 1940, the NAACP raised the constitutional violations of allowing the federally funded USES and other programs to discriminate by race.[227] At the same time, Randolph leveraged wartime labor needs in 1941 by threatening Roosevelt with mass demonstrations on Washington by organized Black workers. Unconstrained by Southern Democrats during the war, Roosevelt forged a new alliance with the NAACP and Randolph, beginning with ordering the federal takeover of all USES offices and the issuing of new USES antidiscrimination policies and practices. As part of reforming the USES, Roosevelt renamed the "Negro Placement Service Unit" as the "Racial Relations Unit" in 1941, placed it under federal control, and ordered it to report directly to the USES director. Roosevelt's most important antidiscrimination measure was Executive Order 8802, issued on June 25,

1941. This required all employers and trades unions to "provide for the full and equitable participation of all workers in defense industries, without discrimination because of race, creed, color, or national origin."

Roosevelt simultaneously created the Fair Employment Practice Committee (FEPC) to implement his executive order, monitor discrimination, provide a forum for complaints, and gather data on Black employment in government departments. Federal control over jobs expanded dramatically under the War Manpower Commission (WMC), formed the following year in 1942. Roosevelt ensured that Blacks benefited from the wartime boom in jobs by creating the Minority Groups Service and ordering the USES to report directly to the FEPC. In 1943, he issued Executive Order 9346 (in 1943) to increase the staffing of the FEPC and further strengthen his wartime antidiscrimination directive on all employers, adding the requirement that government agencies include a nondiscrimination provision in all of their subcontracts.[228] FEPC was highly effective as a mechanism for increasing Black employment because it had jurisdiction over war industries, government contracts, government employment, and trade unions.

Wartime presidential powers enabled temporary expansions in federal jurisdiction over states and localities. Under federal control, Bulletin No. USES C-45 in 1942 required all local USES offices "to forward reports about employers submitting discriminatory specifications in any vacancy notices they received."[229] Yet, states and localities – especially those in the South – resisted by simply failing to submit reports. To ensure some measure of federal enforcement, the NAACP engaged the local USES offices across the country and worked as an additional reporting source for Roosevelt. In 1943, the NAACP wrote to the WMC that "complaints have been received from various sections of the country by the Association in which Negroes complain that local offices of the USES refuse to furnish applications, or consider them, for skilled, professional, or White-collar jobs in war industries. Negroes are required to use separate entrances and are interviewed in segregated offices."[230] The FEPC also actively encouraged local contractors to use Black workers by holding hearings in Los Angeles (October 1941), Chicago (January 1942), New York (February 1942), and Birmingham (June 1942).[231]

The concentration of WWII military training camps in the South provoked even more clashes among local Whites, White soldiers, and Black soldiers (many of whom grew up in Northern cities and were experiencing Southern racism for the first time). As Desmond King notes, wartime increases in Black soldiers training in Southern military camps placed tremendous strain on segregated transportation.[232] Moreover, when defense industry jobs exploded demands for labor during World War II, a White countermovement escalated into the "bloody summer" of 1943, where Whites engaged in striking and rioting in order to prevent Blacks from being employed.[233]

Conflict also emerged within the federal government. President Truman "issued a circular to all heads of government departments, agencies, and independent establishments urging them to ensure no discrimination occurred as the number of personnel was reduced."[234] Increased Black employment imposed by Roosevelt's USES and FEPC led to a countermovement by federal agencies and departments of enacting Jim Crow segregation policies. The year 1943 saw the Machine Records Branch of the War Department and the Geological Survey Unit in the Department of Interior, among a number of other agencies, become formally segregated.[235] On August 7, 1944, 6,000 White employees of the Philadelphia Transportation Company led a massive strike in response to the hiring and training of eight Black workers under Roosevelt's non-discrimination policy, which expanded into a citywide race riot.[236] With strong resistance from states and localities and from within federal agencies, President Roosevelt and Truman's progressive actions on Black employment rights had limited sway against the massive edifices of regressive state citizenship that had been built over decades.

Return to Jim Crow Employment

National gains in rights to human capital formation under Roosevelt and Truman were built on fragile ground. Racial tensions resulting from Roosevelt's equal opportunity and antidiscrimination policies during World War II further alienated Northern Whites from the Black civil rights movement. Truman sought to formalize the civil rights gains of his predecessor, and he faced continued pressure from A. Philip Randolph and the NAACP, who led a "Double-V Campaign" (victory for democracy at home as well as abroad) to desegregate the US Armed Forces and provide equal employment opportunities (Dimension 3). More than 3 million Black people had registered to serve and nearly 500,000 served overseas during World War II.[237] A. Philip Randolph told Truman in 1947 that "Negroes do not want to shoulder a gun to fight for democracy abroad unless full democracy is obtained at home," a warning that Truman took seriously.[238]

In response, President Truman issued Executive Order 9808 on December 5, 1946, establishing a Committee on Civil Rights to investigate the status of civil rights in the country and propose measures to strengthen and protect them, which included a subcommittee on fair employment practices. Reporting in December 1947, the committee recommended that a permanent commission be established to monitor employment practices in both private sectors and federal agencies. It also recommended that a subcommittee be created within the "Civil Service Commission and the personnel departments of the various agencies" to monitor job training programs and discriminatory practices in hiring, promoting, and transferring of federal employees.[239] Truman's leadership, however, was constrained: the Fair Employment Board (1948–1955) and the Committee on Government Employment Policy (1955–1961) were created to monitor and report on racial discrimination in employment practices, not to enforce Black rights with regard to employment (Dimension 3). Moreover, the window for presidential leadership was relatively short and faced stiff congressional resistance.

As V. O. Key explains, the most important issue at the Democratic Party's 1944 national convention, as the war was coming to an end, was preventing a permanent FEPC from being established and blocking all civil rights legislation.[240] Congress introduced bills in 1944 and 1945 that would have excluded Black veterans from being considered a priority for civil service positions alongside their White counterparts.[241] Unable to gain the legislative majority for these bills to pass, Congress instead fought to return the USES to state and local control, essentially accomplishing the same goal. Congress removed temporary federal appointments given to Blacks during the war and terminated the FEPC and the WMC. This weakened the USES by no longer requiring employers to hire through public employment offices.[242]

Unable to prevent the USES from returning to states' control, the NAACP and Randolph's labor union turned to state governors in 1946 "requesting their assurance and support that USES offices would practice non-discrimination," with little effect.[243] They also continued to place pressure on Congress through mobilizing international pressure on civil rights, demanding the federal government to mandate state and local compliance on USES antidiscrimination policies. Without federal action, the USES issued a policy of nondiscrimination in 1953 knowing that it would never be enforced by the states. This included a provision that banned federal employment practices based on "racial, color, religious or nationality discrimination" and directed USES offices to actively encourage other federal agencies to include similar nondiscrimination clauses on their government-issued contracts. Congress supported the change in USES policy because it gave the appearance of racial equality but was unenforceable on states, localities, or private employers .[244]

Meanwhile, President Truman's progressive legislative attempts were blocked by a coalition of Southern Democrats and Northern Republicans throughout his presidency. In 1948, Truman failed to gain Congressional support for a permanent FEPC, anti-lynching legislation, and legislative ban on the poll tax in federal elections. When Republicans gained control of the House and the Senate in 1950, approving a permanent FEPC bill in the House, Southern Democrats defeated the bill through filibustering in the Senate. Only progressive states were capable of passing FEPC laws modelled after Roosevelt's wartime presidency, including New York, New Jersey, Massachusetts, Connecticut, and Washington. Meanwhile, at the national level, conservative Democratic candidates won against moderates by running campaigns against President Truman's Fair Deal and civil rights programs in 1951.[245]

Progress on the right to human capital formation (Dimension 3) remained limited. After abolishing the FEB, in 1955 President Eisenhower issued Executive Order 10590, which created the Committee on Government Employment Policy in order to assist government departments and agencies to implement equal opportunity. In 1965, President Johnson issued an executive order directing the USCSC to similarly address racial discrimination. President Carter in 1978 passed the Civil Service Reform Act, which replaced the USCSC with the Office of Personnel Management to monitor equal employment opportunity and treatment in the government.[246] Despite these presidential orders, Congress remained unwilling to provide strong leadership on the issue of equal employment. By the 1970s, the National Urban Coalition reported major concerns about racism within the USES, the primary agency charged with helping Americans find jobs.[247]

Jim Crow's Hold on Education, Housing, and Marriage

During Reconstruction and the late 1800s, residential segregation began as an informal practice. Once disenfranchisement laws spread in the late 1890s and early 1900s, states and cities across the country began to adopt zoning laws to prevent Blacks from purchasing housing in White neighborhoods. City councils began to pass zoning laws to separate residential areas into Black and White neighborhoods, beginning first with Richmond and Baltimore in 1911 and followed by Winston-Salem (1912), Atlanta (1913), and Louisville (1914). These spread across Northern cities in response to the Great Migration from 1910 up to World War I. In 1917, the US Supreme Court in *Buchanan v. Warley* struck down a law in Louisville, Kentucky, that forbade a "colored" person from moving into a home in a neighborhood with a majority of White residents. The court ruled that such racial zoning laws violated the Fourteenth Amendment's due protection clause and the freedom to enter into a private contract between Whites and Blacks.[248] While *Buchanan* marked a victory in the battle against racial segregation, it focused on upholding property rights, not affirming equal protection under the law. This left the door open for regressive practices: Buchanan only applied to legal statues by state or local governments, not private agreements. Even then, New Orleans and Indianapolis passed similar ordinances, in 1924 and 1926, respectively, which were struck down in *Harmon v Tyler* (1927).[249]

Importantly, the US Supreme Court ruling in the *Civil Rights Cases* (1883) that struck down the Civil Rights Act of 1875 enabled racial housing covenants to proceed: it ruled that the Fourteenth Amendment and other constitutional rights were not enforceable on individuals, only on states. The right to residency and homeownership in 1883 thus became the exclusive jurisdiction of states, who sanctioned racial covenants and made private contracts enforceable in court.[250] At the same time as state and local zoning laws emerged, racial covenants began to form, first in California in 1882 during the height of its (and federal) anti-Chinese movement (see Chapter 5). Once Jim Crow rolled out across the South, private racial covenants emerged in Virginia (1904), Missouri and Washington, DC (1905), Louisiana (1907), and Georgia (1912). According to Michael Jones-Correa, the national diffusion in the timing of racial covenants was caused by the "interplay of changing demographics of cities at the time and critical events like the riots of 1917–1921."[251] Covenants continued to spread, making their way to Michigan and Ohio by 1922 and New York by 1928.[252]

Reaffirming the 1883 precedent on how federalism shapes enforcement authority, the US Supreme Court upheld racial restrictive covenants in *Corrigan v. Buckley* (1926), noting that they were a form of private contract between buyers and sellers of property. Within the contract itself, these exclusions "took the form of an appendix or article in the deed not to sell, rent, or lease property to minority groups, usually Blacks, but also, depending on the part of the country, Jews, Chinese, Japanese, Mexicans, or any non-Caucasians."[253] The Court argued in *Corrigan*:

The constitutional right of a Negro to acquire, own, and occupy property does not carry with it the constitutional power to compel sale and conveyance to him of any particular private property. The individual citizen, whether he be black or white, may refuse to sell or lease his property to any particular individual or class of individuals. The state alone possesses the power to compel a sale or taking of private property, and that only for public use. The power of these property owners to exclude one class of citizens implies the power of the other class to exercise the same prerogative over property which they may own. What is denied one class may be denied the other. There is, therefore, no discrimination within the civil rights clauses of the Constitution.[254]

The federal New Deal provided the opening of the federal government to enter the housing market in 1933 for the first time, but, much like the other public benefits, federal housing assistance supported rather than prevented racial covenants.[255]

The federal Home Owner's Loan Act passed in 1933, run by Federal Home Loan Bank Board, assisted homeowners facing foreclosure by reducing their mortgages.[256] Soon after, the National Housing Act of 1934 created the Federal Housing Administration, to assist both prospective private homeowners and larger public developments. Consistent with other federal programs during the New Deal, these loan programs benefited White homeowners and accelerated the speed with which long-term racial disparities in affordable housing and residential segregation unfolded. Indeed, by 1940, an estimated 80 percent of property in Chicago and Los Angeles had restrictive covenants barring Black families.[257]

When the US Supreme Court in *Shelley v. Kraemer* (1948) struck down racial covenants, separate and unequal neighborhoods were already well established.[258] In addition, real estate boards and neighborhood associations continued to prohibit the purchase, lease, or occupation of property to racial minorities through other mechanisms. On February 4, 1950, the NAACP's Counsel Thurgood Marshall wrote to the federal commissioner of the Public Housing Administration, John Egan, that the *Buchanan* (1917) ruling prevents the federal government from placing local housing authorities in charge of federally funded housing projects.[259] Meanwhile, the NAACP urged the FHA to withhold funding from any local community found to segregate or discriminate in housing projects.[260]

The logic of White supremacy that underpinned residential segregation also directly shaped other elements of Blacks' right to human capital formation, including anti-miscegenation laws and school segregation laws that spread immediately following the end of the Civil War (Dimension 3). Once Blacks gained their freedom in 1865, White supremacy gained a new face in the South, particularly in terms of control over intimacy and close physical proximity. White power under slavery relied broadly on the ability to control Black sexual identity, marriage, children, literacy, and religion. The collapse of slavery meant that new rules needed to be devised. As Joel Williamson explains, "slavery necessitated a constant, physical intimacy" between Whites and Blacks, while emancipation necessitated their separation.[261] Restrictions on interracial marriage emerged first in Georgia, Mississippi, Alabama, and South Carolina in 1865 but continued to spread through 1908. The US Supreme Court in *Pace v. Alabama* (1883) unanimously rejected equal protection and expressly denied that Alabama's anti-miscegenation law discriminated on the basis of race.[262] Importantly, Blacks (and later LGBT individuals) were criminalized for interracial sexual acts as a felony offense under state sodomy laws.

Like anti-miscegenation laws, state laws segregating public schools emerged in the South immediately following the Civil War, beginning in Tennessee (1866) and followed by Alabama and Louisiana (in 1877). In the North, segregated schooling had antebellum origins but emerged again alongside housing segregation in the late 1800s and early 1900s. At the same time, there was some progress on education integration during the pre–Civil Rights era. In 1938, in *Missouri ex rel. Gaines v. Canada*, the US Supreme Court struck down a Missouri law allowing the state university to bar state residents who were Black from being admitted.[263] Importantly, the court rejected the state's offer to pay out-of-state fees for Black students to attend a peer institution outside of Missouri as an inadequate defense of equal protection under the Fourteenth Amendment. *Gaines* was a stepping stone to reversing "separate but equal," but it did not itself rule segregated schooling unconstitutional. A decade later, Mexican immigrants' right to attend California's public schools was also upheld by the US Court of Appeals for the Ninth Circuit ruled in *Mendez v. Westminster* (1947), which ruled: "By enforcing the segregation of school children of Mexican descent against their will and contrary to the laws of California, respondents have violated the federal law as provided in the Fourteenth Amendment to the Federal Constitution by depriving them of liberty and property without due process of law and by denying to them the equal protection of the laws."[264]

Gaines was later used as precedent in a similar case of admission to a Texas law school in *Sweatt v. Painter* (1950) and, even more remarkable, served as precedent in *McLaurin v. Oklahoma State Regents for Higher Education* (1950) to strike down separate classroom, library, and dining tables for Black students at the University of Oklahoma.[265] In the landmark *Brown v. Board of Education in Topeka* (1954), the Supreme Court built on these Fourteenth Amendment precedents to abolish the Plessy "separate but equal" doctrine, but equal protection remained narrowly applied to public education only.[266] To uproot Southern regimes of regressive state citizenship, the United States would need social movement activism, legislative action, and national enforcement on the order of a "Second Reconstruction."

THE CIVIL RIGHTS REVOLUTION – AND BACKSLIDING

Progress emerged first from presidential executive orders in the 1950s, in the wake of World War II and Supreme Court decisions, such as *Brown v. Board of Education* in 1954, which faced continued resistance from Southern Democrats in the US Senate and from Southern states refusing to desegregate schools. When Congress passed the Civil Rights Act of 1957, originally intended to provide federal protections to Black voting rights, South Carolina's Strom Thurmond led the Senate filibuster to effectively strip the law of its enforcement mechanism prior to its passage. Thus, the 1957 law established the Commission on Civil Rights and the office of assistant attorney general for civil rights to investigate voter rights infringements, but its original enforcement mechanism was entirely removed, including empowering federal courts to oversee cases and the US attorney general to pursue legal actions against violators. States, rather than the federal government, maintained control over Black citizenship rights as a result. Constant pressure from the civil rights movement led to the Civil Rights Act of 1960, which authorized federal judges to oversee racial discrimination by requiring local authorities to maintain and provide comprehensive voting records, but overcoming Southern resistance still required stronger mechanisms.

Meaningful civil rights reform really took hold only after the sustained mass protests of the civil rights movement prompted the passage of landmark legislation in 1964 and 1965. The Civil Rights Act of 1964 provided the legal framework needed to preempt state and local laws, ending Jim Crow segregation nationwide. It banned discrimination (based on race, color, religion, sex, or national origin); segregation in schools, employment, and public accommodations; and unequal use of voter registration requirements. That same year, Congress ratified the Twenty-Fourth Amendment to ban poll taxes in federal elections, which was soon extended to state and local elections by the US Supreme Court in *Harper v. Virginia State Board of Elections* (1966).[267] Finally, the Voting Rights Act (VRA) of 1965 stopped all voter restrictions for a five-year period in jurisdictions with histories of voter suppression, created federal "preclearance" with the Justice Department placed in charge of authorizing new electoral rules, and appointed federal officials to monitor compliance. As we explained in Chapter 3, vigorous enforcement of these civil rights measures held the forces of regressive state citizenship at bay for nearly five decades, even as the Republican Party began pursuing a "Southern strategy" to woo White Democrats back toward the Republican Party and proposing mechanisms to dilute Black voting power after gaining control of various Southern statehouses.

Alongside federal legislative actions, the US Supreme laid a foundation for a rights-based interpretation of the Constitution that would also end important areas of Jim Crow regressive state citizenship. The court unanimously ruled in *McLaughlin v. Florida* (1964) that a criminal statute prohibiting an unmarried interracial couple from habitually living in and occupying the same room at night violated the Fourteenth Amendment's equal protection clause, with Justice White explaining that racial classifications can only be sustained by a compelling state interest.[268] Three years later, in *Loving v. Virginia* (1967), the court expanded its interpretation on interracial cohabitation to invalidate similar prohibitions of interracial marriage.[269] It is important to note: *Bowers v. Hardwick* (1986) upheld state sodomy laws to regulate and criminalize LGBT individuals, who were not legally allowed to marry (in Chapter 3, we reviewed the change in 2003 and 2013 overturning these laws).[270] Following these successes, the Fair Housing Act of 1968 prohibited discrimination concerning the sale, rental, and financing of housing based on race, religion, national origin, or sex.

It is clear that the civil rights movement made significant headway from the 1950s to the 1980s in reestablishing national rights for Blacks that severely punctured holes in state regimes of regressive citizenship. Yet state citizenship continues to vary and hold tremendous power in shaping the rights of Blacks, even today. The conservative backlash on Black rights expansions fully unfolded in the 1980s under President Reagan, releasing previous constraints on state citizenship by ending the Fourteenth Amendment's equal protection from extending to race-conscious policies and practices. As a result, in 1996, California was able to pass Proposition 209, amending its constitution to prohibit state public employment, public contracting, and public education from considering race, sex, or ethnicity. Even as the courts rolled back civil rights protections, the federal government expanded its role in exclusionary citizenship by building up the carceral state, its War on Drugs, and the apparatus of immigration enforcement. These federal actions have allowed states to retrench Black access to key dimensions of rights and, in many ways, have ushered in a new era of regressive state citizenship across much of the United States.

In the following section, we focus on two of the five dimensions of rights to illustrate how regressive and progressive forms of state citizenship are reemerging today: voting rights (Dimension 4) and legal protection and due process (Dimension 2). Importantly, the regressive and exclusionary forms of state citizenship emerging today do not parallel Jim Crow, but they do demonstrate a pressing contemporary concern for Black citizenship rights. Constitutional interpretation, legislative action, and executive action still remain critical to preserving a strong baseline of rights. As we will show, in its sweeping decision, the US Supreme Court in *Shelby v. Holder* (2013) constrained federal action and opened the doors to regressive state election laws.[271] Meanwhile, federal criminal justice since the 1960s has targeted communities of color and incentivized cooperative arrangements with states and localities that have led to exclusionary rather than inclusionary forms of reinforcing state citizenship. Dramatic expansions and contractions in Black citizenship rights continue to occur, with progressive state citizenship beginning to surface again, as a model for inclusion.

Expansions and Contractions in Federal Voting Rights

The 1965 Voting Rights Act (VRA) marks the formal transition into the Civil Rights period, with important implications for the US Constitution and federalism. The VRA suspended voting tests and systems in state and local jurisdictions with less than 50 percent registration or turnout of their resident voting-age population during the recent 1964 election and put in place a system of federal oversight over state election rules.[272] Section 5 required all new subfederal jurisdictions with known legacies of voter suppression to submit any new voting rules to the Justice Department for "preclearance." The VRA, as a result of its enforcement sections, struck at the heart of regressive state voting laws that had epitomized White supremacy's hold on political parties and formal government through the Jim Crow period. It fundamentally shifted power over voting rights to the federal government, without actually ending states' control over the voting process for federal, state, and local elections.

It is no coincidence that the Civil Rights period was ushered in by the courts having to uphold the VRA against challenges by Southern states on the grounds that it violated Tenth Amendment protections of state prerogatives. In *South Carolina v. Katzenbach* (1966), the Warren Court, with a near unanimous decision, ruled that the Voting Rights Act was a valid exercise of Congress's power under the enforcement clause of the Fifteenth Amendment, which gave Congress full powers to stop discrimination in voting.[273] Importantly, the Court rejected the claims of South Carolina and state attorneys general from Virginia, Louisiana, Alabama, Mississippi, and Georgia that the law lacked a rational basis and intruded on state prerogatives protected by the Tenth Amendment. In a companion case, *Katzenbach v. Morgan* (1966), the US Supreme Court also upheld Section 4(e)'s protection, for those with limited English proficiency, of the right to register and vote.[274] A decade later, the US Supreme Court held in *White v. Regester* (1973) that a 1970 redistricting scheme for two urban counties in Texas represented a form of "vote dilution" affecting Mexican Americans and African Americans that violated the VRA and the Fifteenth Amendment.[275] Looking at the "totality of circumstances," the court considered the historic political and economic discrimination against those in these local jurisdictions to strike down the entire state reapportionment scheme.

Still, voting remains hotly contested. The renewals of the VRA in 1970, 1975, 1982, 1992, and 2006 were followed by erosions in voting rights at the state level. In 1975, Congress added provisions to the VRA to protect Latinos, Asian Americans, and Native Americans as "language minority groups" and set a nationwide requirement for states and local governments to provide bilingual "registration of voting notices, forms, instructions, assistance, or other materials of information relating to the electoral process, including ballots."[276] The VRA's preclearance requirement was also expanded in 1975 to include "tests or devices" involving any jurisdiction that provided English-only election information, when the jurisdiction had a single language minority group constituting more than 5 percent of its total voting-age population. Pressured by a coalition of civil rights organizations, in 1982 Congress amended the VRA to overturn the US Supreme Court decision in *Mobile v. Bolden* (1980), which ruled that Section 2 only prohibited *purposeful* discrimination, which Congress amended in Section 2 to explicitly and more broadly ban all voting practices that had a discriminatory *effect*.[277] Court protection of voting rights would last another two decades, after which conservative moves by various states in the post-9/11 period would chip away at voting rights and bring much of it crumbling down.

State Citizenship in the Era of Shelby v. Holder

In response to the contested presidential election of 2000, due to inconsistent voting technology, Congress passed the Help America Vote Act (HAVA) of 2002. However, states responded to HAVA in the context of the September 11, 2001, terrorist attacks, passing laws requiring first-time registrants to present photo identification at the polls if registering by mail, rather than seeking to redress unreliable voting technology. In 2005, Georgia and Indiana became the first two states to require voters to present specific forms of photo identification every time they vote, which was soon upheld by the US Supreme Court in *Crawford v. Marion County* (2008).[278] Arizona and Kansas took restrictions on voting rights even further, aided by the work of Kris Kobach, who found a loophole in federal election law that allows states to impose "proof of citizenship" requirements for registration to vote in state elections, including the provision of birth certificates for those born in the United States, even though federal law does not require such proof of registration to vote in federal elections.[279] While the Supreme Court had invalidated Arizona's Proposition 200's requirement of US citizenship for registration in federal elections in a 2013 decision, it explicitly allowed states to pursue more stringent voter registration requirements for state elections.[280]

Even more consequential in 2013, however, was the Court's *Shelby County v. Holder* ruling, which opened the floodgates of voter restrictions in Southern states. The *Shelby* ruling invalidated the need for Southern states to get preclearance from the federal government before making any changes to voting rights laws, such as switching from district to at-large systems or adding new requirements to the processes of voter registration and voting. This, in turn, allowed Southern states to pass more stringent laws on voter identification cards, voter registration purges, and use of unreliable databases to verify identity. The same day that the US Supreme Court issued its ruling, Texas passed the first restrictive photo identification law, which had previously been denied by the Department of Justice under preclearance.[281] Three weeks later, the Republican-controlled state legislature of North Carolina passed a law reducing early voting, restricting same-day registration, and eliminating a set of voter registration initiatives.[282] States throughout the country, including Arizona, Nebraska, and Ohio, soon followed by restricting early and absentee voting.[283] In July 2017, Georgia led in the largest voter purge in history, cancelling more than 500,000 voter registrations which, in addition to long lines and faulty voting equipment, likely cost Stacy Abrams the 2018 gubernatorial race.[284] In addition, a report by the Leadership Conference on Civil Rights revealed that, since the 2013 *Shelby* ruling, Southern states have closed over 1,200 polling locations that disproportionately affect low-income and Black-majority areas.[285]

Voter purges and the closing of polling locations are just two manifestations of voting rights erosions over the last two decades. Equally important, the VRA and the build-up of voting rights since the 1960s left other areas entirely unaddressed. Regressive elements of state citizenship have persisted through felon disenfranchisement laws, which have always remained controlled by the states even under the VRA. Indeed, the pervasiveness of this form of exclusion from voting rights is illustrated by the fact that every state in 2016, except for Maine and Vermont, imposed either temporary or permanent restrictions on voting by people with felony convictions. As Bernard Fraga explains, in the 2016 election, "approximately 2.5 percent of citizen voting-age adults" and "7.4 percent for African Americans nationwide" were ineligible to vote as a result of felon disenfranchisement laws.[286]

While the larger trend over the past two decades has been regressive in nature, some states are beginning to expand voting rights – providing a new model of progressive state citizenship in the wake of *Shelby*. Modelled after Michigan's early effort to facilitate voter registration, in 1993 President Bill Clinton signed the National Voter Registration Act (NVRA), requesting states to allow individuals to register to vote by mail, at public agencies, and when applying for a driver's license. Beginning with Oregon in 2016, a few states that same year exceeded the federal baseline on voting rights by passing laws that create automatic or automated voter registration, all just in time for the presidential election. This progressive development expanded between 2016 and 2018, with twelve states (Alaska, California, Colorado, Connecticut, Illinois, Maryland, New Jersey, Oregon, Rhode Island, Vermont, Washington, and West Virginia) and the District of Columbia enacting automatic voter registration systems.[287] California has passed perhaps the most comprehensive array of electoral reforms aimed at increasing voter registration and participation, including automated voter registration with driver's license renewals, preregistration of sixteen- and seventeen-year-olds, expanded early voting, drop-box voting, and same-day voter registration.[288] These reforms have enabled the state to achieve a voter registration rate of 80 percent for the first time since 1952, a remarkable feat given the relatively higher concentrations of low-propensity voters such as those with low incomes, immigrants, and members of communities of color in the state.[289]

State Citizenship in the Era of Mass Incarceration

When major reforms of the 1960s were pushing the nation forward on Black citizenship rights, a parallel exclusionary development was also underway. Beginning as early as the 1950s, under what Vesla Weaver calls "frontlash," were punitive developments in criminal justice at both federal and state levels of governance, from legalizing the death penalty to abolishing parole and imposing mandatory minimum sentencing, allowing juveniles to be incarcerated in adult prisons, passing state felon disenfranchisement laws, and practicing chain-gang labor.[290] In short, the civil rights gains of the 1950s and 1960s fueled a new focus toward crime and punitive conceptions of law and order. Indeed, as we show earlier in this chapter, Jim Crow spread in the 1920s and the 1930s because lynching in the South was strategically tied to combating riots in Northern cities. Rather than expand the right of legal protection and due process, "law and order" became the dominant political frame justifying states' rights under Jim Crow.

More alarming, when the 1960s civil rights and voting rights laws were being passed, which required strong presidential leadership by President Johnson to ensure full Democratic support in Congress, the federal government was simultaneously taking on a new role in crime control by passing the Law Enforcement Assistance Act on 1965. This new federal law authorized the US attorney general to provide grants for the training of state and local law enforcement and to fund projects designed to expand law enforcement responsibilities. Soon after, Congress passed the Crime Control and Safe Streets Act of 1968 and new Federal Sentencing Guidelines, which significantly altered criminal justice into a more expansion punitive system.[291]

When President Nixon took office in 1969, conservative backlash in the form of the War on Drugs and mass incarceration fully opened the door for exclusionary reinforcing state citizenship in policing and crime and also allowed for pervasive state regressive developments that linked criminal status to all five core dimensions of citizenship rights. These developments deepened under Ronald Reagan's presidency and found renewed vigor with Bill Clinton's enactment of the 1994 Federal Crime Bill, which created harsher criminal sentences and incentivized states to build more prisons and pass tougher sentencing laws. The Democratic Party under President Clinton's leadership sought to wrest control of crime issues from the Republicans and had abandoned the push for progress on Blacks' rights in the process.

As a result, many states started going down the path of regressive citizenship: denying rights across the spectrum, including the right to free movement while on parole or after being released and enacting policies of racial profiling such as "stop and frisk" (Dimension 1); passing mandatory sentencing laws, three-strikes legislation, and juvenile incarceration (Dimension 2); denying ex-convicts the right to housing, the right to child custody, and employment opportunities (Dimension 3); banning voting and jury service (Dimension 4); and constructing the idea of Black criminality and young "superpredators," as well as characterizing ex-felons as undeserving of rights (Dimension 5).[292]

The total number of people incarcerated increased from roughly 500,000 in 1980 to over 2.2 million in 2015, with Blacks making up the majority of the incarcerated and correctional populations.[293] Sweeping national gains during the 1960s in civil rights and subsequent court interpretations provided significant progress in Black citizenship rights, but regressive state citizenship has still reappeared, albeit in a weaker and more indirect form than during Jim Crow. In *Batson v. Kentucky* (1985), the US Supreme Court ruled that jurors cannot be dismissed based on race under the equal protection clause of the Fourteenth Amendment but generally upheld state and local power to dismiss jurors, including excluding all persons with past criminal charges or convictions (Dimension 2).[294] Moreover, the imprisoned population in the United States, as a result of the US Census's usual-residence rule, is counted as residents of the jurisdiction where they are being held for their incarceration (Dimension 4). As Michelle Alexander highlights, this politically advantages "predominately white, rural areas, white communities" where prisons are more often built, and politically harms "urban, overwhelmingly minority communities" where prisoners previously lived.[295]

Our conceptual framework of state citizenship reveals how and why criminal justice is so pervasive an issue for Black citizenship today. Even more so than on the issue of voting rights – where backsliding is also occurring – criminal justice has become the primary pathway for states to enact regressive or progressive forms of citizenship. More alarming, while the onus of mass incarceration is placed at the state level with 90 percent (out of a total of 2.3 million in 2019) of the incarcerated population today under state or local prisons, Republican and Democratic leaders have led in the legislative actions to federally incentivize incarceration, with little to no consideration of the consequences for Black citizenship rights.[296]

State limitations on the right to free movement has also extended well beyond incarceration to include other aspects of policing. Thus, for example, the New York Police Department's stop-and-frisk policy allowed a police officer to stop, question, and search any pedestrian if they "reasonably suspect" that the pedestrians may commit, or have already committed, a crime. Framed as a policy to maintain law and order, stop- and-frisk significantly erodes the right to free movement for Blacks and other minorities. Indeed, from 2001 to 2010, New York City created and enforced an electronic database of the names and addresses of individuals subject to a stop-and-frisk, regardless of whether they were charged with any crimes. In *Floyd, et al. v. City of New York, et al.* (2013), the federal district court even called stop-and-frisk a "policy of indirect racial profiling," ruling that the New York Police Department violated the Fourth Amendment (through unreasonable searches) and the Fourteenth Amendment's equal protection clause.[297] Indeed, in their study of NYC's stop-and-frisk policy, Andrew Gelman, Jeffrey Fagan, and Alex Kiss show that persons of African and Hispanic descent were stopped much more frequently than whites. Judge Shira A. Scheindlin ordered the creation of an independent monitor to oversee NYPD's reform efforts.[298]

As we have shown in this chapter, Jim Crow laws limited the free movement rights of Blacks by keeping them separate from Whites in private and public spaces, including public transportation, housing, workplaces, restaurants, parks, and swimming pools. In a similar manner, present-day policies like stop-and-frisk and racial profiling at traffic stops disproportionately limit the right to free movement (Dimension 1) of Black and Brown residents. These regressive policies take away rights that are supposed to be guaranteed by the federal government and the equal protections provision of the Fourteenth Amendment. The political implications of racial profiling and the violation of "free movement" rights also extend to many other groups, including Muslims, who are disproportionately more likely to face surveillance on city streets and near places of worship, and Latinos, who are more likely to be stopped for identification checks.

There is hope, however. Repressive arrangements in federalism on criminal justice are being challenged by civil rights organizations and activism at the state levels, including the ACLU's 2019 fifty-state blueprint to end mass incarceration.[299] Key states are also stepping up to sever their role in punitive criminal justice and to provide leadership on reforms that are creating a much-needed move towards progressive state citizenship. This progress on criminal justice is not exclusive to Democratic states. In the early 2000s, states with large incarceration rates, beginning first with the conservative state of Texas, began slowing spending on new prisons. A series of reforms have been enacted by conservative Republican states like Texas and Florida, and in progressive states like California, with similar goals of reducing the overcrowded and overwhelmed prison systems. Democratic- and Republican-controlled states alike, with thirty-five states between 2010 and 2018 in total, have passed ban-the-box legislation requiring employers to consider job applicants' qualifications prior to checking their criminal history, expanding the right to human capital formation (Dimension 3).[300]

Democratic states, however, have gone much further by passing state laws that mandate the removal of conviction history questions from job applications for private employers.[301] As on other dimensions of state citizenship rights, California is pushing the farthest. Until 2011, the state had been zealous in pushing for more punitive sentencing, including the 1994 Three Strikes Law that imposed a mandatory twenty-five-years-to-life sentence on third felonies and Proposition 21 in 2000 that imposed higher penalties for juvenile offenses. These policies prompted a dramatic increase in the state's prison population, and the Supreme Court ruled in its 2011 *Brown v. Plata* decision that prison overcrowding and lack of access to health care violated the constitutional rights of state inmates.[302] The Court mandated a significant reduction of the state prison population, which opened opportunities for criminal justice reform advocates to successfully push for changes such as reduction in drug crime penalties (Proposition 47 in 2014), reductions in juvenile sentences and early release of nonviolent inmates (Proposition 57 in 2016), reductions of high school suspensions for "willful disobedience," and the closing of juvenile prisons and to more broadly transition the Division of Juvenile Justice (from within Corrections) to the California Health and Human Services Agency – creating the Department of Youth and Community Restoration by July 2020.[303] Given the strong racial disparities in youth discipline and prison sentencing, these reforms go a long way in advancing the citizenship rights of Black and Latinx populations in the state. Thus, a progressive form of Black state citizenship is beginning to form in California that breaks away from the federal criminal justice approach to build a more inclusionary model of crime prevention that is rehabilitative in focus.[304]

CONCLUSIONS

It is clear that the United States entered a new era of national citizenship in the 1960s, with constitutional and federal safeguards on Black rights that remain even today. It is also clear, however, that states continue to hold sway in the provision of rights that disproportionately affect Black residents. These include the *right to free movement* (with variation in state policies on policing); *rights to due process and legal protection* (with variation in state policies on criminal justice, including policing and sentencing regulations); the *right to develop human capital* (in employment, public and charter schools, and housing); the *right of participation and representation* (in voting rules and administration, including those related to voter ID, felon disenfranchisement, and redistricting); and the *right to identify and belong* (as reflected in state policies regarding monuments to the Confederacy, including flags and statutes on public property). States like California, after having undergone a period of racially conservative propositions in the 1980s and 1990s, have begun to enact policies of inclusionary citizenship for Black residents after 2010, including ending "three-strikes legislation," decriminalizing marijuana possession, and passing legislation preventing employers from asking applicants about their history of incarceration.[305] Still, bans on affirmative action in education and employment remain in California and many other states, blunting moves toward progressive state citizenship for Blacks. As we shall see in the next chapter, California has forged a very different trajectory with respect to state citizenship for immigrants, potentially pointing to a similar pathway for advancement in Black rights in the years to come.

5

Worst to First

California's Evolution from Regressive to Progressive State Citizenship

"California Becomes 'Sanctuary State' in Rebuke of Trump Immigration Policy."[1] So declared a headline in the *Los Angeles Times* on October 5, 2017, outlining the state's passage of legislation (SB 54) that would place strong limits on state and local cooperation with federal immigration agencies. The same article framed the so-called sanctuary law as part of a larger scale effort to resist the Trump administration's moves on immigration enforcement, quoting the bill's sponsor and State Senate President Pro Tem Kevin De León, who remarked that "California is building a wall of justice against President Trump's xenophobic, racist and ignorant immigration policies." Similar stories covered California's legislative deliberation and passage of the state sanctuary bill, in sources as varied as CNN,[2] the *Washington Post*,[3] the progressive blog *Think Progress*,[4] and local television news in California.[5]

The narrative of a state sanctuary push driven by resistance to the Trump administration captures important aspects of immigration federalism today. At the same time, this narrative is misleading and ahistorical when applied to California, glossing over the state's strategic leadership on immigrant integration over two decades. Indeed, even on the question of "sanctuary policies," the state had passed two prior laws limiting state cooperation with federal immigration authorities: the TRUST Act in Fall 2013 and the TRUTH Act in Fall 2016. California passed each of these laws under the Obama administration and, in the case of the TRUST Act, overcame vigorous opposition from Democratic appointees at the Department of Homeland Security and a reluctant Democratic governor who had previously vetoed the bill in September 2012.[6] Importantly, California's passage of the TRUST Act prompted the Obama administration to abandon the Secure Communities program in Fall 2014 and to announce a new set of priorities in immigration enforcement that shifted in light of California's action.[7] Contrary to some recent accounts, California was in the business of resisting key aspects of federal immigration enforcement and expanding immigrant rights well before Trump got elected. We show in this chapter that California had already advanced immigrant rights to a sufficient degree that it had crystallized a progressive form of state citizenship in 2015.

Here, we carefully assess where California currently stands with respect to state citizenship, and we situate the present moment in a sweep of the state's history, using the framework of state citizenship that we outlined in Chapter 2. As we detail in this chapter, California was a pioneer of *regressive state citizenship* for much of the nineteenth century, pushing for restrictions on immigrants that went well beyond those at the federal level. It continued with exclusionary regimes of both *regressive* and *reinforcing state citizenship* for most of the twentieth century, peaking with the passage of Proposition 187 in 1994 and Proposition 209 in 1998. Starting in 1999, however, the state began a dramatic reversal, pushing for modest policy victories through 2003, followed by a period of policy stasis and movement infrastructure-building during a Republican gubernatorial administration. Soon after the election of Democratic Governor Jerry Brown, the legislative push for pro-immigrant policies began anew, starting as a ripple and soon accelerating into a wave that dramatically expanded immigrant access to many types of rights at the state level. We pay detailed attention to the post-1999 period in California, exploring important milestones in the advancement of immigrant rights, and pinpoint 2015 as the year in which *progressive state citizenship* became crystallized.

Applying our explanatory framework (laid out in Chapter 3), we trace the key factors that incubated and enabled this development of a progressive regime of state citizenship in California. We show that voter backlash against racial propositions and subsequent shifts in party control made a shift to progressive state citizenship more likely after 2010. In addition to partisanship,[8] two other factors were essential to the development of this shift: evolving dynamics of federalism conflict involving Congress and the Obama administration; and coordinated, long-term investment strategies by private foundations in California to develop a cross-regional network of immigrant advocacy organizations. Absent these two factors, the crystallization of progressive state citizenship in California would have not occurred or would have been delayed considerably.

CALIFORNIA AS ANTI-IMMIGRANT PIONEER

The move toward immigrant integration was not inevitable in California. In fact, history paints quite the opposite picture: California led the nation in restrictive measures on immigration, from its very establishment as a state in 1850 through the mid-1990s, when it passed a series of laws that were racially divisive and restricted immigrant rights in myriad ways. Its state citizenship was strongly regressive in nature during its first few decades, targeting Asian immigrants and going well beyond any federal government restrictions on these populations. Indeed, California was pioneering anti-Chinese immigrant legislation at a time when the federal government was largely silent on immigration enforcement. Once the federal government entered the field of immigration restriction more fully – with the passage of the Page Act in 1875 and the Chinese Exclusion Act in 1882 – California's regressive citizenship policies adopted a mix of exclusionary reinforcing elements (with some policies mirroring federal restrictions and applying them at the state and local level, while other policies such as the Alien Land Law continued to exceed federal restrictions on immigrant populations).

With a sizable increase in Mexican migration during the 1910s and the 1920s, and with the consolidation of Asian exclusion by Congress in 1924, California began to pass policies aimed primarily at Mexican immigrants, restricting access to important types of rights that lasted through 1998. Meanwhile, federal immigration policy changed in important ways, most notably with the period of Mexican repatriation, the rise and fall of the Bracero program, and the 1965 passage of the Immigration and Nationality Act that inaugurated a new era of unauthorized immigration. Throughout this period, California continued to contract immigrant rights by tinkering with its combination of reinforcing and regressive state citizenship policies, often pushing the boundaries of what was permissible and sparking court and Congressional pushback.

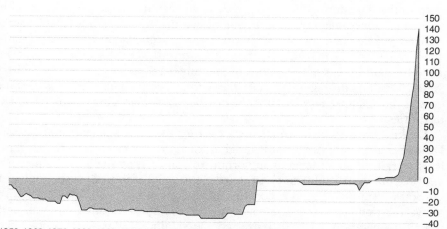

FIGURE 5.1 Running tally of state citizenship in California
Note: Totals across dimensions of citizenship as noted in Chapter 2 (see Appendix for indicator scoring).

In Figure 5.1, we provide a visualization of state citizenship policies with respect to immigrants, with a cumulative score of inclusion and exclusion based on the five dimensions of state citizenship rights we outlined in Chapter 2. For ease of exposition, we save a detailed methodological discussion of indicators and policy coding for the Appendix. As our running tally on state citizenship indicates, the last two decades in California are remarkable and exceptional when compared to a nearly 150-year history of restricting immigrant rights. The overwhelming record of California with respect to immigrant rights is one of erosion of rights, with distinct periods marked not only by the changing targets of state exclusionary policies – Asians, followed by Mexicans – but also by changes in the role of the federal government with respect to immigration control. Additionally, Table 5.1 provides a summary of how our concept of citizenship is applied to California throughout this chapter, in terms of both classifying policies within the five core dimensions and tracing developments in citizenship subtypes in each of the three historical periods of American political development (as we laid out in Chapters 2 and 3).

STATEHOOD AND CALIFORNIA'S EARLY RACIAL ORDER

California made gold, and gold made the state of California, vaulting it from territory to statehood in record time. The region certainly sparked colonial interest before the discovery of gold, as Spain subjugated the local Native populations and established a system of townships (*pueblos*), religious centers (*missions*), and fortifications (*presidios*) in the eighteenth century as part of Alta California.[9] And American settlers and military expeditions had encroached in parts of the state during the 1840s, even as the region struggled for power with the central government of Mexico. Still, it was the discovery of gold at Sutter's Mill on January 24, 1848 – days prior to the conclusion of the Mexican-American War – that sealed the fate of California. The discovery of gold in 1849 brought in tens of thousands of migrants from other parts of the United States, upending the region's racial order and accelerating its entry as a US state even as the country grappled with the question of slavery's expansion into new territories.

Looking back to California's first governor's state of the state address, on December 21, 1849, Governor Peter H. Burnett made it clear that the first state legislature held an undeniably important role in crafting the legal framework and machinery of California's regressive state citizenship. Burnett implored quickness, stating that the constitutional convention and first legislature "have the right to proceed, at once, to put the State machine into full and practical operation." He also stressed the significance of state policies for shaping statehood and state citizenship, saying, "Either a brilliant destiny awaits California, or one of the most sordid and degraded. She will be marked by strong and decided characteristics. Much will depend upon her early legislation."[10]

TABLE 5.1 *Immigrant state citizenship in the United States*

A. Immigrant citizenship in a multidimensional framework of rights

1) Free movement	State entry ban or bond/tax, state-led removal (*Period I*); Repatriation (*Period II*); immigration enforcement with federal anti-harboring enforcement laws, driver's licenses (*Period III*)
2) Due process and legal protection	Court testimony ban (*Period I*); noncooperation with enforcing immigration law; state ban on privatized prisons (*Period III*)
3) Develop human capital	Employment ban, foreign miner's tax, anti-vagrancy laws (*Period I*) debt peonage; mining license to work, fishing ban, housing ban, alien land law, education ban (*Period II*); work relief ban, general/cash assistance ban, welfare assistance ban, healthcare ban, employer sanctions (*Period II* and *Period III*)
4) Participate and be Represented	Immigrant voting rights (*Period I*); poll tax, literacy tests (*Period II*); noncitizen local voting eligibility and office holding (*Period III*)
5) Identify and belong	Alienating language in laws, English-only laws, Office of Immigrant Affairs (all three periods of immigration federalism)

B. Immigrant citizenship subtypes in a federated framework

Progressive state citizenship	California on all dimensions (*Period III*)
Reinforcing (inclusionary) state citizenship	White immigrant homesteaders during westward expansion (*Period I*); White immigrant voting in national, state, and local elections; New Deal welfare in Northeastern states with White immigrant populations (*Period II*)
Reinforcing (exclusionary) state citizenship	Restrictions on international or internal migration (*Period I*); racialized New Deal welfare in all Southwest states with large non-White immigrant populations; Bracero program of Mexican labor in California, Arizona, and Texas (*Period II*); employer sanctions; cooperative arrangements in enforcing immigration laws such as detainer requests (*Period III*)
Regressive state citizenship	Chinese exclusion before federal law enacted (end of *Period I*); criminalization of unlawful presence; ban on professional licenses, postsecondary education and public benefits (*Period III*)

Note: Periods are indicated in italics: *Period I* (1789–1878), *Period II* (1879–1964), and *Period III* (1965–present).

It was soon apparent that the promise of a new California wouldn't be shared equally by all. The discovery of gold and the influx of miners gave Whites the upper hand and, in doing so, enabled state leaders to institute a regime of regressive state citizenship very soon after the state's founding. As we shall soon see, the state built much of its machinery of regressive citizenship on Chinese exclusion. The state also deepened and formalized White supremacy in its racial order more generally, diluting the rights of Blacks and Hispanics and leveraging already-existing power dynamics between Mexican settlers and Native Americans to advantage White control, particularly over labor (see Table 5.2).

Blacks

Frontier life in America was particularly promising for Blacks, offering the opportunity to gain a greater measure of autonomy and freedom. Moreover, news of the discovery of gold reached throughout the country and encouraged many free Blacks to leave the East Coast. Blacks were as anxious as Whites to strike gold and achieve the American dream, and formed small free Black communities in different parts of the state, with Black churches, schools, and societies.[11] Some Blacks were explorers themselves and actively served the United States during the Mexican-American war.[12] Moreover, as the nation faced increased sectional tensions over slavery, Frederick Douglass and the abolitionist newspaper *The Liberator* promoted the successes of Blacks in California, sparking further migration to the state.[13] Douglass targeted his critique of the American Colonization Society's efforts to send Blacks to Liberia, arguing that they instead should use their resources to send Blacks to California.[14]

California's early promise of opportunity and equality proved to be an illusion. During the first set of constitutional debates in California, Whites sought to form an exclusionary form of citizenship that prevented their contact with Blacks – alleged to be "one of the greatest evils that society can be afflicted with."[15] In the first year of statehood, officials pushed for a law that would have banned all Blacks from migrating to the state.[16] However, the bill failed due to strong opposition from slave owners, who brought their slaves to the state to work in mines. The following year, California passed a law that gave one year of protection to slave owners; it then extended this protection again in 1853 and 1854. At the same time, it enacted in 1852 its own Fugitive Slave Law, requiring the return of runaway slaves from California to slave owners. Whites used these state laws not only to bring in more Blacks held in legal bondage but also to hold Blacks lacking proof of freedom in near-slavery conditions, despite California's constitutional ban on slavery.[17] Perhaps what mattered most for the Black population in California during this period was the legal impact of the foreign miner's tax, which was imposed and brutally enforced on Blacks, Native Americans, and other groups. Rather than slavery law, California's miner's law

TABLE 5.2 *California's state-building period, 1846–1855*

Policy type	Citizenship Dimensions 1–5*	Citizenship type**	Blacks	Native Americans	Mexican Americans	Immigrants
Voting ban	4	*Regressive*	1850 Constitution	1850 Constitution		
Office-holding ban	4	*Regressive*	1850 Constitution	1850***		
Court testimony ban	2	*Regressive*	1850 Constitution	1851 / 1852		
Court decision appeal ban	2	*Regressive*		1851 / 1852		
Presumed criminal status	2	*Specific to policy/ group* ↑	*Reinforcing* 1852	*Regressive* 1850		
Indenture Law	1, 2, 3, 5	*Specific to policy/ group* ↑	*Reinforcing* 1852***	*Regressive* 1846 / *Regressive* 1850		
Foreign miner's tax	1, 2, 3, 5	*Regressive*	1851	1850	1850***	1850
Anti-vagrancy Law	1, 2, 3, 5	*Regressive*	1855	1855	1855	1855

* The provision of rights to: (1) free movement; (2) due process and legal protection; (3) develop human capital; (4) participate and be represented; and (5) identify and belong.

** Citizenship types: regressive; restrictive; progressive.

*** Distinguishes de facto policy (differential access to rights). Meanwhile, the table's baseline is de jure policy (provision of rights).

dictated who could labor freely. Whites believed that non-Whites laboring in the mines devalued their labor – mining was considered to be an "honorable" form of work.[18] Several hundred Blacks worked the mines, including in about two dozen specific mining sites throughout the state.[19] However, the vast majority of Blacks during this early period (roughly 2,000, or 1 percent of the state's population in 1852[20]) engaged in menial service-related occupations as cooks, porters, boot-polishers, farmers, ranchers, blacksmiths, and businessmen.

Native Americans

Mexico abolished slavery in 1823 after declaring independence from Spain, and the 1824 Mexican Constitution formally granted Black and Native Americans citizenship. Nevertheless, under Mexico's rule, California's governor Mariano Chico established an Indian pass program in 1836. This program – modelled after slave passes in Latin America and the US South – ordered that "every Indian, found away from his residence without licenses from the *alcalde*, administrator or missionary, should be arrested and sentenced to labor on the public works."[21] Thus, Native Americans were formally citizens of Mexico but were denied the same rights as other Mexicans to human capital formation (Dimension 3 of our framework). Control and exploitation of Indian labor was instrumental to the strength of California's early pre-US ranchero economy. Although we do not push the historical connection too far, regressive citizenship in California can be viewed as initially forming under Mexico rule, with punitive elements applied to the Indigenous population.

The exploitation and exclusion of Native Americans continued during the Mexican-American War and its aftermath. John C. Frémont, who served as California's first US senator, led the Sacramento River massacre, killing several hundred Wintu in 1846 before the war, and made it a general order for his unit "to shoot Indians on sight."[22] Once the Mexican-American War began, the US government ordered Frémont back to California, and he continued to massacre California's Native population and forced them to leave their lands. On September 15, 1846, US Navy captain John B. Montgomery issued the first US government's Indian Policy in California, which was framed as part of the wartime effort. Montgomery proclaimed, "All [p]ersons so holding or detaining Indians, shall release them, and permit them to return to their own homes, unless they can make a legal contract with them, which shall be acknowledged before the nearest Justice of Peace." Furthermore, Montgomery explained, "The Indian population must not be looked upon in the light of slaves, but it is deemed necessary that the Indians within the settlements, shall have employment with the right of choosing their own masters or employer."[23] This wartime proclamation set up Native American indentured servitude status without term limitations, making their release dependent on the express permission of a master, employer, or justice of the court.

Following Montgomery's order, officials in Monterey (Mexican California's capital city) enacted an ordinance in January 1847 stating that "no person whatever shall ... hire or take into his service any Indians without a certificate from the former employer of that Indian stating that the said employer has no claims on the services of that Indian for wages advanced," adding a fine of up to $20 for each violation.[24] San Francisco's magistrate Washington A. Bartlett followed suit. In November 1847, California's Secretary of State Henry W. Halleck established an Indian pass system, requiring Native Americans to show proof that they are employed by non-Indians and indentured, as well as defining those without passes as runaway laborers or criminals, subject to arrest and punishment as stock rustlers.[25]

Using our multidimensional framework of citizenship rights, laid out in Chapter 2, Native Americans in California had even less right to free movement and to human capital formation than Blacks (see Table 5.2). The end of the war and the push for statehood opened up the possibility for California's Indian policy to turn progressive. Indeed, the Treaty of Guadalupe Hidalgo guaranteed to all former Mexican citizens who were residents of California, including Native Americans, the full panoply of rights as US citizens. It was soon apparent, however, that these were relatively empty promises. California's 1850 constitution expressly denied the right to vote to Blacks and to Native Americans (Dimension 4), preventing them from participating in approving the new constitution, from electing the state's first body of legislators, and from shaping California's early policies. In addition, the federal act admitting the state of California on September 9, 1850, made no reference to Native American land rights.[26] To make matters worse, the federal government took actions that strengthened regressive state citizenship even further: the federal Land Claims Act of 1851 extinguished aboriginal titles and required all land claims from the Spanish and Mexican governments to be filed within two years.

After statehood, regressive citizenship in California for Native Americans emerged in multiple ways. It included a set of *de facto* restrictions, ones that were debated in constitutional debates and strategically left out, particularly on Native American rights. Soon, however, these restrictions on Native American rights were institutionalized as a *de jure* set of exclusionary constitutional provisions and state laws. On April 22, 1850, the first state legislature passed the "Act for the Government and Protection of Indians," also referred to as the Indian Indenture Act. This law established indenture servitude through custodianship of Indian minors and convict leasing, banning Native Americans from vagrancy, and denying Native Americans due process rights by making them criminals until proven innocent.[27] The law separated Native American children and adults from their "families, languages, and cultures" by indenturing them to Whites and punished them for vagrancy by charging a bond for their release or "hiring" them out at a public auction.[28]

Within a very short span of time, Native American were formally excluded from nearly all five dimensions of citizenship. In 1850 and 1851, California enacted laws banning Native Americans and Blacks from providing "evidence in favor of, or against, any White person," defining as Indian anyone having one-half (in 1850) and later one-fourth (in 1851) Indian blood. Native Americans could make complaints before a justice of the peace, but they could not provide testimony against a White man, and they could not appeal cases to a higher court.[29] During California's early period, the federal government was moving toward a more inclusive approach, but it lacked the will to formalize or enforce a type of inclusionary national citizenship that overcame state resistance: it negotiated eighteen treaties with 119 California tribes and created nineteen protected California reservations. California's US senators, however, led in opposing all treaties, and on July 8, 1852, the US Senate placed the federal treaties under an "injunction of secrecy" that was ultimately lifted only in 1905.[30] Thus, lacking any meaningful federal rights and protections during the period of early statehood, Native Americans in California faced increased state-level restrictions and growing White animosity over land possession that turned the 1850s into a decade of dispossession, exploitation, and large-scale massacres.[31]

Mexican Americans

The discovery of gold in 1848 sparked a major wave of migration, not only from various parts of the United States but also from across the newly established US–Mexico border. Demographically, northern California became predominantly White with the influx of prospective miners, while southern California remained heavily Mexican and dependent on agriculture. The state's large size and these demographic and economic divisions even sparked some early debate over splitting the state in two.[32] Perhaps most consequential, the massive migration of Whites to California had significantly altered political power, enough to reverse gains in federal and state rights for Mexican Americans. Under the Treaty of Guadalupe Hidalgo that concluded the Mexican-American War, Californios were given the same rights as US citizens. Mexican Americans provided eight of the forty-eight delegates to California's 1849 state constitutional convention, and all state laws were translated into Spanish. Mexican Americans ran for elected office and, helped by their numerical majority in many parts of Southern California, were able to win many state, county, and local seats.[33]

Despite their access to US citizenship, Mexican Americans quickly lost political power when the state rapidly shifted to a majority White population. Soon, Mexican Americans were unable to prevent state laws targeting immigrants that were enforced in ways that also hurt Mexican Americans who had formal access to US citizenship. Even after naturalizing as US citizens, Mexican Americans under California state laws lost their voting rights (Dimension 4), trial-by-jury rights (Dimension 2), and property rights (Dimension 3).[34] Lacking both constitutional protection and federal action to protect existing rights, California's regime of regressive state citizenship emerged unimpeded. When the federal government signed the Treaty of Guadalupe Hidalgo in 1848, granting US citizenship rights to 80,000 Mexican nationals, it classified them as "White." Threatened by this federal racial classification, California linked Mexican American citizens to their *mestizo* descent (Indian or Spanish descent), making them non-White and excluding them from voting under the state constitution.[35] California also set up commissions and courts to remove land from Mexican Americans and then legally banned them from owning property (Dimension 3), despite their US citizenship status.[36] As one scholar put it, "[d]espite de jure [US] citizenship status, Mexicans could not exercise the franchise [in California] with anything close to the same ease of lighter-skinned Angelenos."[37] Thus, while the federal treaty of 1848 was inclusive of Mexican nationals, California reclassified its Mexican residents as a non-White racial caste subject to its exclusionary state policies.[38]

Two prominent examples of regressive state citizenship policies during this early period pertained to the foreign miner's tax in 1850 and the anti-vagrancy law of 1855. Under federal law, mines in California were open to everyone – US citizens, Mexican Americans, Blacks, Native Americans, and immigrants. California quickly moved to end this open-access policy, making the right to human capital a keystone dimension of its regime of exclusion. The large influx of Latin American (and especially Mexican) immigrants to California shaped early debates and laws on how to regulate public lands and mining. California Senator Thomas Jefferson Green introduced the foreign miner's tax as a bill levying a monthly $16 license fee on all foreign-born miners and including enforcement provisions for those refusing to pay to be subject to eviction, jail time, and heavy fines.[39] "An Act for the Better Regulation of the Mines and the Government of Foreign Miners" passed in 1850 and increased Green's proposed levy to $20.[40] Importantly, Green framed the law as an issue of free labor, specifically seeking to restrict foreign capitalists' employment of Mexican "peons" in California's mines.[41] Those of Mexican origin were considered unfree forms of labor, posing a similar "danger" to free White labor as enslaved and indentured Blacks and Native Americans.[42]

Cast in the White supremacist racial order, California's foreign miner's tax was a legislative restriction on immigrants, but it was also enforced as a racial restriction on Mexican Americans.[43] Whites were able to employ state law to target and expel both US citizens and immigrants of Mexican origin. After the tax was in place, in May 1850 an estimated 4,000 foreign-born miners – made up of Mexicans, Chileans, Peruvians, French, German, and English miners – confronted the new tax collector in Sonora, California. The tax collector formed a large posse of armed White US citizens, violently ending the protest and leading many foreigners to abandon the mines. Similar conflicts led to several thousand foreigners abandoning the mines in 1850 and 1851.[44] A group of White Sonoran merchants, who directly benefited from Mexican American and immigrant business, challenged the legality of the foreign miner's tax, arguing that California lacked constitutional power to tax federal mineral lands and that the tax violated the Treaty of Guadalupe Hidalgo's extension of equal citizenship rights. In *The People, ex. rel. The Attorney General v. Naglee* (1850), the California supreme court upheld the state law and the power of California to regulate the activities of foreigners within its own borders.[45] Extensive lobbying by the merchants led the state legislature to repeal the law in March 1851.[46]

In 1855, California went further in targeting Mexican Americans by enacting a universal anti-vagrancy law that popularly became known as the Greaser Act, based on a derogatory racial epithet, thereby expanding its regressive state citizenship along Dimensions 1, 3, and 5 of our framework.[47] The 1855 law stated: "All persons except Digger Indians, who have no visible means of living, who in ten days do not seek employment, nor labor when employment is offered to them, all healthy beggars, who travel with written statements of their misfortunes, all persons who roam about from place to place without any lawful business, all lewd and dissolute persons who live in and about houses of Ill-Fame; all common prostitutes and common drunkards *may be committed to jail and sentenced to hard labor for such time as the Court, before whom they are convicted shall think proper, not exceeding ninety days* [emphasis added]."[48] Furthermore, the Act specifically called out "persons who are commonly known as 'Greasers' or the issue of Spanish and Indian blood,"[49] and the law was implemented in a way that disproportionately targeted Mexican Americans.

CALIFORNIA'S ANTI-ASIAN PERIOD (1852–1912)

After quickly rising to statehood and restricting the provision of rights to Blacks, Native Americans, and Mexicans, the dominant thrust of California's regressive state citizenship turned to Chinese immigrants. California's foreign miner's tax, while short-lived, irreversibly and physically removed Mexican-American citizens and immigrants from California's mines. Within just a year of the law's repeal in 1851, Chinese "coolies" took the place of Mexican "peons," and Whites soon began to attack this new perceived threat to their labor. The California Assembly's powerful Committee on Mines and Mining Interests met in the spring of 1852 and proclaimed that foreign immigration – particularly by Chinese – was the greatest threat to the state's prosperity.[50] The state's concern over Chinese immigrants would prove to be enduring and would establish a robust regime of regressive state citizenship for decades to come.

Anti-Asian legislation became the major focus in part because Black migration remained severely constrained after being banned in the 1860s, the Native American population dramatically decreased due to violent massacres and removal campaigns, and Mexican immigration was limited until the early 1900s. At the same time, the United States was advancing a more inclusive approach, signing a treaty in 1868 with China and actively recruiting Chinese labor to work on the transcontinental railroad. While White labor groups in California vociferously objected to the arrival of Chinese immigrants, others saw the opportunity to further develop mining, railroad construction, manufacturing, and farming in the state. State officials thus directed their legislative efforts toward passing a range of anti-Chinese policies that benefited its continued economic growth while controlling all aspects of Chinese life.

In this section, we unpack the development and full range policies of California's *regressive citizenship* during this period. Our primary focus is on anti-Chinese policies from 1852 to 1885, but the section ties this to the state's broader anti-Asian movement that extended to 1912, with policies denying Japanese and Indian immigrants the right to land ownership. As we will argue, the 1900s ushered California into a new period of regressive citizenship, fueled by developments in federal immigration law and the national ban on Asian migration (in 1882, 1917, 1921, and 1924). California responded to these federalism dynamics, shifting its focus away from Asian groups and toward a new anti-Mexican focus – with policies targeting US citizens, legal immigrants, and undocumented immigrants (see Figure 5.2).

It wasn't long before California's leaders and public began to resent the growth of the state's Chinese population, especially in mining districts. In January 1852, Governor John McDougal praised Chinese labor for "draining

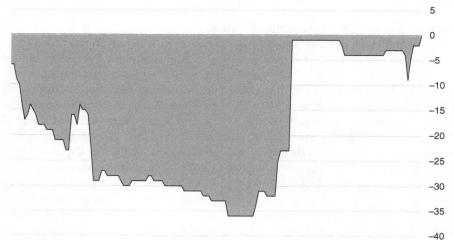

FIGURE 5.2 California's 150 years of exclusionary state citizenship

California's immense swamplands."[51] Days after this speech, however, John Bigler replaced McDougal as California's governor and spent much of his first year delivering anti-Asian speeches to the state legislature, characterizing Chinese immigrants as a "tide" of "coolie labor" that threatened White American workers.[52] An 1852 report by the state's Committee on Mines and Mining Interests added fuel to the anti-Chinese movement, exhaling that the "vast numbers of the Asiatic races, and of the inhabitants of the Pacific Islands, and of many other dissimilar from ourselves in customs, language and education" threatened the state. Political leaders framed Chinese as a "servile labor by foreign capitalists" "held to labor under contracts not recognized by American law."[53]

Removing Rights to Due Process and to Legal Protections

California's regressive citizenship began to form in the early 1850s by extending restrictions already placed on Blacks in the 1849 constitution and other early laws to establish the first exclusions on Chinese. While denied the right to vote, Chinese residents in 1850 could testify in most California courts. The state's criminal statute in 1850 provided only that "[n]o Black or mulatto person, or Indian, shall be permitted to give evidence in favor of, or against, any White person." Only some state courts excluded Chinese as witnesses.[54] This changed when three Chinese witnesses were placed on a criminal court case in 1853 that led to the sentencing of a White US citizen, George W. Hall, who was charged to be hanged for the murder of Ling Sing, a Chinese miner from Nevada County. In *People v. Hall* (1854), Chief Justice Hugh C. Murray of the California supreme court ruled that Chinese testimony was banned under state law. Chinese were of the same "ethnic stock" as Indians, Murray argued, and were therefore excluded under the state's criminal statute.[55]

The first years of California statehood ensured Chinese were excluded from most core dimensions of state citizenship. Chinese miners were often under foreign mining companies' labor contracts, which were not recognized under federal or state law.[56] The ban placed on testimony essentially stripped all Chinese residents of their right to legal recourse and protection in court, for labor contracts or any other matter. The exclusion was intentional: in the *Hall* (1854) ruling, Chief Justice Murray further argued that recognizing Chinese testimony might lead to their eventual participation at the "polls, in the jury box, upon the bench, and in our legislative halls."[57] The *Hall* decision was soon applied in *Speer v. See Yup Co.* (1859) to ban Chinese testimony in all civil cases in the state, in addition to criminal cases. Notably, Reconstruction-era expansions in Black rights (detailed in Chapters 3 and 4) began to place some constraints on the regressive elements of California's state citizenship. For example, the federal government passed the Civil Rights Act of 1870, provided that all persons had the same right in every state and territory to "make and enforce contracts, to sue, be parties, give evidence, and to the full and equal benefit of all laws and proceedings for the security of person and property as is enjoyed by white citizens."[58] In response, California removed all racial bans on who could testify in court in 1872, but several other restrictions on the rights of Chinese Americans would remain in place.[59]

Restricting Rights to Human Capital Formation

California's restriction on Chinese rights also extended to human capital formation (Dimension 3), particularly with respect to housing, education, and employment. In 1866, the state passed a law declaring "Chinese" houses of prostitution to be public nuisances and providing a variety of remedies for their abatement.[60] Section 1 of the Act provided that "common repute" should serve as competent evidence of the character of the house. To avoid equal protection concerns under the Fourteenth Amendment (1868), this law was amended in 1874 by removing "Chinese" and declaring all houses of prostitution public nuisances.[61] Common repute, however, remained the deciding factor, and Chinese households and businesses remained the primary target of the state's anti-prostitution law. Two years later, in 1876, California passed another law to restrict Chinese residents from housing, known as the "cubic air law."[62] This state law was modelled after San Francisco's 1870 ordinance, which "made it a misdemeanor for anyone to let rooms or apartments that should contain less than five hundred cubic feet of air for each adult person sleeping or dwelling in them and made it a crime as well for any tenant to dwell or sleep in such a room or apartment."[63]

The state expanded restrictions on Chinese residents' right to develop human capital in 1860, passing a law that segregated "Negroes, Mongolians, and [American] Indians" and prevented the right to attend any public school. It empowered school superintendents to withhold funds from districts that violated state law and placed them in charge of creating separate segregated schools.[64] In 1866, a new law required superintendents to establish separate schools "if the parents or guardians of ten such children should apply for them" and permitted districts to admit non-White children to White schools if White parents did not object.[65] California specified in a comprehensive school law passed in 1870 that children of African and American Indian descent were to be segregated in separate schools, but it failed to mention Chinese children.[66]

Following the lead of Massachusetts, California's supreme court ruled in *Ward v. Flood* (1874) that segregation school laws were considered a special police power of the state.[67] It did not violate the Thirteenth Amendment or the equal protection clause of the Fourteenth Amendment. The court further explained that state constitutional rights guaranteed that children in the state were entitled to attend public schools and that "colored children" could only be restricted from attending White schools when separate segregated schools existed in their district.[68] In 1880, California overhauled its education law as Section 1662 of the Political Code, striking out the word "White," and stated instead that "[e]very school, unless otherwise provided by law, must be open for the admission of all children between six and twenty-one years of age, residing in the district."[69]

Chinese were not specified in California's laws. However, by 1885, the state had made it clear that Chinese residents did not have the right to a public education, either in White or in segregated schools. In 1884, Joseph Tape attempted to enroll his daughter (who was half White, half Chinese) in San Francisco's Spring Valley Primary School, but they were denied access by school officials. Tape complained to the District Superintendent Andrew J. Moulder and then to State Superintendent of Public Instruction William Welcker. The latter did not defend Tape's daughter's right to a public education under the state law enacted in 1880; instead, Welcker argued that "Mongolian children" were excluded from attending California's public school under any circumstances. He referred to California's 1879 constitution as reserving public education for residents who were legally able to become US citizens. Welcker further exclaimed that offering Chinese residents the right to public education would encourage their migration, and California's laws were intended to discourage this.[70] Moulder and the San Francisco school board passed a resolution in 1884 "prohibiting [officials], under pain of immediate dismissal, from admitting any 'Mongolian child,' either male or female, to any public school in the city."[71]

The Tape family, represented by Attorney Gibson, filed for a writ of mandate in the superior court of the city and county to order the principal of the school to admit their daughter. Judge James Maguire issued the mandate and said he would hold any board member that dismissed a principal for admitting Tape's daughter in contempt of court.[72] The San Francisco school board formed a Legislative Committee with other education officials throughout the state and decided to appeal to the state supreme court.[73] In *Tape v. Hurley* (1885), the California supreme court upheld the superior court's decision, ruling that state law was universal in its provision of the right to public education and did not explicitly deny Chinese or other groups from this right.[74] State law only empowered trustees' discretion to exclude "children of vicious habits or suffering from contagious disease," and Tape's daughter did not fit these two exclusions.[75] School officials quickly turned to the state legislature in 1885 to amend Section 1662 to empower trustees to "establish separate schools for children of Mongolian or Chinese descent" and deny them access to White schools.[76]

Segregation remained California's de jure policy until Section 1662 was repealed. In *Gong Lum v Rice* (1927), the US Supreme Court ruled that the creation and maintenance of a public schools was an exclusive state power and upheld segregation under *Plessy v Ferguson*'s (1896) "separate but equal" doctrine.[77] Section 1662 devolved decision-making power over segregation to school boards, which meant that some Chinese, Japanese, and members of other minority groups were able to attend all White schools. After the Federal Ninth

Circuit Court of Appeals in *Westminster School Dist. of Orange County v. Mendez* (1947) ruled that segregating students of Mexican descent "against their will and contrary to the laws of California violated the Fourteenth Amendment," the issue of segregation was revisited in California.[78] The San Francisco School Board and state officials had begun to change their anti-Chinese views as a result of strong Chinese American support during World War II, which encouraged them to go beyond *Westminster* to end segregation for all racialized groups by removing Section 1662 in 1947.[79]

Even during the heyday of regressive state citizenship, Chinese immigrants had some success in fighting exclusionary state policies on human capital formation. District associations assisted Chinese immigrants in finding employment and shelter, arbitrated disputes, and financed their debts. The Six Companies served as the coordinating council to these associations and primary intermediary between California's Chinese community and the larger White society. Following the enactment of California's 1852 anti-Chinese laws, the state's Committee on Mines and Mining Interests was tasked with considering several bills to increase licensing fees and a possible ban on all foreigners from working in mines. Six Companies pressured state officials and provided a full report to California's legislature asking for "fair promise of its safe and profitable employment."[80] In 1853, the Committee backed down from supporting a bill to exclude all Chinese from mining, but it passed a state law that raised the mining licensing fee by $1 and began the state's incremental approach of gradually pushing Chinese miners out. In 1855, a new state law further increased the license fee to $6 per month, with a provision to add an additional $2 per month each subsequent year. On April 19, 1856, external pressure from businesses led the state legislature to repeal the 1855 law and reset the foreign miners' license fee to the 1853 level of $4 per month.[81] The following year, in *People v. Downer* (1857), the state supreme court struck down the 1852, 1853, and 1855 mining fees as preempted by federal control over foreign commerce.[82]

In the early 1860s, the courts began to limit what California could do to restrict the right to develop human capital. Republican Governor Leland Stanford successfully pressured the state legislature to discourage immigration by the "degraded" Chinese immigrants and pass the state's Anti-Coolie Act of 1862, which was a tax placed on Chinese workers to "protect Free White Labor," despite the fact that Stanford employed Chinese workers as cheap labor on his farms and railroad enterprise.[83] This state law effectively reestablished and went beyond past restrictions placed on Chinese miners, restrictions that were all ruled unconstitutional in 1857. It charged a $2.50 license fee each month on Chinese workers to "protect Free White Labor," leaving only those employed in growing tea, rice, coffee, or sugar untaxed. Not surprisingly, the California supreme court quickly ruled the new law preempted by federal power over foreign commerce in *Lin Sing v Washburn* (1862), calling the law a "measure of special and extreme hostility to the Chinese."[84]

California's attorney general at the time, Frank M. Pixley, exclaimed that "[t]he Police of the ocean belongs to Congress. The Police of the land belongs to the States."[85] Nevertheless, the court ruled that singling out one group of foreigners for taxation discouraged immigration and thus infringed on Congress's power over foreign commerce.

Restricting Rights to Free Movement

Regressive state citizenship emerged in parallel to national citizenship and federal immigration law. In the *Passenger Cases* (1849), the Supreme Court ruled that federal exclusivity over foreign commerce preempted New York and Massachusetts state laws imposing an entry tax on alien passengers arriving from foreign ports.[86] Despite the constitutional decision, federal inaction enabled California to pass two anti-Chinese laws in 1852 that effectively restricted the entry of Chinese immigrants into the state (Dimension 1) and expanded its exclusions on the right to due process (Dimension 2) and the right to human capital formation (Dimension 3). It passed a law to deter all new immigration, especially from China, by requiring shipmasters to pay $500 per alien passenger or pay a commutation fee of $5 to the state hospital fund, which could be increased at the discretion of the commissioner on immigration up to $1,000. Another 1852 law set up a state mining license used to charge Chinese miners a monthly tax of $3, split equally between the state and mining counties, and authorized local sheriffs to enforce tax collection. Furthermore, California's mining license law was the first step toward denying due process, by banning any Chinese person without a license from access to state and local courts (Dimension 2).[87] In *People v. Hall* (1854), California's supreme court not only uniformly banned Chinese testimony throughout the state, but it also restricted free movement by creating an identification document to be used by the state and counties to control the movement of Chinese residents and their labor.

Recognizing possible legal concerns over its entry bonds, California passed a resolution in 1854 for the state legislature to ask the US Congress for permission to enact future entry bonds. It nevertheless proceeded without Congressional guidance to enact a new commutation tax in 1855, which added an additional $50 bond per alien passenger on top of the $500 bond established in 1852. In 1858 and again in 1862, California passed laws prohibiting any Chinese or Mongolian from entering the state, but these were quickly declared invalid by the state court. California's entry bond remained in force until the California supreme court in *People v. SS Constitution* (1872) ruled, according to the *Passenger Cases*, that it was unconstitutional and preempted by federal exclusivity over matters of foreign commerce.[88]

The need for labor led to a large influx of Chinese immigrants, despite entry restrictions and limits on free movement under state law. City governments, popular tribunals, and local vigilantism picked up where the state left off.

Residential segregation laws confined where Blacks, Chinese, and other non-White groups could reside, creating early ghettos. Moreover, criminal justice was in the hands of White citizens, who formed popular tribunals outside of official government courts and vigilante groups to target Chinese immigrants. As Paul Spitzzeri explains, Los Angeles, San Francisco, and other cities were frontier societies with fluid open borders that made moving in and out especially easy for criminals.[89] Lacking official law enforcement officers created a perceived need for these tribunals and vigilantism, but what emerged were government-sanctioned contractions on free movement (Dimension 1) as well as due process and legal protection (Dimension 2), targeting Chinese and other marginalized groups. Vigilante groups were led by local elites, officials and, business owners, and they operated "in the guise of supporters of the law, claiming they had stepped in only when the courts and statutes failed."[90]

With segregation and vigilantism in place, Chinese immigrants were physically vulnerable and legally unprotected. In 1871, a shooting between Chinese in the Los Angeles grew into a larger massacre after a White spectator was accidentally shot and killed. A large White crowd mobilized and surrounded the Chinese quarters, leaving no room to escape. They rioted, looted Chinese homes and businesses, and killed at least nineteen Chinese Americans – some of whom were lynched in public. The Workingmen's Party led similar riots, looting and burning Chinese houses and businesses in Yreka, Chico, Weaverville, and other cities in the early 1870s, often forcing Chinese residents to flee to other cities.[91] Meanwhile, in 1878, San Francisco enacted a law to increase the size of the police, but police commissioners prohibited them from protecting businesses and property within the Chinese Quarter.[92]

California's Regressive State Citizenship and 1879 Constitution

As we have already laid out, California developed a regime of regressive citizenship early in its statehood, with restrictions on rights affecting various racial groups (see Tables 5.1 and 5.3). However, it reached new heights in 1879 when California passed its new state constitution, which alone included provisions that spanned all five core dimensions of citizenship. A total of 152 delegates were selected to the state constitutional convention in 1878, fifty-two of whom belonged to the Workingmen's Party, which was vigorously anti-Chinese. The convention established a Committee on the Chinese to draft provisions related directly to Chinese exclusions to be placed in the new constitution.[93] The committee's report recommended an article with nine provisions that would have prohibited all future Chinese immigration into California and excluded Chinese residents in the state from nearly all aspects of life. Many, but not all, of these recommendations were integrated into the state constitution or subsequently passed as state laws.

TABLE 5.3 *California's anti-Asian period, 1852–1943*

Policy type	Citizenship Dimensions 1–5*	Citizenship type**	Years enacted	Year of repeal or preemption
State-led removal	1, 2, 5	*Regressive*	1879 Constitution 1880	
Entry bond/tax	1, 5	*Regressive*	1852 1855	1862 *Preempted* 1875 *Preempted*
Entry ban	1, 5	*Regressive*	1858 1862	1862 1872
Court testimony ban	2	*Regressive*	1852 miners only 1854 criminal cases 1859 civil cases	1870 *Preempted*
License/fee to work	1, 2, 3, 5	*Regressive*	1852 1853 1855 1856***	1857 1939 mining license *Repealed*
Employment ban	3	*Regressive*	1879 Constitution 1880	1880 *Preempt* (statute only)
Business license ban	3	*Regressive*	1880	
Fishing ban	3	*Regressive*	1880 (Chinese) 1943 (Japanese)	1948 *Preempted*
Housing ban	3	*Regressive*	1866 anti-prostitution 1874 anti-prostitution 1876 anti–cubic air	
Public education ban	3, 5	*Regressive*	1860 1866*** 1870 1874*** 1880*** 1885 segregated	1954 *Repealed*
Alien Land Law	1, 2, 3, 5	*Regressive*	1913 1920 1923	1948 *Preempted*

* The provision of rights to: (1) free movement; (2) due process and legal protection; (3) develop human capital; (4) participate and be represented; and (5) identify and belong.

** Citizenship types: regressive; restrictive; progressive.

*** Expanded rights for Blacks and other minorities, not Chinese.

Ultimately, the Workingmen's Party prevailed in getting the state constitution to devote an entire article to Chinese exclusion, which is worth reading in full:

Article Xix. CHINESE.

SECTION 1. The Legislature shall prescribe all necessary regulations for the protection of the State, and the counties, cities, and towns thereof, from the burdens and evils arising from the presence of aliens who are or may become vagrants, paupers, mendicants, criminals, or invalids afflicted with contagious or infectious diseases, and from aliens otherwise dangerous or detrimental to the well-being or peace of the State, and to impose conditions upon which persons may reside in the State, and to provide the means and mode of their removal from the State, upon failure or refusal to comply with such conditions; *provided,* that nothing contained in this section shall be construed to impair or limit the power of the Legislature to pass such police laws or other regulations as it may deem necessary.

SEC. 2. No corporation now existing or hereafter formed under the laws of this State, shall, after the adoption of this Constitution, employ directly or indirectly, in any capacity, any Chinese or Mongolian. The Legislature shall pass such laws as may be necessary to enforce this provision.

SEC. 3. No Chinese shall be employed on any State, county, municipal, or other public work, except in punishment for crime.

SEC. 4. The presence of foreigners ineligible to become citizens of the United States is declared to be dangerous to the well-being of the State, and the Legislature shall discourage their immigration by all the means within its power. Asiatic coolieism is a form of human slavery, and is forever prohibited in this State, and all contracts for coolie labor shall be void. All companies or corporations, whether formed in this country or any foreign country, for the importation of such labor, shall be subject to such penalties as the Legislature may prescribe. The Legislature shall delegate all necessary power to the incorporated cities and towns of this State for the removal of Chinese without the limits of such cities and towns, or for their location within prescribed portions of those limits, and it shall also provide the necessary legislation to prohibit the introduction into this State of Chinese after the adoption of this Constitution. This section shall be enforced by appropriate legislation.[94]

Article XIX, by its very existence and framing, attacked the right of Chinese to identify and belong in the state of California (Dimension 5). In addition, Section 1 of the Article severely limited immigrants' rights to free movement (Dimension 1) and due process (Dimension 2), allowing the state to remove anyone deemed to be detrimental to the well-being of the state and to impose conditions on those who are allowed to remain. Sections 2 and 3 curtailed the right of human capital formation (Dimension 3), barring Chinese from being employed by any corporation or government entity. Section 4 allowed cities and towns to expel Chinese immigrants and to specify the areas where they could reside, further diminishing the right to free movement and due process (Dimensions 1 and 2). Other parts of the 1879 constitution curtailed the right of Chinese to hold property, by narrowing them to US citizens and immigrants of White or African descent eligible for US citizenship (Article 1, Section 17) (Dimension 3). It also limited the right to participate and be represented (Dimension 4), noting in Article 2, Section 1 that "no native of China, no idiot, insane person, or person convicted of any infamous crime ... shall ever exercise the privileges of an elector in this State."[95]

Soon after the constitution was enacted, the state legislature added two new sections to the Penal Code to implement the constitutional provision that forbade corporations from employing Chinese (Dimension 3). They made it a misdemeanor – punishable by fine or imprisonment in the county jail – for any officer, director, or agent of a corporation to employ "any Chinese or Mongolian" in any capacity or for any work. They also made the second conviction of employing any Chinese person a crime with the severe consequence of corporations forfeiting their charter, franchise, and all corporate rights.[96] In *In re Tiburcio Parrott* (1880), Judges Sawyer and Hoffman of the United States Circuit Court for the District of California ruled that these two state laws, which implemented the state's constitutional ban on employing Chinese, unconstitutional.[97]

A week after *Tiburcio Parrott*, the state passed a law to implement the constitution's mandate that local governments actively remove "Chinese residents beyond town or city limits or in the alternative to set aside discrete portions of the city for Chinese residence."[98] That same month, the state passed two more anti-Chinese laws: one banning aliens who are considered ineligible to become a state elector from obtaining a license to transact any business or pursue any occupation in the state; and another law forbidding them from catching fish in the state's waters for purposes of sale.[99]

To summarize, the completion of the transcontinental railroad, the slowdown in gold mining, and the economic recession followed by increased White migration to California all inflamed the anti-Chinese movement in 1877. On July 23, 1877, thousands of Whites organized to riot and burn the city's Chinese quarter and docks to prevent the transportation of new Chinese immigrants to San Francisco. City officials waited two days before having police and others step in to stop the rioting. After this event, Denis Kearney organized the Workingmen's Party in October 1877 under the slogan "The Chinese must go," which led to the anti-Chinese state constitution in 1879 and continued rioting and expulsion campaigns through the 1880s. In 1881, following the 1879 constitution, sixty Chinese buildings were destroyed by fires in Dutch Flat, which became a common – and now explicitly sanctioned via the state constitution – means of expelling Chinese from cities throughout the 1880s.[100] Kearney traveled the country, bringing his message as far as Boston, and pushing Congress to pass the 1882 Chinese Exclusion Act.

Federalism Conflicts and Resolution

Developments simultaneously emerged at the federal level on federal preemption, international treaties, and civil rights, which all posed a conflict with California's regressive laws. The US Supreme Court ruled state taxes or bonds violated the US Constitution's allocation of the power to regulate foreign commerce and immigrant admission to the federal government alone in three separate cases: *Passenger Cases* (1849), *Henderson v. Mayor of the City of New York* (1875), and *Chy Lung v. Freeman* (1875).[101] In addition, the federal government played a significant role in facilitating migration after the Civil War, largely to replace workers that had been lost and to establish new labor for building the transcontinental railroad linking California to the Midwest and the eastern seaboard.[102] It entered into the Burlingame Treaty of 1868 with China, which recognized "the mutual advantage of the free migration and emigration" of peoples of the two nations "for purposes of curiosity, of trade, or as permanent residents." It also established that "Chinese subjects visiting or residing in the United States, shall enjoy the same privileges, immunities, and exemptions in respect to travel or residence, as may there be enjoyed by the citizens or subjects of the most favored nation."[103] This federal treaty conflicted with most of California's existing anti-Chinese laws and sparked significant backlash in the state, ranging from rioting and lynching to new legislative efforts to prevent Chinese migration to California.

The Radical Republican Congress that had pushed for the end of slavery with the Thirteenth Amendment also began to set up, for the first time, civil rights under federal law – including the Civil Rights Bill of 1866 and the Fourteenth Amendment in 1868 – that had some impact on California's regressive citizenship. Partially in response to California's treatment of Chinese immigrants, Congress passed the Civil Rights Act of 1870 to ensure that all people, including newly freed African Americans and Chinese residents, were given the same legal protections as White citizens. Section 16 of the 1870 federal law applied the Fourteenth Amendment's equal protection:

That all persons within the jurisdiction of the United States, Indians not taxed or excepted, shall have the same right in every State and Territory in the United States to make and enforce contracts, to sue, be parties, give evidence, and to the full and equal benefit of all laws and proceedings for the security of person and property as is enjoyed by white citizens, and shall be subject to like punishments, pains, penalties, taxes, licenses, and exactions of every kind and none other, any law, statute, ordinance, regulations, or custom to the contrary notwithstanding. No tax or charge shall be imposed or enforced by any State upon any person emigrating thereto from a foreign country which is not equally imposed and enforced upon every person emigrating to such State from any other foreign country, and any law of any State in conflict with this provision is hereby declared null and void.

In *Yick Wo v. Hopkins* (1886), the first such case to squarely present the question of discrimination against Chinese, the court struck down a San

Francisco ordinance regulating laundry establishments in the city for violating the Fourteenth Amendment's equal protection clause.[104] Importantly, the nature of equal protection jurisprudence itself evolved (and continues to evolve) from the time of *Yick* Wo to present day, with major constitutional changes occasioned by *Brown v. Board of Education* (1954) and *Washington v. Davis* (1976).[105]

Soon, however, conflicts between California's regressive citizenship laws and federal law began to resolve, with the state successfully pushing the federal government to add more exclusionary provisions. Thus, the first major federal immigration laws resembled California's laws and, in large measure, helped the state achieve its goals of Chinese exclusion. Anti-Chinese laws in California suffered some defeat in cases like *Chy Lung v Freeman* (1875), which struck down its entry bond and tax law. However, these same restrictions soon emerged in federal law. The very same year as *Chy Lung*, Congress passed the Page Act of 1875, which essentially replaced California's 1870 law making it unlawful to bring into the state any "Mongolian, Chinese, or Japanese female" without first presenting to the commissioner of immigration evidence of their good character.

As early as 1867, Congressman Johnson of California introduced a resolution in the House of Representatives, directing the Judiciary Committee to inquire whether the US Congress could by legislation prevent the immigration of "Chinese and other inferior races" into the country.[106] On the ten-year anniversary of the Burlingame Treaty, the California Senate sent a memorial to the US Congress seeking a federal law limiting the total number of Chinese passengers who could be landed by vessel at any US port to ten persons.[107] One year later, in 1879, the US Congress passed the "Fifteen Passenger Bill," limiting the number of Chinese passengers who might be brought to the United States in any one vessel to fifteen.[108] President Hayes vetoed the Fifteen Passenger Bill as an attempt to nullify the treaty and, on November 17, 1880, amended the Burlingame Treaty's free emigration provision to allow the "US government, whenever it determined that it should be in its interest to do so, to *suspend* for a reasonable period of time, but not absolutely to prohibit, the coming of Chinese laborers into the United States." The amended treaty reaffirmed the right of Chinese laborers in the United States to "go and come of their own free will" and guaranteed them all the "rights, privileges, immunities, and exemptions" accorded to the citizens or subjects of the most favored nation.[109]

In 1882, the US Congress proposed an immigration bill to ban new Chinese laborers for twenty years and establish an internal passport system to control the movement of those already residing inside the country. President Hayes vetoed this bill, and the US Congress subsequently revised the ban to ten years and removed the passport control provision. On May 6, 1882, President Chester A. Arthur signed "An Act to execute certain treaty stipulations relating to Chinese," also known as the Chinese Exclusion Act of 1882.[110] It made it a criminal and civil crime for anyone to violate the federal ban on Chinese laborers, including miners.[111] In 1884, after many federal court cases prompted questions about rules on reentry, Congress passed a second exclusion act, which amended the certification procedures for all Chinese immigrant residents, requiring that they show "the individual, family, and tribal name of the laborer and when and where he had pursued his occupation," among other provisions, and made it clear that the certificate would be "the only evidence permissible" for Chinese immigrants to establish the right of reentry.[112] It also specified that these exclusions applied to all Chinese and subjects of China, not just laborers. Finally, even though the 1882 Chinese Exclusion Act did not call for the expulsion of Chinese immigrants already living in the United States, state authorities stood idly as nativists engaged in widespread acts of arson and rioting in Chinese settlements across the state.[113]

In 1888, the federal government revised its treaty with China, adding a twenty-year ban on new immigration and reaffirming federal protection and rights for Chinese immigrants residing inside the US. Soon after, the federal government passed the Scott Act of 1888, permanently banning immigration from Chinese laborers and their reentry, irrespective of former residence in the US. California leaders celebrated and continued to urge the US Congress to pass even harsher laws, one of which would require lawful Chinese residents to register and carry certificates of identification or face immediate deportation.[114] The Scott Act was severe. It prevented Chinese laborers from having any right to visit China and then return to the US, thereby permanently separating Chinese families. In *Chae Chan Ping v. United States* (1889), the US Supreme Court upheld the Scott Act and the US Congress's power to enact exclusions on Chinese immigration.[115]

This new era in immigration federalism made entry/exit and removal powers exclusive to the federal government, significantly constraining how California's regressive citizenship would evolve in the twentieth century. In 1891, California passed a state law – "An Act to prevent Chinese Migration" – that stopped migration of Chinese persons and required registration and certificates for those Chinese already residing within the state. The supreme court of California that same year, in *Ex Parte Ah Cue* (1894), struck down the law, stating that was "plainly in excess of the power of the state, and in conflict with the Constitution of the United States." It was preempted by exclusive federal authority over immigration law.[116] Nevertheless, California continued to push for added restrictions at the federal level, including the 1892 Geary Act (named after the California congressman), which extended the Chinese ban another ten years and created an internal passport system that required all Chinese to be photographed.[117] Without an identity document, any person suspected of being Chinese was presumed to be in the country unlawfully and subject to immediate deportation. Furthermore, the Geary Act restricted Chinese testimony in deportation cases (allowing only White witnesses to defend Chinese), denied bail to Chinese defendants, and made "illicit residence" in the country a federal crime punishable by up to one year of imprisonment and hard labor.[118] In *Fong Yue Ting v. United States* (1893), the US Supreme Court upheld the constitutionality of the Geary Act.[119] We will have more to say about the role of Congress and the Supreme Court in channeling and constraining California's regressive citizenship in Chapter 6.

By 1900, the Chinese population in California had dwindled to about 60 percent of what it had been at the high point of immigration (Figure 5.3).[122] Discrimination continued for many years, but the state and federal restrictions began to shift. Japanese immigration to California began in the early 1880s and picked up steam over the subsequent two decades. Unlike the early wave of Chinese immigrants, who worked in mining and railroad construction, Japanese immigrants specialized in agriculture and succeeded in all aspects of the industry, from cultivation to warehousing, distribution, and retail. Far from welcoming these economic contributions, California began to push for a series of restrictions on land ownership to curtail the perceived economic power of Japanese immigrants. In 1913, the state passed its first Alien Land Law, which limited ownership of land to three-year leaseholds by persons ineligible to citizenship, which included not only Chinese and Japanese but also the growing number of Sikh immigrants who had taken up farming in the state.[123] In 1920, California passed a second Alien Land Law, further amended in 1923, which ended its three-year lease provision, banned Asian immigrants from owning stock in companies that acquired agricultural land, and established an annual report requirements to track their labor activities. In

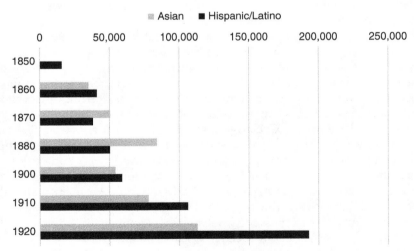

FIGURE 5.3 Asian and Hispanic share of California's population, 1850–1920
Note: Most population records from the 1890 Census were destroyed by a fire in the Commerce Department building in 1921.[121]
Source: Census data from IPUMS-USA[120]

1920, the California State Board of Control prepared a report, entitled *California and the Oriental*, for Governor William D. Stephens on persons of Asian descent living in the state, primarily focusing on concerns raised by the increase in Japanese residents. Stephens sent this report and a letter to the US secretary of state calling for the passage of a federal Japanese exclusion act, much like the Chinese act.[124] Responding to this pressure, in 1924, President Coolidge signed a very restrictive immigration act that forbade any further Japanese immigration to the United States.[125]

World War II marked a quick expansion in regressive citizenship, with California spearheading national efforts to place Japanese residents and US citizens into internment or concentration camps. California's Joint Immigration Committee strategically targeted Japanese in a propaganda campaign in newspapers, painting a negative popular image of them as un-American and unassimilable and portraying them as loyal to Japan and threats to the United States.[126] Moreover, the California committee were supported by White supremacist organizations, including the Native Sons and Daughters of the Golden West, which urged the state government to place all Japanese into concentration camps. Taking their cue, Attorney General of California Earl Warren began to place pressure on the federal government to remove all ethnic Japanese. All Japanese in the country were deemed "an enemy race" and were stripped of all federal and state rights on February 19, 1942, when President Roosevelt signed Executive Order No. 9066 ordering that Japanese residents be physically detained and placed into internment camps.[127]

Soon after the end of World War II, California's push for regressive citizenship involving Asian immigrants would largely draw to a close. In 1943, California amended its fish and game policies to deny commercial fishing licenses to "aliens ineligible for citizenship," which meant any Asian immigrant.[128] In *Takahashi v. Fish and Game Commission* (1948), the US Supreme Court struck down California's 1943 fishing license law.[129] That same year, in *Oyama v. California* (1948), it struck down California's Alien Land Laws, but only as they applied to US citizens of Japanese dissent.[130] Four years later, in *Sei Fujii v. California* (1952), the supreme court of California ruled that the Alien Land Laws (of 1913, 1920, and 1923) violated the equal protection clause of the Fourteenth Amendment and were thus unconstitutional.[131] This ruling, however, did not mean the end of regressive citizenship in California. The state continued to push for new ways to limit the right of immigrants well into the twentieth century, with Mexican-origin residents as the primary target.

THE ANTI-MEXICAN PERIOD (1930–1998)

In the 1890s, Mexican immigrants were recruited for the first time by the Santa Fe and Southern Pacific Railway companies to construct their southern railway lines, beginning a new period of cross-border migration. Having closed the doors to Asian labor, California's agricultural economy in the 1910s relied on Mexican-American citizens and immigrants as the state's primary source of seasonal farm workers.[132] Meanwhile, wartime efforts during World War I, which formally began for the US in 1917, added another significant "pull factor" for Mexican migration, as the needs of the wartime economy and the deployment of working-age adults to Europe created massive labor shortages in the United States. Across the border, the ongoing Mexican Revolution during this time (1910–1920) added a major push factor, as Mexican nationals crossed the border in search of work as well as safety. Thus, from 1917 to 1921, an estimated 74,000 Mexican immigrant workers entered the country through temporary labor contracts, and hundreds of thousands more entered without documentation.[133]

Finally, growing nativism in the US pushed the federal government to ban nearly all immigration in 1921 and 1924, with stringent caps on southern and eastern Europe for the first time. These federalism dynamics would shape the future of state citizenship in California for years to come (see Figure 5.4): federal law remained silent on Mexican immigration, creating even greater pull factors across the US southern border during the Roaring Twenties, a time of rapid economic expansion. Thus, Mexican migration became an essential part of California's economy. For example, by 1928 an estimated 84 percent of agricultural workers in Southern California were Mexicans of varying legal statuses.[134] In California's prior periods and treatment of Blacks, Native Americans, and Chinese, state policies racialized Mexican migrants and exploited them, establishing a regime of regressive state citizenship (see Chapter 2, Figure 2.9). The new era of federal plenary power in immigration

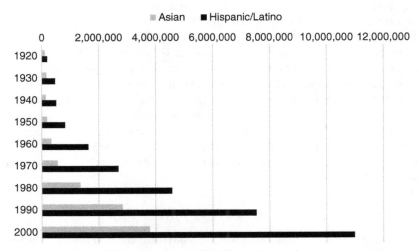

FIGURE 5.4 Asian and Hispanic share of California's population, 1920–1980

law, which began in 1882, added greater complexity to the control that California would try to exert over its Mexican American and Mexican immigrant populations. Rather than constraining regressive state policies, federal immigration law in many ways actually opened a new pathway for California to develop an exclusionary form of state citizenship, one that mirrored federal law and enforcement practices, while also continuing to expand its *regressive* state policies that went below the federal baseline on immigrant rights.

Established in 1924, the US border patrol was small in number but was nevertheless able to selectively target Mexicans who were US citizens or immigrants of varying statuses alike for removal. Already subjected to racialized exploitation, Mexican Americans faced significant hostility from Whites during the Great Depression beginning in 1929. A period of mass expulsion soon followed, with nearly 400,000 Mexican nationals forcibly and immediately removed, with the peak year, 1931, seeing 138,000 removals.[135] Repatriation was a race-based program targeting all Mexicans, and it ignored the fact that more than half of the people removed were US citizens. Moreover, it ushered in a new era of California's state citizenship, through a new type of exclusionary and *reinforcing* policy applied jointly by federal, state, and local officials. Repatriation denied Mexicans access to their existing rights – to free movement (Dimension 1), due process and legal protection (Dimension 2), and identify and belonging (Dimension 5) – and kick-started California's century of anti-Mexican policies.

Federalism dynamics were key to this century of state citizenship. Expansions in social welfare under President Roosevelt's New Deal created new spaces for California to reinforce and entrench its racialized, regressive state citizenship. Prior to federal relief and social welfare, California's county-level relief offices from the 1900s to the 1930s used social welfare to control farm workers, making them dependent on employers. As Jess Walsh explains, growers and county relief offices worked together to manipulate relief rolls in way that constructed "a fluid and mobile population of farm workers sustained in the off-seasons but ready to be deployed at harvest time."[136] Seasonal agricultural workers often headed to cities during their off-season to temporarily work in urban industries, like canneries, textiles, garments, and construction, where they had access to other forms of relief and cash assistance.[137] However, many local relief agencies began to require proof of US citizenship and denied Mexican immigrants access to these forms of relief.[138]

Even before the onset of the Great Depression, the California legislature passed a joint resolution in 1929 calling on Congress to restrict immigration from Mexico. California's Governor Young, in particular, had been on a fact-finding mission from 1924 to 1928 and used statistics to argue that Mexicans were disproportionately reliant on relief, depleting the state of resources.[139] While public officials in California and Texas pushed for national restrictions in the late 1920s, agricultural businesses testified to the House Committee on Immigration and Naturalization that the benefits outweighed the costs, especially since Mexican immigrants did not seek to naturalize or remain in the US permanently.

Federal relief during the Great Depression emerged at the height of California's anti-Mexican sentiment (see Table 5.4). In 1932, President Hoover signed the Emergency Relief and Construction Act, offering state and local governments loans to pay for relief. The largest relief program, the Federal Emergency Relief Administration (FERA), was established in 1933, appropriating $500 million to states (as matching grants) to spend on either direct relief or work relief. Importantly, all immigrants were included as part of the American population who should be given access to state relief using FERA funds. Franklin D. Roosevelt's New Deal of the 1930s denied access to Blacks in the South but did not require US citizenship or federal legal status.[140] As Cybelle Fox highlights, federal officials sent a memo to all state relief administrators stating that "[t]here shall be no discrimination because of race, religion, color, non-citizenship, political affiliation or because of membership in any special or selected group" when administering FERA funds, giving Blacks and Mexicans "unprecedented" access to relief.[141]

Nevertheless, South and Southwest local relief offices purposely shut down during harvest seasons in order to secure growers' control over Black and immigrant labor. FERA relief funds were under the control of appointed state emergency relief administrator.[142] This enabled Governor James Rolph of California to appoint an anti-immigrant conservative, Archbishop Hanna, who advocated restricting Mexican immigration.[143] By contrast, it also enabled Illinois to protect White immigrants from discrimination by social workers and relief administrators.[144] Failing to push for federal restrictions on immigration from Mexico, anti-immigrant activists in California turned their efforts to federal restriction on social welfare. They succeeded in leading a coalition of Southern and Southwestern congressmen to push for adding industry-specific exclusions on Black and immigrant workers in agriculture, domestic service, retail, and restaurants in the Fair Labor Standards Act of 1938 (FLSA), denying these groups important labor rights and protections. They also changed existing federal New Deal policy by adding new restrictions in 1936 to Work Projects Administration (WPA) projects, banning the employment of "unauthorized" immigrants and, three years later in 1939, banning the employment of all immigrants.[145]

Mexican labor was intimately tied to California's federal and state leadership on immigration. Removing immigrant labor from WPA projects and banning immigrants from being able to receive federal relief was strategic: it worked in the favor of California's large farming and agricultural sectors during the Great Depression by creating a class of exploitable workers who were denied basic labor rights (Dimension 3). Soon this state model was mirrored at the federal level. With economic expansion fully underway by 1940, these same sectors in

TABLE 5.4 *California's anti-Mexican period, 1890–1998*

Policy type	Citizenship Dimensions 1–5*	Citizenship type**	US citizen	Legal immigrant	Undocumented	Repealed or preempted
State-led removal	1, 2, 5	*Restrictive*	1920s repatriation***	1920s Repatriation***	1920s	
Immigration enforcement with Fed.	1, 5	*Restrictive*	Repatriation***	Repatriation***	1994 (Proposition 187)	1994 *Preempted*
Work relief ban	3	*Regressive*	1933 (FERA)	1933 (FERA)	1933 (FERA)	
General/cash assistance ban	3	*Regressive*	1934 (OAA) 1935 (ADC)	1934 (OAA) 1935 (ADC)	1934 (OAA) 1935 (ADC)	
Labor contract	1, 2, 3, 5	*See specific group/policy→*	*Regressive* 1890–1920 debt peonage 1942–1964 Bracero *Reinforcing* UFW contract *Progressive*	*Regressive* 1890–1920 debt peonage 1942–1964 Bracero *Reinforcing* UFW contract *Progressive*	*Regressive* 1890–1920 debt peonage 1942–1964 Bracero *Reinforcing* UFW contract *Progressive*	
Welfare assistance ban	3	*Regressive*		1900–1933***	1900–1933*** 1969***	
Employer sanctions	3, 5	*Regressive*			1971	1986 *Preempted*

(continued)

TABLE 5.4 (*continued*)

Policy type	Citizenship Dimensions 1–5*	Citizenship type**	US citizen	Legal immigrant	Undocumented	Repealed or preempted
Public benefits ban	3	*Regressive*		1970s 1994 (Proposition 187)	1970s 1994 (Proposition 187)	1994 *Preempted*
Health care ban	3	*Regressive*		1994 (Proposition 187)	1994 (Proposition 187)	1994 *Preempted*
K–12 education ban	3	*Regressive*			1994 (Proposition 187)	1994 *Preempted*
Bilingual education ban	3, 5	*See specific group/ policy*→	*Regressive* 1998	*Regressive* 1998	*Regressive* 1998	*Progressive* 2016
Driver's license ban	1, 3, 5	*See specific group/ policy*→			*Regressive* 1993	*Progressive* 2013

* The provision of rights to: (1) free movement; (2) due process and legal protection; (3) develop human capital; (4) participate and be represented; and (5) identify and Belong.

** Citizenship types: regressive; restrictive; progressive.

*** Distinguishes de facto policy (differential access to rights). Meanwhile, the table's baseline is de jure policy (provision of rights).

California, Texas, and Arizona requested that the federal Immigration Service allow them to continue bringing in Mexican immigrant labor.[146] This led to the federal creation of the Bracero Program in 1942. President Truman negotiated a bilateral agreement with Mexico to provide for seasonal migration of "braceros," a program that continued from 1942 until 1964. In the 1940s, the program brought in fewer than 100,000 workers per year but then increased in the 1950s to more than 400,000 per year.[147]

In 1952 and in 1965, Congress comprehensively overhauled federal immigration as part of the broader civil rights revolution, eliminating explicit racial barriers to immigration and naturalization. This significant shift in federal law had a profound impact on California's regressive state citizenship, particularly in how it would begin to target undocumented immigrants. New federal floors were established that provided Mexican Americans and legal immigrants new rights and protections while simultaneously cracking down on undocumented immigrants, thereby opening pathways for California to push both regressive and reinforcing state citizenship policies with respect to its Mexican immigrant population. During this federal shift, Congress instituted per-country limitations on every migrant-sending country, which had profound effects on countries of high migration to the United States. Most notably, for the first time, limits were placed on legal migration from Mexico, which were especially drastic as they followed on the heels of the dismantling of the Bracero Program.[148] Congress's decision to discontinue the Bracero program, largely in anticipation of the 1965 INA amendments, disrupted the agricultural system on which both US employers and Mexican laborers and their dependents had grown to rely.

These dramatic shifts in federal policy caused a marked change in unlawful migration, including its magnitude, meaning, and political and legal importance. One of the major consequences of the 1965 amendments to federal law was a significant increase in lawful migration from Asia, with a concurrent limitation on lawful migration from Mexico and Central America that ballooned the unauthorized immigrant population in the state.[149] This prompted a push in regressive legislation and state administration of welfare policy. In the 1970s, California was the first state to pass an employer sanction law, which was followed by major court decisions upholding the law and congressional responses trying to preempt it. The state was also an early adopter of policies limiting access to welfare benefits, thus instituting a regressive form of citizenship with respect to human capital formation.

After the US Supreme Court in *Shapiro v. Thompson* (1969) held state laws denying welfare assistance to persons who are residents unconstitutional, California began to limit access through immigrant specific restrictions.[150] California's State Social Welfare Board urged Governor Reagan to bar applicants who were either "temporary" or "illegal immigrants."[151] This led Reagan to pass the Accountability Act of 1971, overhauling the state's welfare system, which included a provision "designed to prevent the granting of aid to illegal aliens and temporary foreign visitors" and "set up a mechanism for communication between county welfare offices and INS to identify illegal aliens on welfare."[152]

In *Graham v. Richardson* (1971), the US Supreme Court invalidated welfare schemes in Pennsylvania and Arizona that barred recently immigrated lawful permanent residents from accessing public benefits, ruling it violating their Fourteenth Amendment equal protection right.[153] Prior to *Graham*, most state and local restrictions on noncitizen employment and participation in economic activities restrictions survived judicial scrutiny. The *Graham* court invalidated state welfare schemes that barred recently immigrated lawful permanent residents from accessing public benefits. On the equal protection claim, the Court treated the legal permanent resident challengers as a discrete and insular minority requiring heightened judicial scrutiny by the Court. On the preemption claim, the Court found that the welfare restrictions tended to influence migration decisions and therefore impermissibly intruded into a statutory field occupied by the federal government. In reaction, several states began to remove such restrictions on legal immigrants. At the same time, the Court let stand state restrictions on the employment of unauthorized immigrants, signaling the limits to its equal protection approach.[154]

These federalism dynamics had important consequences in California, whose economy faced a recession in 1970–1971 and where anti-immigrant political leaders began their push for the first employer sanctions law, AB 528, banning the hiring of undocumented immigrant labor.[155] California Assemblyman Pete Chacon, a prominent member of the Assembly Committee on Labor Relations, attacked the issue of employment, arguing that "for too many years the illegal entrant has been the tool of unscrupulous employers who capitalize on his willingness to work long hours for minimum wages. The widespread use of illegal entrant workers ... deprives unskilled and semi-skilled Mexican-Americans, citizens and aliens alike, black and white workers, of decent employment."[156] State leaders attacked illegal immigration as the primary cause of California's economic problems and the reason for regulating who can be employed in the state.[157] Sectors of the labor movement also supported restricting the hiring of undocumented workers, including the California Teamsters, California's Federation of Labor (AFL-CIO), the UFWOC, and the California Rural Legal Assistance, Inc (CRLA).[158]

On November 8, 1971, California Governor Ronald Reagan signed AB 528 into law, which stated: "No employer shall knowingly employ an alien who is not entitled to lawful residence in the United States if such employment would have an adverse effect on lawful resident workers."[159] California's effort led ten other states to pass similar laws and was passed in the context of increasing undocumented migration following the US Congress's dismantling of the Bracero Program, federal immigration law instituting severe limits on Mexican migration, and the effects of an economic recession at the time. The irony of AB 528 is that it did not prevent employers from hiring undocumented labor and, instead, increased an employer's control over immigrant labor. It empowered employers and growers with the option of threatening to report employees' immigration status to officials for possible deportation.[160] In *De Canas v. Bica* (1976), the court left California's 1971 employer sanction law in place, until federal law superseded it in 1986.[161]

Federalism dynamics shaped California's role beyond welfare changes at the state level during the 1970s. California leaders mobilized around new federal restrictions to pressure the US Congress to contract rights in other areas of federal welfare policy, succeeding on many fronts.[162] The federal Supplemental Security Income (SSI) program established in 1972 barred unauthorized immigrants from its benefits, and the Social Security Administration, also established in 1972, barred them from receiving Social Security numbers. Moreover, in 1973, the secretary of the Department of Health, Education and Welfare began, for the first time, a ban on undocumented immigrants receiving Medicaid and AFDC. The US Department of Agriculture in 1974 limited food stamp benefits to US citizens and permanently residing aliens, and this restriction was ratified by the US Congress in 1977. And in 1976, the US Congress amended federal unemployment insurance law barring access undocumented immigrants. Thus, for the first time at the federal level and thanks to significant pressure from California lawmakers, many applicants for public assistance became subject to status verification through the INS.[163]

Diffusion of California's policies continued as a result of new federalism dynamics. Congress looked to California's 1971 employment verification law as a model for its 1986 Immigration Reform and Control Act (IRCA), which established the first federal employer sanction law and made it unlawful for undocumented immigrants to work inside the United States. Notably, alongside this federal enforcement scheme, the IRCA expressly forbade "any State or local law imposing civil or criminal sanctions (other than through licensing and similar laws) upon those who employ ... unauthorized persons," thereby replacing California's policy in this area.[164] This shifted California's employer sanctions law from regressive to reinforcing, as the federal government matched California's exclusionary policy on employment and preempted it.

The final wave of reinforcing and regressive state legislation in California occurred in the 1990s. In the early part of that decade, California was suffering disproportionately from the economic recession, as military base closures and cuts in defense spending after the end of the Cold War eliminated hundreds of thousands of jobs in the state. To make matters worse, cities and counties in California began filing for bankruptcy, causing even deeper job cuts and loss of economic confidence.[165] Anti-immigrant activists in Southern California successfully mobilized a widespread political movement out of this economic anxiety. As petition gatherers began to collect thousands of signatures on immigration restriction measures, the state legislature moved to address voter anger by passing a raft of regressive and reinforcing measures in 1993. The state passed laws barring unauthorized immigrants from obtaining driver's licenses, mandating cooperation between state prisons and federal immigration authorities, and requiring employment agencies to verify immigration status. In 1994, California reached an important transition point with the passage of Proposition 187 (Prop. 187). Taken up by Governor Pete Wilson's reelection campaign, Prop. 187 garnered significant financial and political support from the Republican Party and was enacted by voters in November 1994 by a very wide margin of 59 percent to 41 percent.[166] It sought to limit access to public services for undocumented persons, required state officials at all levels to report suspected unlawful presence, and barred primary and secondary education for undocumented children. Thus, Proposition 187 contained both regressive elements, denying rights to public education that the Supreme Court had upheld in *Plyler v. Doe* (1982) and reinforcing elements by mirroring federal restrictions to control access to rights at the state level.

In many ways, however, Prop. 187 was the beginning of the end of regressive citizenship in California. A federal district court held most of Prop. 187 unconstitutional.[167] Its verification, notification, and cooperation/reporting requirements were preempted by federal immigration law. Its denial of education to undocumented children violated equal protection. Ultimately, the state abandoned its defense of the law entirely and came to a mediated settlement.[168]

CALIFORNIA'S DRAMATIC TURN TO PROGRESSIVE STATE CITIZENSHIP (1998–PRESENT)

The shift to *progressive state citizenship* in California did not occur suddenly after the court defeat of Proposition 187. As we detail here, this process emerged over two decades – gradually at first, with some early policy victories on education and health care between 1997 and 2002, followed by a period of policy stasis and movement infrastructure-building from 2003 to 2010, and then a period of accelerated policy change (Figure 5.5). By 2015, pro-immigrant integration policies had advanced sufficiently across all five dimensions of state citizenship that they had crystallized into a robust regime of progressive state citizenship. Still, if we view the past two decades in light of the state's 150-year history of exclusion, the shift toward progressive state citizenship has been very quick indeed. The only other period of rapid change in citizenship regimes in California occurred in the early years of the state's founding, when, between 1852 and 1879, the state rapidly advanced exclusionary anti-Chinese policies across all five dimensions, similarly crystallizing a robust regime of regressive state citizenship.

These two disparate periods in California state citizenship share some important similarities. Federalism conflicts emerged in the 1860s between the

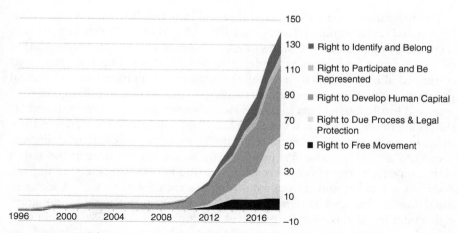

FIGURE 5.5 California's move toward progressive state citizenship
Note: Totals by dimension of citizenship as noted in Chapter 2 (see Appendix for indicator scoring).

US government intent on importing Chinese labor to work on the railroads and nativist movements in California aiming to isolate Chinese immigrants and kick them out of the country. From California's very founding, proslavery Democrats controlled state government and had general public support to pass many anti-Chinese laws that were being pushed by White nativist labor groups. These groups got considerably stronger when the federal government signed the Burlingame Treaty with China in 1868, with the Workingmen's Party under Kearney consolidating grassroots power in the 1870s and pushing for even harsher laws and a state constitutional revision in 1879 that crystallized California's regime of regressive state citizenship.

As we elaborate in this section on contemporary California, federalism conflicts have had a symbiotic relationship with the growing strength of social movement actors after 1996, and both have played a significant role in propelling California rapidly toward a progressive regime of state citizenship. The state's immigrant rights movement became energized over the fight over Proposition 187 and exclusionary moves in federal immigration reform in 1996, and the movement drew renewed energy during the massive immigration rallies of 2006 following the passage of harsh immigration legislation in the US House of Representatives.[169] Meanwhile, coordinated investments by philanthropic organizations in the state helped the movement grow in geographic reach and sophistication, placing constant pressure on the state to enact pro-immigrant policies. However, pressure from social movement actors and Democratic lawmakers did not lead inevitably to policy change: federalism dynamics were key to the timing and sequencing of when these policies passed, and especially so for the rapid movement toward progressive state citizenship after 2012.

Key federalism dynamics during this period included: (1) federal immigration reform and social welfare reform under IIR-IRA and the PWORA in 1996 that set up new opportunities for states to engage in policymaking; (2) an escalation of immigration enforcement under the second Bush administration that continued during the first term of the Obama administration; (3) federal programs such as 287(g) agreements and Secure Communities that compelled state and local governments to cooperate on immigration enforcement; and (4) the failure of the DREAM Act in 2010 and comprehensive immigration reform in 2013–2014 that made even reluctant Democrats realize that California needed to act. Thus, while Proposition 187 was a key moment in the state's shift away from regressive citizenship, we should not overstate its impact. Federalism conflict and movement strength were critical to early success in immigrant rights and remained critical to the proliferation of immigrant rights once the Democratic Party gained full control in 2010. We explain how federalism dynamics, movement-building, and party control linked up together – in specific years and involving particular issues – to shape the timing and sequencing of progressive state policies.

Before we proceed with a chronological account of California's shift to progressive state citizenship from 1996 to today, it is important to set the context for federal policy and state social movement activity in the mid-1990s. In the wake of Proposition 187's passage and subsequent defeat in federal court, the US Congress passed two major pieces of legislation that set the stage for California's immigrant rights movement: the 1996 Illegal Immigration Reform and Immigrant Responsibility Act (IIR-IRA) and the Personal Responsibility and Work Opportunity Reconciliation Act (PRWORA, also referred to as welfare reform). IIR-IRA significantly boosted immigration enforcement, dramatically increasing the number of crimes that would land legal immigrants in deportation proceedings, preventing unauthorized immigrants from arguing their case before a judge if they were apprehended within 100 miles of the US border and excluding them from reentry to the United States for up to ten years.[170] It also enabled states and localities to receive delegated authority from the federal government to engage in immigration enforcement under Section 287(g) of the Immigration and Nationality Act.[171] The PRWORA added new federal restrictions on immigrant access to welfare and devolved welfare decisions to the states, including public benefits, professional licenses, and educational benefits. Importantly, however, both welfare reform and immigration reform in 1996 allowed states to be more generous than the federal government toward their noncitizen populations, with the proviso that any prior benefits would be "wiped clean" and would require enactments by new state law after August 22, 1996.[172]

Through welfare reform, the federal government devolved many new powers to states, which aligned with important political and demographic changes underway in California. As early as the 1980s, California labor groups and multiracial coalitions were partnering with immigrants in large cities, and new immigrant rights organizations were forming in rural and exurban areas. By the 1990s, hundreds of thousands of Latinx became eligible for naturalization, many of them beneficiaries of legalization under IRCA in 1986. Republican backing for Proposition 187 and other racially divisive propositions such as Prop. 209 in 1996 (banning affirmative action) and Prop. 227 in 1998 (banning bilingual education programs) energized this growing Latino electorate and turned them decisively against the Republican Party.[173] These propositions also convinced a new generation of Latino community organizers to run for political office, propelling the Latino Caucus to be a powerful force in the state legislature.[174]

The development of local organizational capacity was also critical during this period, as Ruth Milkman and Manuel Pastor have shown.[175] Major national labor unions like the AFL-CIO, the SEIU, and Unite-HERE saw immigrants as a rapidly growing part of their membership, prompting them to change their stance from being exclusionary or neutral on immigration to becoming strongly pro-immigrant.[176] The AFL-CIO began to help immigrants in preparing amnesty applications and created the Labor Immigrant Assistance Project (LIAP) and the California Immigrant Workers Association (CIWA), both based in Los Angeles.[177] The SEIU led a "Justice for Janitors" campaign that staged a successful strike in 1990 and partnered with Los Angeles Mayor Tom Bradley to achieve multiyear contracts and higher wages for janitors. Around the same time, Pastor and colleagues have shown that strong coalitions in Los Angeles formed between African Americans and immigrants, successfully pushing for reforms such as reducing mass transit costs and increasing access, expanding job training support, establishing community benefits agreements with large commercial developers, increasing school funding, and expanding drug treatment programs.[178]

Immigrant rights organizations also began to emerge, including the Coalition for Humane Immigrant Rights of Los Angeles (CHIRLA), the Koreatown Immigrant Workers Association (KIWA), the National Day Laborer Organizing Network (NDLON), the South Asian Network (SAN), and the Central American Resource Center (CARECEN). They fought to protect undocumented day laborers and domestic workers through an emergency hotline and offering support services.[179] The strong local organizational capacity that developed in the 1990s was leveraged by philanthropic organizations, who began to help build a coordinated network of immigrant advocacy groups across the state.[180] These developments would prove critical in the two decades following the passage of Proposition 187, as they spawned a new generation of Latino lawmakers in Sacramento who introduced legislation to improve the lives of unauthorized immigrants, won support from their Democratic colleagues with the help of a robust network of immigrant advocacy groups across the state, and ultimately convinced a moderate Democratic governor to sign a string of measures in 2013 and

2014 that were symbolically bold and substantively far-reaching, propelling California toward a progressive regime of state citizenship.

EARLY POLICY VICTORIES (1998–2002)

Movement toward progressive reforms in the late 1990s were very limited. California's efforts during this period either sought to restore to immigrants prior benefits that had been stripped away by federal reforms or to build momentum from city-level policy victories. California immediately restored some welfare benefits, such as temporary prenatal health care for legal immigrants, that were rescinded by the Personal Work Opportunity and Reform Act of 1996. The state soon enacted laws to create emergency welfare benefits of its own, including food assistance in 1998 and cash assistance in 1999. It further expanded prenatal care to undocumented immigrant women in 2002 by extending CHIP coverage to unborn children, after the US Department of Health and Human Services gave states the option to do so. Similarly, the state led in passing AB 540 in 2001, offering in-state tuition benefits to undocumented students, which had been denied under federal law a short time earlier in 1996.

In the 1990s, the Coalition for Humane Immigrant Rights of Los Angeles (CHIRLA) and the Mexican American League Defense and Education Fund (MALDEF) fought to repeal anti–day labor ordinances, which had spread across localities in the state. After gaining some local successes, these organizations turned their efforts toward worker protections at the state level, passing AB 633 in 1999, a law that held retailers, manufacturers, and contractors liable for federal labor-law violations.[181] Immigrant rights organizations fought for restoring driver's licenses to undocumented immigrants and, in 2003, managed to get Democratic Governor Gray Davis to pass AB 60, but this success was very short-lived. Davis faced a voter recall, and Republican Arnold Schwarzenegger, who won the election, pressured lawmakers to repeal the measure and vetoed further attempts to restore driver's licenses.[182]

MOVEMENT INFRASTRUCTURE-BUILDING (2003–2009)

The Schwarzenegger administration was opposed to most pro-immigrant legislation, particularly since the state was still recovering from its 2001 financial crisis and the governor had run on a vow to repeal driver's licenses for undocumented immigrants. On the other hand, the immigrant rights movement succeeded during this period in boosting its organizational capacity, networked strength, and political sophistication, setting up for future legislative victories. Statewide funders invested in the movement's regional infrastructure, which provided immigrant rights organizations with greater capacity to coordinate acts of civil disobedience by immigrant youth, outreach to business organizations and clergy, and research messaging strategies to better sway public opinion.[183] This network helped elect a new generation of pro-immigrant champions in the state legislature and also held other elected officials accountable in places well beyond Los Angeles and San Francisco. Another important development during this period was the growth of the National Day Labor Organizing Network (NDLON), which was established in 2001. NDLON found itself at the forefront of local-level battles over day labor centers throughout the state and soon also expanded its scope to resisting increases in federal enforcement under the 287(g) program.[184]

Finally, the Schwarzenegger years also saw the growing strength of California Immigrant Policy Center, which had evolved from being a collaborative project of Los Angeles and Bay Area–based immigrant rights organizations (named the California Immigrant Welfare Collaborative), into an independent organization with strong regional partnerships in the state's other major regions, including the Central Valley, Central Coast, Inland Empire, Orange County, and San Diego. These regional partners would prove critical to building statewide legislative support for immigration rights, as well as ensuring accountability in the implementation of legislative reforms. Thus, while there was very little room for pro-immigrant legislation from 2003 to 2009, the movement itself grew in strength, reach, and sophistication.[185]

While California's pro-immigrant movement was growing, the state became entangled at the local level with larger federalism dynamics, fueling pockets of anti-immigrant mobilization in parts of Southern California. One of the most restrictive federal reform bills, HR 4437 (Sensenbrenner, R-WI), passed in the House in December 2005. HR 4437 sought to criminalize unlawful presence in the country, to criminalize the act of associating with undocumented immigrants, and to revise "the definition of 'aggravated felony' to include all smuggling offenses, and illegal entry and reentry crimes."[186] Sensenbrenner failed in the Senate, but he had two important legacies for the immigrant rights movement in California. First, over 1 million protesters marched in cities across California in Spring 2006, with organizations as varied as labor unions, the Catholic Church, other faith-based organizations, Spanish radio personalities, and the television network Univision playing an important role in shaping both the mobilization and the messaging behind the rallies.[187] These rallies not only demonstrated the reach of the immigrant rights movement in regions across California; they also strengthened movement organizations in Orange County and various parts of inland California, including the Central Valley and Inland Empire. Private foundations saw the opportunity to strengthen the movement even further. Instead of creating one immigrant rights coalition for the entire state or dissipating their investments across small-scale local initiatives throughout the state, they chose a middle ground – to coordinate their philanthropic activities and to support and grow a robust ecosystem of regional and statewide immigrant rights organizations that would work in concert with each other and that would work on engaging local constituents and state representatives alike.[188] These efforts would take years of patient investing, something that funders were willing to do in anticipation of a different political opportunity structure after Governor Schwarzenegger's two terms in office.

Anti-immigrant actors also leveraged Sensenbrenner's failure in 2005 and 2006, arguing for a concerted push in state and local legislation to contract immigrant rights. In 2006, the city of San Bernardino pushed for a comprehensive local ordinance they called the "Illegal Immigration Relief Act," seeking to mandate English-only for all city-related business and banning day labor centers, day labor work solicitation, any hiring of unauthorized workers, and any renting of properties to undocumented immigrants.[189] Pro-immigrant activists, the ACLU of Orange County, and the Mexican American Legal Defense and Educational Fund (MALDEF) quickly mobilized and provided legal support to the pro-immigrant mayor and city councilmembers, who voted down the ordinance by a vote of 4–3.[190] Joseph Turner, author of the restrictive ordinance, turned his efforts to placing the ordinance as a voter initiative during the November 2006 general election but was blocked by San Bernardino County superior court Judge A. Rex Victor, who ruled that Turner did not acquire the needed signatures to qualify the measure for a public vote.[191]

Framed within the federal debate over unlawful presence, this restrictive ordinance and others that followed were intended to drive undocumented persons out of their respective jurisdictions by contracting their right to free movement (Dimension 1) and right to develop human capital (Dimension 3). Although San Bernardino's ordinance failed, city councils from across the country followed suit. Landlord ordinances were part of a larger onslaught of exclusionary laws championed by conservative organizations like NumbersUSA, FAIR, and its legal arm Immigration Reform Law Institute led by Kris Kobach and Michael Hethmon.[192] Over 100 cities across the country followed San Bernardino's failed ordinance, and at least six cities in California (Apple Valley, Costa Mesa, Escondido, Lancaster, Santa Clarita, and Vista) enacted anti-immigrant ordinances on matters ranging from day laborers to employers and landlords.[193]

On October 17, 2006, Southern California's city of Escondido approved an ordinance that made it illegal to rent property to "illegal aliens."[194] Unlike San Bernardino's failed attempt, Escondido succeeded in enacting its ordinance. Before Escondido's law was officially enforced, MALDEF, the ACLU of San Diego, People for the American Way, the Fair Housing Council of San Diego, and several private-law firms challenged the ordinance and pressured Judge John Houston of the United States District Court for the Southern District of California in San Diego to issue a temporary injunction. The City Council reconsidered and rescinded its ordnance.[195] While Escondido's ordinance was short-lived, it nevertheless had a lasting impact on the state's progressive movement. Landlords in other California cities were prompted by

Escondido's 2006 ordinance, even as it failed, to begin screening prospective applicants for immigration status. Complaints from landlords throughout the state on the legality of immigration status screenings were taken up by the Apartment Association of California Cities, who partnered with the ACLU to quietly and successfully push for a state law, AB 976 (2007).

Governor Schwarzenegger had previously resisted pro-immigrant policies such as driver's licenses, but pro-immigrant forces succeeded in passing AB 976 by enlisting the support of business interests and by pushing legislation quietly and with little fanfare. AB 976 created legal uniformity and certainty for businesses. The Assembly Judiciary report highlighted legal challenges posed by federal immigration law against local ordinances like Escondido, as well as conflicts with federal and state antidiscrimination law. For example, the state's Unruh Civil Rights Acts requires full and equal accommodations in all business establishments, and the federal Fair Employment and Housing Act makes housing discrimination and harassment unlawful.[196]

AB 976 was a rare but important progressive policy victory, signaling the state's departure from restrictive movements taking place in a few California cities and across many other states. It was still a quiet campaign waged behind closed doors, which prevented inflaming debate over the immigration issue.[197] In the end, the Apartment Association and the ACLU were able to achieve a progressive policy victory without tapping into the growing immigrant rights movement in California or relying on Democratic control. For our purposes, AB 976 also has important consequences for state citizenship, particularly on the right to develop human capital, as it prohibits local governments from requiring landlords to check on the immigration or citizenship status of tenants and prohibits landlords from independently doing the same.[198] The governor signed AB 976 but remained steadfastly opposed to providing driver's licenses to unauthorized immigrants. Moreover, the 2008 financial crisis and its aftermath left little room for advocates to push for state policies that would advance immigrant rights. It was not until the electoral victory of Democratic Governor Jerry Brown in 2010 that the policy window for pro-immigrant legislation began to open up.

ACCELERATION OF PRO-IMMIGRANT POLICIES (2010–2012)

Unlike in 2003 to 2009, political conditions beginning in 2010 were ripe for policy innovation on immigration. Democrats had gained full control of the state, with the newly Democratic Governor Jerry Brown and a Democratic majority in both the state senate and the state assembly. In addition, voters had approved Proposition 25 in November 2010, which reduced the threshold for passing a state budget from a two-thirds supermajority to a simple majority. This simple rule change meant that Republican lawmakers in Sacramento could no longer threaten to withhold support for a budget resolution in order to extract concessions from other pieces of progressive legislation.[199] Finally, nearly fifteen years of movement-building had created a cross-regional infrastructure that connected immigrant rights organizations to each other and to local constituencies that could apply pressure on lawmakers outside of San Francisco and Los Angeles. Still, some Democrats feared that state-level efforts might hurt progress on federal reforms.

The failure of the DREAM Act in 2010 was a wake-up call, however, as Democrats could not manage to push for a popular bill in Congress with a near–filibuster-proof majority. Recognizing the futility of federal reform, the immigrant rights movement began to fully engage in state policy proliferation where possible.[200] These efforts included ways to mitigate or resist federal enforcement efforts and other ways to improve the lives of undocumented residents. Most notably, California proceeded again on bills improving the lives of immigrant youth and passed the California Dream Act in 2011 through two bills: AB 130 granted non–state-funded scholarships for public colleges and universities; and AB 131 granted state-funded financial aid such as institutional grants, community college fee waivers, the Cal Grant, and the Chafee Grant.

The state also made tremendous progress on worker rights. California passed a resolution in 2010 for a Domestic Workers Bill of Rights, not taking statutory action but highlighting the work done by domestic workers in the state and the labor violations faced by these workers. More importantly, it began to carve out new worker protections and standards under state law while expanding its enforcement of federal labor law. The Wage Theft Protection Act passed in 2011 required employers to provide each employee written notice of their wages, hours, and working conditions. It also increased state penalties and strengthened the enforcement of federal and state laws protecting workers from nonpayment and underpayment of wages. The following year, in 2012, the state passed a Domestic Workers Bill of Rights, guaranteeing basic work standards and protections for domestic workers.

Taking on the issue of federal legal status and rights of undocumented workers, California also passed AB 1236 in 2011, preventing state and local jurisdictions from being able to mandate that private employers use E-Verify, a federal database that electronically verifies the identity and work authorization of employees.[201] State law cannot prevent employers' voluntary use of the database, and other federal laws that prohibit employment of unauthorized workers still apply. Nevertheless, California's labor protections and anti-E-Verify law greatly expanded the rights of undocumented workers.[202] The following year, the state further expanded the right of undocumented residents to develop human capital by explicitly granting them access to professional business licenses. In 2012, the California supreme court was presented with an undocumented applicant who had completed law school and passed the state's bar exam.[203] Weeks after oral argument in the case, and following guidance from the federal government about state statutory requirements for expansion of alien benefits under the 1996 IIR-IRA law,[204] the California legislature stepped in and enacted a law expressly allowing undocumented applicants to become members of the state bar.[205] Relying on that statute, the state supreme court ruled to admit the undocumented applicant.[206]

The state also made meaningful progress in 2011 toward expanding access to the right of free movement. Governor Brown was not receptive to State Senator Gil Cedillo's push for driver's licenses, but Cedillo nevertheless managed to score a legislative victory through the passage of AB 353 in 2011. This law allows an unlicensed person stopped at a DUI checkpoint to call for a licensed driver to retrieve their cars if their only offense is driving without a license. With a deep anti-immigrant history and onslaught of restrictive local ordinances in the early 2000s, police and sheriff's departments in California often impounded cars at DUI checkpoints if the driver did not have a license, severely restricting the ability of undocumented immigrants to move freely to work, to school, or for various errands. Impounding was a fairly widespread practice in California at the time, as local governments saw it as a means of raising revenue in the name of ensuring public safety. For example, Escondido was receiving as much as $400,000 a year from city contracts with towing companies.[207] Ending car impounds was a major priority for many of the regional immigrant rights coalitions in the state's politically conservative regions such as the Central Valley and Inland Empire. Of course, AB 353 did not provide driver's licenses to undocumented immigrants, nor did it expressly limit state or local cooperation in enforcing immigration law. Still, it ended car impounds from being employed as a financial threat over immigrants and other marginalized communities and, in doing so, meaningfully expanded the right to free movement in California.[208]

As 2012 drew to a close, there was one more notable expansion in the right to free movement in California, one that would prove critical in even further expansions in 2013 and beyond. On June 15, 2012, President Obama announced, in a Rose Garden ceremony at the White House, "Effective immediately, the Department of Homeland Security is taking steps to lift the shadow of deportation from these young people. Over the next few months, eligible individuals who do not present a risk to national security or public safety will be able to request temporary relief from deportation proceedings and apply for work authorization."[209] As the president announced the Deferred Action for Childhood Arrivals (DACA) program, he intended the program to be temporary, putting pressure on Congress to pass the DREAM Act or comprehensive immigration reform. Running for reelection, President Obama was also facing immense pressure from immigration rights activists to provide some meaningful form of deportation relief, including acts of civil disobedience from DREAMers who occupied Obama's candidate offices in Denver and staged sit-ins throughout the country, pushing the president to pass administrative relief.[210] DACA was thus a national policy response to national-level political and policy dynamics. Soon, however, the executive action also put pressure on states to reform their policies on driver's licenses, in-state tuition, and more – serving as an exogenous shock to state action, as Gulasekaram and Ramakrishnan have noted.[211] The shock was certainly felt in California, as Gil Cedillo quickly pushed a driver's license bill (AB 2189) in August 2012 that got overwhelming support among state legislators and won Governor Brown's signature a few weeks later. The passage of "DACA licenses" would set the stage for even greater expansions in state citizenship rights, nudging a moderate Democratic governor to start taking bolder stances on immigration.

A TIPPING POINT (2013)

As California and the rest of the nation took stock of the 2012 presidential election, it seemed like comprehensive immigration reform might finally get passed at the national level. The Republican National Committee viewed Romney's disastrous showing among Latinos with grave concern and commissioned a lengthy report (Growth and Opportunity Project) that called on the party to move quickly in favor of comprehensive immigration reform.[212] Party leaders in the House like Eric Cantor and Paul Ryan lent their support for immigration reform, and even conservative commentators like Bill O'Reilly and Sean Hannity starting voicing their support for legalization, even as they called it an "amnesty."[213] Prospects for immigration reform looked even brighter as the US Senate produced a bill (S744) that passed in June 2013 by an overwhelming margin, sixty-eight to thirty-two, with fourteen Republican Senators voting in favor. Soon, however, it was apparent that federal immigration reform would ground to a halt once again. The Republican-controlled House called the Senate bill "dead on arrival" in early July,[214] and, by late September, Senate Republicans had managed to shut down the federal government in an attempt to prevent implementation of the Affordable Care Act.[215]

It was against this federal backdrop that California state legislators pushed a series of bills in summer 2013 that advanced various dimensions of immigrant rights, including the right to *free movement* (AB60 providing driver's licenses to undocumented immigrants), *due process* (AB4 severely limiting federal immigration detainers and AB524 enabling charges of extortion against individuals who threaten to report the immigration status of an individual), and *human capital formation* (AB1024 allowing unauthorized immigrants to practice law and SB666 enabling the suspension or revocation of business licenses for employers for retaliation against employees on the basis of their citizenship or immigration status). Importantly, Governor Brown was no longer signaling to pro-immigrant lawmakers that he would veto the TRUST Act. Federalism dynamics thus loomed large over California's actions in 2013, and the state was finally ready to start taking big leaps on immigration reform – not simply as a last-ditch effort to spur Congressional action but also to serve as a substitute for federal immigration reform.[216]

As far as progressive state citizenship is concerned, California's moves on driver's licenses and immigration detainers were perhaps the most consequential. AB 60, the Safe and Responsible Driver's Act, marked a dramatic expansion in the right to free movement by granting undocumented residents driver's licenses. The law created a new driver's license with special markings limiting it to state functions and free movement, separate from California's federally compliant driver's license. To protect undocumented residents, immigrant rights organizations pushed to include antidiscrimination provisions in the bill, making it illegal for state or local officials to use the AB 60 license to "consider an individual's citizenship or immigration status as a basis for a criminal investigation, arrest, or detention."[217] During his signing of the law, Governor Jerry Brown proclaimed, "No longer are undocumented people in the shadows," and added, "They are alive and well and respected in the state of California."[218] Moreover, given this historic moment, Brown held two signing ceremonies, one on the South Lawn of Los Angeles City Hall and another at Fresno City College in the Central Valley.[219]

While AB 60 was an important legislative achievement by itself, it also signaled larger developments in federalism that tipped the scales in California's immigrant rights trajectory. Just days after AB 60 was signed, Governor Brown also signed California's first state-level noncooperation law called the Transparency and Responsibility Using State Tools (TRUST) Act, which stipulates that state and local law enforcement officers can only enforce federal immigration detainers issued by the US Immigration and Customs Enforcement (ICE) for persons convicted of serious crimes.[220] More than AB 60, signing the TRUST Act in 2013 represented a significant change in Brown's thinking on state immigration policy and set the stage for him to be an integral part of the "advocacy coalition" pushing California toward a progressive regime of state citizenship.

Before Brown was governor, he served as attorney general of California from 2007 to 2011. Beginning in 2008, the federal government under President Obama launched its Secure Communities (S-Comm) program, which established a federal partnership with state and local jails by using federal immigration and criminal databases to identify and track unauthorized immigrants for deportation.[221] Brown not only supported S-Comm prior to becoming governor; as the state's attorney general, he was also the person who signed California's memorandum to enter into the program. Brown's early move had set the state along a path of balancing progress on immigrant rights while continuing to actively partner in enforcing immigration law.

In 2011, Brown's first year as governor, Assemblyman Tom Ammiano introduced the TRUST Act for the first time in any state (AB 1081), and the bill was a major legislative priority for the National Day Labor Organizing Network (NDLON), which cosponsored the bill along with the Asian Law Caucus.[222] Ammiano and Democratic allies saw record numbers of deportations under S-Comm and were concerned that low-level offenders were being targeted, despite President Obama's policy of only targeting unauthorized immigrant with records of serious crimes.[223] Through a Freedom of Information Act request, advocacy organizations gained access to ICE data that revealed these suspicions. It also revealed damaging evidence that partnering with S-Comm created adverse chilling effects on the immigrant population's reporting of crime, either as victims or witnesses, because of possible deportation consequences.[224] Advocates argued that "ICE's own data shows that in California 7 out of 10 of the over 67,900 individuals deported under S-Comm had no convictions or were accused only of minor offenses."[225] This meant that families with no criminal history were being separated, and state and local law enforcement were actively involved in these deportation consequences.

It is important to note that movement capacity and pressure were critical to the push for AB 1081, which was built on an earlier detainer resistance movement across several county, city, and law enforcement jurisdictions that NDLON had led across the country. Founded in California in 2001, NDLON had been an early leader on protecting day laborers and other undocumented immigrants. They warned California leaders of the S-Comm program and partnered with the California Immigrant Policy Center, the Asian Law Caucus, and Senators Tom Ammiano and Kevin De León to draft an early version of the TRUST Act in 2011, which would have blocked state and local law enforcement from sharing fingerprints with ICE. This was a major step forward in the formation of an "advocacy coalition," per the framework in theories of policy change, as sympathetic legislators were working intimately with advocacy organizations to push legislation that both saw as urgent and consequential.

As the bill wended its way through the legislature, advocates realized that they had to water down some of the provisions in order to gain Governor Brown's support. Ammiano amended the bill to block state and local law enforcement officers from complying with detainer requests only for people that do not have a history of a violent or serious felony. AB 1081 read, "Unlike criminal detainers, which are supported by a warrant and require probable cause, there is no requirement for a warrant and no established standard of proof, such as reasonable suspicion or probable cause, for issuing an ICE detainer request. Immigration detainers have erroneously been placed on United States citizens as well as immigrants who are not deportable."[226] It sought to prevent these negative consequences by narrowing enforcement partnerships and protect immigrants who were nonviolent offenders.

It was soon clear, however, that Governor Brown was not party to the "advocacy coalition" on immigration reform. On September 30, 2012, he vetoed the TRUST Act. He recognized undocumented immigrants as an important labor source for California's economy, but he then explained:

"Comprehensive immigration reform – including a path to citizenship – would provide tremendous economic benefits and is long overdue. Until we have immigration reform, federal agents shouldn't try to coerce local law enforcement officers into detaining people who've been picked up for minor offenses and pose no reasonable threat to their community."[227] Importantly, federalism dynamics in 2012 had restrained Brown from acting. Top federal officials had privately lobbied Brown to veto the legislation, in order to preserve any momentum toward federal reform. According to emails obtained by Advancing Justice–Asian Law Caucus and the National Day Laborer Organizing Network, senior ICE officials in Washington, DC, asked "that Brown hold off approving the bill while the federal agency developed an alternative pilot program in California to limit which immigrants police and sheriffs could detain. They said the program would influence national policy."[228]

No matter the reason for Governor Brown's hesitation in 2012, he was fully on board with California's advocacy coalition by summer of the following year. NDLON and others in the immigrant rights movement continued to place pressure on the state, and federalism dynamics had changed significantly by 2013. As noted earlier, the heady optimism for national immigration reform that followed President Obama's reelection had worn off by early summer, as it was abundantly clear that the US House of Representatives was very unlikely to pass immigration reform. This freed Brown from his fixation on federal reform, and he no longer viewed state reforms on immigration as piecemeal and inadequate. Indeed, he was starting to call California's moves "immigration reform."[229] This is the backdrop to understanding why Brown signed California's 2013 immigration bills in such a dramatic manner – first signing the driver's license bill in prominent public ceremonies in Los Angeles as well as Fresno and subsequently signing a raft of pro-immigrant measures timed to coincide with massive nationwide protests on federal immigration reform on October 5, 2013. Of course, Brown was not the only vital member of the state's advocacy coalition on immigrant rights. The vitality and reach of the immigrant rights movement had allowed it to place constant pressure on Sacramento to enact driver's licenses and the TRUST Act, among other policies, and these created ideal conditions for federalism dynamics in Washington to powerfully and quickly effect Governor Brown's shift from skepticism to full-throttled support for state level immigration reform.

Impressive as the gains were in 2013, they were not adequate to fully establish progressive citizenship in the state (Figure 5.6). The raft of legislation passed that year made critical advancements in three dimensions of citizenship: (1) the right to free movement; (2) the right to due process and legal protection; and (3) the right to develop human capital. The advocacy coalition had reached a tipping point, however, as it had built considerable strength and cross-sector support within the state, and it no longer viewed federal

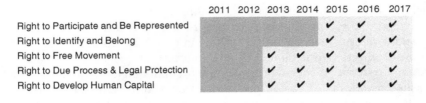

FIGURE 5.6 California's transition to progressive state citizenship, 2013–2015

immigration reform as a realistic option. This set in motion the proliferation of even more state policies from 2014 onward, deepening progress along key dimensions such as due process and human capital formation and expanding access to the right to participate the right to identify and belong. It would only take another two years for California to fully establish progressive state citizenship as a durable and meaningful form of rights-based membership.

THE CRYSTALLIZATION OF PROGRESSIVE STATE CITIZENSHIP BY 2015

California followed a momentous legislative year on immigration in 2013 with continued zeal for further reform (see Table 5.5). Advocates pushed for the passage of SB 1210 in 2014, which established a State DREAM Loan Program for undocumented students at the University of California and California State University systems.[230] California also expanded access to professional licensing one step further in 2014, when Governor Jerry Brown signed SB1159 into law requiring "all 40 licensing boards under the California Department of Consumer Affairs to consider applicants regardless of immigration status by 2016."[231] This was a powerful move, as it affected not only high-salary occupations like doctors and licensed engineers but also licensing for beauty salon workers and realtors, which are much larger occupation groups for unauthorized immigrants in the state. California also meaningfully advanced the right to due process and the right to human capital formation by passing AB 2751 in 2014, protecting workers' rights to update their personal information based on a lawful change of name, social security number, or federal employment authorization document, without fear of retaliation by the employer. The state also granted extensive worker protections in 2015, passing SB 588 – the "California Fair Day's Pay Act" – which gave the California Labor Commissioner tough new enforcement rights against

TABLE 5.5 *California's progressive period, 1996–2019*

Policy type	Citizenship Dimensions 1–5*	Undocumented (asterisks denote number of laws passed per year, if more than one)
Access to driving	1	2011 (ban on car impounds) 2012 (driver's license) – DACA only 2013 (driver's license)
Access to safe spaces	1	2017*** 2019
Access to government buildings	1	2017
Not asked about federal legal status	2	2011 2013 2015 2017***
Noncooperation	2	2013 2017***** 2019
Enforcement information shared (with fed.)	2	2017
Informed of detainer request	2	2016
Due process	2	2012 2014 2015**** 2017** 2019
Reduced sentencing to prevent immigration consequences	2	2014 2015** 2016** 2017***
Immigration legal services	2	2015** 2016 ("One California" – $15 million) 2017 ("One California" – $30 million) 2018 ("One California" – $45 million)
Office of immigrant affairs	3, 5	2015
Health care	3	1996 1997 1998 2012 (Medi-Cal) – DACA only 2013** (Medi-Cal)

(continued)

Policy type	Citizenship Dimensions 1–5*	Undocumented (asterisks denote number of laws passed per year, if more than one)
		2015 (Health for All Children)
		2016 ($145 budget for children health care)
		2017
		2019 (Medi-Cal for young adults)
Education	3	2001 (in-state tuition)
		2011** (Dream Act)
		2012
		2013 (professional licenses)
		2014
		2015 (public employment)
		2017****
Work	3	1999
		2011 (anti e-verify)
		2013*****
		2014***
		2015***
		2018 (state public employment)
Shelter	3	2007 (ban on landlord exclusions)
Right to family reunification	3	2012
Vote in local elections	4	2016 (San Francisco)
Hold political office	4	2015 (local appointment)
		2016 (state appointment) – DACA only
		2018 (state appointment)
		2019 (boards and commissions)
Public accommodation	5	2017
Removing/apologizing for alienating language in policy	5	2005
		2014 (Prop. 187 apology)
		2015 (removed "alien" from labor code)
		2017**
Absence of English-only language	5	2017***
Identification document	5	2013 (state ID) – DACA only

* The Provision of Rights to: (1) free movement; (2) due process and legal protection; (3) develop human capital; (4) participate and be represented; and (5) identify and belong.
  DACA only – noted at the end of policy/year if a policy expands a right for only DACA residents.

employers who steal employees' wages, and SB 623 – the "Worker's Compensation Equity for All" Act – which ensured that all injured workers, regardless of legal status, receive workers compensation benefits from the Uninsured Employers Benefits Trust Fund or the Subsequent Injuries Benefits Trust Fund. Finally, California also made significant advancements in human capital rights by expanding access to health insurance for all undocumented children in 2015 (SB 4).[232]

California had also made significant progress in the right to identify and belong (Dimension 5). On June 23, 2014, Senator De León led California in passing SB 396, removing all inactive passages from Proposition 187 from California's education, health and safety, and welfare codes. De León explained that Prop. 187, even when inactive, has a "damaging and lasting impact on the immigrant communities because it further stigmatized an already vulnerable population," noting that, even today, "the immigrant population fears interacting with government officials and, as a result, is often hesitant to become civically engaged and cooperate with the police."[233] While SB 396 built on prior efforts by California to provide an important right to identify and belong, including an official act of apology for Repatriation of Mexican American and immigrants in the early twentieth century, the state was still short of the minimum threshold for progressive state citizenship by the end of 2014.

This changed in 2015, as the chair of the Senate Labor and Industrial Labor Relations Committee, Senator Tony Mendoza, introduced SB 432, removing the word "alien" from the state's labor code. The Senate Rules Committee justified the law, stating that "any derogative references to foreign-born individuals be repealed from state law" and that "the word 'alien' has no place in the laws of our state and more importantly, should never be the basis of an employment hiring protocol."[234] Passed on August 10, 2015, SB 432 deleted the outdated and discriminatory reference to alien in state law, marking an progressive leap forward in welcoming and embracing immigrants as integral to California's culture, society, and economy. This law pushed California above the minimum threshold on all dimensions of state citizenship, solidifying for all immigrants in the state a general right to identify and belong – a remarkable achievement for a state that had pioneered anti-immigrant discrimination by devoting an entire constitutional article to it in 1879.

The year 2015 was important for more reasons than the removal of "alien" from California labor code, as the state also began to see meaningful increases in the right to participate. In August 2015, the city of Huntington Park appointed two long-term residents to serve on local commissions. It appointed to its parks and recreation commission Julian Zatarian, who had arrived from Sinaloa, Mexico, in 2007 as a thirteen-year-old and had resided as undocumented in California ever since, attending Huntington Park High School and Santa Monica College. The city also appointed to its health and education commission Francisco Medina, also undocumented and originally from Mexico.[235]

City Council member Jhonny Pineda led in making these appointments; he explained, "They've always given to the community ... [T]hey just happen to be undocumented." Pineda's background as an immigrant farm worker at the age of thirteen made these appointments especially meaningful: he said the appointments showed that Huntington Park is "a city of opportunity and a city of hope."[236] Some public outrage occurred in the city council meeting following their appointments, with accusations of Pineda and the city "breaking the law." Pineda explained that no law exists that bars their appointments and that both appointees underwent full background checks as required of any other official. Mayor Karina Macias further defended the city's appointments, arguing, "They have every right to be at that table, because they are part of our community, and I'll leave it at that."[237] Importantly, these two appointments did not provoke any opposition from California's governor or attorney general, and there were no moves in the state legislature to preempt these moves by passing statewide legislation banning the appointment of undocumented immigrants to state or local government commissions. These two city-level appointments were made the same month that the word "alien" was statutorily removed from the state's labor code, crystallizing California's progressive regime of state citizenship.

Progressive citizenship in California has meant that undocumented citizens of California, like Zatarian and Medina, not only have access to in-state tuition, postsecondary financial assistance, driver's licenses, and a range of protections from immigration enforcement but also have the right to participate as appointed government officials. Medina's story illustrates the significance of being undocumented in California and having meaningful rights to participate in positions of public leadership. He graduated from California State University Dominguez Hills, interned for former state Assembly member Gil Cedillo, and is now an active political leader in local government.[238] The following year, in 2016, Governor Brown appointed Jorge Reyes Salinas, who has temporary legal status under DACA, to the California State University board of trustees as a student trustee, deepening California's progressive state citizenship even further.[239] Finally, in 2018, California's Senate Rules Committee appointed Lizbeth Mateo, a thirty-three-year-old practicing attorney who is undocumented, to serve on the California Student Opportunity and Access Program Project Grant Advisory Committee. Mateo and the committee will advise the California Student Aid Commission on ways to increase college access to low-income or underserved communities.[240]

The crystallization of progressive state citizenship in 2015 does not mean that it ceases to deepen or expand. Crystallization continues to form as a synergistic and constitutive strengthening of state citizenship rights across all five dimensions. The TRUST Act was implemented in 2014, setting a floor for how the state would mitigate immigration enforcement that would allow localities to go further, even fully opting out of compliance with ICE detainer requests.[241] San Francisco and the counties of Contra Costa, Alameda, and San Mateo announced in 2014 that they would no longer cooperate with any ICE detention requests of possible unauthorized immigrants in local jails.[242] State and local noncooperation layered on top of one another and fundamentally deepened the right to due process and legal protection among other rights. This had a notable impact on enforcement by lowering deportations considerably and on federal law, being a reason for President Obama's ending of the Secure Communities program in 2014.[243]

California's progressive citizenship has continued to deepen since 2015, through new, robust noncooperation laws (passing the TRUTH Act in 2016 and the so-called state sanctuary bill of SB 54 in 2017), lowering state crimes and convictions to prevent immigration implications from happening (passing AB 813 and SB 1242 in 2016, and passing SB 180 in 2017), banning new immigrant detention center contracts from being made with the federal government (passed in the 2017 budget), and protecting immigrant workers from preventable worksite raids by requiring employers to ask for warrants (passing AB 450 in 2017). California's commitment to protecting immigrants now extends into deportation cases, providing due process rights by requiring ethical representation and confidentiality from attorneys (passing AB 60 in 2015) and providing financial assistance for legal counsel (passing AB 1476 in 2014 and SB 78 in 2015), and establishing a Deportation Defense Services Fund of $15 million in 2017.

Finally, California has also created new offices and programs that help improve immigrant access to various rights, including due process rights guaranteed under both federal and state law. In 2014, Senator Lara introduced SB 1392 "Office of New American Integration," but the bill died in committee.[244] The following year, SB 10 similarly proposed creating an "Office of New Americans," which turned into a budget line item and passed.[245] Placed under the Attorney General of California, the Office of Immigrant Assistance provides outreach and education to inform immigrant communities about state laws to streamline implementation of the robust set of progressive policies. This was an important addition to California's progressive regime, strengthening immigrant access to rights and formalizing some relationships between community organizations and government agencies. For example, it connects immigrant rights organizations to the California Department of Justice, which enforces criminal and civil law violations – many of which now include protections for undocumented workers. While the Office of Immigrant Assistance does not advocate for new progressive policies, it formalizes the implementation process of the California's robust set of existing policies, making immigrant rights real.

The creation of a state Office of Immigrant Assistance was paired with significant state investments to improve immigrant access to legal protections.

Governor Brown approved a $3 million state budget investment to fund legal help for Central American child migrants in 2014, in response to a surge in children crossing the border to flee violence.[246] In 2015, Governor Brown passed SB 79 authorizing the California Department of Social Services (CDSS) and its Immigration Branch to fund nonprofits for immigration services related to DACA, naturalization, other legal status changes, and legal defense for unaccompanied undocumented minors. In 2015 alone, just over $14 million was offered to sixty-one nonprofits for these purposes.[247] Governor Brown also passed a Budget Act in 2016 that invested $15 million to create the One California program, which he placed under the CDSS's control. In 2017 and 2018, Brown passed Budget Acts investing $30 million and $45 million, respectively, into One California.[248] Cities have also followed suit, especially in response to President Trump's electoral win in 2016. Immigrant rights organization led by CHIRLA sent a letter in November 2016 to Los Angeles Mayor Garcetti, the City Council and the County Board of Supervisors "calling for more aggressive action in the face of possible deportations."[249] The city established a $10 million L.A. Justice Fund in 2017 for undocumented immigrants that face deportation.

Newsom and the Deepening of Progressive Citizenship

Governor Brown went from being a skeptic on immigrant rights when he assumed office in 2010 to an enthusiastic champion and national leader by 2015. Gavin Newsom entered office as an even stronger progressive champion, on matters ranging from criminal justice reform (as we saw in Chapter 4) to immigrant rights. Newsom moved quickly after taking office to sign AB 917, expediting the certification process for victims seeking to obtain T-Visas or U-Visas.[250] During the crisis of migrants being released from federal custody with no federal support, Newsom quickly mobilized California's $25 million budget for Rapid Response to open new migrant family shelters in San Diego and worked with organizations like the San Diego Alliance to transport migrants to temporary housing with relatives or friends. During his first month in office, Newsom also redirected California's National Guard from the border to focus on aiding migrants within the state, while actively leading lawsuits against the Trump administration on the "public charge" rule and proposed citizenship question on the 2020 Census.

Newsom also took the opportunity early in his administration to stake out a contrasting vision of immigrant rights and foreign policy vis-à-vis the Trump administration. Within his first six months of office, he made an official three-day fact-finding visit to El Salvador and then invited the country's leaders to send a delegation to meet with California businesses. As he explained, "Helping stabilize El Salvador directly helps California by mitigating the border challenges, by mitigating migration, by tempering the rhetoric with the Trump administration."[251] Contrasting President Trump's threat to cancel federal aid to El Salvador and build a wall along the USA–Mexico border, as well as restrictive asylum policies such as Remain in Mexico, Governor Newsom of California was actively forging international ties with El Salvador in businesses, tourism, and addressing the migration crisis.

It is becoming clear that California is entering a new era, one where the governor is as enthusiastic a champion of immigrant rights as are leaders in the state legislature. Newsom's championing of immigrant rights starkly contrasts Brown's hesitant and sympathetic approach. In addition to his executive actions, Newsom signed SB 225 allowing all Californians, regardless of their legal immigration status, to serve on state and local public boards and commissions – a bill nearly identical to SB 174 that Governor Brown had vetoed in 2018.[252] Like the prior bill that Brown had vetoed, SB 225 formally laid out the concept of "citizens of the state" to mean "(a) All persons born in the state and residing within it, except the children of alien public ministers and consuls. (b) All persons born out of the state who are citizens of the United States and residing within the state."[253] Thus, SB 225 formalized what was already clear in California by 2015: citizenship was a state matter, not only a federal one.

The "Citizens of the state" law was part of a larger package of progressive immigration laws signed by Newsom in October 2019, which together protected immigrants from being arrested by ICE at courthouses (AB 668) and prohibited noncriminal information from the state databases from being used for immigration enforcement purposes (AB 1747), and expanding the state's support and resources for undocumented students through establishing a Dreamer Resource Liaisons at its colleges and universities (AB 1645). Even earlier in 2019, Newsom had already expanded California's postsecondary resources for undocumented students through establishing the Cal Grant B Services Incentive Grant Program (AB 540) and expanding eligibility for the California DREAM loan program (SB 354).[254] Finally, Newsom continued to expand immigrant access to health care, signing a law that would provide health insurance access to all state residents age twenty-five and younger (SB 104).

CONCLUSIONS

California formally declared through state law in 2019 what was already apparent by 2015, when the state had passed, cumulatively over a decade, a package of immigration reforms that amounted to a robust form of state citizenship.[255] As this chapter has shown, California has made tremendous progress for its immigrant residents on all five dimensions of citizenship rights – the right to free movement, to due process and legal protection, to develop human capital, to participate and be represented, and to identify and belong.

At the same time, regimes of state citizenship need not push solely in a progressive direction, expanding on rights provided at the federal level. Indeed, during the first few decades after its founding, California pushed strongly and decisively toward a regressive regime of state citizenship, writing discrimination into its state constitution by 1879. The rapidity of the shift toward regressive state citizenship has been matched only recently, and in reverse. California has made tremendous leaps in the last two decades and now provides a meaningful and durable regime of progressive state citizenship. In both periods, political parties and social movements played a significant role, with state legislators and governors testing the limits of what is constitutionally possible (state-level factors that fall under "legislative actions" and "executive actions" in our explanatory framework; see Figure 3.1 and Table 3.1). At the same time, constitutional opportunities, presidential action and congressional action were also critical, linking up with social movement-building and party control to shape the timing, content, and sequencing of citizenship expansion and contraction.

The dominant explanation for California's progressive turn in recent years has been a story about Proposition 187 and the rise of Democratic party control. Prop. 187 prompted a major increase in immigrant naturalization and brought new Latino leaders into state government, enabling progressive citizenship policies to proliferate. This argument captures an important part of California's move to progressive state citizenship but is limited in two important respects. As this chapter has shown, California's immigrant rights policies were shaped by the interplay between party control, a strong and widespread social movement infrastructure – built not only in reaction to Proposition 187 but also through coordinated actions and philanthropic investments – and important federalism dynamics that included Congressional legislation in 1996 enabling state expansion of immigrant rights, as well as subsequent conflicts that spurred state action.

Another limitation of the Proposition 187 story is that it problematically paints California as being sui generis, or unique with respect to all other states. California is not alone. Currently, sixteen other states and the District of Columbia offer driver's licenses to undocumented residents, and their legislative trajectories were similarly driven by the interplay between federalism dynamics and state politics. The rollout of DACA licenses across all states similarly spotlights the role of federalism dynamics in structuring the expansion of important rights such as free movement. As we shall see in Chapter 6, the timing and sequencing of other expansions and contractions in state citizenship rights have had a similar interplay elsewhere as in California, with constitutional opportunities, executive actions, and legislative actions by parties and social movement actors playing important roles.

6

State Citizenship and Immigration Federalism

In March 2018, President Trump hosted a roundtable discussion at the White House on immigration sanctuary cities. As the *Los Angeles Times* noted about the meeting:

[C]onservative politicians and law enforcement officials from across the country and the federal government took turns one-upping each other with disgust over California's "sanctuary city" law.

But one elected leader bested them all. Rep. Martha McSally, an Arizona Republican, said Trump's famous promise to build a wall along the Mexican border should be extended – to protect her state from the liberals to the west.

"As we look in Arizona, we often look into the dangers of the southern border," McSally said. "But if these dangerous policies continue out of California, we might need to build a wall between California and Arizona as well."[1]

Some muted laughter ensued, and Rep. McSally continued. "But seriously, they cannot just provide sanctuary for these criminals."

To be clear, America's version of federalism would ensure that any wall erected between Arizona and California would purely be a symbolic one. The Privileges and Immunities clause of the US Constitution, the Fourteenth Amendment, and congressional regulations on interstate commerce would all ensure that the wall would be porous, enabling the free flow of goods and people across states. At the same time, Rep. McSally's point underscores an important dynamic in American federalism today: the border between California and Arizona marks the strongest contrast involving immigration federalism, and there is little love lost between the two neighbors with respect to their competing visions of state citizenship. In Chapter 5, we detailed how California reached a critical moment in 2015, consolidating a robust regime of progressive state citizenship that provides expanded protections on all major dimensions of citizenship rights.

If California had a foil, it would be Arizona, which has enacted some of the most restrictive policies regulating the lives of undocumented immigrants in the country. Some of Arizona's laws have been struck down in federal court, including its mirror scheme of state immigration enforcement (SB 1070) and denial of state driver's licenses to DACA recipients, while others have been upheld, including the Legal Arizona Worker's Act, which revokes the licenses of business who refuse to comply with the federal E-Verify system. And several other laws – including those preventing undocumented immigrants from accessing health care, in-state tuition, driver's licenses, and professional licenses – remain in place and have faced limited legal challenge.

The contrast between Arizona and California citizenship is stark, but it has only emerged relatively recently. For the majority of California's history, as we saw in Chapter 5, the state led the country on regressive state citizenship, starting with restrictions on Chinese residents and then extending exclusions to other immigrant groups and the Mexican-American population. Similarly, Arizona pursued anti-immigrant policies since its founding in 1912, in a bid to ensure White resident control over Mexican labor, and learned from California's regressive model up through the 1990s. Pratheepan Gulasekaram and Karthick Ramakrishnan note: "Prior to [Proposition 187's] demise, and concurrent with efforts to overhaul federal immigration legislation in 1996, activists in other states including Florida, Texas, and Arizona consulted with the proponents of Prop. 187 in hopes of passing their own versions of the law."[2] Eight years later, in 2004, Arizona passed Proposition 200 over the opposition of its Democratic governor and Republican US senators, inaugurating a new wave of restrictive state laws targeting immigrants in the state.

While there is much to be learned from contrasting Arizona and California in their opposite trajectories on state citizenship, it is important to also include other states and see the fuller range of immigration policies. Figure 6.1 places all fifty states on an aggregate scale, accounting for the full range of policies enacted on all five dimensions of our concept of citizenship. In this chapter, we situate various states along a continuum, from the most inclusive to the most exclusionary on each dimension of citizenship rights. We describe how our citizenship framework (as laid out in Chapter 2) helps to make sense of the full range of policies enacted across all fifty states from 1996 to 2019. After unpacking each dimension descriptively, we briefly explain how constitutional opportunities, legislative action, and executive action have shaped their developments over time.

As Gulasekaram and Ramakrishnan have noted, immigration federalism in the United States can be roughly divided into three eras, with the first two lasting about a century each. The first era, which Gerald Newman has dubbed the "lost century of American immigration law," was a period when states played a far greater role than the federal government in controlling immigration and, as Anna Law has shown, Northeastern states paid particular attention to prevent the entry of indigent and disabled immigrants.[3] The second era of immigration federalism, according to Gulasekaram and Ramakrishnan, lasted from the 1870s through the 1960s, with federal law and US Supreme Court decisions

Policy Spread Score on All 5 Dimensions

	Net Score (Exclusionary)								Net Score (Inclusionary)						
Count of States	-60	-50	-40	-30	-20	-10	-1	0	1	10	20	30	40	50	140
1	AZ	AL	GA	SC	IN	AR	AK	DC	CO	CT					CA
2			TN	UT	MS	FL	IA	WI	DE	IL					
3					TX	ID	KY		HI	NJ					
4						KS	MA		MD	NY					
5						LA	ME		NM	OR					
6						MI	MN		NV	WA					
7						MO	MT		RI						
8						NC	ND		VT						
9						NE	NH								
10						OK	OH								
11						VA	PA								
12							SD								
13							WV								
14							WY								

FIGURE 6.1 Exclusionary and inclusionary citizenship for immigrants across states, 2019

establishing federal exclusivity over setting immigration law. Since the 1970s, however, and accelerating after 2001, states have taken on more significant roles with regard to immigration policymaking. Thus, state citizenship for immigrants takes on a very new meaning in the contemporary period than during the first century of immigration law. As we explore in this chapter, California and Arizona are pulling in opposite directions on progressive and regressive state citizenship with respect to their immigrant populations. With this in mind, we conclude this chapter by conducting a fifty-state cross-sectional analysis to identify the reasons why some states have proceeded farther than others in the development of progressive state citizenship.

THE THIRD ERA OF IMMIGRATION FEDERALISM

As we explained in Chapter 3, the US Constitution sets the frame for state citizenship, producing the baseline of rights against which progressive, regressive, and reinforcing citizenship can be measured. State citizenship is further constrained in the case of immigrants. Since the 1870s, the Supreme Court has granted the federal government exclusive authority to determine who can enter the United States and the conditions under which foreign-born individuals can be allowed to stay or be forced to leave the country. The rise and dominance of the federal government in controlling immigration law and immigrant rights coincided with its growing constitutional authority and administrative capacity under Reconstruction, as well as its growing involvement in international affairs, most notably in Asia.

The twin developments of American nation-building and international treaty-making intertwined notably with the signing of the 1868 Burlingame Treaty. As we discussed in Chapter 5, the treaty established trading relations between the United States and China, as well as the right of Chinese nationals to freely immigrate to the United States and be able to travel and receive protections while living there. The United States needed Chinese labor to build the transcontinental railroad, but its nation-building interests soon collided with the mobilization of white nativists in California determined to remove Chinese laborers from the country. California ultimately succeeded in getting the federal government to impose a ban on Chinese immigration starting in 1882, but a series of federal laws and Supreme Court decisions in the ensuing years ensured that states would no longer have any control over *immigration law*. However, they could still exercise considerable authority when it came to *alienage law*, meaning how immigrants would get treated with respect to their access to rights and benefits at the state level. As Gulasekaram and Ramakrishnan have noted, this division of labor remained fairly stable for nearly a century, constituting the "second era" of immigration federalism where the federal government was supreme on most aspects of immigration control.

Then, in 1965, Congress overhauled federal immigration law through revisions to the Immigration and Naturalization Act (INA) and capped migration from the Western hemisphere for the first time. This altered the landscape of state and local lawmaking, as states increasingly began using alienage law as an instrument to deter immigration.[4] New legal limits placed on Mexican migration occurred immediately after the United States ended the Bracero Program in 1964, which was supplying employers with hundreds of thousands of Mexican laborers per year. Dependence on Mexican labor, when paired with restrictions on migration in the INA, led to a new phenomenon of mass unauthorized immigration. States soon began enacting laws trying to deter unauthorized immigration by imposing cuts to welfare eligibility and imposing stiff penalties on employers. On November 8, 1971, California Governor Ronald Reagan signed AB 528 into law, stating: "No employer shall knowingly employ an alien who is not entitled to lawful residence in the United States if such employment would have an adverse effect on lawful resident workers."[5] Other states followed suit, creating a patchwork of policies that concerned business organizations and Congress alike for their lack of uniformity. Thus, in writing the Immigration Reform and Control Act (IRCA) in 1986, Congress not only passed a national amnesty for unauthorized immigrants but also preempted state laws on employer sanctions by making it exclusive to the federal government.

State activity on regulating immigrants then entered a period of fits and starts. In 1994, California once again led the country by passing Proposition 187, a law barring unauthorized immigrants from most public benefits and services, and creating a state-level immigration enforcement scheme (that was ruled unconstitutional). Like in the 1970s, California's policy moves prompted changes in federal policy. Congress passed the Personal Responsibility and Work Opportunity Reconciliation Act (PWORA) of 1996, barring states from using federal funds to provide Medicaid and welfare to legal and undocumented immigrants, among other exclusions.[6] It also passed the Illegal Immigration Reform and Immigrant Responsibility Act (IIR-IRA) of 1996, restricting states' ability to provide postsecondary education benefits on the basis of state residency, unless US citizens from other states could also be eligible for that benefit.[7]

IIR-IRA criminalized many aspects of immigrant lives, expanded border enforcement, enhanced penalties and enforcement against smuggling and document fraud, and heightened interior enforcement to deport unlawfully residing immigrants. Importantly, the legislation also expanded the possibility of state-level involvement in immigration enforcement, creating a program through Section 287(g) of the INA that enabled the federal government to deputize state and local law enforcement agencies to enforce immigration law.[8] That same year, in 1996, containing strongly anti-immigrant legislation concealed in anti-terrorism language, the Anti-Terrorism and Effective Death Penalty Act (AEDPA) limited the constitutional rights and protections formerly offered to immigrants even further. As Lisa Solbakken explains, the AEDPA removed due process rights from both legal and undocumented immigrants by getting rid of a "judicial review after a final deportation order premised upon an enumerated conviction" as well as extending the crimes eligible for a deportation order.[9] Furthermore, as Gulasekaram and Ramakrishnan explain, September 11, 2001, fueled the spread of restrictive legislation, as states took advantage of the 1996 changes in federal law that loosened prior constraints on states and localities.

Taking hold of this new immigration federalism context, beginning early in the 2000s, Kris Kobach led an effort to involve states and localities in exclusionary state legislation. While working in the Department of Justice in 2002, Kobach authored a memo seeking to change the department's enforcement policy so that local police could make arrests for civil violations of immigration law, which was soon adopted by the Office of Legal Counsel. A few years later in 2004, Kobach turned his sights on working with conservative national organizations like FAIR and NumbersUSA, who had previously been focused entirely on federal laws. FAIR's legal wing, the Immigration Reform Law Institute (IRLI), worked with Kobach to influence states like Arizona and localities like Hazelton, Pennsylvania, with legal counsel and model restrictive legislation that often tested the boundaries of federal constitutionality.[10] Thus, openings created by Congress in 1996, combined with conservative social movement activity at the federal and state level, enabled Arizona and other states to proliferate exclusionary forms of state citizenship.

Arizona's Proposition 2000, the "Arizona Taxpayer and Citizen Protection Act," was one of the first anti-immigrant laws passed in 2004, kickstarting the restrictive wave of policies.[11] FAIR had funded the signature-gathering campaign and then pushed the courts in the state to enforce the law broadly.[12] The law changed voter registration in the state by requiring residents to prove US citizenship prior to registering to vote; it also banned undocumented immigrants from access to public benefits by requiring state and local agencies to use strict identification standards that checked for legal immigration status.[13] Proposition 200 also mandated that state and local officials report violations of federal immigration law and made it a misdemeanor to not follow state law in reporting such violations.[14]

Gulasekaram and Ramakrishnan mark September 11, 2001, as the point of origin for the spread of state and local laws, which was only made possible by federal legislative actions in immigration law that opened legislative space for states and localities to become more active. The IRCA in 1986 preempted state employer sanctions but left open the possibility for states to punish employers through their ability to regulate business licenses. The most explicit invitations to state activity on immigration regulation came in 1996, as Congress passed legislation expanding federal–state cooperation on immigration enforcement via Section 287(g) of the Immigration and National Act and also wiped the slate clean on state laws expanding welfare eligibility to immigrant residents and requiring them to pass such laws anew. In response, many states passed laws reestablishing health and welfare benefits to legal permanent residents. Texas and California also led in the effort to expand undocumented resident's access to in-state tuition in 2001. Nine states soon followed between 2002 and 2006.

The next major movement on immigration federalism occurred after 2005. The Border Protection, Antiterrorism, and Illegal Immigration Control Act of 2005 (HR 4437), also called the Sensenbrenner bill, accelerated state and local policymaking. HR 4437 sought to criminalize both unlawful presence in the country and associating with any person inside the country who was unauthorized.[15] Section 202 of the bill imposed criminal penalties to anyone who "assists, encourages, directs, or induces a person to reside in or remain in the United States ... knowing or in reckless disregard of the fact that such person is an alien who lacks lawful authority to reside in or remain in the United States."[16] This federal bill passed the House but was defeated in the Senate, providing a new opportunity for Kris Kobach and FAIR to push Republican-controlled states and cities on enacting their own forms of immigration enforcement bills. State laws grew exponentially as a result, from fifteen passed in 2005 to forty-nine in 2006 and ninety-eight in 2007 – most of which were restrictive in nature and modeled after one another.[17]

National immigration debates in 2005 and 2006 also sparked a nationwide protest movement by pro-immigrant activists.[18] Yet, progressive philanthropies were slow to invest in state-level legislative activity.[19] Instead, they were much more likely to support national groups, like the National Immigration Law Center, America's Voice, and the National Immigration Forum, who were all focused exclusively on comprehensive immigration reform at the national level. Absent much social movement strength or pressure, Democratic leaders at the state level remained hesitant to fully pursue state- or local-level strategies, fearing that they might harm national reforms efforts. Thus, when compared to restrictive policies, pro-immigrant policies emerged and spread comparatively slower across states and localities.

In line with our explanatory framework developed in Chapter 3, court rulings, Congressional legislation, and presidential actions created opportunities for state-level reforms on inclusionary and exclusionary forms of citizenship to emerge. At the same time, state-level legislative actions by parties and social movements drove changes in state citizenship regimes. Changes to federal law on immigration and welfare in 1996, combined with the rise of White nationalism post-9/11, gave conservatives an early lead on pushing exclusionary and regressive forms of state citizenship (see Figure 2.9). By 2012, however, the tide had turned, as the Supreme Court overturned key aspects of exclusionary state policies and President Obama headed down the path of taking more executive actions on immigration in the face of Congressional stalemate.[20] Once these federalism dynamics became clear, California's social movement activists and progressive champions in the state legislature were able to push for robust and sweeping reforms (see Chapter 5). California was not alone in building a grassroots infrastructure essential to pursuing progressive state citizenship. Growth of statewide organizations and networks had also emerged in places like New York (the New York Immigration Coalition), Illinois (the Illinois Coalition for Immigrant and Refugee Rights), Massachusetts (the Massachusetts Immigrant and Refugee Advocacy Coalition), and Oregon (CAUSA). Most of these statewide networks were not as well resourced as California's. Still, early in 2010, these statewide organizations and eight others joined forces to form the National Partnership for New Americans (NPNA), seeking to promote cross-regional efforts at immigrant integration.[21] The dynamism of federalism also fueled a conservative countermovement, which started to regain strength by 2015 in opposition to President Obama's executive actions on immigration.

President Trump's elections and executive orders have only deepened state legislative action on immigration, among progressives and conservatives alike. Figure 6.2 provides a snapshot of where all fifty states land with respect to passing exclusionary or inclusionary laws, across all five of our citizenship dimensions: (1) the right to free movement; (2) the right to due process and legal protection; (3) the right to develop human capital; (4) the right to

The Right to Free Movement (Dimension 1)

Count of States	\-19	\-10	\-9	\-8	\-5	\-4	\-3	\-2	\-1	0	1	2	3	4	9
	Net Score (Exclusionary)										Net Score (Inclusionary)				
1	AZ	IN	AL	SC	GA	UT	KY	FL	AK		DE	CT	CO	OR	CA
2							ME	IA	AR		DC	HI	NV	NJ	
3							MO	ID	KS		IL	VA		NY	
4							NC	MS	LA		MD	WA			
5							NE	MT	MA		NM				
6								RI	MI		VT				
7								SD	MN						
8								TN	ND						
9								TX	NH						
10									OH						
11									OK						
12									PA						
13									WI						
14									WV						
15									WY						

FIGURE 6.2 Immigrant inclusion on Dimension 1: rights to free movement

participate and be represented; and (5) the right to identify and belong. Our original dataset accounts for all state policies enacted from 1996 to 2019. Scoring included classification of all of the provisions within states' policies on indicators within our multidimensional citizenship framework, with a score of -1 representing a regressive or reinforcing exclusionary provision within a single policy and a score of +1 representing a progressive or reinforcing inclusionary provision within a single policy. Rather than treating each policy equally, our scoring of provisions within each policy more accurately captures the full dimensionality taking place across all fifty states (for more details on our policy dataset and scoring, please see Appendix A).

RIGHT TO FREE MOVEMENT (DIMENSION 1)

"You are now free to move about the country." So goes a famous television advertising slogan for Southwest Airlines in the United States.[22] Clearly, however, not everyone has the same freedom to move about the country (as we saw in Chapter 4), and state laws play a significant role in regulating the right to free movement among immigrants. While the American passport has become the predominant form of national identification since World War I, its primary function is to protect citizens and regulate movement across national borders.[23] By contrast, states have considerable leeway in controlling the free movement rights of immigrants. States today can provide expansions in the right to free movement through laws granting access to driver's licenses and auto insurance, laws limiting the impounding of cars for those without driver's licenses, and laws expanding access to public transportation, public buildings, and safe spaces from federal immigration enforcement. At the same time, states can also contract these rights by passing laws to restrict access to state government buildings, by denying driver's licenses (as well as criminalize those driving without licenses), and by linking state and local cooperation with federal immigration enforcement during routine traffic stops. More extreme measures have directly criminalized unlawful presence under state law in varying ways. Figure 6.2 places all fifty states on an aggregate scale, from most restrictive to most progressive, accounting for the full range of policies enacted on Dimension 1.

Between 2003 and 2010, at least seven states that previously granted driving privileges to undocumented immigrants either rescinded those policies or overturned them. Following the congressional passage of REAL ID in 2005, many states revoked driver's licenses that were previously issued to undocumented residents and began to enact new requirements on driver's license applicants, including providing proof of US citizenship, a valid social security number, and proof of lawful immigration status. The provision of driver's licenses to undocumented immigrants opened deep divisions in even progressive states: in 2007, through a gubernatorial executive order, Oregon revoked access to driver's licenses for undocumented immigrants.[24] The following year, in 2008, the state legislature of Oregon passed a law requiring driver's license applicants to prove either US citizenship status or legal residence under US immigration law. As we shall explore more deeply in Chapter 7, California and New York had long, tortuous journeys on expanding access to driver's licenses, even with Democratic governors at the helm. And even though Pennsylvania had a Democratic governor in Ed Rendell in 2009, its Pennsylvania Department of Transportation retroactively canceled thousands of immigrants' driver's licenses and implemented a new practice requiring a Social Security number or proof of lawful immigration status. New Mexico was the lone exception in the decade following 9/11, expanding access to driver's licenses in 2003 after a successful mobilization and lobbying campaign by immigrant rights activists.[25]

Just as 9/11 provided an exogenous shock that enabled restriction on state driver's licenses, President Obama's announcement of the Deferred Action for Childhood Arrivals (DACA) program was an "exogenous policy shock" that pushed in the opposite direction. As Gulasekaram and Ramakrishnan note, the White House did not intend to push state driver's license policy when formulating the DACA program, but it soon became apparent that DACA recipients would need driver's licenses to be able to go to work.[26] Forty-six of the fifty states moved quickly to offer driver licenses to DACA recipients, with Kansas and Arizona remaining steadfastly opposed. In 2014, the Ninth Circuit court ruled that, because Arizona provided driver licenses to other legal immigrants groups, it was required to issue them to DACA recipients under the Fourteenth Amendment's equal protection clause.[27] Momentum created by DACA licenses also paved the way for a more general push for driver's licenses for undocumented immigrants. Seven states, along with Washington, DC, successfully pushed for expanded driver's licenses in 2013, followed by another two states in 2015 and three more in 2019. Thus, using our explanatory framework in Chapter 3, executive actions at the federal level via DACA helped enable two waves of state legislative action on immigrant driver's licenses – on DACA licenses at first, and on more general driver's licenses in the years that followed.

Not all driver's license expansion policies are the same, however. The federalism conflicts that arise from driver's licenses as a form of identification may lead to immigration status inquiries at traffic stops or in other areas. California's AB 60 (2013) policy includes an antidiscrimination provision to help safeguard the right to free movement, making it a state crime for state and local officials, including law enforcement, to target or investigate drivers with new licenses for possible immigration violations. Even prior to its inclusive driver's license law, California passed AB 353 (2011) allowing an unlicensed person stopped at a DUI checkpoint to call for a licensed driver to retrieve their cars if their only offense is driving without a license, preventing the use of car impounds for immigration purposes by local officials in the state. Nevada's 2013 driver's license law also protects against information in DMV databases being released to federal officials for "any purpose relating to the enforcement of immigration laws."[28] Delaware's 2015 law "ensure[s] the public trust of the Delaware undocumented population that will utilize the driving privilege card for its intended purposes, [by making] all personal identifiable information collected during the application process ... confidential."[29]

State organizational capacity by immigrant activists was critical to both California's passage of AB 60 driver's licenses in 2013 and New York's more recent passage of driver's licenses in 2019, as we detail in Chapter 7. Andrea Silva's case study of Oregon, however, highlights that capacity-building alone does not guarantee success.[30] Oregon's statewide immigrant rights organization (CAUSA) partnered with stakeholders in 2013, such as agricultural groups, labor unions, police chiefs, and clergy, to support a series of pro-integration measures, but the coalition was unable to overcome a ballot referendum that repealed the driver's license measure in 2014.[31] Nevertheless, Oregon has continued to expand in other areas, including expansions in health coverage to undocumented children in 2017 and an executive order that same year declaring the state a sanctuary. The state's immigrant rights advocacy coalition also succeeded in getting the legislature to pass driver's licenses again in 2019, although opponents have vowed to repeal it once more through the ballot box.[32] In addition to Oregon, New York and New Jersey expanded access to driver's licenses in 2019, and Colorado – which already provides licenses – passed an additional law to increase the number of DMV locations issuing those licenses.

Despite gains in several states, California remains far ahead on the right to free movement (Dimension 1), which expanded significantly in 2017 when the legislature enacted SB 54 – the California Values Act – that not only prohibited cooperation with federal officials on immigration enforcement but also included a "safe spaces" provision that made California schools, health facilities, libraries, courthouses, and the Division of Labor Standards Enforcement safe and accessible to all California residents, regardless of immigration status. The law required each of these institutions to make public policies of their own that limit assistance with immigration enforcement to the fullest extent possible without violating federal law.[33] Building on these safeguards, California's SB 1194, passed in 2018, prohibits all lodging and bus transportation agencies from disclosing private information to any third party, such as an immigration enforcement agent, without a court-issued subpoena, warrant, or order.[34] Thus, building on its state constitutional provision from 1972, which secures the right to privacy for all Californians, and on existing state consumer protection laws, SB 1194 uses its power to regulate businesses in the state to expand and enforce a more inclusive vision of free movement and presence.

In stark contrast to these inclusionary developments, several states are pushing toward the opposite end of the spectrum of free movement: criminalizing driving without a license, enforcing immigration checks at traffic stops, and overstepping what is constitutionally permissible by criminalizing unlawful presence. The state of Georgia enacted SB 529 in 2006, requiring all of its residents to possess a valid form of federal identification. Two years later, Georgia lawmakers enacted SB 350 (2008), creating a new felony-level crime upon the fourth conviction in a five-year period for driving without a valid license. It also required state and local officials in jails to engage in a reasonable effort to determine the nationality of any person held who was convicted of driving without a license, charged with a felony, or charged with driving under the influence. Thus, state provisions on free movement go well beyond driver's license policy to include their authority over regular traffic stops and arrests, as well as their ability to determine safe spaces for immigrant residents and protect immigrant access to public transportation.

Arizona's notorious SB 1070 law of 2010 pushed the legal scope of what state and local government could and could not do with respect to the rights of immigrants. On free movement, it made it a misdemeanor crime for noncitizens to be in the state without identity documents (*struck down by the courts*); made it a crime for anyone in the state to shelter, hire, or transport undocumented immigrants (*struck down*); and required local law enforcement to check the immigration status of anyone they suspected of being undocumented (*upheld*). The "show me your papers" provision expanded the role of state and local law enforcement agencies over federal unlawful presence, within the boundaries of what is constitutional, by making it their added responsibility to identify and apprehend any person they suspected to be residing in the country in violation of US immigration law at routine traffic stops. Originally, SB 1070's provision was more expansive: it authorized and required local officers to identify and apprehend suspected undocumented person anywhere in the state. This was quickly amended by HB 2162 (2011) to traffic stops. In the wake of Arizona's SB 1070, Alabama, Georgia, Utah and South Carolina all enacted similar laws, including the notorious "show me your papers" provision.

Several states are also layering federal ID requirements on top of their "show me your papers" provisions. Following Arizona's lead, South Carolina made it a state crime to not carry federal identification that would verify one's legal status. Section 5 of South Carolina's SB 20 (2011) makes it a state misdemeanor for any person eighteen years or older to "fail to carry" "a certificate of alien registration or alien registration receipt card," punishable by a fine up to $100, up to thirty days' imprisonment, or both. Moreover, subsection 6(B)(2) made it unlawful for any person to display or possess a counterfeit or false ID for the purpose of proving one's lawful presences in the United States, with different punishments set for first and second offenses. Section 4 of South Carolina's law laid out even more extreme measures that criminalized unlawful presence by making self-harboring – defined as simply residing in the state, moving within the state, or entering public or private buildings – a state-level crime. Additionally, it criminalized the act of harboring, transporting or shielding an undocumented person, which applied to family members and children. Violations were made punishable by a fine up to $5,000, a prison sentence of up to five years, or both.[35]

Federalism Dynamics and Dimension 1 Rights for Immigrants

Constitutional opportunities, congressional action, and presidential action have all shaped federalism dynamics related to the ability of states to expand or constrain the free movement rights of immigrants. As we noted earlier, there is no universal federal identification document in the United States that establishes legal presence; in addition to temporary visas and green cards, federal visa waiver programs allow for some immigrants to remain in the country without a formal ID, and asylum applicants reside inside the country without express authorization and then proceed to take steps to legalize their presence under refugee policy.[36] In 2005, President Bush signed the REAL ID Act into law, marking a landmark change by creating minimum federal standards for state-issued licenses and identification cards if those cards are to be used for federal purposes, such as access to federal buildings, identification for airline travel, and proof of identity for accessing federal benefits. Importantly, REAL ID provides states with the discretion to issue federally approved licenses to unlawfully present persons who are recipients of deferred action.

Using their statutory discretion, many states maintained a policy even prior to 2012 of allowing temporary immigrants and undocumented persons who had received deferred action and obtained employment authorization documents, or EADs, from the federal government to apply for driver's licenses. States, however, may maintain more stringent standards than the minimum allowed by REAL ID or may choose to provide licenses that fail to meet the minimum federal status-verification standard with the understanding that such licenses may not be acceptable for federal purposes once the REAL ID Act becomes fully implemented. States have authority over free movement within their jurisdiction, partly because the federal government cannot mandate that state or local government enforce federal immigration laws. States can therefore issue state driver's licenses, ban car impoundments, regulate local law enforcement during traffic stops, and regulate access to public institutions and spaces – all of which directly expand or contract the right to free movement (Dimension 1).[37]

Courts have set significant limits on the ability of states to restrict unlawful presence. The US Supreme Court in *Arizona v. United States* (2012), explained, when upholding SB 1070's Section 2(B) "show me your papers" provision, that "Congress has done nothing to suggest it is inappropriate for states to communicate with the federal government regarding immigration matters."[38] It went further, explaining that "[c]onsultation between federal and state officials is an important feature of the immigration system" and that federal law "has encouraged the sharing of information about possible immigration violations."[39] What distinguished "show me your papers" from federal immigration enforcement, according to the court, was that traffic stops were a routine matter in state and local governance. As long as the stop was lawful and not exclusively to check for immigration status, then this routine in local governance could lead to legitimate forms of legal status checks. The court held that "if Section 2(B) only requires state officers to conduct a status check during the course of an authorized, lawful detention or after a detainee has been released, the provision would likely survive preemption – at least absent some showing that it has other consequences that are adverse to federal law and its objectives."[40]

When Georgia enacted HB 87 in 2011, the American Civil Liberties Union and the Georgia Latino Alliance for Human Rights challenged the law, claiming that "provisions of the law would violative of the Fourth Amendment in all circumstances, that it would penalize the exercise of the right to travel, that HB 87 facially restricts access to government service on the basis of national origin, or that the Act on its face deprives individuals of a property interest protected by the Fourteenth Amendment," in addition to preemption claims under INA.[41] Following the *Arizona* (2012) ruling, the Eleventh Circuit Court lifted the injunction on HB 87 to allow local law enforcement in Georgia to begin enforcing the "show me your papers" provision. Also in line with the *Arizona* ruling, the court held that only Section 7 of Georgia's law was preempted by federal immigration law because it "sought to create three new criminal violations: (1) transporting or moving an illegal alien; (2) concealing or harboring an illegal alien; and (3) inducing an illegal alien to enter the state of Georgia," all considered exclusive federal regulations and federal crimes under INA.[42]

South Carolina faced similar court challenges linked to *Arizona* after it passed SB 20 in 2011. Civil action led the United States government and the Lowcountry Immigration Coalition (the National Immigration Law Center, the Southern Poverty Law Center, and the American Civil Liberties Union of South Carolina) to challenge various sections of the Act, largely on preemption grounds. A district judge placed a temporary injunction on Sections 4, 5, and 6(B)(2), preventing them from being enforced.[43] Before the Fourth Circuit Court heard the state of South Carolina's appeal, the US Supreme Court in *Arizona*, struck down several of the same provisions in SB 1070, which made it a state crime for an alien to fail to carry an alien registration document and for an unauthorized alien to apply for, solicit, or perform work. SB 20 was remanded back to the district court, which upheld its injunction of Sections 4, 5, and 6(B)(2) citing *Arizona*.[44]

The South Carolina case was appealed to the Fourth Circuit Court, which in 2013 rejected the state's argument that its provisions in SB 20 were proper exercises of its state police powers.[45] The court argued that it was "hard-pressed to see how an unlawfully present alien, going about her normal daily life, would be able to avoid violating Sections 4(A) and (C) of the Act. Simply staying in one's home could be viewed as an attempt to 'shelter' oneself from detection. Taking a bus or driving home at the end of the workday would be 'transport[ing]' oneself to the shelter of one's home to avoid detection. The broad sweep of these sections violates the clear rule of Arizona that unlawful presence is not a criminal offense."[46] SB 20's Sections 4(A) and (C) had effectively criminalized unlawful presence and were therefore preempted by federal law. Alabama's HB 56 (2011), written by Kris Kobach and modeled after SB 1070, faced similar constitutional challenge. The courts upheld the "show me your papers" provision requiring the local law enforcement to make a reasonable attempt to determine a person's immigration status if they had a 'reasonable suspicion" that the person was unlawfully present in the United States during a legal stop, detention, or arrest (unless the action would hinder an official investigation of some kind).

Since federal law provides a comprehensive scheme for unlawful presence and harboring, transporting, or shielding undocumented immigrants, it preempts state laws that criminalize unlawful presence through these varying means. Under federal law, the penalty for harboring is a fine and/or imprisonment of not more than five years (see note on history of federal law).[47] The maximum sentence is increased to ten years if the harboring was done "for the purpose of commercial advantage or private financial gain," to twenty years if serious bodily injury occurs or a life is placed "in jeopardy" during or in relation to the offense, and to life imprisonment or capital punishment if death results from the offense.

State laws criminalizing the harboring of undocumented immigrants have only been addressed at the federal circuit levels. The Eleventh Circuit Court enjoined Alabama's HB 568 (2012), which criminalized the harboring of unauthorized aliens and other related crimes.[48] The following year, in 2013, the Ninth Circuit enjoined a similar anti-harboring provision in Arizona's SB 1070.[49] Even with these court-imposed limits, states hold tremendous power. Alabama's HB 56, Section 30 (2011) was upheld by the Eleventh Circuit Court (2012) with little scrutiny and upheld enormous state power over the right to free movement, beyond requiring local law enforcement to check the status of persons at traffic stops. It criminalized as a Class C felony the act by undocumented persons (or third parties on their behalf) of entering into or attempting to enter into a business transaction with the state or any political subdivision, "including, but not limited to, applying for or renewing a motor vehicle license plate, applying for or renewing a driver's license or nondriver identification card, or applying for or renewing a business license." Outside the domain of federal immigration law, business transactions and licensing have wielded an important space for states to expand rights, to contract rights, and even to criminalize free movement and presence.

RIGHT TO DUE PROCESS AND LEGAL PROTECTION (DIMENSION 2)

States today have nowhere near the power to control immigration that they exercised during America's first century (see Figure 6.3). Nevertheless, they play a central role in shaping immigrant access to due process and legal protection, given the low federal standard on immigrant rights in this area.

As in the case of free movement, California leads the way on state provisions of due process and legal protections to immigrants. In 2013, California passed the Transparency and Responsibility Using State Tools (TRUST) Act, providing that officers can only enforce immigration detainers issued by ICE for persons convicted of serious crimes.[50] In 2014, when California's TRUST Act went into effect, the city of San Francisco and the counties of Contra Costa, Alameda, and San Mateo followed the lead set by the state, announcing that they would no longer cooperate with any ICE detention requests of possible unauthorized immigrants in local jails.[51] Together, California's state and local sanctuary policies resulted in a major decrease in deportations by ICE after 2014, increasing pressure on President Obama, under the direction of Homeland Security Secretary Jeh Johnson, to end S-Comm that same year.[52] As we argued in Chapter 5, Democratic control of the state, and partnerships between officials and immigrant rights organizations, paved the road for California to expand its sanctuary-type protections exponentially since 2014, including passing the TRUTH Act in 2016 and the California Values Act (AB 54) in 2017.

By limiting who state and local law enforcement can hold, question, and transfer to federal immigration authorities, the California Values Act considerably expands immigrant rights to due process and legal protection. It also prohibits local law enforcement, school police, and security departments from using money or personnel to investigate or arrest persons for immigration enforcement purposes. The law also requires that the state's attorney general publish model policies for limiting assistance with immigration enforcement for use by public schools, public libraries, and public health facilities. While other states have not enacted as strong a sanctuary policy as the California Values Act, they have followed suit with regard to limiting local law enforcement's cooperation. Connecticut passed its TRUST Act in 2013, followed by Illinois in 2017, Oregon in 2017, and New Jersey's governor issuing an executive order in 2018 reversing the state's stance to "pro-sanctuary."[53] As we noted in Chapter 1, Oregon had enacted a form of state sanctuary in 1987, well before California, and those protections got strengthened through its more recent passage of a TRUST Act.

In addition to being able to limit their engagement in federal enforcement, states also have significant authority and control over legal representation. Thus, for example, undocumented persons lacking federal due process protections in immigration court can still have their rights expanded under

The Right to Due Process & Legal Protection (Dimension 2)

Count of States		Net Score (Exclusionary)																	Net Score (Inclusionary)			
	-22	-17	-16	-15	-14	-12	-10	-9	-6	-5	-4	-2	-1	0	1	2	3	4	6	7	49
1	AZ	GA	TN	AL	MS	TX	VA	UT	OK	NC	IN	AR	FL	DC	AK	CO	NJ	IL	CT	RI	CA
2		SC										MI	KS	DE	HI		NY	NV	OR	WA	
3												MO		IA	MN		VT				
4													ND	ID	NM						
5														KY							
6														LA							
7														MA							
8														MD							
9														ME							
10														MT							
11														NE							
12														NH							
13														OH							
14														PA							
15														SD							
16														WI							
17														WV							
18														WY							

FIGURE 6.3 Immigrant inclusion on Dimension 2: rights to due process & legal protection

state policies. These include limiting holds to forty-eight hours, informing people in their custody of a detainer request, creating legal protections of attorney confidentiality, and revising state or local criminal sentencing guidelines to protect immigrants. States have passed these measures in order to prevent undocumented immigrants from being transferred from state and local custody to federal custody.

As with sanctuary, California has paved an impressive inroad for expanding due process and legal protections to its undocumented residents, even creating new categories of protection for unlawful status under state law. For example, recently enacted state law bars state or local agencies from sharing information on legal status with federal officials; prohibits their resources from being used toward any investigation or enforcement activity related by the federal government (SB 31 in 2017); and adds special protections to victims or witnesses of hate crimes with regard to information-sharing (AB 493 in 2017). California's legal protections have gone beyond bans on information sharing: undocumented persons also have the right not to be asked about their legal status by any state or local public official (AB 1195 in 2013), and the right to be informed of any immigration detainer request submitted by the federal government to local law enforcement and jails (AB 2792 in 2016).

States have also taken important steps to ensure the protection of immigrants within sensitive locations and in attorney–client representation. Even states that are pushing for exclusion have enacted minimal protection by barring "notarios" from falsely claiming that they can provide legal representation as immigration attorneys. California further expands these protections by requiring state bars to regulate and oversee immigration attorneys and to share any violations committed by attorneys with the general public (AB 60 in 2015, AB 1159 in 2013); requiring courts prior to accepting a guilty or nolo contendere by a defendant to notify them of any immigration consequences (AB 1343 in 2015); and requiring local law enforcement to provide detained undocumented custodial parents the right to make telephone calls when in detention (AB 2015 in 2012). California has also enacted laws prohibiting the disclosure of a person's immigration status as it pertains to juvenile, civil, and criminal proceedings (AB 899 in 2015, AB 2159 in 2017, and SB 785 in 2018).

California and other states have reformed other aspects of their criminal justice system in order to reduce even more harmful consequences to immigrants. Some have reduced criminal sentencing to 364 days in order to sever possible immigration violation consequences. Similarly, California law prohibits sharing information from its state gang database for federal immigration law purposes; it also authorizes the state's Department of Justice to suspend or revoke access to the state database for any violators (AB 90 in 2017). Finally, California is the only state so far allowing parolees to be eligible for a pardon, commutation, or certificate of rehabilitation without regard to their immigration status (AB 2845 in 2018) and to specifically expand community treatment or rehabilitation programs for undocumented inmates (SB 1021 in 2012).

Outside of their own criminal justice system, states can also use their power over public contracts to end state and local resources and officials from having any role in the deportation practices or holds of undocumented persons. In California, state and local law enforcement agencies are prohibited from contracting with the federal government for use of their facilities to house individuals as federal detainees for purposes of civil immigration custody (AB 110 in 2018), and the state budget bans any contracts from being formed with immigrant detention centers or entering into similar contracts with the federal government (SB 112 in 2017). The state has also banned ICE and other federal agencies from making civil arrests at state and local courthouses (AB 668 in 2019). Finally, California and a few other states have provided financial assistance for undocumented persons to gain attorney representation. Thus, in the absence of federal guarantees of due process and legal protection for undocumented immigrants, states have found various ways to expand this citizenship right for their resident populations.

On the other side of the spectrum, immigration federalism today also enables states to reinforce federal capacity on immigration enforcement and to tighten the link between state criminal justice and immigrant deportation. Arizona has taken the lead in this regard. SB 1070's "show me your papers" provision contracts rights along both Dimensions 1 and 2, by requiring "state and local law enforcement agencies and officers to make a 'reasonable attempt' to determine the immigration status of any person, who they have 'reasonable suspicion' to believe, is unlawfully present in the United States." Thus, an undocumented person can have their legal status checked by local law enforcement following minor traffic violations, without being provided additional due process protections. After a stop, the provision in Arizona's law requires the officer to contact federal immigration officers and to hold any person unable to provide sufficient proof of their legal status for up to forty-eight hours, until federal agents take over custody of them. Additionally, Section 2(C) and (D) requires that state and local law enforcement transfer known undocumented immigrants to federal custody and even allows for them to transport the person directly to a federal facility. Similar to Section 2(B), Section 6 (*struck down*) created an even more direct role in immigration enforcement: law enforcement officers were able to make warrantless arrests whenever they had probable cause to believe that an individual had committed a deportable offense.

While Section 2(B) has gained national attention from the US Supreme Court decision in 2012, other unchallenged provisions of SB 1070 have set the basic contours of the state's exclusionary reinforcing citizenship. Two other parts of Section 2 bar all state and local agencies and officials from adopting a policy that would limit or restrict their cooperation in enforcing federal immigration law (Section 2(A)), and it also requires "sending, receiving or maintaining" legal status information to federal, state, or local agencies and officials whenever requested (Section 2(F)).[54] Thus, SB 1070 established the first comprehensive anti-sanctuary law for reinforcing federal immigration enforcement initiatives. Additionally, Section 2(E) empowers any private person to sue state and local agencies and officials in state court for either adopting a sanctuary policy or not implementing SB 1070 to its fullest extent.[55]

Several states followed Arizona's lead after 2010. The following year, Alabama (2011), Utah (2011), South Carolina (2011), and Georgia (2011) all passed comprehensive laws, modeled after SB 1070, that combined anti-sanctuary provisions with enforcement provisions (other states proposed laws that failed, including Kansas (HB 2576), Mississippi (HB 488 and SB 2090), Missouri (SB 590), Rhode Island (HB 7313), and West Virginia (SB 64)). Generally, restrictive laws on due process and legal protections have required state and local public institutions to verify legal status and to share this information with other state and federal law enforcement agencies. In addition, provisions within these laws have authorized both government and private actors to file civil lawsuits against any suspected violator.

Meanwhile, regressive state laws are able to erode the federal baseline set on criminal justice rights – by denying suspected undocumented immigrants the right to post bail, to parole, to pre-trial release, or to pardons for their state-level crimes. These contractions in rights have layered on top of comprehensive schemes in Arizona, Alabama, South Carolina, and other states that reinforce federal level exclusions. For example, Arizona's Proposition 100 (2006) amended its state constitution to prohibit bail for individuals who both are charged with committing a serious felony offense and have entered or remain in the United States illegally. Regressive laws have also emerged in unusual states, where progressive immigrant integration policies have spread, most notably in Oregon (2011) – which passed HB 3508 prohibiting the governor from pardoning any individual subject to an outstanding deportation.

Indeed, while immigration law is exclusive to the federal government, states are developing a reinforcing capacity as well as denying basic due process and legal protections within their own criminal justice systems. Section 6 of Alabama's HB 56 (2011) places the attorney general in charge of overseeing compliance with the law and threatens violators with the removal of state funds, grants, or appropriations. Also, Section 20 establishes the Alabama Department of Homeland Security to head the state's coordination effort to transfer all known undocumented immigrants to federal custody, but only after their sentence for state or local crimes are served. Section 4 requires the state's attorney general to "negotiate the terms of a Memorandum of Agreement between the State of Alabama and the United States Department of Homeland Security," in order to provide a federal–state partnership that would deputize state law enforcement officers to focus exclusively on immigration enforcement, under the direction of the state attorney general.

Similarly, South Carolina established an "Illegal Immigration Enforcement Unit" in SB 20 (2011), which empowers officers with "the same power to serve criminal processes against offenders as sheriffs of the various counties and also the same power as those sheriffs to arrest without warrants and to detain persons found violating or attempting to violate immigration laws. The officers also shall have the same power and authority held by deputy sheriffs for the enforcement of the criminal laws of the State."[56] Other states have taken the approach of empowering federal agents rather than developing a reinforcing state capacity in immigration enforcement. North Dakota passed HB 1467 (2015), extending to US Customs and Border Protection officers' authority under state law to arrest people without a warrant for certain crimes committed in their presence. Similarly, Texas passed SB 150 (2011) and SB 530 (2011), granting federal agents power to arrest, search and seizure under state laws.

Federalism Dynamics and Dimension 2 Rights for Immigrants

As with free movement (Dimension 1), constitutional opportunities and changes in federal legislation and executive action have shaped state variation in immigrant rights to due process and legal protection. Federal immigration law makes unauthorized entry and reentry (after being previously formally removed from the country) a misdemeanor and possible felony, with up to two years' imprisonment. Contrary to popular belief, however, undocumented presence in the United States is not a crime. The proposed Border Protection, Antiterrorism, and Illegal Immigration Control Act of 2005 (HR 4437) sought to criminalize unlawful presence in the United States, but it failed to pass.[57] Moreover, not all undocumented immigrants actually enter the country illegally. A large number of immigrants overstay their temporary visas, or they find employment that is not authorized by their visa. Federal immigration law treats unlawful presence as a civil violation subject to removal from the country but not as a criminal offense.

Most importantly, while the federal government can incentivize and encourage state and local compliance, they cannot compel state or local officials to use their own resources and personnel to apprehend, detain, or keep noncitizens in their custody.[58] The formal separation of federal and state sovereignty under the Tenth Amendment's anti-commandeering principle prevents the federal government from being able to mandate states and localities to become immigration enforcers. The Second Circuit, in *City of New York v. United States* (1999), clarified the limits of sanctuary policies as a form of resistance to federal enforcement of immigration law. It held that states and localities could not directly prevent communication of information previously obtained about legal status to federal immigration officers, but it also preserved state and local power to not inquire about immigrant's legal status in the first place ("don't ask") under the Tenth Amendment. Today, *City of*

New York remains the only limit on sanctuary resistance by states and localities; they cannot actively obstruct federal enforcement, but they can sever their connection from immigration enforcement entirely.[59]

Beyond questions of preemption and commandeering, enforcement of federal immigration law by state and local jurisdictions also runs the risk of producing constitutional violations of rights for citizens and noncitizens alike.[60] In *Galarza v. Lehigh County* (2014), the Third Circuit held that states and localities are not required to imprison people based on ICE detainers.[61] Since Lehigh County, Pennsylvania, was free to disregard the ICE detainer, the ACLU interpreted the decision as suggesting that states and localities "shares in the responsibility for violating Galarza's Fourth Amendment and due process rights."[62] Following the case, the Lehigh County Board of Commissions ended its policy of imprisoning people on ICE detainers.[63] In *Miranda-Olivares v. Clackamas County*, the US District Court of Oregon added that honoring ICE detainers without probable cause is a violation of the Fourth Amendment.[64]

At the same time, laws in Arizona, Alabama, South Carolina, and elsewhere continue to reinforce key aspect of federal immigration enforcement and, in the process, to exclude immigrants from basic due process. There are several ways for states to proactively engage and cooperate with federal immigration authorities. The Criminal Alien Program (CAP), emerging out of the Immigration Reform and Control Act (IRCA) of 1986, makes it a high priority for federal enforcement agencies to identify, detain, and deport non-US citizens in federal, state, and local prisons and jails.[65] IRCA also enabled the creation of the State Criminal Alien Assistance Program (SCAAP), which reimburses state and local governments for the costs they incur from incarcerating or detaining immigrants.[66] More recently, the Illegal Immigration Reform and Immigration Responsibility Act (IIR-IRA), passed in 1996, created Section 287(g) (of the Immigration and Nationality Act), granting the Department of Homeland Security the ability to enter into agreements with local law enforcement agencies to deputize local officers to engage in immigration enforcement.[67] Finally, an even bigger shift occurred in 2008 with the creation of the Secure Communities (S-Comm) program, which effectively nationalized state–federal cooperation on immigration enforcement. Under S-Comm, jurisdictions are mandated to share fingerprint data with the Department of Homeland Security of every person booked into state and local jails. This would then trigger ICE to issue detainer requests to local jails for those immigrants they identify as residing in the country unlawfully. Thus, in cases like *Arizona v. United States* (2012), the courts have upheld state laws and provisions that reinforce, but do not overstep, their role in partnering with the federal government to enforce immigration law.

It is important to note that S-Comm also places limits on the actions of states with progressive citizenship regimes. While several states have chosen not to comply with detainer requests, they are still obligated to share fingerprint data with the Department of Homeland Security as a condition of accessing any federal criminal biometric database system.[68] This was true even when the Obama administration phased out S-Comm in favor of the Priority Enforcement Program (PEP), which narrowed the focus of ICE on those convicted of serious crimes but still kept the information-sharing requirements in place. And the limits of state resistance are even greater today, after the Trump administration revived S-Comm through executive order in 2017 and did away with the Obama administration's system of targeted priorities for deportation.

Finally, some states have attempted to erode due process protections in even more fundamental ways. In 2011, Kris Kobach helped Alabama craft HB 56, which included a provision on contracts that would strike at the heart of due process rights. HB 56 held in Section 27 (a) that "No court of this state shall enforce the terms of, or otherwise regard as valid, any contract between a party and an alien unlawfully present in the United States, if the party had direct or constructive knowledge that the alien was unlawfully present in the United States at the time the contract was entered into."[69] The United States filed suit soon after HB56 was enacted, challenging the constitutionality of the law's multiple provisions, including the invalidation of contracts based on a person's immigrant legal status. The Eleventh Circuit court agreed. It found the statute to be "extraordinary and unprecedented" and criticized its broad sweep: "Essentially, the ability to maintain even a minimal existence is no longer an option for unlawfully present aliens in Alabama."[70] In finding the section preempted, the court also noted that it burdened "a capability that, in practical application, is essential for an individual to live and conduct daily affairs."[71] Thus, even as executive actions from the Trump administration have expanded states' abilities to facilitate immigrant detention and deportation, federal courts have kept in place some fundamental due process rights, including the general right to enter into contracts.

RIGHT TO HUMAN CAPITAL FORMATION (DIMENSION 3)

Courts have also kept in place some key elements of rights to human capital formation, including the right to a K–12 public education. Building on the landmark decision of *Brown v. Board of Education* (1954) that struck down Jim Crow laws in public education, the US Supreme Court ruled in *Plyler v. Doe* (1982) that the Fourteenth Amendment's equal protection clause safeguards the right to K–12 public education for all undocumented children. In fact, as Hiroshi Motomura unpacks in great detail, the *Plyler* Court cited the *Brown* decision in arguing that K–12 education is fundamental to their integration, to their formation of human capital, and to the state and national interest.[72] Federal courts have reaffirmed the equal protection provisions of *Plyler* time and again, including issuing a permanent injunction on Proposition 187 in 1994 over its ban on allowing undocumented students in public K–12 schools and blocking a provision in Alabama's HB 56 in 2012 that required school officials to check and report on newly enrolled K–12 students' immigration status.[73] At the same time, federal courts have stopped short of extending the equal protection framework for immigrant rights in other arenas, including for higher education. On these and other features of human capital formation, state control over the rights of undocumented immigrants have led to very divergent policy outcomes (Figure 6.4).

Today, twenty-three states and the District of Columbia provide in-state tuition to undocumented students who attend an in-state high school for a specified period, usually between one and three years. In 2001, Texas and California were the first two states to grant in-state tuition to undocumented residents. Nine states followed between 2002 and 2006, including New York, Utah, Washington, Oklahoma, Illinois, Kansas, New Mexico, and Nebraska. A notable gap in state legislation existed between 2007 and 2011, as Congress grappled with passing the DREAM Act and many states followed Arizona's lead on enacting exclusionary immigration laws.[74] Momentum started again after the 2010 DREAM Act failed to pass during a lame-duck session of Congress. Connecticut passed in-state tuition in 2011, and, in 2014, California expanded its in-state policy by allowing any combination of elementary and secondary schooling within the state to fulfill its three-year residency requirement. Finally, in eight additional states, college and university systems have passed their own policies granting in-state tuition to undocumented students, even though their state governments have not passed similar enabling legislation.[75] Thus, it is fairly common for states to exceed the federal standard on human capital rights for immigrants, with a majority of states today providing access to in-state tuition (either through state laws or through policies in their public university systems).

States have also advanced the human capital rights of undocumented immigrants by expanding access to financial aid. Ten states today provide undocumented students access to some form of aid, including scholarships and grants from state and private funds.[76] In 2011, California passed the California Dream Act through two bills: AB 130 granted non–state-funded scholarships for public colleges and universities; AB 131 granted state-funded financial aid such as institutional grants, community college fee waivers, the Cal Grant, and the Chafee Grant. In 2014, California added even more aid provisions, establishing a State DREAM Loan Program through SB 1210 for undocumented students at the University of California and California State University systems. This same year, a few California colleges and universities also joined a national program, TheDream.US, which offered scholarships to low-income undocumented students.[77] While the financial aid programs in Texas and New Mexico do not go as far as do California's, they actually passed several years prior (in 2001 and 2005, respectively), while Minnesota and Washington passed their laws soon after California. Finally, Maryland,

The Right to Develop Human Capital (Dimension 3)

	Net Score (Exclusionary)														Net Score (Inclusionary)									
Count of States	-27	-18	-17	-12	-11	-9	-8	-7	-6	-5	-4	-3	-2	-1	0	1	2	3	4	5	6	8	9	57
1	AL	GA	TN	AZ	MO	NE	MS	FL	AR	LA	ND	CO	AK	DC	DE	HI	KY	MA	MD	OR	CT	NY	IL	CA
2							UT		ID	MI	TX	MN	ME	MT	IA			NM		WA				
3									SC	IN	NC	PA	NV	OH	RI			NJ						
4												NH	VA	SD	OK	VT								
5											WV			WY	WI									

FIGURE 6.4 Immigrant inclusion on Dimension 3: right to develop human capital

Oregon, and New Jersey granted state financial aid in 2018, followed by New York and Illinois in 2019.

Not all moves on higher education have been in a inclusive direction. Six states have expressly denied in-state tuition to legal immigrants; these include Alabama, Arizona, Georgia, Indiana, Missouri, and South Carolina.[78] In addition, three states – Alabama, Georgia, and South Carolina – have taken a further step of prohibiting unlawfully present immigrants from attending any state institution of higher learning. One state took an even more extreme position: In 2002, Virginia's Attorney General Jerry Kilgore issued a memo advising Virginia's public colleges and universities to deny admission to undocumented students and to report them to federal immigration authorities.[79] It is unclear whether any university did so, but Virginia's state government was clearly sending a message to undocumented immigrants that they were not welcome in the state's public universities.[80] Finally, Kris Kobach sought to scuttle Kansas's in-state tuition law by helping to bring a lawsuit against the state in 2007.[81] Kobach and plaintiffs argued that the in-state tuition law was a violation of IIR-IRA because it created a benefit for undocumented immigrants that were unavailable to US citizens from other states. The Tenth Circuit ruling rejected the argument, noting that the residency requirement for unauthorized immigrants also applied to US citizens. Kobach tried again in 2011, this time appealing a California Supreme Court decision unanimously upholding in-state tuition for state residents, regardless of their federal legal status. The Supreme Court denied cert soon thereafter, thus firmly establishing the ability of states to provide residents with human capital rights that exceed the federal floor.

Employment Rights for Immigrants

While courts have constrained the ability of states to deny public education to undocumented immigrants, they have placed very few constraints on the authority of states to regulate immigrant rights to employment. Indeed, immigration federalism enables states to either require or limit employer use of a federal database, E-Verify, that uses both Department of Homeland Security and Social Security Administration databases to electronically verify the identity and work authorization of employees.

Illinois passed the first anti–E-Verify state law in 2007, led by advocates arguing that the E-Verify system was often inaccurate and led to many wrongful employment ineligibility outcomes. HB 1743 (2007) outlined specific procedures to be used by employers while participating in E-Verify in order to protect the civil rights of employees, and a second bill, HB 1744 (2007), prevented all government jurisdictions in the state from requiring employers to use any employment verification system for any reason. It further mandated procedures and responsibilities for proper use by private employers, including posting notices and alerting employees of the employer's participation in

E-Verify and of existing antidiscrimination protections in the state. When the provision of HB 1744 prohibiting employers from using E-Verify was overturned in federal court, in 2009, Illinois passed an amended version to create stricter standards regulating how employers use E-Verify, adding requirements on employer training, posting of legal notices, and antidiscrimination procedures in the workplace.

Following Illinois's lead, California passed AB 1236 (2011) prohibiting states and localities from mandating the use of E-Verify, "except as required by federal law or as a condition of receiving federal funds." More recently, it passed AB 622 (2015) expanding the reach of its anti–E-Verify law by limiting all employers, private and public, to checking the status of only workers that have received a conditional offer of employment, and it prohibits verification of already employed workers. The only exception is if checking one's status is required by federal law or as a condition of receiving federal funds. These policies cannot prevent employers from voluntarily using E-Verify, and other federal laws that prohibit employment of unauthorized workers still apply.[82] Nevertheless, Illinois and California's anti–E-Verify laws create a firewall between immigration and labor enforcement at the state level.

Relatedly, states have employed their authority over business licenses to expand and protect the rights of undocumented professionals to form their own businesses, to become a licensed attorney under the state bar, or to gain professional licenses in other industries regulated by state or local governments. In 2012, the California Supreme Court was presented with an undocumented applicant who had completed law school and passed the state's bar exam and whose admission was recommended by the state bar association.[83] Just weeks after oral argument in the case, the California legislature enacted a law expressly allowing undocumented applicants to become members of the state bar.[84] Relying on that statute, the state supreme court ruled to admit the undocumented applicant.[85]

A similar dynamic occurred in Florida, where the state supreme court initially rejected the application of an undocumented bar applicant,[86] but that decision was made moot when the Florida legislature passed a bill, in accordance with federal law, that granted undocumented immigrants the ability to become members of the bar.[87] New York has failed to pass legislation similar to California's and Florida's, although the state supreme court ruled in June 2015 that DACA recipients could practice law in the state without the need for any new state law affirming this benefit.[88] California expanded access to professional licensing one step further in October 2014, when Governor Jerry Brown signed SB 1159 into law requiring "all 40 licensing boards under the California Department of Consumer Affairs to consider applicants regardless of immigration status by 2016."[89] Building on these progressive employment rights, a few states, including California, Illinois, and New York, have passed a range of workforce protection laws that prohibit employer retaliation by using an employee's legal status against them for any reason; a domestic worker bill of rights that provides the same level of workplace protections to undocumented workers as given to citizens and legal immigrants; wage theft and equal remedies against employer abuse; and antidiscrimination laws in the workplace and in contracts.

By contrast, twenty-two states today have enacted some form of E-Verify compliance law, with varying restrictions and penalties. Georgia's SB 529 (2006) demands E-Verify compliance of all employees hired by the state, state contractors, and subcontractors; requires employers to withhold 6 percent of paid compensation as state income tax for employees lacking a taxpayer identification number or is a nonresident alien; prohibits employers from claiming paid wages that exceed $600 as business expenses; and empowers the Commissioner of the Georgia Department of Labor to make any rules and regulations necessary to ensure compliance. As an early state to enact such requirements, SB 529 was enforced in phases, beginning with employers of 500 or more employees in 2007 and subsequently extending to employers with more than 100 employees in 2008 and those with fewer than 100 employees in 2009.[90]

From 2009 to 2011, Georgia passed three laws amending its requirements for E-Verify compliance by requiring all public subcontractors to show proof that newly hired employees were verified (HB 2 in 2009) and barring noncompliant private contractors from any public project (SB 447 in 2010). Rather than criminalizing noncompliance, however, Georgia's approach to employment has been to make it more costly for employers to hire undocumented workers. In passing HB 87 in 2011, Georgia began to lessen this burden by exempting businesses with ten or fewer employees and allowing noncompliant businesses under "good faith" to make corrections within thirty days without facing any penalties. Louisiana has enacted three laws between 2011 and 2012, all mirroring the restrictions in Georgia's focus on public contracts and delegating authority to the state workforce commission to notify state authorities to suspend the license of and fine the person in violation.

Alabama's HB 56 (2011), unlike Georgia's phasing in and exceptions-based approach, prohibited all business entities, employers, and public employers from knowingly employing, hiring for employment, or continuing to employ "an unauthorized alien to perform work within the State of Alabama," as described in federal law (8 USC § 1324a) and required the use of E-Verify to enforce the law. South Carolina's HB 4400 (2008) came before Alabama's law and went much further to prohibit all public and private employers from hiring undocumented workers by not only requiring E-Verify compliance but also issuing a South Carolina employment license. In 2011, South Carolina amended its law, when passing SB 20, to require any complaints of noncompliance in E-Verify to be investigated by state officials, ordering them to notify ICE of any suspected undocumented worker, to inform state and local law enforcement agencies, and for the state official to conduct a full audit of the employer. The law also imposed employer penalties that range from probationary periods that require regular reports to the state to having a state employment licenses suspended or revoked.

Beyond E-Verify, which reinforces federal exclusions, the most regressive states have further eroded rights by prohibiting state or local government entering into any form of business transaction with undocumented immigrants. The same provision of Alabama's HB 56 (2011) that we highlight as being a significant exclusion on the right to free movement, Section 30, also criminalizes attempts by undocumented immigrants (or a third party on their behalf) to enter into a business transaction with the state or any political subdivision, including "applying for or renewing a business license" anywhere in the state. Similarly, North Dakota's HB 1367's (2011) Alien Agricultural Land Ownership law prohibits "any illegal alien," with the exception of Canadian citizens, from being "eligible to acquire agricultural land" and made violations a Class A misdemeanor. Even in progressive states, exclusions have been carved into licensing laws. For example, New York's AB 9706 (2010) amended real estate law in the state to require that any person seeking a real estate broker license be legally permitted to work in the United States.

Public Benefits, Health Care, and Housing for Immigrants

The right to human capital formation (Dimension 3) is also being shaped by states expanding or contracting immigrant access to health care. Today, twenty-seven states provide "legal" immigrant children access to CHIP, and six of these states – California, Illinois, Massachusetts, New York, Oregon, Washington – as well as the District of Columbia provide immigrant children access to health insurance regardless of legal status.[91] While the Affordable Care Act (ACA) of 2010 considers DACA individuals ineligible, states are able to grant low-income lawfully present immigrants as well as DACA individuals' eligibility for Medi-Cal benefits by defining their status as Permanent Residence Under Color of Law (PRUCOL).[92]

In states like New York and California, local benefits expansion preceded state expansion. In 2015, for example, Healthy Way LA "Unmatched," Healthy San Francisco, and Alameda County HealthPAC were available to immigrants regardless of legal status, including benefits such as primary care, emergency care, mental health services, and prescription drugs. Thirteen California counties participated in the Healthy Kids program, an insurance program funded by both public and private sources that provides comprehensive medical, dental, and vision coverage to low-income uninsured county residents regardless of legal status. Similar coverage to all immigrants was provided by the Kaiser Permanente Child Health Program, which offered premium subsidies for uninsured California children regardless of immigration status and currently covers thirty counties across the state.[93]

In 2015, California proposed a new bill SB 1005 – The Health for All Act – that would expand health insurance coverage to all undocumented immigrants in the state. Currently, the ACA specifically excludes undocumented immigrants from being insured under California's health care exchange system. SB 1005 would have created a new exchange system, the California Health Benefit Exchange Program for All Californians (regardless of legal status), and extended Medi-Cal benefits to low-income undocumented immigrants in the state.[94] While this comprehensive health care bill did not pass, California has achieved major victories: in 2015, it passed a state law that expands health care to all undocumented children (eighteen years old or younger);[95] more recently, in 2019, California passed a law providing access to the state's Medicaid program to qualifying low-income undocumented adults who are twenty-five years old or younger.[96] California entered 2020 set to extend Medicaid coverage to all undocumented seniors, but this was tabled by Governor Gavin Newsom after having to spend the state's fiscal reserves on COVID-19 relief. Meanwhile, Governor JB Pritzker signed the 2021 budget, making Illinois the first in the country to extend health insurance to low-income (but not all) seniors residents, regardless of immigration status.[97]

By contrast, states have enacted exclusionary reinforcing laws that apply federal standards to all health care and public benefits. Nebraska in 2011, for example, repealed its state-funded public benefits for legal immigrants that do not qualify for assistance under federal guidelines or with federal dollars, including TANF, SNAP, Medicaid, and aid to the aged, blind, and disabled. In 2010, Minnesota enacted two laws essentially excluding adults and children from health-related benefits: SB 460 (2010) excluded undocumented residents from the right to general assistance medical care such as mental health care and consultation, while SB 2505 (2010) prohibited undocumented young children from early childhood education programs provided by the state. Georgia, Alabama, and Arizona have fully excluded undocumented persons from receiving any public benefit and have imposed strict penalties on state or local officials violating state law.

In addition to health care, housing adds another important element to human capital rights. California became the only state to overrule and stop the emergence of local restrictions in housing when it passed AB 976 (2007), prohibiting local governments from requiring that landlords check the legal status of tenants and prohibiting landlords from independently doing the same.[98] After the US Congress failed to pass the Sensenbrenner bill in 2005 and 2006, anti-immigrant actors made a concerted push in restrictive local legislation. In 2006, the city of San Bernardino pushed for a comprehensive local ordinance they called the "Illegal Immigration Relief Act," seeking to mandate English-only for all city-related business and banning day labor centers, day labor work solicitation, any hiring of unauthorized workers, and any renting of properties to undocumented immigrants.[99] Pro-immigrant activists quickly mobilized and provided legal support to the pro-immigrant mayor and city council members to defeat the ordinance.[100] At the state level,

California moved to pass AB 976 (2007) after six cities within its jurisdiction succeeded in enacting anti-immigrant ordinances.[101]

Outside of California, in 2006, the mayor of Hazleton, Pennsylvania, said that he wanted to make his city "the toughest place on illegal immigrants in America."[102] The city became the first in the country to enact a local law, called the Illegal Immigration Relief Act, that imposed a $1,000-per-day fine on landlords who rent to undocumented immigrants and revoked the business licenses of employers for five years if they hired undocumented workers. Following Hazelton's lead, Tom Macklin, the mayor of Avon Park, Florida, pushed for a similar ordinance (but failed), urging, "If we address the housing issue – make it as difficult as possible for illegals to find safe haven in Avon Park – then they are going to have to find someplace else to go."[103] Soon, however, these local restrictions were preempted by federal law.

Federalism Dynamics and Dimension 3 Rights for Immigrants

The constitutional and federal legislative landscape for states' role in providing the right to human capital formation (Dimension 3) is more mixed, when compared to free movement rights (Dimension 1). On the one hand, *Plyler v Doe* (1982) clearly establishes a baseline constitutional right to K–12 education and federal labor law sets a floor that also applies to undocumented immigrants. At the same time, many undocumented immigrants face the risk of deportation when they seek to exercise their rights.[104] Research shows that undocumented immigrants do not make workplace claims, despite having federal rights to do so.[105] Employers prefer hiring immigrant workers because they are exploitable, and have no incentive to ensure safe working conditions.[106] Recently, the Supreme Court ruled in *Hoffman Plastic Compounds, Inc. v. National Labor Relations Board* (2002) that undocumented workers are not entitled to back pay, making them more vulnerable to employer abuse and severing immigrants from access to rights established under the National Labor Relations Act of 1935. Moreover, in 1996, IIR-IRA generally prohibited states from conferring a "public benefit" (including professional licenses) to an unauthorized immigrant unless the state affirmatively enacted a state law providing the benefit after 1996.[107] Thus, court interpretation and federal action have tended to lower the existing federal baseline on the right to human capital formation, but they have also given states new opportunities to expand those rights above a meager federal baseline.

In 1996, the federal government's Personal Work Opportunity and Reform Act (PWORA) made many groups of noncitizens ineligible for important federal health care benefits, including federally funded public benefit programs: Temporary Assistance for Needy Families (TANF), Supplemental Nutrition Assistance Program (SNAP, often referred to as "food stamps"), Supplemental Security Income (SSI), Medicaid, and the Children's Health Insurance Program (CHIP).[108] While unauthorized immigrants and temporary immigrants were ineligible for these programs prior to 1996, this new federal law expanded restrictions by placing a five-year ineligibility period for new lawful immigrant residents in the US. Further, individuals granted DACA status under President Barack Obama's 2012 executive order were also ineligible for these federal programs. Enabling state to expand and contract these rights, the 1996 law devolved some decision-making over noncitizen eligibility for jointly funded federal–state programs and state-only public assistance programs to state governments, and it also *required* states that desired to provide public assistance to unauthorized immigrants to do so through enactment of affirmative legislation after 1996.[109] This allows states to spend their own resources to cover nonqualifying legal and unauthorized immigrants without a federal match in funds. States have done this in two key areas: prenatal care and child health care.

Ineligible immigrants have minimal access to prenatal health care only in emergencies under federal law. In particular, the Emergency Medical Treatment and Active Labor Act (EMTALA) of 1986 prevents hospitals from turning away any uninsured patient in need of emergency treatment, including labor and delivery, as well as other "emergency" health care services related to childbirth. However, this federal law does not provide access to routine prenatal care, and under PWORA, noncitizens are ineligible for regular prenatal care. In 2002, the US Department of Health and Human Services gave states the option to provide prenatal care to undocumented immigrant women by extending CHIP coverage to unborn children.

Today, states have expanded immigrant access to prenatal health care in three ways: laws granting access to CHIP for unborn children; laws granting access to presumptive eligibility (PE) for pregnant women to obtain immediate temporary Medicaid coverage; and states setting up more comprehensive low-income insurance for pregnant women through state-funded programs. In particular, thirty-two states provide access to CHIP regardless of legal status, thirty states provide access to PE (with seventeen of these states offering access to PE regardless of legal status), and three states have comprehensive state-funded insurance programs for low-income pregnant women regardless of legal status.[110]

Since the late 1970s, federal courts have also generally cleared the way for states to impose restrictions on the ability of unauthorized immigrants to access welfare benefits, state driver's licenses, and postsecondary education. The Illegal Immigration Reform and Immigrant Responsibility Act (IIR-IRA) of 1996 restricted states' ability to provide postsecondary education benefits on the basis of state residency, unless a US citizen from another state would also be eligible for that benefit.[111] This change in federal law spurred state legislative action on education, and federal courts have upheld both progressive laws – such as the ones in California and Oregon allowing any state resident to receive in-state tuition and state financial aid – and regressive laws banning unauthorized immigrants gaining admissions to state colleges and universities.[112]

On the other end of the spectrum, in *Chamber of Commerce of the United States v. Whiting* (2011), the US Supreme Court upheld Arizona's 2007 law requiring the use of E-Verify by Arizona employers and made punishable by suspension or revocation of the employer's business license. In a 5–3 vote, the court explained that "although Congress had made the program voluntary at the national level, it had expressed no intent to prevent States from mandating participation."[113] It also ruled that the 1986 Immigration Reform and Control Act prevented states from imposing fines on employers, but it expressly left open the possibility for states to continue regulating employers through the issuance of business licenses. With the federal government constitutionally unable to mandate state or local participation in E-Verify, the federal program's voluntary design and state control over licensing employers has created an important legislative space for states to directly expand and contract undocumented worker's right to find employment. Criminalizing and penalizing employers of unauthorized workers, federal law, under the Immigration Reform and Control Act of 1986 (IRCA), only preempts state or local laws that would create subfederal-level crimes or civil sanctions upon employers.[114]

By contrast, in *Arizona* (2012), the US Supreme Court struck out the only remaining provision in Section 5: as amended by HB 2162, Section 5(C) made it a Class 1 misdemeanor crime "for a person who is unlawfully present in the United States and who is an unauthorized alien to knowingly apply for work, solicit work in a public place or perform work as an employee or independent contractor in this state" (HB 2162, Section 5). The state of Arizona argued to the court that this provision criminalized undocumented *employees*, not employers (as under IRCA), and was valid because it did not infringe on existing federal law.[115] However, the court ruled that the employment of undocumented workers generally fell within the field of federal immigration law, established by IRCA in 1986, and was also preempted.

Court interpretation has also constrained other elements of regressive citizenship developments on human capital rights. In *Valle del Sol v. Whiting* (2013), the Ninth Circuit Court of Appeals took on another two provisions of SB 1070, arguing that they "singled out day labor solicitation for a harsh penalty while leaving other types of solicitation speech that blocks traffic unburdened" and adding that the law only "emphasizes that its purpose is to encourage self-deportation by stripping undocumented immigrants of their livelihood."[116] The court upheld a preliminary injunction that blocked the enforcement Section 5(A)(B) that penalized day laborers from soliciting work, ruling that they likely violated their First Amendment right to free speech.[117]

Finally, state legislative activity on housing rights have pushed in both inclusionary and exclusionary directions. For example, California's AB 976 (2007), which bans local landlord ordinances, expanded immigrant inclusion by adapting both federal and state antidiscrimination law. This includes California's Unruh Civil Rights Acts (1959) that protects full and equal accommodations in all business establishments, as well as the California Fair Employment and Housing Act (also passed in 1959) that makes housing discrimination and harassment unlawful.[118] Several jurisdictions, however, moved in an opposite direction on housing rights, requiring landlords to check on the legal status of their tenants. The Third Circuit Court finally got a chance to weigh in on the constitutionality of landlord audiences in 2013 with *Lozano v. Hazleton*, and it struck down the ordinance, ruling that federal immigration law preempted the ability of state or local policies requiring landlords to verify legal status.[119]

RIGHT TO POLITICAL PARTICIPATION AND REPRESENTATION (DIMENSION 4)

The contrast between immigrant citizenship rights and Black citizenship rights at the state level is most visible on Dimension 2, particularly with respect to the long fight for enforcing the Fifteenth Amendment on voting rights and the broader civil rights struggle for office holding and full representation. For undocumented residents, while no state currently provides the right to vote in state elections, many states allow for local legislation to expand voting rights. Indeed, states today are acting to increase their autonomy much like states in early America, who at the time defined their own civic and political identities in conferring local political membership to noncitizens (see Figure 6.5). In 1968, New York City passed the first local law in the country allowing noncitizen parents (of schoolchildren) the right to vote in community school board elections and to hold office on school boards.[120] Chicago, Illinois, and Takoma Park, Maryland, allow lawfully residing immigrants to vote in local elections.[121] In 1992, Takoma Park formally amended its municipal charter in order to give all of its residents, including noncitizens, the right to vote and run for office in local elections, motivated primarily by concerns over fairness, since a large immigrant population resided in the city and was subject to the same obligations as citizens of paying taxes and military conscription.[122] Two other cities – New York City and Burlington, Vermont – as well as Washington, DC, have recently proposed similar bills.[123]

San Francisco began its fight for local voting rights, when the state was transitioning toward progressive policies in response to Proposition 187 (1994). In February 1996, San Francisco Supervisor Mabel Teng sponsored a proposal to grant two groups of legal permanent residents (LPRs, or Green Card holders) the right to vote, including giving parents the right to vote in school board elections and community college students the right to vote for city college trustees.[124] Teng explained that his motivation was "to extend the right to legal residents who live here, work here, have kids that go to school here, or who go to school themselves" and "encourage people to participate in the political process."[125] San Francisco's 1996 attempt, and another two ballot measures in 2004 and 2010, failed to pass, largely due to failures in strategic campaigning and public opinion. In 2004, the San Francisco Board of

The Right to Participate & Be Represented (Dimension 4)

Count of States	Net Score (Exclusionary)							Net Score (Inclusionary)	
	−6	−5	−4	−3	−2	−1	0	1	9
1	UT	VA	GA	AL	AK	AR MT	IL	WA	CA
2		NH	KS	ND	LA	AZ NC	MD		
3			OK		MA	CO NE	NJ		
4					MS	CT NM	OR		
5					TN	DC NV			
6					TX	DE NY			
7						FL OH			
8						HI PA			
9						IA RI			
10						ID SC			
11						IN SD			
12						KY VT			
13						ME WI			
14						MI WV			
15						MN WY			
16						MO			

FIGURE 6.5 Immigrant inclusion on Dimension 4: rights to participate & be represented

Supervisors voted 9–2 to place a measure on the November ballot to amend the language in the city charter on voter qualifications, but it did not receive the needed majority votes to pass. After two decades, in 2016, San Francisco succeeded in passing Proposition N, which allows all immigrant parents the right to vote in school board elections.

Despite not having voting rights at the state level, multiple states have enacted laws that help to make voting for eligible minorities more accessible in addition to allowing local voting rights for immigrants. California has permitted other local inclusionary measures on participation and representation, including passing AB 817 (2013), which authorized county elections officials to appoint a person who is a lawful permanent resident in the United States and who is otherwise eligible to register to vote – except for their lack of US citizenship – to serve as a precinct board member. In 2016, Governor Brown appointed Jorge Reyes Salinas, who has temporary legal status under DACA, to the California State University board of trustees as a student trustee.[126] Finally, in 2018, California's Senate Rules Committee appointed Lizbeth Mateo, a thirty-three-year-old practicing attorney who is undocumented, to serve on the California Student Opportunity and Access Program Project Grant Advisory Committee.[127] This move prompted

California's state legislature to propose a law in 2018 (vetoed by Governor Brown) and again in 2019 (passed by Governor Newsom) that formalized the political inclusion of undocumented immigrants with regard to serving on state and local boards and commissions (see Chapter 5).

Finally, the right to participate and be represented has continued to expand, beyond the right to vote and serve on appointed state and local positions. Passing AB 2592 (2018), California has become the first state to lead in public outreach to all of its residents to promote awareness of, and encourage participation in, the US Census – which includes counting undocumented residents for purposes of apportionment and calculations on federal and state grantmaking. Washington State has also found ways to increase immigrant participation in public policy, including creating a legislative task force on community policing in the state (under HB 2098 in 2016), with representation from the Northwest immigration rights project.

By contrast, Arizona's Proposition 200, the "Arizona Taxpayer and Citizen Protection Act," was one of the first state anti-immigrant laws passed after 9/11, and it kickstarted a big new wave of restrictive policies.[128] FAIR had funded the signature-gathering campaign and then pushed the courts in the state to enforce the law broadly.[129] The law changed voter registration in the state by requiring residents to provide documentary proof of US citizenship while registering to vote, whereas previously a mere oath of affirmation sufficed. It also banned undocumented immigrants from access to public benefits by requiring state and local agencies to use strict identification standards that checked for legal immigration status. The US Supreme Court struck down Prop 200's voter registration provision in a 7–2 ruling on *Arizona v. Inter Tribal Council of Ariz., Inc.* (2013), noting that the National Voter Registration Act requires states to accept and use a uniform federal voter registration form. However, the court also noted that the NVRA "also authorizes States, '[i]n addition to accepting and using the' Federal Form, to create their own, state-specific voter-registration forms."[130] This meant that the state could create a separate registration process for state and local elections requiring documentary proof of US citizenship, which it then proceeded to do.

To date, nine states have enacted laws to require proof of national citizenship in state and local elections, many of which include provisions to use E-Verify or other federal databases to verify eligibility. Virginia, for example, passed SB 315 (2015), requiring the State Board of Elections to delete from its record of registered voters the names of voters who are known not to be US citizens and requiring checking for national citizenship status of all registering voters using the federal Systematic Alien Verification for Entitlements (SAVE) Program. North Dakota, which also requires national citizenship for voting, passed HB 1389 (2015) to create a legislative management study relating to verification of citizenship status for voting, with a focus on examining the feasibility of requiring the Department of Transportation to include a notation on a driver's license or nondriver identification card indicating the individual is not a US citizen. Kansas has gone much further: SB 34 (2015) criminalized "voting without being qualified" as a severity-level-7 nonperson felony. Adding to voter restrictions and criminalization, states have prohibited contributions for any election, caucus, or convention from foreign nationals residing in their jurisdictions as well as foreign governments, corporations, organizations. They have also gone the opposite direction of California by expressly prohibiting undocumented residents from being appointed to state or local positions and from serving on juries.

Federalism Dynamics and Dimension 4 Rights for Immigrants

While federal law restricts voting in national elections to US citizens, neither the Constitution nor federal law prevent states and localities from providing voting rights to immigrants in state or local elections or in school board elections.[131] Today, Section 216 of IIR-IRA makes it a crime for any noncitizen to vote in a federal election, but the Constitutional framework leaves open state or local voting rights. Indeed, Gerald Rosberg argues that the Fourteenth Amendment's equal protection clause makes it possible for noncitizens to gain voting rights.[132] Scholars also note that while the Fourteenth, Fifteenth, Nineteenth, Twenty-Fourth, and Twenty-Sixth Amendments prevent states from denying national citizens the right to vote, the "one person, one vote" jurisprudence on suffrage leaves open whether or not states can expand voting rights to residents who are not US citizens.[133]

At the same time, federal law and constitutional interpretation also allow states to impose additional restrictions on citizens seeking voter registration. As we have shown for Black voting rights, federal courts have allowed voter ID laws and felon disenfranchisement laws to stand, even if they pose disproportionate burdens on low-income communities and communities of color (see Chapters 3 and 4). Documentary proof of citizenship laws go one step further, requiring residents to provide copies of birth certificates, passports, naturalization documents, or other documents such as driver's licenses that have, in turn, determined documentary proof of US citizenship. Thus, despite the Fifteenth Amendment and the Voting Rights Act of 1965, court interpretation and state legislative actions have helped promulgate regressive forms of state citizenship.

RIGHT TO IDENTIFY AND BELONG (DIMENSION 5)

On June 23, 2014, Senator Kevin de León led California in passing SB 396, removing all inactive passages from Proposition 187 from California's education, health and safety, and welfare codes. De León explained that Prop. 187, even when inactive, has a "damaging and lasting impact on the immigrant communities because it further stigmatized an already vulnerable population," noting that even today "the immigrant population fears interacting with

State Citizenship and Immigration Federalism

government officials and, as a result, is often hesitant to become civically engaged and cooperate with the police."[134] The contrast between California's position today and its position two decades earlier is stark, which makes state laws and acts of apologies an important step in developing a state citizenship that is inclusive. As we noted in Chapter 5, the state has passed additional legislation establishing immigrants' right to belong, including SB 432 (2015) which removed all mentions of the word "alien" from the state's labor code, and SB 225 (2019), which formally laid out the concept of "citizens of the state," including all citizens born in the state and residing within it. While most other states have not yet followed in passing these resolutions, there is a large number that have removed, or have refrained from passing, English-only provisions in their state constitutions (see Figure 6.6).

Of course, California is not alone in its provision of the right to identify and belong. Illinois passed HR 115 (2017), condemning President Trump's actions barring refugees from the US during his first year in office, and HR 587 (2017), calling on Trump and the US Department of Homeland Security to preserve protections under DACA, which it grounds in the values of both the United States and the state of Illinois. In addition, a few states have advanced the right to identify by providing identification documents to undocumented immigrants

The Right to Identify & Belong (Dimension 5)

Count of States	Net Score (Exclusionary)							Net Score (Inclusionary)				
	-9	-5	-4	-3	-2	-1	0	1	2	3	4	18
1	AZ	TX	AL	LA	GA	AK	CT	CO	DE	IL	NV	CA
2	TN		MI	SD	MA	AR	IN	DC	OR			
3				UT	NE	HI	ND	FL	WA			
4				VA	KY	IA	VT	MD				
5					WY	ID		ME				
6						KS		MN				
7						MO		NC				
8						MS		NH				
9						MT		NJ				
10						NY		NM				
11						OH		OK				
12						RI		PA				
13						SC		WI				
14						WV						

FIGURE 6.6 Immigrant inclusion on Dimension 5: rights to identify & belong

that are separate from driver's licenses. Vermont's SB 38 (2013) not only provided the right to drive: it also gave undocumented resident the right to a separate identification card provided by the state. Notably, California has yet to pass a state identification card separate from a driver's license.

Representing the other end of the spectrum, Tennessee praised Arizona's anti-immigrant law, SB 1070, by passing JHR 1253 in 2010 to honor and commend "the State of Arizona and its government officials on the upcoming commemoration of Arizona's Centennial and salutes the initiative and the courage of the Arizona State Legislature and Governor Jan Brewer in their actions to protect their citizens and the borders of our great nation through the passage of immigration legislation." Since then, Tennessee has passed multiple resolutions specifically to recognize anti-immigrant actors such as Joe Carr, describing him as a "Renaissance man" and "illustrious" for leading the state's effort to pass "the toughest illegal immigration laws in the country."[135] Exclusionary state resolutions have also been enacted to show support of funding and building the border wall. Finally, some states have attempted to invalidate and penalize the use of foreign identification documents altogether, although, as we note in the next section, federal courts have struck these down. Meanwhile, others have enacted English-only language laws in education and have made English the official language of the state, effectively denying many immigrants the right to identify with, and belong to, the state and its institutions.

Federalism Dynamics and Dimension 5 Rights for Immigrants

While states have been given fairly wide latitude in passing resolutions that contain welcoming or alienating language vis-à-vis their immigrant populations, there are limits to how far they can go in constraining the right to identify and belong. In 2011, Indiana sought to push the limits of what is possible on the right to identify and belong, passing SB 590 in the wake of other comprehensive and exclusionary measures in Arizona, Alabama, and South Carolina. Section 18 of Indiana's law created a new infraction for any person (other than a police officer) who knowingly or intentionally offers or accepts a consular identification card as a valid form of identification for any purpose. On May 25, 2011, three foreign residents of Indiana – represented by the ACLU of Indiana, the national ACLU's Immigrants' Rights Project, the National Immigration Law Center, and private counsel – filed a class action lawsuit in the US District Court for the Southern District of Indiana.

In addition to challenging other provisions of SB 590, the plaintiffs claimed that Section 18, which made the use of consular identification cards for identification within the state a civil infraction punishable by fine, was preempted by federal law and in violation of the Fourteenth Amendment's guarantee of due process. Mexico, Brazil, Guatemala, El Salvador, and Columbia all filed an amicus on behalf of plaintiffs. Judge Sarah Evans

Barker, on June 24, 2011, granted the plaintiffs' motion for a preliminary injunction in *Buquer v. City of Indianapolis* (2011).[136] On March 28, 2013, Judge Barker permanently enjoined Section 18 of 590 under a preemption ruling and Section 20 of 590 under both federal preemption and Fourteenth Amendment due process grounds.[137] Since the United States is a signatory to the Vienna Convention on Consular Relations (VCCR), which provides that a foreign consulate may issue travel documents, visas, or other appropriate documents to protect and assist its citizens in the foreign country, states and localities are not able to criminalize foreign identification documents. They are, however, still able to prohibit their use for federal, state, or local resources or benefits.

EXPLAINING VARIATION IN STATE CITIZENSHIP

Our analysis in Chapter 5 revealed that the consolidation of Democratic Party control was a critical factor in the push for progressive state citizenship. California made virtually no progress on state citizenship for immigrant residents when Arnold Schwarzenegger was governor and, indeed, experienced some backsliding when the Republican governor first took office and compelled the legislature to repeal its short-lived provision on driver's licenses to undocumented immigrants. Still, Democratic Party control did not guarantee progress on immigrant rights. It would take the combined force of a strong immigrant rights movement, legislative champions in both chambers, and key windows of opportunity generated by federal tensions (such as the issuance of DACA in 2012 and legislative obstruction by House Republicans in 2013) for California to make good on its promises of progressive state citizenship.

What does the story look like when we move our analysis beyond California to include not only other states pushing in a progressive direction but also others moving in a regressive or exclusionary direction? While we are not able to conduct a similarly detailed, historical institutional analysis for all fifty states with respect to immigrant citizenship rights, we are able to consider the relevance of timing and state-level factors predictive of inclusive versus exclusive regimes of state citizenship. First, with respect to timing: most states passed progressive policies on state citizenship after California, with the exception of DACA driver's licenses, which were all passed within a year of DACA's announcement. Thus, the same kind of federalism dynamics relevant for California were also present for other states that passed pro-immigrant laws.

To what extent, then, does party control matter for the passage of inclusionary and exclusionary laws on state citizenship rights? We conducted a cross-sectional, fifty-state analysis of state laws affecting immigrant citizenship rights, both in the aggregate and for each of our five dimensions of state citizenship (see Appendix B for more details). We hypothesized that Democratic Party control would matter in our fifty-state analysis, with respect to either our combined measure or our individual dimensions of state citizenship. We tested for the predictive significance of this factor after controlling for other factors, such as the density of civil rights organizations in the state (as a rough proxy for immigrant social movement activity), the proportion of non-White registered voters in the state (where we would expect greater support for inclusionary policies in states with higher shares of non-White voters), and the growth of the foreign-born population in the state (which may account for greater exclusionary policies).

As the results indicate (see Appendix B), Democratic Party control predicts more inclusionary citizenship policies overall, and for each dimension of state citizenship with the exception of Dimension 5 (right to identify and belong), where the variable is in the anticipated direction but not statistically significant. None of the other factors in our model have a statistically significant relationship. This is not to say, of course, that social movement activity at the state level does not matter. We do not have precise measures of immigrant social movement strength across all fifty states. However, as we shall see in our final chapter, a qualitative analysis of the push for state sanctuaries suggests that the strength and strategic action of social movement actors play a critical role in capitalizing on the windows of policy opportunity to push for advancements in progressive state citizenship.

7

Enabling Progress on State Citizenship

If California is a bellwether on state citizenship, what can we expect in the rest of the country? The depth of California's progressive state citizenship today is a remarkable achievement, one that consolidated in a relatively short span of time considering the state's long anti-immigrant history. As we have shown in Chapter 5, the passage of Proposition 187 in 1994 had important consequences for building an advocacy coalition over time, energizing Latino voters, increasing naturalizations, and prompting many activists to run for elected office. All of these factors strengthened the immigrant rights movement and the power of the Latino Legislative Caucus, which were important partners in an "advocacy coalition" that spanned nonprofit organizations and state legislators alike. The legacy effects of Proposition 187 also helped make the state solidly Democratic, with the notable exception of the 2003 to 2010 period, when a Republican celebrity got elected following an energy crisis and the subsequent recall of a sitting governor. However, Proposition 187 was, by itself, insufficient to produce a strong, widespread, and effective immigrant rights movement – it would take significant investments in movement-building infrastructure by private foundations to ensure that immigrant advocates across the state were effective partners in an advocacy coalition for immigration reform.

In addition to movement strength and party control, federalism dynamics, including conflicts, tensions, and openings, also made a critical difference. Indeed, these three factors linked up together – in specific years and involving particular issues – to shape the timing and sequencing of progressive state policies. For example, federal immigration reform and social welfare reform under IIRIRA and PWORA in 1996 constrained immigrant access but opened new opportunities for California to extend emergency health care in 1996 and 1997 and adopt an anti-sweatshop law in 1999. Similarly, failure of the federal Dream Act in 2001 fueled California's expansion of in-state tuition to undocumented immigrants in 2001, but only because movement pressure and

Democratic control was able to mobilize around the federal failure. This interplay continued to shape the timing, speed, and specific issues taken on during California's progressive period of policy proliferation.

In this final chapter, we take a deeper look at the dynamics producing advancements in progressive state citizenship, with examples from both the historical and the contemporary periods. We argue that some of the most notable legislative advancements in progressive state citizenship occurred because of the intersection of two key factors: *state advocacy coalitions* that unite strong social movement actors and legislative champions alike, combined with *policy openings* created by federalism tensions that enable or propel state governors to act. We provide a detailed look at California and New York's two-decade push for driver's licenses to illustrate our argument. We also examine the timing and spread of state sanctuary laws on immigration across several states. Finally, we also provide a historical look at the development of progressive state citizenship in the antebellum North, focusing on states' protection of runaway slaves, to show that advocacy coalitions and federalism tensions were key to the spread of progressive state citizenship. After reviewing these examples, we end our book by offering thoughts on the future of state citizenship in a politically polarized United States.

ADVOCACY COALITIONS AND IMMIGRANT DRIVER'S LICENSES IN CALIFORNIA AND NEW YORK

Movement strength and Democratic party control have been key factors shaping state expansions in the right to immigrant free movement, and it is instructive to take a deeper look at the cases of California and New York to understand not only why both factors are important but also how movement actors and legislators acting in concert through advocacy coalitions helped overcome opposition to immigrant driver's licenses.

The immigrant rights movement in California has been a strong and consistent source of political pressure since 1999, and Democratic state legislator Gil Cedillo proposed numerous bills on the driver's license issue, with support from numerous colleagues in the Latino Legislative Caucus. Together, they succeeded in 2003 by getting Governor Gray Davis to sign SB 60, but this success was built on fragile foundations. A recall election replaced Davis with a Republican governor, who quickly led in the repeal of SB 60 before it was ever implemented. The federal REAL ID Act passed in 2005, setting up a potential federalism conflict, but immigrant rights activists and their legislative champions adapted their legislation to make state driver's licenses compliant with REAL ID. While this adaptation was in line with Governor Schwarzenegger's position on the issue, but he still vetoed the bill and remained adamantly opposed to immigrant driver's licenses throughout his administration.

The election of Governor Jerry Brown in 2010 removed one of the key barriers to driver's license reform, as Democrats controlled the executive and legislative branch. While unified party control may have been necessary to pass driver's license reform in California, it was by no means sufficient. Brown had signalled his opposition to immigrant driver's licenses, preferring to wait for federal immigration reform. Thus, even as movement pressure remained consistent, and Cedillo aimed to propose legislation in 2011 and 2012, the anticipation of a likely veto from Governor Brown persuaded Democratic leaders to table the measure. It was only after Brown fully aligned himself with the advocacy coalition for immigration reform in 2013 – as hopes for federal reform were looking increasingly dim – that Cedillo and others finally succeeded in their decade-long effort to pass immigrant driver's licenses. Thus, there were many years (especially in 2004, 2005, 2011, and 2012) when driver's licenses could have passed, either as a result of the timing in federalism dynamics, movement strength, or Democratic party control. However, these three factors were not all simultaneously present. In 2013, however, these three factors came into alignment, allowing state driver's licenses to be passed alongside other meaningful moves toward progressive state citizenship.

Nearly twenty years of California history shows us just how remarkable an achievement the passage of AB 60 was. Governor Pete Wilson signed SB 976 in 1993, barring undocumented immigrants from applying for driver's licenses. Additionally, SB 1758 passed in 1994, allowing local law enforcement officers to impound the cars of unlicensed drivers for thirty days and charge a fine to reclaim the car.[1] Notably, Democratic as well as Republican lawmakers supported these measures, which passed by overwhelming margins as legislators tried to dissipate voter anger over the extended economic recession in California and the effective mobilization of anti-immigration forces in the state. The tide began to turn starting in 1999, as Gilbert Cedillo led the first effort among fourteen different attempts to expand immigrant access to driver's licenses. First, in 1999, Cedillo partnered with the Coalition for Humane Immigrant Rights in Los Angeles (CHIRLA) to draft and introduce AB 1463, a bill that would have expanded legal immigrants' access to driver's license (but not the undocumented). The law would have provided an exception to providing a Social Security Number, allowing legal immigrants to sign an affidavit about their residency and immigration status. Vetoing the bill in 2000, Governor Gray Davis stated:

Requiring the DMV to issue a driver's license or I.D. card merely on the basis of the applicant providing a "receipt" from the INS that an application or petition for lawful immigration status has been initiated is an invitation for fraud. Moreover, the states of Arizona, Florida, New Mexico, and Texas all require that a social security number be provided to their Department of Motor Vehicles. California should not embrace a weaker standard than those imposed by other southern border states ... There is no question that a driver's license is often the key document used to acquire other documentation and to qualify for various services and services.[2]

Davis vetoed another one of Cedillo's driver's license bills in 2002, sparking the outrage of the Latino legislative caucus, who refused to endorse him for reelection.[3] Clearly, Democratic party control of the legislature and governor's office was not sufficient to pass driver's license reform. Federalism dynamics were not favorable for driver's license reform in the immediate post-9/11 context, and the advocacy coalition of immigrant rights activists and allied legislators was not yet sufficiently large or strong to overcome a gubernatorial veto. There was one temporary exception to this dynamic in 2003, as Gray Davis signed SB 60, changing his stance on driver's licenses in a last-ditch effort to garner Latino voter support and avoid being recalled.[4] After Davis lost the election, Republican Governor Arnold Schwarzenegger successfully pushed for the repeal of SB 60 even before it could get implemented, raising post-9/11 security concerns. Cedillo and the Democratic legislature conceded, against the wishes of immigrant advocacy groups like CHIRLA, in an attempt to preserve goodwill with the new governor and to set a foundation for bipartisan dealmaking.

Schwarzenegger encouraged this line of thinking by promising Cedillo and others that he would work together on a new driver's license bill, with the stipulation that there be an identifying mark on licenses provided to undocumented residents. In 2004, Cedillo proposed SB 1160 and Nuñez proposed AB 2895, bills that were joined and renamed the "Immigrant and Security Act," adding security measures requiring undocumented residents to pay for extensive background checks and to be fingerprinted before acquiring a driver license. The governor was unmoved. In his veto message, Schwarzenegger stated, "This bill does not adequately address the security concerns that my Department of Homeland Security and I have, and I cannot support it."[5] The governor framed his concerns around post-9/11 security and anti-terrorism, arguing that there should be a special driver's licenses with a clear identification marker for noncitizens. Schwarzenegger's resistance encouraged California's minority Republican party to frame pro-integration state proposals as undermining national security and the rule of law. In 2004, State Senator Tom McClintock argued, "Illegal immigrants are in direct violation of our federal immigration laws. These laws require them to be deported, not accommodated."[6]

The next window of opportunity for immigrant driver's licenses opened up in 2005. Congress passed the REAL ID Act in 2005, creating a minimum standard for state-issued licenses and identification cards to be used for federal purposes, and providing states the discretion to issue federally approved licenses to unlawfully present persons who are recipients of deferred action. Seizing opportunity around this federal law, Cedillo proposed SB 60 in 2005, emphasizing the bill's security measures, compliance with federal law, and alignment with Governor Schwarzenegger's primary concern of adding a noncitizen identification. Indeed, security and compliance with federal law were stressed in the Senate Transportation and Housing Committee bill report, which noted:

This urgency bill would require the State of California to comply with the federal "Real ID Act of 2005," a recently enacted measure which established standards and procedures for the issuance of driver's licenses and identification cards, and authorized the states to issue driver's licenses and identification cards to undocumented immigrants, providing that the license or identification card (1) clearly states that it may not used for any other official purpose, and (2) uses an unique design or color.[7]

The senate committee placed these security provisions of SB 60 within the context of the 9/11 Commission's recommendations to Congress to enact the REAL ID Act and attempted to leverage the urgency around terrorism and securitization to get a driver's license bill passed. Schwarzenegger still vetoed the 2005 bill, as well as subsequent bills in 2006 and 2007. When another bill was vetoed in 2008, the governor had made it clear that legalization at the federal level was the only path for undocumented immigrants in California to obtain a driver's license, stating in his veto message that "he could not sign such a bill until Congress adopts a comprehensive immigration reform plan and a method is found to validate the identity of undocumented immigrants."[8]

It may seem as though the ultimate arbiter of immigrant driver's licenses was political party, given Governor Schwarzenegger's consistent use of his veto pen. If this were true, then driver's licenses would have been immediately adopted once Governor Jerry Brown assumed office on January 3, 2011. Brown's administration ushered in a new era of uniform party control in California, which layered on top of a decade of movement and capacity building in immigrant advocacy. Brown was sympathetic to pro-immigrant policies, but, as we have argued earlier, he was not yet fully aligned with the immigrant rights advocacy coalition, let alone be a member of it. That coalition was still comprised largely of the powerful Latino Legislative Caucus and a strong network of immigrant advocacy organizations around the state, and it was pushing for bold reforms that were sometimes in open conflict with the Obama administration and its Department of Homeland Security. It would take another round of failure in federal immigration reform for Brown to align himself more centrally with California's advocacy coalition on immigrant rights.

As Brown took office in 2011, Cedillo scored a legislative victory on DUI checkpoints by passing AB 353, which allows an unlicensed person stopped at a checkpoint to call for a licensed driver to retrieve their car if their offense is driving without a license. Cedillo was still hoping to pass a driver's license bill before being termed out of the state legislature, and he tried to introduce a bill in 2011 (AB 260) and reserved two placeholder measures in early 2012 to achieve his goal. Governor Brown, however, was not on board. As the *Los Angeles Times* noted, "Brown has voiced opposition to such licenses."[9] Cedillo's efforts failed to gain any traction among his Democratic colleagues, with some deriding his efforts as quixotic by calling him "one bill Gil,"[10] and he was forced to scrap his plans in 2011 as well as 2012.

Federalism dynamics began to tip the scales, however, beginning in 2012 as President Obama announced the Deferred Action for Childhood Arrivals program in June that year. Democrats soon mobilized to pass "DACA licenses," which had two important effects on Cedillo's long-standing quest. First, DACA sucked the wind out of any effort to push for universal driver's licenses in California, but it also accorded Cedillo the opportunity to take credit for passing driver's licenses for DACA beneficiaries. The state deadline to introduce a new bill had passed long before DACA's rollout, but Cedillo quickly maneuvered to make a bill possible by employing a "gut and amend" strategy of taking an existing bill and dramatically altering it. AB 2189 was originally a bill that would require a photograph rather than a signature as proof of identification when renting a car, but Cedillo and the Democratic party turned it into the DACA driver's license bill, which had widespread support and passed.[11]

Importantly, DACA also shaped the long-run development of future immigrant rights policies, including the extension of universal driver's licenses in 2013. It did so through three mechanisms: (1) DACA licenses predisposed Governor Brown to be favorable on the issue by 2013; (2) state legislators were able to carry momentum from DACA licenses to undocumented licenses; and (3) the Department of Motor Vehicles was prepared for such a change, since implementation around DACA licenses made expansion of licenses to all undocumented immigrants more feasible from implementation and administration perspectives.[12] DACA's failure to spur federal immigration reform by summer 2013 also helped ensure the passage of AB 60: Democratic party control, Brown's rapprochement with the immigrant advocacy coalition, and federalism dynamics all combined to finally make driver's licenses a reality in 2013.

Ironically, Cedillo was no longer in the state legislature to put his name on universal driver's licenses (AB 60) because of legislative term limits. Nevertheless, he handed off the bill to Assemblyman Luis Alejo, who partnered with a well-established and robust cross-regional immigrant advocacy network, especially CIPC, CHIRLA, and Asian Americans Advancing Justice (AAAJ) on a statewide and grassroots campaign for AB 60. Alejo could also count on the help of legislative colleagues in the Assembly as well as the State Senate, including Sen. Ricardo Lara, who was a long-time immigrant rights champion.[13] The advocacy coalition spearheaded strategic coordination across the state's different regions on advocacy and framing and created a Drive California campaign with more than forty separate affiliated groups, each with their separate regional infrastructure and resources. CIPC framed AB 60 around universalistic concerns of expanding workforce development and increasing public safety by ensuring that every person had a license, went through driver training, and had auto insurance.[14] As a result, it gained wide support from various stakeholders, including business interests and even the California Police Chiefs Association and the California Highway

Patrol (CHP). Julie Powell of the CHP stated: "It has nothing to do with if they're in the country legally or illegally ... Our main concern is that the people of California are safe, and one way to assist in accomplishing that mission is to make sure California drivers are tested, trained and insured."[15]

Importantly, Alejo drove the passage of universal driver's licenses in 2013 alongside his renewed efforts on the TRUST Act, which Brown had vetoed in 2012.[16] The key difference in securing passage for both bills was not Alejo; it was Governor Jerry Brown, who has shifted his position on immigration as a direct result of what was happening at the national level. During his 2010 campaign for Governor, Brown said that he opposed driver's licenses because it was a piecemeal solution to federal immigration reform.[17] He had also vetoed the 2012 TRUST Act under significant pressure from the Obama administration.

As we noted earlier, however, the lack of meaningful progress on federal immigration reform in 2013 convinced Brown to go bold on immigration policy. Indeed, Brown's press release on driver's licenses in October 2013 reflected his newfound resolve – to pass measures that value the state's immigrant population and to serve notice to the rest of the country on how to treat unauthorized immigrants: "When a million people without their documents drive legally and with respect in the state of California, the rest of this country will have to stand up and take notice ... No longer are undocumented people in the shadows. They are alive and well and respected in the state of California."[18] Two days later, the governor would do one better. His press release announcing a raft of other immigration measures encapsulated the moment and its significance perfectly: "While gridlock continues in Washington, California continues to move forward on immigration reform."[19]

Overcoming New York's "Third Rail" on Immigrant Rights

While Republican intransigence on comprehensive immigration reform in 2013 helped push California's Jerry Brown toward embracing driver's licenses, the same was not true in New York, where legislators and governors were much more reluctant to embrace such measures. Part of the reason lay in the strong association between driver's licenses and security measures to fight terrorism: in response to the September 11, 2001, attacks on the World Trade Center, New York's Governor George E. Pataki (Republican) issued an executive order requiring all driver's license applicants to provide a Social Security number – effectively barring undocumented residents from this right to drive. Compounding the problem was the fact that subsequent attempts to provide immigrant driver's licenses went down in spectacular defeat, making many Democratic legislators reluctant to support such measures. Indeed, the director of the New York Immigrant Coalition (NYIC), the largest immigrant rights advocacy group in the state, has called driver's licenses the "third rail of New York state politics," making any seemingly controversial measure on rights expansion dead on arrival.[20]

As we detail here, it was only when Democrats had full control of the state legislature in 2019, and when the immigrant rights movement had cross-regional strength outside of New York City, that the NYIC and its legislative allies were able to finally pass driver's licenses in the state. And even then, federalism tensions lent a helping hand, as opposition to President Trump helped to flip Republican districts into Democratic hands in 2018, emboldening progressive legislators to exercise more leadership and exerting greater pressure on Governor Andrew Cuomo, a moderate Democrat, to live up to his anti-Trump talk by signing the so-called Green Light Law.[21]

When the New York Immigrant Coalition began its campaign in 2005 to pass a state law providing driver's licenses to all residents, it faced strong opposition from both Republicans and moderate Democrats in the State Senate. The immigrant rights movement in New York State at the time was primarily concentrated in New York City, with very little grassroots strength in Long Island, Westchester Valley, and other parts of upstate New York.[22] Coming out of the national marches in support of Dreamers in 2006, the NYIC and other advocacy coalitions in New York were optimistic about making progress on driver's licenses. After repeated failures, however, they realized that building a statewide advocacy coalition was critical.

Some of the biggest hurdles to passing driver's licenses came from moderate Democrats in upstate New York, who were concerned about winning elections in highly competitive districts. For example, Democrat Kathy Hochul led in speaking against expanding the right to driver's licenses, both as a county clerk from 2007 to 2011 and as the first Democrat in forty years to win the US House seat in Erie County in 2011. Thus, when Democratic Governor Eliot Spitzer announced an executive order in 2007 that would roll back Governor Pataki's rules on driver's license restrictions, advocacy coalitions, both within the state legislature and in the immigrant rights movement, were thus relatively weak.[23] Soon thereafter, Spitzer faced significant backlash from fellow Democrats in the state, including Hillary Clinton, who was then a US Senator and 2008 presidential candidate,[24] as well as key Congressional leaders like Kirsten Gillibrand.[25] National media personalities like Lou Dobbs quickly mobilized against Spitzer's proposal, adding fuel to a fire already sparked by various anti-immigrant activists and state officials in upstate New York. Within two months, Spitzer dropped the driver's license measure, and the issue soon became etched in the minds of many New York legislators and advocates as the "third rail" of state politics.[26]

Advances in immigrant rights did not look promising when Democrat Andrew Cuomo became governor in 2011. Even as Cuomo began to forge coalitions with labor groups to move legislation in Albany, he considered immigrant driver's licenses to be off the table. This set New York apart from other progressive states and the California story of driver's license expansions. When DACA was enacted in 2012, the vast majority of states had moved quickly that same year to expand driver's licenses to DACA recipients and mobilized the following year in 2013 to go one step further by expanding licenses to undocumented residents. By contrast, New York allowed so-called DACA licenses through administrative action, and there was no corresponding legislative momentum on more general driver's licenses or other immigrant rights expansions. Thus, even though both California and New York faced the same federalism opportunities with DACA in 2012 and Republican intransigence on comprehensive immigration reform in 2013, the presence (or absence) of a strong, cross-regional advocacy coalition played a critical difference.

Failure to pass federal immigration reform in 2013 accelerated California's moves toward progressive state citizenship, but only because the California Immigrant Policy Center, its regional networks, and other movement allies had built a robust statewide advocacy coalition. By contrast, New York state lacked a similar cross-regional network, leaving Democratic legislators from upstate New York unwilling to support even relatively popular provisions as financial assistance for undocumented college students. Against this backdrop, attempts to pass even more comprehensive omnibus bills – such as the New York is Home Act in 2015 that included voting rights – proved futile and, indeed, might have left the impression that the immigrant-rights advocacy coalition was not sophisticated enough to sequence legislation in a strategic manner.[27] Thus, for more than a decade, New York's immigrant advocacy coalitions were unable to build a strong statewide network to make even incremental progress on immigrant rights. Divisions between moderate and progressive Democratic legislators, lack of philanthropic investment in cross-regional movement building, and a deeply skeptical and unsupportive governor made the prospects of even seemingly easy legislation very difficult. Thus, unlike in California, federalism dynamics related to DACA were unable to spark the needed change in New York.

The 2016 presidential elections, however, provided an impetus in unexpected ways. In December 2015, New York played host to the annual National Immigrant Integration Conference in Brooklyn. Hillary Clinton, then a presidential candidate, had agreed to speak at the event, and immigrant rights organizers in New York state used the occasion to lay out a strategic roadmap for movement-building and policy coordination across regions. Thus, NYIC found a greater receptivity among funders and movement organizations alike to begin building a cross-regional movement in the state with strategic policy aims. This development proved critical to building support for more progressive Democratic candidates and to countering conservative opposition among moderate Democrats and Republicans in upstate New York. For the next four years, from 2015 to 2019, the New York Immigrant Coalition built an advocacy coalition of allied groups and state legislators from across the state – paralleling, in many ways, what California had done a decade earlier.

In 2017, with a robust statewide movement infrastructure built up, the NYIC launched its plans to push for driver's licenses once again.[28] Its Greenlight Campaign remained an uphill battle however, until after the 2018 statewide elections, when Democrats took control of both the state Senate and Assembly. As Steve Choi explains, this shift was dramatic: a new group of Democratic leaders such as Julia Salazar were elected to Senate in the conservative strongholds of Long Island, and the NYIC was able to turn the Senate into an ally of the movement. The newly active Senate prompted the Assembly, which had historically been led by Democrats and more progressive than the governor, to become even more energetic on immigrant rights. The NYIC also leveraged state politics in important ways. When the State Legislature passed the Dream Act in early 2019, the NYIC used the death of legislator Jose Peralta (who had advocated for driver's licenses) to push legislators to transition immediately from its success on the Dream Act to begin acting on driver's licenses – utilizing the frame: "Dream Bigger." At the press hearing for the signing of the state's Dream Act, NYIC took control to declare driver's licenses as the next important step.

The NYIC spent much of 2019 mobilizing its statewide advocacy coalition with the Greenlight bill as its highest priority, with a clear focus on winning support among moderate state senators and forcing the hand of Governor Cuomo. Cuomo, having previously served as the state attorney general under Spitzer, still remained politically opposed to passing driver's licenses. What he did not anticipate, however, was that the immigrant advocacy coalition would leverage his opposition to Trump – a central theme of his reelection campaign – to make good on his promises to defend immigrant New Yorkers. Indeed, Cuomo provided added fodder to the immigrant rights coalition in early 2019 when he delivered his third inaugural address from Ellis Island, pledging to "pursue a 'new justice agenda' that would confront a 'cancer' of hatred and division" that threatened the nation.[29] The NYIC sensed an opening and pounced on it. Cuomo could no longer take an oppositional stance to Trump without contradicting his political position as a leader on immigrant rights.

The NYIC expanded and strengthened the immigrant rights coalition even more and was able to gain critical support from business partners, including Airbnb and the conservative Business Council, among others, who spoke in support of the driver's licenses bill. Many district attorneys and county sheriffs also came on board, giving the coalition even broader appeal with public safety as a critical frame. Still, Cuomo seemed unpersuaded, and, indeed, his allies mobilized behind the scenes in the state senate to try and scuttle the bill.[30] In a last-ditch effort, Cuomo asked the state's first Black attorney general, Letitia James, to examine the negative impact of a driver's license bill passing.[31] The NYIC quickly and successfully mobilized to pressure James to express her full support for the bill, forcing Governor Cuomo and his allies in the state senate to pass the bill into law. On June 17, 2019, New York became the thirteenth state to provide driver's licenses to its undocumented residents, after a two-decade political fight.

In the end, the alignment of strong statewide advocacy coalitions and the timing of federalism conflicts led to the passage of state driver's licenses in both California and New York. Party control of state government is clearly important to explaining the general pro- or anti-immigrant stance of states across the country, but, as Governors Brown and Cuomo both illustrate, unified Democratic control is clearly not sufficient to pass progressive legislation on immigrant rights. As we highlight in the case of driver's licenses, it is also necessary to have a strong advocacy coalition that includes not only statewide legislative leaders and movement champions but also regional partners who can push reluctant legislators and even governors across the finish line. In addition, federalism conflict played a critical role in the timing of successful policy developments. California was able to leverage DACA in 2012 and the failure of immigration reform in 2013 to enact its driver's licenses and to more broadly enact a range of other progressive policies. New York did not have unified party government in 2013, nor did it have an immigrant rights movement that was strong across the state. Trumpism helped move the state on both of these dimensions after 2017, allowing driver's licenses to finally break free from being considered the state's policy "third rail."

Much more needs to be done on immigrant rights in New York (and in Illinois, New Jersey, Connecticut, and elsewhere) before they can attain California's level of progressive state citizenship. If we continue to see patient philanthropic investments in these states and strategic, cross-regional, and cross-sectoral work that capitalizes on party control and federalism conflict, we will likely see more states accelerate progress toward progressive state citizenship.

ADVOCACY COALITIONS AND THE GROWTH OF IMMIGRANT SANCTUARY LAWS

The importance of advocacy coalitions involving movement activists as well as state legislative champions is also evident in the spread of immigrant sanctuary laws.[32] Immediately following the failed attempt by Republicans to push through HR 4437 in 2005, coordinated mobilizations occurred across the country, with an estimated 5 million people marching in over 300 demonstrations in 2006 alone.[33] Immigrants and their allies used these demonstrations to place pressure on Washington, DC, to move toward a bipartisan approach to reforming federal immigration law, with a pathway to citizenship for all immigrants.[34] Meanwhile, smaller local immigrant right organizations and the National Day Labor Organizing Network (NDLON), with its deep grassroots ties across the country, began to exert pressure on cities to pass sanctuary policies.

Los Angeles, California, where NDLON is headquartered, was the first city to pass a sanctuary policy in 2006, which references its opposition to the

Sensenbrenner bill.[35] Over the next several months, multiple cities passed similar sanctuary laws in opposition to enforcement-heavy federal immigration bills. With a strong push from advocacy organizations, on March 1, 2007, San Francisco became the first city after 2005 to legally resist entangling local law enforcement with immigration law.[36] The Office of the Mayor issued an executive order that reaffirmed its 1980s status as a sanctuary city, stating: "No department, agency, commission, officer or employee of the City and County of San Francisco may assist Immigration and Customs Enforcement (ICE) investigation, detention or arrest proceedings," nor "require information about or disseminate information regarding the immigration status of an individual when providing services or benefits."[37] A few policies mirroring San Francisco's spread across the country from 2007 to 2011, after which a new focus on resisting immigration detainer requests began to define the sanctuary movement, led by NDLON partnering with local advocacy and city officials.[38]

In 2008, the US Department of Homeland Security created a new collaborative information program, Secure Communities (S-Comm), that effectively co-opted local law enforcement and jails into automatically providing the federal government information on all arrested individuals.[39] When S-Comm first began to spread across the country, NDLON and its allies in California (including the Asian Law Caucus, California Immigrant Policy Center, SIREN, and CHIRLA) led resistance by formulating and championing model legislation across cities and states.[40] Sanctuary policies evolved to prevent local law enforcement from entering into 287(g) agreements or honoring ICE detainer requests.[41] By constraining local law enforcement through severing local ties, these sanctuary policies had a significant and visible impact on decreasing deportations.[42] Santa Clara County, California, moved first on anti-detainer policies, passing a resolution in 2010 preventing local officials and resources from investigating, questioning, apprehending, or arresting any person for immigration purposes.[43] The following year, it enacted a much more specific policy limiting local law enforcement from honoring ICE detainer requests.[44] Over the next few years, anti-detainer sanctuary policies began to spread across cities and counties, and local law enforcement agencies began to issue similar sanctuary policies as public statements or official department policies.

From 2010 to 2013, as local sanctuary policies began to evolve into important forms of resistance to federal law and protections for undocumented residents, national advocacy organizations remained focused on federal reforms, with hopes that President Obama be able to gain enough Republican support to pass a comprehensive measure while Democrats were the majority in the House and Senate. National organizations like the ACLU, MALDEF, and the NILC were also focused on defeating the spread of Arizona SB 1070 copycats through litigation beginning in 2011.

Even with a heavily Democrat-controlled state, Governor Brown of California remained resistant to the idea of a state sanctuary, vetoing the California TRUST Act in 2012. Brown recognized undocumented immigrants as an important labor source for California's economy, but then explained: "Comprehensive immigration reform – including a path to citizenship – would provide tremendous economic benefits and is long overdue. Until we have immigration reform, federal agents shouldn't try to coerce local law enforcement officers into detaining people who've been picked up for minor offenses and pose no reasonable threat to their community."[45] Federalism dynamics in 2012 had restrained Brown from acting. Top federal officials had privately lobbied Brown to veto the legislation, in order to preserve any momentum toward federal reform. According to emails obtained by Advancing Justice – Asian Law Caucus and NDLON, senior ICE officials in Washington, DC, asked "that Brown hold off approving the bill while the federal agency developed an alternative pilot program in California to limit which immigrants police and sheriffs could detain. They said the program would influence national policy."[46]

California's immigrant rights movement continued to place pressure on the state, and federalism dynamics had changed significantly by 2013. As noted earlier, the heady optimism following President Obama's reelection had worn off by early summer, as it was abundantly clear that the US House of Representatives was very unlikely to pass immigration reform. This freed Brown from his fixation on federal reform, and he no longer viewed state reforms on immigration as piecemeal and inadequate. Indeed, he was starting to refer to California's moves as "immigration reform."[47] This is the backdrop to understanding why Brown signed California's 2013 immigration bills in such a dramatic manner – first signing the driver's license bill in prominent public ceremonies in Los Angeles and in Fresno, and subsequently signing a raft of pro-immigrant measures timed to coincide with massive nationwide protests on federal immigration reform on October 5, 2013.

In 2013, California passed the Transparency and Responsibility Using State Tools (TRUST) Act, providing that officers can only enforce immigration detainers issued by ICE for persons convicted of serious crimes.[48] In 2014, when California's TRUST Act went into effect, the city of San Francisco and the counties of Contra Costa, Alameda, and San Mateo announced that they would no longer cooperate with any ICE detention requests of possible unauthorized immigrants in local jails.[49] California's state and local sanctuary policies resulted in a major decrease in deportations by ICE after 2014 and caused President Obama, under the direction of Homeland Security Secretary Jeh Johnson, to end S-Comm that same year.[50] Democratic control of the state, and partnerships between officials and immigrant rights organizations, have paved the road for California to expand its sanctuary-type protections exponentially since 2014, including passing the TRUTH Act in 2016 and the Values Act in 2017.

As we explained in Chapter 6, the formation of the National Partnership for New Americans (NPNA) in 2010 by twelve of the country's largest statewide immigrant advocacy organizations had connected the advocacy coalitions across the states.[51] That network of state advocacy coalitions helped to proliferate policies through learning, momentum-building, and seizing opportunities created by federalism conflict. Meanwhile, House Republicans' obstruction on creating a pathway to citizenship and the ongoing enforcement actions of the Obama administration signaled to immigrant advocacy leaders that they would need to pass protective measures at the state level. Thus, following the failure of comprehensive immigration reform (CIR) in 2013, California and Connecticut were among others who proposed similar policies that same year. The Massachusetts Immigrant and Refugee Advocacy Coalition (MIRA) proposed a Trust Act and a Driver's License bill, but these failed to pass due to the lack of Democratic party control and politically powerful "movement allies" in the state legislature.[52]

In 2013, Colorado passed HB 1258 repealing a statute that formerly compelled its local officials to participate in federal immigration issues, which emphasized the importance of "public safety by building trust between immigrant communities and local police and to ensure equal protection and safety for all members of Colorado communities, including witnesses and victims of crime." The following year, in a joint statement, every jail in the state of Colorado said that they would not honor ICE detainer requests.[53] Meanwhile, Maryland's governor and Secretary Hershberger of Maryland's Department of Public Safety and Correctional Services clarified the state's policy as limiting compliance with ICE detainers, requiring clear probable cause and a judicial warrant.

Divided party control delayed progress in Illinois, where an impressive immigrant rights movement had scored significant early progressive victories like limiting the use of E-Verify in 2010, even before California had passed a similar law. The election of Republican Governor Bruce Rauner delayed any further progress, however. It took Democratic legislators and a Republican governor a few years to get aligned in their vision for governance; the state infamously operated for 736 days without a budget in place because of intense interparty disagreements.[54] Still, the advocacy coalition for immigrant rights was able to capitalize on new federalism tensions after Donald Trump's election. Rauner was eager to separate himself from Trump and get reelected in 2018, and advocates found a strategic opening to continue their push to pass the TRUST Act in August 2017.[55] Energized, the advocacy coalition continued pushing more immigrant protection bills, including an immigrant victims' rights bill that passed with an override of the governor's veto in November 2018.[56] Having strengthened its advocacy coalition, and with a new Democratic governor after January 2019, Illinois is continuing to expand its scope of immigrant protections, much like California has done ever since passing its Trust Act in 2013.[57]

Finally, courts have played a critical role in ensuring the gains made by advocacy coalitions on state and local sanctuary laws. In contrast to striking down Arizona's SB 1070 and its copycats, the courts have upheld and even protected California's 2017 sanctuary policy. On January 25, 2017, President Trump attacked "sanctuary cities" by issuing an executive order that targeted jurisdictions with the threat of removing federal funding.[58] In response, Santa Clara filed a motion for a preliminary injunction, arguing that "the Executive Order has created a cloud of financial uncertainty so overwhelming that it irreparably harms the Country's ability to budget, govern and ultimately provide services to the residents it serves."[59] Santa Clara was not alone. Four other cities filed lawsuits challenging the executive order.[60] On April 25, 2017, a federal judge joined the Santa Clara and San Francisco motions, ruling that the executive order likely violated the Spending Clause by removing federal funding from sanctuary jurisdictions; the judge therefore ordered a nationwide preliminary injunction.[61] On August 1, 2018, the United States Court of Appeals for the Ninth Circuit, in *City and County of San Francisco v. Trump*, lifted the nationwide injunction and allowed President Trump's anti-sanctuary order to go into effect even as it faced judicial review through federal court appeals.[62]

Importantly, the Ninth Circuit preserved the injunction on the executive order for California, because the court considered there was sufficient evidence of federal intent to injure the state and its localities.[63] According to the court, "the district court noted that California and its cities, especially San Francisco, were visible targets of the Administration's intent to defund sanctuary jurisdictions."[64] It then found that there was not sufficient evidence that other states and localities would be similarly targeted and injured in order for a nationwide injunction to be justified.[65] Consistent with the Ninth Circuit ruling, the United States District Court for the Eastern District of California denied a motion to strike down California's TRUST Act, stating that the state sanctuary law was not an "obstacle" to federal enforcement.[66] Kevin de León, leader on immigrant rights and then-Senate Pro Tem, responded to the ruling to uphold sanctuary, stating: "California is under no obligation to assist Trump [in] tear[ing] families apart."[67] Current litigation has upheld the constitutional legitimacy of city and state sanctuary laws.

ADVOCACY COALITIONS AND FEDERALISM TENSIONS IN THE ANTEBELLUM NORTH

The importance of state advocacy coalitions bridging movement actors and political insiders is not confined to the contemporary period, nor is it confined to immigrant rights. Movement actors exploited federalism tensions to productive effect in the early eighteenth century in Pennsylvania and Massachusetts. The US Constitution's fugitive slave clause did not specify the responsible entity or procedures for enforcing recaption; however, early federal law clearly established that slave owners had a right to reclaim any runaway slave in Northern states or federal territories, effectively making the movement and presence of runaway slaves illegal in the North. The Fugitive Slave Act of 1793 clarified the rights of slave owners to recapture runaway slaves in Northern states and federal territories, while also establishing an anti-harboring provision making it unlawful to aid fugitive slaves in any way.[68]

Attuned to opportunities at national and state levels, Northern abolitionists sought ways to expand citizenship rights to runaway slaves. As we explain in Chapters 3 and 4, reforming federal law to abolish slavery was politically unrealistic. The number of free and slave states were purposely balanced to ensure equal numbers in US Senate seats, and slaves were counted for apportionment to expand Southern Congressional seats in the federal government: this entrenched federal stalemate on issues regarding slavery and Black rights. Roadblocks to abolitionist's federal reforms, together with state-level movement-building and alliances with state officials, had paved the way for Northern state legislation to become the only beacon of hope for runaway slaves prior to the Civil War.

In 1820, and again in 1826, Pennsylvania passed the North's first state personal liberty law, which banned all state officials and state resources from being used to enforce the 1793 fugitive slave law. As we will show, these two laws emerged after the nationally oriented abolitionist organization based in Pennsylvania had failed to secure federal reforms and in response to federalism tensions over the rendition of runaway slaves within its jurisdiction. While federalism helps to explain the emergence of Northern personal liberty laws, it is not sufficient. Critical to Pennsylvania's inaugural law was the organizational capacity of its abolitionists and the ability of White movement leaders to cultivate critical allies in the state's legislature during moments when federalism tensions emerged. Other Northern states faced the same sectional tensions caused by the federal fugitive slave law, but they were unable to pass personal liberty laws until after abolitionists similarly built up their statewide capacity – and only when federalism events helped to direct their focus to the state level.

Quakers established the Pennsylvania Abolition Society (PAS) in 1775, to discuss the abolition of slavery and protection of free Blacks prior to American Independence. It soon emerged as the strongest anti-slavery organization in the nation, leading the push for Pennsylvania to become the first Northern state to pass a gradual emancipation law in 1780. PAS also sought to enforce the rights of free Blacks. In 1791, when slave catchers kidnapped a free Black citizen in Pennsylvania, the organization led the fight to pressure Pennsylvania's governor to request that the slave catchers be extradited to Pennsylvania to be tried in court for kidnapping, but a federal law protecting free Blacks did not exist.[69] For the next few decades, PAS led federal attempts to pressure the US Congress to pass an anti-kidnapping bill. Its first effort in 1791 backfired. Congress, under Southern control, dropped the bill entirely and instead passed an even more exclusionary Fugitive Slave Law of 1793, with an anti-harboring provision making it a federal crime to aid runaway slaves seeking freedom.

In 1796, another kidnapping occurred in Pennsylvania, with four Black citizens being arrested and removed from Philadelphia by slave catchers. PAS responded in 1797 by leading a petition campaign to pressure Congress to pass a federal anti-kidnapping bill, which was tabled indefinitely.[70] Two years later, in 1799, Philadelphia's Black abolitionists petitioned the US Congress to recognize free Blacks as "admitted to partake of the liberties and unalienable rights therein held forth [in the US Constitution]" and asked for federal laws that would end the slave trade and amend the Fugitive Slave Law adding an anti-kidnapping protections to free Blacks.[71] Throughout the early 1800s, PAS continued to petition for a national anti-kidnapping law, but it succeeded in having a Congressional bill considered in committee only once in 1817.[72] In the US Senate that year, Southern officials entirely revised the bill in order to advance their slavery interests, strengthening the enforcement mechanisms of federal law with no mention of protecting free Blacks at all. PAS responded by quickly mobilizing Northern Congressional opposition to defeat the bill.

Realizing the futility of achieving federal reform after several attempts, PAS turned its focus on expanding the rights of free Blacks by passing more state-level policies. Led mostly by White abolitionists with strong allies in state government, PAS was able to build a statewide coalition that could mobilize popular support in the state around major national slavery events. Two weeks after the Missouri Compromise passed (1820), extending slavery into federal territories and allowing Missouri to enter the Union as a slave state, PAS launched a massive petition campaign to pressure the state legislature to pass an immediate emancipation law, an anti-kidnapping law, and the first Northern law to sever the state's role in enforcing the federal fugitive slave law.[73] Total abolition in the state remained elusive, but Pennsylvania achieved a major transformation by providing rights to free Blacks and ending its role in capturing runaway slaves.[74]

Similar federalism tensions sparked other states' passage of personal liberty laws, but it would take many years to build similar, strong statewide coalitions. More than two decades after Pennsylvania's 1820 law, Massachusetts became the second Northern state to sever its enforcement of fugitive slave law. This required more than a decade of organization-building in the state. In 1831, William Lloyd Garrison began publishing the *Liberator*, marking the beginning of immediate abolitionism, which followed the motto "No union with Slaveholders." Garrison also formed the New England Anti-Slavery Society (NEASS) in 1832 and the American Anti-Slavery Society (AASS) in 1833, officially marking Massachusetts's entrance into a national leadership role. Indeed, Garrison articulated new ideas about freedom and formed a mass abolitionist movement across the North, but he also led the NEASS and the

AASS to reject traditional forms of political activism that were essential to PAS's success in Pennsylvania.[75]

The NEASS was renamed the Massachusetts Anti-Slavery Society (MASS) in 1834, with a new direction set by Elizur Wright to form allies in the state legislature. Having already grown not only throughout the state but also through ties across the North forged by Garrison, Wright's direction of MASS to begin pushing for state legislation was quickly successful. The state passed a law in 1836 automatically emancipating slaves brought into the state by slave owners, referred to as slaves in transit.[76] Again, in 1837, MASS successfully petitioned for a due process law providing all Blacks the right of trial by jury in the state. Wright formally broke ties with Garrison and MASS in 1839 to form the Massachusetts Abolition Society (MAS) and the state's Liberty party, in order to achieve an even stronger foothold in state politics. The timing of these state-level development in Massachusetts's advocacy coalition aligned with key federalism tensions over fugitive slave law, leading to the state's personal liberty being passed in 1843 modelled after Pennsylvania.

Months after the US Supreme Court's ruling in *Prigg v. Pennsylvania* (1842) had sparked national attention on the issue of fugitive slave law (see Chapter 4 for more details on this ruling), a slave named George Latimer and his pregnant wife escaped from Norfolk, Virginia, to Boston, Massachusetts. Shortly thereafter, Latimer was arrested and returned to slavery.[77] The state's Liberty party and MAS immediately responded by establishing a Latimer Committee, purchased Latimer's freedom, and led in a targeted state petition campaign that received over 64,000 signatures for new state legislation to protect runaway slaves. This led Massachusetts to pass its first personal liberty law in 1843.

The deep tension caused by federal law and sectionalism continued to shape the legislative strategy of advocacy coalitions in Northern states. The infamous 1854 rendition case of Anthony Burns, who escaped in 1853 and was recognized and detained the following year in Boston, led MAS to push for a second, much more robust personal liberty law. During his hearing, abolitionists stormed the courthouse to physically remove Burns from federal custody. President Franklin Pierce responded by sending more than 2,000 US troops to enforce the Fugitive Slave Act of 1850, demonstrating the federal government's resolve to enforce its laws and to use the rendition of Burns as an example of federal plenary power. The case ended with Burns's removal, but the Massachusetts state legislature partnered with abolitionists in 1855 to pass the North's most comprehensive personal liberty law.

Despite having established statewide organizational capacity to pressure the legislature through grassroots tactics, and having representation through the state's Liberty party, MAS was unable to enact a proposed personal liberty law in 1851. The capture and removal of Burns provided a critical window of opportunity for MAS to lead a massive petition campaign and mobilize state legislators. Following Burn's removal, MAS sent more than 8,000 individual petitions to the standing committee on Federal Relations in the state legislature.[78] Soon after, the state reintroduced the 1851 bill, amended and passed the most comprehensive runaway protection bill in the North. It included a provision forbidding state officials from enforcing the federal fugitive slave law, a strict anti-kidnapping provision, and additional due process protections, including appointing special state commissioners to defend runaway slaves in court, placing the burden of proof on slave owners, and providing all Blacks with the right of habeas corpus, trial by jury, and testimony against Whites.[79]

The examples of state liberty laws in the antebellum North, state sanctuary laws, and driver's license laws in the contemporary period all indicate the critical importance of two factors: federalism tensions that open windows of policymaking opportunity; and the prior construction of state advocacy coalitions that can take advantage of such opportunities. These federalism tensions can be precipitated by prominent events such as the capture and rendition of Anthony Burns. More frequently, however, these enabling federalism tensions have taken the form of Congressional gridlock preventing the passage of citizenship expansion (such as in the early 1800s on anti-kidnapping provisions or in 2013 on immigrant legalization) or of legislative or executive actions that run counter to the demands of state and local activists (as with the case of the 1820 Missouri Compromise, the 1850 Fugitive Slave Act, and President Trump's "Muslim ban"). These explanatory factors make intuitive sense. Pressures for state-level reforms grow when advocacy coalitions feel stymied at the federal level; indeed, successful federal reforms would largely obviate the need for state-level reforms. At the same time, federalism tensions only open up windows of opportunity. In order for states to effectively capitalize on them, movement activists need to have built up sufficient organizational capacity and alliances with state legislators and governors to pass progressive laws on state citizenship.

THE FUTURE OF STATE CITIZENSHIP IN A POLARIZED AMERICA

Just as citizenship is predominantly viewed as an exclusively national phenomenon, so too is the view of American progress on citizenship rights, whether it be Black civil rights or immigrant rights. By contrast, the assertion of states' rights is viewed primarily through the lens of the Jim Crow South, with governors and state legislatures enacting laws to restrict or erode rights guaranteed by federal law and the US Constitution. Yet, as we show throughout this book, states have also been important venues for rights expansion.

Indeed, the availability of key federal rights today, ranging from women's suffrage to reproductive rights to gay rights, grew out of successful efforts to expand state-level rights that subsequently built political momentum for national reform. Abolitionists in the free North were one of the first to build advocacy coalitions linking mass movements with key political allies in state legislatures, which in turn pushed strategically for state-level reforms during moments of federalism tension. As a result, many Northern states ended their enforcement of federal fugitive slave laws and passed a range of state laws protecting runaway slaves from recaption. Notably, these abolitionist successes were deeply linked to the national battle over abolition and were profoundly influential in securing state-level citizenship protections under the Fourteenth Amendment.[80] Similarly, the push for women's suffrage was stymied in Congress and was ultimately achieved only after suffragists built strong state-level movements, combining insider and outsider political strategies to pass state constitutional amendments that built political momentum toward ratification of the Nineteenth Amendment.

Immigrant citizenship rights in the United States are at a similar crossroads today. For nearly two decades, advocates for immigrant rights have been holding out hope for immigrant legalization at the national level. The White House and a bipartisan coalition of members in the US Congress started the push for comprehensive immigration reform in 2001, only to see it waylaid time and again – first getting sidetracked after 9/11, then failing to pass a Republican-controlled House in 2006, failing to break a Senate filibuster in 2007, failing to get on the legislative agenda during President Obama's first term, and failing to pass the Republican-controlled House in 2013 even after securing over two-thirds support in the US Senate. The only significant form of federal relief from immigrant enforcement has been the Deferred Action for Childhood Arrivals program, and even that relief has been temporary and limited in its scope. Meanwhile, advancement in state citizenship rights for immigrant residents have proceeded apace, including the right to free movement (such as through driver's licenses), right to due process (by limiting cooperation on immigration enforcement and providing public legal assistance for immigrant detainees), and right to develop human capital (such as through in-state tuition, student scholarships, health care expansion, and professional licensing).

Progressive state citizenship will likely remain the best possible mechanism to safeguard immigrant rights for the foreseeable future, particularly as the US Senate increasingly becomes less representative of high-population, urbanized states with large immigrant populations. We are also much more likely to see advancements in the rights of transgendered persons, the formerly incarcerated, and other disenfranchised groups at the state level prior to any significant advancements in their federally guaranteed rights. Even among groups that already enjoy a broad range of rights, progressive state citizenship can help deepen advancements along particular dimensions of rights (e.g., by expanding the right to develop human capital by guaranteeing access to postsecondary education or affordable housing). Finally, expansions in state citizenship rights might also capitalize on the increasingly ambitious and assertive stances of US states, particularly with respect to exercising their policing powers in light of the COVID-19 pandemic.

As we have shown throughout this book, state citizenship does not signify secession or inherent conflict with federal citizenship. Indeed, the the two are often complementary, even as states test the limits of what is constitutionally permissible and politically probable. Advocates would thus be well advised to push for rights expansions in both arenas. Securing national rights, particularly with the promise of setting a fifty-state floor on protections via the guarantees of the Fourteenth Amendment, can still reap significant rewards. National legislation is also essential for states to enact certain types of reforms such as providing their own work authorization, as advocates of "Heartland visas" have sought to do. At the same time, civil rights and immigrant rights advocacy coalitions – including social movement organizations, legislative champions, governors, and philanthropists – should refrain from pinning all their hopes on federal reform and ignore the provision of state-level rights.

Not only does state-level engagement help safeguard against the erosion of federally guaranteed rights – it is also the most likely pathway to build momentum towards expanding rights at the national level, whether by winning support from Senators in the thirty or so states needed to overcome a filibuster, from legislatures in the thirty-eight or more states needed to ratify a US Constitutional amendment, or from massive shifts in public opinion and lower-court jurisprudence that can sway decisions by the US Supreme Court. The last century has seen significant examples of rights expansions through all these mechanisms, and American states are likely to remain important players in shaping citizenship rights in the decades to come.

Appendix A

PROCESS TRACING METHODS

We employ process tracing in Chapters 4, 5, and 7 to unpack the interacting parts of our theory of advocacy coalitions as a type of causal mechanism that, we argue, explains the development of reinforcing, regressive, and progressive state citizenship throughout American history for Black citizenship and immigrant citizenship. John Gerring explains that investigating causal mechanisms enables us to go further in examining causal relationships than correlation by "peering into the box of causality to locate the intermediate factors lying between some structural cause and its purported effect."[1] Specifically, our use of process tracing uncovers how advocacy coalition-building and federalism conflict shape the timing and sequencing of federal and state-level policy proposal and enactments. We track when social movements (abolitionist groups, immigrant rights groups, and countermovements) gain both sympathetic allies and champions with legislators and executives at the national and state levels, and then we examine how these coalitions shape the timing and sequencing of policy reforms across all five dimensions of rights from our conceptual framework (developed in Chapter 2). Testing our theory of advocacy coalitions is done by showing that each part of the hypothesized causal mechanism is *present*.[2] We draw from both primary and secondary sources to provide evidence of the *presence* or *absence* of coalition-building and reform efforts at both national and state levels.

A benefit of process tracing is being able to reveal and then explain how advocacy coalitions form and how they mobilize around federalism conflicts. We further complement our process tracing methodology conducted in Chapters 4, 5, and 7 with a cross-sectional quantitative analysis in Chapter 6 of policy enactments across all fifty states to test for the key factors of our advocacy coalition theory (partisan control and social movements) and alternative demographic explanations (see Appendix B for more detail).

STATE POLICY DATASET

Historical policy data on Black rights (Chapter 4, 1700 to present) and on immigrant rights in California (Chapter 5, 1850 to present), compiled from a combination of primary and secondary scholarship, is intended to provide a broad sketch of the state policies enacted across the five dimensions of rights laid out in our conceptual framework (Chapter 2). Contemporary policy data on immigrant rights is compiled systematically, in order to conduct both process tracing and quantitative analysis in Chapters 5, 6, and 7 of our advocacy coalition theory. Specifically, we compiled a comprehensive dataset of all passed policies across the fifty states from 1996 to 2019, using multiple sources, including the National Conference of State Legislature (NCSL) (using their complete 2008 through 2018 datasets), the National Immigration Law Center, state legislature websites, American Civil Liberties Union, LatinoJustice PRLDEF, the Fair Immigration Reform Movement, the Migration Policy Institute, internal policy agendas and published blueprints of organizations like the California Immigrant Policy Center and the New York Immigrant Coalition, and secondary literature. The NCSL is searchable beginning only in 2008, and the other datasets focus on specific policy areas; we therefore conducted news searches of state policies from 1996 to 2019 using LexisNexus and ProQuest and monitored contemporary news stories.

SCORING ON POLICY INDICATORS

We apply an additive scoring scheme on the indicators – "+1" for expansions in rights and "-1" for contractions in rights – for each provision of a state law that fits one of the five dimensions of our conceptual framework. This means that, if a law contracts or expands rights on more than one dimension or more than one indicator within the same dimension of rights, we provide a score of greater than "1" to account for all relevant indicators. We also provide adaptive scoring to show any change in state citizenship over time, from 1850 to 2019: we apply a score of "-1" or "+1" on years where a state law is either repealed, overruled, or preempted by state/federal courts and by newly enacted federal laws that supersede prior state law.

SCORING SENATE BILL NO. 54, THE CALIFORNIA VALUES ACT (2017)

SB 54 established a comprehensive expansion in the state's provision of: the right to free movement (Dimension 1); the right to due process and legal protection (Dimension 2); and the right to identify and belong (Dimension 5). For illustrative purposes, it is helpful to look at SB 54, which states:

Existing law provides that when there is reason to believe that a person arrested for a violation of specified controlled substance provisions may not be a citizen of the United States, the arresting agency shall notify the appropriate agency of the United States having charge of deportation matters.

This bill would repeal those provisions [Dimension 2 – sharing of information].

Existing law provides that whenever an individual who is a victim of or witness to a hate crime, or who otherwise can give evidence in a hate crime investigation, is not charged with or convicted of committing any crime under state law, a peace officer may not detain the individual exclusively for any actual or suspected immigration violation or report or turn the individual over to federal immigration authorities [Dimension 2 – unconstitutional detentions (forty-eight-hour holds)].

This bill would, among other things and subject to exceptions, prohibit state and local law enforcement agencies, including school police and security departments, from using money or personnel to investigate, interrogate, detain, detect, or arrest persons for immigration enforcement purposes, as specified, and would, subject to exceptions, proscribe other activities or conduct in connection with immigration enforcement by law enforcement agencies [Dimension 2 – noncooperation]. The bill would apply those provisions to the circumstances in which a law enforcement official has discretion to cooperate with immigration authorities. The bill would require, by October 1, 2018, the Attorney General, in consultation with the appropriate stakeholders, to publish model policies limiting assistance with immigration enforcement to the fullest extent possible for use by public schools, public libraries, health facilities operated by the state or a political subdivision of the state, and courthouses [Dimension 1 – safe spaces], among others. The bill would require, among others, all public schools, health facilities operated by the state or a political subdivision of the state, and courthouses to implement the model policy, or an equivalent policy. The bill would state that, among others, all other organizations and entities that provide services related to physical or mental health and wellness, education, or access to justice, including the University of California, are encouraged to adopt the model policy. The bill would require that a law enforcement agency that chooses to participate in a joint law enforcement task force, as defined, submit a report annually pertaining to task force operations to the Department of Justice, as specified. The bill would require the Attorney General, by March 1, 2019, and annually thereafter, to report on the types and frequency of joint law enforcement task forces, and other information, as specified, and to post those reports on the Attorney General's Internet Web site. The bill would require law enforcement agencies to report to the department annually regarding transfers of persons to immigration authorities. The bill would require the Attorney General to publish guidance, audit criteria, and training recommendations regarding state and local law enforcement databases, for purposes of limiting the availability of information for immigration enforcement, as specified [Dimension 2 – sharing of information]. The bill would require the Department of Corrections and Rehabilitation to provide a specified written consent form in advance of any interview between a person in department custody and the United States Immigration and Customs Enforcement regarding civil immigration violations.

This bill would state findings and declarations of the Legislature relating to these provisions.

By imposing additional duties on public schools and local law enforcement agencies, this bill would impose a state-mandated local program.

The California Constitution requires the state to reimburse local agencies and school districts for certain costs mandated by the state. Statutory provisions establish procedures for making that reimbursement.

This bill would provide that, if the Commission on State Mandates determines that the bill contains costs mandated by the state, reimbursement for those costs shall be made pursuant to the statutory provisions noted above.

TABLE A1 *SB 54 scoring procedure illustration*

Dimension 1: Right to free movement	Indicator	Score applied	Preempted
Right to access safe spaces from federal enforcement	Present	Score +1	

Dimension 2: Right to due process and legal protection	Indicator	Threshold	Preempted
Right not to be asked about legal status	Absent		
Noncooperation in federal immigration enforcement	Present	Score +1	
Absence of state and local deportation practices	Absent		
Right not to have enforcement information shared (with federal government)	Present	Score +1	
Right to be informed of immigration detainer request	Absent		
Prevents unconstitutional detentions (48-hour hold)	Present	Score + 1	
Cumulative total score on policy		**Score +4**	

In 1994, California passed Proposition 187, another comprehensive law. In contrast to the SB 54 (see Table A1), however, this law was regressive with an additive negative score. Many parts of the law were also blocked by a court injunction until they were eventually struck down. Judge Mariana Pfaelzer issued a permanent injunction of Prop. 187 in December 1994, the same year the state law was enacted, blocking all provisions except those dealing with higher education and false documents. Here we provide Sections 1–4 in full and 5–7 in part, to illustrate other aspects of our scoring procedure.

Proposition 187 (1994) read:

SECTION 1. Findings and Declaration. The People of California find and declare as follows: That they have suffered and are suffering economic hardship caused by the presence of illegal aliens in this state. That they have suffered and are suffering personal injury and damage caused by the criminal conduct of illegal aliens in this state. That they have a right to the protection of their government from any person or persons entering this country unlawfully. Therefore, the People of California declare their intention to provide for cooperation between their agencies of state and local government with the federal government, and to establish a system of required notification by and between such agencies to prevent illegal aliens in the United States from receiving benefits or public services in the State of California [Dimension 5 – alienating language in policy].

SEC 2. Manufacture, Distribution or Sale of False Citizenship or Resident Alien Documents: Crime and Punishment. Section 113 is added to the Penal Code, to read: *113. Any person who manufactures, distributes or sells false documents to conceal the true citizenship or resident alien status of another person is guilty of a felony, and shall be punished by imprisonment in the state prison for five years or by a fine of seventy-five thousand dollars ($75,000)* [Dimension 5 – identification documents].

SEC 3. Use of False Citizenship or Resident Alien Documents: Crime and Punishment.

Section 114 is added to the Penal Code, to read: 114. *Any person who uses false documents to conceal his or her true citizenship or resident alien status is guilty of a felony, and shall be punished by imprisonment in the state prison for five years or by a fine of twenty-five thousand dollars ($25,000)* [Dimension 5 – identification documents].

SEC 4. Law Enforcement Cooperation with INS. Section 834b is added to the Penal Code, to read: *834b. (a) Every law enforcement agency in California shall fully cooperate with the United States Immigration and Naturalization Service regarding any person who is arrested if he or she is suspected of being present in the United States in violation of federal immigration laws* [Dimension 2 – noncooperation]. *(b) With respect to any such person who is arrested, and suspected of being present in the United States in violation of federal immigration laws, every law enforcement agency shall do the following: (1) Attempt to verify the legal status of such person as a citizen of the United States, an alien lawfully admitted as a permanent resident, an alien lawfully admitted for a temporary period of time or as an alien who is present in the United States in violation of immigration laws. The verification process may include, but shall not be limited to, questioning the person regarding his or her date and place of birth, and entry into the United States, and demanding documentation to indicate his or her legal status* [Dimension 2 – asked about legal status]. *(2) Notify the person of his or her apparent status as an alien who is present in the United States in violation of federal immigration laws and inform him or her that, apart from any criminal justice proceedings, he or she must either obtain legal status or leave the United States* [Dimension 1 – free movement]. *(3) Notify the Attorney General of California and the United States Immigration and Naturalization Service of the apparent illegal status and provide any additional information that may be requested by any other public entity. (c) Any legislative, administrative, or other action by a city, county, or other legally authorized local governmental entity with jurisdictional boundaries, or by a law enforcement agency, to prevent or limit the cooperation required by subdivision (a) is expressly prohibited* [Dimension 2 – noncooperation].

SEC 5. Exclusion of Illegal Aliens from Public Social Services. Section 10001.5 is added to the Welfare and Institutions Code, to read: *10001.5. (a) In order to carry out the intention of the People of California that only citizens of the United States and aliens lawfully admitted to the United States may receive the benefits of public social services and to ensure that all persons employed in the providing of those services shall diligently protect public funds from misuse, the provisions of this section are adopted* [Dimension 3 – right to health care].

SEC 7. Exclusion of Illegal Aliens from Public Elementary and Secondary Schools. Section 48215 is added to the Education Code, to read: *48215. (a) No public elementary* [Dimension 3 – right to K–12 education] *or secondary school shall admit, or permit the attendance of, any child who is not a citizen of the United States, an alien lawfully admitted as a permanent resident, or a person who is otherwise authorized under federal law to be present in the United States* [Dimension 3 – right to postsecondary education].

48215. (b) Commencing January 1, 1995, each school district shall verify the legal status of each child enrolling in the school district for the first time in order to ensure the enrollment or attendance only of citizens, aliens lawfully admitted as permanent residents, or persons who are otherwise authorized to be present in the United States [Dimension 1 – safe spaces; Dimension 2 – right not to be asked about legal status].

48215. (e) Each school district shall provide information to the State Superintendent of Public Instruction, the Attorney General of California, and the United States Immigration and Naturalization Service regarding any enrollee or pupil, or parent or guardian, attending a public elementary or secondary school in the school district determined or reasonably suspected to be in violation of federal immigration laws within forty-five days after becoming aware of an apparent violation. The notice shall also be provided to the parent or legal guardian of the enrollee or pupil, and shall state that an existing pupil may not continue to attend the school after ninety calendar days from the date of the notice, unless legal status is established [Dimension 2 – noncooperation].

TABLE A2 *Proposition 187 scoring procedure illustration*

Dimension 1: Right to free movement	Indicator	Score applied	Preempted
Right to free movement	Present	Score −1	Score +1
Right to access government buildings	Present	Score −1	Score +1
Right to access safe spaces from federal enforcement	Present	Score −1	Score +1
Dimension 2: Right to due process and legal protection	**Indicator**	**Threshold**	**Preempted**
Right not to be asked about legal status	Present	Score −2	Score +2
Noncooperation in federal immigration enforcement	Present	Score −3	Score +3
Dimension 3: Right to develop human capital	**Indicator**	**Threshold**	**Preempted**
Right to K–12 education	Present	Score −1	Score +1
Right to public higher education	Present	Score −1	*LULAC*
Right to health care	Present	Score −1	*LULAC*
Dimension 5: Right to identify and belong		**Threshold**	**Preempted**
Right to identification document	Present	Score −2	*LULAC*
Alienating language in policy	Present	Score −1*	
Cumulative total score on policy (after preemption)		**Score −5**	

* We provide a score of −1 on alienating language in policy because the federal injunction zeroed out the scores on most other provisions. This scoring rule helps capture regressive state developments at a minimal level that would otherwise be hidden because of federal preemption occurring in the same year as the state law being enacted. In this table, we also illustrate how the scoring is applied to specific provisions of the state law across dimensions and indicators, with federal-level preemption considerations being scored at the same time. In the end, Prop. 187 scored a −5.

The following year, *LULAC v. Wilson* (1995) ruled Prop. 187 unconstitutional, including the identification document, education, and health care provisions. We score 1995 across these dimension/indicators to zero out the negative scoring applied to Prop. 187 in 1994, adding a cumulative total score of +4 in 1995 (see *LULAC* quadrants of Table A2). Notably, we leave a −1 score on dimension 5 – "alienating language in policy" – until California officially repealed the unenforceable sections of Proposition 187, passing SB 396 in 2014.

Appendix B

TABLE A3 *Predictors of state citizenship rights involving immigrants, 2019*

	All dimensions	Dim 1	Dim 2	Dim 3	Dim 4	Dim 5
Democratic party control	64.82** [26.04]	11.06*** [3.71]	22.14** [9.42]	21.84** [10.09]	3.68* [1.92]	6.11* [3.53]
Density of civil rights organizations	−93.55 [477.35]	−64.06 [68.07]	−31.26 [172.65]	34.55 [184.92]	−15.25 [35.17]	−17.53 [64.74]
Nonwhite share of registered voters	0.29 [0.29]	0.06 [0.04]	0.03 [0.11]	0.13 [0.11]	0.03 [0.02]	0.04 [0.04]
Growth in foreign-born, 2010–2017	17.82 [37.24]	5.98 [5.31]	6.41 [13.47]	5.31 [14.43]	−0.48 [2.74]	0.61 [5.05]
Constant	−47.36** [17.69]	−8.53*** [2.52]	−13.80** [6.40]	−16.80** [6.85]	−3.74*** [1.30]	−4.48* [2.40]
Observations	49	49	49	49	49	49
R-squared	0.147	0.215	0.115	0.132	0.136	0.093
Standard errors in brackets						

* significant at 10 percent; ** significant at 5 percent; *** significant at 1 percent

Note: Democratic party control is derived from the "Ranney Index," which measures state party control based on the party of the governor and the party in control of each legislative chamber. The measure has a null value for Nebraska, which has a unicameral legislature.

Dependent variable is net inclusionary citizenship rights, with exclusionary rights taking on negative values.

Notes

1 INTRODUCTION

1. Julia Preston, "Thousands Rally Nationwide in Support of an Immigration Overhaul," *The New York Times*, October 6, 2013, Section A; Column 0; National Desk; p. 16.
2. Joy Powell, "Diverse Crowd Rallies for Immigration Reform," *Star Tribune* (Minneapolis, MN), October 6, 2013, NEWS; p. 3B; Jacob Piekarski, "Minnesotans March for Immigration Reform," *Twin Cities Daily Planet* (blog), October 7, 2013, www.tcdailyplanet.net/minnesotans-march-immigration-reform/.
3. Preston, "Thousands Rally Nationwide in Support of an Immigration Overhaul."
4. Anthony Orozco, "Rally in Reading for Immigration Reform," *Reading Eagle* (Pennsylvania), October 6, 2013, State and Regional News.
5. California Legislative Information, "AB-4 State Government: Federal Immigration Policy Enforcement," 2013, https://leginfo.legislature.ca.gov/faces/billNavClient.xhtml?bill_id=201320140AB4.
6. Office of Governor Edmund G. Brown Jr., "Governor Brown Signs Immigration Legislation – Governor Edmund G. Brown Jr.," October 5, 2013, www.gov.ca.gov/2013/10/05/news18253/.
7. Patrick McGreevy, "Signing Trust Act Is Another Illegal-Immigration Milestone for Brown," *Los Angeles Times*, October 5, 2013, www.latimes.com/local/la-me-brown-immigration-20131006-story.html.
8. Office of Governor Edmund G. Brown Jr., "Governor Brown Signs Immigration Legislation – Governor Edmund G. Brown Jr."
9. National Immigration Law Center, "State Laws Providing Access to Driver's Licenses or Cards, Regardless of Immigration Status, Last Updated August 19." www.nilc.org/wp-content/uploads/2015/11/drivers-license-access-table.pdf, accessed July 26, 2020
10. Graber, Lena, and Krsna Avila, with Nikki Marquez and Sharon Hing. *Growing the Resistance: How Sanctuary Laws and Policies Have Flourished During the Trump Administration*. San Francisco, CA: Immigrant Legal Resource Center, 2019.
11. Seth Freed Wessler, "Connecticut Limits Cooperation With Secure Communities," Text, Colorlines, June 3, 2013, www.colorlines.com/articles/connecticut-limits-cooperation-secure-communities.

12. Legislative Counsel Committee, *Chapter 181 – State Police; Crime Reporting and Records; Public Safety Standards and Training; Sex Offender Reporting; Private Security Services*, www.oregonlegislature.gov/bills_laws/ors/2013ors181.html (2013), accessed April 27, 2014.

13. Conrad Wilson, "30 Years After Its Passing, Oregon's 'Sanctuary State' Law Serves As A Model For Others," April 17, 2017, www.opb.org/news/article/oregon-sanctuary-city-state-donald-trump-immigration/.

14. Wilson, "30 Years After."

15. Wilson, "30 Years After."

16. For a brief overview of urban citizenship in relation to immigrant integration, please see Monica Varsanyi, "Interrogating 'Urban Citizenship' Vis-à-Vis Undocumented Migration," *Citizenship Studies* 10, no. 2 (2006): 229–249, https://doi.org/10.1080/13621020600633168.

17. Michael Javen Fortner, "Urban Autonomy and Effective Citizenship," in *Urban Citizenship and American Democracy*, edited by Amy Bridges and Michael Javen Fortner, 23–64 (Albany, NY: State University of New York Press, 2016).

18. Rogers M. Smith, "American Cities and American Citizenship," in Bridges and Fortner, *Urban Citizenship and American Democracy*, 211–222.

19. David Jacobson, *Rights Across Borders: Immigration and the Decline of Citizenship* (Baltimore, MD: Johns Hopkins University Press, 1996); Yasemin Nuhoğlu Soysal, *Limits of Citizenship: Migrants and Postnational Membership in Europe* (Chicago, IL: University of Chicago, 1994).

20. T. H. Marshall, *Class, Citizenship, and Social Development: Essays by T. H. Marshall* (New York: Doubleday, 1965), 78.

21. Elizabeth F. Cohen, *Semi-Citizenship in Democratic Politics* (Cambridge: Cambridge University Press, 2009).

22. Irene Bloemraad, Anna Korteweg, and Gökçe Yurdakul, "Citizenship and Immigration: Multiculturalism, Assimilation, and Challenges to the Nation-State," *Annual Review of Sociology* 34, no. 1 (2008): 155–156, https://doi.org/10.1146/annurev.soc.34.040507.134608.

23. Natasha Behl, *Gendered Citizenship: Understanding Gendered Violence in Democratic India*, Oxford Studies in Gender and International Relations (Oxford and New York: Oxford University Press, 2019); Gershon Shafir, *The Citizenship Debates: A Reader* (University of Minnesota Press, 1998); Will Kymlicka, *Multicultural Citizenship: A Liberal Theory of Minority Rights* (Oxford: Oxford University Press, 1996), www.oxfordscholarship.com/view/10.1093/0198290918.001.0001/acprof-9780198290919; Soysal, *Limits of Citizenship: Migrants and Postnational Membership in Europe*; Iris Marion Young, "Polity and Group Difference: A Critique of the Ideal of Universal Citizenship," *Ethics* 99, no. 2 (1989): 250–74; Ruth Lister, "What Is Citizenship?," in *Citizenship: Feminist Perspectives*, ed. Ruth Lister and Jo Campling (London: Macmillan Education UK, 2003), 13–42, https://doi.org/10.1007/978-0-230-80253-7_2; Ruth Lister, "Citizenship: Towards a Feminist Synthesis," *Feminist Review* 57, no. 1 (September 1, 1997): 28–48, https://doi.org/10.1080/014177897339641.

24. William H. Riker, *Federalism: Origin, Operation, Significance* (Boston, MA: Little, Brown, 1964), 155.

25. Riker, *Federalism*; Robert C. Lieberman and John S. Lapinski, "American Federalism, Race and the Administration of Welfare," *British Journal of Political Science* 31, no. 2

(April 2001): 303–329, https://doi.org/10.1017/S0007123401000126; Michael K. Brown, "Ghettos, Fiscal Federalism and Welfare Reform," in *Race and The Politics of Welfare Reform*, ed. Sanford F. Schram, Joe Soss, and Richard C. Fording (Ann Arbor: University of Michigan Press, 2003); Robert C. Lieberman, *Shaping Race Policy: The United States in Comparative Perspective* (Princeton, NJ: Princeton University Press, 2005); Dara Z. Strolovitch, Dorian T. Warren, and Paul Frymer, "Katrina's Political Roots and Divisions: Race, Class, and Federalism in American Politics," *Understanding Katrina: Perspectives from the Social Sciences: Social Science Research Council* (blog), 2006, http://understandingkatrina.ssrc.org /FrymerStrolovitchWarren/; Lisa L. Miller, *The Perils of Federalism: Race, Poverty, and the Politics of Crime Control* (Oxford: Oxford University Press, 2008); Deborah E. Ward, *The White Welfare State: The Racialization of U.S. Welfare Policy* (Ann Arbor: University of Michigan Press, 2005); Joe Soss, Richard C. Fording, and Sanford F. Schram, *Disciplining the Poor: Neoliberal Paternalism and the Persistent Power of Race* (Chicago, IL: University of Chicago Press, 2011).

26. Soss, Fording, and Schram, *Disciplining the Poor*, 112–115.

27. Miller, *The Perils of Federalism*.

28. David Brian Robertson, *Federalism and the Making of America* (Abingdon: Routledge, 2012), 39.

29. Robertson, *Federalism and the Making of America*, 57.

30. Jamila Michener, *Fragmented Democracy: Medicaid, Federalism, and Unequal Politics* (Cambridge: Cambridge University Press, 2018), 8.

31. Daniel R. Biggers and Michael J. Hanmer, "Understanding the Adoption of Voter Identification Laws in the American States," *American Politics Research* 45, no. 4 (July 1, 2017): 560–588, https://doi.org/10.1177/1532673X16687266.a.

32. Eileen L. McDonagh, "The 'Welfare Rights State' and the 'Civil Rights State': Policy Paradox and State Building in the Progressive Era," *Studies in American Political Development* 7, no. 2 (September 1993): 226, https://doi.org/10.1017/S0898588X00 001103.

33. Margaret Weir, "States, Race, and the Decline of New Deal Liberalism," *Studies in American Political Development* 19, no. 2 (October 2005): 171, https://doi.org/10 .1017/S0898588X05000106.

34. Weir, "States, Race, and the Decline of New Deal Liberalism," 158.

35. Weir, "States, Race, and the Decline of New Deal Liberalism," 161.

36. James T. Patterson, *The New Deal and the States: Federalism in Transition* (Princeton, NJ: Princeton University Press, 1969).

37. Cybelle Fox, Three Worlds of Relief: Race, Immigration, and the American Welfare State from the Progressive Era to the New Deal (Princeton, NJ: Princeton University Press, 2012).

38. Suzanne Mettler, *Dividing Citizens: Gender and Federalism in New Deal Public Policy* (Ithaca, NY: Cornell University Press, 1998).

39. Richard Bensel, "Southern Leviathan: The Development of Central State Authority in the Confederate States of America," *Studies in American Political Development* 2 (March 1987): 68–136, https://doi.org/10.1017/S0898588X00001735; Daniel Kato, "Strengthening the Weak State: Politicizing the American State's 'Weakness' on Racial Violence," *Du Bois Review: Social Science Research on Race* 9, no. 2 (2012): 457–580, https://doi.org/10.1017/S1742058X12000306; Robert C. Lieberman, "Weak State, Strong Policy: Paradoxes of Race Policy in the United States, Great Britain, and

France," *Studies in American Political Development* 16, no. 2 (October 2002): 138–161, https://doi.org/10.1017/S0898588X0200007X; Megan Ming Francis, *Civil Rights and the Making of the Modern American State* (Cambridge: Cambridge University Press, 2014); Robert Mickey, *Paths Out of Dixie: The Democratization of Authoritarian Enclaves in America's Deep South, 1944–1972* (Princeton, NJ: Princeton University Press, 2015).

40. Kimberly S. Johnson, *Governing the American State: Congress and the New Federalism, 1877–1929* (Princeton, NJ: Princeton University Press, 2007); Richard D. Freeman and Joel Rogers, "The Promise of Progressive Federalism," in *Remaking America: Democracy and Public Policy in an Age of Inequality*, ed. Joe Soss, Jacob S. Hacker, and Suzanne Mettler (New York: Russell Sage Foundation, 2007); Miller, *The Perils of Federalism*; Lisa L. Miller, "The (Dys)Functions of American Federalism," *Tulsa Law Review* 49 (2013): 267; Joe Soss, "Lessons of Welfare: Policy Design, Political Learning, and Political Action," *American Political Science Review* 93, no. 2 (1999): 363–380, https://doi.org/10.2307/2585401; Soss, Fording, and Schram, *Disciplining the Poor*.

41. Freeman and Rogers, "The Promise of Progressive Federalism."

42. Lenny Mendonca and Laura Tyson, "The Progressive Resurgence of Federalism," Stanford Social Innovation Review, 2018; Mendonca, Lenny T., and Laura D. Tyson. "The New Era of Progressive Federalism." New America, February 2018. http://newamerica.org/new-america/policy-papers/new-era-progressive-federalism/.

43. Heather K. Gerken, "Federalism as the New Nationalism: An Overview," *Yale Law Journal* 123 (2014): 1889; Jessica Bulman-Pozen, "From Sovereignty and Process to Administration and Politics: The Afterlife of American Federalism," *Yale Law Journal* 123 (2014): 1920; Heather K. Gerken, "Loyal Opposition, The," *Yale Law Journal* 123 (2014): 1958; Abbe R. Gluck, "Our [National] Federalism," *Yale Law Journal* 123 (2014): 1996; Alison L. LaCroix, "The Shadow Powers of Article I," *Yale Law Journal* 123 (2014): 2044; Cristina M. Rodriguez, "Negotiating Conflict through Federalism: Institutional and Popular Perspectives," *Yale Law Journal* 123 (2014): 2094–2133.

44. Gerken, "Federalism as the New Nationalism," 1893.

45. Michael Jonas, "Progressive Politics from the Ground up," *CommonWealth Magazine*, July 11, 2017, https://commonwealthmagazine.org/politics/progressive-politics-from-the-ground-up/.

46. Jonas, "Progressive Politics from the Ground Up."

47. Bulman-Pozen, "From Sovereignty and Process to Administration and Politics"; Jessica Bulman-Pozen, "Partisan Federalism," *Harvard Law Review* 127 (2014): 1077–1146.

48. Heather K. Gerken, "Foreword: Federalism All the Way Down," *Harvard Law Review* 123, no. 1 (2010): 4–74.

49. Robert Cover, "Federalism and Administrative Structure," *Yale Law Journal* 92 (1983).

50. Jessica Bulman-Pozen and Heather K. Gerken, "Uncooperative Federalism," *Yale Law Journal* 118, no. 7 (2009): 1256–1310. As they explain, "[w]hen states are challenging federal power, we tend to depict them as autonomous sovereigns. When states are implementing federal mandates, we generally think they should act as cooperative servants. We have not, in short, fully explored the possibilities associated with what we call *uncooperative federalism*" (Bulman-Pozen and Gerken, "Uncooperative Federalism," 1256).

51. Peter L. Markowitz, "Undocumented No More: The Power of State Citizenship," *Stanford Law Review* 67 (2015): 1–42.
52. We say more about regressive and reinforcing state citizenship in Chapter 2.
53. Keith E. Whittington, "'Interpose Your Friendly Hand': Political Supports for the Exercise of Judicial Review by the United States Supreme Court," *American Political Science Review* 99, no. 4 (2005): 583–596.
54. Anna O. Law, "Lunatics, Idiots, Paupers, and Negro Seamen – Immigration Federalism and the Early American State," *Studies in American Political Development* 28, no. 2 (October 2014): 107–128.
55. James H. Kettner, *Development of American Citizenship, 1608–1870*, Reprint edition (Chapel Hill: University of North Carolina Press, 1978).
56. Scott v. Sandford ("*Dred Scott*"), 60 US 393, 405 (1857); For a full discussion of this legal history, see Markowitz, "Undocumented No More," 13–16.
57. Richard M. Valelly, *The Two Reconstructions: The Struggle for Black Enfranchisement*, American Politics and Political Economy (Chicago, IL: University of Chicago Press, 2004).
58. Vesla M. Weaver, "Frontlash: Race and the Development of Punitive Crime Policy," *Studies in American Political Development* 21, no. 2 (September 2007): 230–265, https://doi.org/10.1017/S0898588X07000211; Michelle Alexander, *The New Jim Crow: Mass Incarceration in the Age of Colorblindness*, Revised ed. (New York: The New Press, 2012); Michener, *Fragmented Democracy*.
59. *Clinton v Cedar Rapids and the Missouri River Railroad*, 24 Iowa 455 (1868).
60. *Hunter v. Pittsburgh*, 207 U.S. 161 (1907).
61. *Community Communications v. City of Boulder*, 455 U.S. 40 (1982).
62. Catherine E. Shoichet, "These States Have Banned Sanctuary Cities," *CNN*, May 8, 2017, www.cnn.com/2017/05/08/politics/sanctuary-city-state-bans/index.html.
63. The court blocked only the provision of the law that punishes local officials for "endorsing" policies that limit enforcement of immigration laws. Judge Edith Jones argued, "The state cannot regulate [through the law's 'endorse' provision] the substance of elected officials' speech under the First Amendment without passing the strict scrutiny test."
64. Josh Gerstein, "Appeals Court Overturns Block on Texas Anti-Sanctuary Law," *Politico*, March 13, 2018, http://politi.co/2DpCrIF; Julián Aguilar, "Appeals Court Allows More of Texas 'Sanctuary Cities' Law to Go into Effect," *Texas Tribune*, September 25, 2017, www.texastribune.org/2017/09/25/appeals-court-allows-more-texas-sanctuary-cities-law-go-effect/.
65. Pratheepan Gulasekaram and S. Karthick Ramakrishnan, *The New Immigration Federalism* (New York: Cambridge University Press, 2015), 60.
66. Karen Orren and Stephen Skowronek, *The Search for American Political Development* (Cambridge and New York: Cambridge University Press, 2004), 123.
67. Law, "Lunatics, Idiots, Paupers, and Negro Seamen – Immigration Federalism and the Early American State."
68. Valelly, *The Two Reconstructions*.
69. N. D. B. Connolly, "This, Our Second Nadir," *Boston Review*, February 21, 2018, http://bostonreview.net/forum/remake-world-slavery-racial-capitalism-and-justice/n-d-b-connolly-our-second-nadir.

70. William J. Barber and Jonathan Wilson-Hartgrove, *The Third Reconstruction: Moral Mondays, Fusion Politics, and the Rise of a New Justice Movement* (Boston, MA: Beacon Press, 2016).

71. Desmond S. King and Rogers M. Smith, "Racial Orders in American Political Development," *American Political Science Review* 99, no. 1 (February 1, 2005): 75–92; Desmond S. King and Rogers M. Smith, "Strange Bedfellows? Polarized Politics? The Quest for Racial Equity in Contemporary America," *Political Research Quarterly* 61, no. 4 (December 1, 2008): 686–703, https://doi.org/10.1177/1065912908322410; Rogers M. Smith, "Beyond Tocqueville, Myrdal, and Hartz: The Multiple Traditions in America.," *American Political Science Review* 87, no. 3 (1993): 549–566, https://doi.org/10.2307/2938735; Rogers M. Smith, *Civic Ideals: Conflicting Visions of Citizenship in U.S. History* (New Haven, CT: Yale University Press, 1997); Orren and Skowronek, *The Search for American Political Development*; Ira Katznelson, *When Affirmative Action Was White: An Untold History of Racial Inequality in Twentieth-Century America* (New York: W. W. Norton, 2006).

72. King and Smith, "Racial Orders in American Political Development."

73. Richard M. Valelly, "LGBT Politics and American Political Development," *Annual Review of Political Science* 15, no. 1 (May 11, 2012): 317, https://doi.org/10.1146/annurev-polisci-061709-104806.

74. Daniel Tichenor, *Dividing Lines: The Politics of Immigration Control in America*, Princeton Studies in American Politics (Princeton, NJ: Princeton University Press, 2002); Cybelle Fox, *Three Worlds of Relief: Race, Immigration, and the American Welfare State from the Progressive Era to the New Deal* (Princeton, NJ: Princeton University Press, 2012); Francis, *Civil Rights and the Making of the Modern American State*.

2 CITIZENSHIP IN A FEDERATED FRAMEWORK

1. Pratheepan Gulasekaram and S. Karthick Ramakrishnan, *The New Immigration Federalism* (New York: Cambridge University Press, 2015).

2. Elizabeth F. Cohen and Cyril Ghosh, *Citizenship* (Cambridge: Polity Press, 2019), 9–47.

3. J. G. A. Pocock, "The Idea of Citizenship Since Classical Times," in *Theorizing Citizenship*, ed. Ronald S. Beiner (Albany: State University of New York Press, 1995), 29–52; Ulrich K. Preuß, "Problems of a Concept of European Citizenship," *European Law Journal* 1, no. 13 (1995): 267–281; Christian Joppke and Ewa Morawska, "Integrating Immigrants in Liberal Nation-States: Policies and Practices," in *Toward Assimilation and Citizenship: Immigrants in Liberal Nation-States*, ed. Christian Joppke and Ewa Morawska, Migration Minorities and Citizenship (London: Palgrave Macmillan, 2014), 1–36, www.palgrave.com/us/book/9781403904911.

4. J. G. A. Pocock, "The Ideal of Citizenship since Classical Times," in *The Citizenship Debates: A Reader*, ed. Gershon Shafir (University of Minnesota Press, 1998), 37.

5. Rainer Bauböck, "Reinventing Urban Citizenship," *Citizenship Studies* 7, no. 2 (July 1, 2003): 139, https://doi.org/10.1080/1362102032000065946.

6. Michael Ignatieff, "The Myth of Citizenship," in *Theorizing Citizenship* (Albany: State University of New York Press, 1995), 53–77.

7. John Locke, *Second Treatise of Government* (New York: Barnes & Noble Publishing, 2004 [1690]).

8. Willem Maas, ed., *Multilevel Citizenship* (Philadelphia: University of Pennsylvania Press, 2013), 8.

9. H. H. Gerth and C. Wright Mills, *From Max Weber: Essays in Sociology* (New York: Oxford University Press, 1946), 83.

10. In addition to political citizenship, Weber also explored types of citizenship other than political citizenship, including social citizenship and class citizenship. See Max Weber, *Economy and Society: an Outline of Interpretive Sociology* (New York: Bedminster Press, 1968).

11. Charles Tilly, ed., *The Formation of National States in Western Europe*, Studies in Political Development 8 (Princeton, NJ: Princeton University Press, 1975), 42.

12. Tilly, *The Formation of National States in Western Europe*, 42.

13. Charles Tilly, *Coercion, Capital and European States: AD 990–1992* (Cambridge, MA: Blackwell Publishers Inc., 1992), 10.

14. Charles Tilly, *Citizenship, Identity, and Social History* (Cambridge, MA: Cambridge University Press, 1996), 8; emphasis added.

15. Tilly, *Citizenship, Identity, and Social History*, 8.

16. Rogers Brubaker, *Citizenship and Nationhood in France and Germany* (Cambridge, MA: Harvard University Press, 2009), 31.

17. Brubaker, *Citizenship and Nationhood in France and Germany*, 27.

18. Brubaker, *Citizen and Nationhood in France and Germany*, 28.

19. John Torpey, "Coming and Going: On the State Monopolization of the Legitimate 'Means of Movement,'" *Sociological Theory* 16, no. 3 (1998): 239–259; John Torpey, *The Invention of the Passport: Surveillance, Citizenship, and the State*, Cambridge Studies in Law and Society (Cambridge: Cambridge University Press, 2000).

20. Stein Rokkan, "Dimensions of State-Formation and Nation-Building: A Possible Paradigm for Research on Variations within Europe," in *The Formation of National States in Western Europe*, ed. Charles Tilly (Princeton, NJ: Princeton University Press, 1975), 589.

21. Sarah Wallace Goodman, *Immigration and Membership Politics in Western Europe* (New York: Cambridge University Press, 2014), 5.

22. Goodman, *Immigration and Membership Politics*, 7.

23. See Rainer Bauböck and Christian Joppke, eds., *How Liberal Are Citizenship Tests?*, vol. 2010/41, EUI Working Papers (Florence, Italy: Robert Schuman Centre for Advanced Studies, EUI, 2010); Amitai Etzioni, "Citizenship in a Communitarian Perspective," *Ethnicities* 11, no. 3 (2011), 336–349; Christian Joppke, *Citizenship and Immigration* (Immigration & Society series) (Cambridge, MA: Polity, 2010); Dora Kostakopoulou, "The Anatomy of Civic Integration," *Modern Law Review* 73, no. 6 (2010): 933–958; Phil Triadafilopoulos, "Illiberal Means to Liberal Ends? Understanding Recent Immigrant Integration Policies in Europe," *Journal of Ethnic and Migration Studies* 37, no. 6 (2011), 861–880; Liav Orgad, "Illiberal Liberalism: Cultural Restrictions on Migration and Access to Citizenship in Europe," *American Journal of Comparative Law* 58, no. 1 (2010), 53–105; Keith Banting and Will Kymlicka, "Is There Really a Retreat from Multiculturalism Policies? New

Evidence from the Multiculturalism Policy Undex," *Comparative European Politics* 11, no. 5 (2013), 577–598; Jeanine Klaver and A. W. M. Odé, *Civic Integration and Modern Citizenship: The Netherlands in Perspective* (Groningen: Europa Law Publishing, 2009). See also Anita Böcker and Tineke Strik, "Language and Knowledge Tests for Permanent Residence Rights: Help or Hindrance for Integration?," *European Journal of Migration and Law* 13, no. 2 (2011), 157–184; Elspeth Guild, Kees Groenendijk, and Sergio Carrera, eds., *Illiberal Liberal States: Immigration, Citizenship, and Integration in the EU* (Farnham: Ashgate, 2009); Ricky van Oers, Eva Ersbøll, and Theodora Kostakopoulou, *A Re-definition of Belonging? Language and Integration Tests in Europe* (Boston, MA: Martinus Nijhoff Publishers, 2010); Tineke Strik et al., "Synthesis Report," in *The INTEC Project: Integration and Naturalisation Tests: The New Way to European Citizenship* (Nijmegen, Netherlands: Centre for Migration Law, Radboud University, 2010); Ricky van Oers, *Deserving Citizenship: Citizenship Tests in Germany, the Netherlands and the United Kingdom* (Leiden: Martinus Nijhoff Publishers, 2013).

24. Marc Morjé Howard, "Comparative Citizenship: An Agenda for Cross-National Research," *Perspectives on Politics* 4, no. 3 (September 2006): 443–455, https://doi .org/10.1017/S1537592706060294; Sara Wallace Goodman, "Conceptualizing and Measuring Citizenship and Integration Policy: Past Lessons and New Approaches," *Comparative Political Studies* 48, no. 14 (December 1, 2015): 1905–1941, https://doi .org/10.1177/0010414015592648; Sara Wallace Goodman, *Immigration and Membership Politics in Western Europe* (New York: Cambridge University Press, 2014), http://ebookcentral.proquest.com/lib/asulib-ebooks/detail.action?docID=177 5901; Sara Wallace Goodman, "Integration Requirements for Integration's Sake? Identifying, Categorising and Comparing Civic Integration Policies," *Journal of Ethnic & Migration Studies* 36, no. 5 (May 2010): 753–772, https://doi.org/10.1080 /13691831003764300; Ruud Koopmans and Ines Michalowski, "Why Do States Extend Rights to Immigrants? Institutional Settings and Historical Legacies Across 44 Countries Worldwide," *Comparative Political Studies* 50, no. 1 (January 1, 2017): 41–74, https://doi.org/10.1177/0010414016655533; Rainer Bauböck, "Studying Citizenship Constellations," *Journal of Ethnic and Migration Studies* 36, no. 5 (May 1, 2010): 847–859, https://doi.org/10.1080/13691831003764375; Vink and Rainer Bauböck, "Citizenship Configurations: Analysing the Multiple Purposes of Citizenship Regimes in Europe," *Comparative European Politics* 11, no. 5 (2013): 621–648, http://dx.doi.org.ezproxy1.lib.asu.edu/10.1057/cep.2013.14.

25. Brubaker, *Citizenship and Nationhood in France and Germany*; Peter Schuck, *Citizens, Strangers, and In-Betweens: Essays on Immigration and Citizenship* (Boulder, CO: Westview Press, 2008); Peter H. Schuck, "Citizenship in Federal Systems," *The American Journal of Comparative Law* 48, no. 2 (April 1, 2000): 195–226; Peter H. Schuck, "Membership in the Liberal Polity: The Devaluation of American Citizenship," *Georgetown Immigration Law Journal* 3 (1989): 1.

26. Peter H. Schuck, "Taking Immigration Federalism Seriously," *University of Chicago Legal Forum* (2007): 59.

27. Schuck, "Taking Immigration Federalism Seriously," 65.

28. Peter J. Spiro, *Beyond Citizenship: American Identity after Globalization* (New York: Oxford University Press, 2008), 19–32, 67–79, 131.

29. Spiro, *Beyond Citizenship: American Identity after Globalization*, 30.

30. Peter J. Spiro, "The States and Immigration in an Era of Demi-Sovereignties," *Virginia Journal of International Law* 35 (1994–1995): 121.
31. Hiroshi Motomura, *Immigration Outside the Law* (Oxford: Oxford University Press, 2014); Hiroshi Motomura, *Americans in Waiting: The Lost Story of Immigration and Citizenship in the United States* (Oxford: Oxford University Press, 2006); Hiroshi Motomura, "The Curious Evolution of Immigration Law: Procedural Surrogates for Substantive Constitutional Rights," *Columbia Law Review* 92, no. 7 (1992): 1625–1704; Linda Bosniak, *The Citizen and the Alien: Dilemmas of Contemporary Membership* (Princeton, NJ: Princeton University Press, 2008); Linda Bosniak, "Universal Citizenship and the Problem of Alienage," *Immigration and Nationality Law Review* 21 (2000): 373; Linda Bosniak, "Citizenship Denationalized," *Indiana Journal of Global Legal Studies* 7, no. 2 (April 1, 2000): 447–509; Linda S. Bosniak, "Ethical Territoriality and the Rights of Immigrants," in *Amsterdam Law Forum*, vol. 1, 2008, http://papers.ssrn.com/sol3/papers.cfm?abstract_id=1480139; Linda S. Bosniak, "Immigrants, Preemption and Equality," *Virginia Journal of International Law* 35 (1994): 179; Linda Bosniak, "Constitutional Citizenship through the Prism of Alienage," *Ohio State Law Journal* 63 (2002): 1285; Michael Scaperlanda, "Partial Membership: Aliens and the Constitutional Community," *Iowa Law Review* 81 (1995): 707.
32. Steve Patrick Ercolani, "Why Are Immigrants Being Deported for Minor Crimes?," *The Atlantic*, November 20, 2013, www.theatlantic.com/national/archive/2013/11/why-are-immigrants-being-deported-for-minor-crimes/281622/; "A Legal Permanent Resident Committed a Crime More than 20 Years Ago. Now He Faces Deportation," *Denverite*, March 21, 2017, www.denverite.com/legal-permanent-resident-committedcrime-20-years-ago-now-faces-deportation-30970/.
33. Michael Javen Fortner, "Urban Autonomy and Effective Citizenship," in *Urban Citizenship and American Democracy*, ed. Amy Bridges and Michael Javen Fortner (Albany, NY: State University of New York Press, 2016), 24.
34. Rogers Smith, "American Cities and American Citizenship," in *Urban Citizenship and American Democracy*, ed. Amy Bridges and Michael Javen Fortner (Albany, NY: State University of New York Press, 2016), 215.
35. Rainer Bauböck and Liav Orgad, eds., *Cities vs States: Should Urban Citizenship Be Emancipated from Nationality?* European University Institute, 2019. http://globalcit.eu/cities-vs-states-should-urban-citizenship-be-emancipated-from-nationality/?fbclid=IwAR3I2pxdoPRsy65i8l1Z-_okEoUZieOtjtVw6M6-fCgxmrkaG_HuIaLXu1A.
36. David Jacobson, *Rights Across Borders: Immigration and the Decline of Citizenship* (Baltimore, MD: Johns Hopkins University Press, 1996); Yasemin Nuhoğlu Soysal, *Limits of Citizenship: Migrants and Postnational Membership in Europe* (Chicago, IL: University of Chicago, 1994).
37. Saskia Sassen, "The Repositioning of Citizenship: Emergent Subjects and Spaces for Politics," *Berkeley Journal of Sociology* 46 (2002): 80.
38. Rose Cuison Villazor, "Sanctuary Cities and Local Citizenship," *Fordham Urban Law Journal* 37 (2010): 581.
39. Villazor, "Sanctuary Cities and Local Citizenship."
40. Peter L. Markowitz, "Undocumented No More: The Power of State Citizenship," *Stanford Law Review* 67 (2015): 1–42.

41. Els de Graauw, "Municipal ID Cards for Undocumented Immigrants Local Bureaucratic Membership in a Federal System," *Politics & Society* 42, no. 3 (September 1, 2014): 310.
42. De Graauw, "Municipal ID Cards," 310, 312.
43. Els de Graauw, Making Immigrant Rights Real: Nonprofits and the Politics of Integration in San Francisco (Ithaca, NY: Cornell University Press, 2016).
44. Cristina Rodriguez, "Enforcement, Integration, and the Future of Immigration Federalism," *Journal on Migration and Human Security* 5 (2017): 532.
45. Maas, *Multilevel Citizenship*.
46. Willem Maas, "Varieties of Multilevel Citizenship," in Maas (ed.), *Multilevel Citizenship*, 2.
47. Elizabeth F. Cohen and Jenn Kinney, "Multilevel Citizenship in a Federal State: The Case of Noncitizens' Rights in the United States," in Maas, ed., *Multilevel Citizenship*, 70.
48. Rogers Smith, "Attrition through Enforcement in the '"Promiseland"': Overlapping Memberships and the Duties of Governments in Mexican America," in Maas, ed., *Multilevel Citizenship*, 43–69.
49. Irene Bloemraad, Anna Korteweg, and Gökçe Yurdakul, "Citizenship and Immigration: Multiculturalism, Assimilation, and Challenges to the Nation-State," *Annual Review of Sociology* 34, no. 1 (2008): 153–79, https://doi .org/10.1146/annurev.soc.34.040507.134608.
50. Bloemraad, Korteweg, and Yurdakul, "Citizenship and Immigration," 154.
51. Bloemraad, Korteweg, and Yurdakul, "Citizenship and Immigration," 166.
52. Bloemraad, Korteweg, and Yurdakul, "Citizenship and Immigration," 154.
53. Rainer Bauböck, Transnational Citizenship: Membership and Rights in International Migration (Cheltenham: Edward Elgar, 1994); Jacobson, Rights Across Borders; Soysal, Limits of Citizenship.
54. Bloemraad, Korteweg, and Yurdakul, "Citizenship and Immigration," 155–156.
55. We say more about root concepts later in this chapter.
56. Jane Jenson and Martin Papillon, "Challenging the Citizenship Regime: The James Bay Cree and Transnational Action," *Politics & Society* 28, no. 2 (June 1, 2000): 245–64, https://doi.org/10.1177/0032329200028002005; Gøsta Esping-Andersen, *The Three Worlds of Welfare Capitalism* (Princeton, NJ: Princeton University Press, 1990).
57. Aude-Claire Fourot, Mireille Paquet, and Nora Nagels, "Citizenship as a Regime," in *Citizenship as a Regime: Canadian and International Perspectives* (Montreal and Kingston: McGill-Queen's University Press, 2018), 19.
58. Jenson and Papillon, "Challenging the Citizenship Regime," 246.
59. Deborah J. Yashar, "Contesting Citizenship: Indigenous Movements and Democracy in Latin America," *Comparative Politics* 31, no. 1 (1998): 23–42, https://doi.org/10.2307/422104; Deborah J. Yashar, *Contesting Citizenship in Latin America: The Rise of Indigenous Movements and the Postliberal Challenge* (Cambridge: Cambridge University Press, 2005).
60. Elizabeth F. Cohen, *Semi-Citizenship in Democratic Politics* (Cambridge: Cambridge University Press, 2009), 24.
61. Cohen, *Semi-Citizenship in Democratic Politics*, 25.
62. T. H. Marshall, *Class, Citizenship, and Social Development: Essays by T. H. Marshall* (New York: Doubleday, 1965), 78.

63. Bosniak, *The Citizen and the Alien*, 4–5.

64. Cohen, *Semi-Citizenship in Democratic Politics*, 14

65. Cohen, *Semi-Citizenship in Democratic Politics*, 15.

66. Cohen, *Semi-Citizenship in Democratic Politics*, 25.

67. Cohen, *Semi-Citizenship in Democratic Politics*, 36.

68. Pratheepan Gulasekaram and S. Karthick Ramakrishnan, *The New Immigration Federalism* (New York: Cambridge University Press, 2015); Monica Varsanyi, ed., *Taking Local Control: Immigration Policy Activism in U.S. Cities and States* (Stanford: Stanford University Press, 2010); Monica W. Varsanyi, Paul G. Lewis, Doris Marie Provine, and Scott Decker, "A Multilayered Jurisdictional Patchwork: Immigration Federalism in the United States," *Law & Policy* 34, no. 2 (April 1, 2012): 138–158. For scholarship showing how immigration federalism shapes the lives of undocumented immigrants in the United States, see Angela S. García, *Legal Passing: Navigating Undocumented Life and Local Immigration Law* (Oakland: University of California Press, 2019); Robert G. Gonzales, *Lives in Limbo: Undocumented and Coming of Age in America* (Oakland: University of California Press, 2015); Robert G. Gonzales, "Learning to Be Illegal Undocumented Youth and Shifting Legal Contexts in the Transition to Adulthood," *American Sociological Review* 76, no. 4 (August 1, 2011): 602–619, https://doi.org/10.1177/0003122411411901.

69. Giovanni Sartori, "Concept Misformation in Comparative Politics," *American Political Science Review* 64, no. 4 (December 1, 1970): 1033–1053, https://doi.org/10.2307/1958356.

70. Sartori, "Concept Misformation in Comparative Politics," 1038.

71. David Collier and Steven Levitsky, "Democracy with Adjectives: Conceptual Innovation in Comparative Research," *World Politics* 49, no. 3 (April 1997): 430–451, https://doi.org/10.1353/wp.1997.0009.

72. David Collier and Steven Levitsky, "Democracy: Conceptual Hierarchies in Comparative Research," in *Concepts & Method in Social Science: The Tradition of Giovanni Sartori*, ed. David Collier and John Gerring (New York: Routledge, 2009), 269–288; S. Karthick Ramakrishnan, "Incorporation versus Assimilation: The Need for Conceptual Differentiation," in *Outsiders No More? Models of Immigrant Political Incorporation*, ed. Jennifer L. Hochschild, et al. (Oxford: Oxford University Press, 2013).

73. Cohen, *Semi-Citizenship in Democratic Politics*; Cohen and Ghosh, *Citizenship*; Irene Bloemraad, Anna Korteweg, and Gökçe Yurdakul, "Citizenship and Immigration: Multiculturalism, Assimilation, and Challenges to the Nation-State," *Annual Review of Sociology* 34, no. 1 (2008): 153–179, https://doi.org/10.1146/annurev.soc.34.040507.134608.

74. Goodman, *Immigration and Membership Politics in Western Europe*, 19.

75. Michael Walzer, *Spheres of Justice: A Defense of Pluralism and Equality* (New York: Basic Books, 1983), 30.

76. Bosniak, *The Citizen and the Alien*, 19.

77. Locke, *Second Treatise of Government*.

78. Hannah Arendt, *The Origins of Totalitarianism* (New York: Houghton Mifflin Harcourt, 1973 [1951]).

79. Bosniak, *The Citizen and the Alien*.

80. De Graauw, "Municipal ID Cards for Undocumented Immigrants Local Bureaucratic Membership in a Federal System."

81. Kimberle Crenshaw, "Mapping the Margins: Intersectionality, Identity Politics, and Violence against Women of Color," *Stanford Law Review* 43, no. 6 (1991): 1241–1299, https://doi.org/10.2307/1229039; Ange-Marie Hancock, "When Multiplication Doesn't Equal Quick Addition: Examining Intersectionality as a Research Paradigm," *Perspectives on Politics* 5, no. 1 (March 2007): 63–79, https://doi.org/10.1017/S1537592707070065; Rita Kaur Dhamoon, "Considerations on Mainstreaming Intersectionality," *Political Research Quarterly* 64, no. 1 (March 1, 2011): 230–243, https://doi.org/10.1177/1065912910379227.

82. Peter B. Evans, Dietrich Rueschemeyer, and Theda Skocpol, *Bringing the State Back In* (Cambridge and New York: Cambridge University Press, 1985).

83. Oxford English Dictionary, www.oed.com/view/Entry/102156?redirectedFrom=jurisdiction#eid (Subscription required).

84. Torpey, "Coming and Going"; Torpey, *The Invention of the Passport*.

85. Jane Caplan and John Torpey, eds., *Documenting Individual Identity: The Development of State Practices in the Modern World* (Princeton, NJ: Princeton University Press, 2001); Craig Robertson, *The Passport in America: The History of a Document* (New York: Oxford University Press, 2010); Mark B. Salter, *Rights of Passage: The Passport in International Relations* (Boulder, CO: Lynne Rienner Publishers, 2003).

86. Robertson, *The Passport in America*; Craig Robertson, "A Documentary Regime of Verification," *Cultural Studies* 23, no. 3 (2009): 329–354, https://doi.org/10.1080/09502380802016253.

87. Gerald L. Neuman, "The Lost Century of American Immigration Law (1776–1875)," *Columbia Law Review* 93, no. 8 (December 1, 1993): 1848–1849.

88. Neuman, "The Lost Century," 1849–1851, 1961–1862; Kunal M. Parker, "State, Citizenship, and Territory: The Legal Construction of Immigrants in Antebel," *Law and History Review* 19, no. 3 (September 2001): 583–643; Kunal M. Parker, *Making Foreigners: Immigration and Citizenship Law in America, 1600–2000* (New York: Cambridge University Press, 2015); Anna O. Law, "Lunatics, Idiots, Paupers, and Negro Seamen – Immigration Federalism and the Early American State," *Studies in American Political Development* 28, no. 2 (October 2014): 107–128.

89. Sally E. Hadden, *Slave Patrols: Law and Violence in Virginia and the Carolinas*, Harvard Historical Studies, v. 138 (Cambridge, MA: Harvard University Press, 2001).

90. Allan Colbern, "Today's Runaway Slaves: Unauthorized Immigrants in a Federalist Framework" (Riverside: University of California, Riverside, 2017), 12.

91. Roger L. Ransom and Richard Sutch, *One Kind of Freedom: The Economic Consequences of Emancipation*, 2nd ed. (Cambridge and New York: Cambridge University Press, 2001); Douglas A. Blackmon, *Slavery by Another Name: The Re-Enslavement of Black Americans from the Civil War to World War II* (London: Icon Books, 2013).

92. Richard M. Valelly, *The Two Reconstructions: The Struggle for Black Enfranchisement*, American Politics and Political Economy (Chicago, IL: University of Chicago Press, 2004); Megan Ming Francis, *Civil Rights and the Making of the Modern American State* (New York: Cambridge University Press, 2014).

93. C. Vann Woodward, *The Strange Career of Jim Crow* (Oxford: Oxford University Press, 2001), Introduction.

94. Massachusetts, "1855 Chap. 0489. An Act to Protect the Rights and Liberties of the People of the Commonwealth of Massachusetts," 1855, http://archives .lib.state.ma.us/handle/2452/97312.

95. Michelle Alexander, *The New Jim Crow: Mass Incarceration in the Age of Colorblindness* (New York and Jackson, TN: New Press, distributed by Perseus Distribution, 2010).

96. See http://assembly.state.ny.us/leg/?default_fld=%0D%0A&bn=A11177&term= 2009&Summary=Y&Actions=Y&Memo=Y&Text=Y.

97. *Floyd v. City of N.Y.*, 959 F. Supp. 2d 540 (S.D.N.Y. 2013).

98. Andrew Gelman, Jeffrey Fagan, and Alex Kiss, "An Analysis of the New York City Police Department's 'Stop-and-Frisk' Policy in the Context of Claims of Racial Bias," *Journal of the American Statistical Association* 102, no. 479 (September 1, 2007): 813–823, https://doi.org/10.1198/016214506000001040.

99. Charles R. Epp, Steven Maynard-Moody, and Donald P. Haider-Markel, *Pulled Over: How Police Stops Define Race and Citizenship* (Chicago, IL: University of Chicago Press, 2014).

100. Cohen, *Semi-Citizenship in Democratic Politics*, 9.

101. Elizabeth F. Cohen, *The Political Value of Time: Citizenship, Duration, and Democratic Justice* (Cambridge: Cambridge University Press, 2018), 48.

102. Leonard C. Feldman, *Citizens Without Shelter: Homelessness, Democracy, and Political Exclusion* (Ithaca, NY: Cornell University Press, 2006), 18.

103. Kathe Newman and Elvin K. Wyly, "The Right to Stay Put, Revisited: Gentrification and Resistance to Displacement in New York City," *Urban Studies* 43, no. 1 (January 1, 2006): 23–57, https://doi.org/10.1080/00420980500388710.

104. Colbern, "Today's Runaway Slaves: Unauthorized Immigrants in a Federalist Framework."

105. Francis, *Civil Rights and the Making of the Modern American State*.

106. Henry Shue, *Basic Rights: Subsistence, Affluence, and U.S. Foreign Policy* (Princeton, NJ: Princeton University Press, 1980).

107. Amartya Sen, *Inequality Reexamined* (New York and Cambridge, MA: Russell Sage Foundation and Harvard University Press, 1992); Amartya Sen, *Development as Freedom* (Oxford and New York: Oxford University Press, 2001).

108. Shannon Gleeson, *Precarious Claims: The Promise and Failure of Workplace Protections in the United States* (Oakland: University of California Press, 2016); Shannon Gleeson, "'They Come Here to Work': An Evaluation of the Economic Argument in Favor of Immigrant Rights," *Citizenship Studies* 19, no. 3–4 (April 3, 2015): 400–420, https://doi.org/10.1080/13621025.2015.1006173; Jacqueline Vaughn Switzer and Jacqueline Vaughn, *Disabled Rights: American Disability Policy and the Fight for Equality* (Washington, DC: Georgetown University Press, 2003).

109. T. H. Marshall, *Citizenship and Social Class* (Cambridge: Cambridge University Press, 1950), 30; Keith Aoki, "No Right to Own: The Early Twentieth-Century Alien Land Laws as a Prelude to Internment Symposium: The Long Shadow of Korematsu," *Boston College Law Review* 40 (1998): 37–72.

110. Feldman, *Citizens Without Shelter*; Wiley, Hannah. "California 'Right to Housing' Proposal Dies in Capitol." The Sacramento Bee, January 23, 2020; Savage, David G. "Supreme Court Lets Stand Ruling That Protects Homeless People Who Sleep on Sidewalk." Los Angeles Times, December 16, 2019.

111. Martha C. Nussbaum, "A Right to Marry?," *California Law Review* 98, no. 3 (2010): 667–696.
112. Christopher D. Jozwiak, "Lofton v. Secretary of the Department of Children & (and) Family Services: Florida's Gay Adoption Ban under Irrational Equal Protection Analysis," *Law and Inequality: A Journal of Theory and Practice* 23 (2005): 407–428.
113. *Brown v. Board of Education of Topeka*, 347 US 483 (1954).
114. Motomura, *Immigration Outside the Law*, 7–8; *Plyler v. Doe*, 457 US 202 (1982).
115. Motomura, *Immigration Outside the Law*, 8.
116. Gulasekaram and Ramakrishnan, *The New Immigration Federalism*, 48.
117. 42 U.S. Code § 1395dd – Examination and Treatment for Emergency Medical Conditions and Women in Labor.
118. Nancy Denton and Douglas S. Massey, *American Apartheid: Segregation and the Making of the Underclass* (Cambridge, MA: Harvard University Press, 1993).
119. Kenneth B. Clark, *Dark Ghetto: Dilemmas of Social Power* (Middletown, CT: Wesleyan University Press, 1989), 11.
120. Kimberly Morland et al., "Neighborhood Characteristics Associated with the Location of Food Stores and Food Service Places," *American Journal of Preventive Medicine* 22, no. 1 (January 1, 2002): 23–29, https://doi.org/10.1016/S0749-3797(01)00403-2.
121. US Commission on Civil Rights, "Understanding Fair Housing," *Clearinghouse Publication* (Washington, DC: US Government Printing Office, February 1973). *Corrigan v. Buckley* 271 U.S. 323 (1926).
122. *Jones v. Alfred H. Mayer Co.*, 392 U.S. 409 (1968)
123. *Pace v. Alabama*, 106 U.S. 583 (1883).
124. *Loving v. Virginia*, 388 U.S. 1 (1967).
125. *Lawrence v. Texas*, 539 US 558 (2003).
126. *Obergefell v. Hodges*, 135 S. Ct. 2584 (2015).
127. Hollis-Brusky, Amanda. "The Supreme Court Closed the Door on LGBTQ Employment Discrimination. But It Opened a Window." *Washington Post*, June 16, 2020. https://www.washingtonpost.com/politics/2020/06/16/supreme-court-closed-door-lgbtq-employment-discrimination-it-opened-window/.
128. *Obergefell*, 135 S. Ct. at 2601.
129. US Department of State – Bureau of Consular Affairs, "Adoption by Non-U.S. Citizens Living in the U.S.," accessed March 22, 2018, https://travel.state.gov/content/travel/en/Intercountry-Adoption/Adoption-Process/before-you-adopt/adoption-by-non-us-citizens-living-in-us.html.
130. Alexander Keyssar, *The Right to Vote: The Contested History of Democracy in the United States* (New York: Basic Books, 2009).
131. Ron Hayduk, *Democracy for All: Restoring Immigrant Voting Rights in the U.S.* (New York: Routledge, 2012); Ron Hayduk, "Give Noncitizens the Right to Vote? It's Only Fair," *Los Angeles Times*, December 22, 2014, www.latimes.com/opinion/op-ed/la-oe-hayduk-let-noncitizens-vote-20141223-story.html; Ron Hayduk, "Democracy for All: Restoring Immigrant Voting Rights in the US," *New Political Science* 26, no. 4 (December 1, 2004): 499–523, https://doi.org/10.1080/0739314042000297478; Ron Hayduk, "Political Rights in the Age of Migration: Lessons from the United States," *Journal of International Migration and Integration* 16, no. 1 (April 25, 2014): 99–118, https://doi.org/10.1007/s12134-014-0336-6.

132. Gerald M. Rosberg, "Aliens and Equal Protection: Why Not the Right to Vote?," *Michigan Law Review* 75, no. 5/6 (April 1, 1977): 1092–1136, https://doi.org/10.2307/1288026.

133. Jamin B. Raskin, "Legal Aliens, Local Citizens: The Historical, Constitutional and Theoretical Meanings of Alien Suffrage," *University of Pennsylvania Law Review* 141, no. 4 (April 1, 1993): 1391–1470, https://doi.org/10.2307/3312345.

134. Daniels R. Gilda, "Lining Up: Ensuring Equal Access to the Right to Vote" (Advancement Project and the Lawyers' Committee for Civil Rights Under Law, August 22, 2013), http://b.3cdn.net/advancement/666cb8d8d9d4a9a169_kxm6yslwk.pdf.

135. Hayduk, *Democracy for All*, 2012.

136. William Seltzer, "Excluding Indians Not Taxed: Federal Censuses and Native-Americans in the 19th Century," in *1999 Proceedings of the Government and Social Statistics Section of the American Statistical Association*, 2000, 161–166.

137. U.S. Supreme Court, "*Evenwel v. Abbott*," Legal Information Institute, Cornell University, 2016, www.law.cornell.edu/supremecourt/text/14-940; *Reynolds v. Sims*, 377 US 533 (1964); *Evenwel v. Abbott*, 578 US ___ (2016).

138. Hayduk, *Democracy for All*, 2012.

139. De Graauw, "Municipal ID Cards for Undocumented Immigrants Local Bureaucratic Membership in a Federal System."

140. "H.Res.683 – Expressing the Regret of the House of Representatives for the Passage of Laws that Adversely Affected the Chinese in the United States, Including the Chinese Exclusion Act." (2012), www.congress.gov/bill/112th-congress/house-resolution/683/actions.

141. Cohen, *Semi-Citizenship in Democratic Politics*, 79–80.

142. David Collier and John Gerring, *Concepts & Method in Social Science: The Tradition of Giovanni Sartori* (New York, NY: Routledge, 2009).

143. Sartori, "Concept Misformation in Comparative Politics"; David Collier and James E. Mahon, "Conceptual 'Stretching' Revisited: Adapting Categories in Comparative Analysis," *The American Political Science Review* 87, no. 4 (December 1, 1993): 845–855, https://doi.org/10.2307/2938818

144. David Collier and Steven Levitsky, "Democracy: Conceptual Hierarchies in Comparative Research," in *Concepts and Method in Social Science: The Tradition of Giovanni Sartori*, ed. David Collier and John Gerring (New York and London: Routledge, 2009), 271.

145. Collier and Levitsky, "Democracy: Conceptual Hierarcies in Comparative Research."

146. Jamila Michener, *Fragmented Democracy: Medicaid, Federalism, and Unequal Politics* (New York: Cambridge University Press, 2018), 8.

147. William H. Riker, *Federalism: Origin, Operation, Significance* (Boston, MA: Little, Brown, 1964), 155.

148. Pratheepan Gulasekaram and S. Karthick Ramakrishnan, "Immigration Federalism: A Reappraisal," *New York University Law Review* 88 (2013): 2074–2319; Carissa Hessick, "Mirror Image Theory in State Immigration Regulation," *SCOTUSblog* (blog), July 13, 2011, www.scotusblog.com/2011/07/mirror-image-theory-in-state-immigration-regulation/.

149. Kris W. Kobach, "Reinforcing the Rule of Law: What States Can and Should Do to Reduce Illegal Immigration," *Georgetown Immigration Law Journal* 22 (2007):

459–483; Kris W. Kobach, "Attrition through Enforcement: A Rational Approach to Illegal Immigration," *Tulsa Journal of Comparative and International Law* 15 (2007): 155–163; Kris W. Kobach, "Quintessential Force Multiplier: The Inherent Authority of Local Police to Make Immigration Arrests, The," *Albany Law Review* 69 (2005): 179–235.

150. See Chapter 1 for a discussion of the contemporary literature on progressive federalism, which we argue is largely focused on their implications for national politics and policies.

151. Ryan Gabrielson, "Sobriety Checkpoints Catch Unlicensed Drivers," *New York Times*, February 13, 2010, www.nytimes.com/2010/02/14/us/14sfcheck.html

152. Laura E. Enriquez, Daisy Vazquez Vera, and S. Karthick Ramakrishnan, "On the Road to Opportunity: Racial Disparities in Obtaining AB 60 Driver Licenses," *Boom California* (blog), November 28, 2017, https://boomcalifornia.com/2017/11/28/on-the-road-to-opportunity/.

153. "An Act to Amend Sections 7282 and 7282.5 of, and to Add Chapter 17.25 (Commencing with Section 7284) to Division 7 of Title 1 of, the Government Code, and to Repeal Section 11369 of the Health and Safety Code, Relating to Law Enforcement" (2017), https://leginfo.legislature.ca.gov/faces/billNavClient.xhtml?bill_id=201720180SB54.

154. Jazmine Ulloa, "Gov. Jerry Brown and Senate Leader Kevin De León Strike Deal on Changes to 'Sanctuary State' Legislation," *Los Angeles Times*, September 11, 2017.

155. Hayduk, *Democracy for All*.

156. Hayduk, *Democracy for All*, 76.

157. Tara Kini, "Sharing the Vote: Noncitizen Voting Rights in Local School Board Elections," *California Law Review* 93, no. 1 (January 1, 2005): 271–321.

158. Hayduk, "Political Rights in the Age of Migration."

159. Michael Martinez and Jaqueline Hurtado, "Undocumented Immigrants Picked for City Posts Say U.S. 'Progressing,'" CNN, August 8, 2015, www.cnn.com/2015/08/08/us/huntington-park-undocumented-immigrants-city-commission-appointees/index.html.

160. Taryn Luna and Billy Kobin, "Undocumented Immigrant Appointed to State Post in California," *Sacramento Bee*, March 15, 2018, www.sacbee.com/news/politics-government/capitol-alert/article205249624.html.

161. Tony Mendoza, "Senate Bill No. 432" (2015), https://leginfo.legislature.ca.gov/faces/billTextClient.xhtml?bill_id=201520160SB432.

3   NATIONAL AND STATE CITIZENSHIP IN THE AMERICAN CONTEXT

1. Paul Clement and Neal Katyal, "On the Meaning of Natural Born Citizen," *Harvard Law Review Forum* 128 (2015): 161–164. Clement and Katyal note: "Congress has made equally clear from the time of the framing of the Constitution to the current day that, subject to certain residency requirements on the parents, someone born to a U.S. citizen parent generally becomes a U.S. citizen without regard to whether the birth takes place in Canada, the Canal Zone, or the continental United States" (161).

2. Article IV, Section 2, of US Constitution.

3. Article III, Section 2, of US Constitution.

4. Karen Orren and Stephen Skowronek, *The Search for American Political Development* (Cambridge and New York: Cambridge University Press, 2004), 123.

5. Eric Foner, The Second Founding: How the Civil War and Reconstruction Remade the Constitution (New York: W. W. Norton, 2019); Paul Finkelman, Slavery and the Founders: Race and Liberty in the Age of Jefferson (Abingdon: Routledge, 2014); David Brian Robertson, Federalism and the Making of America (Abingdon: Routledge, 2012); James H. Kettner, Development of American Citizenship, 1608–1870, Reprint Edition (Chapel Hill: The University of North Carolina Press, 1978).

6. Anna O. Law, "The Historical Amnesia of Contemporary Immigration Federalism Debates," *Polity* 47, no. 3 (July 2015): 309.

7. Robertson, *Federalism and the Making of America*, 19.

8. William H. Riker, *Federalism: Origin, Operation, Significance* (Boston, MA: Little, Brown, 1964).

9. David A. Bateman, *Disenfranchising Democracy: Constructing the Electorate in the United States, the United Kingdom, and France* (New York: Cambridge University Press, 2018); David A. Bateman, Ira Katznelson, and John S. Lapinski, *Southern Nation: Congress and White Supremacy after Reconstruction* (Princeton, NJ: Princeton University Press, 2018); David Collier and Steven Levitsky, "Democracy with Adjectives: Conceptual Innovation in Comparative Research," *World Politics* 49, no. 3 (April 1997): 430–451, https://doi.org/10.1353/wp.1997.0009; David Collier and Robert Adcock, "Democracy and Dichotomies: A Pragmatic Approach to Choices about Concepts," *Annual Review of Political Science* 2, no. 1 (1999): 537–565, https://doi.org/10.1146/annurev.polisci.2.1.537; David Collier and Steven Levitsky, "Democracy: Conceptual Hierarcies in Comparative Research," in *Concepts and Method in Social Science: The Tradition of Giovanni Sartori*, ed. David Collier and John Gerring (New York and London: Routledge, 2009), 269–288; Gøsta Esping-Andersen, *The Three Worlds of Welfare Capitalism* (Princeton, NJ: Princeton University Press, 1990); Kathleen Thelen, "Timing and Temporality in the Analysis of Institutional Evolution and Change," *Studies in American Political Development* 14, no. 1 (April 2000): 101–108, doi:10.1017/S0898588X00213035; James Mahoney, ed., *Comparative Historical Analysis in the Social Sciences* (Cambridge and New York: Cambridge University Press, 2003); James Mahoney and Kathleen Thelen, eds., *Explaining Institutional Change: Ambiguity, Agency, and Power* (Cambridge: Cambridge University Press, 2009); Adam Przeworski, *Democracy and Development: Political Institutions and Well-Being in the World, 1950–1990* (Cambridge: Cambridge University Press, 2000); Orren and Skowronek, *The Search for American Political Development*; Desmond S. King and Rogers M. Smith, "Racial Orders in American Political Development," *American Political Science Review* 99, no. 1 (February 1, 2005): 75–92; Desmond S. King and Rogers M. Smith, *Still a House Divided: Race and Politics in Obama's America* (Princeton, NJ: Princeton University Press, 2013); Rogers M. Smith, *Civic Ideals: Conflicting Visions of Citizenship in U.S. History* (New Haven, CT: Yale University Press, 1997); Robert W. Mickey, "The Beginning of the End for Authoritarian Rule in America: Smith v. Allwright and the Abolition of the White Primary in the Deep South, 1944–1948," *Studies in American Political Development* 22, no. 2 (September 2008): 143–182, https://doi.org/10.1017/S0898588X08000096; Robert Mickey, *Paths Out of Dixie: The Democratization of Authoritarian Enclaves in America's Deep South, 1944–1972* (Princeton, NJ: Princeton University Press, 2015); Mireille Paquet, Nora Nagels, and Aude-Claire Fourot, *Citizenship as a Regime: Canadian and*

International Perspectives (Montreal and Kingston: McGill-Queen's University Press, 2018).

10. Richard M. Valelly, *The Two Reconstructions: The Struggle for Black Enfranchisement*, American Politics and Political Economy (Chicago, IL: University of Chicago Press, 2004).

11. Jeffery A. Jenkins, Justin Peck, and Vesla M. Weaver, "Between Reconstructions: Congressional Action on Civil Rights, 1891–1940," *Studies in American Political Development* 24, no. 1 (2010): 57–89.

12. Paul Frymer, *Uneasy Alliances: Race and Party Competition in America* (Princeton, NJ: Princeton University Press, 2010).

13. Bateman, Katznelson, and Lapinski, *Southern Nation*; Bateman, *Disenfranchising Democracy*; Mickey, *Paths Out of Dixie*; J. Morgan Kousser, *The Shaping of Southern Politics: Suffrage Restriction and the Establishment of the One-Party South, 1880–1910* (New Haven, CT: Yale University Press, 1974).

14. Kimberley S. Johnson, "The Color Line and the State: Race and American Political Development," in *The Oxford Handbook of American Political Development*, ed. Richard M. Valelly, Suzanne Mettler, and Robert C. Lieberman (Oxford: Oxford University Press, 2016), 593–624; Kimberly Johnson, *Reforming Jim Crow: Southern Politics and State in the Age Before Brown* (Oxford: Oxford University Press, 2010); Kimberley S. Johnson, "Racial Orders, Congress, and the Agricultural Welfare State, 1865–1940," *Studies in American Political Development* 25, no. 2 (2011): 143–161, https://doi.org/10.1017/S0898588X11000095; Amy E. Lerman and Vesla M. Weaver, *Arresting Citizenship: The Democratic Consequences of American Crime Control* (Chicago, IL: University of Chicago Press, 2014); Vesla M. Weaver, Jacob S. Hacker, and Christopher Wildeman, "Detaining Democracy? Criminal Justice and American Civic Life," *ANNALS of the American Academy of Political and Social Science* 651, no. 1 (January 1, 2014): 6–21, https://doi.org/10.1177/0002716213504729; Amy E. Lerman and Vesla Weaver, "Staying out of Sight? Concentrated Policing and Local Political Action," *ANNALS of the American Academy of Political and Social Science* 651, no. 1 (January 1, 2014): 202–219, https://doi.org/10.1177/0002716213503085; Vesla M. Weaver, "Frontlash: Race and the Development of Punitive Crime Policy," *Studies in American Political Development* 21, no. 2 (September 2007): 230–265, https://doi.org/10.1017/S0898588X07000211; Eduardo Bonilla-Silva, *Racism without Racists: Color-Blind Racism and the Persistence of Racial Inequality in America* (New York: Rowman & Littlefield Publishers, 2013), http://ebookcentral.proquest.com/lib/asulib-ebooks/detail.action?docID=1246203; Moon-Kie Jung et al., *State of White Supremacy: Racism, Governance, and the United States* (Stanford, CA: Stanford University Press, 2011), http://ebookcentral.proquest.com/lib/asulib-ebooks/detail.action?docID=683285; Michelle Alexander, *The New Jim Crow: Mass Incarceration in the Age of Colorblindness*, Revised Edition (New York and Jackson, TN: New Press; Distributed by Perseus Distribution, 2012); Daniel Martinez HoSang, *Racial Propositions: Ballot Initiatives and the Making of Postwar California* (Berkeley: University of California Press, 2010); Douglas S. Massey, "Racial Formation in Theory and Practice: The Case of Mexicans in the United States," *Race and Social Problems* 1, no. 1 (March 1, 2009): 12–26, https://doi.org/10.1007/s12552-009-9005-3.

15. Chloe N. Thurston, *At the Boundaries of Homeownership: Credit, Discrimination, and the American State* (Cambridge: Cambridge University Press, 2018); Chloe N. Thurston, "Policy Feedback in the Public–Private Welfare State: Advocacy Groups and Access to Government Homeownership Programs, 1934–1954," *Studies in American Political Development* 29, no. 2 (October 2015): 250–267, https://doi.org/10.1017/S0898588X15000097; Megan Ming Francis, *Civil Rights and the Making of the Modern American State* (Cambridge: Cambridge University Press, 2014); Sidney M. Milkis and Daniel J. Tichenor, *Rivalry and Reform: Presidents, Social Movements, and the Transformation of American Politics* (Chicago, IL: University of Chicago Press, 2019).

16. Milkis and Tichenor, *Rivalry and Reform.*

17. Megan Ming Francis, *Civil Rights and the Making of the Modern American State* (Cambridge: Cambridge University Press, 2014).

18. Chloe N. Thurston, "Black Lives Matter, American Political Development, and the Politics of Visibility," *Politics, Groups, and Identities* 6, no. 1 (January 2, 2018): 163, https://doi.org/10.1080/21565503.2017.1420547.

19. Thurston, *At the Boundaries of Homeownership.*

20. W. E. B. Du Bois and David Levering Lewis, Black Reconstruction in America (the Oxford W. E. B. Du Bois): An Essay Toward a History of the Part Which Black Folk Played in the Attempt to Reconstruct Democracy in America, 1860–1880, ed. Henry Louis Gates (Cary, NC: Oxford University Press, 2007); W. E. B. Du Bois, "Reconstruction and Its Benefits," *American Historical Review* 15, no. 4 (1910): 781–799, https://doi.org/10.2307/1836959; W. E. B. Du Bois, The Problem of the Color Line at the Turn of the Twentieth Century: The Essential Early Essays, ed. Nahum Dimitri Chandler (New York: Fordham University Press, 2014).

21. Jessica Bulman-Pozen, "Partisan Federalism," *Harvard Law Review* 127 (2014): 1077–1146.

22. Shanna Rose and Cynthia J. Bowling, "The State of American Federalism 2014–15: Pathways to Policy in an Era of Party Polarization," *Publius: The Journal of Federalism* 45, no. 3 (July 1, 2015): 351–379.

23. Pratheepan Gulasekaram and S. Karthick Ramakrishnan, *The New Immigration Federalism* (New York: Cambridge University Press, 2015).

24. Orren and Skowronek, *The Search for American Political Development*, 123.

25. Stephen Skowronek, *Building a New American State: The Expansion of National Administrative Capacities, 1877–1920* (Cambridge and New York: Cambridge University Press, 1982), 14–31.

26. Anna O. Law, "Lunatics, Idiots, Paupers, and Negro Seamen – Immigration Federalism and the Early American State," *Studies in American Political Development* 28, no. 2 (October 2014): 110.

27. Law, "Lunatics, Idiots, Paupers, and Negro Seamen – Immigration Federalism and the Early American State," 110; Brian Balogh, *A Government Out of Sight: The Mystery of National Authority in Nineteenth-Century America* (Cambridge: Cambridge University Press, 2009).

28. This went beyond going beyond what Congress had prescribed in the Alien and Sedition Acts of 1798. See Law, "Lunatics, Idiots, Paupers, and Negro Seamen – Immigration Federalism and the Early American State," 111; Jerry L. Mashaw,

"Reluctant Nationalists: Federal Administration and Administrative Law in the Republican Era, 1801–1829," *Yale Law Journal* 116 (2007): 1636–1741.

29. Law, "Lunatics, Idiots, Paupers, and Negro Seamen – Immigration Federalism and the Early American State"; Law, "The Historical Amnesia of Contemporary Immigration Federalism Debates"; Gerald L. Neuman, "The Lost Century of American Immigration Law (1776–1875)," *Columbia Law Review* 93, no. 8 (December 1, 1993): 1833–1901; Gerald L. Neuman, *Strangers to the Constitution: Immigrants, Borders, and Fundamental Law* (Princeton, NJ: Princeton University Press, 2010); Hidetaka Hirota, "'The Great Entrepot for Mendicants': Foreign Poverty and Immigration Control in New York State to 1882," *Journal of American Ethnic History* 33, no. 2 (2014): 5–32, https://doi.org/10.5406/jamerethnhist.33.2.0005; Hidetaka Hirota, "The Moment of Transition: State Officials, the Federal Government, and the Formation of American Immigration Policy," *Journal of American History* 99, no. 4 (March 1, 2013): 1092–1108.

30. Robert C. Lieberman, Shifting the Color Line: Race and the American Welfare State (Cambridge, MA: Harvard University Press, 2001); Suzanne Mettler, *Dividing Citizens: Gender and Federalism in New Deal Public Policy* (Ithaca, NY: Cornell University Press, 1998); Richard Franklin Bensel, *Yankee Leviathan: The Origins of Central State Authority in America, 1859–1877* (Cambridge and New York: Cambridge University Press, 1990); Richard Franklin Bensel, *Sectionalism and American Political Development, 1880–1980* (Madison: University of Wisconsin Press, 1987); Ira Katznelson, *When Affirmative Action Was White: An Untold History of Racial Inequality in Twentieth-Century America* (New York: W. W. Norton, 2006); Cybelle Fox, *Three Worlds of Relief: Race, Immigration, and the American Welfare State from the Progressive Era to the New Deal* (Princeton, NJ: Princeton University Press, 2012).

31. Desmond King, "Forceful Federalism against American Racial Inequality," *Government and Opposition* 52, no. 2 (April 2017): 356–382, https://doi.org/10.1017/gov.2016.52.

32. Orren and Skowronek, *The Search for American Political Development*, 121.

33. Valelly, *The Two Reconstructions*; Frymer, *Uneasy Alliances*; Daniel Tichenor, *Dividing Lines: The Politics of Immigration Control in America*, Princeton Studies in American Politics (Princeton, NJ: Princeton University Press, 2002); Sidney M. Milkis and Daniel J. Tichenor, "Reform's Mating Dance: Presidents, Social Movements, and Racial Realignments," *Journal of Policy History* 23, no. 4 (October 2011): 451–490, https://doi.org/10.1017/S0898030611000261; Smith, *Civic Ideals*; Rogers M. Smith, "Substance and Methods in APD Research," *Studies in American Political Development* 17, no. 1 (April 2003): 111–115, https://doi.org/10.1017/S0898588X0300004X; King and Smith, "Racial Orders in American Political Development"; Orren and Skowronek, *The Search for American Political Development*.

34. Valelly, *The Two Reconstructions*; C. Vann Woodward, *The Strange Career of Jim Crow* (Oxford: Oxford University Press, 2001); Michelle Alexander, *The New Jim Crow: Mass Incarceration in the Age of Colorblindness*, Revised Edition (New York and Jackson, TN: New Press; Distributed by Perseus Distribution, 2012); Vesla M. Weaver, "Frontlash: Race and the Development of Punitive Crime Policy," *Studies in American Political Development* 21, no. 2 (2007): 230–265; Vesla M. Weaver and Amy E. Lerman, "Political Consequences of the Carceral State,"

    American Political Science Review 104, no. 4 (November 2010): 817–833, https://doi.org/10.1017/S0003055410000456.

35. Gulasekaram and Ramakrishnan, *The New Immigration Federalism.*

36. King and Smith, *Still a House Divided,* 16–17.

37. Robertson, *Federalism and the Making of America,* 23.

38. Robertson, *Federalism and the Making of America,* 23.

39. *Brown v. Board of Education of Topeka,* 347 US 483 (1954).

40. *Loving v. Virginia,* 388 US 1 (1967).

41. *Roe v. Wade,* 410 US 113 (1973).

42. *Plyler v. Doe,* 457 US 202 (1982).

43. *Obergefell v. Hodges,* 576 US 644 (2015).

44. *New York v. United States,* 505 US 144 (1992).

45. *Printz v. United States,* 521 US 898 (1997).

46. Rose and Bowling, "The State of American Federalism 2014–15," 361; *National Federation of Independent Business v. Sebelius,* 567 US 519 (2012).

47. Robertson, *Federalism and the Making of America,* 20.

48. Oh. Const. of 1802, art. IV § I, reprinted in Thorpe (1909) (Vol. 5), 2901–2913; Middleton (2005), 19–41.

49. *Commonwealth v. Ayes,* 35 Mass. (18 Pick.) 193 (1836); Paul Finkelman, *An Imperfect Union: Slavery, Federalism, and Comity* (Clark, NJ: The Lawbook Exchange, 1981), 101–125; Paul Finkelman, "Prelude to the Fourteenth Amendment: Black Legal Rights in the Antebellum North," *Rutgers Law Journal* 17 (1985): 444.

50. Alexander Keyssar, *The Right to Vote: The Contested History of Democracy in the United States* (New York: Basic Books, 2009).

51. Finkelman, *Slavery and the Founders,* 17–18.

52. Finkelman, *Slavery and the Founders,* 22.

53. Finkelman, *Slavery and the Founders,* 22.

54. US Const. art. IV, § 2, cl. 3.

55. Finkelman, *Slavery and the Founders,* 34.

56. Finkelman, *Slavery and the Founders,* 9.

57. Skowronek, *Building a New American State*; Robertson, *Federalism and the Making of America,* 42–43.

58. Corey M. Brooks, *Liberty Power: Antislavery Third Parties and the Transformation of American Politics* (Chicago, IL: University of Chicago Press, 2016), 17.

59. Brooks, *Liberty Power,* 19–20.

60. Brooks, *Liberty Power,* 18.

61. Martha S. Jones, Birthright Citizens: A History of Race and Rights in Antebellum America (Cambridge: Cambridge University Press, 2018), 27; David Brion Davis, *The Problem of Slavery in the Age of Revolution, 1770–1823* (Ithaca, NY: Cornell University Press, 1975), 35.

62. "Restriction of Slavery," 16th Cong., 2d Sess., 37 Annals of Cong. 23 (November 22, 1820); "Admission of Missouri," 16th Cong., 2d Sess., 37 Annals of Cong. 79–80 (December 9, 1820).

63. *Scott v. Sandford,* 60 US 393, 417 (1857).

64. Martha S. Jones, *Leave of Court: African-American Legal Claims Making in the Era of Dred Scott v. Sandford,* ed. Manisha Sinha and Penny Von Eschen, Contested Democracy: Politics, Ideology, and Race in American History (New York:

Columbia University Press, 2007), 63–64; *Scott v. Sandford*, 60 US 393, 528; *Passenger Cases*, 48 US 283 (1849).

65. Peter L. Markowitz, "Undocumented No More: The Power of State Citizenship," *Stanford Law Review* 67 (2015): 11; Naturalization Act, 1 Stat. 103, 103–104 (1790); *Holmgren v. United States*, 217 US 509 (1910).

66. Robertson, *Federalism and the Making of America*, 33. Robertson explains: "States would retain power over taxes (except on imports or exports), militias, criminal law, property, and contracts, 'corporations civil and religious,' and the creation of cities, counties, courts, schools, 'poor houses, hospitals, and houses of employment.' They could regulate vices, manage politics and elections (including elections to national office), promote their own manufactures, and build roads and canals. Within their borders, then, the state governments had power over labor (including slave labor), capital, land, natural resources, and energy – all the basic elements of a productive economy" (31–32).

67. Robertson, *Federalism and the Making of America*, 28.

68. Lou Falkner Williams, *The Great South Carolina Ku Klux Klan Trials, 1871–1872* (Athens: University of Georgia Press, 2004), 131; *US v. Hall*, 26 Federal Cases, 79–82 (1871).

69. Williams, *The Great South Carolina Ku Klux Klan Trials, 1871–1872*, 62.

70. Ian Haney Lopez, White by Law: The Legal Construction of Race (New York: New York University Press, 2006), 37; Bernard L. Fraga, *The Turnout Gap: Race, Ethnicity, and Political Inequality in a Diversifying America* (Cambridge: Cambridge University Press, 2018), 25–26.

71. *In re Rodriguez*, 81 F. 337 (WD Tex. 1897).

72. *Smith v. Turner*, 48 US 283 (1849).

73. *Chy Lung v. Freeman*, 92 US 275 (1875).

74. *Chae Chan Ping v. United States*, 130 US 581 (1889).

75. *Yick Wo v. Hopkins*, 118 US 356 (1886).

76. *Fong Yue Ting v. United States*, 149 US 698 (1893).

77. Lopez, *White by Law*, 39; Fraga, *The Turnout Gap*, 28; *In re Ah Yup* 1 F. Cas. 223 (C.C.D. Cal. 1878).

78. *United States v. Wong Kim Ark*, 169 US 649 (1898).

79. *Slaughterhouse Cases*, 83 US 36 (1873).

80. *United States v. Reese*, 92 US 214 (1876).

81. *United States v. Cruikshank*, 92 US 542 (1876).

82. James Gray Pope, "Snubbed Landmark: Why United States v. Cruikshank (1876) Belongs at the Heart of the American Constitutional Canon," *Harvard Civil Rights-Civil Liberties Law Review* 49 (2014): 385–448.

83. Valelly, *The Two Reconstructions*, 118.

84. *Civil Rights Cases*, 109 US 3 (1883).

85. *Louisville, New Orleans and Texas Railway Co. v. Mississippi*, 133 US 587 (1890); *Hall v. DeCuir*, 95 US 485 (1877).

86. *Plessy v. Ferguson*, 163 US 537 (1896).

87. *Williams v. Mississippi*, 170 US 213 (1898).

88. *Carter v. Texas*, 177 US 442 (1900) (sustaining an accused Black because the state court would not hear his witnesses to the exclusion of Blacks from a grand jury) and *Rogers v. Alabama*, 192 US 226 (1904) (sustaining an accused Black because the lower court did not examine evidence that a ban on Black voters affected

juror selection) with *Tarrance v. Florida*, 188 US 519 (1903), *Brownfield v. South Carolina*, 189 US 426 (1903), *Martin v. Texas*, 200 US 316 (1906), and *Franklin v. South Carolina*, 218 US 161 (1910) (all finding insufficient evidence of exclusion of Blacks from juries).

89. *Buchanan v. Warley*, 245 US 60 (1917).
90. *Corrigan v. Buckley*, 217 US 323 (1926).
91. *Missouri ex rel. Gaines v. Canada*, 305 US 337 (1938).
92. *Westminster School Dist. of Orange County v. Mendez*, 161 F.2d 774, at 782 (9th Cir. 1947).
93. *Sweatt v. Painter*, 339 US 629 (1950); *McLaurin v. Oklahoma State Regents for Higher Education* 339 US 637 (1950).
94. *Brown v. Board of Education of Topeka Kansas*, 347 US 443 (1954).
95. John David Smith, "Segregation and the Age of Jim Crow," in *When Did Southern Segregation Begin?*, ed. John David Smith (Boston, MA: Bedford/St. Martin's, 2002), 14.
96. Valelly, *The Two Reconstructions*, 70.
97. Michael Grossberg, *Governing the Hearth: Law and the Family in Nineteenth-Century America* (Chapel Hill: The University of North Carolina Press, 1988), 176–177, http://ebookcentral.proquest.com/lib/asulib-ebooks/detail.action?docID=475184.
98. Grossberg, *Governing the Hearth*, 192.
99. *Commonwealth v. Allison*, 227 Mass. 57 (1917).
100. Grossberg, *Governing the Hearth*, 192.
101. Alexander Keyssar, *The Right to Vote: The Contested History of Democracy in the United States* (New York: Basic Books, 2009), 149.
102. Keyssar, *The Right to Vote*, 166.
103. Keyssar, *The Right to Vote*, 170–171.
104. Kristi Andersen, *After Suffrage: Women in Partisan and Electoral Politics Before the New Deal* (Chicago, IL: University of Chicago Press, 1996); Glenda Elizabeth Gilmore, *Gender and Jim Crow, Second Edition: Women and the Politics of White Supremacy in North Carolina, 1896–1920* (Chapel Hill, NC: UNC Press Books, 2019); Ellen Carol DuBois, *Feminism and Suffrage: The Emergence of an Independent Women's Movement in America, 1848–1869* (Ithaca, NY: Cornell University Press, 1999).
105. Gilmore, *Gender and Jim Crow*.
106. Ron Hayduk, *Democracy for All: Restoring Immigrant Voting Rights in the United States* (New York: Routledge, 2012).
107. Jamin B. Raskin, "Legal Aliens, Local Citizens: The Historical, Constitutional and Theoretical Meanings of Alien Suffrage," *University of Pennsylvania Law Review* 141, no. 4 (April 1, 1993): 1395, https://doi.org/10.2307/3312345.
108. Raskin, "Legal Aliens, Local Citizens."
109. Robert K. Murray, *Red Scare: A Study in National Hysteria, 1919–1920* (Minneapolis: University of Minnesota Press, 1955).
110. Woodward, *The Strange Career of Jim Crow*, 2001, Ebook, chapter 4, 173.
111. Daniel J. Tichenor, *Dividing Lines: The Politics of Immigration Control in America*; Aristide Zolberg, *A Nation by Design* (Cambridge, MA: Harvard University Press, 2005).
112. Raskin, "Legal Aliens, Local Citizens."

113. Margo J. Anderson, *The American Census: A Social History* (New Haven, CT: Yale University Press, 1988).
114. As Anderson (1988, 157) notes, the tortured history of the 1920s apportionment debate did incorporate one significant departure from precedent, which was to allow states to malaportion seats within states. The US Supreme Court allowed the provision to stand, not finding any Constitutional or legal basis to strike it down. Only in the early 1960s, with the cases of *Baker v. Carr* (1962), *Reynolds v. Sims* (1964), and *Wesberry v. Sanders* (1964), did the Supreme Court finally enshrine the principle of "one person, one vote" that mandated the drawing of equal districts with respect to population.
115. Christopher S. Parker, *Fighting for Democracy: Black Veterans and the Struggle Against White Supremacy in the Postwar South* (Princeton, NJ: Princeton University Press, 2009), 47.
116. "AN ACT To repeal the Chinese Exclusion Acts, to establish quotas, and for other purposes" (Pub Law 78–199) (known as both the Magnuson Act of 1943 and the Chinese Exclusion Repeal Act of 1943).
117. The Luce–Celler Act of 1946 (Public Law 483).
118. The Immigration and Nationality Act of 1952 (Public Law 82–414) (known as the McCarran–Walter Act).
119. Desmond S. King, *Separate and Unequal: Black Americans and the US Federal Government* (Oxford: Clarendon Press, 1997), 40.
120. Skowronek, *Building a New American State*, 68.
121. Lieberman, *Shifting the Color Line*; Jill Quadagno, *The Color of Welfare: How Racism Undermined the War on Poverty* (Oxford: Oxford University Press, 1996); Katznelson, *When Affirmative Action Was White*; Deborah E. Ward, *The White Welfare State: The Racialization of US Welfare Policy* (Ann Arbor: University of Michigan Press, 2005); Mary Poole, *The Segregated Origins of Social Security: African Americans and the Welfare State* (Chapel Hill: University of North Carolina Press, 2006); Fox, *Three Worlds of Relief*.
122. The Wagner-Peyser Act of 1933 (Public Law 73–30).
123. Parker, *Fighting for Democracy*, 48.
124. Parker, *Fighting for Democracy*, 48.
125. Valelly, *The Two Reconstructions*.
126. *Harper v. Virginia Board of Elections*, 383 US 663 (1966).
127. King and Smith, *Still a House Divided*, 148.
128. Gulasekaram and Ramakrishnan, *The New Immigration Federalism*.
129. Paul Frymer, Black and Blue: African Americans, the Labor Movement, and the Decline of the Democratic Party (Princeton, NJ: Princeton University Press, 2011), 87–88; John David Skrentny, *After Civil Rights: Racial Realism in the New American Workplace* (Princeton, NJ: Princeton University Press, 2014).
130. John David Skrentny, *After Civil Rights: Racial Realism in the New American Workplace* (Princeton, NJ: Princeton University Press, 2014), 4.
131. 42 USC § 2000E–2(a).
132. Charles R. Epp, *The Rights Revolution: Lawyers, Activists, and Supreme Courts in Comparative Perspective* (Chicago, IL: University of Chicago Press, 1998).
133. Valelly, *The Two Reconstructions*; King and Smith, *Still a House Divided*, 170.
134. *South Carolina v. Katzenbach*, 383 US 301 (1966).
135. *South Carolina v. Katzenbach*, 383 US 301, 359–360 (1966).

136. *Katzenbach v. Morgan*, 384 US 641 (1966).
137. *White v. Regester*, 412 US 755 (1973).
138. King and Smith, *Still a House Divided*, 150.
139. *Jones v. Alfred H. Mayer Co.*, 392 US 409 (1968).
140. *Jones v. Alfred H. Mayer Co.*, 392 US 409, 411, 440 (1968).
141. King and Smith, *Still a House Divided*, 150.
142. See, e.g., *Trafficante v. Metropolitan Life Insurance Park Merced Apartments*, 409 US 205 (1972) (holding that White tenants had standing to sue because their landlords' discrimination against non-Whites deprived them of a multiracial living environment); *US v. City of Black Jack*, 508 F. 2d 1179 (1974) (holding that a zoning ordinance banning new multiple-family dwellings had a racially discriminatory effect that violated the Fair Housing Act); *Zuch v. Hussey*, 394 F. Supp. 1028 (1975) (granting injunction against realtors engaged in "blockbusting," seeking to accelerate neighborhood transitions to racial homogeneity); *Hills v. Gautreaux*, 425 US 284 (1976) (where, reinforced by briefs from the National Committee Against Discrimination in Housing, the Lawyers' Committee for Civil Rights Under Law, and the National Education Association, the Court rejected Republican solicitor general Robert Bork's argument that a remedy for discrimination in public housing by the Chicago Housing Authority could not extend to the entire metropolitan area); *Laufman v. Oakley Building and Loan*, 72 F.R.D. 116 (1976) (granting discovery request to gain evidence of "redlining" in home loans); *Dunn v. Midwestern Indemnity*, 88 F. R.D. 191 (1980) (granting discovery request for evidence of racial discrimination in homeowners' insurance).
143. *Griggs v. Duke Power Co.*, 401 US 424 (1971).
144. King and Smith, *Still a House Divided*, 108.
145. *Wards Cove Packing Co. v. Atonio*, 490 US 642 (1989).
146. Frymer, *Black and Blue*, 88.
147. Skrentny, *After Civil Rights*; John David Skrentny, *The Ironies of Affirmative Action: Politics, Culture, and Justice in America* (Chicago: University of Chicago Press, 2018).
148. *Steelworkers v. Weber*, 443 US 193 (1979).
149. King and Smith, *Still a House Divided*, 120.
150. *Fullilove v. Klutznick*, 448 US 448 (1980).
151. *Griswold v. Connecticut*, 381 US 479 (1965).
152. *Eisenstadt v. Baird*, 405 US 438 (1972).
153. *Loving v. Virginia*, 388 US 1 (1967).
154. *Pace v. Alabama*, 106 US 583 (1883).
155. *Obergefell v. Hodges*, 576 US (2015); Sarah A. Soule, "Going to the Chapel? Same-Sex Marriage Bans in the United States, 1973–2000," *Social Problems* 51, no. 4 (2004): 453–477; Caroline Beer and Victor D. Cruz-Aceves, "Extending Rights to Marginalized Minorities: Same-Sex Relationship Recognition in Mexico and the United States," *State Politics & Policy Quarterly* 18, no. 1 (2018): 3–26.
156. *Eisenstadt v. Baird*, 405 US 438 (1972).
157. *Roe v. Wade*, 410 US 113, 153 (1973).
158. *Doe v. Bolton*, 410 US 179 (1973).
159. *Weinberger v. Wiesenfeld*, 420 US 636 (1975).
160. *Stanton v. Stanton*, 421 US 7 (1975).

161. *Orr v. Orr*, 440 US 268 (1979).
162. *Planned Parenthood v. Casey*, 505 US 833 (1992).
163. *Bowers v. Hardwick*, 478 US 186 (1986).
164. *Lawrence v. Texas*, 539 US 558, 560 (2003).
165. *Lawrence v. Texas*, 539 US 558, 564–565 (2003).
166. *Regents of the University of California v. Bakke*, 438 US 265, 407 (1978).
167. Skrentny, *After Civil Rights*, 10.
168. *Grutter v. Bollinger*, 539 US 306 (2003).
169. *Gratz v. Bollinger*, 539 US 244 (2003).
170. *Schuette v. Coalition to Defend Affirmative Action*, 572 US 291 (2014).
171. Gulasekaram and Ramakrishnan, 45; *Graham v. Richardson*, 403 US 365 (1971).
172. *De Canas v. Bica*, 424 US 351 (1976).
173. Gulasekaram and Ramakrishnan, *The New Immigration Federalism*; Kitty Calavita, "California's 'Employer Sanctions' Legislation: Now You See It, Now You Don't," *Politics & Society* 12, no. 2 (June 1, 1983): 205–230, https://doi .org/10.1177/003232928301200204 (documenting the factors that led to the rise of California's AB 528 and the pressures and compromises that eventually led to its disuse and ineffectiveness); Huyen Pham, "The Private Enforcement of Immigration Laws," *Georgetown Law Journal* 96 (2008): 777–826 (noting that Connecticut, Delaware, Florida, Kansas, Maine, Massachusetts, Montana, New Hampshire, Vermont, Virginia, and Las Vegas, Nevada, all had employer sanctions schemes).
174. Gulasekaram and Ramakrishnan, *The New Immigration Federalism*, 47; *Sugarman v. Dougall*, 413 US 634 (1973).
175. Gulasekaram and Ramakrishnan, *The New Immigration Federalism*, 47; *Foley v. Connelie*, 435 US 291 (1978) (upheld a NY law barring noncitizens from becoming state troopers).
176. Gulasekaram and Ramakrishnan, *The New Immigration Federalism*, 48; *Toll v. Moreno*, 458 US 1 (1982).
177. *Plyler v. Doe*, 457 US 202 (1982).
178. Education Code Section 21.031.
179. Hiroshi Motomura, *Immigration Outside the Law* (Oxford and New York: Oxford University Press, 2014), 11.
180. *Chamber of Commerce v. Whiting*, 563 US 582 (2011).
181. *Arizona v. United States*, 567 US 387 (2012).
182. *Hoffman Plastic Compounds, Inc. v. National Labor Relations Board*, 535 US 137 (2002).
183. King and Smith, *Still a House Divided*, 124; *General Building Contractors Association, Inc. v. Pennsylvania*, 458 US 375, 382–384, 388–391, 407–418 (1982).
184. King and Smith, *Still a House Divided*, 126; *Wards Cove Packing Co. v. Atonio*, 490 US 642, 643 (1989).
185. King and Smith, *Still a House Divided*, 108, 126.
186. King and Smith, *Still a House Divided*, 126; *Richmond v. J. A. Croson Co.*, 488 US 469, 477 (1989).
187. *Metro Broadcasting, Inc. v. FCC*, 497 US 547 (1990); *Adarand Constructors, Inc. v. Peña*, 515 US 200 (1995).
188. King and Smith, *Still a House Divided*, 94; *Ricci v. DeStefano*, 557 US 2 (2009).

189. King and Smith, *Still a House Divided*, 94.

190. King and Smith, *Still a House Divided*, 95.

191. Valelly, *The Two Reconstructions*, 193–196; Keyssar, *The Right to Vote*; King and Smith, *Still a House Divided*, 171.

192. Valelly, *The Two Reconstructions*, 201.

193. Valelly, *The Two Reconstructions*, 202.

194. Valelly, *The Two Reconstructions*, 202.

195. Alan I. Abramowitz, *The Great Alignment: Race, Party Transformation, and the Rise of Donald Trump* (New Haven, CT: Yale University Press, 2018); Frymer, *Uneasy Alliances*; Ian Haney-López, *Dog Whistle Politics: How Coded Racial Appeals Have Reinvented Racism and Wrecked the Middle Class* (Oxford: Oxford University Press, 2015); Christopher N. Lasch, "Sanctuary Cities and Dog-Whistle Politics," *New England Journal on Criminal and Civil Confinement* 42 (2016): 159–190.

196. King and Smith, *Still a House Divided*, 148–149.

197. 24 CFR Part 14, Section 100.70(a).

198. King and Smith, *Still a House Divided*, 149.

199. Nancy Denton and Douglas S. Massey, *American Apartheid: Segregation and the Making of the Underclass* (Cambridge, MA: Harvard University Press, 1993), 192–198.

200. Denton and Massey, *American Apartheid*, 46.

201. King and Smith, *Still a House Divided*, 151–152.

202. *Village of Arlington Heights v. Metropolitan Housing Development Corporation*, 429 US 252 (1977).

203. King and Smith, *Still a House Divided*, 88, 114, 109.

204. *Mobile v. Bolden*, 446 US 55 (1980).

205. King and Smith, *Still a House Divided*, 175.

206. King and Smith, *Still a House Divided*, 176.

207. King and Smith, *Still a House Divided*, 176.

208. *Rogers v. Lodge*, 458 US 613, 615 (1982).

209. Justice Brennan stressed three factors aimed to prevent racially exclusionary districting that led to greater minority representation: First, a minority group had to "demonstrate that it is sufficiently large and geographically compact to constitute a majority in a single-member district." Second, it must "show that it is politically cohesive," sharing common political interests that were being thwarted. And third, it had to show "that the White majority votes sufficiently as a bloc to enable it … usually to defeat the minority's preferred candidate." *Thornburg v. Gingles*, 478 US 30, 50–51 (1986).

210. *Shaw v. Reno*, 509 US 630 (1993).

211. See *Holder v. Hall*, 512 US 874 (1994); *Miller v. Johnson*, 515 US 900 (1995); *Bush v. Vera*, 517 US 952 (1996); *Reno v. Bossier Parish School Board*, 528 US 320 (2000); *Georgia v. Ashcroft*, 539 US 461 (2003); *Bartlett v. Strickland*, 129 S. Ct. 1231 (2009).

212. *Miller v. Johnson*, 515 US 900 (1995).

213. *Shelby County v. Holder*, 570 US 529 (2013).

214. Vesla M. Weaver, "Frontlash: Race and the Development of Punitive Crime Policy," *Studies in American Political Development* 21, no. 2 (September 2007): 230, https://doi.org/10.1017/S0898588X07000211.

215. Valelly, *The Two Reconstructions*, 186–193.

216. Fraga, *The Turnout Gap*, 14.
217. King and Smith, *Still a House Divided*, 103.
218. King and Smith, *Still a House Divided*, 104.
219. Milkis and Tichenor, *Rivalry and Reform*.
220. King and Smith, *Still a House Divided*, 150–151.
221. King and Smith, *Still a House Divided*, 153.
222. John David Skrentny, *The Minority Rights Revolution* (Cambridge, MA: Harvard University Press, 2009), 340.
223. King and Smith, *Still a House Divided*, 182.
224. King and Smith, *Still a House Divided*, 159, 161, 165.

4 STATE CITIZENSHIP FOR BLACKS

1. *Dred Scott v. Sandford*, 60 US 39 (1857).
2. Indeed, Dred Scott's lawyers argued that his civil ceremony marriage to Harriet Robinson in the Wisconsin territory was tacit acceptance of his status as a free person (since slave marriages had no legal recognition) and that his daughter Eliza had been born in free territory, on a steamboat between a free state and free territory.
3. Gibson Campbell and Kay Jung, "Historical Census Statistics on Population Totals by Race, 1790 to 1990, and by Hispanic Origin, 1790 to 1990, for the United States, Regions, Divisions, and States." (Washington, DC: US Census Bureau, 2002), Table A-20.
4. *Shelby County v. Holder*, 570 US 529 (2013).
5. National Association for the Advancement of Colored People, "Criminal Justice Fact Sheet," www.naacp.org/criminal-justice-fact-sheet/, accessed November 18, 2019.
6. Odi Ofer and Nicole Zayas Fortier, *Unveiling a State-by-State Plan to End Our Mass Incarceration Crisis* (New York: American Civil Liberties Union, 2019), www.aclu.org/news/smart-justice/unveiling-a-state-by-state-plan-to-end-our-mass-incarceration-crisis/?initms_aff=nat&initms_chan=soc&utm_medium=soc&initms=191018_fb&utm_source=fb&utm_campaign&utm_content=191018&ms_aff=nat&ms_chan=soc&ms=191018_fb.
7. Paul Finkelman, Slavery and the Founders: Race and Liberty in the Age of Jefferson (Abingdon: Routledge, 2014), 17–18.
8. Brian D. Humes, Elaine K. Swift, Richard M. Valelly, Kenneth Finegold, and Evelyn C. Fink, "Representation of the Antebellum South in the House of Representatives: Measuring the Impact of the Three-Fifths Clause," in *Party, Process, and Political Change in Congress: New Perspectives on the History of Congress*, ed. David Brady and Mathew D. McCubbins (Palo Alto, CA: Stanford University Press, 2002), 452–466.
9. Edward Raymond Turner, "Slavery in Pennsylvania" (1911), Chapter V, www.gutenberg.org/files/44579/44579-h/44579-h.htm.
10. Patrick Rael, Eighty-Eight Years: The Long Death of Slavery in the United States, 1777–1865 (Athens: University of Georgia Press, 2015), 65; Edlie L. Wong, Neither Fugitive nor Free: Atlantic Slavery, Freedom Suits, and the Legal Culture of Travel (New York: New York University Press, 2009): Thomas D. Morris, *Free Men All: The Personal Liberty Laws of the North, 1780–1861* (Clark, NJ: The Lawbook Exchange, 1974).

11. Rael, *Eighty-Eight Years*, 48.

12. Rael, *Eighty-Eight Years*, 2; Alice Dana Adams, *The Neglected Period of Anti-Slavery in America, 1808–1831*, Radcliffe College Monographs, No. 14 (Gloucester, MA: Peter Smith, 1964); Arthur Zilversmit, *The First Emancipation: The Abolition of Slavery in the North* (Chicago, IL: The University of Chicago Press, 1967).

13. Philip D. Morgan and Andrew Jackson O'Shaughnessy, "The Arming Slaves in the American Revolution," in *Arming Slaves: From Classical Times to the Modern Age*, ed. Christopher Leslie Brown and Philip D. Morgan (New Haven, CT: Yale University Press, 2006), 198.

14. Rael, *Eighty-Eight Years*, 57.

15. Rael, *Eighty-Eight Years*, 57.

16. Rael, *Eighty-Eight Years*, 64.

17. Turner, "Slavery in Pennsylvania," 80–81.

18. Turner, "Slavery in Pennsylvania," 81.

19. Turner, "Slavery in Pennsylvania," 83–85.

20. Turner, "Slavery in Pennsylvania," 87.

21. Rael, Eighty-Eight Years, 63–64; "September Meeting," *Proceedings of the Massachusetts Historical Society* 10 (1868): 332.

22. Quoted in John D. Cushing, "The Cushing Court and the Abolition of Slavery in Massachusetts: More Notes on the 'Quock Walker Case,'" *American Journal of Legal History* 5, no. 3 (April 1961): 133; "The Commonwealth v. Nathaniel Jennison," *Proceedings of the Massachusetts Historical Society* 13 (1873–1875): 294.

23. Zilversmit, *The First Emancipation*.

24. Rael, *Eighty-Eight Years*, 67.

25. Patrick Rael, "The Long Death of Slavery in New York," in *Slavery in New York*, ed. Ira Berlin and Leslie Harris (New York: New Press, 2005), 122–125.

26. An Act directing the process in Habeas Corpus, Ma. Gen. Laws, March 16, 1785 § 1–13, reprinted in Laws of the Commonwealth of Massachusetts, from November 28, 1780 to February 28, 1807: With the Constitutions of the United States of America and of the Commonwealth, Prefixed, Vol. 1, 3 vols (Boston, MA: J. T. Buckingham, 1807), 236–241, https://babel.hathitrust.org/cgi/pt?id=nyp .33433008587432&view=1up&seq=7; An Act establishing the Right to, and the Form of the Writ De Homine Replegiando, or Writ for replevying a Man, Ma. Gen. Laws, February 19, 1787, reprinted in *Laws of the Commonwealth of Massachusetts, from November 28, 1780 to February 28, 1807: With the Constitutions of the United States of America and of the Commonwealth, Prefixed*, Vol. 1, 3 vols. (Boston, MA: J. T. Buckingham, 1807), 361–365; Thomas D. Morris, *Free Men All: The Personal Liberty Laws of the North, 1780–1861* (Clark, NJ: The Lawbook Exchange, 1974), 11–12.

27. Marion Gleason McDougall, *Fugitive Slaves (1619–1865)* (Boston, MA: Ginn & Company, 1891), 17.

28. Act of February 12, 1793 (1 Stat. 302); *Annals of Congress*, 2nd Cong., 2nd sess. (1793), 1414–1415.

29. *Annals of Congress*, 2nd Cong., 2nd sess. (1793), 1415.

30. Adams, *The Neglected Period of Anti-Slavery in America, 1808–1831*, 107.

31. *Penn. House Journal, 1819–1820*, 339–341, 987, 1069, 1081, 1088; *Penn. Session Laws, 1820*, 104–106; Morris, *Free Men All*, 44–45.

32. Morris, *Free Men All*, 45.
33. *Penn. House Journal, 1825–1826*, 386.
34. An Act to give effect to the provisions of the constitution of the United States, relative to fugitives from labour, for the protection of free people of color, and to prevent kidnapping, Pa. Gen. Laws, March 25, 1826 § 1–11, reprinted in John Purdon *A Digest of the Laws of Pennsylvania from the Year 1700 to the 16th Day of June, 1836*, 5th ed. (Philadelphia, PA: M'Carty & Davis, 1837), 746–749; *Penn. Session Laws, 1826*, 150–155; *Penn. Senate Journal, 1825–1826*, 339, 353–354, 466, 481, 494, 511, 516–517, 522; Morris, *Free Men All*, 46–53.
35. *Prigg v. Com. of Pennsylvania*, 41 US 539 (1842).
36. Christopher N. Lasch, "Rendition Resistance," *North Carolina Law Review* 92 (2013): 175.
37. *Prigg*, 41 US (16 Pet.) at 616.
38. Lawrence B. Goodheart, *Abolitionist, Actuary, Atheist: Elizur Wright and the Reform Impulse* (Kent, OH: Kent State University Press, 1990), 106–108.
39. Robert M. Cover, *Justice Accused: Antislavery and the Judicial Process* (New Haven, CT: Yale University Press, 1975).
40. "Great Massachusetts Petition: To the Senate and House of Representatives of the State of Massachusetts," 1842, Latimer Committee: An Electronic Archive, Massachusetts Historical Society, www.masshist.org/database/viewer.php?item_id=1683&mode=small&img_step=1; *House No. 41, Commonwealth of Massachusetts*, General Court, 1843, 1–2.
41. Bruce Laurie, *Beyond Garrison: Antislavery and Social Reform* (Cambridge and New York: Cambridge University Press, 2005), 80.
42. An Act to protect the Rights and Liberties of the People of the Commonwealth of Massachusetts, Mass. Gen. Laws ch. 0489 § 1–23 (1855), reprinted in *Acts and Resolves Passed by the General Court of Massachusetts, in the Year 1855: Together with the Messages* (Boston, MA: Secretary of the Commonwealth, 1855), 924–929; *Mass. Senate Document No. 162, 1855*; *Mass. Senate Journal, 1855*, Mass. State Library, 76: 801; *Mass. House Journal, 1855*, 77: 1710; Morris, *Free Men All*, 167–170.
43. Morris, *Free Men All*, 166; Norman L. Rosenberg, "Personal Liberty Laws and Section Crisis: 1850–1861," in *Abolitionism and American Law*, History of the American Abolitionist Movement (New York: Garland Publishing, 1999), 328.
44. Leon F. Litwack, *North of Slavery: The Negro in the Free States, 1790–1860* (Chicago, IL: University of Chicago Press, 1961), 98.
45. C. Vann Woodward, *The Strange Career of Jim Crow*, Third Revised Edition (Oxford: Oxford University Press, 1974); Howard N. Rabinowitz, "From Exclusion to Segregation: Southern Race Relations, 1865-1890," *Journal of American History* 63, no. 2 (1976): 325–350, https://doi.org/10.2307/1899640.
46. Gilbert Thomas Stephenson, "The Separation of The Races in Public Conveyances," *American Political Science Review* 3, no. 2 (1909): 180–204, https://doi.org/10.2307/1944727.
47. Litwack, *North of Slavery: The Negro in the Free States, 1790–1860*, 97.
48. Litwack, *North of Slavery*, 100.
49. Louis Ruchames, "Jim Crow Railroads in Massachusetts," *American Quarterly* 8, no. 1 (1956): 68, https://doi.org/10.2307/2710298.
50. Ruchames, "Jim Crow Railroads in Massachusetts," 72.

51. Litwack, *North of Slavery: The Negro in the Free States, 1790–1860,* 78.
52. Litwack, *North of Slavery,* 79.
53. Litwack, *North of Slavery,* 85.
54. Oh. Const. of 1802, art. IV § I, reprinted in Thorpe 1909 (Vol. 5), 2901–2913; Middleton 2005, 19–41.
55. An act to regulate black and mulatto persons, Oh. Laws, January 5, 1804; Stephen Middleton, *The Black Laws in the Old Northwest: A Documentary History,* Contributions in Afro-American and African Studies, no. 152 (Westport, CT: Greenwood Press, 1993), 15–17; Middleton, *The Black Laws,* 49–51.
56. Paul Frymer, "'A Rush and a Push and the Land Is Ours': Territorial Expansion, Land Policy, and US State Formation," *Perspectives on Politics* 12, no. 1 (March 2014): 119–144.
57. An Act to Regulate Black and Mulatto Persons, Oh. Laws, January 25, 1807; Middleton, *The Black Laws,* 17–18; Middleton, *The Black Laws,* 51–52.
58. Middleton, *The Black Laws,* 70–71.
59. An act to prevent kidnapping, Oh. Laws, February 15, 1831; Middleton, *The Black Laws,* 27; Middleton, *The Black Laws,* 52.
60. Morris, *Free Men All,* xi–xii.
61. Middleton, *The Black Laws,* 228–229.
62. Charles Wesley Mann, The Chicago Common Council and the Fugitive Slave Law of 1850: An Address Read Before the Chicago Historical Society at a Special Meeting Held January 29, 1903 (Chicago, IL: Chicago Historical Society, 1903), 85–86; Craig B. Mousin, "Clear View from the Prairie: Harold Washington and the People of Illinois Respond to Federal Encroachment of Human Rights, A," *Southern Illinois University Law Journal* 29 (2005): 285.
63. In. Const. of 1851 Art. 13 § 1, reprinted in Francis Newton Thorpe, The Federal and State Constitutions, Colonial Charters, and Other Organic Laws of the States, Territories, and Colonies, Now or Heretofore Forming the United States of America, Vol. 2 (Washington, DC: Government Printing Office, 1909), 1073–1095; Finkelman, "Prelude to the Fourteenth Amendment: Black Legal Rights in the Antebellum North," *Rutgers Law Journal* 17 (1986): 434–435; Middleton, The Black Laws, 204.
64. An act to enforce the 13th Article of the Constitution, In. Rev. Stat, June 18, 1852; Finkelman, "Prelude to the Fourteenth Amendment," 439–440; Middleton, *The Black Laws,* 204.
65. An act providing for the colonization of Negroes and mulattoes and their descendants, and appropriating 5,000 dollars thereof, constituting the State Board of Colonization, declaring the duties of said board, and of state treasurer and county treasurer in relation thereof, In. Rev. Stat, April 28, 1852 § 1–6; An act providing for the colonization of free Negroes, making appropriations thereof, and establishing a colonization agency, In. Rev. Stat, March 3, 1853 § 1–3; An act to give power to the State Board of Colonization, In. Rev. Stat, March 1, 1855 § 1–4; Middleton, *The Black Laws,* 219–221.
66. An Act to prevent the immigration of free Negroes into this state, Il. Laws, February 12, 1853 § 1–11; Finkelman, "Prelude to the Fourteenth Amendment," 435; Middleton, *The Black Laws,* 299–302.
67. Ira Berlin, *Slaves without Masters: The Free Negro in the Antebellum South* (New York: W. W. Norton, 2007).

68. Ulrich Bonnell Phillips, *American Negro Slavery; A Survey of the Supply, Employment and Control of Negro Labor as Determined by the Plantation Regime,* 1st paperback ed., Louisiana Paperbacks L9 (Baton Rouge: Louisiana State University Press, 1966); Kenneth M. Stampp, *The Peculiar Institution: Slavery in the Ante-Bellum South* (New York: Knopf, 1956); Eugene D. Genovese, *Roll, Jordan, Roll: The World the Slaves Made* (New York: Pantheon Books, 1974).

69. Martha S. Jones, *Birthright Citizens: A History of Race and Rights in Antebellum America* (Cambridge: Cambridge University Press, 2018), 25–26; James Martin Wright, *The Free Negro in Maryland, 1634–1860* (New York: Columbia University, 1921), https://catalog.hathitrust.org/Record/100159569.

70. Jones, *Birthright Citizens,* 25.

71. Jones, *Birthright Citizens,* 21–22.

72. Jones, *Birthright Citizens,* 20.

73. Jones, *Birthright Citizens,* 20.

74. Jones, *Birthright Citizens,* 74; "An ACT to Incorporate Certain Persons in Every Christian Church or Congregation in This State," Maryland Laws of 1802, chap. 111 (passed January 8, 1803).

75. Jones, *Birthright Citizens,* 74.

76. Nicholas May, "Holy Rebellion: Religious Assembly Laws in Antebellum South Carolina and Virginia," *American Journal of Legal History* 49, no. 3 (2007): 237–256; Berlin, *Slaves without Masters,* 73.

77. Jones, *Birthright Citizens,* 20; On banning in-migration of Blacks in the antebellum era, also see David A. Bateman, *Disenfranchising Democracy: Constructing the Electorate in the United States, the United Kingdom, and France* (New York: Cambridge University Press, 2018), 100–101.

78. Jones, *Birthright Citizens,* 79; "A Further Additional Supplement to the Act, Entitled, A Act Relating to the People of Colour of This State," Passed at December session, Maryland Laws of 1831, chap. 281.

79. Jones, *Birthright Citizens,* 46.

80. Jones, *Birthright Citizens,* 48.

81. Maryland Laws of 1832, chap. 323, May 14, 1832.

82. Jones, *Birthright Citizens,* 64–65. Baltimore's free Blacks became increasingly isolated after Maryland turned toward a reinforcing state citizenship in the 1830s. Local resistance offered some reprieve: to circumvent state restrictions on Black religious gatherings, in 1834 Baltimore city passed an ordinance allowing the mayor to issue legal permits authorizing Black religious gatherings. (Jones, *Birthright Citizens,* 79; Maryland Laws of 1834, chap. 160, Ordinances of the Mayor and City Council of Baltimore (Baltimore, MD: John D. Toy, 1838), 462.) Yet, as historian Barbara Fields explains, marketing, processing, the exchange of information, the purchase and sale of slaves, and the provision of food, supplies, and legal advice linked Baltimore with restrictive slavery laws in Maryland and the rest of the South (Barbara Jeanne Fields, *Slavery and Freedom on the Middle Ground: Maryland during the Nineteenth Century,* Yale Historical Publications 123 (New Haven, CT: Yale University Press, 1985), 7).

83. Jeffrey R. Brackett, *The Negro in Maryland: A Study of the Institution of Slavery* (Baltimore, MD: N. Murray, publication agent, Johns Hopkins University, 1889), 224–225. Maryland Laws of 1841, chap. 272, sections 1 and 2. *Index to the Law of*

Maryland: From the Year 1838 to the Year 1845, Inclusive (Annapolis, MD: Riley & Davis, 1846).

84. Martha S. Jones, *Leave of Court: African-American Legal Claims Making in the Era of Dred Scott v. Sandford*, ed. Manisha Sinha and Penny Von Eschen, *Contested Democracy: Politics, Ideology, and Race in American History* (New York: Columbia University Press, 2007), 59.
85. Jones, *Leave of Court*, 59; Brackett, *The Negro in Maryland*, 176.
86. Brackett, *The Negro in Maryland*, 176.
87. *Debates and Proceedings of the Maryland Reform Convention to Revise the State Constitution: To Which Are Prefixed the Bill of Rights and Constitution Adopted*, 2 vols. (Annapolis, MD: William N'Neir, 1851), 1:8.
88. Jones, *Birthright Citizens*, 93.
89. Thomas Cooper and David James McCord, eds., *The Statutes at Large of South Carolina: Containing the Acts from 1682 to 1716, Inclusive*, Vol. 2 (Columbia, SC: A. S. Johnston, 1836), 23.
90. Thomas Cooper and David James McCord, eds., *The Statutes at Large of South Carolina*, Vol. 7 (Columbia, SC: A. S. Johnston, 1836), 343.
91. Sally E. Hadden, *Slave Patrols: Law and Violence in Virginia and the Carolinas*, Harvard Historical Studies, v. 138 (Cambridge, MA: Harvard University Press, 2001), 18.
92. Cooper and McCord, *The Statutes at Large of South Carolina*, Vol. 2: 254–255.
93. Peter H. Wood, *Black Majority: Negroes in Colonial South Carolina from 1670 through the Stono Rebellion*, The Norton Library (New York: Norton, 1975), 102–103.
94. Wood, *Black Majority*, 103.
95. Hadden, *Slave Patrols*.
96. Richard C. Wade, *Slavery in the Cities; The South, 1820–1860* (New York: Oxford University Press, 1964).
97. Walter Johnson, *Soul by Soul: Life Inside the Antebellum Slave Market* (Cambridge, MA: Harvard University Press, 1999).
98. Glenn McNair, *Criminal Injustice: Slaves and Free Blacks in Georgia's Criminal Justice System* (Charlottesville: University of Virginia Press, 2009).
99. Andrew Fede, *People Without Rights: An Interpretation of the Fundamentals of the Law of Slavery in the US South*, Distinguished Studies in American Legal and Constitutional History (New York: Garland Pub, 1992); Andrew Fede, *Roadblocks to Freedom: Slavery and Manumission in the United States South* (New Orleans, LA: Quid Pro Books, 2011); James M Campbell, *Slavery on Trial: Race, Class, and Criminal Justice in Antebellum Richmond, Virginia* (Gainesville: University Press of Florida, 2007); Ariela Julie Gross, *What Blood Won't Tell: A History of Race on Trial in America* (Cambridge, MA: Harvard University Press, 2010); Ariela Julie Gross, *Double Character: Slavery and Mastery in the Antebellum Southern Courtroom* (Princeton, NJ: Princeton University Press, 2000).
100. Rael, *Eighty-Eight Years*, xvi–xvii.
101. Frederick Douglass, "What to the Slave Is the Fourth of July?," in *My Bondage and My Freedom* (New York: Miller, Orton & Mulligan, 1855), 441–445.
102. *Scott v. Sandford*, 60 US 393, 417.
103. Jones, *Leave of Court: African-American Legal Claims Making in the Era of Dred Scott v. Sandford*, 63–64; *Dredd Scott v. Sandford*, 60 US 393, 528 (1957).

104. Congress moved to limit presidential power over reconstruction by passing the Tenure of Office Act (1867), which barred Johnson from removing any appointed officers. Congress then required all military orders related to reconstruction to be issued through the general of the army, Ulysses S. Grant, who had grown loyal to their Radical cause. Tensions between the president and Congress escalated when Johnson decided in February 1868 to remove the secretary of war, Edwin M. Stanton, from his Cabinet. The House of Representatives quickly moved to impeach the president, although the Senate ultimately acquitted him after a protracted trial.

105. David N. Gellman and David Quigley, *Jim Crow New York: A Documentary History of Race and Citizenship, 1777–1877* (New York: New York University Press, 2003), 300.

106. Woodward, *The Strange Career of Jim Crow*, 2001, Ebook Chapter 1.

107. Woodward, *The Strange Career of Jim Crow*, Ebook Chapter 1.

108. John David Smith, "Segregation and the Age of Jim Crow," in When Did Southern Segregation Begin?, ed. John David Smith (Boston, MA: Bedford/St. Martin's, 2002), 13.

109. Gilbert Thomas Stephenson, "The Separation of The Races in Public Conveyances," *American Political Science Review* 3, no. 2 (1909): 180–204, https://doi.org/10.2307/1944727.

110. Woodward, *The Strange Career of Jim Crow*, Ebook Chapter 1.

111. Smith, "Segregation and the Age of Jim Crow," 13; William Cohen, *At Freedom's Edge: Black Mobility and the Southern White Quest for Racial Control, 1861–1915* (Baton Rouge: Louisiana State University Press, 1991), 213–216.

112. Joel Williamson, "The Separation of the Races," in *When Did Southern Segregation Begin?*, ed. John David Smith (Boston, MA: Bedford/St. Martin's, 2002), 78.

113. Cohen, *At Freedom's Edge*, 213–216.

114. Williamson, "The Separation of the Races," 65–66; Joel Williamson, *After Slavery: The Negro in South Carolina During Reconstruction, 1861–1877* (New York: Norton, 1975).

115. James Gray Pope, "Snubbed Landmark: Why United States v. Cruikshank (1876) Belongs at the Heart of the American Constitutional Canon," Harvard Civil Rights-Civil Liberties Law Review 49 (2014): 386.

116. Steven Hahn, *A Nation Under Our Feet: Black Political Struggles in the Rural South from Slavery to the Great Migration* (Cambridge, MA: Belknap Press of Harvard University Press, 2005), 198, 205.

117. Richard M. Valelly, *The Two Reconstructions: The Struggle for Black Enfranchisement*, American Politics and Political Economy (Chicago, IL: University of Chicago Press, 2004), 95.

118. Williamson, "The Separation of the Races," 65–66; Williamson, *After Slavery*.

119. Smith, "Segregation and the Age of Jim Crow," 14.

120. Woodward, *The Strange Career of Jim Crow*, Ebook Chapter 1.

121. Williamson, "The Separation of the Races," 67.

122. Smith, "Segregation and the Age of Jim Crow," 14.

123. Eric Foner, *Reconstruction: America's Unfinished Revolution, 1863–1877* (New York: Harper Collins, 2011), 556 (of 1998 version).

124. Lou Falkner Williams, *The Great South Carolina Ku Klux Klan Trials, 1871–1872* (Athens: University of Georgia Press, 2004), 22.

125. Williams, *The Great South Carolina Ku Klux Klan Trials, 1871–1872*, 105–106. Canada's refusal to extradite KKK members caused President Grant to send secret agents to physically remand them into US custody in 1872.

126. Gellman and Quigley, *Jim Crow New York*, 278–293.

127. Gellman and Quigley, *Jim Crow New York*, 287.

128. Gellman and Quigley, *Jim Crow New York*, 293.

129. Gellman and Quigley, *Jim Crow New York*, 302.

130. Jones, *Birthright Citizens*, 150.

131. Jones, *Birthright Citizens*, 218n9.

132. Jones, *Birthright Citizens*, 149.

133. Jones, *Birthright Citizens*, 149.

134. Jones, *Birthright Citizens*, 150.

135. Finkelman, "Prelude to the Fourteenth Amendment."

136. C. Vann Woodward, *The Strange Career of Jim Crow* (Oxford: Oxford University Press, 2001).

137. Joel Williamson, *The Crucible of Race: Black–White Relations in the American South since Emancipation* (Oxford: Oxford University Press, 1984), 492–493.

138. Valelly, *The Two Reconstructions*, 47.

139. Edward L. Ayers, *The Promise of the New South: Life after Reconstruction* (New York: Oxford University Press, 2007), 8, http://ebookcentral.proquest.com /lib/asulib-ebooks/detail.action?docID=430642.

140. Robert Mickey, *Paths Out of Dixie: The Democratization of Authoritarian Enclaves in America's Deep South, 1944–1972* (Princeton, NJ: Princeton University Press, 2015), 39.

141. *Slaughterhouse Cases*, 83 US 36 (1873).

142. *United States v. Cruikshank*, 92 US 542 (1876).

143. Pope, "Snubbed Landmark."

144. *United States v. Reese*, 92 US 214 (1876).

145. Pope, "Snubbed Landmark," 399. As historian Steven Hahn explains, "White Leaguers surely recognized that the federal government was losing interest in interfering in southern politics and sustaining Republican regimes by military means. But they also responded to the growing assertiveness of African Americans within the Republican party, which showed itself in the rising incidence of black officeholding" (Hahn, *A Nation Under Our Feet*, 296).

146. *Civil Rights Cases*, 109 US 3 (1883).

147. *Plessy v Ferguson*, 163 US 537, 551 (1896).

148. *Plessy v Ferguson*, 163 US 537, 552 (1896).

149. John David Smith, "Segregation and the Age of Jim Crow," in *When Did Southern Segregation Begin?*, edited by John David Smith, 3–42 (Boston, MA: Bedford/St. Martin's, 2002).

150. Michal R. Belknap, *Federal Law and Southern Order: Racial Violence and Constitutional Conflict in the Post-Brown South* (Athens: University of Georgia Press, 1987), 5.

151. Valelly, *The Two Reconstructions*, 144.

152. Cohen, *At Freedom's Edge*, Table 9, p. 211.

153. Ida B. Wells, *Crusade for Justice: The Autobiography of Ida B. Wells* (Chicago: University of Chicago Press, 1970); Patricia A. Schechter, *Ida B. Wells-Barnett and American Reform, 1880–1930*. Chapel Hill: The University of North Carolina Press, 2001.
154. Megan Ming Francis, *Civil Rights and the Making of the Modern American State* (Cambridge: Cambridge University Press, 2014), 3. Francis also explains: "Though a number of important figures and organizations came before the NAACP was established to champion the issue of racial violence (e.g., Ida B. Wells's Antilynching League, The Niagara Movement, Monroe Trotter's National Equal Rights League, T. Thomas Fortune, John Milhollands's Constitution League), they were unable to penetrate any branch of the federal government" (25).
155. Belknap, *Federal Law and Southern Order*, 18.
156. Keith M. Finley, *Delaying the Dream: Southern Senators and the Fight against Civil Rights, 1938–1965* (Baton Rouge: Louisiana State University Press, 2010), 26–27.
157. Belknap, *Federal Law and Southern Order*, 19–20.
158. C. Vann Woodward, *The Strange Career of Jim Crow*, Third Revised Edition (Oxford: Oxford University Press, 1974), 130–131.
159. Belknap, *Federal Law and Southern Order*, 24.
160. Francis, *Civil Rights and the Making of the Modern American State*, 2.
161. Francis, *Civil Rights and the Making of the Modern American State*, 2. *Moore v. Dempsey* 261 US 86 (1923).
162. *Powell v. Alabama* 287 US 45 (1932); *Hollins v. Oklahoma* 295 US 394 (1935); *Brown v. Mississippi* 297 US 278 (1936).
163. *Chambers v. Florida* 309 US 227 (1940).
164. *Smith v. Allwright*, 321 US 649 (1944); *Shelley v. Kraemer*, 334 US 1 (1948); *Sweatt v. Painter*, 339 US 629 (1950); *McLaurin v. Oklahoma State Regents*, 339 US 637 (1950); *Brown v. Board of Education of Topeka*, 347 US 483 (1954).
165. Aldon D. Morris, *The Origins of the Civil Rights Movement* (New York: The Free Press, 1984), 48.
166. Morris, *The Origins of the Civil Rights Movement*, 4.
167. *Morgan v. Virginia*, 328 US 373 (1946).
168. *Henderson v. United States*, 339 US 816 (1950).
169. *Brown v. Board of Education of Topeka*, 347 US 483 (1954).
170. *Boynton v. Virginia*, 364 US 454 (1960).
171. Morris, *The Origins of the Civil Rights Movement*, 54–55.
172. Morris, *The Origins of the Civil Rights Movement*, 57.
173. *Gayle v. Browder*, 352 US 903 (1956).
174. Morris, *The Origins of the Civil Rights Movement*, 65.
175. Morris, *The Origins of the Civil Rights Movement*, 69–70, 72.
176. Aldon Morris explains the historical significance of SCLC, noting: "The SCLC leaders, educated in black colleges, had learned about the great black protest leaders of the past – Denmark Vesey, Nat Turner, Sojourner Truth, Frederick Douglass, Booker T. Washington, Harriet Tubman, and W. E. B. DuBois – and about the [protest] tradition they spearheaded" (Morris, *The Origins of the Civil Rights Movement*, 94).
177. Morris, *The Origins of the Civil Rights Movement*, 88.
178. Woodward, *The Strange Career of Jim Crow*, Ebook Chapter 2 (93).

179. J. Morgan Kousser, *The Shaping of Southern Politics: Suffrage Restriction and the Establishment of the One-Party South, 1880–1910* (New Haven, CT: Yale University Press, 1974), 140.

180. Valelly, *The Two Reconstructions*, 124.

181. Kousser, *The Shaping of Southern Politics*, 140.

182. Kousser, *The Shaping of Southern Politics*, 143.

183. C. W. H. III, "Federal Legislation to Safeguard Voting Rights: The Civil Rights Act of 1960," *Virginia Law Review* 46, no. 5 (1960): 953, https://doi.org/10.2307/1070567.

184. Alexander Keyssar, *The Right to Vote*: The Contested History of Democracy in the United States (New York: Basic Books, 2009), 86–89.

185. Valelly, *The Two Reconstructions*, 131.

186. Valelly, *The Two Reconstructions*, 124. Kousser explains that Black Belt Democrats in Alabama long debated adopting Tennessee (statutory) or Mississippi's (constitutional) restrictions, choosing the later in 1901 (Kousser, *The Shaping of Southern Politics*, 132).

187. W. E. B. du Bois, "Some Efforts of American Negroes For Their Own Social Betterment. Report of an Investigation under the Direction of Atlanta University; Together with the Proceedings of the Third Conference for the Study of the Negro Problems, Held at Atlanta University, May 25–26, 1898" (Atlanta: Atlanta University Press, 1898), https://docsouth.unc.edu/church/duboisau/menu.html.

188. Kousser, *The Shaping of Southern Politics*, 210.

189. Kousser, *The Shaping of Southern Politics*, 210.

190. Alan Sverdlik, "Savannah Tribune," *New Georgia Encyclopedia* (blog), June 8, 2018, www.georgiaencyclopedia.org/articles/arts-culture/savannah-tribune.

191. Ruth Currie McDaniel, "Black Power in Georgia: William A. Pledger and the Takeover of the Republican Party," *Georgia Historical Quarterly* 62, no. 3 (1978): 232–233.

192. Kousser, *The Shaping of Southern Politics*, 211.

193. McDaniel, "Black Power in Georgia," 236.

194. Kousser, *The Shaping of Southern Politics*, 217–221.

195. Mickey, "The Beginning of the End for Authoritarian Rule in America: Smith v. Allwright and the Abolition of the White Primary in the Deep South, 1944–1948," *Studies in American Political Development* 22, no. 2 (September 2008): 148, https://doi.org/10.1017/S0898588X08000096; Kousser, *The Shaping of Southern Politics*, 72–82.

196. Keyssar, *The Right to Vote*, 171.

197. Frymer, *Uneasy Alliances*.

198. Keyssar, *The Right to Vote*, 94–138; Ron Hayduk, *Democracy for All*: Restoring Immigrant Voting Rights in the United States (New York: Routledge, 2012).

199. Keyssar, *The Right to Vote*, 138.

200. Valelly, *The Two Reconstructions*, 141.

201. *Guinn v. United States*, 238 US 347 (1915).

202. Valelly, *The Two Reconstructions*, 141.

203. Keyssar, *The Right to Vote*, 91.

204. *Breedlove v. Suttles*, 302 US 277 (1937).

205. *Smith v. Allwright*, 321 US 649 (1944).

206. *Nixon v. Herndon*, 273 US 536 (1927).

207. *Grovey v. Townsend*, 295 US 45 (1935).
208. Finley, *Delaying the Dream*, 59–60.
209. Finley, *Delaying the Dream*, 62.
210. Nancy Denton and Douglas S. Massey, *American Apartheid: Segregation and the Making of the Underclass* (Cambridge, MA: Harvard University Press, 1993), 28–29.
211. Denton and Massey, *American Apartheid*, 28.
212. Denton and Massey, *American Apartheid*, 29.
213. Desmond S. King, *Separate and Unequal: Black Americans and the US Federal Government* (Oxford: Clarendon Press, 1997), 8.
214. Denton and Massey, *American Apartheid*, 28.
215. David A. Bateman, Ira Katznelson, and John S. Lapinski. *Southern Nation: Congress and White Supremacy after Reconstruction* (Princeton, NJ: Princeton University Press, 2018), 264–322.
216. King, *Separate and Unequal*, 40.
217. Skowronek, *Building a New American State*: The Expansion of National Administrative Capacities, 1877–1920 (Cambridge and New York: Cambridge University Press, 1982), 68.
218. King, *Separate and Unequal*, 46.
219. King, *Separate and Unequal*, 46.
220. King, *Separate and Unequal*, 20–21.
221. King, *Separate and Unequal*, 48.
222. King, *Separate and Unequal*, 10.
223. Ira Katznelson, *When Affirmative Action Was White*: An Untold History of Racial Inequality in Twentieth-Century America (New York: W. W. Norton, 2006).
224. King, *Separate and Unequal*, 51.
225. Valelly, *The Two Reconstructions*, 147.
226. King, *Separate and Unequal*, 96.
227. King, *Separate and Unequal*, 182.
228. King, *Separate and Unequal*, 78–79.
229. King, *Separate and Unequal*, 182.
230. King, *Separate and Unequal*, 176.
231. King, *Separate and Unequal*, 78.
232. King, *Separate and Unequal*, 121.
233. Harvard Sitkoff, "Racial Militancy and Interracial Violence in the Second World War," *Journal of American History* 58, no. 3 (1971): 661, https://doi.org/10.2307/1893729.
234. King, *Separate and Unequal*, 34.
235. King, *Separate and Unequal*, 32.
236. King, *Separate and Unequal*, 32.
237. King, *Separate and Unequal*, 114.
238. King, *Separate and Unequal*, 114.
239. King, *Separate and Unequal*, 61.
240. V. O. Key, *Politics, Parties and Interest Groups*, 3rd ed. (New York: Thomas Y. Crowell Co., 1952), 136.
241. King, *Separate and Unequal*, 88.
242. King, *Separate and Unequal*, 182.
243. King, *Separate and Unequal*, 188.

244. King, *Separate and Unequal*, 185.
245. King, *Separate and Unequal*, 24.
246. King, *Separate and Unequal*, 70-80.
247. King, *Separate and Unequal*, 200.
248. *Buchanan v. Warley*, 245 US 60 (1917).
249. *Harmon v. Tyler*, 273 US 668 (1927).
250. Michael Jones-Correa, "The Origins and Diffusion of Racial Restrictive Covenants," *Political Science Quarterly* 115, no. 4 (2000): 544, https://doi.org/10.2307/2657609; Example of a racial covenant: "In consideration of the premises and the sum of five dollars ($5.00) each to the other in hand paid, the parties hereto do hereby mutually covenant, promise, and agree each to the other, and for their respective heirs and assigns, that no part of the land now owned by the parties hereto, a more detailed description of said property, being given after the respective signatures hereto, shall ever be used or occupied by, or sold, conveyed, leased, rented, or given to, Negroes, or any person or persons of the Negro race or blood. This covenant shall run with the land and bind the respective heirs and assigns of the parties hereto for the period of twenty-one (21) years from and after the date of these presents" (*Corrigan v. Buckley* 299 F. 899; US App. (1924); 55 App. D.C. 30).
251. Jones-Correa, "The Origins and Diffusion of Racial Restrictive Covenants," 551.
252. Jones-Correa, "The Origins and Diffusion of Racial Restrictive Covenants," 545–547.
253. Jones-Correa, "The Origins and Diffusion of Racial Restrictive Covenants," 544.
254. *Corrigan v. Buckley* 271 US 323 (1926) (quoted in Jones-Correa, "The Origins and Diffusion of Racial Restrictive Covenants," 544).
255. Jones-Correa, "The Origins and Diffusion of Racial Restrictive Covenants," 563.
256. King, *Separate and Unequal*, 189.
257. US Commission on Civil Rights, "Understanding Fair Housing," Clearinghouse Publication (Washington, DC: US Government Printing Office, February 1973).
258. *Shelley v. Kraemer*, 334 US 1 (1948).
259. King, *Separate and Unequal*, 194.
260. King, *Separate and Unequal*, 194.
261. Williamson, *After Slavery*.
262. Andrew Koppelman, "The Miscegenation Analogy: Sodomy Law as Sex Discrimination," *Yale Law Journal* 98, no. 1 (1988): 150, https://doi.org/10.2307/796648; *Pace v. Alabama*, 106 US 583 (1883).
263. *Missouri ex rel. Gaines v. Canada* 305 US 337 (1938).
264. *Westminster School Dist. of Orange County v. Mendez*, 161 F.2d 774, at 782 (9th Cir. 1947).
265. *Sweatt v. Painter* 339 US 629 (1950); *McLaurin v. Oklahoma State Regents for Higher Education*, 339 US 637 (1950).
266. *Brown v. Board of Education of Topeka Kansas*, 347 US 443 (1954).
267. *Harper v. Virginia Board of Elections*, 383 US 663 (1966)
268. Koppelman, "The Miscegenation Analogy," 151; *McLaughlin v. Florida*, 379 US 184 (1964).
269. *Loving v. Virginia*, 388 US 1 (1967).
270. *Bowers v. Hardwick*, 478 US 186 (1986).
271. *Shelby County v. Holder*, 570 US 529 (2013).

272. Valelly, *The Two Reconstructions*; King and Smith, *Still a House Divided*, 170.
273. *South Carolina v. Katzenbach*, 383 US 301 (1966).
274. *Katzenbach v. Morgan*, 384 US 641 (1966).
275. *White v. Regester*, 412 US 755 (1973).
276. Bernard L. Fraga, *The Turnout Gap: Race, Ethnicity, and Political Inequality in a Diversifying America* (Cambridge: Cambridge University Press, 2018), 32–33; 42 USC § 1973aa–1a(b) (1976) (S 203(b) of Act).
277. *Mobile v. Bolden*, 446 US 55 (1980).
278. Fraga, *The Turnout Gap*, 177; *Crawford v. Marion County Election Board*, 553 US 181 (2008).
279. Jeremy Duda, "Few Voters Use Federal-Only Ballots," *Arizona Mirror*, January 1, 2019, www.azmirror.com/blog/few-voters-use-federal-only-ballots/; Staff and Wire Reports, "US Supreme Court Won't Review Kansas, Arizona Voter Registration Appeal, Leaving in Place Two-Tier Voting System," *Topeka Capital-Journal*, June 29, 2015, www.cjonline.com/article/20150629/NEWS/306299738.
280. Rebecca Beitsch, "'Proof of Citizenship' Voting Laws May Surge Under Trump," Pew Charitable Trusts, *Stateline* (blog), November 16, 2017, http://pew.org /2zKkGDN.
281. Tomas Lopez, "'Shelby County': One Year Later," Brennan Center for Justice, 2014, www.brennancenter.org/our-work/research-reports/shelby-county-one-year-later.
282. Lopez, "'Shelby County'"; Ari Berman, *Give Us the Ballot: The Modern Struggle for Voting Rights in America* (New York: Farrar, Straus and Giroux, 2015), 294.
283. Fraga, *The Turnout Gap*, 185.
284. Molly Olmstead, "Georgia Is Purging Voter Rolls Again," *Slate*, October 30, 2019, https://slate.com/news-and-politics/2019/10/georgia-election-purge-voter-rolls.html.
285. Andy Sullivan, "Southern US States Have Closed 1,200 Polling Places in Recent Years: Rights Group," Reuters, September 10, 2019, www.reuters.com/article/us-usa-election-locations-idUSKCN1VV09J.
286. Fraga, *The Turnout Gap*, 173.
287. Fraga, *The Turnout Gap*, 191.
288. Danielle Root and Liz Kennedy, "Increasing Voter Participation in America" (Center for American Progress, July 11, 2018), www.americanprogress.org/issues/democracy/reports/2018/07/11/453319/increasing-voter-participation-america/; John Myers, "Californians Can Register to Vote on Election Day at Any Polling Place under New Law," *Los Angeles Times*, October 9, 2019, www.latimes.com/california/story/2019-10-08/californians-register-to-vote-any-polling-place-2020-new-law.
289. John Wildermuth, "California Hits Highest Voter Totals Since 1952, and Dems Are Way Out in Front," *San Francisco Chronicle*, November 7, 2019, www.sfchronicle.com/politics/article/California-hits-highest-voter-totals-since-1952-14818066.php.
290. Vesla M. Weaver, "Frontlash: Race and the Development of Punitive Crime Policy," Studies in American Political Development 21, no. 2 (September 2007): 230, https://doi.org/10.1017/S0898588X07000211.
291. Weaver, "Frontlash," 230.
292. Frank R. Baumgartner, Derek A. Epp, and Kelsey Shoub, *Suspect Citizens: What 20 Million Traffic Stops Tell Us About Policing and Race* (New York: Cambridge University Press, 2018); Joe Soss and Vesla Weaver, "Police Are

Our Government: Politics, Political Science, and the Policing of Race–Class Subjugated Communities," *Annual Review of Political Science* 20, no. 1 (2017): 565–591, https://doi.org/10.1146/annurev-polisci-060415-093825; Amy E. Lerman and Vesla M. Weaver, *Arresting Citizenship: The Democratic Consequences of American Crime Control* (Chicago, IL: University of Chicago Press, 2014); Charles R. Epp, Steven Maynard-Moody, and Donald P. Haider-Markel, *Pulled Over: How Police Stops Define Race and Citizenship* (Chicago, IL: University of Chicago Press, 2014); Amy E. Lerman and Vesla Weaver, "Staying out of Sight? Concentrated Policing and Local Political Action," *ANNALS of the American Academy of Political and Social Science* 651, no. 1 (January 1, 2014): 202–219, https://doi.org/10.1177/0002716213503085; Vesla M. Weaver and Amy E. Lerman, "Political Consequences of the Carceral State," *American Political Science Review* 104, no. 4 (November 2010): 817–833, https://doi.org/10.1017/S0003055410000456; Michelle Alexander, *The New Jim Crow: Mass Incarceration in the Age of Colorblindness*, Revised Edition (New York and Jackson, TN: New Press, 2012); Murakawa, Naomi. *First Civil Right: How Liberals Built Prison America* (New York: Oxford University Press, 2014); Marie Gottschalk, *Caught: The Prison State and the Lockdown of American Politics* (Princeton, NJ: Princeton University Press, 2014).

293. National Association for the Advancement of Colored People, "Criminal Justice Fact Sheet."

294. *Batson v. Kentucky*, 476 US 79 (1986).

295. Michelle Alexander, *The New Jim Crow*, Revised Edition (New York: The New Press, 2012), 193.

296. Wendy Sawyer and Peter Wagner, "Mass Incarceration: The Whole Pie 2019," *Prison Policy Initiative* (blog), March 19, 2019, www.prisonpolicy.org/reports/pie2019.html.

297. *Floyd v. City of NY*, 959 F. Supp. 2d 540 (2013).

298. Andrew Gelman, Jeffrey Fagan, and Alex Kiss, "An Analysis of the New York City Police Department's 'Stop-and-Frisk' Policy in the Context of Claims of Racial Bias," *Journal of the American Statistical Association* 102, no. 479 (September 1, 2007): 813–823, https://doi.org/10.1198/016214506000001040.

299. Ofer and Fortier, *Unveiling a State-by-State Plan to End Our Mass Incarceration Crisis*.

300. Beth Avery, "Ban the Box: US Cities, Counties, and States Adopt Fair Hiring Policies," *National Employment Law Project* (blog), accessed November 19, 2019, www.nelp.org/publication/ban-the-box-fair-chance-hiring-state-and-local-guide/.

301. Avery, "Ban the Box."

302. *Brown v. Plata*, 563 US 493 (2011).

303. Tim Arango, "In California, Criminal Justice Reform Offers a Lesson for the Nation," *New York Times*, January 21, 2019, sec. US, www.nytimes.com/2019/01/21/us/california-incarceration-reduction-penalties.html; Charlotte West, "As Newsom Rethinks Juvenile Justice, California Reconsiders Prison for Kids," *CalMatters* (blog), June 13, 2019, https://calmatters.org/justice/2019/06/california-juvenile-justice-system-gavin-newsom/; Dana Goodyear, "How Far Will California Take Criminal-Justice Reform?," *New Yorker*, October 5,

2019, www.newyorker.com/news/california-chronicles/how-far-will-california-take-criminal-justice-reform.

304. Gabrielle Canon, "Once Known for 'Three Strikes' Law, California Is Now Embracing Criminal Justice Reform," *USA Today*, September 18, 2019, www.usatoday.com/story/news/politics/2019/09/18/about-californias-criminal-justice-reform-bills/2353853001/.

305. "California Will Allow up to 4,000 Nonviolent Third-Strike Criminals with Life Sentences to Seek Parole," *Los Angeles Times*, October 18, 2018, www.latimes.com/local/california/la-me-california-three-strikes-prop-57-20181018-story.html; Arango, "In California, Criminal Justice Reform Offers a Lesson for the Nation"; Thomas Fuller, "Californians Legalize Marijuana in Vote That Could Echo Nationally," *New York Times*, November 9, 2016, sec. US, www.nytimes.com/2016/11/09/us/politics/marijuana-legalization.html; Dennis Romero, "New Law Says Employers Can't Ask Applicants About Criminal Past," *LA Weekly*, October 17, 2017, www.laweekly.com/new-law-says-employers-cant-ask-applicants-about-criminal-past/.

5 WORST TO FIRST

1. Jazmine Ulloa, "California Becomes 'Sanctuary State' in Rebuke of Trump Immigration Policy," *Los Angeles Times*, October 5, 2017, www.latimes.com/politics/la-pol-ca-brown-california-sanctuary-state-bill-20171005-story.html.

2. Madison Park, "California's Senate Passes Sanctuary State Bill," CNN.com, April 4, 2017, www.cnn.com/2017/04/04/politics/california-sanctuary-state-bill-sb-54/index.html.

3. Kristine Phillips, "In Message of Defiance to Trump, Lawmakers Vote to Make California a Sanctuary State," *Washington Post*, September 16, 2017, sec. Politics, www.washingtonpost.com/news/politics/wp/2017/09/16/in-message-of-defiance-to-trump-lawmakers-vote-to-make-california-a-sanctuary-state/.

4. Esther Yu Hsi Lee, "California Sends Strong Rebuke to Trump Administration, Becomes 'Sanctuary State,'" October 5, 2017, https://thinkprogress.org/california-passes-sanctuary-state-law-79164e77783a/.

5. Rob Hayes, "Trump Policies Spurring 'Sanctuary State Bill' on in CA," *ABC7 Los Angeles*, June 20, 2017, http://abc7.com/2124312/.

6. Jazmine Ulloa, "How California's Trust Act Shaped the Debate on the New 'Sanctuary State' Proposal," latimes.com, accessed February 19, 2018, www.latimes.com/politics/la-pol-ca-trust-act-sanctuary-state-immigration-20170910-htmlstory.html; Ulloa, "California Becomes 'Sanctuary State' in Rebuke of Trump Immigration Policy."

7. Kate Linthicum, "Obama Ends Secure Communities Program as Part of Immigration Action," latimes.com, accessed February 19, 2018, www.latimes.com/local/california/la-me-1121-immigration-justice-20141121-story.html.

8. We build on the established literature in immigration federalism that accounts partisanship's role in explaining restrictive and integrationist approaches to state- and local-level immigration policies, adding the role of both social movements and federalism dynamics as essential for explaining the timing and overall spread of state laws. Importantly, and building on the partisanship arguments in immigration

federalism, our argument challenges demographic explanations of state policymaking in the immigration context. See Pratheepan Gulasekaram, and S. Karthick Ramakrishnan, *The New Immigration Federalism* (New York: Cambridge University Press, 2015); Alexandra Filindra, "Is 'Threat' in the Eye of the Researcher? Theory and Measurement in the Study of State-Level Immigration Policymaking," *Policy Studies Journal* 47, no. 3 (2019): 517–543, https://doi.org/10.1111/psj.12264; Adam M. Butz and Jason E. Kehrberg, "Anti-Immigrant Sentiment and the Adoption of State Immigration Policy." *Policy Studies Journal* 47, no. 3 (2019): 605–623, https://doi.org/10.1111/psj .12326; Joshua N. Zingher, "The Ideological and Electoral Determinants of Laws Targeting Undocumented Migrants in the U.S. States," *State Politics & Policy Quarterly* 14, no. 1 (March 1, 2014): 90–117, https://doi.org/10.1177 /1532440014524212; James E. Monogan, "The Politics of Immigrant Policy in the 50 US States, 2005–2011," *Journal of Public Policy* 33, no. 1 (April 2013): 35–64, https://doi.org/10.1017/S0143814X12000189; Jill Nicholson-Crotty and Sean Nicholson-Crotty, "Industry Strength and Immigrant Policy in the American States," *Political Research Quarterly* 64, no. 3 (2011): 612–624; Graeme Boushey and Adam Luedtke, "Immigrants across the U.S. Federal Laboratory: Explaining State-Level Innovation in Immigration Policy," *State Politics & Policy Quarterly* 11, no. 4 (December 1, 2011): 390–414, https://doi .org/10.1177/1532440011419286; Timothy Marquez and Scot Schraufnagel, "Hispanic Population Growth and State Immigration Policy: An Analysis of Restriction (2008–12)," *Publius: The Journal of Federalism* 43, no. 3 (July 1, 2013): 347–367, https://doi.org/10.1093/publius/pjt008; Vickie D. Ybarra, Lisa M. Sanchez, and Gabriel R. Sanchez, "Anti-Immigrant Anxieties in State Policy: The Great Recession and Punitive Immigration Policy in the American States, 2005–2012," *State Politics & Policy Quarterly*, September 28, 2015, https://doi.org/10.1177/1532440015605815.

9. State of California Office of Historic Preservation, ed., *Five Views: An Ethnic Sites Survey of California* (Sacramento: State of California – the Resources Agency, Department of Parks and Recreation, Office of Historic Preservation, 1988).

10. Governor Peter H. Burnett, "State of the State Address," December 21, 1849, http://governors.library.ca.gov/addresses/s_01-Burnett1.html.

11. Rudolph M. Lapp, *Blacks in Gold Rush California* (New Haven, CT: Yale University Press, 1977).

12. Sylvia Alden Roberts, *Mining for Freedom: Black History Meets the California Gold Rush* (Bloomington, IN: iUniverse, 2008), 6.

13. Lapp, *Blacks in Gold Rush California*, 13.

14. Lapp, *Blacks in Gold Rush California*, 16.

15. A quote from Oliver Wozencraft, taken from J. Ross Browne, "Report of the Debates of the Counties of California, on the Formation of the State Constitution, in September and October, 1849," (Washington, 1850), 137–147.

16. Lapp, *Blacks in Gold Rush California*, 130.

17. State of California Office of Historic Preservation, ed., *Five Views*, 64.

18. Roberts, *Mining for Freedom*, 12.

19. A map of these Black mining sites was prepared by Joe Moore for the National Park Service. See Roberts, *Mining for Freedom*, 19.

20. Lapp, *Blacks in Gold Rush California*, 22.

21. Benjamin Madley, *An American Genocide: The United States and the California Indian Catastrophe, 1846–1873* (New Haven, CT: Yale University Press, 2016), chapter 5, 4.
22. Thomas E. Breckinridge, *Thomas E. Breckenridge Memoirs*, Western Historical Manuscripts Collection (Columbia: University of Missouri at Columbia, n. d.), 55.
23. Madley, *An American Genocide: The United States and the California Indian Catastrophe, 1846–1873*, E-book chapter 5.
24. Madley, An American Genocide, E-book chapter 5.
25. Madley, *An American Genocide*, E-book chapter 5.
26. California Act of Admission, 9 Stat. 452 (1850).
27. An Act for the Government and Protection of Indians, Act of April 22, 1850, ch. 133, *SC*, at 408–410.
28. Kimberly Johnston-Dodds, "Early California Laws and Policies Related to California Indians," *California State Library, California Research Bureau Reports*, CRB02-014, 2002, 1, https://digitalcommons.csumb.edu/hornbeck_usa_3_d/34.
29. Johnston-Dodds, "Early California Laws and Policies Related to California Indians," 6.
30. Madley, *An American Genocide*, E-book chapter 5.
31. Jack Norton, *Genocide in Northwestern California: When Our Worlds Cried* (San Francisco, CA: Indian Historian Press, 1979).
32. State of California Office of Historic Preservation (ed.), *Five Views*, 209.
33. State of California Office of Historic Preservation (ed.), *Five Views*, 209.
34. Maria E. Montoya, *Translating Property: The Maxwell Land Grant and the Conflict over Land in the American West, 1840–1900* (Lawrence: University Press of Kansas, 2002), 157–190; see Laura E. Gómez, "Race, Colonialism, and Criminal Law: Mexicans and the American Criminal Justice System in Territorial New Mexico," *Law & Society Review* 34, no. 4 (2000): 1132, who states: "In California, European-Americans succeeded in disenfranchising Mexicans and Indians fairly quickly [after the 1848 treaty], but Mexicans in New Mexico dominated legislatures and constitutional conventions in the postwar era." Also see Martha Menchaca, "Chicano Indianism: A Historical Account of Racial Repression in the United States," *American Ethnologist* 20, no. 3 (1993): 583–603. Paul Frymer, "Building an American Empire: Territorial Expansion in the Antebellum Era," *UC Irvine Law Review* 1 (2011): 947, states: "Land commissioners were created by the federal government on a number of occasions – such as in the aftermath of the Mexican-American War for the purpose of adjudicating disputes between indigenous and settler rights in new territories. As mentioned earlier, these commissions tended to bias their findings toward American settlers."
35. Richard Griswold del Castillo, *The Treaty of Guadalupe Hidalgo: A Legacy of Conflict* (Norman: University of Oklahoma Press, 1992), 69–72; Gulasekaram and Ramakrishnan, *The New Immigration Federalism*, 19; Martha Menchaca, *The Mexican Outsiders: A Community History of Marginalization and Discrimination in California* (Austin: University of Texas Press, 2010); Natalia Molina, *How Race Is Made in America: Immigration, Citizenship, and the Historical Power of Racial Scripts* (Berkeley: University of California Press, 2014), 26.
36. Laura E. Gómez, Manifest Destinies: The Making of the Mexican American Race (New York: New York University Press, 2007); Miroslava Chavez-Garcia,

Negotiating Conquest: Gender and Power in California, 1770s to 1880s (Tucson: University of Arizona Press, 2004); William Deverell, *Whitewashed Adobe: The Rise of Los Angeles and the Remaking of Its Mexican Past* (Berkeley: University of California Press, 2004); Martha Menchaca, *The Mexican Outsiders: A Community History of Marginalization and Discrimination in California* (Austin: University of Texas Press, 2010). For the history of territorial conquest, or land and property ownership in California, see Lisbeth Haas, *Conquests and Historical Identities in California, 1769–1936* (Berkeley: University of California Press, 1995).

37. Deverell, *Whitewashed Adobe*, Chapter 1.
38. Gómez, *Manifest Destinies*. For a good review of the literature on Mexican's racial status after 1848, see Molina, *How Race Is Made in America*, 24–28.
39. An Act for the Better Regulation of the Mines and the Government of Foreign Miners, Act of April 13, 1850, ch. 97, *SC*, at 221–23; *Alta California*, April 5, 1850. The bill in its final form would call for a $20 monthly tax.
40. State of California, *Journal of the Assembly*, 1st sess. (1849/50), 1147, 1165; State of California, *Journal of the Senate*, 1st sess. (1849/50), 257–258; Act of April 13, 1850, ch. 97, *SC*, at 221–223.
41. Stacey L. Smith, *Freedom's Frontier: California and the Struggle over Unfree Labor, Emancipation, and Reconstruction* (Chapel Hill: The University of North Carolina Press, 2013), 87.
42. For the debates over federal mineral lands and the status of foreigners working on them, see State of California, *Journal of the Assembly*, 1st sess. (1849/50), 802–817; and *Congressional Globe*, 31st Cong., 1st sess., 1850, appendix, 1362–1373.
43. State of California Office of Historic Preservation, ed., *Five Views*, 210.
44. Smith, *Freedom's Frontier*, 93.
45. *The People, ex. rel. The Attorney General v. Naglee*, 1 Cal. 232 (1850).
46. An Act to Repeal an Act for the Better Regulation of the Mines, and the Government of Foreign Miners, Act of March 14, 1851, ch. 108, *SC*, at 424.
47. Steven Bender, *Greasers and Gringos: Latinos, Law, and the American Imagination* (New York: New York University Press, 2003).
48. 1855 Cal. Stat. ch 175 § 1.
49. 1855 Cal. Stat. ch 175 § 1.
50. Smith, *Freedom's Frontier*, 80.
51. Charles J. McClain Jr., "The Chinese Struggle for Civil Rights in Nineteenth Century America: The First Phase, 1850–1870," *California Law Review* 72 (1984): 535.
52. McClain, "The Chinese Struggle for Civil Rights in Nineteenth Century America," 536–537.
53. Assembly Commission on Mines and Mining Interests, Report, Cal. Assembly, 3d Sess., Appendix to the Journals 829 (1852), cited in McClain, "The Chinese Struggle for Civil Rights in Nineteenth Century America," 536.
54. Act of Apr. 16, 1850, ch. 99, § 14, 1850 Cal. Stat. 229, 230, amended by Act of Mar. 18, 1863, ch. 70, 1863 Cal. Stat. 69, repealed by omission from codification CAL. PENAL CODE § 1321 (1872) (officially repealed, Act of Mar. 30, 1955, ch. 48, § 1, 1955 Cal. Stat. 488, 489). A parallel, but not identical provision, applied to testimony in civil cases. Civil Practice Act of 1851, ch. 5, § 394(3), 1851 Cal. Stat. 51, 114, amended by Act of Mar. 16, 1863, ch. 68, 1863 Cal. Stat. 60, repealed by

omission from codification CAL. CIV. PROC. CODE §§ 8, 1880 (1872) (officially repealed, Act of Mar. 30, 1955, ch. 33, § 1, 1955 Cal. Stat. 475, 475).

55. *People v. Hall*, 4 Cal. at 400 (1854). In *People v. Awa 27 Cal. 638* (1865), the court reversed the appellant's manslaughter conviction on the grounds that testimony by his Chinese witness had been improperly excluded under the 1863 statute forbidding Chinese testimony against White persons. The statute prohibited a Chinese person from testifying only against a White person, and, since the opposing party in the case (the state) clearly was not a "white person" within the statute's terms, the court reversed the conviction and remanded the cause for a new trial.

56. McClain, "The Chinese Struggle for Civil Rights in Nineteenth Century America," 536.

57. People v. Hall, 4 Cal. at 404 (1854).

58. Library of Congress, "Statutes at Large: 41st Congress, Session 2, Chapter 114: An Act to enforce the Right of Citizens of the United States to vote in the several States of this Union, and for other Purposes" (Washington, DC: United States Congress), www.loc.gov/law/help/statutes-at-large/41st-congress.php.

59. Shirley Ann Wilson Moore, "'We Feel the Want of Protection': The Politics of Law and Race in California, 1848–1878," *California History* 81, no. 3/4 (2003): 120, https://doi.org/10.2307/25161701.

60. Act of Mar. 31, 1866, ch. 505, 1866 Cal. Stat. 641–642.

61. Act of Feb. 7, 1874, ch. 76, 1874 Cal. Stat. 84.

62. Charles J. McClain, *In Search of Equality: The Chinese Struggle against Discrimination in Nineteenth-Century America* (Berkeley: University of California Press, 1994), 310n102; Statute of Apr. 3, 1876, Cal. Legis., 21st Sess., ch. 496, p. 759.

63. McClain, *In Search of Equality*, 45.

64. Act of Apr. 28, 1860, ch. 329, 1860 Cal. Stat. 321–422.

65. Act of Mar. 24, 1866, ch. 342, 1866 Cal. Stat. 398.

66. Act of Apr. 14, 1870, ch. 556, 1869–1870 Cal. Stat. 839.

67. *Ward v. Flood*, 48 Cal. 36 (1874).

68. Ward v. Flood, 48 Cal. 36, 52–56 (1874).

69. McClain, *In Search of Equality*, 136; Act of Apr. 7, 1880, ch. 80, 1880 Cal. Stat. 142–143, 152.

70. McClain, *In Search of Equality*, 137.

71. McClain, *In Search of Equality*, 138–139.

72. McClain, *In Search of Equality*, 140.

73. McClain, *In Search of Equality*, 140–141.

74. *Tape v. Hurley*, 66 Cal. 473 (1885).

75. McClain, *In Search of Equality*, 142.

76. Act of Mar. 12, 1885, ch. 97, 1885 Cal Stat. 99–100.

77. *Gong Lum v Rice* 275 US 78 (1927); *Plessy v Ferguson* 163 US 537 (1896).

78. *Westminster School Dist. of Orange County v. Mendez*, 161 F.2d 774, 781 (9b Cir. 1947).

79. Joyce Kuo, "Excluded, Segregated and Forgo En: A Historical View of the Discrimination of Chinese Americans in Public Schools," *Asian American Law Journal* 5 (1998): 181–212.

80. McClain, "The Chinese Struggle for Civil Rights in Nineteenth Century America," 543.

81. McClain, "The Chinese Struggle for Civil Rights in Nineteenth Century America," 548.

82. *People v. Downer*, 7 CaL 169 (1857).

83. Daniel J. Tichenor and Alexandra Filindra, "Raising Arizona v. United States: Historical Patterns of American Immigration Federalism," *Lewis & Clark Law Review* 16 (2012): 1226.

84. McClain, "The Chinese Struggle for Civil Rights in Nineteenth Century America," 556; *Lin Sing v Washburn*, 20 Cal. 534 (1862).

85. McClain, "The Chinese Struggle for Civil Rights in Nineteenth Century America," 556.

86. *Passenger Cases*, 48 US 283 (1849).

87. McClain, "The Chinese Struggle for Civil Rights in Nineteenth Century America," 539.

88. *People v. SS Constitution*, 42 Cal. 578 (1872).

89. Paul R. Spitzzeri, "Judge Lynch in Session: Popular Justice in Los Angeles, 1850–1875," *Southern California Quarterly* 87, no. 2 (2005): 83, https://doi.org/10.2307/41172258.

90. Spitzzeri, "Judge Lynch in Session: Popular Justice in Los Angeles, 1850–1875," 84.

91. State of California Office of Historic Preservation, ed., *Five Views*, 116.

92. State of California Office of Historic Preservation, ed., *Five Views*, 117.

93. McClain, *In Search of Equality*, 316n6.

94. California Secretary of State, "1878–1879 Constitutional Convention Working Papers," 2018, www.sos.ca.gov/archives/collections/constitutions/1879/.

95. California Constitution of 1879, art. II, § 1.

96. Act of Feb. 13, 1880, ch. 10, 1880 Cal. Stat. 6.

97. *In re Tiburcio Parrott*, 1 F. 481 (C.C.D. Cal. 1880).

98. Act of Apr. 3, 1880, ch. 66, 1880 Cal. Stat. 114–115.

99. Act of Apr. 12, 1880, ch. 102, 1880 Cal. Stat. 192; Act of Apr. 23, 1880, ch. 226, 1880 Cal. Stat. 388–389.

100. State of California Office of Historic Preservation, ed., *Five Views*, 118.

101. *Passenger Cases*, 48 US 283 (1849); *Henderson v. Mayor of City of New York*, 92 US 259 (1875); *Chy Lung v. Freeman*, 92 US 275 (1875).

102. Gulasekaram and Ramakrishnan, *The New Immigration Federalism*, 18.

103. The Burlingame Treaty, July 28, 1868, United States–China, 16 Stat. 739 (1869–1871).

104. *Yick Wo v. Hopkins*, 118 US 356 (1886).

105. *Brown v. Board of Education of Topeka*, 347 US 483; *Washington v. Davis*, 426 US 229 (1976).

106. McClain, *In Search of Equality*, 147.

107. "Memorial of the Senate of California to the Congress of the United States, August 13, 1877," 22nd Sess., Cal. Legis., Appendix to the Journals of the Senate and Assembly, vol. 3, at 8–9.

108. H. R. 2433, 45th Cong., 3d Sess. (1879).

109. McClain, *In Search of Equality*, 148.

110. Act of May 6, 1882, ch. 126, § 14, 22 Stat. 58.

111. Act of May 6, 1882, ch. 126, § 14, 22 Stat. 58, § 1. The act made clear that the term "skilled" laborers included those engaged in mining. Act of May 6, 1882, ch. 126, § 15.
112. McClain, *In Search of Equality*, 159.
113. McClain, *In Search of Equality*, 149.
114. McClain, *In Search of Equality*, 193.
115. *Chae Chan Ping v. United States*, 130 US 581 (1889).
116. *Ex Parte Ah Cue*, 101 Cal. 197, 198 (1894).
117. Act of May 5, 1892, ch. 60, 27 Stat. 25.
118. McClain, *In Search of Equality*, 203.
119. *Fong Yue Ting v. United States*, 149 US 698 (1893).
120. Steven Ruggles et al., "IPUMS-USA: Integrated Public Use Microdata Series: Version 7.0 [Dataset]," 2017.
121. US Census Bureau, "Availability of 1890 Census – History," 2018, www.census.gov/history/www/genealogy/decennial_census_records/availability_of_1890_census.html.
122. McClain, *In Search of Equality*, 282.
123. Ronald T. Takaki, *Strangers from a Different Shore: A History of Asian Americans* (Boston: Little, Brown, 1989).
124. McClain, *In Search of Equality*, 283.
125. Immigration and Nationality Act of 1924, ch. 190, 43 Stat. 153, 162, § 13(c).
126. Andrew E. Taslitz, "Stories of Fourth Amendment Disrespect: From Elian to the Internment," *Fordham Law Review* 70 (2002): 2307.
127. Taslitz, "Stories of Fourth Amendment Disrespect," 2307.
128. Gulasekaram and Ramakrishnan, *The New Immigration Federalism*, 36.
129. *Takahashi v. Fish & Game Commission*, 334 US 410 (1948).
130. *Oyama v. State of California*, 332 US 633 (1948).
131. *Sei Fujii v. State of California*, 38 Cal.2d 718 (1952).
132. M. H. Lewis, "Migratory Labor in California" (California: State Relief Administration of California, Division of Special Surveys and Studies, 1936); Carey McWilliams and Matt S. Meier, *North From Mexico: The Spanish-Speaking People of the United States*, Updated by Matt S. Meier, 2nd ed. (New York: Praeger, 1990); Mark Reisler, *By the Sweat of Their Brow: Mexican Immigrant Labor in the United States, 1900–1940* (Westport, CT: Praeger, 1976).
133. Rodolfo Acuña, *Occupied America: A History of Chicanos*, 3rd ed. (New York: Harper Collins Publishers, 1988), 160.
134. Lewis, "Migratory Labor in California," 29.
135. Abraham Hoffman, *Unwanted Mexican Americans in the Great Depression: Repatriation Pressures, 1929–1939* (Tucson: University of Arizona Press, 1974).
136. "This interdependence of the agricultural sector and urban relief resources manifested itself in Southern California as early as 1908. In that year, the presence of farm workers in Los Angeles in the winter seasons, considered a pervasive problem, prompted the establishment of a Housing Commission under the Los Angeles City Health Department. The Commission focused in particular on conditions 'among Mexican laborers who made their headquarters in Los Angeles during the winter and in the spring migrated to the rural districts to follow the fruit.'" Jess Walsh, "Laboring at the Margins: Welfare and the

Regulation of Mexican Workers in Southern California," *Antipode* 31, no. 4 (October 1, 1999): 403, https://doi.org/10.1111/1467-8330.00111.

137. Douglas Monroy, "An Essay on Understanding the Work Experience of Mexicans in Southern California, 1900–1939," *Aztlan: A Journal of Chicano Studies* 12, no. 1 (1981): 59–74.

138. For a brief history of residency laws placed on Mexican Americans and immigrants in the Southwest, see Sarah Deutsch, *No Separate Refuge: Culture, Class, and Gender on an Anglo-Hispanic Frontier in the American Southwest, 1880–1940* (Oxford: Oxford University Press, 1989).

139. Walsh, "Laboring at the Margins," 404.

140. On White and Black access to social welfare, see Frances Fox Piven and Richard A. Cloward, *Regulating the Poor: The Functions of Public Welfare* (New York: Knopf Doubleday Publishing Group, 2012); Felicia Ann Kornbluh, *The Battle for Welfare Rights: Politics and Poverty in Modern America* (Philadelphia: University of Pennsylvania Press, 2007); Brian Steensland, *The Failed Welfare Revolution: America's Struggle over Guaranteed Income Policy* (Princeton, NJ: Princeton University Press, 2011); Vincent J. Burke and Vee Burke, *Nixon's Good Deed: Welfare Reform* (New York: Columbia University Press, 1974); Martin Gilens, *Why Americans Hate Welfare: Race, Media, and the Politics of Antipoverty Policy* (Chicago, IL: University of Chicago Press, 2009); Jill Quadagno, *The Color of Welfare: How Racism Undermined the War on Poverty* (Oxford: Oxford University Press, 1996); Thomas Byrne Edsall and Mary D. Edsall, *Chain Reaction: The Impact of Race, Rights, and Taxes on American Politics* (New York: W. W. Norton, 1992); Jonathan Rieder, *Canarsie: The Jews and Italians of Brooklyn Against Liberalism* (Cambridge, MA: Harvard University Press, 2009); Michael Katz, *Undeserving Poor* (New York: Knopf Doubleday, 2011); Ira Katznelson, *When Affirmative Action Was White*: An Untold History of Racial Inequality in Twentieth-Century America (New York: W. W. Norton, 2006); Mary Poole, *The Segregated Origins of Social Security: African Americans and the Welfare State* (Chapel Hill: University of North Carolina Press, 2006).

141. Cybelle Fox, *Three Worlds of Relief*: Race, Immigration, and the American Welfare State from the Progressive Era to the New Deal (Princeton, NJ: Princeton University Press, 2012), 190.

142. "FERA regulations prohibited discrimination on the basis of citizenship status. And while southern and southwestern officials defied federal orders against discrimination on the basis of race and color, northeastern and midwestern officials did not discriminate on the basis of citizenship. As a result, European aliens generally had the same sort of access to relief as naturalized European immigrants or even native-born Whites. Where the promise of equal treatment on the basis of race or color was radical in the context of the times, FERA's promise of equal treatment regardless of citizenship status was not. In fact, it was more or less in line with how aliens had always been treated by relief officials." Fox, *Three Worlds of Relief*, 201.

143. Fox, *Three Worlds of Relief*, 197.

144. "Where European immigrants were more numerous, social workers and relief administrators often had local and state policies prohibiting discrimination, and they were more likely to follow up on cases of discrimination when they did occur. In Chicago, this official local-level policy of non-discrimination even extended to

blacks and Mexicans. The director of the Cook County Bureau of Public Welfare maintained that "the relief given to all applicants, whether white or colored, native born or foreign born, aliens or citizens, is on the identical basis." The state's attorney of Cook County noted in 1934 that "no discrimination on account of race or color can exist in the public institutions of this state with legal justification or excuse." The state even passed a law in 1935 that made discrimination in the hiring of individuals for work relief on the basis of race, color, or creed a misdemeanor, with a possible jail term of thirty days to six months for public officials (or their agents) who violated it." Fox, *Three Worlds of Relief*, 199–200.

145. Fox, *Three Worlds of Relief*, 215.
146. Kitty Calavita, *Inside the State: The Bracero Program, Immigration, and the I. N. S.* (New York: Routledge, 1992).
147. US Senate Committee on the Judiciary, A Report on Temporary Worker Programs: Background and Issues, US Government Printing Office, 1980, 36.
148. Gulasekaram and Ramakrishnan, *The New Immigration Federalism*, 44.
149. Douglas Massey, Jorge Durand, and Nolan J. Malone, *Beyond Smoke and Mirrors: Mexican Immigration in an Era of Economic Integration* (New York: Russell Sage Foundation, 2002).
150. *Shapiro v. Thompson*, 394 US 618 (1969).
151. Cybelle Fox, "Unauthorized Welfare: The Origins of Immigrant Status Restrictions in American Social Policy," *Journal of American History* 102, no. 4 (2016): 1063.
152. Fox, "Unauthorized Welfare," 19.
153. Gulasekaram and Ramakrishnan, *The New Immigration Federalism*, 45; *Graham v. Richardson*, 403 US 365 (1971).
154. Gulasekaram and Ramakrishnan, *The New Immigration Federalism*, 41.
155. Kitty Calavita, "California's 'Employer Sanctions' Legislation: Now You See It, Now You Don't," *Politics & Society* 12, no. 2 (June 1, 1983): 209, https://doi.org/10.1177/003232928301200204.
156. Calavita, "California's 'Employer Sanctions' Legislation," 211.
157. Alejandro Portes, "Labor Functions of Illegal Aliens," *Society* 14, no. 6 (1977): 36, https://doi.org/10.1007/BF02712515.
158. Calavita, "California's 'Employer Sanctions' Legislation," 213.
159. Calavita, "California's 'Employer Sanctions' Legislation." According to Calavita, eleven states and one city followed California's lead in adopting employer sanctions: Connecticut, Delaware, Florida, Kansas, Maine, Massachusetts, Montana, New Hampshire, New Jersey, Vermont, Virginia, and the city of Las Vegas, Nevada (Calavita, 226n3).
160. Two weeks after its passage, Judge Charles Church of the superior court for the county of Los Angeles granted an injunction in the *Dolores Canning Company, Inc. vs. Howard* case, and in 1975, the California appellate court ruled AB 528 unconstitutional under federal preemption (California Court of Appeals, Los Angeles, 40 Cal. App. 3rd 676–688, *115 Cal. Rptr.* 435 (1974)). The Supreme Court, in *DeCanas and Canas vs. Bica* (1976), reversed the California ruling and upheld AB 528 as an area of law to protect workers within the state, within the State's police power.
161. *De Canas v. Bica*, 424 US 351 (1976).

162. "Frustrated with the consequences of federal restriction, state and local officials demanded federal relief – to little avail. On behalf of elderly immigrants like Mrs. Cardenas, Congressman Edward Roybal, who in 1962 was the first Mexican American elected to Congress from California since 1879, wrote to the Commissioner of Social Security, urging the federal government provide SSI to a 'small number of aliens' 'whose public assistance was terminated.' The county grant supporting Cardenas had 'been helpful,' Roybal wrote, but 'it is my firm belief that the Federal government bears the responsibility for a permanent, nationwide solution to the problem.' In 1977, Congress held hearings on legislation designed to reimburse medical facilities that provided care to unauthorized immigrants. HEW opposed the legislation, preferring to wait for comprehensive immigration reform and national health insurance before promising to cover such costs. By the early 1980s, New York City sued HEW, charging that the regulation denying Medicaid benefits to unauthorized immigrants violated the Social Security Act." Fox, "Unauthorized Welfare," 29–30.

163. Fox, "Unauthorized Welfare," 11–12.

164. 8 USC $1324(a)(h)(2).

165. Gulasekaram and Ramakrishnan, *The New Immigration Federalism*, 51.

166. Gulasekaram and Ramakrishnan, *The New Immigration Federalism*, 54.

167. *LULAC v. Wilson*, 908 F. Supp. 755 (C.D. Cal. 1995).

168. Gulasekaram and Ramakrishnan, *The New Immigration Federalism*, 52–53.

169. Kim Voss and Irene Bloemraad, eds., *Rallying for Immigrant Rights* (Berkeley: University of California Press, 2010).

170. 104th Congress, "Illegal Immigration Reform and Immigrant Responsibility Act of 1996," Pub. L. No. 104–208 (1996), www.gpo.gov/fdsys/pkg/PLAW-104publ208/html/PLAW-104publ208.htm.

171. Office of Inspector General, "The Performance of 287(g) Agreements" (Washington, DC: Department of Homeland Security, March 4, 2010).

172. 8 USC § 1621(d), 1623(a). See also Gulasekaram and Ramakrishnan, *The New Immigration Federalism*, 130.

173. S. Karthick Ramakrishnan, *Democracy in Immigrant America: Changing Demographics and Political Participation* (Stanford, CA: Stanford University Press, 2005), www.loc.gov/catdir/toc/ecip0417/2004009114.html.

174. Melanie Mason and Patrick McGreevy, "Latino Lawmakers Move to Reverse Decades of Anti-Immigrant Legislation," *Los Angeles Times*, June 22, 2014, www.latimes.com/local/la-me-pol-legislature-latinos-20140622-story.html#page=1.

175. Ruth Milkman, LA Story: Immigrant Workers and the Future of the US Labor Movement (New York: Russell Sage Foundation, 2006); Manuel Pastor, *State of Resistance: What California's Dizzying Descent and Remarkable Resurgence Mean for America's Future* (New York: The New Press, 2018).

176. Ruth Milkman, *LA Story: Immigrant Workers and the Future of the US Labor Movement* (New York: Russell Sage Foundation, 2006).

177. Robert Lazo, "Latinos and the AFL-CIO: The California Immigrant Workers Association as an Important New Development," *La Raza Law Journal* 4 (1991): 22.

178. Manuel Pastor, "How Immigrant Activists Changed L.A.," *Dissent Magazine*, Winter 2015, www.dissentmagazine.org/article/how-immigrant-activists-changed-los-

angeles; Manuel Pastor and Michele Prichard, "L.A. Rising: The 1992 Civil Unrest, the Arc of Social Justice Organizing, and the Lessons for Today's Movement Building" (Los Angeles, CA: USC Program for Environmental & Regional Equity, 2012), http://dornsife.usc.edu/pere/larising/.

179. Pastor and Prichard, "L.A. Rising," 7.
180. Cathy Cha, "Lessons for Philanthropy from the Success of California's Immigrant Rights Movement," *Responsive Philanthropy*, Winter 2014.
181. Janice Ruth Fine, *Worker Centers: Organizing Communities at the Edge of the Dream* (Ithaca, NY: Cornell University Press, 2006), 90.
182. Gulasekaram and Ramakrishnan, *The New Immigration Federalism*, 146.
183. Gulasekaram and Ramakrishnan, *The New Immigration Federalism*, 119–150.
184. Organizational interview with NDLON, January 22, 2015.
185. Gulasekaram and Ramakrishnan, *The New Immigration Federalism*, 146; Cha, "Lessons for Philanthropy from the Success of California's Immigrant Rights Movement."
186. F. James Sensenbrenner Jr., "H.R.4437 – 109th Congress (2005–2006): Border Protection, Antiterrorism, and Illegal Immigration Control Act of 2005," webpage, January 27, 2006, www.congress.gov/bill/109th-congress/house-bill /4437.
187. Voss and Bloemraad, *Rallying for Immigrant Rights*; Chris Zepeda-Millán, *Latino Mass Mobilization: Immigration, Racialization, and Activism* (Cambridge: Cambridge University Press, 2017).
188. Cha, "Lessons for Philanthropy from the Success of California's Immigrant Rights Movement"; Allan Colbern and S. Karthick Ramakrishnan, "State Policies on Immigrant Integration: An Examination of Best Practices and Policy Diffusion," *UCR School of Public Policy Working Paper Series*, February 2016, 1–20.
189. City of San Bernardino, Illegal Immigration Relief Act Ordinance, $$ 4, 5, 6, 7, and 8, available at www.ailadownloads.org/advo/SanBernardinoIllegalImmigration Ordinance.pdf.
190. Kristina Campbell, "Local Illegal Immigration Relief Act Ordinances: A Legal, Policy, and Litigation Analysis," *Denver University Law Review* 84 (March 1, 2007).
191. Campbell, "Local Illegal Immigration Relief Act Ordinances."
192. Gulasekaram and Ramakrishnan, *The New Immigration Federalism*, 59–64.
193. Gulasekaram and Ramakrishnan, *The New Immigration Federalism*, 82.
194. Escondido, California Ordinance No. 2006-38R, An Ordinance Establishing Penalties For the Harboring of Illegal Aliens in the City of Escondido (Oct. 18, 2006).
195. Campbell, "Local Illegal Immigration Relief Act Ordinances," 10–11.
196. "Assembly Bill No. 976, Assembly Judiciary Committee Report" (2007), https:// leginfo.legislature.ca.gov/faces/billAnalysisClient.xhtml? bill_id=200720080AB976.
197. "Assembly Bill No. 976, Assembly Judiciary Committee Report." Interview with senior staff member, ACLU Immigrants' Rights Project, March 2010.
198. California Legislative Information, "AB-976 Tenancy: Tenant's Characteristics," https://leginfo.legislature.ca.gov/faces/billTextClient.xhtml?bill_id=200720080 AB976, accessed February 18, 2018.

199. *Los Angeles Times* (editorial), "Prop. 25 Changes Everything," *Los Angeles Times*, November 4, 2010, sec. Editorial, http://articles.latimes.com/2010/nov/04/opinion/la-ed-props-20101104.

200. Gulasekaram and Ramakrishnan, *The New Immigration Federalism*, 120.

201. Notably, federal law requires some employers, such as federal contractors, to use E-Verify.

202. 8 USC § 1324 (making employment of unauthorized aliens unlawful, and providing federal employer sanctions scheme); 8 USC § 1373 ("a Federal, State, or local government entity … may not prohibit, or in any way restrict, any government entity or official from sending to, or receiving from, [federal immigration authorities] information regarding the citizenship or immigration status … of any individual."). See also the passage of three laws in 2013: AB 524, SB 666, and AB 263.

203. Jordan Fabian, "Sergio Garcia: USA's First Undocumented Lawyer," *National Journal*, January 6, 2014.

204. Gulasekaram and Ramakrishnan, *The New Immigration Federalism*, 136–137.

205. Cal. Bus. & Prof. Code § 6064 (b) (2014).

206. *In re Sergio C. Garcia on Admission*, S202512 (Cal. Jan. 2, 2014).

207. Sasha Bronner, "California Checkpoint Impounds To Stop Under New Law Signed By Gov. Brown," *Huffington Post*, October 11, 2011, sec. LA, www.huffingtonpost.com/2011/10/11/california-checkpoint-impound_n_1005607.html.

208. Contractions in the right to free movement through restricting driving has a much longer and racialized history in California, originating in the early twentieth century. See Genevieve Carpio, *Collisions at the Crossroads: How Place and Mobility Make Race* (Oakland: University of California Press, 2019).

209. Obama White House, "Remarks by the President on Immigration," whitehouse.gov, June 15, 2012, https://obamawhitehouse.archives.gov/the-press-office/2012/06/15/remarks-president-immigration.

210. John Ingold, "Immigration Activists Stage Sit-in at Denver Obama Office," *Denver Post*, June 5, 2012, www.denverpost.com/ci_20791243/immigration-activists-stage-sit-at-denver-obama-office; Julia Preston, "Dream Act Gives Young Immigrants a Political Voice," *New York Times*, November 30, 2012, sec. US, www.nytimes.com/2012/12/01/us/dream-act-gives-young-immigrants-a-political-voice.html.

211. Gulasekaram and Ramakrishnan, *The New Immigration Federalism*.

212. Republican National Committee, "Growth & Opportunity Project," GOP, 2013, https://gop.com/growth-and-opportunity-project.

213. Chris Haynes, Jennifer Lee Merolla, and S. Karthick Ramakrishnan, *Framing Immigrants: News Coverage, Public Opinion, and Policy* (New York: Russell Sage Foundation, 2016), 44.

214. Chris Carroll, "US House Declares Immigration Bill 'Dead on Arrival,'" *Times Free Press*, July 1, 2013, www.timesfreepress.com/news/local/story/2013/jul/01/tennessee-house-declares-immigration-bill-dead-on/112138/.

215. Jonathan Weisman and Jeremy W. Peters, "Government Shuts Down in Budget Impasse," *New York Times*, September 30, 2013, sec. Politics, www.nytimes.com/2013/10/01/us/politics/congress-shutdown-debate.html.

216. Office of Governor Edmund G. Brown Jr., "Governor Brown Signs Immigration Legislation – Governor Edmund G. Brown Jr.," October 5, 2013, www.gov.ca.gov/2013/10/05/news18253/.
217. California Legislative Information. 2013. "AB-60 Driver's Licenses: Eligibility: Required Documentation," https://leginfo.legislature.ca.gov/faces/billNavClient.xhtml?bill_id=201320140AB60, accessed February 24, 2018.
218. Jessica Calefati, "Gov. Jerry Brown Signs Law Allowing Illegal Immigrants to Drive Legally," *San Jose Mercury News*, October 3, 2013, www.lexisnexis.com/lnacui2api/api/version1/getDocCui?lni=59H1-V8P1-DYT4-V06Y&csi=8411&hl=t&hv=t&hnsd=f&hns=t&hgn=t&oc=00240&perma=true.
219. Rick Orlov, "Gov. Jerry Brown Signs Driver S License Bill for Undocumented Immigrants," *Whittier Daily News* (California), October 3, 2013, www.lexisnexis.com/lnacui2api/api/version1/getDocCui?lni=59H4-FJC1-DYT4-V3HX&csi=8411&hl=t&hv=t&hnsd=f&hns=t&hgn=t&oc=00240&perma=true.
220. The Trust Act of 2013 Cal. Stat. 4650 (codified at CAL. GOV'T CODE §§ 7282–7282.5 (West Supp. 2014))
221. Adam B. Cox and Thomas J. Miles, "Policing Immigration," *University of Chicago Law Review* 80, no. 1 (January 1, 2013): 87–136; Hiroshi Motomura, *Immigration Outside the Law* (Oxford and New York: Oxford University Press, 2014), 78–80.
222. California Legislative Information, "AB-1081 State Government: Federal Immigration Policy Enforcement," 2012, https://leginfo.legislature.ca.gov/faces/billAnalysisClient.xhtml?bill_id=201120120AB1081.
223. Ulloa, "How California's Trust Act Shaped the Debate on the New 'Sanctuary State' Proposal."
224. Michael J. Mishak, "Bill Would Let Counties Opt out of US Immigration Enforcement Program," *Los Angeles Times*, May 31, 2011, http://articles.latimes.com/2011/may/31/local/la-me-immigration-20110531; "National Day Laborer Organizing Network, Immigrant Rights Groups Call for Transparency as They Serve FOIA Request to Uncover the Truth about ICE's 'Discontinuation' of Secure Communities," 2015, https://ndlon.org/immigrant-rights-groups-call-for-transparency-as-they-serve-foia-request-to-uncover-the-truth-about-ice-s-discontinuation-of-se-communities-3/.
225. Senator Tom Ammiano, "Assembly Bill No. 1081, Senate Floor Bill Analysis" (2012), https://leginfo.legislature.ca.gov/faces/billAnalysisClient.xhtml?bill_id=201120120AB1081.
226. "Assembly Bill No. 1081" (2011), https://leginfo.legislature.ca.gov/faces/billNavClient.xhtml?bill_id=201120120AB1081.
227. Governor Jerry Brown, "Assembly Bill No. 1081, Governor Brown's Veto Message" (2012), www.gov.ca.gov/wp-content/uploads/2017/09/AB_1081_Veto_Message.pdf.
228. Ulloa, "How California's Trust Act Shaped the Debate on the New 'Sanctuary State' Proposal."
229. Office of Governor Edmund G. Brown Jr., "Governor Brown Signs Immigration Legislation – Governor Edmund G. Brown Jr."
230. "Senate Bill No. 1210" (2014), https://leginfo.legislature.ca.gov/faces/billNavClient.xhtml?bill_id=201320140SB1210.

231. Josie Huang, "Immigrants without Legal Status Able to Apply for Professional Licenses in CA," *Southern California Public Radio* (2014), www.scpr.org/blogs/multiamerican/2014/09/29/17360/immigrants-professionally-licensed-california/, last accessed January 20, 2015.

232. "Senate Bill 4" (2015), https://leginfo.legislature.ca.gov/faces/billNavClient.xhtml?bill_id=201520160SB4.

233. "Senate Bill No. 396, Senate Floor Analysis" (2014), 396, https://leginfo.legislature.ca.gov/faces/billAnalysisClient.xhtml?bill_id=201320140SB396.

234. Tony Mendoza, "Senate Bill No. 432" (2015), https://leginfo.legislature.ca.gov/faces/billTextClient.xhtml?bill_id=201520160SB432.

235. Michael Martinez and Jaqueline Hurtado, "Undocumented Immigrants Picked for City Posts Say US 'Progressing,'" CNN, August 8, 2015, www.cnn.com/2015/08/08/us/huntington-park-undocumented-immigrants-city-commission-appointees/index.html.

236. Martinez and Hurtado, "Undocumented Immigrants Picked for City Posts Say US 'Progressing.'"

237. Leslie Berestein Rojas, "Huntington Park Appointing 2 New Commissioners Who Don't Have Legal Status," *Southern California Public Radio*, August 3, 2015, www.scpr.org/news/2015/08/03/53546/huntington-park-to-appoint-commissioners-who-don-t/.

238. Rojas, "Huntington Park Appointing 2 New Commissioners Who Don't Have Legal Status."

239. Rosanna Xia, "Campus Conversation: Jorge Reyes Salinas, California State University Student Trustee," *Los Angeles Times*, October 5, 2017, www.latimes.com/local/lanow/la-me-cal-state-student-trustee-jorge-campus-convo-20171005-htmlstory.html.

240. Taryn Luna and Billy Kobin, "Undocumented Immigrant Appointed to State Post in California," *Sacramento Bee*, March 15, 2018, www.sacbee.com/news/politics-government/capitol-alert/article205249624.html.

241. The Trust Act of 2013 Cal. Stat. 4650 (codified at CAL. GOV'T CODE §§ 7282–7282.5 (West Supp. 2014)).

242. "San Francisco Joins Neighboring Counties In Suspending Undocumented Immigrant Jail Holds," accessed December 7, 2014, http://sanfrancisco.cbslocal.com/2014/05/29/san-francisco-joins-neighboring-counties-in-suspending-undocumented-immigrant-jail-holds/.

243. Amy Taxin and Elliot Spagat, "California Immigration Holds Drop Significantly Under Trust Act," Associated Press, June 6, 2014.

244. "Senate Bill N. 1392" (2014), http://leginfo.legislature.ca.gov/faces/billStatusClient.xhtml?bill_id=201320140SB1392.

245. S. Karthick Ramakrishnan and Allan Colbern, "The California Package: Immigrant Integration and the Evolving Nature of State Citizenship," *Policy Matters* 6, no. 3 (2015): 9.

246. Dakota Smith and Cindy Carcamo, "Responding to Trump, L.A. Proposes $10-Million Legal Defense Fund for Immigrants Facing Deportation," *Latimes.com*, December 19, 2016, www.latimes.com/local/lanow/la-me-ln-lafund-20161219-story.html.

247. California Department of Social Services, "Immigration Branch Immigration Services Funding Tentative Award Announcement" (Sacramento, CA,

December 9, 2015), www.cdss.ca.gov/Portals/9/Immigration/2015–16%20Final %20Immigration%20Award%20Announcement%2012–9-15.pdf? ver=2017–09-20–120446-477.

248. California Department of Social Services, "Immigration Services Funding Fact Sheet" (Sacramento, CA, July 2017), www.cdss.ca.gov/Portals/9/Immigration/ ISF%20Fact%20Sheet%20July%202017.pdf?ver=2017–11-28–195256-543.

249. Smith and Carcamo, "Responding to Trump, L.A. Proposes $10-Million Legal Defense Fund for Immigrants Facing Deportation."

250. Eloise Gómez Reyes, "Expedited Certification Process for U Visa and T Visa Applicants Signed into Law," October 11, 2019, https://a47.asmdc.org/press- releases/20191011-expedited-certification-process-u-visa-and-t-visa-applicants- signed-law.

251. Taryn Luna, "Gov. Gavin Newsom Pledges to Help Build up El Salvador to Reduce Migration," *Los Angeles Times*, April 15, 2019, www.latimes.com/politics/la-pol- ca-el-salvador-gavin-newsom-20190415-story.html.

252. Karthick Ramakrishnan testified in favor of SB-174 (2018) "Citizens of the state" law introduced by Senator Ricardo Lara that would have allowed state residents without US citizenship to serve on state boards and commissions. See https:// leginfo.legislature.ca.gov/faces/billTextClient.xhtml?bill_id=201720180SB174.

253. "Senate Bill 225" (2019) ("Citizens of the state"), https://leginfo.legislature.ca.gov /faces/billCompareClient.xhtml?bill_id=201920200SB225&showamends=false#.

254. Phil Willon, "California Extends New Protections to Immigrants under Laws Signed by Newsom," *Los Angeles Times*, October 14, 2019, www.latimes.com /california/story/2019–10-14/california-new-protections-immigrants-laws-signed -gavin-newsom.

255. Karthick Ramakrishnan and Allan Colbern, "Op-Ed: Immigration Reform: 'The California Package,'" *Los Angeles Times*, June 24, 2015, sec. Opinion; Melanie Mason, "California Gives Immigrants Here Illegally Unprecedented Rights, Benefits, Protections," *Los Angeles Times*, August 11, 2015, sec. California.

6 STATE CITIZENSHIP AND IMMIGRATION FEDERALISM

1. Noah Bierman, "Arizona Candidate Jokingly (?) Calls for a Border Wall with California," *Los Angeles Times*, February 20, 2018, www.latimes.com/politics/la- na-pol-essential-washington-updates-arizona-candidate-jokingly-calls-for -1521573433-htmlstory.html.

2. Pratheepan Gulasekaram and S. Karthick Ramakrishnan, *The New Immigration Federalism* (New York: Cambridge University Press, 2015), 53.

3. Gerald L. Neuman, "The Lost Century of American Immigration Law (1776–1875)," *Columbia Law Review* 93, no. 8 (December 1, 1993): 1833–1901; Anna O. Law, "Lunatics, Idiots, Paupers, and Negro Seamen – Immigration Federalism and the Early American State," *Studies in American Political Development* 28, no. 2 (October 2014): 110.

4. Gulasekaram and Ramakrishnan, *The New Immigrant Federalism*, 43.

5. Calavita, Kitty. "California's 'Employer Sanctions' Legislation: Now You See It, Now You Don't." *Politics & Society* 12, no. 2 (June 1, 1983): 205–230, https://doi .org/10.1177/003232928301200204. According to Calavita, eleven states and one

city followed California's lead in adopting employer sanctions: Connecticut, Delaware, Florida, Kansas, Maine, Massachusetts, Montana, New Hampshire, New Jersey, Vermont, Virginia, and the city of Las Vegas, Nevada (226n3).

6. For scholarship on immigrants and public benefits in the 1990s, see Kitty Calavita, "The New Politics of Immigration: 'Balanced-Budget Conservatism' and the Symbolism of Proposition 187," *Social Problems* 43, no. 3 (1996): 284–305, https://doi.org/10.2307/3096979; Robin Dale Jacobson, *The New Nativism: Proposition 187 and the Debate over Immigration* (Minneapolis: University of Minnesota Press, 2008); Lynn Fujiwara, *Mothers Without Citizenship: Asian Immigrant Families and the Consequences of Welfare Reform* (Minneapolis: University of Minnesota Press, 2008); Cybelle Fox, "Unauthorized Welfare: The Origins of Immigrant Status Restrictions in American Social Policy," *Journal of American History* 102, no. 4 (2016): 1052–1053.

7. 8 USC § 1623(a).

8. Gulasekaram and Ramakrishnan, *The New Immigration Federalism*, 50.

9. Lisa C. Solbakken, "The Anti-Terrorism and Effective Death Penalty Act: Anti-Immigration Legislation Veiled in an Anti-Terrorism Pretext Notes," *Brooklyn Law Review* 63 (1997): 1382–1383.

10. Gulasekaram and Ramakrishnan, *The New Immigration Federalism*, 100–103.

11. *See* Arizona Taxpayer and Citizen Protection Act, Ariz. Rev. Stat. § 46-140.01 (through 2nd Reg Sess. 50th Leg. 2012) (verifying applicants for public benefits), www.azleg.gov/viewdocument/?docName=https://www.azleg.gov/ars/46/00140-0 1.htm (https://perma.cc/L64R-33G9).

12. Gulasekaram and Ramakrishnan, *The New Immigration Federalism*, 111.

13. This provision was held unconstitutional. See *Arizona v. Inter Tribal Council of Ariz., Inc.*, 570 US 1 (2013).

14. Gulasekaram and Ramakrishnan, *The New Immigration Federalism*, 60.

15. Border Protection, Antiterrorism, and Illegal Immigration Control Act of 2005, HR 4437, 109th Cong. (2005), www.congress.gov/bill/109th-congress/house-bill /04437 (https://perma.cc/6C5J-EGTB).

16. Tom K. Wong, *The Politics of Immigration: Partisanship, Demographic Change, and American National Identity* (New York: Oxford University Press, 2016), 8.

17. Gulasekaram and Ramakrishnan, *The New Immigration Federalism*, 114.

18. Irene Bloemraad, Kim Voss, and Taeku Lee, "The Protests of 2006: What Were They, How Do We Understand Them, Where Do We Go?," in *Rallying for Immigrant Rights: The Fight for Inclusion in 21st Century America*, ed. Kim Voss and Irene Bloemraad (Berkeley: University of California Press, 2011), 3–43.

19. Gulasekaram and Ramakrishnan, *The New Immigration Federalism*, 95–117.

20. Gulasekaram and Ramakrishnan, *The New Immigration Federalism*, 3–8.

21. Gulasekaram and Ramakrishnan, *The New Immigration Federalism*, 147.

22. Lewis Lazare, "Southwest Airlines Debuts Dramatically Different Ad Campaign," *Chicago Business Journal*, March 19, 2013, www.bizjournals.com/chicago/news/ 2013/03/19/southwest-airlines-ready-to-welcome.html.

23. Craig Robertson, *The Passport in America: The History of a Document* (New York: Oxford University Press, 2010); John Torpey, *The Invention of the Passport: Surveillance, Citizenship, and the State*, Cambridge Studies in Law and Society (Cambridge and New York: Cambridge University Press, 2000).

24. Oregon Exec. Order No. 07-22, Nov. 16, 2007, available at www.oregon.gov/gov/pdf/eoo722.pdf.

25. Erika Davila, "Panel OKs Bill to Make It Easier for Immigrants to Get Licenses," *Santa Fe New Mexican* (New Mexico), February 13, 2003; Katy June-Friesen. "May I See Some Identification?" *Weekly Alibi*, August 2005; Erika Davila, "State Sets Hearing on Issuing Licenses to Foreign Residents," *Santa Fe New Mexican* (New Mexico), May 23, 2002.

26. Gulasekaram and Ramakrishnan, *The New Immigration Federalism*, 132.

27. *Ariz. Dream Act Coal. v. Brewer*, No. 13 – 16248 (9th Cir. July 7, 2014).

28. Nevada "Senate Bill 303" (2013), www.leg.state.nv.us/Session/77th2013/Bills/SB/SB303_EN.pdf

29. Delaware "Senate Bill 59" (2015), https://legis.delaware.gov/BillDetail?legislationId=24774.

30. Andrea Silva, "Undocumented Immigrants, Driver's Licenses, and State Policy Development: A Comparative Analysis of Oregon and California," *UCLA Institute for Research on Labor & Employment*, May 1, 2015, https://escholarship.org/uc/item/3sd3mo6k.

31. Gulasekaram and Ramakrishnan, *The New Immigration Federalism*, 147.

32. Rachel Monahan, "Opponents to Oregon Driver's Licenses for Undocumented Immigrants Refile Initiative Petition," *Willamette Week*, October 27, 2019, www.wweek.com/news/state/2019/10/27/opponents-to-oregon-drivers-license-for-undocumented-immigrants-refile-initiative-petition/.

33. California "Senate Bill 54" (2017), https://leginfo.legislature.ca.gov/faces/billNavClient.xhtml?bill_id=201720180SB54.

34. California "Senate Bill 1194" (2018), https://leginfo.legislature.ca.gov/faces/billTextClient.xhtml?bill_id=201720180SB1194.

35. Act 69, 2011 S.C. Acts (SB 20), Section 4(A)(B)(C)(D). *See also United States v. South Carolina*, 720 F.3d 518, at 6–7 (4th Cir. 2013).

36. Huyen Pham, "The Private Enforcement of Immigration Laws," *Georgetown Law Journal* 96 (2008): 782.

37. Robertson, *The Passport in America*.

38. *Arizona v. United States*, 567 US 387 (2012).

39. *Arizona*, 132 S. Ct. at 2508 (citing 8 USC § 1357(g)(10(A)).

40. *Arizona*, 132 S. Ct. at 2509.

41. *Georgia Latino Alliance for Human Rights v. Deal*, 793 F. Supp. 2d 1317, 1336–1339 (N.D. Ga. 2011).

42. O.C.G.A. §§ 16-11- 200–202; *Georgia Latino Alliance for Human Rights v. Governor of Georgia*, 691 F.3d 1250, 1263 (11th Cir. 2012).

43. *United States v. South Carolina*, 840 F. Supp. 2d 898, 904 (DSC 2011).

44. *United States v. South Carolina*, 906 F. Supp. 2d 463, 466–469, 473–474 (DSC 2012).

45. *United States v. South Carolina*, 720 F.3d 518, at 41 (4th Cir. 2013).

46. *United States v. South Carolina*, 720 F.3d 518, at 23–24 (4th Cir. 2013).

47. Congress first added the misdemeanor crime of "harboring" to the statutes that govern federal immigration in 1917 but did not specifically provide for a penalty. In 1952, harboring became a felony; willfulness or knowledge was required, and employers were exempted (Act of Mar. 12, 1851, Pub. L. No. 283, 66 Stat. 26 (amending 8 USC § 144). In 1986, the requirement was reduced to "knowing or in

reckless disregard," and employers were no longer exempted (Immigration Reform and Control Act of 1986, Pub. L. No. 99-603, sec. 112, § 274(a), 100 Stat. 3359, 3381–3383 (codified as amended at 8 USC § 1324 (2012)). Congress increased the penalties for harboring in 1994, 1996, and 2004, but throughout its history there has never been a definition of "harboring" in the statute.

48. *United States v. Alabama*, 691 F.3d 1269, 1285 (11th Cir. 2012).
49. *Valle del Sol Inc. v. Whiting*, 732 F.3d 1006, 1024–1026 (9th Cir. 2013); See also *Villas at Parkside Partners v. City of Farmers Branch*, 726 F.3d 524, 539 (5th Cir. 2013) (holding city ordinance criminalizing harboring invalid on preemption grounds).
50. The Trust Act of 2013, A.B. 4, 2013–2014 Gen. Assemb., Reg. Sess. (Cal. 2013).
51. See *San Francisco Joins Neighboring Counties in Suspending Undocumented Immigrant Jail Holds*, CBS San Francisco (May 29, 2014), http://sanfrancisco .cbslocal.com/2014/05/29/san-francisco-joins-neighboring-counties-in-suspending-undocumented-immigrant-jail-holds/ (https://perma.cc/249B-LCQ9).
52. Gulasekaram and Ramakrishnan, *The New Immigration Federalism*, 130.
53. HB 6659, 2013 Gen Assemb., Reg. Sess. (Conn. 2013), www.cga.ct.gov/2013/act/pa/ 2013PA-00155-R00HB-06659-PA.htm (https://perma.cc/328V-KZQX); SB 0031, 100th Gen. Assemb. (Ill. 2017), www.ilga.gov/legislation/billstatus.asp?DocNum= 31&GAID=14&GA=100&DocTypeID=SB&LegID=98874&SessionID=91(https:// perma.cc/3TV2-HBFT); HB 3464, 79th Gen. Assemb., Reg. Sess. (Or. 2017), https:// olis.leg.state.or.us/liz/2017R1/Downloads/MeasureDocument/HB3464/Enrolled (https://perma.cc/45L4-UH8Z); Office of the NJ Attorney General, Attorney General Law Enforcement Directive No. 2018-6 (2018), www.nj.gov/oag/dcj/agguide/ directives/ag-directive-2018-6.pdf (https://perma.cc/55JJ-7KUB).
54. Section 2(A): (anti-sanctuary provision) "No official or agency of this state or a county, city, town or other political subdivision of this state may adopt a policy that limits or restricts the enforcement of federal immigration laws to less than the full extent permitted by federal law."
55. Section 2(G) empowers any person to bring "an action in superior court to challenge any official or agency of this state" that "adopts or implements a policy that limits or restricts the enforcement of federal immigration laws less than the full extent permitted by federal law." The civil penalty for violating the law is set at $1,000 (minimum) and $5,000 (maximum) per each day after the action is filed. If the person who brings suit prevails, that person may be entitled to reimbursement of court costs and reasonable attorney fees. Section 2 (I) adds that law enforcement officers are to be compensated by their agency for incurred legal costs, unless the officer is shown to have acted in bad faith.
56. SB 20, Section 17 (C)(2)(c).
57. Tom K. Wong, *The Politics of Immigration: Partisanship, Demographic Change, and American National Identity* (New York: Oxford University Press, 2016), 7.
58. The federal court of appeals for the Third Circuit recently adopted this reasoning in holding that Lehigh County, PA, was not obligated to comply with an ICE detainer that resulted in the unlawful detention of a US citizen: *Galarza v. Lehigh County*, No. 12-3991 (3rd Cir. Mar. 4, 2014) (holding that immigration detainers are requests and cannot be mandatory pursuant to the Supreme Court's "anti-commandeering" interpretation of the 10th Amendment). Also see Allan Colbern, Melanie Amoroso-Pohl, and Courtney Gutiérrez. "Contextualizing

Sanctuary Policy Development in the United States: Conceptual and Constitutional Underpinnings, 1979 to 2018." *Fordham Urban Law Journal* 46, no. 3 (January 1, 2019): 489–547.

59. *City of New York v. United States*, 179 F.3d 29 (2d Cir. 1999).
60. Annie Lai and Christopher N. Lasch, "Crimmigration Resistance and the Case of Sanctuary City Defunding," *Santa Clara Law Review* 57 (2017): 543.
61. *Galarza v. Szalczyk*, 745 F.3d 634, 639–645 (3d Cir. 2014).
62. *Galarza v. Szalczyk*, ACLU, www.aclu.org/cases/immigrants-rights/galarza-v-szalczyk (https://perma.cc/FN2N-MA44). *See Galarza*, 745 F.3d at 644–645. See also Lai and Lasch, "Crimmigration Resistance and the Case of Sanctuary City Defunding," 547 (referencing the federal court decisions as "suggesting that jurisdictions that elected to hold people could be liable for violating their Fourth Amendment rights").
63. See Res. 2014-36, 2014 (Lehigh Cty. Bd. of Comm'rs, Pa. 2014).
64. See *Miranda-Olivares v. Clackamas County*, No. 3:12-CV-02317-ST, 2014 WL 1414305 (D. Or. Apr. 11, 2014) (ruling that Clackamas County violated the Fourth Amendment by solely relying on the ICE detainer request to hold a noncitizen for two weeks).
65. American Immigration Council. "The Criminal Alien Program (CAP): Immigration Enforcement in Prisons and Jails" (Washington, DC: American Immigration Council, August 1, 2013), www.americanimmigrationcouncil.org/research/criminal-alien-program-cap-immigration-enforcement-prisons-and-jails.
66. National Conference of State Legislatures. "The State Criminal Alien Assistance Program (SCAAP)," April 13, 2013, www.ncsl.org/research/immigration/state-criminal-alien-assistance-program.aspx.
67. See Illegal Immigration Reform and Immigration Responsibility Act, Pub. L. No. 104–208, § 287(g), 110 Stat. 3009, 3009-563 (codified at 8 USC § 1357(g) (2012)).
68. National Immigration Law Center. "Untangling the Immigration Enforcement Web." Washington, DC: National Immigration Law Center, September 2017, www.nilc.org/issues/immigration-enforcement/untangling-immigration-enforcement-web/; Christopher N. Lasch, "Enforcing the Limits of the Executive's Authority to Issue Immigration Detainers Immigration Law," *William Mitchell Law Review* 35 (2008): 173.
69. Legiscan, 2011, "Bill Text: Alabama House Bill 56 (2011), Enrolled," https://legiscan.com/AL/text/HB56/id/321074.
70. *United States v. Alabama*, 691 F.3d 1269, 1296, at 1293 (11th Cir. 2012).
71. *United States v. Alabama*, 691 F.3d 1269, 1296, at 1294 (11th Cir. 2012).
72. Hiroshi Motomura, *Immigration Outside the Law* (Oxford and New York: Oxford University Press, 2014).
73. Lynn Schnaiberg, "Judge Rejects Prop 187 Bans on Calif. Services," *Education Week*, November 29, 1995, www.edweek.org/ew/articles/1995/11/29/13prop.h15.html; Lesli A. Walsh and Mark Maxwell, "Court Rules That Ala. Can't Check Students' Immigration Status," *Education Week*, August 29, 2012, www.edweek.org/ew/articles/2012/08/29/02alabama.h32.html.
74. Wisconsin enacted a tuition equity law in 2009 but repealed it in 2011.
75. These include the University of Hawaii Board of Regents, the Kentucky Council on Postsecondary Education, the University of Maine Board of Trustees, the University of Michigan Board of Regents, the Ohio Board of Regents, the Oklahoma State

Regents for Higher Education, and Rhode Island's Board of Governors for Higher Education, plus The University of Delaware and Delaware Technical Community College. National Conference of State Legislatures, "Tuition Benefits for Immigrants," (2020), www.ncsl.org/research/immigration/tuition-benefits-for-immigrants.aspx, accessed March 29, 2020.

76. National Conference of State Legislatures, "Tuition Benefits for Immigrants."
77. Carla Rivera, "Two Long Beach Colleges Will Offer Dream Scholarships." *Los Angeles Times*, February 4, 2014, www.latimes.com/local/lanow/la-me-ln-college-dream-20140204-story.html.
78. National Conference of State Legislatures, "Tuition Benefits for Immigrants."
79. Office of the Att'y Gen., Commonwealth of Va., Immigration Law Compliance Update 1 (Sept. 5, 2002), available at http://schev.virginia.gov/AdminFaculty/ImmigrationMemo9-5-02APL.pdf.
80. Peter Whoriskey, "Illegal Immigrants Still Being Enrolled at NVCC," *Washington Post*, December 1, 2002.
81. *Day v. Sebelius*, 376 F. Supp. 2d 1022 (D. Kan. 2005); *Day v. Bond*, 500 F.3d 1127 (10th Cir. 2007).
82. 8 USC § 1324 (making employment of unauthorized aliens unlawful, and providing federal employer sanctions scheme); 8 USC § 1373 ("a Federal, State, or local government entity ... may not prohibit, or in any way restrict, any government entity or official from sending to, or receiving from, [federal immigration authorities] information regarding the citizenship or immigration status ... of any individual").
83. Jordan Fabian, "Sergio Garcia: USA's First Undocumented Lawyer," *National Journal*, January 6, 2014.
84. Cal. Bus. & Prof. Code § 6064 (b) (2014).
85. *In re Sergio C. Garcia on Admission*, S202512 (Cal. Jan. 2, 2014).
86. Florida Board of Bar Examiners Re: Question as to Whether Undocumented Immigrants are Eligible for Admission to the Florida Bar, N. SC11-2568 (Fla. Mar. 6, 2014).
87. Katie Mettier, "Undocumented Immigrant Jose Godinez-Samperio Tells of Becoming a Lawyer," *Tampa Bay Times*, October 21, 2014.
88. Liz Robbins, "New York Court Rules for Immigrant in Fight to Become Lawyer," *New York Times*, June 4, 2015.
89. Josie Huang, "Immigrants without Legal Status Able To Apply for Professional Licenses in CA," Southern California Public Radio (2014), www.scpr.org/blogs/multiamerican/2014/09/29/17360/immigrants-professionally-licensed-california/, last accessed January 20, 2015.
90. Pham, "The Private Enforcement of Immigration Laws," 791.
91. "MAPS: Health Coverage for Immigrant Children and Pregnant Women," *National Immigration Law Center*, January 6, 2015, www.nilc.org/healthcoveragemaps.html.
92. See Claire D. Brindis, Max W. Hadler, Ken Jacobs, Laurel Lucia, Nadereh Pourat, Marissa Raymond-Flesch, Rachel Siemons, and Efrain Talamantes, "Realizing the Dream for Californians Eligible for Deferred Action for Childhood Arrivals (DACA): Demographics and Health Coverage" (Berkeley: University of California Berkeley Labor Center, February 1, 2014), http://laborcenter.berkeley.edu/realizing-the-dream-for-californians-eligible-for-deferred-action-for-childhood-arrivals-daca-demographics-and-health-coverage/#endnote15.

93. See Brindis et al., "Realizing the Dream for Californians Eligible for Deferred Action for Childhood Arrivals (DACA)."
94. See California "Senate Bill 1005" (2013), https://legiscan.com/CA/bill/SB1005/2013.
95. California "Senate Bill 75" (2015), https://leginfo.legislature.ca.gov/faces/billNavClient.xhtml?bill_id=201520160SB75.
96. California "Senate Bill 104" (2019), https://leginfo.legislature.ca.gov/faces/billNavClient.xhtml?bill_id=201920200SB104.
97. Gutierrez, Melody. "California Coronavirus Cases: Tracking the Outbreak." *Los Angeles Times*, January 8, 2020. https://www.latimes.com/projects/california-coronavirus-cases-tracking-outbreak/embed/; Pardo, Daniel. "LA Legislator Vows to Fight for Undocumented Seniors to Receive Healthcare," May 24, 2020. https://spectrumnews1.com/ca/la-west/politics/2020/05/24/la-legislator-vows-to-fight-for-undocumented-seniors-to-receive-healthcare-; Heather, Kade. "Illinois to Become 1st State to Provide Medicaid Regardless of Immigration Status." *The State Journal-Register*, May 27, 2020. https://www.sj-r.com/news/20200527/illinois-to-become-1st-state-to-provide-medicaid-regardless-of-immigration-status.
98. California Legislative Information., "AB-976 Tenancy: Tenant's Characteristics," https://leginfo.legislature.ca.gov/faces/billTextClient.xhtml?bill_id=200720080AB976, accessed February 18, 2018.
99. City of San Bernardino, Illegal Immigration Relief Act Ordinance, $$ 4, 5, 6, 7, and 8, available at www.ailadownloads.org/advo/SanBernardinoIllegalImmigrationOrdinance.pdf.
100. Kristina Campbell, "Local Illegal Immigration Relief Act Ordinances: A Legal, Policy, and Litigation Analysis," *Denver University Law Review* 84 (March 1, 2007).
101. Gulasekaram and Ramakrishnan, *The New Immigration Federalism*, 82.
102. Michael Powell and Michelle García, "Pa. City Puts Illegal Immigrants on Notice," *Washington Post*, August 22, 2006, www.washingtonpost.com/archive/politics/2006/08/22/pa-city-puts-illegal-immigrants-on-notice-span-classbankheadthey-must-leave-mayor-of-hazleton-says-after-signing-tough-new-lawspan/b3e1ecfc-124a-4e05-a3b0-1edbec01bf3b/.
103. Pham, "The Private Enforcement of Immigration Laws," 791.
104. For wage and hour abuses, see Wendy Williams, "Model Enforcement of Wage and Hour Laws for Undocumented Workers: One Step Closer to Equal Protection under the Law," *Columbia Human Rights Law Review* 37 (2005): 755; Katherine Loh and Scott Richardson, "Foreign-Born Workers: Trends in Fatal Occupational Injuries, 1996–2001," *Monthly Labor Review* 127 (2004): 42; Bruce Nissen, Alejandro Angee, and Marc Weinstein, "Immigrant Construction Workers and Health and Safety: The South Florida Experience," *Labor Studies Journal* 33, no. 1 (March 1, 2008): 48–62, https://doi.org/10.1177/0160449X07312075; Diana Vellos, "Immigrant Latina Domestic Workers and Sexual Harassment," *American University Journal of Gender and the Law* 5 (1996): 407; Gloria González-López, "Heterosexual Fronteras: Immigrant Mexicanos, Sexual Vulnerabilities, and Survival," *Sexuality Research & Social Policy* 3, no. 3 (2006): 67–81, https://doi.org/10.1525/srsp.2006.3.3.67.
105. Shannon Gleeson, "Labor Rights for All? The Role of Undocumented Immigrant Status for Worker Claims Making," *Law & Social Inquiry* 35, no. 3 (June 1, 2010): 561–602, https://doi.org/10.1111/j.1747-4469.2010.01196.x.

106. Roger Waldinger and Michael I. Lichter, *How the Other Half Works: Immigration and the Social Organization of Labor*, 1st ed. (Berkeley: University of California Press, 2003); Katherine M. Donato and Carl L. Bankston III, "The Origins of Employer Demand for Immigrants in a New Destination: The Salience of Soft Skills in a Volatile Economy," in *New Faces in New Places: The Changing Geography of American Immigration*, ed. Douglas S. Massey (New York: Russell Sage Foundation, 2008); Jennifer Gordon, *Suburban Sweatshops: The Fight for Immigrant Rights* (Cambridge, MA: Belknap Press, 2007).

107. 8 USC § 1621(d).

108. 8 USC § 1601 et. seq.

109. 8 USC § 1622; 8 USC § 1621(d).

110. Rachel Fabi, "Undocumented Immigrants in the United States: Access to Prenatal Care," *The Hastings Center: Undocumented Patients Project*, September 29, 2014, www.undocumentedpatients.org/issuebrief/undocumented-immigrants-in-the-united-states-access-to-prenatal-care/.

111. 8 USC § 1623(a).

112. See *Equal Access Educ. v. Merten*, 305 F. Supp. 2d 585, 614 (E.D. Va. 2004).

113. *Chamber of Commerce v. Whiting* 131 S. Ct. 1968 (2011)

114. 8 USC 1324a(h).

115. Daniel J. Tichenor and Alexandra Filindra, "Raising Arizona v. United States: Historical Patterns of American Immigration Federalism," *Lewis & Clark Law Review* 16 (2012): 1221.

116. *Valle del Sol v. Whiting*, 709 F.3d 808, at 6 (9th Cir. 2013).

117. Gulasekaram and Ramakrishnan, *The New Immigration Federalism*, 199; *Valle del Sol v. Whiting*, 709 F.3d 808 (9th Cir. 2013).

118. California, "Assembly Bill No. 976, Assembly Judiciary Committee Report" (2007), https://leginfo.legislature.ca.gov/faces/billAnalysisClient.xhtml?bill_id=200720080AB976.

119. *Lozano v. City of Hazelton*, 724 F.3d 297 (2013).

120. Ron Hayduk, *Democracy for All: Restoring Immigrant Voting Rights in the US* (New York: Routledge, 2012), 76.

121. Pamela Constable, "D.C., Other Cities Debate Whether Legal Immigrants Should Have Voting Rights," *Washington Post*, February 9, 2015, www.washingtonpost.com/local/should-legal-immigrants-have-voting-rightscontentious-issue-comes-to-dc-other-cities/2015/02/09/85072440-abof-11e4-ad71-7b9ebaof87d6_story.html.

122. Jamin B. Raskin, "Legal Aliens, Local Citizens: The Historical, Constitutional and Theoretical Meanings of Alien Suffrage," *University of Pennsylvania Law Review* 141, no. 4 (April 1, 1993): 1463, https://doi.org/10.2307/3312345.

123. Ron Hayduk, "Give Noncitizens the Right to Vote? It's Only Fair," *Los Angeles Times*, December 22, 2014, www.latimes.com/opinion/op-ed/la-oe-hayduk-let-noncitizens-vote-20141223-story.html.

124. Tara Kini, "Sharing the Vote: Noncitizen Voting Rights in Local School Board Elections," *California Law Review* 93, no. 1 (January 1, 2005): 271–321.

125. Diana Walsh, "Bold Plan to Let Noncitizens Vote on School Items," *SFGate.Com*, February 6, 1996, www.sfgate.com/news/article/Bold-plan-to-let-noncitizens-vote-on-school-items-3159327.php.

126. Rosanna Xia, "Campus Conversation: Jorge Reyes Salinas, California State University Student Trustee," *Los Angeles Times*, October 5, 2017, www .latimes.com/local/lanow/la-me-cal-state-student-trustee-jorge-campus-convo -20171005-htmlstory.html.

127. Taryn Luna and Billy Kobin, "Undocumented Immigrant Appointed to State Post in California," *Sacramento Bee*, March 15, 2018, www.sacbee.com/news/politics- government/capitol-alert/article205249624.html.

128. See Arizona Taxpayer and Citizen Protection Act, Ariz. Rev. Stat. § 46-140.01 (through 2nd Reg Sess. 50th Leg. 2012) (verifying applicants for public benefits), www.azleg.gov/viewdocument/?docName=https://www.azleg.gov/ars/46/00140- 01.htm (https://perma.cc/L64R-33G9).

129. Gulasekaram and Ramakrishnan, *The New Immigration Federalism*, 111.

130. *Arizona v. Inter Tribal Council of Ariz., Inc.*, 570 US 1 (2013).

131. Kini, "Sharing the Vote."

132. Gerald M. Rosberg, "Aliens and Equal Protection: Why Not the Right to Vote?," *Michigan Law Review* 75, no. 5/6 (April 1, 1977): 1092–1136, https://doi.org/10 .2307/1288026.

133. Jamin B. Raskin, "Legal Aliens, Local Citizens: The Historical, Constitutional and Theoretical Meanings of Alien Suffrage," *University of Pennsylvania Law Review* 141, no. 4 (April 1, 1993): 1391–1470, https://doi.org/10.2307/3312345.

134. California "Senate Bill No. 396, Senate Floor Analysis" (2014), 396, https://leginfo .legislature.ca.gov/faces/billAnalysisClient.xhtml?bill_id=201320140SB396.

135. HJR 896 (2014); SJR 729 (2018).

136. *Buquer v. City of Indianapolis*, 797 F. Supp. 2d 905 (SD Ind. 2011).

137. *Buquer v. City of Indianapolis et al.*, 1:11-cv-00708-SEB-MJD (SD Ind. 2013).

7   ENABLING PROGRESS ON STATE CITIZENSHIP

1. Violeta Campos, *Restoring the Right to Drive: Re-Licensing the Undocumented Community in California* (Los Angeles, CA: Occidental College, 2014), 15, www .oxy.edu/sites/default/files/assets/UEP/Comps/2014/Campus% 2CVioleta_Restoring%20the%20Right%20to%20Drive.pdf.

2. Davis Gray, *AB 1463 Veto Message*, LegInfo.Ca.Gov., 2000, www.leginfo.ca.gov /pub/99-00/bill/asm/ab_1451-1500/ab_1463_vt_20000929.html.

3. Dan Morain, "Latino Caucus Won't Support Davis Reelection," *Los Angeles Times*, October 5, 2002.

4. Kimberly Edds, "No Driver's Licenses for Calif. Illegal Immigrants," *Washington Post*, September 24, 2004, www.washingtonpost.com/wp-dyn/articles/A45651- 2004Sep23.html.

5. Edds, "No Driver's Licenses for Calif. Illegal Immigrants."

6. Edds, "No Driver's Licenses for Calif. Illegal Immigrants."

7. "Senate Bill No. 60, Senate Transportation & Housing Committee Report" (2005), www.leginfo.ca.gov/pub/09-10/bill/sen/sb_0051-0100/sb_60_cfa_20090409_144 957_sen_comm.html

8. Patrick McGreevy, "Cedillo Vows to Try Driver's License Immigration Bill Again," *LA Times Blogs – L.A. NOW* (blog), October 3, 2008, http://latimesblogs .latimes.com/lanow/2008/10/cedillo.html.

9. Patrick McGreevy, "Assemblyman Tries Again on Licenses for Illegal Immigrants," *Los Angeles Times*, February 25, 2012, http://articles.latimes.com/2012/feb/25/local/la-me-drivers-license-20120225.

10. George Skelton, "Lawmaker Fulfills Pledge to Late Wife with Legislative Victory," *Los Angeles Times*, September 5, 2012, http://articles.latimes.com/2012/sep/05/local/la-me-cap-cedillo-20120906; Araceli Martínez, "La Historia Detrás De Las Licencias Para Indocumentados," *La Opinión* (blog), December 30, 2014, https://laopinion.com/2014/12/30/la-historia-detras-de-las-licencias-para-indocumentados/. Cedillo noted in his interview on *La Opinión* that he had sponsored over 100 laws in the state of California.

11. Nanette Asimov, "Bill Would Give Young Immigrants Licenses," *San Francisco Chronicle*, August 26, 2012, www.sfgate.com/news/article/Bill-would-give-young-immigrants-licenses-3815663.php.

12. Interview with legislative staff member, February 12, 2015.

13. Pratheepan Gulasekaram and S. Karthick Ramakrishnan, *The New Immigration Federalism* (New York: Cambridge University Press, 2015), 259n152.

14. Allan Colbern and S. Karthick Ramakrishnan, "State Policies on Immigrant Integration: An Examination of Best Practices and Policy Diffusion," *UCR School of Public Policy Working Paper Series*, February 2016, 7.

15. Jeremy B. White, "California Immigrants Soon Can Seek Driver's Licenses," *Sacramento Bee*, December 15, 2014, www.sacbee.com/news/politics-government/article4486973.html.

16. Claudia Mendez Salazar, "Alejo Reintroduces Legislation Allowing Undocumented Immigrants to Get a Driver's License," *Monterey County Herald* (California), December 4, 2012, sec. LOCAL, www.lexisnexis.com/lnacui2api/api/version1/getDocCui?lni=576G-4MK1-DYT4-V47M&csi=270944,270077,11059,8411&hl=t&hv=t&hnsd=f&hns=t&hgn=t&oc=00240&perma=true.

17. Rick Orlov, "Gov. Jerry Brown Signs Driver's License Bill for Undocumented Immigrants," *Whittier Daily News* (California), October 3, 2013, www.lexisnexis.com/lnacui2api/api/version1/getDocCui?lni=59H4-FJC1-DYT4-V3HX&csi=8411&hl=t&hv=t&hnsd=f&hns=t&hgn=t&oc=00240&perma=true.

18. Office of Governor Edmund G. Brown Jr., "Governor Brown Signs AB 60 – Governor Edmund G. Brown Jr.," October 3, 2013, www.gov.ca.gov/2013/10/03/news18246/.

19. Office of Governor Edmund G. Brown Jr., "Governor Brown Signs Immigration Legislation – Governor Edmund G. Brown Jr."

20. Christina Goldbaum, "County Clerks Revolt Over N.Y. Licenses for Undocumented Immigrants," *New York Times*, November 14, 2019, sec. New York, www.nytimes.com/2019/11/14/nyregion/immigrants-drivers-license.html; interview with Steven K. Choi, executive director of the New York Immigration Coalition, November 2019.

21. Vivian Wang, "Progressives Vowed Driver's Licenses for the Undocumented. Then the Suburbs Spoke Up," *New York Times*, June 16, 2019, sec. New York, www.nytimes.com/2019/06/16/nyregion/undocumented-immigrants-drivers-licenses-ny.html.

22. Interview with Steven K. Choi, executive director of the New York Immigration Coalition, November 2019.

23. Nina Bernstein, "Spitzer Grants Illegal Immigrants Easier Access to Driver's Licenses," *New York Times*, September 22, 2007, sec. N.Y./Region, www.nytimes.com/2007/09/22/nyregion/22licenses.html.
24. Elise Foley, "Eliot Spitzer Says Hillary Clinton's 2008 Camp Urged Him Not to Give Driver's Licenses to Undocumented Immigrants," *HuffPost*, October 29, 2015, www.huffpost.com/entry/eliot-spitzer-hillary-clinton-drivers-licenses-undocumentedn563 25e1be4b00aa54a4d3864.
25. Kirk Semple, "Gillibrand's Immigration Views Draw Fire," *New York Times*, January 27, 2009, sec. Politics, www.nytimes.com/2009/01/28/us/politics/28immigration.html.
26. Danny Hakim, "Spitzer Dropping His Driver's License Plan," *New York Times*, November 14, 2007, sec. N.Y./Region, www.nytimes.com/2007/11/14/nyregion/14spitzer.html.
27. Allan Colbern and S. Karthick Ramakrishnan, "State Policies on Immigrant Integration: An Examination of Best Practices and Policy Diffusion," 1–20.
28. New York Immigration Coalition, "Blueprint for Immigrant New York," November 8, 2017, www.thenyic.org/userfiles/file/nyic_Blueprint_for_ImmigrantNY_v5.pdf.
29. Shane Goldmacher, "At Inauguration, Cuomo Rallies State Against Trump," *New York Times*, January 1, 2019.
30. Vivian Wang, "Progressives Vowed Driver's Licenses for the Undocumented. Then the Suburbs Spoke Up," *New York Times*, June 16, 2019.
31. Dan M. Clark, "NY AG Says Undocumented Drivers' License Bill Is Constitutional, Sidestepping Cuomo Request," *New York Law Journal*, June 17, 2019.
32. Our explanatory framework (see Chapter 3) captures the role of social movements and connects the development of sanctuary policies to broader historical policy developments in immigration federalism, while also building on scholarship around sanctuary policies and partisanship. See Loren Collingwood and Benjamin Gonzalez O'Brien, *Sanctuary Cities: The Politics of Refuge* (Oxford: Oxford University Press, 2019).
33. Irene Bloemraad, Kim Voss, and Taeku Lee, "The Protests of 2006: What Were They, How Do We Understand Them, Where Do We Go?," in *Rallying for Immigrant Rights: The Fight for Inclusion in 21st Century America*, ed. Kim Voss and Irene Bloemraad (Berkeley: University of California Press, 2011), 3–43.
34. Tom K. Wong, *The Politics of Immigration*: Partisanship, Demographic Change, and American National Identity (New York: Oxford University Press, 2016), 7–16.
35. Allan Colbern, Sanctuary Policy Dataset (on file with author).
36. Exec. Directive 07–01 (City & Cty. S.F., Mar. 1, 2007); Colbern, Sanctuary Policy Dataset (on file with author).
37. Exec. Directive 07–01 (City & Cty. S.F., Mar. 1, 2007).
38. Colbern, Sanctuary Policy Dataset (on file with author).
39. *See Secure Communities: Overview*, US Immigration & Customs Enforcement, www.ice.gov/secure-communities (https://perma.cc/6VYU-M47W).
40. Gulasekaram and Ramakrishnan, *The New Immigration Federalism*, 129.
41. Res. 10–00530 (Common Council of the City of Madison, Wis. 2010); Colbern, Sanctuary Policy Dataset (on file with author).
42. Gulasekaram and Ramakrishnan, *The New Immigration Federalism*, 130.
43. Res. No. 2010–316 (Santa Clara Bd. of Supervisors, Cal. 2010); Colbern, Sanctuary Policy Dataset (on file with author).

44. Res. No. 2011–504 (Santa Clara County, Cal. Oct. 18, 2011); Colbern, Sanctuary Policy Dataset (on file with author).

45. Governor Jerry Brown, "Assembly Bill No. 1081, Governor Brown's Veto Message" (2012), www.gov.ca.gov/wp-content/uploads/2017/09/AB_1081_Veto_Message.pdf.

46. Jazmine Ulloa, "How California's Trust Act Shaped the Debate on the New 'Sanctuary State' Proposal," *Los Angeles Times*, September 10, 2017, www.latimes.com/politics/la-pol-ca-trust-act-sanctuary-state-immigration-20170910-htmlstory.html.

47. Office of Governor Edmund G. Brown Jr., "Governor Brown Signs Immigration Legislation – Governor Edmund G. Brown Jr."

48. The Trust Act of 2013, A.B. 4, 2013–2014 Gen. Assemb., Reg. Sess. (Cal. 2013).

49. See "San Francisco Joins Neighboring Counties in Suspending Undocumented Immigrant Jail Holds," CBS San Francisco (May 29, 2014), http://sanfrancisco.cbslocal.com/2014/05/29/san-francisco-joins-neighboring-counties-in-suspending-undocumented-immigrant-jail-holds/ (https://perma.cc/249B-LCQ9).

50. Gulasekaram and Ramakrishnan, *The New Immigration Federalism*, 130.

51. Gulasekaram and Ramakrishnan, *The New Immigration Federalism*, 147.

52. "Why Immigrant-Friendly Legislation Has Stalled in Mass," *WBUR News*, April 9, 2014, www.wbur.org/news/2014/04/09/immigration-bills-massachusetts.

53. S. Karthick Ramakrishnan and Allan Colbern, "The California Package: Immigrant Integration and the Evolving Nature of State Citizenship," *Policy Matters* 6, no. 3 (2015): 7.

54. Monique Garcia, Rick Geiger, and Kim Pearson, "Illinois House Overrides Rauner Vetoes of Income Tax Increase, Budget," *Chicago Tribune*, July 7, 2017, www.chicagotribune.com/politics/ct-madigan-rauner-illinois-house-tax-increase-override-met-0707-20170706-story.html.

55. Shelby Bremer, "Rauner Signs 'Illinois Trust Act' on Immigration," *NBC Chicago* (blog), August 28, 2017, www.nbcchicago.com/blogs/ward-room/rauner-signs-illinois-trust-act-immigration-bill-442015923.html.

56. Sam Dunklau, "Immigrants Get Their 'Voice': Illinois House Overrides Voices Act Veto," *NPR Illinois* (blog), November 28, 2018, www.nprillinois.org/post/immigrants-get-their-voice-illinois-house-overrides-voices-act-veto.

57. For example, Illinois recently passed a law on par with California's Values Act called the "Keep Illinois Families Together Act" (2019) that severs state and local resources from engaging in immigration enforcement and begins to create safe spaces from enforcement.

58. Exec. Order No. 13768, 82 Fed. Reg. 8,799 (Jan. 25, 2017) www.federalregister.gov/documents/2017/01/30/2017–02102/enhancing-public-safety-in-the-interior-of-the-united-states (https://perma.cc/N5XB-28HM).

59. See *Motion for Preliminary Injunction* at 23–24, County of Santa Clara, No. 17-cv-00574 (N.D. Cal Feb. 3, 2017); see also Annie Lai and Christopher N. Lasch, "Crimmigration Resistance and the Case of Sanctuary City Defunding," *Santa Clara Law Review* 57, no. 9 (2018).

60. See Complaint, *City & County of San Francisco v. Donald J. Trump*, 275 F. Supp. 3d 1196 (N.D. Cal. Jan. 31, 2017) (No. 3:17-cv-00485); Complaint, *County of Santa Clara v. Donald J. Trump*, No. 5:17-cv-00574 (N.D. Cal. Feb. 3, 2017); Complaint, *City of Chelsea & City of Lawrence v. Donald J. Trump*, No. 1:17-cv-10214 (D. Mass. Feb. 8, 2017); Complaint, *City of Richmond v. Donald J. Trump*,

No. 3:17-cv-01535 (N.D. Cal. Feb. 22, 2017); Complaint, *City of Seattle v. Donald J. Trump*, No. 2:17-cv-00497 (W.D. Wash. Mar. 29, 2017).

61. See *County of Santa Clara v. Donald J. Trump*, 250 F. Supp. 3d 497 (N.D. Cal. 2017) (order granting the County of Santa Clara's and City and County of San Francisco's Motions to Enjoin Section 9(a) of Exec. Order 13768).

62. See *City & County of San Francisco v. Donald J. Trump*, 897 F.3d 1225, 1231 (9th Cir. 2018).

63. See *City & County of San Francisco v. Donald J. Trump*, 1344–1345.

64. See *City & County of San Francisco v. Donald J. Trump*, 1238.

65. See *City & County of San Francisco v. Donald J. Trump*, 1244.

66. *United States v. California*, 314 F. Supp. 3d 1077, 1104 (E.D. Cal. 2018).

67. Thomas Fuller, "Judge Rules for California over Trump in Sanctuary Law Case," *New York Times*, July 5, 2018, www.nytimes.com/2018/07/05/us/california-sanctuary-law-ruling.html (https://perma.cc/B67R-LGPM).

68. Act of February 12, 1793 (1 Stat. 302); *Annals of Congress*, 2nd Cong., 2nd sess. (1793), 1414–1415.

69. Marion Gleason McDougall, *Fugitive Slaves (1619–1865)* (Boston: Ginn & Company, 1891), 17.

70. McDougall, *Fugitive Slaves (1619–1865)*, 19.

71. The Petition of the People of Colour, free men, within the City and Suburbs of Philadelphia, December 30, 1799, 6A.G1.1 (House Records), National Archives; Thomas D. Morris, *Free Men All: The Personal Liberty Laws of the North, 1780–1861* (Clark, NJ: The Lawbook Exchange, 1974), 31.

72. Jesse Torrey, *American Slave Trade; Or, An Account of the Manner in Which the Slave Dealers Take Free People from Some of the United States of America, and Carry Them Away, and Sell Them as Slaves in Other of the States; and of the Horrible Cruelties Practiced in the Carrying on of This Most Infamous Traffic: With Reflections on the Project for Forming a Colony of American Blacks in Africa, and Certain Documents Respecting That Project* (London: C. Clement and published by J. M. Cobbett, 1822), 66.

73. Alice Dana Adams, *The Neglected Period of Anti-Slavery in America, 1808–1831*, Radcliffe College Monographs, No. 14 (Gloucester, MA: Peter Smith, 1964), 107.

74. *Pennsylvania House Journal, 1819–1820*, 339–341, 987, 1069, 1081, 1088; *Pennsylvania Session Laws, 1820*, 104–106; Morris, *Free Men All*, 44–45.

75. Bruce Laurie, *Beyond Garrison: Antislavery and Social Reform* (Cambridge and New York: Cambridge University Press, 2005).

76. Commonwealth v. Ayes, 35 Mass. (18 Pick.) 193 (1836); Paul Finkelman, *An Imperfect Union: Slavery, Federalism, and Comity* (Clark, NJ: The Lawbook Exchange, 1981), 101–125; Paul Finkelman, "Prelude to the Fourteenth Amendment: Black Legal Rights in the Antebellum North," *Rutgers Law Journal* 17 (1985): 444.

77. Robert M. Cover, *Justice Accused: Antislavery and the Judicial Process* (New Haven, CT: Yale University Press, 1975).

78. Joel Parker, *Personal Liberty Laws and Slavery in the Territories* (Boston: Wright & Potter, 1861), 32–33.

79. An Act to protect the Rights and Liberties of the People of the Commonwealth of Massachusetts, Mass. Gen. Laws ch. 0489 § 1–23 (1855), reprinted in *Acts and Resolves Passed by the General Court of Massachusetts, in the Year 1855: Together*

with the Messages (Boston, MA: Secretary of the Commonwealth, 1855), 924–929; *Mass. Senate Document No. 162, 1855*; *Mass. Senate Journal, 1855*, Mass. State Library, 76:801; *Mass. House Journal, 1855*, 77:1710; Morris, *Free Men All*, 167–170.

80. Guy Gugliotta, "Civil War Toll Up by 20 Percent in New Estimate," *New York Times*, April 2, 2012, www.nytimes.com/2012/04/03/science/civil-war-toll-up-by-20-percent-in-new-estimate.html.

APPENDIX A

1. John Gerring, *Case Study Research* (Cambridge, MA: Cambridge University Press, 2007), 45.
2. Derek Beach and Rasmus Brun Pedersen, *Process-Tracing Methods: Foundations and Guidelines* (Ann Arbor: University of Michigan Press, 2013), 3.

Select References

Abramowitz, Alan I. *The Great Alignment: Race, Party Transformation, and the Rise of Donald Trump*. New Haven, CT: Yale University Press, 2018.

Acuña, Rodolfo. *Occupied America: A History of Chicanos*. 3rd ed. New York: Harper Collins, 1988.

Adams, Alice Dana. *The Neglected Period of Anti-Slavery in America, 1808–1831*. Radcliffe College Monographs, No. 14. Gloucester, MA: Peter Smith, 1964.

Alexander, Michelle. *The New Jim Crow: Mass Incarceration in the Age of Colorblindness*. Revised ed. New York: The New Press, 2012.

Andersen, Kristi. *After Suffrage: Women in Partisan and Electoral Politics Before the New Deal*. Chicago, IL: University of Chicago Press, 1996.

Anderson, Margo J. *The American Census: A Social History*. New Haven, CT: Yale University Press, 1988.

Aoki, Keith. "No Right to Own: The Early Twentieth-Century Alien Land Laws as a Prelude to Internment Symposium: The Long Shadow of Korematsu." *Boston College Law Review* 40 (1998): 37–72.

Arango, Tim. "In California, Criminal Justice Reform Offers a Lesson for the Nation." *New York Times*, January 21, 2019, sec. US. www.nytimes.com/2019/01/21/us/california-incarceration-reduction-penalties.html.

Avery, Beth. "Ban the Box: U.S. Cities, Counties, and States Adopt Fair Hiring Policies." *National Employment Law Project* (blog). www.nelp.org/publication/ban-the-box-fair-chance-hiring-state-and-local-guide/, accessed November 19, 2019.

Ayers, Edward L. *The Promise of the New South: Life after Reconstruction*. 15th anniversary ed. New York: Oxford University Press, 2007. http://ebookcentral.proquest.com/lib/asulib-ebooks/detail.action?docID=430642.

Balogh, Brian. *A Government Out of Sight: The Mystery of National Authority in Nineteenth-Century America*. Cambridge: Cambridge University Press, 2009.

Barber, William J., and Jonathan Wilson-Hartgrove. *The Third Reconstruction: Moral Mondays, Fusion Politics, and the Rise of a New Justice Movement*. Boston, MA: Beacon Press, 2016.

Bateman, David A. *Disenfranchising Democracy: Constructing the Electorate in the United States, the United Kingdom, and France*. New York: Cambridge University Press, 2018.

Bateman, David A., Ira Katznelson, and John S. Lapinski. *Southern Nation: Congress and White Supremacy after Reconstruction*. Princeton, NJ: Princeton University Press, 2018.

Bauböck, Rainer. "Reinventing Urban Citizenship." *Citizenship Studies* 7, no. 2 (July 1, 2003): 139–160. https://doi.org/10.1080/1362102032000065946.

"Studying Citizenship Constellations." *Journal of Ethnic and Migration Studies* 36, no. 5 (May 1, 2010): 847–859. https://doi.org/10.1080/13691831003764375.

Transnational Citizenship: Membership and Rights in International Migration. Cheltenham: Edward Elgar, 1994.

Bauböck, Rainer, and Liav Orgad, eds. *Cities vs States: Should Urban Citizenship Be Emancipated from Nationality?* European University Institute, 2019. http://globalcit.eu/cities-vs-states-should-urban-citizenship-be-emancipated-from-nationality/?fbclid=IwAR3I2pxdoPRsy65i8l1Z-_okEoUZieOtjtVw6M6-fCgxmrkaG_HuIa LXu1A.

Baumgartner, Frank R., Derek A. Epp, and Kelsey Shoub. *Suspect Citizens: What 20 Million Traffic Stops Tell Us About Policing and Race*. New York: Cambridge University Press, 2018.

Behl, Natasha. *Gendered Citizenship: Understanding Gendered Violence in Democratic India*. Oxford Studies in Gender and International Relations. Oxford: Oxford University Press, 2019.

Beitsch, Rebecca. "'Proof of Citizenship' Voting Laws May Surge Under Trump." Pew Charitable Trusts. *Stateline* (blog), November 16, 2017. http://pew.org/2zKkGDN.

Belknap, Michal R. *Federal Law and Southern Order: Racial Violence and Constitutional Conflict in the Post-Brown South*. Athens: University of Georgia Press, 1987.

Bender, Steven. *Greasers and Gringos: Latinos, Law, and the American Imagination*. New York: New York University Press, 2003.

Bensel, Richard Franklin. *Sectionalism and American Political Development, 1880–1980*. Madison: University of Wisconsin Press, 1987.

"Southern Leviathan: The Development of Central State Authority in the Confederate States of America." *Studies in American Political Development* 2 (1987): 68–136. https://doi.org/10.1017/S0898588X00001735.

Yankee Leviathan: The Origins of Central State Authority in America, 1859–1877. Cambridge: Cambridge University Press, 1990.

Berlin, Ira. *Slaves without Masters: The Free Negro in the Antebellum South*. New York: W. W. Norton, 2007.

Berman, Ari. *Give Us the Ballot: The Modern Struggle for Voting Rights in America*. New York: Farrar, Straus and Giroux, 2015.

Bernstein, Nina. "Spitzer Grants Illegal Immigrants Easier Access to Driver's Licenses." *New York Times*, September 22, 2007, sec. N.Y./Region. www.nytimes.com/2007/09/22/nyregion/22licenses.html.

Bierman, Noah. "Arizona Candidate Jokingly (?) Calls for a Border Wall with California." *Los Angeles Times*, February 20, 2018. www.latimes.com/politics/la-na-pol-essential-washington-updates-arizona-candidate-jokingly-calls-for-1521573433-htmlstory.html.

Biggers, Daniel R., and Michael J. Hanmer. "Understanding the Adoption of Voter Identification Laws in the American States." *American Politics Research* 45, no. 4 (2017): 560–588. https://doi.org/10.1177/1532673X16687266.a.

Blackmon, Douglas A. *Slavery by Another Name: The Re-Enslavement of Black Americans from the Civil War to World War II*. London: Icon Books, 2013.

Bloemraad, Irene, Anna Korteweg, and Gökçe Yurdakul. "Citizenship and Immigration: Multiculturalism, Assimilation, and Challenges to the Nation-State." *Annual Review of Sociology* 34, no. 1 (2008): 153–179. https://doi.org/10.1146/annurev.soc.34.040507.134608.

Bloemraad, Irene, Kim Voss, and Taeku Lee. "The Protests of 2006: What Were They, How Do We Understand Them, Where Do We Go?" In *Rallying for Immigrant Rights: The Fight for Inclusion in 21st Century America*, edited by Kim Voss and Irene Bloemraad, 3–43. Berkeley: University of California Press, 2011.

Bonilla-Silva, Eduardo. *Racism without Racists: Color-Blind Racism and the Persistence of Racial Inequality in America*. New York: Rowman & Littlefield, 2013.

Bosniak, Linda. *The Citizen and the Alien: Dilemmas of Contemporary Membership*. Princeton, NJ: Princeton University Press, 2008.

"Citizenship Denationalized." *Indiana Journal of Global Legal Studies* 7, no. 2 (April 1, 2000): 447–509.

"Universal Citizenship and the Problem of Alienage," *Immigration and Nationality Law Review* 21 (2000): 373–424.

Boushey, Graeme, and Adam Luedtke. "Immigrants across the U.S. Federal Laboratory: Explaining State-Level Innovation in Immigration Policy." *State Politics & Policy Quarterly* 11, no. 4 (December 1, 2011): 390–414. https://doi.org/10.1177/1532440011419286.

Brackett, Jeffrey R. *The Negro in Maryland: A Study of the Institution of Slavery*. Baltimore, MD: N. Murray, publication agent, Johns Hopkins University, 1889.

Bremer, Shelby. "Rauner Signs 'Illinois Trust Act' on Immigration." *NBC Chicago*, August 28, 2017. www.nbcchicago.com/blogs/ward-room/rauner-signs-illinois-trust-act-immigration-bill-442015923.html.

Brooks, Corey M. *Liberty Power: Antislavery Third Parties and the Transformation of American Politics*. Chicago, IL: University of Chicago Press, 2016.

Brubaker, Rogers. *Citizenship and Nationhood in France and Germany*. Cambridge, MA: Harvard University Press, 2009.

Bulman-Pozen, Jessica. "From Sovereignty and Process to Administration and Politics: The Afterlife of American Federalism." *Yale Law Journal* 123 (2014): 1920–1957.

"Partisan Federalism." *Harvard Law Review* 127 (2014): 1077–1146.

Bulman-Pozen, Jessica, and Heather K. Gerken. "Uncooperative Federalism." *Yale Law Journal* 118, no. 7 (2009): 1256–1310.

Butz, Adam M., and Jason E. Kehrberg. "Anti-Immigrant Sentiment and the Adoption of State Immigration Policy." *Policy Studies Journal* 47, no. 3 (2019): 605–623. https://doi.org/10.1111/psj.12326.

"California Will Allow up to 4,000 Nonviolent Third-Strike Criminals with Life Sentences to Seek Parole." *Los Angeles Times*, October 18, 2018. www.latimes.com/local/california/la-me-california-three-strikes-prop-57-20181018-story.html.

Calavita, Kitty. "California's 'Employer Sanctions' Legislation: Now You See It, Now You Don't." *Politics & Society* 12, no. 2 (June 1, 1983): 205–230. https://doi.org/10.1177/003232928301200204.

Inside the State: The Bracero Program, Immigration, and the I. N. S. New York: Routledge, 1992.

"The New Politics of Immigration: 'Balanced-Budget Conservatism' and the Symbolism of Proposition 187." *Social Problems* 43, no. 3 (1996): 284–305. https://doi.org/10.2307/3096979.

Campbell, Gibson, and Kay Jung. *Historical Census Statistics on Population Totals by Race, 1790 to 1990, and by Hispanic Origin, 1790 to 1990, for the United States, Regions, Divisions, and States.* Washington, DC: US Census Bureau, 2002.

Campbell, James M. *Slavery on Trial: Race, Class, and Criminal Justice in Antebellum Richmond, Virginia.* Gainesville: University Press of Florida, 2007.

Campbell, Kristina. "Local Illegal Immigration Relief Act Ordinances: A Legal, Policy, and Litigation Analysis." *Denver University Law Review* 84 (March 1, 2007): 1041.

Campos, Violeta. *Restoring the Right to Drive: Re-Licensing the Undocumented Community in California.* Los Angeles, CA: Occidental College, 2014. www.oxy.edu/sites/default/files/assets/UEP/Comps/2014/Campus%2CVioleta_Restoring%20the%20Right%20to%20Drive.pdf.

Canon, Gabrielle. "Once Known for 'Three Strikes' Law, California Is Now Embracing Criminal Justice Reform." *USA Today*, September 18, 2019. www.usatoday.com/story/news/politics/2019/09/18/about-californias-criminal-justice-reform-bills/2353853001/.

Carpio, Genevieve. *Collisions at the Crossroads: How Place and Mobility Make Race.* Oakland: University of California Press, 2019.

Cha, Cathy. "Lessons for Philanthropy from the Success of California's Immigrant Rights Movement." *Responsive Philanthropy* (Winter 2014): 1, 13–14.

Chadbourn, James Harmon. *Lynching and the Law.* Clark, NJ: The Lawbook Exchange, 2008.

Chavez-Garcia, Miroslava. *Negotiating Conquest: Gender and Power in California, 1770s to 1880s.* Tucson: University of Arizona Press, 2004.

Clement, Paul, and Neal Katyal. "On the Meaning of Natural Born Citizen." *Harvard Law Review Forum* 128 (2015): 161–164.

Cohen, Elizabeth F. *Semi-Citizenship in Democratic Politics.* Cambridge: Cambridge University Press, 2009.

Cohen, Elizabeth F., and Cyril Ghosh. *Citizenship.* Cambridge: Polity Press, 2019.

Cohen, Elizabeth F., and Jenn Kinney. "Multilevel Citizenship in a Federal State: The Case of Noncitizens' Rights in the United States." In *Multilevel Citizenship*, edited by Willem Maas, 77–88. Philadelphia: University of Pennsylvania Press, 2013.

Cohen, William. *At Freedom's Edge: Black Mobility and the Southern White Quest for Racial Control, 1861–1915.* Baton Rouge, LA: LSU Press, 1991.

Colbern, Allan. *Today's Runaway Slaves: Unauthorized Immigrants in a Federalist Framework.* Riverside: University of California, Riverside, 2017.

Colbern, Allan, Melanie Amoroso-Pohl, and Courtney Gutiérrez. "Contextualizing Sanctuary Policy Development in the United States: Conceptual and Constitutional Underpinnings, 1979 to 2018." *Fordham Urban Law Journal* 46, no. 3 (January 1, 2019): 489–547.

Colbern, Allan, and Karthick Ramakrishnan. "State Policies on Immigrant Integration: An Examination of Best Practices and Policy Diffusion." *UCR School of Public Policy Working Paper Series*, 2016, 1–20.

Collier, David, and Robert Adcock. "Democracy and Dichotomies: A Pragmatic Approach to Choices about Concepts." *Annual Review of Political Science* 2, no. 1 (1999): 537–565. https://doi.org/10.1146/annurev.polisci.2.1.537.

Collier, David, and John Gerring. *Concepts & Method in Social Science: The Tradition of Giovanni Sartori*. New York: Routledge, 2009.

Collier, David, and Steven Levitsky. "Democracy: Conceptual Hierarcies in Comparative Research." In *Concepts and Method in Social Science: The Tradition of Giovanni Sartori*, edited by David Collier and John Gerring, 269–288. New York: Routledge, 2009.

"Democracy with Adjectives: Conceptual Innovation in Comparative Research." *World Politics* 49, no. 03 (April 1997): 430–451. https://doi.org/10.1353/wp.1997.0009.

Collier, David, and James E. Mahon. "Conceptual 'Stretching' Revisited: Adapting Categories in Comparative Analysis." *American Political Science Review* 87, no. 4 (December 1, 1993): 845–855. https://doi.org/10.2307/2938818.

Collingwood, Loren, and Benjamin Gonzalez O'Brien. *Sanctuary Cities: The Politics of Refuge*. Oxford: Oxford University Press, 2019.

Connolly, N. D. B. "This, Our Second Nadir." *Boston Review*, February 21, 2018. http://bostonreview.net/forum/remake-world-slavery-racial-capitalism-and-justice/n-d-b-connolly-our-second-nadir.

Cover, Robert. "Federalism and Administrative Structure." *Yale Law Journal* 92 (1983): 1342–1343.

Cover, Robert M. *Justice Accused: Antislavery and the Judicial Process*. New Haven, CT: Yale University Press, 1975.

Cox, Adam B., and Thomas J. Miles. "Policing Immigration." *University of Chicago Law Review* 80, no. 1 (January 1, 2013): 87–136.

Cushing, John D. "The Cushing Court and the Abolition of Slavery in Massachusetts: More Notes on the 'Quock Walker Case.'" *American Journal of Legal History* 5, no. 3 (April 1961): 118–144.

C. W. H. III. "Federal Legislation to Safeguard Voting Rights: The Civil Rights Act of 1960." *Virginia Law Review* 46, no. 5 (1960): 945–75. https://doi.org/10.2307/1070567.

Davis, David Brion. *The Problem of Slavery in the Age of Revolution, 1770–1823*. Ithaca, NY: Cornell University Press, 1975.

De Graauw, Els. *Making Immigrant Rights Real: Nonprofits and the Politics of Integration in San Francisco*. Ithaca, NY: Cornell University Press, 2016.

"Municipal ID Cards for Undocumented Immigrants Local Bureaucratic Membership in a Federal System," *Politics & Society* 42, no. 3 (September 1, 2014): 309–330.

Denton, Nancy, and Douglas S. Massey. *American Apartheid: Segregation and the Making of the Underclass*. Cambridge, MA: Harvard University Press, 1993.

Deutsch, Sarah. *No Separate Refuge: Culture, Class, and Gender on an Anglo-Hispanic Frontier in the American Southwest, 1880–1940*. Oxford: Oxford University Press, 1989.

Deverell, William. *Whitewashed Adobe: The Rise of Los Angeles and the Remaking of Its Mexican Past*. Berkeley: University of California Press, 2004.

Douglass, Frederick. "What to the Slave Is the Fourth of July?" In *My Bondage and My Freedom*, 441–445. New York: Miller, Orton & Mulligan, 1855.

DuBois, Ellen Carol. *Feminism and Suffrage: The Emergence of an Independent Women's Movement in America, 1848–1869*. Cornell University Press, 1999.

Du Bois, W. E. B. *The Problem of the Color Line at the Turn of the Twentieth Century: The Essential Early Essays*. Ed. Nahum Dimitri Chandler. New York: Fordham University Press, 2014.

"Reconstruction and Its Benefits." *American Historical Review* 15, no. 4 (1910): 781–799. https://doi.org/10.2307/1836959.

"Some Efforts of American Negroes For Their Own Social Betterment. Report of an Investigation under the Direction of Atlanta University; Together with the Proceedings of the Third Conference for the Study of the Negro Problems, Held at Atlanta University, May 25–26, 1898." Atlanta, GA: Atlanta University Press, 1898. https://docsouth.unc.edu/church/duboisau/menu.html.

Du Bois, W. E. B., and David Levering Lewis. *Black Reconstruction in America (the Oxford W. E. B. Du Bois): An Essay Toward a History of the Part Which Black Folk Played in the Attempt to Reconstruct Democracy in America, 1860–1880.* Edited by Henry Louis Gates. Cary, NC: Oxford University Press, 2007.

Duda, Jeremy. "Few Voters Use Federal-Only Ballots." *Arizona Mirror*, January 1, 2019. www.azmirror.com/blog/few-voters-use-federal-only-ballots/.

Dunklau, Sam. "Immigrants Get Their 'Voice': Illinois House Overrides Voices Act Veto." *NPR Illinois*, November 28, 2018. www.nprillinois.org/post/immigrants-get-their-voice-illinois-house-overrides-voices-act-veto.

Enriquez, Laura E., Daisy Vazquez Vera, and S. Karthick Ramakrishnan. "On the Road to Opportunity: Racial Disparities in Obtaining AB 60 Driver Licenses." *Boom California* (blog), November 28, 2017. https://boomcalifornia.com/2017/11/28/on-the-road-to-opportunity/.

Epp, Charles R. *The Rights Revolution: Lawyers, Activists, and Supreme Courts in Comparative Perspective.* Chicago, IL: University of Chicago Press, 1998.

Epp, Charles R., Steven Maynard-Moody, and Donald P. Haider-Markel. *Pulled Over: How Police Stops Define Race and Citizenship.* Chicago, IL: University of Chicago Press, 2014.

Esping-Andersen, Gøsta. *The Three Worlds of Welfare Capitalism.* Princeton, NJ: Princeton University Press, 1990.

Evans, Peter B., Dietrich Rueschemeyer, and Theda Skocpol. *Bringing the State Back In.* Cambridge and New York: Cambridge University Press, 1985.

Fede, Andrew. *People Without Rights: An Interpretation of the Fundamentals of the Law of Slavery in the U.S. South.* Distinguished Studies in American Legal and Constitutional History. New York: Garland Publishing, 1992.

Roadblocks to Freedom: Slavery and Manumission in the United States South. New Orleans, LA: Quid Pro Books, 2011.

Feldman, Leonard C. *Citizens Without Shelter: Homelessness, Democracy, and Political Exclusion.* Ithaca, NY: Cornell University Press, 2006.

Fields, Barbara Jeanne. *Slavery and Freedom on the Middle Ground: Maryland during the Nineteenth Century.* Yale Historical Publications 123. New Haven, CT: Yale University Press, 1985.

Filindra, Alexandra. "Is 'Threat' in the Eye of the Researcher? Theory and Measurement in the Study of State-Level Immigration Policymaking." *Policy Studies Journal* 47, no. 3 (2019): 517–543. https://doi.org/10.1111/psj.12264.

Fine, Janice Ruth. *Worker Centers: Organizing Communities at the Edge of the Dream.* Ithaca, NY: Cornell University Press, 2006.

Finkelman, Paul. *An Imperfect Union: Slavery, Federalism, and Comity.* Clark, NJ: The Lawbook Exchange, 1981.

"Prelude to the Fourteenth Amendment: Black Legal Rights in the Antebellum North." *Rutgers Law Journal* 17 (1985): 415.

Slavery and the Founders: Race and Liberty in the Age of Jefferson. Abingdon: Routledge, 2014.

Finley, Keith M. *Delaying the Dream: Southern Senators and the Fight against Civil Rights, 1938–1965.* Baton Rouge: Louisiana State University Press, 2010.

Foley, Elise. "Eliot Spitzer Says Hillary Clinton's 2008 Camp Urged Him Not to Give Driver's Licenses to Undocumented Immigrants." *HuffPost*, October 29, 2015. www .huffpost.com/entry/eliot-spitzer-hillary-clinton-drivers-licenses-undocumented_n_56 325e1be4b00aa54a4d3864.

Foner, Eric. *Reconstruction: America's Unfinished Revolution, 1863–1877.* New York: Harper Collins, 2011.

The Second Founding: How the Civil War and Reconstruction Remade the Constitution. New York: W. W. Norton, 2019.

Fortner, Michael Javen. "Urban Autonomy and Effective Citizenship." In *Urban Citizenship and American Democracy*, edited by Amy Bridges and Michael Javen Fortner, 23–64. Albany, NY: State University of New York Press, 2016.

Fourot, Aude-Claire, Mireille Paquet, and Nora Nagels. "Citizenship as a Regime." In *Citizenship as a Regime: Canadian and International Perspectives*, 3–23. Montreal and Kingston: McGill-Queen's University Press, 2018.

Fox, Cybelle. *Three Worlds of Relief: Race, Immigration, and the American Welfare State from the Progressive Era to the New Deal.* Princeton, NJ: Princeton University Press, 2012.

"Unauthorized Welfare: The Origins of Immigrant Status Restrictions in American Social Policy." *Journal of American History* 102, no. 4 (2016): 1051–1074.

Fraga, Bernard L. *The Turnout Gap: Race, Ethnicity, and Political Inequality in a Diversifying America.* New York: Cambridge University Press, 2018.

Fragomen, Austin T. "The Illegal Immigration Reform and Immigrant Responsibility Act of 1996: An Overview." *International Migration Review* 31, no. 2 (June 1, 1997): 438–460. https://doi.org/10.1177/019791839703100208.

Francis, Megan Ming. *Civil Rights and the Making of the Modern American State.* New York: Cambridge University Press, 2014.

Freeman, Richard D., and Joel Rogers. "The Promise of Progressive Federalism." In *Remaking America: Democracy and Public Policy in an Age of Inequality*, edited by Joe Soss, Jacob S. Hacker, and Suzanne Mettler, 205–227. New York: Russell Sage Foundation, 2007.

Frymer, Paul. *Black and Blue: African Americans, the Labor Movement, and the Decline of the Democratic Party.* Princeton, NJ: Princeton University Press, 2011.

Frymer, Paul. "Building an American Empire: Territorial Expansion in the Antebellum Era." *UC Irvine Law Review* 1 (2011): 913–954.

"'A Rush and a Push and the Land Is Ours': Territorial Expansion, Land Policy, and U.S. State Formation." *Perspectives on Politics* 12, no. 1 (March 2014): 119–144.

Uneasy Alliances: Race and Party Competition in America. Princeton, NJ: Princeton University Press, 2010.

Fujiwara, Lynn. *Mothers Without Citizenship: Asian Immigrant Families and the Consequences of Welfare Reform.* Minneapolis: University of Minnesota Press, 2008.

Fuller, Thomas. "Californians Legalize Marijuana in Vote That Could Echo Nationally." *New York Times*, November 9, 2016, sec. US. www.nytimes.com/ 2016/11/09/us/politics/marijuana-legalization.html.

García, Angela S. *Legal Passing: Navigating Undocumented Life and Local Immigration Law.* Oakland: University of California Press, 2019.

Garcia, Monique, Rick Pearson, and Kim Geiger. "Illinois House Overrides Rauner Vetoes of Income Tax Increase, Budget." *Chicago Tribune,* July 7, 2017. www .chicagotribune.com/politics/ct-madigan-rauner-illinois-house-tax-increase-override-met-0707-20170706-story.html.

Gelman, Andrew, Jeffrey Fagan, and Alex Kiss. "An Analysis of the New York City Police Department's 'Stop-and-Frisk' Policy in the Context of Claims of Racial Bias." *Journal of the American Statistical Association* 102, no. 479 (September 1, 2007): 813–823. https://doi.org/10.1198/016214506000001040.

Gellman, David N., and David Quigley. *Jim Crow New York: A Documentary History of Race and Citizenship, 1777–1877.* New York: New York University Press, 2003.

Genovese, Eugene D. *Roll, Jordan, Roll: The World the Slaves Made.* New York: Pantheon Books, 1974.

Gerken, Heather K. "Federalism as the New Nationalism: An Overview." *Yale Law Journal* 123 (2014): 1889–1919.

"Foreword: Federalism All the Way Down." *Harvard Law Review* 123, no. 1 (2010): 4–74.

"Loyal Opposition, The." *Yale Law Journal* 123 (2014): 1958–1995.

Gilens, Martin. *Why Americans Hate Welfare: Race, Media, and the Politics of Antipoverty Policy.* Chicago, IL: University of Chicago Press, 2009.

Gilmore, Glenda Elizabeth. *Gender and Jim Crow, Second Edition: Women and the Politics of White Supremacy in North Carolina, 1896–1920.* Chapel Hill: University of North Carolina Press Books, 2019.

Gleeson, Shannon. "Labor Rights for All? The Role of Undocumented Immigrant Status for Worker Claims Making." *Law & Social Inquiry* 35, no. 3 (June 1, 2010): 561–602. https://doi.org/10.1111/j.1747-4469.2010.01196.x.

Precarious Claims: The Promise and Failure of Workplace Protections in the United States. Oakland: University of California Press, 2016.

"'They Come Here to Work': An Evaluation of the Economic Argument in Favor of Immigrant Rights." *Citizenship Studies* 19, no. 3–4 (April 3, 2015): 400–420. https://doi.org/10.1080/13621025.2015.1006173.

Gómez, Laura E. *Manifest Destinies: The Making of the Mexican American Race.* New York: New York University Press, 2007.

"Race, Colonialism, and Criminal Law: Mexicans and the American Criminal Justice System in Territorial New Mexico." *Law & Society Review* 34, no. 4 (2000): 1129–1202.

Gluck, Abbe R. "Our [National] Federalism." *Yale Law Journal* 123 (2014): 1996–2043.

Goldbaum, Christina. "County Clerks Revolt Over N.Y. Licenses for Undocumented Immigrants." *New York Times,* November 14, 2019, sec. New York. www .nytimes.com/2019/11/14/nyregion/immigrants-drivers-license.html.

Gonzales, Roberto G. "Learning to Be Illegal Undocumented Youth and Shifting Legal Contexts in the Transition to Adulthood." *American Sociological Review* 76, no. 4 (August 1, 2011): 602–619, https://doi.org/10.1177/0003122411411901.

Lives in Limbo: Undocumented and Coming of Age in America. Oakland: University of California Press, 2015.

Goodheart, Lawrence B. *Abolitionist, Actuary, Atheist: Elizur Wright and the Reform Impulse*. Kent, OH: Kent State University Press, 1990.

Goodman, Sara Wallace. "Conceptualizing and Measuring Citizenship and Integration Policy: Past Lessons and New Approaches." *Comparative Political Studies* 48, no. 14 (December 1, 2015): 1905–1941. https://doi.org/10.1177/0010414015592648.

Immigration and Membership Politics in Western Europe. New York: Cambridge University Press, 2014. http://ebookcentral.proquest.com/lib/asulib-ebooks/detail .action?docID=1775901.

"Integration Requirements for Integration's Sake? Identifying, Categorising and Comparing Civic Integration Policies." *Journal of Ethnic & Migration Studies* 36, no. 5 (May 2010): 753–772. https://doi.org/10.1080/13691831003764300.

Goodyear, Dana. "How Far Will California Take Criminal-Justice Reform?" *New Yorker*, October 5, 2019. www.newyorker.com/news/california-chronicles/ how-far-will-california-take-criminal-justice-reform.

Gordon, Jennifer. *Suburban Sweatshops: The Fight for Immigrant Rights*. Cambridge, MA: Belknap Press, 2007.

Gottschalk, Marie. *Caught: The Prison State and the Lockdown of American Politics*. Princeton, NJ: Princeton University Press, 2014.

Gross, Ariela Julie. *Double Character: Slavery and Mastery in the Antebellum Southern Courtroom*. Princeton, NJ: Princeton University Press, 2000.

What Blood Won't Tell: A History of Race on Trial in America. Cambridge, MA: Harvard University Press, 2010.

Grossberg, Michael. *Governing the Hearth: Law and the Family in Nineteenth-Century America*. Chapel Hill: The University of North Carolina Press, 1988. http:// ebookcentral.proquest.com/lib/asulib-ebooks/detail.action?docID=475184.

Gugliotta, Guy. "Civil War Toll Up by 20 Percent in New Estimate." *New York Times*, April 2, 2012. www.nytimes.com/2012/04/03/science/civil-war-toll-up-by-20- percent-in-new-estimate.html.

Gulasekaram, Pratheepan, and S. Karthick Ramakrishnan. *The New Immigration Federalism*. New York: Cambridge University Press, 2015.

"Immigration Federalism: A Reappraisal." *New York University Law Review* 88 (2013): 2074–2319.

Haas, Lisbeth. *Conquests and Historical Identities in California, 1769–1936*. Berkeley: University of California Press, 1995.

Hadden, Sally E. *Slave Patrols: Law and Violence in Virginia and the Carolinas*. Harvard Historical Studies, v. 138. Cambridge, MA: Harvard University Press, 2001.

Hahn, Steven. *A Nation Under Our Feet: Black Political Struggles in the Rural South from Slavery to the Great Migration*. Cambridge, MA: Belknap Press of Harvard University Press, 2005.

Hakim, Danny. "Spitzer Dropping His Driver's License Plan." *New York Times*, November 14, 2007, sec. N.Y./Region. www.nytimes.com/2007/11/14/nyregion/ 14spitzer.html.

Haney-López, Ian. *Dog Whistle Politics: How Coded Racial Appeals Have Reinvented Racism and Wrecked the Middle Class*. New York: Oxford University Press, 2015.

Hayduk, Ron. *Democracy for All: Restoring Immigrant Voting Rights in the U.S.* New York,: Routledge, 2012.

Haynes, Chris, Jennifer Lee Merolla, and S. Karthick Ramakrishnan. *Framing Immigrants: News Coverage, Public Opinion, and Policy.* New York: Russell Sage Foundation, 2016.

Hirota, Hidetaka. "'The Great Entrepot for Mendicants': Foreign Poverty and Immigration Control in New York State to 1882." *Journal of American Ethnic History* 33, no. 2 (2014): 5–32. https://doi.org/10.5406/jamerethnhist.33.2.0005.

"The Moment of Transition: State Officials, the Federal Government, and the Formation of American Immigration Policy." *Journal of American History* 99, no. 4 (March 1, 2013): 1092–1108.

Hoffman, Abraham. *Unwanted Mexican Americans in the Great Depression: Repatriation Pressures, 1929–1939.* Tucson: University of Arizona Press, 1974.

HoSang, Daniel Martinez. *Racial Propositions: Ballot Initiatives and the Making of Postwar California.* Berkeley: University of California Press, 2010.

Howard, Marc Morjé. "Comparative Citizenship: An Agenda for Cross-National Research." *Perspectives on Politics* 4, no. 3 (September 2006): 443–455. https://doi.org/10.1017/S1537592706060294.

Humes, Brian D., Elaine K. Swift, Richard M. Valelly, Kenneth Finegold, and Evelyn C. Fink. "Representation of the Antebellum South in the House of Representatives: Measuring the Impact of the Three-Fifths Clause." In *Party, Process, and Political Change in Congress: New Perspectives on the History of Congress*, edited by David Brady and Mathew D. McCubbins, 452–466. Palo Alto, CA: Stanford University Press, 2002.

Ignatieff, Michael. "The Myth of Citizenship." In *Theorizing Citizenship*, edited by Ronald Beiner, 53–78. Albany: State University of New York Press, 1995.

Jacobson, David. *Rights Across Borders: Immigration and the Decline of Citizenship.* Baltimore, MD: Johns Hopkins University Press, 1996.

Jacobson, Robin Dale. *The New Nativism: Proposition 187 and the Debate over Immigration.* Minneapolis: University of Minnesota Press, 2008.

Jenkins, Jeffery A., Justin Peck, and Vesla M. Weaver. "Between Reconstructions: Congressional Action on Civil Rights, 1891–1940." *Studies in American Political Development* 24, no. 1 (April 2010): 57–89. https://doi.org/10.1017/S0898588X10000015.

Jenson, Jane, and Martin Papillon. "Challenging the Citizenship Regime: The James Bay Cree and Transnational Action." *Politics & Society* 28, no. 2 (June 1, 2000): 245–264. https://doi.org/10.1177/0032329200028002005.

Johnson, Kevin R. "Immigration and Civil Rights: Is the New Birmingham the Same as the Old Birmingham." *William & Mary Bill of Rights Journal* 21 (2012): 367–397.

Johnson, Kimberly S. "The Color Line and the State: Race and American Political Development." In *The Oxford Handbook of American Political Development*, edited by Richard M. Valelly, Suzanne Mettler, and Robert C. Lieberman, 593–624. Oxford: Oxford University Press, 2016.

Governing the American State: Congress and the New Federalism, 1877–1929. Princeton, NJ: Princeton University Press, 2007.

"Racial Orders, Congress, and the Agricultural Welfare State, 1865–1940." *Studies in American Political Development* 25, no. 2 (2011): 143–161. https://doi.org/10.1017/S0898588X11000095.

Reforming Jim Crow: Southern Politics and State in the Age Before Brown. Oxford: Oxford University Press, 2010.

Johnson, Walter. *Soul by Soul: Life Inside the Antebellum Slave Market.* Cambridge, MA: Harvard University Press, 1999.

Johnston-Dodds, Kimberly. "Early California Laws and Policies Related to California Indians." *California State Library, California Research Bureau Reports, CRB02-014,* 2002, 1. https://digitalcommons.csumb.edu/hornbeck_usa_3_d/34.

Jones, Martha S. *Birthright Citizens: A History of Race and Rights in Antebellum America.* New York: Cambridge University Press, 2018.

"Leave of Court: African-American Legal Claims Making in the Era of Dred Scott v. Sandford." In *Contested Democracy: Politics, Ideology, and Race in American History,* edited by Manisha Sinha and Penny Von Eschen, 54–74. New York: Columbia University Press, 2007.

Jones-Correa, Michael. "The Origins and Diffusion of Racial Restrictive Covenants." *Political Science Quarterly* 115, no. 4 (2000): 541–568. https://doi.org/10.2307/2657609.

Joppke, Christian. *Citizenship and Immigration.* Cambridge, MA: Polity, 2010.

Kato, Daniel. "Strengthening the Weak State: Politicizing the American State's 'Weakness' on Racial Violence." *Du Bois Review: Social Science Research on Race* 9, no. 2 (2012): 457–580. https://doi.org/10.1017/S1742058X12000306.

Katz, Michael. *Undeserving Poor.* New York: Knopf Doubleday, 2011.

Katznelson, Ira. *When Affirmative Action Was White: An Untold History of Racial Inequality in Twentieth-Century America.* New York: W. W. Norton, 2006.

Kettner, James H. *Development of American Citizenship, 1608–1870.* Reprint ed. Chapel Hill: The University of North Carolina Press, 1978.

Key, V. O. *Politics, Parties and Interest Groups.* 3rd ed. New York: Thomas Y. Crowell Co., 1952.

Keyssar, Alexander. *The Right to Vote: The Contested History of Democracy in the United States.* New York: Basic Books, 2009.

King, Desmond. "Forceful Federalism against American Racial Inequality." *Government and Opposition* 52, no. 2 (April 2017): 356–382. https://doi.org/10.1017/gov.2016.52.

King, Desmond S. *Separate and Unequal: Black Americans and the US Federal Government.* Oxford: Clarendon Press, 1997.

King, Desmond S., and Rogers M. Smith. "Racial Orders in American Political Development." *The American Political Science Review* 99, no. 1 (February 1, 2005): 75–92.

Still a House Divided: Race and Politics in Obama's America. Princeton, NJ: Princeton University Press, 2013.

"Strange Bedfellows? Polarized Politics? The Quest for Racial Equity in Contemporary America." *Political Research Quarterly* 61, no. 4 (2008): 686–703. https://doi.org/10.1177/1065912908322410.

Kini, Tara. "Sharing the Vote: Noncitizen Voting Rights in Local School Board Elections." *California Law Review* 93, no. 1 (January 1, 2005): 271–321.

Koopmans, Ruud, and Ines Michalowski. "Why Do States Extend Rights to Immigrants? Institutional Settings and Historical Legacies Across 44 Countries Worldwide." *Comparative Political Studies* 50, no. 1 (January 1, 2017): 41–74. https://doi.org/10.1177/0010414016655533.

Koppelman, Andrew. "The Miscegenation Analogy: Sodomy Law as Sex Discrimination." *The Yale Law Journal* 98, no. 1 (1988): 145–164. https://doi.org/10.2307/796648.

Kousser, J. Morgan. *The Shaping of Southern Politics: Suffrage Restriction and the Establishment of the One-Party South, 1880–1910*. New Haven, CT: Yale University Press, 1974.

Kuo, Joyce. "Excluded, Segregated and Forgo En: A Historical View of the Discrimination of Chinese Americans in Public Schools." *Asian American Law Journal* 5 (1998): 181–212.

Kymlicka, Will. *Multicultural Citizenship: A Liberal Theory of Minority Rights*. Oxford: Oxford University Press, 1996.

Lai, Annie, and Christopher N. Lasch. "Crimmigration Resistance and the Case of Sanctuary City Defunding." *Santa Clara Law Review* 57 (2017): 539–610.

Lapp, Rudolph M. *Blacks in Gold Rush California*. New Haven, CT: Yale University Press, 1977.

Lasch, Christopher N. "Enforcing the Limits of the Executive's Authority to Issue Immigration Detainers Immigration Law." *William Mitchell Law Review* 35 (2008): 164–196.

"Rendition Resistance." *North Carolina Law Review* 92 (2013): 149.

"Sanctuary Cities and Dog-Whistle Politics." *New England Journal on Criminal and Civil Confinement* 42 (2016): 159–190.

Lasch, Christopher N., R. Linus Chan, Ingrid V. Eagly, Dina Francesca Haynes, Annie Lai, Elizabeth M. McCormick, and Juliet P. Stumpf. "Understanding Sanctuary Cities." *Boston College Law Review* 59 (2018): 1703–1774.

Laurie, Bruce. *Beyond Garrison: Antislavery and Social Reform*. Cambridge and New York: Cambridge University Press, 2005.

Law, Anna O. "Lunatics, Idiots, Paupers, and Negro Seamen—Immigration Federalism and the Early American State." *Studies in American Political Development* 28, no. 2 (October 2014): 107–128.

"The Historical Amnesia of Contemporary Immigration Federalism Debates." *Polity* 47, no. 3 (July 2015): 302–319.

Lazare, Lewis. "Southwest Airlines Debuts Dramatically Different Ad Campaign." *Chicago Business Journal*, March 19, 2013. www.bizjournals.com/chicago/news/2013/03/19/southwest-airlines-ready-to-welcome.html.

Lazo, Robert. "Latinos and the AFL-CIO: The California Immigrant Workers Association as an Important New Development." *La Raza Law Journal* 4 (1991): 22–43.

Lerman, Amy E., and Vesla M. Weaver. *Arresting Citizenship: The Democratic Consequences of American Crime Control*. Chicago, IL: University of Chicago Press, 2014.

"Staying out of Sight? Concentrated Policing and Local Political Action." *ANNALS of the American Academy of Political and Social Science* 651, no. 1 (January 1, 2014): 202–219. https://doi.org/10.1177/0002716213503085.

Lieberman, Robert C. *Shaping Race Policy: The United States in Comparative Perspective*. Princeton, NJ: Princeton University Press, 2005.

Shifting the Color Line: Race and the American Welfare State. Cambridge, MA: Harvard University Press, 2001.

"Weak State, Strong Policy: Paradoxes of Race Policy in the United States, Great Britain, and France." *Studies in American Political Development* 16, no. 2 (October 2002): 138–161. https://doi.org/10.1017/S0898588X0200007X.

Lieberman, Robert C., and John S. Lapinski. "American Federalism, Race and the Administration of Welfare." *British Journal of Political Science* 31, no. 2 (April 2001): 303–329. https://doi.org/10.1017/S0007123401000126.

Lister, Ruth. "Citizenship: Towards a Feminist Synthesis." *Feminist Review* 57, no. 1 (September 1, 1997): 28–48. https://doi.org/10.1080/014177897339641.

"What Is Citizenship?" In *Citizenship: Feminist Perspectives*, edited by Ruth Lister and Jo Campling, 13–42. London: Macmillan Education UK, 2003. https://doi.org/10.1007/978-0-230-80253-7_2.

Litwack, Leon F. *North of Slavery: The Negro in the Free States, 1790–1860*. Chicago, IL: University of Chicago Press, 1961.

Locke, John. *Second Treatise of Government*. New York: Barnes & Noble Publishing, 2004 [1690].

Lopez, Ian Haney. *White by Law: The Legal Construction of Race*. New York: New York University Press, 2006.

Lopez, Tomas. "'Shelby County': One Year Later." *Brennan Center for Justice*, 2014.

Luna, Taryn. "Gov. Gavin Newsom Pledges to Help Build up El Salvador to Reduce Migration." *Los Angeles Times*, April 15, 2019. www.latimes.com/politics/la-pol-ca-el-salvador-gavin-newsom-20190415-story.html.

Luna, Taryn, and Billy Kobin. "Undocumented Immigrant Appointed to State Post in California." *Sacramento Bee*, March 15, 2018. www.sacbee.com/news/politics-government/capitol-alert/article205249624.html.

Maas, Willem. *Multilevel Citizenship*. Philadelphia: University of Pennsylvania Press, 2013.

"Varieties of Multilevel Citizenship." In *Multilevel Citizenship*, edited by Willem Maas, 1–21. Philadelphia: University of Pennsylvania Press, 2013.

Madley, Benjamin. *An American Genocide: The United States and the California Indian Catastrophe, 1846–1873*. New Haven, CT: Yale University Press, 2016.

Mahoney, James, ed. *Comparative Historical Analysis in the Social Sciences*. Cambridge and New York: Cambridge University Press, 2003.

Mahoney, James, and Kathleen Thelen, eds. *Explaining Institutional Change: Ambiguity, Agency, and Power*. Cambridge and New York: Cambridge University Press, 2009.

Mann, Charles Wesley. *The Chicago Common Council and the Fugitive Slave Law of 1850: An Address Read Before the Chicago Historical Society at a Special Meeting Held January 29, 1903*. Chicago, IL: Chicago Historical Society, 1903.

Markowitz, Peter L. "Undocumented No More: The Power of State Citizenship." *Stanford Law Review* 67 (2015): 1–42.

Marquez, Timothy, and Scot Schraufnagel. "Hispanic Population Growth and State Immigration Policy: An Analysis of Restriction (2008–12)." *Publius: The Journal of Federalism* 43, no. 3 (July 1, 2013): 347–367. https://doi.org/10.1093/publius/pjt008.

Marshall, T. H. *Citizenship and Social Class*. Cambridge: Cambridge University Press, 1950.

Class, Citizenship, and Social Development: Essays by T. H. Marshall. New York: Doubleday, 1965.

Mashaw, Jerry L. "Reluctant Nationalists: Federal Administration and Administrative Law in the Republican Era, 1801–1829." *Yale Law Journal* 116 (2007): 1636–1741.

Massey, Douglas S. "Racial Formation in Theory and Practice: The Case of Mexicans in the United States." *Race and Social Problems* 1, no. 1 (March 1, 2009): 12–26. https://doi.org/10.1007/s12552-009-9005-3.

Massey, Douglas S., Jorge Durand, and Nolan J. Malone. *Beyond Smoke and Mirrors: Mexican Immigration in an Era of Economic Integration.* New York: Russell Sage Foundation, 2002.

May, Nicholas. "Holy Rebellion: Religious Assembly Laws in Antebellum South Carolina and Virginia." *The American Journal of Legal History* 49, no. 3 (2007): 237–356.

McClain, Charles J. "The Chinese Struggle for Civil Rights in Nineteenth Century America: The First Phase, 1850–1870." *California Law Review* 72 (1984): 529–568.

In Search of Equality: The Chinese Struggle against Discrimination in Nineteenth-Century America. Berkeley: University of California Press, 1994.

McDaniel, Ruth Currie. "Black Power in Georgia: William A. Pledger and the Takeover of the Republican Party." *The Georgia Historical Quarterly* 62, no. 3 (1978): 225–239.

McDonagh, Eileen L. "The 'Welfare Rights State' and the 'Civil Rights State': Policy Paradox and State Building in the Progressive Era." *Studies in American Political Development* 7, no. 2 (1993). https://doi.org/10.1017/S0898588X00001103.

McDougall, Marion Gleason. *Fugitive Slaves (1619–1865).* Boston, MA: Ginn & Company, 1891.

McNair, Glenn. *Criminal Injustice: Slaves and Free Blacks in Georgia's Criminal Justice System.* Charlottesville: University of Virginia Press, 2009.

McWilliams, Carey, and Matt S. Meier. *North from Mexico: The Spanish-Speaking People of the United States.* Updated by Matt S. Meier, 2nd ed. New York: Praeger, 1990.

Menchaca, Martha. "Chicano Indianism: A Historical Account of Racial Repression in the United States." *American Ethnologist* 20, no. 3 (1993): 583–603.

The Mexican Outsiders: A Community History of Marginalization and Discrimination in California. Austin: University of Texas Press, 2010.

Mettler, Suzanne. *Dividing Citizens: Gender and Federalism in New Deal Public Policy.* Ithaca, NY: Cornell University Press, 1998.

Michener, Jamila. *Fragmented Democracy: Medicaid, Federalism, and Unequal Politics.* Cambridge: Cambridge University Press, 2018.

Mickey, Robert W. "The Beginning of the End for Authoritarian Rule in America: Smith v. Allwright and the Abolition of the White Primary in the Deep South, 1944–1948." *Studies in American Political Development* 22, no. 2 (September 2008): 143–182. https://doi.org/10.1017/S0898588X08000096.

Paths Out of Dixie: The Democratization of Authoritarian Enclaves in America's Deep South, 1944–1972. Princeton, NJ: Princeton University Press, 2015.

Middleton, Stephen. *The Black Laws in the Old Northwest: A Documentary History.* Contributions in Afro-American and African Studies, no. 152. Westport, CT: Greenwood Press, 1993.

The Black Laws: Race and the Legal Process in Early Ohio. Athens: Ohio University Press, 2005.

Milkis, Sidney M., and Daniel J. Tichenor. "Reform's Mating Dance: Presidents, Social Movements, and Racial Realignments." *Journal of Policy History* 23, no. 4 (October 2011): 451–490. https://doi.org/10.1017/S0898030611000261.

Rivalry and Reform: Presidents, Social Movements, and the Transformation of American Politics. Chicago, IL: University of Chicago Press, 2019.

Milkman, Ruth. *LA Story: Immigrant Workers and the Future of the US Labor Movement.* New York: Russell Sage Foundation, 2006.

Miller, Lisa L. *The Perils of Federalism: Race, Poverty, and the Politics of Crime Control*. Oxford: Oxford University Press, 2008.

Molina, Natalia. *How Race Is Made in America: Immigration, Citizenship, and the Historical Power of Racial Scripts*. Berkeley: University of California Press, 2014.

Monahan, Rachel. "Opponents to Oregon Driver's Licenses for Undocumented Immigrants Refile Initiative Petition." *Willamette Week*, October 27, 2019. www.wweek.com/news/state/2019/10/27/opponents-to-oregon-drivers-license-for-undocumented-immigrants-refile-initiative-petition/.

Monogan, James E. "The Politics of Immigrant Policy in the 50 US States, 2005–2011." *Journal of Public Policy* 33, no. 1 (April 2013): 35–64. https://doi.org/10.1017/S0143814X12000189.

Monroy, Douglas. "An Essay on Understanding the Work Experience of Mexicans in Southern California, 1900–1939." *Aztlan: A Journal of Chicano Studies* 12, no. 1 (1981): 59–74.

Montoya, Maria E. *Translating Property: The Maxwell Land Grant and the Conflict over Land in the American West, 1840–1900*. Lawrence: University Press of Kansas, 2002.

Moore, Shirley Ann Wilson. "'We Feel the Want of Protection': The Politics of Law and Race in California, 1848–1878." *California History* 81, no. 3/4 (2003): 96–125. https://doi.org/10.2307/25161701.

Morgan, Philip D., and Andrew Jackson O'Shaughnessy. "Arming Slaves in the American Revolution." In *Arming Slaves: From Classical Times to the Modern Age*, edited by Christopher Leslie Brown and Philip D. Morgan, 180–208. New Haven, CT: Yale University Press, 2006.

Morris, Aldon D. *The Origins of the Civil Rights Movement*. New York: The Free Press, 1984.

Morris, Thomas D. *Free Men All: The Personal Liberty Laws of the North, 1780–1861*. Clark, NJ: The Lawbook Exchange, 1974.

Motomura, Hiroshi. *Americans in Waiting: The Lost Story of Immigration and Citizenship in the United States*. Oxford: Oxford University Press, 2006.

"The Curious Evolution of Immigration Law: Procedural Surrogates for Substantive Constitutional Rights." *Columbia Law Review* 92, no. 7 (1992): 1625–1704.

Immigration Outside the Law. Oxford and New York: Oxford University Press, 2014.

Mousin, Craig B. "Clear View from the Prairie: Harold Washington and the People of Illinois Respond to Federal Encroachment of Human Rights, A." *Southern Illinois University Law Journal* 29 (2005): 285.

Murakawa, Naomi. *First Civil Right: How Liberals Built Prison America*. New York: Oxford University Press, 2014.

Murray, Robert K. *Red Scare a Study in National Hysteria, 1919–1920*. Minneapolis: University of Minnesota Press, 1955.

Myers, John. "Californians Can Register to Vote on Election Day at Any Polling Place Under New Law." *Los Angeles Times*, October 9, 2019. www.latimes.com/california/story/2019-10-08/californians-register-to-vote-any-polling-place-2020-new-law.

National Association for the Advancement of Colored People. "Criminal Justice Fact Sheet." www.naacp.org/criminal-justice-fact-sheet/, accessed November 18, 2019.

Neuman, Gerald L. *Strangers to the Constitution: Immigrants, Borders, and Fundamental Law*. Princeton, NJ: Princeton University Press, 2010.

"The Lost Century of American Immigration Law (1776–1875)." *Columbia Law Review* 93, no. 8 (December 1, 1993): 1833–1901.

New York Immigration Coalition. "Blueprint for Immigrant New York," November 8, 2017. www.thenyic.org/userfiles/file/nyic_Blueprint_for_ImmigrantNY_v5.pdf.

Nicholson-Crotty, Jill, and Sean Nicholson-Crotty. "Industry Strength and Immigrant Policy in the American States." *Political Research Quarterly* 64, no. 3 (2011): 612–624.

Norton, Jack. *Genocide in Northwestern California: When Our Worlds Cried.* San Francisco, CA: Indian Historian Press, 1979.

Nussbaum, Martha C. "A Right to Marry?" *California Law Review* 98, no. 3 (2010): 667–696.

Ofer, Odi, and Nicole Zayas Fortier. *Unveiling a State-by-State Plan to End Our Mass Incarceration Crisis.* New York: American Civil Liberties Union, 2019. www.aclu .org/news/smart-justice/unveiling-a-state-by-state-plan-to-end-our-mass-incarceration-crisis/?initms_aff=nat&initms_chan=soc&utm_medium=soc&initms=191018_fb& utm_source=fb&utm_campaign&utm_content=191018&ms_aff=nat&ms_chan= soc&ms=191018_fb.

Olmstead, Molly. "Georgia Is Purging Voter Rolls Again." *Slate*, October 30, 2019. https:// slate.com/news-and-politics/2019/10/georgia-election-purge-voter-rolls.html.

Orren, Karen, and Stephen Skowronek. *The Search for American Political Development.* Cambridge and New York: Cambridge University Press, 2004.

Parker, Christopher S. *Fighting for Democracy: Black Veterans and the Struggle Against White Supremacy in the Postwar South.* Princeton, NJ: Princeton University Press, 2009.

Parker, Joel. *Personal Liberty Laws and Slavery in the Territories.* Boston, MA: Wright & Potter, 1861.

Parker, Kunal M. *Making Foreigners: Immigration and Citizenship Law in America, 1600–2000.* New York: Cambridge University Press, 2015.

Parker, Kunal M. "State, Citizenship, and Territory: The Legal Construction of Immigrants in Antebellum Massachusetts." *Law and History Review* 19, no. 3 (September 2001): 583–643.

Pastor, Manuel. *State of Resistance: What California's Dizzying Descent and Remarkable Resurgence Mean for America's Future.* New York: The New Press, 2018.

Patterson, James T. *The New Deal and the States: Federalism in Transition.* Princeton, NJ: Princeton University Press, 1969.

Pham, Huyen. "The Private Enforcement of Immigration Laws." *Georgetown Law Journal* 96 (2008): 777–826.

Phillips, Ulrich Bonnell. *American Negro Slavery; A Survey of the Supply, Employment and Control of Negro Labor as Determined by the Plantation Regime.* 1st paperback ed. Louisiana Paperbacks L9. Baton Rouge: Louisiana State University Press, 1966.

Piven, Frances Fox, and Richard A. Cloward. *Regulating the Poor: The Functions of Public Welfare.* New York: Knopf Doubleday, 2012.

Pocock, J. G. A. "The Ideal of Citizenship since Classical Times." In *The Citizenship Debates: A Reader,* edited by Gershon Shafir, 29–52. Minneapolis: University of Minnesota Press, 1998.

Poole, Mary. *The Segregated Origins of Social Security: African Americans and the Welfare State*. Chapel Hill: University of North Carolina Press, 2006.

Pope, James Gray. "Snubbed Landmark: Why United States v. Cruikshank (1876) Belongs at the Heart of the American Constitutional Canon." *Harvard Civil Rights-Civil Liberties Law Review* 49 (2014): 385–448.

Powell, Michael, and Michelle García. "Pa. City Puts Illegal Immigrants on Notice." *Washington Post*, August 22, 2006. www.washingtonpost.com/archive/politics/2006/08/22/pa-city-puts-illegal-immigrants-on-notice-span-classbankheadthey-must-leave-mayor-of-hazleton-says-after-signing-tough-new-lawspan/b3e1ecfc-124a-4e05-a3b0-1edbec01bf3b/.

Przeworski, Adam. *Democracy and Development: Political Institutions and Well-Being in the World, 1950–1990*. 1st ed. Cambridge: Cambridge University Press, 2000.

Quadagno, Jill. *The Color of Welfare: How Racism Undermined the War on Poverty*. Oxford: Oxford University Press, 1996.

Rabinowitz, Howard N. "From Exclusion to Segregation: Southern Race Relations, 1865-1890." *Journal of American History* 63, no. 2 (1976): 3256350. https://doi.org/10.2307/1899640.

Rael, Patrick. *Eighty-Eight Years: The Long Death of Slavery in the United States, 1777–1865*. Athens: University of Georgia Press, 2015.

"The Long Death of Slavery in New York." In *Slavery in New York*, edited by Ira Berlin and Leslie Harris, 111–145. New York: New Press, 2005.

Ramakrishnan, S. Karthick. *Democracy in Immigrant America: Changing Demographics and Political Participation*. Stanford, CA: Stanford University Press, 2005.

"Incorporation versus Assimilation: The Need for Conceptual Differentiation." In *Outsiders No More? Models of Immigrant Political Incorporation*, edited by Jennifer L. Hochschild, Jacqueline Chattopadhyay, Claudine Gay, and Michael Jones-Correa, 27–42. Oxford: Oxford University Press, 2013.

Ramakrishnan, S. Karthick, and Allan Colbern. "The California Package: Immigrant Integration and the Evolving Nature of State Citizenship." *Policy Matters* 6, no. 3 (2015): 1–19.

Raskin, Jamin B. "Legal Aliens, Local Citizens: The Historical, Constitutional and Theoretical Meanings of Alien Suffrage." *University of Pennsylvania Law Review* 141, no. 4 (April 1, 1993): 1391–1470. https://doi.org/10.2307/3312345.

"Legal Aliens, Local Citizens: The Historical, Constitutional and Theoretical Meanings of Alien Suffrage." *University of Pennsylvania Law Review* 141, no. 4 (April 1, 1993): 1391–1470. https://doi.org/10.2307/3312345.

Reisler, Mark. *By the Sweat of Their Brow: Mexican Immigrant Labor in the United States, 1900–1940*. Westport, CT: Praeger, 1976.

Reyes, Eloise Gómez. "Expedited Certification Process for U Visa and T Visa Applicants Signed into Law," October 11, 2019. https://a47.asmdc.org/press-releases/20191011-expedited-certification-process-u-visa-and-t-visa-applicants-signed-law.

Riker, William H. *Federalism: Origin, Operation, Significance*. Little, Brown, 1964.

Roberts, Sylvia Alden. *Mining for Freedom: Black History Meets the California Gold Rush*. Bloomington, IN: iUniverse, 2008.

Robertson, Craig. *The Passport in America: The History of a Document*. New York: Oxford University Press, 2010.

Robertson, David Brian. *Federalism and the Making of America*. Abingdon: Routledge, 2012.

Rodriguez, Cristina M. "Enforcement, Integration, and the Future of Immigration Federalism." *Journal on Migration and Human Security* 5 (2017): 509–540.

"Negotiating Conflict through Federalism: Institutional and Popular Perspectives." *Yale Law Journal* 123 (2014): 2094–2133.

Romero, Dennis. "New Law Says Employers Can't Ask Applicants About Criminal Past." *LA Weekly*, October 17, 2017. www.laweekly.com/new-law-says-employers-cant-ask-applicants-about-criminal-past/.

Rosberg, Gerald M. "Aliens and Equal Protection: Why Not the Right to Vote?" *Michigan Law Review* 75, no. 5/6 (April 1, 1977): 1092–1136. https://doi.org/10.2307/1288026.

Root, Danielle, and Liz Kennedy. "Increasing Voter Participation in America." Center for American Progress, July 11, 2018. www.americanprogress.org/issues/democracy/reports/2018/07/11/453319/increasing-voter-participation-america/.

Rose, Shanna, and Cynthia J. Bowling. "The State of American Federalism 2014–15: Pathways to Policy in an Era of Party Polarization." *Publius: The Journal of Federalism* 45, no. 3 (July 1, 2015): 351–379.

Rosenberg, Norman L. "Personal Liberty Laws and Section Crisis: 1850–1861." In *Abolitionism and American Law*, edited by John R. McKivigan, 320–340. History of the American Abolitionist Movement. New York: Garland Publishing, 1999.

Ruchames, Louis. "Jim Crow Railroads in Massachusetts." *American Quarterly* 8, no. 1 (1956): 61–75. https://doi.org/10.2307/2710298.

Salter, Mark B. *Rights of Passage: The Passport in International Relations*. Boulder, CO: Lynne Rienner Publishers, 2003.

Sartori, Giovanni. "Concept Misformation in Comparative Politics." *American Political Science Review* 64, no. 4 (December 1, 1970): 1033–1053. https://doi.org/10.2307/1958356.

Sassen, Saskia. "The Repositioning of Citizenship: Emergent Subjects and Spaces for Politics." *Berkeley Journal of Sociology* 46 (2002): 4–26.

Sawyer, Wendy, and Peter Wagner. "Mass Incarceration: The Whole Pie 2019." *Prison Policy Initiative* (blog), March 19, 2019. www.prisonpolicy.org/reports/pie2019.html.

Schechter, Patricia A. *Ida B. Wells-Barnett and American Reform, 1880–1930*. Chapel Hill: The University of North Carolina Press, 2001.

Schuck, Peter H. "Citizenship in Federal Systems." *American Journal of Comparative Law* 48, no. 2 (April 1, 2000): 195–226.

"Membership in the Liberal Polity: The Devaluation of American Citizenship." *Georgetown Immigration Law Journal* 3 (1989): 1–18.

"Taking Immigration Federalism Seriously." *University of Chicago Legal Forum* (2007): 57–92.

Semple, Kirk. "Gillibrand's Immigration Views Draw Fire." *New York Times*, January 27, 2009, sec. Politics. www.nytimes.com/2009/01/28/us/politics/28immigration.html.

Sen, Amartya. *Development as Freedom*. Oxford and New York: Oxford University Press, 2001.

Inequality Reexamined. New York and Cambridge, MA: Russell Sage Foundation and Harvard University Press, 1992.

Shafir, Gershon. *The Citizenship Debates: A Reader*. Minneapolis: University of Minnesota Press, 1998.

Sitkoff, Harvard. "Racial Militancy and Interracial Violence in the Second World War." *The Journal of American History* 58, no. 3 (1971): 661–681. https://doi.org/10.2307/1893729.

Skowronek, Stephen. *Building a New American State: The Expansion of National Administrative Capacities, 1877–1920*. Cambridge and New York: Cambridge University Press, 1982.

Skrentny, John David. *After Civil Rights: Racial Realism in the New American Workplace*. Princeton, NJ: Princeton University Press, 2014.

The Ironies of Affirmative Action: Politics, Culture, and Justice in America. Chicago, IL: University of Chicago Press, 2018.

The Minority Rights Revolution. Cambridge, MA: Harvard University Press, 2009.

Smith, John David. "Segregation and the Age of Jim Crow." In *When Did Southern Segregation Begin?*, edited by John David Smith, 3–42. Boston, MA: Bedford/St. Martin's, 2002.

Smith, Rogers M. "American Cities and American Citizenship." In *Urban Citizenship and American Democracy*, edited by Amy Bridges and Michael Javen Fortner, 211–222. Albany, NY: State University of New York Press, 2016.

"Attrition through Enforcement in the '"Promiseland"': Overlapping Memberships and the Duties of Governments in Mexican America." In *Multilevel Citizenship*, edited by Willem Maas, 43–69. Philadelphia: University of Pennsylvania Press, 2013.

"Beyond Tocqueville, Myrdal, and Hartz: The Multiple Traditions in America." *American Political Science Review* 87, no. 3 (1993): 549–566. https://doi.org/10.2307/2938735.

Civic Ideals: Conflicting Visions of Citizenship in U.S. History. New Haven, CT: Yale University Press, 1997.

"Substance and Methods in APD Research." *Studies in American Political Development* 17, no. 1 (April 2003): 111–115. https://doi.org/10.1017/S0898588X0300004X.

Smith, Stacey L. *Freedom's Frontier: California and the Struggle over Unfree Labor, Emancipation, and Reconstruction*. Chapel Hill: The University of North Carolina Press, 2013.

Solbakken, Lisa C. "The Anti-Terrorism and Effective Death Penalty Act: Anti-Immigration Legislation Veiled in an Anti-Terrorism Pretext Notes." *Brooklyn Law Review* 63 (1997): 1381–1410.

Soss, Joe. "Lessons of Welfare: Policy Design, Political Learning, and Political Action." *American Political Science Review* 93, no. 2 (1999): 363–380. https://doi.org/10.2307/2585401.

Soss, Joe, Richard C. Fording, and Sanford F. Schram. *Disciplining the Poor: Neoliberal Paternalism and the Persistent Power of Race*. Chicago, IL: University of Chicago Press, 2011.

Soss, Joe, and Vesla Weaver. "Police Are Our Government: Politics, Political Science, and the Policing of Race–Class Subjugated Communities." *Annual Review of*

Political Science 20, no. 1 (2017): 565–591. https://doi.org/10.1146/annurev-polisci-060415-093825.

Soysal, Yasemin Nuhoğlu. *Limits of Citizenship: Migrants and Postnational Membership in Europe.* Chicago, IL: University of Chicago Press, 1994.

Spiro, Peter J. *Beyond Citizenship: American Identity after Globalization.* New York: Oxford University Press, 2008.

"The States and Immigration in an Era of Demi-Sovereignties." *Virginia Journal of International Law* 35 (1994): 121–178.

Spitzzeri, Paul R. "Judge Lynch in Session: Popular Justice in Los Angeles, 1850–1875." *Southern California Quarterly* 87, no. 2 (2005): 83–122. https://doi.org/10.2307/41172258.

Staff and Wire Reports. "U.S. Supreme Court Won't Review Kansas, Arizona Voter Registration Appeal, Leaving in Place Two-Tier Voting System." *Topeka Capital-Journal,* June 29, 2015. www.cjonline.com/article/20150629/NEWS/306299738.

Stampp, Kenneth M. *The Peculiar Institution: Slavery in the Ante-Bellum South.* New York: Knopf, 1956.

Stephenson, Gilbert Thomas. "The Separation of The Races in Public Conveyances." *American Political Science Review* 3, no. 2 (1909): 180–204. https://doi.org/10.2307/1944727.

Strolovitch, Dara Z., Dorian T. Warren, and Paul Frymer. "Katrina's Political Roots and Divisions: Race, Class, and Federalism in American Politics." *Understanding Katrina: Perspectives from the Social Sciences: Social Science Research Council* (blog), 2006. http://understandingkatrina.ssrc.org/FrymerStrolovitchWarren/.

Sullivan, Andy. "Southern U.S. States Have Closed 1,200 Polling Places in Recent Years: Rights Group." *Reuters,* September 10, 2019. www.reuters.com/article/us-usa-election-locations-idUSKCN1VVo9J.

Sverdlik, Alan. "Savannah Tribune." *New Georgia Encyclopedia* (blog), June 8, 2018. www.georgiaencyclopedia.org/articles/arts-culture/savannah-tribune.

Taslitz, Andrew E. "Stories of Fourth Amendment Disrespect: From Elian to the Internment." *Fordham Law Review* 70 (2002): 2257–2360.

Takaki, Ronald T. *Strangers from a Different Shore: A History of Asian Americans.* Boston, MA: Little, Brown, 1989.

Thelen, Kathleen. "Timing and Temporality in the Analysis of Institutional Evolution and Change." *Studies in American Political Development* 14, no. 1 (April 2000): 101–108.

Thurston, Chloe N. *At the Boundaries of Homeownership: Credit, Discrimination, and the American State.* Cambridge: Cambridge University Press, 2018.

"Black Lives Matter, American Political Development, and the Politics of Visibility." *Politics, Groups, and Identities* 6, no. 1 (January 2, 2018): 163. https://doi.org/10.1080/21565503.2017.1420547.

"Policy Feedback in the Public–Private Welfare State: Advocacy Groups and Access to Government Homeownership Programs, 1934–1954." Studies in American Political Development 29, no. 2 (October 2015): 250–267.

Tichenor, Daniel. *Dividing Lines: The Politics of Immigration Control in America.* Princeton Studies in American Politics. Princeton, NJ: Princeton University Press, 2002.

Tichenor, Daniel J., and Alexandra Filindra. "Raising Arizona v. United States: Historical Patterns of American Immigration Federalism." *Lewis & Clark Law Review* 16 (2012): 1215.

Tilly, Charles. *Citizenship, Identity, and Social History*. Cambridge, MA: Cambridge University Press, 1996.

    Coercion, Capital and European States: AD 990–1992. Cambridge, MA: Blackwell, 1992.

    The Formation of National States in Western Europe. Studies in Political Development 8. Princeton, NJ: Princeton University Press, 1975.

Torpey, John. *The Invention of the Passport: Surveillance, Citizenship, and the State*. Cambridge Studies in Law and Society. Cambridge and New York: Cambridge University Press, 2000.

Torrey, Jesse. *American Slave Trade; Or, An Account of the Manner in Which the Slave Dealers Take Free People from Some of the United States of America, and Carry Them Away, and Sell Them as Slaves in Other of the States; and of the Horrible Cruelties Practiced in the Carrying on of This Most Infamous Traffic: With Reflections on the Project for Forming a Colony of American Blacks in Africa, and Certain Documents Respecting That Project*. London: C. Clement and published by J. M. Cobbett, 1822.

Turner, Edward Raymond. "Slavery in Pennsylvania," 1911. www.gutenberg.org/files/44579/44579-h/44579-h.htm.

Ulloa, Jazmine. "How California's Trust Act Shaped the Debate on the New 'Sanctuary State' Proposal." *Los Angeles Times*, September 10, 2017. www.latimes.com/politics/la-pol-ca-trust-act-sanctuary-state-immigration-20170910-htmlstory.html.

Valelly, Richard M. "LGBT Politics and American Political Development." *Annual Review of Political Science* 15, no. 1 (2012): 317. https://doi.org/10.1146/annurev-polisci-061709-104806.

    The Two Reconstructions: The Struggle for Black Enfranchisement. American Politics and Political Economy. Chicago, IL: University of Chicago Press, 2004.

Varsanyi, Monica. "Interrogating 'Urban Citizenship' Vis-à-Vis Undocumented Migration." *Citizenship Studies* 10, no. 2 (2006): 229–249. https://doi.org/10.1080/13621020600633168.

    ed. *Taking Local Control: Immigration Policy Activism in U.S. Cities and States*. Stanford, CA: Stanford University Press, 2010.

Varsanyi, Monica W., Paul G. Lewis, Doris Marie Provine, and Scott Decker. "A Multilayered Jurisdictional Patchwork: Immigration Federalism in the United States." *Law & Policy* 34, no. 2 (April 1, 2012): 138–158.

Villazor, Rose Cuison. "Sanctuary Cities and Local Citizenship." *Fordham Urban Law Journal* 37 (2010): 573–598.

Vink, Maarten Peter, and Rainer Baubock. "Citizenship Configurations: Analysing the Multiple Purposes of Citizenship Regimes in Europe." *Comparative European Politics* 11, no. 5 (2013): 621–648. http://dx.doi.org.ezproxy1.lib.asu.edu/10.1057/cep.2013.14.

Voss, Kim, and Irene Bloemraad, eds. *Rallying for Immigrant Rights*. Berkeley: University of California Press, 2010.

Wade, Richard C. *Slavery in the Cities; The South, 1820–1860*. New York: Oxford University Press, 1964.

Waldinger, Roger, and Michael I. Lichter. *How the Other Half Works: Immigration and the Social Organization of Labor*. Berkeley: University of California Press, 2003.

Walsh, Jess. "Laboring at the Margins: Welfare and the Regulation of Mexican Workers in Southern California." *Antipode* 31, no. 4 (October 1, 1999): 398–420. https://doi.org/10.1111/1467-8330.00111.

Wang, Vivian. "Progressives Vowed Driver's Licenses for the Undocumented. Then the Suburbs Spoke Up." *New York Times*, June 16, 2019, sec. New York. www.nytimes.com/2019/06/16/nyregion/undocumented-immigrants-drivers-licenses-ny.html.

Ward, Deborah E. *The White Welfare State: The Racialization of U.S. Welfare Policy.* Ann Arbor: University of Michigan Press, 2005.

Weir, Margaret. "States, Race, and the Decline of New Deal Liberalism." Studies in American Political Development 19, no. 2 (2005): 157–172. https://doi.org/10.1017/S0898588X05000106.

Weaver, Vesla M. "Frontlash: Race and the Development of Punitive Crime Policy." *Studies in American Political Development* 21, no. 2 (September 2007): 230–265. https://doi.org/10.1017/S0898588X07000211.

Weaver, Vesla M., Jacob S. Hacker, and Christopher Wildeman. "Detaining Democracy? Criminal Justice and American Civic Life." *ANNALS of the American Academy of Political and Social Science* 651, no. 1 (January 1, 2014): 6–21. https://doi.org/10.1177/0002716213504729.

Weaver, Vesla M., and Amy E. Lerman. "Political Consequences of the Carceral State." *American Political Science Review* 104, no. 4 (November 2010): 817–833. https://doi.org/10.1017/S0003055410000456.

Wells, Ida B. *Crusade for Justice: The Autobiography of Ida B. Wells.* Chicago, IL: University of Chicago Press, 1970.

West, Charlotte. "As Newsom Rethinks Juvenile Justice, California Reconsiders Prison for Kids." *CalMatters* (blog), June 13, 2019. https://calmatters.org/justice/2019/06/california-juvenile-justice-system-gavin-newsom/.

"Why Immigrant-Friendly Legislation Has Stalled In Mass." *WBUR News*, April 9, 2014. www.wbur.org/news/2014/04/09/immigration-bills-massachusetts.

Wildermuth, John. "California Hits Highest Voter Totals Since 1952, and Dems Are Way Out in Front." *San Francisco Chronicle*, November 7, 2019. www.sfchronicle.com/politics/article/California-hits-highest-voter-totals-since-1952-14818066.php.

Williams, Lou Falkner. *The Great South Carolina Ku Klux Klan Trials, 1871–1872.* Athens: University of Georgia Press, 2004.

Williamson, Joel. *After Slavery: The Negro in South Carolina During Reconstruction, 1861–1877.* New York: W. W. Norton, 1975.

 The Crucible of Race: Black-White Relations in the American South since Emancipation. Oxford: Oxford University Press, 1984.

 "The Separation of the Races." In *When Did Southern Segregation Begin?*, edited by John David Smith, 61–83. Boston, MA: Bedford/St. Martin's, 2002.

Willon, Phil. "California Extends New Protections to Immigrants under Laws Signed by Newsom." *Los Angeles Times*, October 14, 2019. www.latimes.com/california/story/2019-10-14/california-new-protections-immigrants-laws-signed-gavin-newsom.

Wong, Edlie L. *Neither Fugitive nor Free: Atlantic Slavery, Freedom Suits, and the Legal Culture of Travel.* New York: New York University Press, 2009.

Wong, Tom K. *The Politics of Immigration: Partisanship, Demographic Change, and American National Identity.* New York: Oxford University Press, 2016.

Wood, Peter H. *Black Majority: Negroes in Colonial South Carolina from 1670 through the Stono Rebellion.* The Norton Library. New York: W. W. Norton, 1975.

Woodward, C. Vann. *The Strange Career of Jim Crow.* Oxford: Oxford University Press, 2001.

Wright, James Martin. *The Free Negro in Maryland, 1634–1860.* New York: Columbia University, 1921. https://catalog.hathitrust.org/Record/100159569.

Yashar, Deborah J. *Contesting Citizenship in Latin America: The Rise of Indigenous Movements and the Postliberal Challenge.* Cambridge: Cambridge University Press, 2005.

"Contesting Citizenship: Indigenous Movements and Democracy in Latin America." *Comparative Politics* 31, no. 1 (1998): 23–42. https://doi.org/10.2307/422104.

Ybarra, Vickie D., Lisa M. Sanchez, and Gabriel R. Sanchez. "Anti-Immigrant Anxieties in State Policy: The Great Recession and Punitive Immigration Policy in the American States, 2005–2012." *State Politics & Policy Quarterly*, September 28, 2015. https://doi.org/10.1177/1532440015605815.

Young, Iris Marion. "Polity and Group Difference: A Critique of the Ideal of Universal Citizenship." *Ethics* 99, no. 2 (1989): 250–274.

Zepeda-Millán, Chris. *Latino Mass Mobilization: Immigration, Racialization, and Activism.* Cambridge: Cambridge University Press, 2017.

Zilversmit, Arthur. *The First Emancipation: The Abolition of Slavery in the North.* Chicago, IL: The University of Chicago Press, 1967.

Zingher, Joshua N. "The Ideological and Electoral Determinants of Laws Targeting Undocumented Migrants in the U.S. States." *State Politics & Policy Quarterly* 14, no. 1 (March 1, 2014): 90–117. https://doi.org/10.1177/1532440014524212.

Zolberg, Aristide. *A Nation by Design.* Cambridge, MA: Harvard University Press, 2005.

Index